Library of
Davidson College

CONDITIONAL RELATIONS
(PAṬṬHĀNA)

VOL. I

Pali Text Society

TRANSLATION SERIES No. 37

CONDITIONAL RELATIONS (PAṬṬHĀNA)

Being Vol. I of the Chaṭṭhasaṅgāyana Text of
The Seventh Book of the Abhidhamma Piṭaka

A Translation
by
U NĀRADA

MŪLA PAṬṬHĀNA SAYADAW
(of Rangoon, Burma)

Originator of Abhidhamma Charts

Assisted by
THEIN NYUN

LONDON
Published for the Pali Text Society
BY
LUZAC & COMPANY, LTD.
46 GREAT RUSSELL STREET, W.C.1
1969

All rights reserved

PRINTED BY STEPHEN AUSTIN AND SONS, LTD., HERTFORD, ENGLAND

GENERAL CONTENTS

	PAGE
Foreword by Dr. I. B. Horner	vii
Introduction by Sayadaw U Nārada	xi
Contents of Conditional Relations	cxi

CONDITIONAL RELATIONS

I. Enumeration of the Conditions	1
II. Analytical Exposition of the Conditions	2
III. Question Chapter	13
IV. Answers :—	
1. faultless triplet	22
2. feeling triplet	318
3. resultant triplet	362
4. clinging triplet	429
5. corrupt triplet	502

FOREWORD

The P.T.S. Translation Series entered on another phase in 1962 with the publication of "Discourse on Elements", a translation of Dhātukathā, the third book of the Abhidhamma-piṭaka, by Mūla Paṭṭhāna Sayadaw U Nārada of Rangoon. An Abhidhamma book dealing with Triplets and Couplets of Dhammasaṅgaṇi, and with the Aggregates, Bases, Elements, Truths, Faculties, Dependent Origination, etc., of Vibhaṅga, was thus put within reach of the English-speaking student. Moreover, the immense clarity and consistency both of the translation and of the method of exposition, together with the Charts, of which the Mūla Paṭṭhāna Sayadaw is the originator, make it hard to imagine that this book could ever be superseded. Exactly the same may be said, but with even more emphasis, of this present work. Called "Conditional Relations", it is a translation of the first volume of the enormously long and extremely intricate Paṭṭhāna, the seventh and final book of the Abhidhamma-piṭaka. As the Mūla Paṭṭhāna Sayadaw says at the end of his Introduction, his translation is based on the Sixth Synod or Chaṭṭha Saṅgāyana text, 1955, 5 vols., to which he refers now and again as Synod Text or Synod. The subjects dealt with in each of these vols. are given in the Introduction.

It is not proposed that the same translator will translate the Synod vols. II, III, IV or V. The basis for their translation is contained in this present work, and can be undertaken by any competent scholar of Pali Buddhism. As the treatment is similar, what he would need to do would be to relate the remaining 17 Triplets, the 100 Couplets and their many inter-relationships, to the system of the 24 Conditional Relations by the methods generally obtaining in the five examples detailed in this present translation. If that scholar be as conversant with all the categories of Abhidhamma analysis as U Nārada is clearly seen to be, then he should be capable of applying these methods and completing the remaining sections of this incredibly complicated work.

As the province of Paṭṭhāna is one of Omniscience, the sphere of Buddhas only (see Intr. p. cii), a faithful exposition of this "ocean of method" could be made intelligible only by someone who had devoted years of deep study and reflexion to it, and had had the additional purpose of finding the right approach to display its vast complexities and unique content in a form that could be grasped by students. To enable such a study to be more fully pursued, the Ven. Sayadaw is compiling a Guide to Paṭṭhāna. It will be a companion volume to this present translation, and is to be published by P.T.S. His exceptional qualifications and eminence in this field guarantee the reliability and authoritativeness of all his statements and explanations. This vol. of Paṭṭhāna and the Guide to it may be studied therefore with every confidence. They are a magnificent example of a complete comprehension of what the Buddhavacana meant *then*, at the time it was uttered, and of a rare power to convey this meaning to students some 2,500 years later in the sense that was intended then. They will find that the venerable verities still exist today.

In the Anāgatavaṁsa and some of the Pali Commentaries it is stated that as time goes on and on the Buddha's Dhamma will decay owing to five "disappearances" affecting its survival. In the "disappearance of learning", the Great Paṭṭhāna itself will decay first, other parts of the Piṭaka following till all have fallen into oblivion. It is largely to delay such an eventuality that the Mūla Paṭṭhāna Sayadaw and his fellow-worker, U Thein Nyun, feel it important to devote so much of their time and effort to translating the Abhidhamma. They believe that if Paṭṭhāna can be understood in the West "as it really is" (yathābhūta), a means of keeping it alive for an additional length of time will have been achieved; hence the survival of the rest of the Abhidhamma-piṭaka, of the Sutta-piṭaka and of the Vinaya-piṭaka will be assured also.

It remains for me to record the deep sense of gratitude the Society entertains towards the Venerable Mūla Paṭṭhāna

Sayadaw U Nārada for offering it for publication the works I have mentioned in this Foreword. These translations would not have been possible without the generous help given by U Thein Nyun. The P.T.S. offers him likewise its warm thanks for his many valuable labours, and is glad to note that he is assisting with the preparation of the Guide to Paṭṭhāna.

I. B. HORNER.

London.
December 1967.

INTRODUCTION

The Buddha expounded the Abhidhamma in the Tāvatiṁsā World of the Devas. After He completed the Yamaka, which forms the Sixth Book of Abhidhamma Piṭaka, He continued with the Paṭṭhāna where various methods, deep and wide as the ocean, were provided.

WHAT IS PAṬṬHĀNA ?

Paṭṭhāna (Conditional Relations) deals with the 22 Triplets and 100 Couplets of the Dhammasaṅgaṇī, i.e. all the ultimate realities, both singly and in combinations, with reference to the 24 conditions to show how the causes and their effects are related.

In the methods of the Four Noble Truths and Dependent Origination, only the manifested causes and effects are considered. But in Paṭṭhāna, the forces that bring about the relations between the causes and effects are also taken into account and it is with these forces that this subject is primarily concerned. Hence statements such as " Visible object-base is related to eye-consciousness element and its associated states by object condition " are met with in the Text. This means that visible object-base, a state as the condition, is related to eye-consciousness element and its associated states, the states as the conditioned, by the force of object condition or the conditioning force of object. Although the states, as causes and effects, have to be unavoidably mentioned, stress is laid on the underlying forces that bring about the relations between them.

DEFINITIONS

Condition (paccaya). It is that which must precede the operation of a cause. Root condition and object condition are generic terms for all the six roots and all the objects respectively. But the root, greed, is a specific root condition and the object, visible object-base, is a specific object condition. This applies to all the conditions.

Conditioning state (paccaya dhamma). It is the state which is the cause on which the effect is dependent. It is the cause that is related to an effect and without which there can be no effect. Thus greed is a conditioning state of root condition and visible object-base is a conditioning state of object condition.

Conditioned state (paccayuppanna dhamma). It is the state which is the effect that results from a cause. It is the effect which is related by a cause. Thus, in the example of the relation given above, eye-consciousness element and its associated states are the conditioned states of object condition.

Non-conditioned state (paccanīya dhamma). In the first six chapters, it is the state which is not a conditioned state of the positive conditions. But in the Investigation chapter it is the state which is not common to the conditioning states and conditioned states of the same or different groups of conditions.

Related (upakāraka). This means that when a state is present, the other states that are connected with it will (1) arise if they have not arisen, (2) continue to exist if they have already arisen, or (3) gradually develop while in existence. The ultimate states of reality cannot make efforts on their own or plan to do so. But if one of them is present, the accomplishments of the connected states are brought about. This is what is meant when it is said that a state is related to one or more states.

Force (satti). It is that which has the power to bring about or accomplish. Just as the hotness of chilli is inherent in it and cannot exist apart from it and as the sweetness of sugar is inherent in it and cannot exist apart from it, so also, the conditioning forces inherent in the states cannot exist apart from those states. For example, in root condition, the force of root condition (conditioning force) inherent in the state of greed, which is one of the six roots, cannot exist apart from that state. Here the root conditioning state is greed and the conditioning force of greed is also greed. Therefore, the force and the state which possesses that force cannot be considered

Introduction xiii

apart from each other. It has to be remembered, however, that a state can possess many conditioning forces. For instance, the root, non-delusion, a conditioning state of root condition, possesses, besides the conditioning force of root, those of predominance, conascence, mutuality, dependence, resultant, faculty, path, association, dissociation, presence and non-disappearance.

THE ORDER OF PAṬṬHĀNA EXPOSITION

The order of the Paṭṭhāna Text is as follows :—

I. *The Introduction.* Here the Enumeration of the 24 conditions such as " root condition ", " object condition " and so on is first given and then an Analytical Exposition, neither too brief nor too detailed, of these conditions such as " The roots are related to the states which are associated with roots, and the matter produced thereby, by (the force of) root condition " and so on.

II. *The Main Body of the Exposition.* Here all the ultimate realities are treated by the four methods, namely :

1. Positive Method.
2. Negative Method.
3. Positive-Negative Method.
4. Negative-Positive Method.

These form the four Great Divisions of Paṭṭhāna.

In each of them, the subject-matter consists of :

(i) Triplets.
(ii) Couplets.
(iii) Couplet-Triplet Combinations.
(iv) Triplet-Couplet Combinations.
(v) Triplet-Triplet Combinations.
(vi) Couplet-Couplet Combinations.

This gives the 24 Divisions of Paṭṭhāna.

xiv   Conditional Relations

Each of these Triplets, Couplets, and their Combinations is dealt with under the seven Chapters, namely :

I. " Dependent " Chapter.
II. " Conascent " Chapter.
III. " Conditioned " Chapter.
IV. " Supported " Chapter.
V. " Conjoined " Chapter.
VI. " Associated " Chapter.
VII. " Investigation " Chapter.

Again, each of these Chapters treats of the relations between the conditioning states and conditioned states of the conditions that are involved in each case. The conditions are taken " Singly " (" By Ones "), " By Twos ", " By Threes " and so on. Since the four methods given above are also applied to the conditions, each Chapter has four sections, namely :

1. Positive Conditions.
2. Negative Conditions.
3. Positive–Negative Conditions.
4. Negative–Positive Conditions.

The contents of each Chapter are divided into Questions and Answers about these conditions.

QUESTIONS

From the short outline of the contents of Paṭṭhāna given above, it will be seen that the Text begins with the Positive Method Division, i.e. the Positive states, and first deals with the Faultless * Triplet, the first of the 22 Triplets of the Dhammasaṅgaṇī, and considers it under the first Chapter, the " Dependent " Chapter, with reference to root condition, the first of the Positive conditions. Questions are, therefore, asked in this connection in the first instance.

Since the Faultless Triplet consists of Faultless,* Faulty and Indeterminate † states, these can be taken in seven ways and

---

* The reasons for translating " kusala " as " faultless " are given at the end of this Introduction.
† This means neither faultless nor faulty.

form seven sections, namely : (i) faultless, (ii) faulty, (iii) indeterminate, (iv) faultless, indeterminate, (v) faulty, indeterminate, (vi) faultless, faulty, and (vii) faultless, faulty, indeterminate. Taking each of these sections as reference, questions are asked with respect to each of them. For example, taking (i) faultless as reference, there are the following questions :

Dependent on faultless state, may there arise

(1) faultless state by root condition ?
(2) faulty state by root condition ?
(3) indeterminate state by root condition ?
(4) faultless and indeterminate states by root condition ?
(5) faulty and indeterminate states by root condition ?
(6) faultless and faulty states by root condition ?
(7) faultless, faulty, and indeterminate states by root condition ?

When the rest of the seven sections are each taken as reference, by turns, there is a set of $7 \times 7 = 49$ questions for root condition alone. For the 24 conditions taken singly, therefore, there are $49 \times 24 = 1,176$ questions. From this it can be judged that the number of questions for the whole of Paṭṭhāna must be of a very high order. According to the Commentary, the figure is 404,948,533,248 and the Subcommentary, 388,778,713,344. In the Pali Text, however, all the questions are not included, but only those that are necessary for illustrating the types of the questions. These are given at the beginning of the " Dependent " Chapter. If all of them were to be put into print, it would need over 3 crores of books of 400 pages each.

In the Expositor, Vol. I, p. 16, it is stated that the rays of six colours issued from The Buddha's body only when, with His Omniscience, He contemplated the limitless Paṭṭhāna. " Now not even on a single day during the interval of twenty-one days were rays emitted from the Teacher's body. During the fourth week he sat in a jewel house in the north-west direction. The jewel house here does not mean a house made of the seven jewels but the place where he contemplated the seven books. And while he contemplated the contents of the

Dhammasaṅgaṇī, his body did not emit rays: and similarly with the contemplation of the next five books. But when, coming to the Great Book (Paṭṭhāna), he began to contemplate the twenty-four causal relations of condition, of presentation, and so on, his omniscience certainly found its opportunity therein. For as the great fish Timiratipiṅgala finds room only in the great ocean eighty-four thousand yojanas in depth, so his omniscience truly finds room only in the Great Book. Rays of six colours—indigo, golden, red, white, tawny, and dazzling—issued from the Teacher's body, as he was contemplating the subtle and abstruse Law by his omniscience which had found such opportunity."

Answers

After all the possible questions were indicated, the answers are provided. Since every question does not provide an answer, the total number of answers is less than that of the questions. Here also, the order of exposition of the answers is the same as that for the questions. So it begins with the Positive Method Division where the Faultless Triplet is dealt with under the " Dependent " Chapter. This is divided into two sub-chapters:

(i) Classification (vibhaṅga), where the states in the answers given are classified.

(ii) Enumeration (saṅkhyā), where the numbers of the answers to the sets of questions are provided.

A. Positive Method Division

1. Faultless Triplet: I. " Dependent " Chapter

1. Positive Conditions   (i) Classification Chapter

The Classification Chapter starts with positive root condition, the first of the 23 conditions which are applicable to the Faultless Triplet. Here there are only five possible sections out of the seven, i.e. (1) Faultless, (2) Faulty, (3) Indeterminate, (4) Faultless, Indeterminate, and (5) Faulty, Indeterminate (the remaining two sections (6) Faultless, Faulty, and (7) Faultless, Faulty, Indeterminate, are not possible because these states never arise together).

Introduction xvii

With (1) Faultless section as reference, the three answers with respect to it are (i) (Faultless–Faultless), (ii) (Faultless–Indeterminate), and (iii) (Faultless–Faultless, Indeterminate). The answer for (i) is given in the Text as :

(i) " Dependent on faultless state, arises faultless state by root condition."

The faultless states in this answer are then classified under the aggregates and given after the answer as :

" Dependent on one faultless aggregate, arise three (faultless) aggregates ; dependent on three (faultless) aggregates, arises one (faultless) aggregate ; dependent on two (faultless) aggregates, arise two (faultless) aggregates."

With (2) Faulty section as reference, there are three similar answers, i.e. (iv) (Faulty–Faulty), (v) (Faulty–Indeterminate), and (vi) (Faulty–Faulty, Indeterminate).

With (3) Indeterminate section as reference, there is only one answer, (vii) (Indeterminate–Indeterminate).

With (4) Faultless, Indeterminate section as reference, there is one answer, (viii) (Faultless, Indeterminate–Indeterminate), and

With (5) Faulty, Indeterminate section as reference, there is also a similar answer, (ix) (Faulty, Indeterminate–Indeterminate). (The Text may be referred to for all these answers and the classifications of the states in them.)

Therefore, for the set of 49 questions with root condition in the Dependent Chapter of the Faultless Triplet there are only nine answers. Thus the enumeration, the number of answers, is nine in this case and this is given in the Enumeration Chapter.

The Method of Determining the Answers in the Classification Chapter

The Text gives the answers in the Classification Chapter for the conditions taken singly but not for the conditions taken " By Twos ", " By Threes ", etc. For these only the numbers of answers are provided in the Enumeration Chapter. Therefore, to know what those answers are, it is necessary to know the method of arriving at the answers in the Classification

B

Chapter. The method will be illustrated with the example of root condition above to show how the nine answers are obtained.

The following information is provided as it is essential for the proper understanding of the method and its application to the first six Chapters :

(*a*) The Conditioning and Conditioned States of the Conditions must be known.

These can be obtained from the relations given in the Analytical Exposition at the beginning of the Text. In the first six Chapters, namely : Dependent, Conascent, Conditioned, Supported, Conjoined and Associated, the conditioning and conditioned states of conascence condition are dealt with in the Dependent and Conascent Chapters ; those of dependence condition in the Conditioned and Supported Chapters, and those of association condition in the Conjoined and Associated Chapters. Since root condition of Dependent Chapter is taken as the example, the conditioning and conditioned states of conascence condition must first be known. These are :

Conditioning states	Conditioned states
89 consciousnesses 52 mental factors 4 great primaries heart-base	89 consciousnesses 52 mental factors 28 matter

Details of these analytical units and their divisions into the three sections, (1) faultless, (2) faulty, (3) indeterminate states of the Faultless Triplet are given in the Compendium of Philosophy.

It will be found that :

(1) The faultless states are 21 faultless consciousnesses and 38 associated mental factors.

(2) The faulty states are 12 faulty consciousnesses and 27 associated mental factors.

(3) The indeterminate states are 36 resultant consciousnesses, 20 functional consciousnesses, 38 associated mental factors, 28 matter and Nibbāna.

Note.—In Paṭṭhāna seven kinds of matter are considered.

Introduction xix

They are (1) mind-produced matter, (2) rebirth kamma-produced matter, (3) external matter, (4) nutriment-produced matter, (5) temperature-produced matter, (6) non-percipient beings' kamma-produced matter, (7) during life kamma-produced matter.

(*b*) The Conditioned States are given Prominence in the Six Chapters.

The conditioned states of root condition, object condition, etc., which are also those of conascence condition, are selected and the conditioning states which are conascent with those conditioned states are found. It is from these conditioning and conditioned states that the answers, the classifications of the states in the answers and the enumerations are obtained. This applies to the conditions dealt with in the Dependent and Conascent Chapters. Similar procedures with the conditioned states of the conditions are adopted in the other Chapters where examples are also given.

(*c*) Postnascence Condition is Excluded in the Six Chapters.

Postnascence condition does not possess the force of production but only that of support. But since in the six Chapters it is the former that is dealt with, this condition is excluded. So only 23 out of the 24 conditions are considered.

Illustration of the Method

1. The totals of the conditioning and conditioned states of conascence condition, as tabulated above, are found out from the relations given for this condition in the Analytical Exposition. There it is stated that :

(i) The four immaterial (i.e. mental) aggregates are mutually related to one another by conascence condition.

Here the four mental aggregates are both conditioning and conditioned states. This means that if one of the four mental aggregates is the conditioning state, the remaining three aggregates are the conditioned states ; if three of the four mental aggregates are the conditioning states, then the remaining one is the conditioned state ; if two of the four mental aggregates are the conditioning states, then the remaining two are the conditioned states.

The four mental aggregates, which are 89 consciousnesses

and 52 mental factors, are classified, as shown above, under the faultless, faulty, resultant indeterminate, and functional indeterminate aggregates. Therefore, when the conditioning states are either one of these classes, the conditioned states must be of the same class.

(ii) The four great primaries are mutually related to one another by conascence condition.

Here the four great primaries are both the conditioning and conditioned states, i.e. if one of them is the conditioning state, then the remaining three are the conditioned states; if three of them are the conditioning states, then the remaining one is the conditioned state; if two of them are the conditioning states, then the remaining two are the conditioned states.

As pointed out above, the four great primaries of the seven kinds of matter are to be taken, i.e. those of mind-produced matter, rebirth kamma-produced matter, external matter, nutriment-produced matter, temperature-produced matter, non-percipient beings' kamma-produced matter and during life kamma-produced matter.

(iii) At the moment of conception, mentality and materiality are mutually related to one another by conascence condition.

Here the mental aggregates at the moment of conception, i.e. 15 rebirth consciousnesses and 35 mental factors, and heart-base are both conditioning and conditioned states in the five-aggregate existences. This means that when the mental aggregates are the conditioning states, heart-base is the conditioned state and vice versa.

(iv) States, consciousness and mental factors, are related to mind-produced matter by conascence condition.

Here the mentality which produces matter, i.e. 75 consciousnesses (exclusive of four immaterial resultant consciousnesses, twice five-fold consciousnesses and Arahatta's death-consciousness in the five-aggregate existences) and 52 mental factors are the conditioning states and mind-produced matter is the conditioned state.

(v) The great primaries are related to derived matter by conascence condition.

Of the 28 matter which form the seven kinds of matter, the

four great primaries are the conditioning states and the remaining 24 derived-matter are the conditioned states.

(vi) The material states are sometimes related to the immaterial states by conascence condition and are sometimes not related by conascence condition.

This merely stresses the fact in (iii) above that heart-base is the conditioning state and rebirth mental aggregates are the conditioned states at the moment of conception but not during life.

When all the conditioning and conditioned states are grouped together, they are found to be :—

Conditioning states	Conditioned states
(1) 89 cons., 52 mental factors comprising (a) 21 faultless cons. and 38 associated mental factors. (b) 12 faulty cons. and 27 associated mental factors. (c) 36 resultant indeterminate cons. and 38 associated mental factors. (d) 20 functional indeterminate cons. and 35 associated mental factors. (2) 4 great primaries of (i) mind-produced matter, (ii) rebirth kamma-produced matter, (iii) external matter, (iv) nutriment-produced matter, (v) temperature-produced matter, (vi) non-percipient beings' kamma-produced matter, (vii) during life kamma-produced matter, (3) heart-base.	(1) 89 cons., 52 mental factors comprising (a) 21 faultless cons. and 38 associated mental factors. (b) 12 faulty cons. and 27 associated mental factors. (c) 36 resultant indeterminate cons. and 38 associated mental factors. (d) 20 functional indeterminate cons. and 35 associated mental factors. (2) 28 matter of (i) mind-produced matter, (ii) rebirth kamma-produced matter, (iii) external matter, (iv) nutriment-produced matter, (v) temperature-produced matter, (vi) non-percipient beings' kamma-produced matter, (vii) during life kamma-produced matter.

2. The conditioned states of root condition are found out from the relation for this condition given in the Analytical Exposition. It is stated there that the roots are related to the states associated with roots, and the matter produced thereby, by root condition. Therefore the conditioned states are :—

(1) States associated with roots. These are 71 rooted

consciousnesses and 52 mental factors excluding delusion from the two delusion-rooted consciousnesses as it is not associated with any root. They comprise :

(a) 21 faultless consciousnesses and 38 associated mental factors ;
(b) 12 faulty consciousnesses and 27 associated mental factors ;
(c) 21 resultant indeterminate consciousnesses and 38 associated mental factors ;
(d) 17 functional indeterminate consciousnesses and 35 associated mental factors.

(2) The matter produced thereby. These are :
(a) rooted mind-produced matter. This is produced by the rooted mentality during life ;
(b) rooted rebirth kamma-produced matter. This is produced by the rooted rebirth mentality at the moment of conception.

(3) The conditioned states of root condition which are also those of conascence condition are found. Or, what amounts to the same thing, the conditioned states of conascence condition are examined and those which are also of root condition are selected. It should be noted that the conditioned states of conascence condition consist of all the ultimate realities and, therefore, the conditioned states of root and all the other conditions are always those of conascence condition. Thus the above conditioned states of root condition are also those of conascence condition.

(4) The conditioning states which are conascent with the conditioned states of root condition have to be found. It has to be remembered that conascence condition is under consideration in the Dependent Chapter and, therefore, only the conditioning and conditioned states of this condition have to be dealt with. In this example with root condition, the question whether, dependent on a conditioning state, a conditioned state of root condition can arise or not, can only be answered by knowing the conditioning states which are conascent with the conditioned states of root condition. On referring to the conditioning and conditioned states of conascence condition and

Introduction

the conditioned states of root condition given above, it will be found that the conditioning states which are conascent with the conditioned states of root condition are :

(1) 71 rooted consciousnesses, 52 mental factors (as the four mental aggregates they are mutually related to one another) ;
(2) rooted mind-produced great primaries (the great primaries are mutually related to one another and also related to derived matter) ;
(3) rooted rebirth kamma-produced great primaries (the same reason as (2) above) ;
(4) heart-base (at the moment of conception it is related to the four mental aggregates that arise at that time and which are included in (1) above).

All the data needed for arriving at the answers, the classifications of the states involved in the answers and the enumeration of the answers are now available. These are the conascent conditioning and conditioned states of root condition and they are tabulated below :

Conditioning states	Conditioned states
(1) 71 rooted cons., 52 m.f. comprising (a) 21 faultless cons., 38 assoc. m.f. (b) 12 faulty cons., 27 assoc. m.f. (c) 21 rooted resultant indeterminate cons., 38 assoc. m.f. (d) 17 rooted functional indeterminate cons., 35 assoc. m.f.	(1) 71 rooted cons., 52 m.f. comprising (a) 21 faultless cons., 38 assoc. m.f. (b) 12 faulty consc., 27 assoc. m.f. (c) 21 rooted resultant indeterminate cons., 38 assoc. m.f. (d) 17 rooted functional indeterminate cons., 35 assoc. m.f.
(2) rooted mind-produced (4) great primaries (indeterminate).	(2) rooted mind-produced matter (indeterminate).
(3) rooted rebirth kamma-produced (4) great primaries (indeterminate).	(3) rooted rebirth kamma-produced matter (indeterminate).
(4) heart-base (indeterminate).	*Note.* Matter consists of the four great primaries and derived matter as the rest.

Abbreviations. cons. = consciousnesses ; m.f. = mental factors ; assoc. = associated.

On examination of the table it is seen that :

(1) With the faultless states, 21 faultless consciousnesses and 38 associated mental factors, taken as reference, these states are found on both sides as conditioning and conditioned states. Since they are conascent states, there is the answer (i) (Faultless–Faultless). This is given in the Text as " Dependent on faultless state (as the conditioning state), arises faultless state (as the conditioned state) by root condition ".

Now the above states can be classified under the four mental aggregates, namely : feeling, perception, mental formation and consciousness aggregates. And if one of these four aggregates, on the side of conditioning states, is the conditioning state, then the remaining three aggregates, on the side of conditioned states, which are conascent arise as the conditioned states. Similarly, if three of them are the conditioning states, then the remaining one which is conascent arises as the conditioned state ; if two of them are the conditioning states, then the remaining two which are conascent arise as the conditioned states. So the classified answer as given in the Text is :

" Dependent on one faultless aggregate, arise three (faultless) aggregates ; dependent on three (faultless) aggregates, arises one (faultless) aggregate ; dependent on two (faultless) aggregates, arise two (faultless) aggregates."

Again, the faultless states on the L.H.S. as the conditioning states are conascent with rooted mind-produced matter (indeterminate) on the R.H.S. as the conditioned state. So there is the answer (ii) (Faultless–Indeterminate). This is given in the Text as :

" Dependent on faultless state, arises indeterminate state by root condition." The states are classified and the classified answer which follows is given as :

" Dependent on faultless aggregates, arises mind-produced matter."

Note.—The word " rooted " before mind-produced matter is left out because the faultless aggregates which produce this matter are always associated with roots.

Also the faultless states on the L.H.S. as the conditioning states are conascent with the faultless states and mind-produced matter (indeterminate) on the R.H.S. as the conditioned states. It is a combination of (i) and (ii) above. This gives the answer (iii) (Faultless–Faultless, Indeterminate) and is found in the Text as:

" Dependent on faultless state, arise faultless and indeterminate states by root condition." The classified answer that follows is:

" Dependent on one faultless aggregate, arise three aggregates and mind-produced matter; dependent on three aggregates, arise one aggregate and mind-produced matter; dependent on two aggregates, arise two aggregates and mind-produced matter."

No other answers are possible with Faultless states alone as reference.

(2) With the faulty states, 12 faulty consciousnesses and 27 associated mental factors, taken as reference, three similar answers as for the faultless states are obtained, i.e. (iv) (Faulty–Faulty), (v) (Faulty–Indeterminate) and (vi) (Faulty–Faulty, Indeterminate).

(3) With the indeterminate states taken as reference, those that arise during life are first taken. These are 21 rooted resultant indeterminate consciousnesses and 38 associated mental factors and 17 rooted functional indeterminate consciousnesses and 35 associated mental factors. These on the L.H.S. as the conditioning states are conascent with the same resultant and functional consciousnesses respectively and mind-produced matter on the R.H.S. as the conditioned states. So there is the answer (vii) (Indeterminate–Indeterminate). In the Text it is stated as:

" Dependent on indeterminate state, arises indeterminate state by root condition." And the classified answer is:

" Dependent on one resultant indeterminate or functional indeterminate aggregate, arise three aggregates and mind-produced matter; dependent on three aggregates, arise one aggregate and mind-produced matter; dependent on two aggregates, arise two aggregates and mind-produced matter."

Then the indeterminate states that arise at the moment of conception are 17 rooted rebirth consciousnesses and 35 associated mental factors which are included in the 21 resultant indeterminate consciousnesses and the 38 associated mental factors. These states on the L.H.S. as the conditioning states are conascent with (*a*) the same states and rooted rebirth kamma-produced matter, (*b*) heart-base on the R.H.S. as the conditioned states. Also heart-base (at the moment of conception) on the L.H.S. as the conditioning state is conascent with the rooted rebirth consciousnesses and associated mental factors (which are included in the 21 resultant indeterminate consciousnesses and 38 associated mental factors) on the R.H.S. as the conditioned states. So there is the same answer (vii) (Indeterminate–Indeterminate) and the classified answer given in the Text is :

" At the moment of conception, dependent on one resultant indeterminate aggregate, arise three aggregates and kamma-produced matter ; dependent on three aggregates, arise one aggregate and kamma-produced matter ; dependent on two aggregates, arise two aggregates and kamma-produced matter ; dependent on aggregates, arises heart-base ; dependent on heart-base, arise aggregates."

Note.—" rooted rebirth " is left out as it is understood as such since the matter is produced by rooted mentality at the moment of conception.

Again, considering indeterminate matter, i.e. rooted mind-produced matter and rooted rebirth kamma-produced matter, it will be found that the great primaries are on both sides as conditioning and conditioned states. Since they are mutually related, if one of the four great primaries on the L.H.S. is the conditioning state, then the remaining three on the R.H.S. are the conditioned states ; if three of them on the L.H.S. are the conditioning states, then the remaining one on the R.H.S. is the conditioned state ; if two of them on the L.H.S. are the conditioning states, then the remaining two on the R.H.S. are the conditioned states. Also, the four great primaries of mind-produced and kamma-produced matter on the L.H.S. as the conditioning states are conascent with the derived matter respectively on the R.H.S. as the conditioned states. Thus there is the same answer (vii) (Indeterminate–Indeterminate). And the classified answer given in the Text is:

" Dependent on one great primary, arise three great primaries; dependent on three great primaries, arises one great primary; dependent on two great primaries, arise two great primaries; dependent on (four) great primaries, arise mind-produced and kamma-produced derived matter."

(4) With the faultless, indeterminate as reference, the states are the faultless states and rooted mind-produced great primaries. These on the L.H.S. as the conditioning states are conascent with rooted mind-produced matter on the R.H.S. as the conditioned state. This gives the answer (viii) (Faultless, Indeterminate–Indeterminate) which is found in the Text as:

" Dependent on faultless and indeterminate state, arises indeterminate state by root condition " and classified as:

" Dependent on faultless aggregates and great primaries, arises mind-produced matter."

(5) With the faulty, indeterminate as reference, the faulty states and rooted mind-produced great primaries are taken and, similar to (viii) above, the answer (ix) (Faulty, Indeterminate–Indeterminate) is obtained and classified.

Thus there are only nine answers to the 49 questions with root condition in the Dependent Chapter of the Faultless Triplet. This is given in the Enumeration Chapter as " With root condition (there are) 9 (answers) ".

Another Example with Object Condition

There is no need to go into details with this example as they have been given with root condition above.

1. The conditioning and conditioned states of conascence condition have been found.

2. The conditioned states of object condition are found out from the relations for this condition given in the Analytical Exposition. In this case they are 89 consciousnesses and 52 mental factors, all materiality being excluded.

3. These conditioned states of object condition are also those of conascence condition.

4. The conditioning states which are conascent with the conditioned states of object condition have to be found. The conditioning states of 89 consciousnesses and 52 mental factors (which are the conditioned states of object condition) are 89 consciousnesses, 52 mental factors and heart-base (at the moment of conception).

The conascent conditioning and conditioned states of object condition are tabulated below:—

Conditioning states	Conditioned states
(1) 89 cons., 52 m.f. (2) heart-base (at the moment of conception)	(1) 89 cons., 52 m.f.

When the appropriate states are chosen to get the answers, as was shown in the case of root condition, it will be seen that there are only three answers (i) (Faultless–Faultless), (ii) (Faulty–Faulty), and (iii) (Indeterminate–Indeterminate) to the 49 questions. The classified answers that are obtained are also given in the Classification Chapter and the enumeration, " With object 3 ", in the Enumeration Chapter.

The method, illustrated with the examples of root and object conditions, is applied to the other conditions to determine the conascent conditioning and conditioned states of each condition and to select the appropriate states for obtaining the answers given in the Classification Chapter and the enumerations in the Enumeration Chapter.

When the conditions are taken " By Twos ", " By Threes ", " By Fours ", etc., the conascent conditioning and conditioned states of each of the conditions under consideration have to be examined to find out those which are common to those conditions and then the appropriate states from the common conditioning and conditioned states are selected to arrive at the answers, the classifications of the states in those answers and the enumerations. As mentioned earlier, there are no Classification Chapters for them but only the Enumeration Chapters.

Note.—The most difficult portions of Paṭṭhāna are the Enumeration Chapters where only figures denoting the numbers of the answers are provided. Therefore, concise methods for determining how these figures are arrived at in the Enumeration Chapters of the seven Chapters are given in the appropriate places in this Introduction. And when they are applied the enumerations can be worked out and this difficult portion understood. The Abhidhamma Teaching is, indeed, difficult and so the Buddha always provided methods wherever necessary. It was because Nāgasena knew these methods and applied them that he could show his prowess in the Abhidhamma to the Arahats. This is stated in the Milinda-pañhā, p. 22, thus: " Then Nāgasena went to the innumerable company of the Arahats and said, ' I should like to expound the whole of the Abhidhamma Piṭaka, without abridgement, arranging it under three heads, good, bad and indifferent qualities.' And they gave him leave. And in seven months the Venerable Nāgasena recited the seven books of Abhidhamma in full."

1. Positive Conditions   (ii) Enumeration Chapter

After the Classification Chapter under the Dependent Chapter of the Faultless Triplet comes the Enumeration Chapter. It is divided into (*a*) Enumerations " By Ones " (Single) where the numbers of answers are given when the conditions are taken singly and (*b*) Enumerations " By Twos ", " By Threes ", etc., where the numbers of answers are given when the conditions are taken by twos, by threes and so on.

(*a*) In this case of Single Enumerations, the method of obtaining them was illustrated with the examples of root and object conditions. The Text states these as " With root (there are) 9 (answers), with object (there are) 3 (answers) " and so on. The figures can also be obtained by totalling the answers which are given in the Classification Chapter for the single conditions.

(*b*) In the case of the Enumerations " By Twos ", " By Threes ", etc., the enumerations of root, object and the other conditions taken together by twos, by threes, etc., are provided. There are 23 of each of them. Root condition is first dealt with in the " By Twos " and there are 22 of them. Here root condition is taken as the reference with object and each of the other conditions as the variant. An example with root and object conditions taken together, to illustrate the method of determining the enumeration, is worked out below. In this Dependent Chapter the conascent conditioning and conditioned states of the two conditions, which were found out in determining the single enumerations, have to be examined to find out those that are common to them. Then the appropriate states of the common conditioning and conditioned states are selected to arrive at the enumeration.

The conascent conditioning and conditioned states of root and object conditions have been found above and may be referred to. For ready reference Chart I is provided. On comparison of the conditioning states it will be seen that with respect to :—

(1) the mental states, root condition has a lesser number and therefore the mental states of that condition are the common conditioning states,

(2) the material states, only heart-base is common to both.

Thus the common conditioning states of root and object conditions are 71 rooted consciousnesses, 52 mental factors and heart-base.

When the conditioned states are compared it will be seen that with respect to :—

(1) the mental states, root condition has a lesser number and therefore the mental states of that condition are the common conditioned states,

(2) the material states, there is no common state.

Thus the common conditioned states of root and object conditions are 71 rooted consciousnesses and 52 mental factors exclusive of delusion from the two delusion-rooted consciousnesses.

The common conditioning and conditioned states are tabulated below :—

Common conditioning states	Common conditioned states
(1) 71 rooted cons., 52 mental factors.	(1) 71 rooted cons., 52 mental factors excluding delusion from the 2 delusion-rooted cons.
(2) heart-base.	

CHART I
Conascent Conditioning and Conditioned States

Conditions	Conditioning States	Conditioned States
Root	71 rooted cons., 52 m.f. (which are the 4 rooted mental aggregates during life and at the moment of conception), rooted mind-produced great primaries, rooted rebirth kamma-produced great primaries, heart-base (at the moment of conception).	71 rooted cons., 52 m.f. excluding delusion from the 2 delusion-rooted cons. (which are the 4 rooted mental aggs. during life and at the moment of conception), rooted mind-produced matter, rooted rebirth kamma-produced matter.
Object	89 cons., 52 m.f. (which are the 4 mental aggs. during life and at the moment of conception), heart-base at the moment of conception.	89 cons., 52 m.f. (which are the 4 mental aggs. during life and at the moment of conception).
Not-root	2 delusion-rooted cons., 18 rootless cons., 12 m.f. (4 mental aggs. during life and at the moment of conception), rootless mind-produced gr. pr., rootless rebirth kamma-produced gr. pr., external gr. pr., nutriment-produced gr. pr., temperature-produced gr. pr., non-percipient beings' kamma-produced gr. pr., during life kamma-produced gr. pr., heart-base (at the moment of rootless conception).	delusion from the 2 delusion-rooted cons., 18 rootless cons., 12 m.f. (4 mental aggs. during life and at the moment of conception), rootless mind-produced matter, rootless rebirth kamma-produced matter, external matter, nutriment-produced matter, temperature-produced matter, non-percipient beings' kamma-produced matter, during life kamma-produced matter.
Not-object	75 cons. exclusive of 4 immaterial resultants, twice fivefold cons. and Arahatta's death-cons., 52 m.f. (4 mental aggs. during life and at the moment of conception in 5-agg. existences), mind-produced great primaries, rebirth kamma-produced gr. pr., external gr. pr., nutriment-produced gr. pr., temperature-produced gr. pr., non-percipient beings' kamma-produced gr. pr., during life kamma-produced gr. pr.	mind-produced matter, rebirth kamma-produced matter, external matter, nutriment-produced matter, temperature-produced matter, non-percipient beings' kamma-produced matter, during life kamma-produced matter.

When the appropriate states are selected for the answers, it is found that the three answers are (i) (Faultless–Faultless), (ii) (Faulty–Faulty), and (iii) (Indeterminate–Indeterminate). This is why the Text states " With root condition and object (there are) 3 (answers)." Then the states in the answers can be classified and the classified answers obtained although they are not provided in the Text.

With root condition as reference, the common conditioning and conditioned states with the other conditions taking them by twos, by threes, etc., for 22 conditions have to be determined. This has to be done with each of the 23 conditions as reference.

Note.—If repetition condition is the reference and resultant condition is the variant, there is no answer because there are no common states between them. The reverse also applies. This is indicated in the Text as " With repetition condition and resultant nil " and " With resultant condition and repetition nil ". These are given in brackets under Repetition and Resultant respectively. Therefore, with root condition as reference in " By Twelves " up to " By Twenty-Two " where repetition is included, resultant is left out. And in " By thirteens " up to " By Twenty-two " where resultant is included, repetition is left out. So although it was stated that 23 conditions are considered in this Dependent Chapter, only 22 conditions can be dealt with here.

All the enumerations are not included in the Text. Even in the case where the " By Twos " are given, and of which each of the 23 conditions has 22 items, it will be seen that there are many elisions. So the Text, as placed before the Synod, is abbreviated to a great extent. But if the reader knows the conditioning and conditioned states of the conditions in the Single Enumerations and applies the method given above, the elisions can be found out. It will then be observed that one of the reasons for these elisions is that they have the same enumerations. And only when the answers can be worked out to find all the enumerations will Paṭṭhāna be appreciated.

2. Negative Conditions   (i) Classification Chapter

The Negative conditions are dealt with after the Positive conditions. Here also there are two sub-chapters, the Classi-

Introduction xxxiii

fication followed by the Enumeration. Not-root condition is the first negative condition that is considered. This is taken as the example to show how the answers and the classifications of the states in them are determined.

The Method.—The method is similar to that for the Positive conditions. The conditioned states of the Negative conditions have to be taken and the conascent conditioning states have to be found. Then from the appropriate conditioning and conditioned states, the answers are obtained.

Conditioned states of not-root condition. In the first six Chapters the conditioned states of the negative conditions are the non-conditioned states which, as defined, are the remainder of the conditioned states of the positive conditions. In the case of root condition the non-conditioned states are those that remain after the conditioned states of that condition are deducted from the possible conditioned states of the positive conditions. The possible conditioned states and the conditioned states of root condition are as follows:—

Possible conditioned states	Conditioned states of root condition
89 cons. and 52 mental factors which are taken appropriately for each cons.	71 rooted cons. and 52 mental factors which are taken appropriately for each cons. (rooted mentality) but excluding delusion from the 2 delusion-rooted cons.
28 matter of mind-produced matter, rebirth kamma-produced matter, external matter, nutriment-produced matter, temperature-produced matter, non-percipient beings' kamma-produced matter, during life kamma-produced matter.	rooted mind-produced matter. rooted rebirth kamma-produced matter.

Therefore, the non-conditioned states of root condition are—

(1) delusion from the two delusion-rooted consciousnesses,
(2) 18 rootless consciousnesses and the 12 mental factors

which are taken appropriately for each consciousness (rootless mentality),

(3) rootless mind-produced matter,
(4) rootless rebirth kamma-produced matter,
(5) external matter,
(6) nutriment-produced matter,
(7) temperature-produced matter,
(8) non-percipient beings' kamma-produced matter,
(9) during life kamma-produced matter.

These are the conditioned states which are not of root condition, i.e. they are the conditioned states of not-root condition.

Conditioning states of not-root condition. The conditioning states which are conascent with the above conditioned states have to be found out since conascence condition is here considered. They are, respectively:—

(1) two delusion-rooted consciousnesses (faulty),
(2) 18 rootless consciousnesses and the 12 mental factors which are taken appropriately for each consciousness (indeterminate),
(3) rootless mind-produced great primaries (indeterminate),
(4) rootless rebirth kamma-produced great primaries (indeterminate),
(5) external great primaries (indeterminate),
(6) nutriment-produced great primaries (indeterminate),
(7) temperature-produced great primaries (indeterminate),
(8) non-percipient beings' kamma-produced great primaries (indeterminate),
(9) during life kamma-produced great primaries (indeterminate),
(10) heart-base (indeterminate).

The conditioning and conditioned states of not-root condition are tabulated in Chart I.

On examination of the conditioning states, it is found that only the faulty and indeterminate sections can be taken as references since faultless states are not included. By taking the appropriate conascent conditioning and conditioned states to get the answers, it will be found that only 2 are possible

(i) (Faulty–Faulty) and (ii) (Indeterminate–Indeterminate). This is why it is stated in the Text as :—

" Dependent on faulty state, arises faulty state by not-root condition. "

This is classified as :—

" Dependent on doubt-accompanied or restlessness-accompanied aggregates (which are the two delusion-rooted consciousnesses and their associated mental factors), arises doubt-accompanied or restlessness-accompanied delusion." The Text may be referred to for the rest.

Another example with not-object condition. The conditioned states of object condition are 89 consciousnesses and the 52 mental factors taken appropriately for each consciousness. The non-conditioned states of object condition are those that remain out of the possible conditioned states of the positive conditions which are given above. They are the seven kinds of matter (i.e. all materiality). The conascent conditioning states are, therefore, 75 consciousnesses (the four immaterial resultant consciousnesses, the twice fivefold consciousnesses and the Arahatta's death-consciousness are excluded as they either do not produce materiality or arise together with materiality) and the 52 mental factors taken appropriately for each consciousness and also the great primaries of the seven kinds of matter. These conditioning and conditioned states of not-object condition are tabulated in Chart I. With them there are five answers (i) (Faultless–Indeterminate), (ii) (Faulty–Indeterminate), (iii) (Indeterminate–Indeterminate), (iv) (Faultless, Indeterminate–Indeterminate), and (v) (Faulty, Indeterminate–Indeterminate). The classified answers are given in the Text.

The rest of the 20 conditions are also dealt with in the Classification Chapter.

Why only 20 conditions are involved. In the Positive conditions, the conditioned states of each of the four conditions, conascence, dependence, presence and non-disappearance are 89 consciousnesses and the 52 mental factors taken appropriately for each consciousness and 28 matter of the seven kinds of matter, i.e. all the possible conditioned states of the positive conditions. Thus there are no non-conditioned states of these conditions. In other words, there are no conditioned states of not-conascence, not-dependence, not-presence and not-non-disappearance. So these four negative conditions out of the 24 are not included here. It should be noted that Nibbāna, the only other ultimate reality, is unconditioned and is therefore not taken into account in the first six Chapters.

2. Negative Conditions   (ii) Enumeration Chapter

This Enumeration Chapter is also divided into (a) Single Enumerations or Enumerations " By Ones " and (b) Enumerations " By Twos ", " By Threes ", etc.

(a) The 20 conditions are dealt with starting with not-root condition and then not-object condition, etc., in serial order. The method of obtaining them was illustrated with the examples of not-root and not-object conditions. The Text states these as " With not-root (there are) 2 (answers), with not-object (there are) 5 (answers) " and so on. As in the case of the Positive conditions, the figures can also be obtained by totalling the answers which are given in the Classification Chapter for the single conditions.

(b) Next comes the enumerations " By Twos ", " By Threes ", etc., totalling 19 for each of the 20 conditions. It starts with " By Twos " of not-root condition and there are 19 items. Here not-root condition is taken as the reference with not-object and the other negative conditions as the variant. An example with not-root and not-object conditions taken together, to illustrate the method of determining the enumeration, is worked out below.

The Method. The method is similar to that for the " By Twos " of the Positive conditions illustrated above. The conascent conditioning and conditioned states of the negative conditions, which were found in determining the single enumerations, have to be examined to find out those that are common to them. Then the appropriate states of the common conditioning and conditioned states are selected to arrive at the enumeration.

Illustration of the Method. The conascent conditioning and conditioned states of not-root and not-object conditions have been found from the examples worked out above and these are tabulated in Chart I. On comparison, it will be found that the

Introduction xxxvii

common conditioning and conditioned states of these two negative conditions are:—

Common conditioning states	Common conditioned states
(1) 8 rootless cons. (i.e. excluding twice fivefold cons. from the 18 rootless cons.) and 12 assoc. m.f.	
(2) rootless mind-produced great primaries.	(1) rootless mind-produced matter.
(3) rootless rebirth kamma-produced great primaries.	(2) rootless rebirth kamma-produced matter.
(4) external great primaries.	(3) external matter.
(5) nutriment-produced great primaries.	(4) nutriment-produced matter.
(6) temperature-produced great primaries.	(5) temperature-produced matter.
(7) non-percipient beings' kamma-produced great primaries.	(6) non-percipient beings' kamma-produced matter.
(8) during life kamma-produced great primaries.	(7) during life kamma-produced matter.

It will be seen that the states are rootless mentality and materiality, all indeterminate states, and therefore, there is only one answer (Indeterminate–Indeterminate). The answer for the Classification Chapter, not given in the Text, is :—

" Dependent on indeterminate state, arises indeterminate state by not-root and not-object conditions.

Dependent on rootless resultant indeterminate or rootless functional indeterminate aggregates, arises rootless mind-produced matter;

At the moment of rootless conception, dependent on resultant indeterminate aggregates, arises kamma-produced matter ;

Dependent on one great primary, arise three great primaries ; dependent on three great primaries, arises one great primary ; dependent on two great primaries, arise two great primaries ; dependent on great primaries, arise mind-produced and kamma-produced derived matter . . . " (the rest being the same as not-object condition).

3. Positive-Negative Conditions (ii) Enumeration Chapter

The Positive-Negative conditions are dealt with after the Negative conditions. In the Positive and Negative conditions above, both the reference and variant were positive and negative respectively. Here the reference is positive and the variant is negative. The 23 conditions (postnascence condition being excluded for the reason given above) are taken " By Twos ", " By Threes ", etc., and so there are 22 of them. It starts with " By Twos " with root condition as reference and there are 15 items. The first is " root condition, not-object ". This will be taken as the example to illustrate the method of determining the enumeration.

The Method. " Root condition, not-object " means that the conditioning and conditioned states are those of root condition but are not of object condition. These states can be found by :—

(1) Taking the conascent conditioning and conditioned states of root and object conditions and deducting those of object condition from root condition or

(2) Taking the conascent conditioning and conditioned states of root and not-object conditions and finding out (*a*) those of not-object condition in root-condition or (*b*) those of root condition in not-object condition. In either case, the common conascent conditioning and conditioned states of root and not-object conditions have to be found.

Once the conditioning and conditioned states of root and not-object conditions are obtained, then the appropriate states are selected to arrive at the enumeration.

Illustration of the Method. The conascent conditioning and conditioned states of root and not-object conditions are tabulated in Chart I. On examination of the conditioning states it will be seen that with respect to :—

(1) the mental states, the analytical units are as follows :—

For root condition	For not-object condition
71 rooted cons., 52 m.f. comprising	75 cons. (exclusive of 4 immaterial resultants, twice fivefold cons. and Arahatta's death-cons.), 52 m.f. comprising
21 faultless cons., 38 assoc. m.f.	21 faultless cons., 38 assoc. m.f.
12 faulty cons., 27 assoc. m.f.	12 faulty cons., 27 assoc. m.f.
	5 rootless cons. (exclusive of twice fivefold cons.), 12 assoc. m.f.
21 rooted resultant cons., 38 assoc. m.f.	17 rooted resultant cons. (exclusive of 4 immaterial resultants and Arahatta's death-cons.), 38 assoc. m.f.
17 rooted functional cons., 35 assoc. m.f.	20 functional cons., 35 assoc. m.f. (i.e. 17 rooted + 3 rootless).

Introduction

From them the common mental states can be found.

(2) the material states, the common states are rooted mind-produced great primaries and rooted rebirth kamma-produced great primaries.

When the conditioned states are examined, it will be seen that with respect to :—

(1) the mental states, there are no common states

(2) the material states, the common states are rooted mind-produced matter and rooted rebirth kamma-produced matter.

Thus the common conditioning and conditioned states of root and not-object conditions as tabulated are as follows :—

Common conditioning states	Common conditioned states
(1) 21 faultless cons., 38 assoc. m.f. (2) 12 faulty cons., 27 assoc. m.f. (3) 17 rooted resultant indeterminate cons. (exclusive of 4 immaterial resultants and Arahatta's death-cons.), 38 assoc. m.f. (4) 17 rooted functional indeterminate cons., 35 assoc. m.f. (5) rooted mind-produced great primaries. (6) rooted rebirth kamma-produced great primaries.	(1) rooted mind-produced matter. (2) rooted rebirth kamma-produced matter.

When the appropriate states are selected to determine the number of answers, i.e. the enumeration, it is found that :—

1. Faultless states (1) on the L.H.S. and rooted mind-produced matter (1) on the R.H.S. are conascent and so there is the answer (i) (Faultless–Indeterminate).

2. Faulty states (2) on the L.H.S. and rooted mind-produced matter (1) on the R.H.S. are conascent and the answer is (ii) (Faulty–Indeterminate).

3. Indeterminate states (3) and (4) on the L.H.S. and rooted mind-produced matter (1) on the R.H.S. are conascent and the answer is (iii) (Indeterminate–Indeterminate).

4. At the moment of conception, rooted rebirth resultant states (included in (3) on the L.H.S.) and rooted rebirth kamma-produced matter (2) on the R.H.S. are conascent and the same answer (iii) (Indeterminate–Indeterminate) is obtained.

5. Great primaries (5) and (6) on the L.H.S. and great primaries and derived matter (1) and (2) on the R.H.S. are respectively conascent and there is the same answer (iii) (Indeterminate–Indeterminate).

6. Faultless states (1) and great primaries (5) on the L.H.S. and great primaries and derived matter (1) on the R.H.S. are conascent and the answer is (iv) (Faultless, Indeterminate–Indeterminate).

7. Taking Faulty states (2) instead of Faultless states in the above the answer is (v) (Faulty, Indeterminate–Indeterminate).

These are the five answers possible and the enumeration is 5. The Text states this as " With root condition, not-object (there are) 5 (answers)." There is no Classification Chapter but the classified answers can be obtained from the above conditioning and conditioned states that were selected to get the answers.

All the enumerations of " By Twos ", " By Threes " and so on up to " By Twenty-Threes " are not given in the Text. The elisions can be found out, however, by application of the method to the conditioning and conditioned states of the conditions concerned.

4. Negative-Positive Conditions   (ii) Enumeration Chapter

Finally, the Negative-Positive conditions are considered in this Dependent Chapter. Here the reference is negative and the variant is positive. As in the case of the Negative conditions, only 20 conditions are involved as reference since, as pointed out before, there are no conditioned states of not-conascence, not-dependence, not-presence and not-non-disappearance conditions. The 20 conditions are taken " By Twos ", " By Threes " and so on up to " By Twenty-ones " and so there are 20 of them. It starts with " By Twos " with not-root condition as reference and there are 21 items. The first is " not-root condition, object ". This will be taken as the example to illustrate the method of determining the enumeration.

The Method. " Not-root condition, object " means that the conditioning and conditioned states are those of object condition but are not of root condition. These states can be found

Introduction

out by taking the common conascent conditioning and conditioned states of not-root and object conditions as shown in the Positive-Negative conditions above. Then the appropriate states are selected to arrive at the enumeration.

Illustration of the Method. The conascent conditioning and conditioned states of not-root and object conditions as found are tabulated in Chart I. On examination it will be seen that with respect to :—

(1) the mental states, not-root condition has the lesser number of conditioning and conditioned states and the common states are those of this condition.

(2) the material states, heart-base is the common conditioning state and there is no common conditioned state.

The common conditioning and conditioned states of not-root and object conditions are therefore :—

Common conditioning states	Common conditioned states
(1) 2 delusion-rooted cons.	(1) delusion from the 2 delusion-rooted cons.
(2) 18 rootless cons., 12 assoc. m.f.	(2) 18 rootless cons., 12 assoc. m.f.
(3) heart-base.	

These are the states of not-root condition in the Negative conditions except that the seven kinds of matter are excluded. And as briefly explained there, only two answers are possible, i.e. (i) (Faulty–Faulty) and (ii) (Indeterminate–Indeterminate).

The same method is applied for the rest of the " By Twos " and also for the " By Threes ", " By Fours ", etc., to determine the enumerations. There is no Classification Chapter but the classified answers can be obtained from the common conditioning and conditioned states that had been selected to find the answers.

Summary of Dependent Chapter. Conascence condition, which is considered in this Chapter, must be thoroughly understood and the conditioning and conditioned states of this condition must first be known. Then the conditioning states which are conascent with the conditioned states of each of the 23 positive conditions and each of the 20 negative conditions have to be found. It is from these conascent conditioning and conditioned states that the answers are obtained. In the case of the conditions taken " By Ones ", all that is necessary is to select the appropriate ones of each condition to get the answers to the 49 questions on each of them. But in the cases where the conditions are taken together as " By Twos ", " By Threes ", etc., with the positive, negative, positive-negative and negative-positive conditions, the conascent conditioning and conditioned states of each of the conditions concerned are compared to find those that are common to them. From the common conditioning and conditioned states the answers are obtained in the same way as above. The number of answers possible for each set of 49 questions is the enumeration which is given in the Enumeration Chapter. The answers and the classifications of the states in those answers form the Classification Chapter.

II. 'CONASCENT' CHAPTER

The Conascent Chapter comes after the Dependent Chapter. The contents of these two Chapters are the same although the words " Conascent with " are substituted for " Dependent on ". This is why there are so many elisions in the Text.

Why the same things are repeated. It is to show that they are interchangeable. When it is stated that " Dependent on sensitive eye and visible object arises eye-consciousness " it does not mean that these states are conascent. And, although derived matter arises together with the great primaries, the former is not conascent with the latter. Here, however, it is to be understood that whatever is said to be dependent is also conascent and vice versa.

Other reasons. (1) It is for the benefit of the audience because The Buddha knew that there are those who will gain deliverance when expounded as dependent and others as conascent. (2) To embellish the Teaching. (3) To show His knowledge of philological analysis (Commentary p. 426).

III. 'CONDITIONED' CHAPTER

The Conditioned Chapter is next dealt with. It is treated in a similar manner to the above Chapters.

The Difference from the Previous Chapters. Here dependence condition, in place of conascence condition, is considered. There are two kinds of dependence condition, namely : (1) conascence-dependence (which is the same as conascence condition dealt with in the above chapters) and (2) base-prenascence-dependence. The relations given for dependence and conascence conditions in the Analytical Exposition may be compared.

The Conditioning and Conditioned States of Dependence Condition. As explained above, these will consist of those for conascence condition given in the Dependent Chapter and those for base-prenascence-dependence condition which are as follows :—

Conditioning states	Conditioned states
(1) eye-base.	(1) eye-cons. element and 7 assoc. m.f.
(2) ear-base.	(2) ear-cons. element and 7 assoc. m.f.
(3) nose-base.	(3) nose-cons. element and 7 assoc. m.f.
(4) tongue-base.	(4) tongue-cons. element and 7 assoc. m.f.
(5) body-base.	(5) body-cons. element and 7 assoc. m.f.
(6) heart-base.	(6) mind-element and mind-cons. element and 52 assoc. m.f. taken appropriately.

The Method. The method of determining the answers, the classifications of the states in the answers and the enumerations is illustrated with the example of root condition. Here the conditioned states of root condition which are also those of dependence condition are first taken. Then the conditioning states on which those conditioned states are dependent are found. As two kinds of dependence condition are involved they will be treated separately to find the conditioning and conditioned states of root condition.

Conascence-dependence. Since this is the same as conascence condition the conditioning and conditioned states of root condition found in the Dependent Chapter are to be taken. So the nine answers and classified answers that were obtained there also apply here.

Base-prenascence-dependence. The 71 rooted consciousnesses and the 52 mental factors excluding delusion from the two delusion-rooted consciousnesses, which are the conditioned states of root condition, are also those of base-prenascence-dependence condition, as they come under mind-consciousness element which is a conditioned state of that condition. The conditioning state, as shown in the table above, is heart-base. It must be noted that heart-base is also a conditioning state of root condition in conascence-dependence above, but there it is applicable only at the moment of conception. Here it is applicable during life as well. Therefore, under the answer (vii) (Indeterminate–Indeterminate) of the nine answers above, another classified answer must be added for heart-base during life. This is given in the Text as :—

" Conditioned by heart-base, arise resultant indeterminate or functional indeterminate aggregates ".

The answers. It will be observed that the conditioning and conditioned states of root condition for this Conditioned Chapter are the same as the Dependent Chapter where they have been tabulated and to which reference must be made. As pointed out above, heart-base during life has to be included. The answers will be taken according to the order of the 49 questions.

1. The first seven answers given for root condition in the Dependent Chapter are in the proper order.

2. Then with heart-base on the L.H.S. and faultless states on the R.H.S. (base-prenascence-dependence) there is the answer (viii) (Indeterminate–Faultless).

(3) When the faulty states are taken for the faultless in the above another answer (ix) (Indeterminate–Faulty) is obtained.

(4) Again, with heart-base and great primaries on the L.H.S. and faultless states and mind-produced matter on the R.H.S. there is the answer (x) (Indeterminate–Faultless, Indeterminate). (Here heart-base with faultless states is base-prenascence-dependence and great primaries with mind-produced matter is conascence-dependence.)

(5) When the faulty states are taken for the faultless in the above another answer (xi) (Indeterminate–Faulty, Indeterminate) is obtained.

(6) Also, with faultless states and heart-base on the L.H.S. and faultless states on the R.H.S. the answer is (xii) (Faultless, Indeterminate–Faultless). (Here faultless with faultless is conascence-dependence and heart-base with faultless is base-prenascence-dependence.)

(7) Then with faultless states and great primaries on the L.H.S. and mind-produced matter on the R.H.S. there is the answer (xiii) (Faultless, Indeterminate–Indeterminate) as given in the Dependent Chapter.

(8) By taking together the states on the L.H.S. in the answers (xii) and (xiii) and also those on the R.H.S. there is the answer (xiv) (Faultless, Indeterminate–Faultless, Indeterminate).

(9) By substituting faulty states for the faultless in (xii), (xiii) and (xiv) above, there are three answers (xv) (Faulty, Indeterminate–Faulty), (xvi) (Faulty, Indeterminate–Indeterminate), and (xvii) (Faulty, Indeterminate–Faulty, Indeterminate).

Thus there are 17 answers for root condition and the enumeration, therefore, is 17. The Text states this as " With root (there are) 17 (answers) ". The classified answers can be obtained from the states involved in the answers and they are given in the Text.

The Classification and Enumeration Chapters. These are provided as in the Dependent Chapter. It will be seen, however, that when the five bases are the conditioning states and the twice fivefold consciousnesses are the conditioned states, the following classified answer has to be inserted under the answer (Indeterminate–Indeterminate) :—

" Conditioned by eye-base, arises eye-consciousness . . . conditioned by body-base, arises body-consciousness." As for the remaining base, heart-base, the classified answers have been shown above.

Summary of Conditioned Chapter. As in the case of Dependent Chapter the conditioning and conditioned states of the conditions have to be found. This time the states are those of dependence condition. Then selection of the states are made to get the answers, the classifications of the states and the enumerations.

IV. 'Supported' Chapter

The contents of Supported Chapter are the same as the Conditioned Chapter which precedes it. But in accordance with its title, the words " Supported by " are employed instead.

V. 'Conjoined' Chapter

Next in order is the Conjoined Chapter. It is also treated similarly as the previous chapters. Here the conditioning and conditioned states of association condition are considered. These are :—

Conditioning states	Conditioned states
89 cons. and 52 m.f. taken appropriately.	89 cons. and 52 m.f. taken appropriately.

The above are all mental states and, therefore, in this chapter materiality is not included. As in the previous chapters, 23 conditions are involved in the Positive conditions, but the conditioning and conditioned states are all mentality. Also, in the Negative conditions, only those conditions that have mentality as their conditioned states are applicable. There are 10 of them, namely: not-root, not-predominance, not-prenascence, not-postnascence, not-repetition, not-kamma, not-resultant, not-jhāna, not-path and not-dissociation. In the case of the other Negative conditions such as not-object, since the conditioned states are all materiality, there are no mental states which can be taken as conditioned states that are also those of association condition.

The Method. The method of determining the answers, the classifications of the states in those answers and the enumerations is similar to that in the previous chapters. Root condition is taken as the example. The conditioned states of root condition which are also those of association condition have to be taken. These are 71 rooted consciousnesses and 52 mental factors excluding delusion from the two delusion-rooted consciousnesses. The conditioning states associated with them are 71 rooted consciousnesses and 52 mental factors. Thus the conditioning and conditioned states of root condition are those in the Dependent Chapter with all materiality excluded. On examination of these mental states, it will be found that there are only three answers (i) (Faultless–Faultless) where faultless states on the L.H.S. are associated with faultless states on the

R.H.S. and likewise, (ii) (Faulty–Faulty) and (iii) (Indeterminate–Indeterminate). In this Chapter of the Faultless Triplet it will be observed that the enumeration is never more than three. This is always the case where only mental states are involved. The states in the answers are then classified in the usual way.

VI. 'Associated' Chapter

This is the last of the six chapters which are treated in similar ways. The contents are the same as the Conjoined Chapter although the word " associated " is used in the place of ' conjoined '.

Summary of the Six Chapters

The method of treatment of the six Chapters is the same. The subject-matter, however, is different. In the Dependent and Conascent Chapters the conditioning and conditioned states are those of conascence condition ; in the Conditioned and Supported Chapters those of dependence condition and in the Conjoined and Associated Chapters those of association condition. So for each positive and negative condition which is applicable, the conditioning and conditioned states which are conascent, dependent or associated, as required for the Chapter, are found as in the examples worked out. Then those states that are faultless, faulty and indeterminate (the three sections of the Faultless Triplet) are taken to find out the answers for the Classification Chapters and the enumerations for the Enumeration Chapters. Where the conditions are taken " By Twos ", " By Threes ", etc., the answers for the Classification Chapters (which are not given in the Text) and the enumerations for the Enumeration Chapters are obtained in the same way from the conditioning and conditioned states which are common to each of the conditions concerned.

It will be seen from the above, that a thorough knowledge of the conditioning and conditioned states of each of the conditions is necessary for the proper understanding of the six Chapters. This is the reason for giving the method to show how the conditioning and conditioned states of the conditions for the six Chapters are determined and how, based on them, the answers for the Classification Chapters are obtained. So the Classification Chapter for the condition gives its conditioning and conditioned states.

VII. 'INVESTIGATION' CHAPTER

The Investigation Chapter is the last chapter of the Faultless Triplet. As in the previous six Chapters, the conditions are dealt with according to the four methods, i.e. Positive, Negative, Positive-Negative and Negative-Positive. There are no questions for this chapter but from the answers it can be deduced that they would be on the following lines:—

" May faultless state be related to faultless state by root condition ? "
and that the order of the questions is the same as that in the Question Chapter. As for the answers there is a Classification Chapter for the Positive conditions only. This gives the conditioning and conditioned states of the 24 conditions which, when expanded, make up 56. They are tabulated in Charts II (B)–(H)[1] where the conditions are arranged in groups according to kind. The rest of the Chapter consists of Enumeration Chapters.

The Differences from the Previous Chapters

1. In the previous chapters the conditioned states are given prominence by showing how they arise. The answers given there, for instance, are " Dependent on (or Supported by or Associated with) faultless state, arises faultless state by root condition ". But here the conditioning states are given prominence by showing how they bring about the conditioned states. An example of such answers is " Faultless state is related to faultless state by root condition ".

2. The enumerations are given in a different way from the previous chapters in the Positive and Positive-Negative conditions. The reasons for this will be given when they are dealt with.

[1] At end of Intr.

1. Positive Conditions (i) Classification Chapter

The Classification Chapter gives the relations between the states due to root condition and the rest of the 24 conditions. In the case of root condition, there are three sections (1) Faultless, (2) Faulty, and (3) Indeterminate.

With (1) Faultless section as reference, the three answers with respect to it are : (i) (Faultless–Faultless), (ii) (Faultless–Indeterminate), and (iii) (Faultless–Faultless, Indeterminate). The first answer is given in the Text as :—

" Faultless state is related to faultless state by root condition ".

The faultless states are then classified and given under this as :—

" Faultless roots are related to (their) associated aggregates by root condition ".

With (2) Faulty section as reference, there are three similar answers: (iv) (Faulty–Faulty), (v) (Faulty–Indeterminate), and (vi) (Faulty–Faulty, Indeterminate).

With (3) Indeterminate section as reference, there is only one answer : (vii) (Indeterminate–Indeterminate). (The Text may be referred to for all the answers and the classifications of the states in them.)

Therefore, for the set of 49 questions with root condition, there are 7 answers, i.e. the enumeration is 7. The Text states this in the Enumeration Chapter under " By Ones " as " With root " (there are) 7 (answers). There can be neither more nor less than 7 answers and proof of this is given below.

The Method of Determining the Answers in the Classification Chapter

Root condition is taken as the example. The relation for this condition in the Analytical Exposition is as follows :

" Roots are related to the states associated with roots, and the matter produced thereby, by root condition." Therefore, the conditioning and conditioned states of root condition are :—

Conditioning states	Conditioned states
6 roots comprising non-greed, non-hate, non-delusion which are either faultless, resultant indeterminate or functional indeterminate. greed, hate, delusion which are faulty.	(1) 71 rooted cons., 52 m.f. excluding delusion from the 2 delusion-rooted cons. comprising 21 faultless cons., 38 m.f. 12 faulty cons., 27 m.f. 21 rooted resultant indeterminate cons., 38 m.f. 17 rooted functional indeterminate cons., 35 m.f. (the above are the states associated with roots). (2) rooted mind-produced matter. (3) rooted rebirth kamma-produced matter (the above (2) and (3) are the matter produced thereby).

Of the six roots, three are faultless, three are faulty and three are indeterminate. So, for these roots as the conditioning states, there are only three sections, faultless, faulty and indeterminate which can be taken as references. Their relations with the conditioned states must now be considered. Since root condition belongs to the conascence group of conditions, the conditioned states to be taken must be those that are related to the conditioning states by conascence condition. On examination of the table it is seen that :—

1. With the Faultless section as reference, the faultless roots (the conditioning states) are related to

(a) 21 faultless consciousnesses and the 38 associated mental factors, i.e. their associated aggregates (the conditioned states), and there is the answer (i) (Faultless–Faultless) ;

(b) mind-produced matter (indeterminate) and the answer is (ii) (Faultless–Indeterminate) ;

(c) their associated aggregates and mind-produced matter (i.e. (a) and (b) combined) and the answer is (iii) (Faultless–Faultless, Indeterminate).

2. Similarly with the Faulty section as reference, where the faulty roots are taken and 12 faulty consciousnesses and the 27 associated mental factors are their associated aggregates, the

answers are (iv) (Faulty–Faulty), (v) (Faulty–Indeterminate), and (vi) (Faulty–Faulty, Indeterminate).

3. With the Indeterminate section as reference, the resultant indeterminate roots are related to 21 rooted resultant indeterminate consciousnesses and the 38 associated mental factors, i.e. their associated aggregates, and mind-produced matter. Also, the functional indeterminate roots are related to 17 rooted functional indeterminate consciousnesses and the 35 associated mental factors, i.e. their associated aggregates, and mind-produced matter. Since they are all indeterminate states, the answer is (vii) (Indeterminate–Indeterminate).

Again, at the moment of conception, the resultant indeterminate roots are related to 17 rooted resultant indeterminate consciousnesses and the 35 associated mental factors, i.e. their associated aggregates, and rebirth kamma-produced matter. The same answer (vii) (Indeterminate–Indeterminate) is obtained.

No other relations are possible between the conditioning and conditioned states and, therefore, no other answers are possible. Thus there can only be seven answers as stated above.

1. Positive Conditions   (ii) Enumeration Chapter

This is divided into (1) Single Enumerations and (2) Mixed Enumerations. The Single Enumerations of the 24 conditions starting with root condition are given. They are also compiled in Charts II (B)–(H). Mixed Enumerations are of two kinds, namely: (i) Common and (ii) Combination. All the 24 conditions are dealt with under them.

COMMON

The Classification Chapter above shows how cause is related to its effect by the force of one condition only such as root or object and so on. But here it shows how they are related by the forces of two conditions. In the previous six Chapters when the causes and effects of the conditions taken together " By Twos ", " By Threes ", etc., up to " By Twenty-threes " were considered, the relations between them were those of one condition which was either conascence, dependence or association. And the commons were determined by selecting the common conditioning and conditioned states of the separate conditions concerned.

In this Investigation Chapter, however, the commons are determined by selecting the common conditioning and conditioned states of those conditions which belong to the same group. The conditions grouped according to kind such as the object group of which there are eight, conascence group of which there are 15 and so on are given in Chart II (A).

Root condition is first dealt with. It is taken as reference and the 11 conditions which are common with it such as predominance, conascence, etc., are each taken as the variant. The method of determining the commons of the conditions and obtaining the enumerations from them is illustrated with the example of root and predominance conditions.

Illustration of the Method. As stated above, the commons are determined by finding out the conditioning and conditioned states which are common to the conditions of the same group. In the case of root condition it belongs to the conascence group. Therefore, when the common states of root and predominance conditions are determined, only those kinds of predominance condition that belong to the conascence group need to be considered. Now, there are two kinds of predominance condition, namely: object-predominance and conascence-predominance. Of the two, object-predominance belongs to the object group and conascence-predominance to the conascence group. So the common conditioning and conditioned states of root and conascence-predominance conditions have to be found. [Please see the Minor conascence group in Chart II (C).]

On examination of the conditioning states of these two conditions, it will be seen that non-delusion of the six roots is of the same nature as investigating-wisdom predominance of the four predominant factors. Thus these two states are the conditioning states. Their conditioned states are as follows:—

Conditioning states	Conditioned states
(1) non-delusion.	47 three-rooted cons., 38 assoc. m.f., rooted mind-produced matter, rooted rebirth kamma-produced matter.
(2) investigating-wisdom predominance.	34 predominant three-rooted impulsions, 37 assoc. m.f. exclusive of wisdom, predominant mind-produced matter.

CHART II (A)

GROUPED CONDITIONS (PACCAYA SAMUHO)

(Conditions Grouped according to Kind)

Cds	Ob group	Cn group	Px-S.D.	Na S.D.	Ba-prn group	Pon group	S.W. Asy-kam group	Phy-nu group	Phy-fa group	Mixed Cn-prn group	Mixed Pon-nu group	Mixed Pon-fa group
Ro		Ro 7										
Ob	*Ob 9											
Pd	Ob- 7	Cn- 7										
Px			*Px 7									
Ct			*Ct 7									
Cn		*Cn 9										
Mu		Mu 3										
Dp	Ba-ob-prn-3	*Cn- 9			*,,-3					*,, 2		
S.D.	Ob- 7		*Px- 7	Na 9								
Prn	Ob- 3				*,, 3							
Pon						*,, 3						
Rp		Rp 3										
Kam		Cn- 7	Px- 1	Asy 2				*,, 2				
Rs		Rs 1										
Nu		Cn- 7						*,, 1				
Fa		Cn- 7			,,-1				*,, 1			
Jh		Jh 7										
Pa		Pa 7										
Ass		Ass 3										
Dss	Ba-ob-prn-3	Cn- 3			*,,-3	*,,-3						
Ps	Ob-prn- 3	*Cn- 9			*,,-3	*,,-3		*,, 1	*,, 1	*,, 2	*,, 2	*,, 2
Ab			*Ab 7									
Dsp			*Dsp 7									
N.D.	Ob-prn- 3	*Cn- 9			*,,-3	*,,-3		*,, 1	*,, 1	*,, 2	*,, 2	*,, 2
56	8	15	7	2	6	4	1	3	3	3	2	2

Since (2) has the lesser number of conditioned states, the common conditioning and conditioned states are those of (2). So the relation to be taken to find the answers is " Investigating-wisdom predominance is related to its associated aggregates and predominant mind-produced matter by root and predominance conditions ". There are four answers, (i) (Faultless–Faultless), (ii) (Faultless–Indeterminate), (iii) (Faultless–Faultless, Indeterminate), and (iv) (Indeterminate–Indeterminate).

How 4 answers are obtained. Root condition has seven answers as found in the example worked out above. But since investigating-wisdom predominance is not concerned with faulty states, the three answers for them in root condition are excluded thus leaving four answers. The Text states this as " With root condition and predominance (there are) 4 (answers) ". The classified answers for them can be obtained in the usual way and can be verified with the ones appropriate to them in the Classification Chapter on predominance condition.

The rest of the commons. The commons for these are determined in a similar way as the above. Only when this method of determining the commons is fully grasped will the extremely difficult Enumeration Chapters that follow be understood.

Combination

Combination. The relations between causes and effects deal not only with two conditions, as in the case of the commons above, but also with three, four, etc., right up to 11 conditions taken together. This is known as combination and it consists of three kinds, namely :—

(1) *Mixed Combination.* Here the conditions of the conascence group are always included along with those of the other groups such as object, base-prenascence and so on;

(2) *Miscellaneous Combination.* Here the conditions of the conascence group are excluded and those of the object group, proximity group, etc., are taken.

(3) *Conascent Combination.* This deals only with the conditions of the conascence group.

Brief Explanation. Root condition belongs to the conascence group and so it comes under conascent combination. Object condition belongs to the object group and so it comes under miscellaneous combination. Predominance condition, however, is of two kinds: object-predominance and conascence-predominance. When both are taken together it comes under mixed combination ; if only object-predominance is taken, it comes under miscellaneous combination ; if only conascence-predominance is taken, it comes under conascent combination. This is how all the conditions are to be taken under these combinations.

Root condition under Conascent Combination—24 *answers.* Since root condition belongs to the conascence group, it comes under conascent combination. This is divided into (1) ordinary combinations—nine answers, (2) with faculty and path —nine answers, and (3) with predominance, faculty and path— six answers, giving a total of 24 answers.

There is nothing extraordinary about these combinations for they are derived from the commons dealt with above. So if the commons are understood there will be no difficulty about the combinations.

An Example. The first of the nine answers of the ordinary conascent combination is " Combination of root, conascence, dependence, presence and non-disappearance (has) 7 (answers) ". This combination has come from the commons where it is given as " With root condition and conascence 7, dependence 7, presence 7, non-disappearance 7 ". Here there are four separate items with root condition as reference and each of the other conditions as the variant for, in the commons, only two conditions are taken together. In combination, however, since the four conditions above are common with root condition, they are all taken together for the combination of five conditions as given above.

The second of the nine answers is " Combination of root, conascence, mutuality, dependence, presence and non-disappearance 3 ". Here root condition is common with mutuality which is given as " With root condition and mutuality 3 ". Since they belong to the conascence group the four conditions, conascence, dependence, presence and non-disappearance, of the Major conascence group are always included in conascent combination.

Object and the Other Conditions. The combinations with object and each of the other conditions as reference are given. There are altogether 415 answers under combination. It must be admitted that these combinations are difficult to understand and even in Burma, in the past, there were very few who could fully grasp this portion. But after the translator had explained them with the aid of his charts, it is now being easily learnt.

SELECTION OF THE CONDITIONS FOR NEGATIVE

In the Negative conditions of Dependent Chapter and the rest of the six Chapters the answers such as " Dependent on faulty state, arises faulty state by not-root condition " and so forth are given and the states classified. But in the Negative conditions of this Investigation Chapter only the numbers of answers such as " With not-root (condition there are) 15 (answers) " and so on are mentioned. So it is very difficult to know what these answers are and how they are obtained. In fact, this is one of the most difficult portions of Paṭṭhāna. Therefore, in order to overcome this difficulty, the Synod authorities provided the selection of conditions in order to understand the Negative conditions. But in the marble inscriptions made after the Fifth Synod, many errors were found by the translator and corrected at the Sixth Synod.

How the Conditions are Selected. Chart III (A) gives the total enumerations for each group of conditions. This has been obtained by totalling the enumerations given for the conditions of each group in the Single Enumerations of Charts II (B)–(H). From Chart III (A) it will be seen that the maximum enumeration is 15. This consists of four for the faultless section, four for the faulty section, three for the indeterminate section, two for the faultless, indeterminate section and two for the faulty, indeterminate section. The groups and the answers have to be taken in the order given there. By reading down the answer column (faultless–faultless) it will be observed that it is obtained with object, conascence and strong-dependence conditions. When the chart is read off in this manner it will be found to be in conformity with the Text.

Explanation. When it is stated that " Faultless state is related to faultless state by object condition, conascence condition, strong-dependence condition " it is a very brief statement of the facts. From the Chart it will be understood that the groups of object, conascence and strong-dependence conditions are to be taken and not just the single conditions. Also, this information is not sufficient for it would mean that

Introduction

CHART III (A)

SELECTION OF THE CONDITIONS FOR NEGATIVE
(Total Enumerations of Each Group of Conditions)

Groups of Conditions	Fls Fls	Fty ,,	Ind ,,	Fls-Ind Fty	Fty ,,	Fls ,,	Ind ,,	Fty-Ind Ind	Ind ,,	Fty ,,	Fls Fls-Ind	Ind ,,	Fty Fty-Ind	Ind ,,	Enumerations
Object	,,	,,	,,		,,	,,	,,		,,	,,	,,				9
Conascence [1]	,,		,,	,,	,,		,,		,,	,,		,,		,,	9
Strong-dependence	,,	,,	,,		,,	,,	,,		,,	,,	,,				9
Prenascence [1]									,,	,,	,,				3
Postnascence [2]		,,							,,	,,					3
S.W. Asynchronous Kamma		,,							,,						2
Physical nutriment [3]									,,						1
Physical life faculty [4]									,,						1
Mixed Conascence-Prenascence												,,		,,	2
Postnascence-nutriment												,,		,,	2
Postnascence-faculty												,,		,,	2

[1] For not-conascence and not-prenascence conditions, mixed conascence-prenascence is excluded.
[2] For not-postnascence, mixed postnascence-nutriment and mixed postnascence-faculty are excluded.
[3] For not-nutriment, mixed postnascence-nutriment is excluded but mixed postnascence-faculty is included.
[4] For not-faculty, mixed postnascence-faculty is excluded but mixed postnascence-nutriment is included.

all the conditions of each of these three groups are applicable. But this isn't so. There are exceptions which can be found out with the help of Chart III (B).[1] This summarizes the Single Enumerations of Chart II giving the different kinds of enumerations for the conditions of the same group and taking together those conditions which have the same enumerations.

For this example where the relation between faultless states (i.e. faultless–faultless) is the answer, the conditions which give this answer can be found from the Chart. It will be observed that in the case of—

1. object condition, out of eight in the group there are only three, namely: object, object-predominance, and object-strong-dependence;

2. conascence condition, out of 15 in the group there are 13,

[1] Next page

CHART III (B)

Selection of the Conditions for Negative (DETAILED)

Conditions 56		Groups-11	Faultless section = 4				Faulty section = 4				Indeterminate = 3			Fls-Ind = 2		Fty-Ind = 2		Enumerations
			Fls	Fty	Ind	Fls-Ind	Fty	Fls	Ind	Fty-Ind	Ind	Fls	Fty	Fls	Ind	Fty	Ind	
Ob.	1	Object 8	,,	,,	,,		,,	,,	,,		,,	,,	,,					9
Ob-pd, Ob-S.D.	2		,,	,,	,,		,,				,,	,,	,,					7
Ob-prn, Ba-Ob-prn...*	5										,,	,,	,,					3
Minor Con [1]	7	Conascence 15	,,		,,	,,	,,		,,	,,	,,							7
Major Con [2]	4		,,		,,	,,	,,		,,	,,	,,				,,		,,	9
Mu, Ass	2		,,				,,				,,							3
Rs	1										,,							1
Con-dss	1			,,				,,			,,							3
Px...*	5	Px-S.D. Strong dependence 9	,,		,,		,,		,,		,,	,,	,,					7
Rp	1		,,				,,				,,							3
Px-kam	1				,,													1
Na S.D.	1	Na S.D.	,,	,,	,,		,,	,,	,,		,,	,,	,,					9
Strong Asy kam	1				,,				,,									2
Ba-prn...*	5	Prenascence 6									,,	,,	,,					3
Ba-prn-fa	1										,,							1
Pon...*	4	Pon 4		,,				,,			,,							3
S.W. Asyn kam	1	Kam 1		,,				,,										2
Phy-nu...*	3	Nu 3									,,							1
Phy-life-fa...*	3	Faculty 3									,,							1
Mixed-Cn-prn...*	3	Cn-prn 3												,,		,,		2
Mixed-pon-nu...*	2	Pon-nu 2													,,		,,	2
Mixed-pon-fa...*	2	Pon-fa 2													,,		,,	2

* Please refer to Chart II (A) for the other conditions.
[1] Please refer to Chart II (C) for the conditions.
[2] Please refer to Chart II (E) for the conditions.

the remaining two, resultant and conascence-dissociation, being excluded ;

3. strong-dependence condition, there are seven in all. These are six of the proximity-strong-dependence kind, namely : proximity, contiguity, proximity-strong-dependence, absence, disappearance and repetition, and one of the natural strong-dependence kind, i.e. natural strong-dependence. So 23 conditions out of the 56 expanded conditions give this answer.

The conditions which give the different answers can be found out in a similar way. This information is essential for finding out how the answers for the Negative conditions are obtained.

2. Negative Conditions   (ii) Enumeration Chapter

As mentioned above, there is no Classification Chapter. The Enumeration Chapter begins with the Single Enumerations and then " By Twos ", " By Threes ", etc. All the 24 conditions are dealt with starting with not-root condition of the Single Enumerations.

Method of Exposition. The Text simply states " With not-root (condition there are) 15 (answers) " and so on for the other negative conditions taken " By Ones ". These enumerations do not convey much. The reader would want to know what these answers are and how they are obtained.

The Method of Finding the Answers

Not-root condition is taken as the example. " Not-root " means all the other conditions excepting root condition. The first thing to do is to find out the group to which root condition belongs. It belongs only to the conascence group. Therefore there is no need to consider the other groups of conditions as the enumerations for them, given in Chart III (A), are to be taken unchanged. As for the conascence group, root condition must be excluded from the conditions of that group. Why is this done ? As an analogy, take the case when 1 is deducted from 16 to leave 15. Everyone knows this but very few would be able to give a satisfactory answer as to why 15 is left. The reason is that in the 16 there is one which is common with 1. And when this common 1 is deducted, 15 is left. So here, also, the common root condition has to be deducted. For in the conascence group of conditions, the root condition there is common with the root condition under consideration. And when this common root condition is deducted, the remaining conditions of the conascence group are ' not-root ' conditions.

The Extraordinary Characteristic of the Enumerations of Paṭṭhāna. In the example given above where the common 1 is excluded from 16, 15 is left. Ordinarily this is so. But in the enumerations of Paṭṭhāna when the common is excluded, the enumerations are not reduced accordingly. For instance, there are nine answers for conascence condition and seven for root condition. Ordinarily, when 7 is deducted from 9, 2 is left. But this does not apply here. It is surprising to find that actually 9 is left. For although in these enumerations figures are dealt with, the deduction is not made between them to leave the remainder in figures but only between the states. And it is from the remaining states that the enumerations are obtained.

Example. When root condition is to be excluded from conascence condition, it is the conditioning and conditioned states of root condition given in Chart II (C) that have to be excluded from those of conascence condition given in Chart II (E). The remaining conditioning and conditioned states are, therefore :—

	Conditioning states	Conditioned states
(a)	4 mental aggregates exclusive of 6 roots during life and at the moment of conception.	4 mental aggregates exclusive of 6 roots during life and at the moment of conception (mutually), mind-produced matter, rebirth kamma-produced matter.
(b)	4 great primaries (each of mind-produced, rebirth kamma-produced, external, nutriment-produced, temperature-produced, non-percipient beings' kamma-produced and during life kamma-produced matter).	(Corresponding) 4 great primaries (mutually) and derived matter.
(c)	4 mental aggregates exclusive of 3 rebirth roots, and heart-base at the moment of conception in 5-aggregate existences.	4 mental aggregates exclusive of 3 rebirth roots, and heart-base at the moment of conception in 5-aggregate existences (mutually).

Introduction lxi

When the answers are determined with these states, the enumeration still remains 9, the same as conascence condition, although the common root condition with enumeration 7 has been deducted. Of course, the classifications of the states in the answers will be slightly different.

How 15 Answers are obtained with 'not-root'. For not-root condition all the conditions of the object group and the other groups except root condition have to be taken. The number of answers is found by totalling the enumerations given for each of those groups in Chart III (A), taking them in the order given there. These are:—

(1) object group of conditions—9,
(2) conascence group of conditions from which root condition is excluded—9 (this was worked out above),
(3) strong-dependence group of conditions—9,
(4) prenascence group of conditions—3,
(5) postnascence group of conditions—3,
(6) strong and weak asynchronous kamma group (one condition)—2,
(7) physical nutriment group of conditions—1,
(8) physical faculty group of conditions—1,
(9) mixed conascence-prenascence group of conditions—2,
(10) mixed postnascence-nutriment group of conditions—2,
(11) mixed postnascence-faculty group of conditions—2.

When the different kinds of enumerations are taken, the total is 15. The Text states this as " With not-root (condition there are) 15 (answers) ". The answers are (faultless–faultless) and so on, the 15 that are given in the columns of the Chart.

The Classified Answers. Next, the states in the 15 answers have to be classified as in the Classification Chapter where the conditions, as expanded, are taken in the order which is the same as the horizontal order of the conditions in Chart II (A). Out of the 167 classified answers in that Chapter, the seven for root condition are excluded and so there are 160 such answers for not-root condition. Again, in those answers, the classified states (i.e. the conditioning and conditioned states) of root condition are excluded, wherever they are found, in those of the conditions of the conascent group.

An Example. Take the case of the answer (faultless–faultless). By looking down this column of Chart III (B) the conditions in the various groups which give this answer can be read off. They are 3 of the object group, 13 of the conascence group and 7 of the strong-dependence group. But, as mentioned above, the conditions must be taken in the order of the Classification Chapter. On reference to Chart II (A) the order is found to be object, predominance, proximity, contiguity, conascence, mutuality, conascence-dependence, natural strong-dependence, repetition, conascence-kamma, conascence-nutriment, conascence-faculty, jhāna, path, association, conascence-presence, absence, disappearance, conascence-non-disappearance. Root condition of the minor conascence group is excluded as not-root conditions are dealt with. There are altogether 19 conditions. So for the answer " Faultless state is related to faultless state by not-root condition ", the classified answers for the 19 conditions given in the Classification Chapter for this (faultless–faultless) relation have to be taken. But, as pointed out above, the classified states of root condition are to be excluded wherever they are found in the conditions of the conascence group. Therefore, in conascence-predominance, investigating-wisdom predominance which is of the same nature as the root, non-delusion, is excluded ; in conascence, mutuality, dependence, association, conascence-presence and conascence-non-disappearance, the three faultless roots are excluded ; in faculty and path, knowledge which is of the same nature as the root, non-delusion, is excluded. The classified answers start with those for object condition as given in item 404 of the Text, i.e. After having offered the offering, having undertaken the precept, having fulfilled the duty of observance, (one) reviews it and so on.

Similarly, classified answers have to be found for each of the other answers (faultless–faulty), etc.

All this is certainly very expansive, complicated, deep and abstruse. But if the method, given briefly above, is applied these enumerations will not only be understood, but the elisions can also be expanded and proper judgment made as to their correctness or otherwise.

"By Twos", "By Threes", etc.

In the case of " By Twos " it starts with not-root condition as reference and each of the other 23 negative conditions as the variant. So there are 23 such items. The first is " With not-root condition and not-object (condition there are) 15 (answers) ". Here, for not-root condition, root condition is excluded from the conascence group as explained above. And for not-object condition, all the conditions of the object-group are excluded. When the answers for the rest of the grouped conditions are totalled, in the way shown above, it comes to 15. This is the same method for " By Threes " and the rest.

The Rule of the Negative Conditions. The example of not-root condition shows that the causes, which are related to the effects, are not of root condition but of object and other conditions. And in the case of not-root and not-object conditions it shows that the causes are not of root and object conditions but of other conditions.

3. Positive-Negative Conditions   (ii) Enumeration Chapter

The Positive-Negative conditions come next. Here also each of the 24 conditions is taken as reference. The enumerations are divided into (1) " By Twos " and (2) Combination. In the case of " By Twos " it starts with root condition as reference and not-object, not-predominance, etc., as the variants. There are only 19 items since the four conditions, conascence, dependence, presence and non-disappearance conditions, are excluded. For when a state is root condition it cannot be not-conascence, not-dependence, not-presence or not-non-disappearance condition.

" By Twos "

Here the states which are root condition but not object, or not predominance, etc., are dealt with.

Root but Not-object Condition. First of all it has to be determined whether the two conditions are common or not. As mentioned earlier, in this Investigation Chapter, the commons are determined by selecting the common conditioning and conditioned states of those conditions which belong to the same group. Since root condition belongs to the conascence group and object condition to the object group, they belong to different groups and so the two conditions are not common. In all such cases, the condition, like object condition in this example, which is not common with the reference condition is taken as zero. And just as zero deducted from seven leaves seven, so also object condition as zero deducted from root condition leaves root condition, i.e. the conditioning and conditioned states of root condition, the enumeration for which is 7 as already worked out. This is why the Text states "With root condition, not-object (condition) 7", the seven answers being those of root condition.

The Classified Answers. The seven answers are then classified. For the first answer " Faultless state is related to faultless state by root condition but not object condition ", the classified answer is " Faultless roots are related to (their) associated aggregates by root condition but not object condition ". Except for the additional words " but not object condition ", all the classified answers are the same as for root condition given as items 401–403 in the Text. It has to be noted that in all these enumeration chapters the conditioning and conditioned states have to be first determined in order to be able to classify the states in the answers.

Root but Not-predominance and so on. The method is the same as above. In the case of not-predominance, investigating-wisdom predominance of conascence-predominance condition must be excluded as it is common with non-delusion of root condition. Only then will the states which are root condition but not-predominance condition be obtained.

Combination

The combinations are dealt with after " By Twos ". These are the same as in the Positive conditions.

Ordinary Combination. For the first combination the relation is " Six roots are related to their associated aggregates, rooted mind-produced matter and rooted rebirth kamma-produced-matter ". All these conditioning and conditioned

states are those of root, conascence, dependence, presence, and non-disappearance conditions but not of object, predominance, proximity . . . disappearance conditions. Therefore, the combinations of these five conditions as reference with the variants are taken in the following way: " Combinations of root, conascence, dependence, presence and non-disappearance conditions, not-object (condition) 7, not-predominance 7 . . . not-disappearance 7 ". Here the states dealt with are those that belong to the five conditions but not to the remaining 19 conditions. In the case of the latter conditions, however, for those that are common with the five conditions such as predominance and others, the states that are common have to be excluded. As for those which are not common such as object condition and others, since they are taken as zero, the states are the same as those for the five conditions.

The Rule of the Positive-Negative Conditions. As its name implies, it shows that the causes, which are related to the effects, are those of root condition and so on but not of object condition and so on.

4. Negative-Positive Conditions (ii) Enumeration Chapter

The Negative-Positive conditions are finally considered. All the 24 negative conditions are dealt with. It starts with " By Twos " and ends with " By Twenty-twos " and so there are 21 of them.

" By Twos "

Not-root but Object Condition. Here all the " By Twos " dealt with in the Positive-Negative conditions are included, the only difference being that they are treated in the reverse order. For instance, the states which are object condition but not root were dealt with there, whereas the states which are not root condition but object are dealt with here.

" By Threes "

The states which are not root and not object conditions but predominance condition is an example in this case. There are two kinds of predominance condition, namely: object-predominance and conascence-predominance. Since the states which are not root condition have to be taken, investigating-wisdom predominance (of conascence-predominance), which belongs to root condition, has to be excluded and only the other three predominant factors are taken. Again, since the states are also not object condition, object-predominance, which is part of object condition, has to be excluded. Therefore, the conditioning and conditioned states of investigating-wisdom predominance and object-predominance have to be excluded from those of predominance condition. This gives the relation " One of the predominant factors, desire, effort and consciousness, is related to its associated aggregates and predominant mind-produced matter by not-root and not-object conditions but predominance condition ". From this the enumeration 7 and the classified answers are obtained. The Text only states " With not-root and not-object conditions, predominance 7 ". The same method is employed to determine the enumerations and classified answers of the rest of the Negative-Positive conditions.

The Rule of the Negative-Positive Conditions. This is the reverse of the Positive-Negative conditions. Here it shows that the causes, which are related to the effects, are those which are not root but object condition, not-root and not-object but predominance condition and so on.

Question. Why is it that (1) commons (i.e. " By Twos ") and combinations and (2) " By Twos " and combinations are dealt with for the Positive and Positive-Negative conditions respectively and " By Twos ", By " Threes ", etc., for the Negative and Negative-Positive conditions ?

Answer. There is no need to consider the " By Twos " as this is given for all the conditions under the four methods. As for the combinations, there are no common states of root and object conditions since they belong to different groups and so these two conditions cannot be taken together. Therefore, it is necessary to select and combine only those conditions of the same group which have common states. So combinations of conditions have to be taken with the Positive and Positive-Negative conditions, With the Negative and Negative-Positive conditions, the states which are not root and not object conditions; not root, not object and not predominance conditions

Introduction lxvii

and so on and the states which are not root, not object but predominance condition; not root, not object, not predominance but proximity condition and so on are respectively considered. In these cases the appropriate conditions and the states which are found to be common are excluded. So the conditions can be taken together consecutively in their serial order such as " By Twos ", " By Threes ", " By Fours ", etc.

All that has been dealt with above come under the Faultless Triplet of the Positive Method Division and is just one of the 129,232 sections of Paṭṭhāna.

2. FEELING TRIPLET

In Paṭṭhāna the Triplets and Couplets of the Dhammasaṅganī, which are mentioned at the beginning of this Introduction, are treated in the same serial order as given there. Therefore, the Feeling Triplet is considered after the Faultless Triplet. This Triplet also consists of the Dependent Chapter and the rest of the seven Chapters as in the Faultless Triplet and are dealt with in the same sequence. As a matter of fact this is the procedure throughout the Paṭṭhāna.

States of the Feeling Triplet. The states of each of the three sections of the Feeling Triplet are:—

Sections	States
(i) States associated with pleasant feeling.	(i) 63 cons. accompanied by pleasure and 46 assoc. m.f. exclusive of feeling, hate, envy, stinginess, worry, and doubt.
(ii) States associated with painful feeling.	(ii) 3 cons. accompanied by pain and 21 assoc. m.f. exclusive of feeling, rapture, greed, wrong view, conceit, and doubt.
(iii) States associated with neither painful nor pleasant feeling.	(iii) 55 cons. accompanied by indifference and 46 assoc. m.f. exclusive of feeling, rapture, hate, envy, stinginess, and worry.

Note.—Materiality, Nibbāna and feeling are not included in this Triplet and in this case they are Triplet-freed, i.e. they are neither conditioning nor conditioned states in this Triplet. As materiality is not included, prenascence, postnascence and dissociation conditions, which have only material states as the conditioning or conditioned states, are not taken into account. So the Dependent Chapter alone serves for the whole of the six Chapters. The reason is that, since mental states only are involved, the conditioning and conditioned states of the conditions are the same for each of the six Chapters. Although prenascence and dissociation conditions are included in these Chapters, the purpose is to determine the conditioning and conditioned states of conascence, dependence and association conditions involved in their respective Chapters.

Enumeration and Analytical Exposition of the Conditions. These are given only for the Faultless Triplet but each serves as a model for application to the whole of Paṭṭhāna. In the Feeling Triplet, the three conditions mentioned above are excluded from the list in the Enumeration of Conditions. For the Analytical Exposition, all material states are left out in the relations for the conditions. For example, for root condition it is " The roots are related to the states which are associated with roots by root condition ".

Dependent Chapter

Classification Chapter. An example of the answers is :—

" (*i*) Dependent on state associated with pleasant feeling, arises state associated with pleasant feeling by root condition.
- (*a*) Dependent on one aggregate associated with pleasant feeling, arise two aggregates ; dependent on two aggregates, arises one aggregate ;
- (*b*) At the moment of conception, dependent on one aggregate associated with pleasant feeling, arise two aggregates ; dependent on two aggregates, arises one aggregate."

It will be observed that only three (mental) aggregates are involved as feeling, the other aggregate, is excluded.

The rest of the six Chapters are just referred to since they are the same as Dependent Chapter. This is also the case with the other five Triplets—Rapture, Limited Object, Path Object, Past Object, Internal Object—which have no material states. The analytical states of the Triplets and Couplets are given in the Discourse on Elements. And it is from these states that the conditioning and conditioned states are selected for the Chapters concerned.

Single Enumerations. The conditioning and conditioned

Introduction

states of each of the 21 conditions of this Triplet are found in the way shown in the Faultless Triplet for determining the single enumerations.

The Other Enumerations. For the enumerations " By Twos ", " By Threes ", etc., of the Positive, Negative, Positive-Negative and Negative-Positive conditions, the common conditioning and conditioned states have to be found to arrive at the enumerations as in the case of the Faultless Triplet.

Investigation Chapter

Classification Chapter. Based upon the method given in the Faultless Triplet, the conditioning and conditioned states of the 21 conditions are to be determined.

Enumeration Chapters. The enumerations for the single conditions and the commons can be determined by applying the methods given in the Faultless Triplet. As regards the combinations, since mental states only are involved in this Triplet, there are no mixed combinations; conditions with material states only are not included in miscellaneous combinations and there are few conascent combinations. For the latter, root condition has six whereas in the Faultless Triplet there are 24.

The selection of the conditions for Negative is given in full, but only a few of the enumerations for the Negative, Positive-Negative and Negative-Positive conditions.

3. RESULTANT TRIPLET

States of the Resultant Triplet. The states of each of the three sections of the Resultant Triplet are :—

Sections	States
(i) Resultant states.	(i) 36 resultant indeterminate cons. and 38 assoc. m.f.
(ii) States producing resultant states.	(ii) 12 faulty cons., 21 faultless cons. and 52 assoc. m.f.
(iii) States which are neither resultant nor producing resultant states.	(iii) 20 functional indeterminate cons., 35 assoc. m.f., 28 matter and Nibbāna.

The Six Chapters

Although the Classification Chapters of the six Chapters are given somewhat in detail, the Enumeration Chapters are very brief.

Investigation Chapter

The Classification Chapter is given in full but as regards the Enumeration Chapter only the Single Enumerations and the commons with root condition are provided. The combinations are not given at all.

The Other Enumerations. The selection of the conditions for Negative is complete but, as is generally the case, there are many elisions in the Enumerations for the Negative, Positive-Negative and Negative-Positive conditions.

4. CLINGING TRIPLET

States of the Clinging Triplet. The states of each of the three sections of the Clinging Triplet are:—

Sections	States
(i) States acquired by clinging and favourable to clinging.	(i) 32 mundane resultant indeterminate cons., 35 assoc. m.f. and 20 kamma-produced matter.
(ii) States not acquired by clinging but favourable to clinging.	(ii) 12 faulty cons., 17 mundane faultless cons., 20 functional indeterminate cons., 52 assoc. m.f., 17 mind-produced matter, 15 temperature-produced matter and 14 nutriment-produced matter.
(iii) States not acquired by clinging and not favourable to clinging.	(iii) 8 supramundane cons., 36 assoc. m.f. and Nibbāna.

5. CORRUPT TRIPLET

States of the Corrupt Triplet. The states of each of the three sections of the Corrupt Triplet are :—

Sections	States
(i) Corrupt and corrupting states.	(i) 12 faulty cons. and 27 assoc. m.f.
(ii) Not corrupt but corrupting states.	(ii) 17 mundane faultless cons., 32 mundane resultant cons., 20 functional cons., 38 assoc. m.f. and 28 matter.
(iii) Not corrupt and not corrupting states.	(iii) 8 supramundane cons., 36 assoc. m.f. and Nibbāna.

Introduction lxxi

The five Triplets given above comprise the subject matter of Volume I now translated. No doubt the reader will find it dull and uninteresting as he goes through the bare statements of facts and figures. This is why some idea of the methods by which they are arrived at is given in this Introduction. But to have a proper understanding of Paṭṭhāna and be able to work out the answers by oneself and also fill in the many elisions, the methods must be known in greater detail. For this purpose it will be necessary to issue a guide to Paṭṭhāna where all the methods in the Faultless Triplet and their applications will be given. This suffices for the rest of Paṭṭhāna as the same techniques are employed.

The remaining 17 Triplets, like the Clinging and Corrupt Triplets of Volume I, are treated very briefly in Volume II. There are numerous elisions and most of the combinations are left out. The translator, by applying the methods of the Faultless Triplet, has expanded all the elisions and given all the combinations in the Triplets and Couplets in a Burmese Text on the methods and explanations of Paṭṭhāna.

General Method of the Triplet Paṭṭhāna. The states of the sections of the 22 Triplets have to be known. Then the appropriate states are taken as conditioning and conditioned states to find out the number of answers for each condition of the Chapter concerned, i.e. the Single Enumerations. Next, the states in those answers are (1) classified for the Classification Chapter for the single conditions and (2) used to find the other answers for the conditions taken " By Twos ", " By Threes ", etc., for the rest of the Enumeration Chapter. The states in the latter answers are also classified for the Classification Chapters which are never given in the Text. Finally, with the information so obtained, the contents of the Classification and Enumeration Chapters for the Negative, Positive-Negative and Negative-Positive conditions of the seven Chapters in each Triplet can be worked out as shown with the Faultless Triplet.

The Remaining 23 Paṭṭhānas

The Triplet Paṭṭhāna (22 Triplets) of the Positive Method Division, the first of the six Paṭṭhānas in this Division, is dealt with in the first two volumes as mentioned above. The remaining 23 Paṭṭhānas are divided in the following way in the next three volumes :

Volume III. Couplet Paṭṭhāna of the Positive Method Division (up to Clinging Clusters, i.e. 74 couplets).

Volume IV. The rest of the Couplet Paṭṭhāna (the other 26 couplets) ; Couplet–Triplet and Triplet–Couplet Paṭṭhānas of the same Division.

Volume V. Triplet–Triplet and Couplet–Couplet Paṭṭhānas of the same Division ; the remaining 18 Paṭṭhānas consisting of the same six Paṭṭhānas each of the Negative, Positive–Negative and Negative–Positive Method Divisions.

The six Paṭṭhānas of the Positive Method Division cover 2,260 pages in the sixth Synod edition but the 18 Paṭṭhānas of the remaining three Divisions cover only 426 pages. This shows the extent to which the 18 Paṭṭhānas were condensed at the Synod recitation. However, they can be expanded in the way shown in the Positive Method Division by applying the methods given there for the Triplets and Couplets.

As this translation deals only with the first volume of Paṭṭhāna, the opportunity is now taken to give the reader a general idea of the whole subject. Hence, the contents of the remaining 23 Paṭṭhānas in the last three volumes will be touched upon. Owing to the limitations of space in an Introduction, the examples will be confined to root condition of the Dependent Chapter with the first of each Paṭṭhāna.

POSITIVE METHOD DIVISION

2. Couplet Paṭṭhāna

All the 100 couplets are dealt with in the Couplet Paṭṭhāna. They are divided under 13 heads, such as root cluster, lesser intermediate couplets and others. The root cluster comes first and consists of six couplets beginning with " states which are roots " followed by " states which have associated roots " and others. The Couplet Paṭṭhāna starts with the first root couplet, i.e. root states (states which are roots) and not-root states (states which are not roots) under the seven Chapters as in the

Faultless Triplet and also begins with the Dependent Chapter. In each of these Chapters there are three sections, (i) root, (ii) not-root, and (iii) root, not-root, as references and the same three sub-sections as variants. So there are only nine questions, three for each of the three sections with the three sub-sections and the order is as follows :

(1) With root section as reference and the three subsections, the three questions are :

Dependent on root state, may there arise root (not-root, root and not-root) state by root condition ?

(2) With not-root section as reference and the three subsections :

Dependent on not-root state, may there arise not-root (root, root and not-root) state by root condition ?

(3) With root, not-root section as reference and the three subsections :

Dependent on root and not-root states, may there arise root (not-root, root and not-root) state by root condition ?

This applies to all the Couplet, Couplet–Triplet and Couplet–Couplet Paṭṭhānas. With the Triplet, Triplet–Couplet and Triplet–Triplet Paṭṭhānas there are 49 questions as in the Faultless Triplet.

Classification Chapter. An example is :

" Dependent on root state, arises root state by root condition.

Dependent on non-greed, arise non-hate and non-delusion ; dependent on non-hate, arise non-greed and non-delusion ; dependent on non-delusion, arise non-greed and non-hate ;

Dependent on greed, arises delusion ; dependent on delusion, arises greed ; dependent on hate, arises delusion ; dependent on delusion, arises hate ;

At the moment of conception, dependent on non-greed, arise non-hate and non-delusion. . . . " (Synod Text, Vol. III., p. 1.)

There are 9 answers, i.e. all the questions have answers.

How the 9 answers are obtained. In the root couplet,

(1) the root states are the six roots and

(2) the not-root states are 89 consciousnesses, 46 mental

factors (the six roots having been excluded), 28 matter and Nibbāna.

When the answers are worked out as shown in the Faultless Triplet, they are found to be (i) 1–1, (ii) 1–2, (iii) 1–1, 2, (iv) 2–2, (v) 2–1, (vi) 2–1, 2, (vii) 1, 2–1, (viii) 1, 2–2, and (ix) 1, 2–1, 2.

The Six Chapters. Unlike the Faultless Triplet, all the six Chapters are not given. There is a Classification Chapter for Dependent Chapter and then the Text directs that Conascent and the rest of the Six Chapters are to be treated similarly. In the Enumeration Chapters only those for root condition are given.

Investigation Chapter. The Classification Chapter is given in full but only the Single Enumerations in the Enumeration Chapter that follows. The selection of the conditions for Negative is complete. With regard to the other Enumeration Chapters, only the Single Enumerations of the Negative conditions and the enumerations " By Twos " with root condition of the Positive–Negative and Negative–Positive conditions are provided.

All the other couplets are treated briefly like root couplet.

General Method of the Couplet Paṭṭhāna. The states of the sections of the Couplets have to be known. These are to be found in the Discourse on Elements. Then, by applying the method given in the Faultless Triplet, the Classification and Enumeration Chapters under the seven Chapters for each couplet, together with the commons and combinations, can be worked out. In this way the Couplet Paṭṭhāna, given very briefly in the Text, can be known completely.

3. Couplet–Triplet Paṭṭhāna

Here each of the 100 couplets is taken as reference with each section of each of the 22 Triplets as variants.

An Example with Root Couplet. The first couplet is " root states " and " not-root states ". This is taken as reference with the faultless section of the faultless triplet. So when root states are taken with faultless states, they are (1) root-faultless states. And when not-root states are taken with faultless states, they are (2) not-root–faultless states. These two form the root couplet-faultless Paṭṭhāna. Therefore, similar to the couplets above, there are three sections, (i) root-faultless, (ii) not-root–faultless, and (iii) root-faultless, not-root–faultless and the same three sub-sections.

The Analytical Units. In this root couplet-faultless Paṭṭhāna, the analytical units for :

(1) root-faultless states are : three faultless roots
(2) not-root–faultless states are : 21 faultless consciousnesses and 35 associated mental factors exclusive of the three faultless roots.

Dependent Chapter. When the appropriate states are taken for root condition under Dependent Chapter, which deals with conascence condition, 9 answers are obtained, i.e. (i) 1–1, (ii) 1–2, (iii) 1–1, 2, (iv) 2–2, (v) 2–1, (vi) 2–1, 2, (vii) 1, 2–1, (viii) 1, 2–2, and (ix) 1, 2–1, 2. (1 = root-faultless ; 2 = not-root–faultless.)

The answers are given but not the classified answers (i.e. the states in the answers are not classified) that usually come after the answers in the Classification Chapters. The full answers with root-faultless as reference are :

(i) Dependent on root-faultless state, arises root-faultless state by root condition. (This is the answer in the Text.)

Dependent on non-greed, arise non-hate and non-delusion ; dependent on non-hate, arise non-greed and non-delusion ; dependent on non-delusion, arise non-greed and non-hate.

(ii) Dependent on root-faultless state, arises not-root–faultless state by root condition. (This is the answer in the Text.)

Dependent on root-faultless state, arise associated aggregates.

(iii) Dependent on root-faultless state, arise root-faultless and not-root–faultless states by root condition. (This is the answer in the Text.)

Dependent on non-greed, arise non-hate, non-delusion and associated aggregates ; dependent on non-hate, arise non-greed, non-delusion and associated aggregates ; dependent on non-delusion, arise non-greed, non-hate and associated aggregates. (Synod Text, IV, p. 195 without the classified answers.)

Similarly, root couplet is taken as reference with the faulty and indeterminate sections of the faultless triplet. Since each of the 100 couplets has to be taken as reference with each of the three sections of the 22 triplets, there are 100 × 3 × 22 = 6,600 sections of the Couplet–Triplet Paṭṭhāna, each with its own seven Chapters.

The classified answers are not generally given but only the Single Enumerations. The translator has worked out all the analytical states including those not given in the Text and all the enumerations of this Couplet–Triplet Paṭṭhāna.

Method of the Couplet–Triplet Paṭṭhāna. The states of the couplet–triplet sections have to be known. Then the appropriate states are selected for the Chapters concerned. This is the general method and will not be mentioned again.

The Difficulty of Paṭṭhāna. From this Paṭṭhāna onwards, the direct answers, without the classified answers, are generally given for root condition only and just the Single Enumerations. This is another reason why Paṭṭhāna is difficult.

4. Triplet–Couplet Paṭṭhāna

Here each of the 22 triplets is taken as reference with each section of the couplets as variants.

An example with Faultless Triplet. The three sections of the faultless triplet are each taken with root states of the root couplet. So there are :

(1) faultless-root states, i.e. the three faultless roots
(2) faulty-root states, i.e. the three faulty roots
(3) indeterminate-root states, i.e. the three indeterminate roots.

These are the three sections to be taken as references with the same three sub-sections.

Dependent Chapter. When the appropriate states are taken for root condition under Dependent Chapter, three answers are obtained, i.e. (i) 1–1, (ii) 2–2, and (iii) 3–3. (1 = faultless-root, 2 = faulty-root and 3 = indeterminate-root). The answers are stated without classifying the states in them. The answers, as usually given in the Classification Chapters, are :

(i) Dependent on faultless-root state, arises faultless-root state by root condition.

Dependent on non-greed, arise non-hate and non-delusion ;

dependent on non-hate, arise non-greed and non-delusion ; dependent on non-delusion, arise non-greed and non-hate.

(ii) Dependent on faulty-root state, arises faulty-root state by root condition.

Dependent on greed, arises delusion ; dependent on delusion, arises greed ; dependent on hate, arises delusion ; dependent on delusion, arises hate.

(iii) Dependent on indeterminate-root state, arises indeterminate-root state by root condition.

(a) The classified answer is the same as (i) above.
(b) At the moment of conception . . . (the same as (i) above).
   (Synod IV, p. 468—the classified answers are not given.)

Here also there are many elisions, only the answers and a few single enumerations being given. They should be expanded as usual for $22 \times 2 \times 100 = 4{,}400$ sections of this Paṭṭhāna.

5. Triplet–Triplet Paṭṭhāna

Here each of the 22 triplets is taken as reference with each section of the other triplets as variants.

An Example with Faultless Triplet. The three sections of the faultless triplet are each taken with the states associated with pleasant feeling, the first section of the feeling triplet. So there are :

(1) faultless states associated with pleasant feeling,
(2) faulty states associated with pleasant feeling,
(3) indeterminate states associated with pleasant feeling.

These are the three sections to be taken as references with the same three sub-sections.

The Analytical Units. The analytical units of the above states are found as follows :

(1) Since the states are faultless and associated with pleasant feeling, out of the 37 faultless consciousnesses as expanded, only those with pleasant feeling have to be taken. They are :

(a) 4 of the 8 great consciousnesses,
(b) 4 of the 9 lofty consciousnesses,
(c) 16 of the 20 Path-consciousnesses,

i.e. a total of 24 faultless consciousnesses. The mental factors associated with them are 37 exclusive of feeling.

(2) Since the states are faulty and associated with pleasant feeling, out of the 12 faulty consciousnesses, those with pleasant feeling are : 4 of the 8 greed-rooted consciousnesses. The mental factors associated with them are 21 exclusive of feeling.

(3) Since the states are indeterminate and associated with pleasant feeling, out of the 72 indeterminate consciousnesses, those with pleasant feeling are :

(a) 3 of the 18 rootless consciousnesses. These are (i) body-consciousness accompanied by pleasure, (ii) investigating-consciousness accompanied by pleasant feeling, and (iii) smile-consciousness of the Arahat,
(b) 8 of the 16 great consciousnesses (four each of resultant and functional),
(c) 8 of the 18 lofty consciousnesses (four each of resultant and functional),
(d) 16 of the 20 Fruition-consciousnesses,

i.e. a total of 35 indeterminate consciousnesses. The mental factors associated with them are 37 exclusive of feeling.

Note.—In the study of Abhidhamma it is very essential to know the analytical units. This is why The Buddha, on expounding the Abhidhamma, gave them in detail at the beginning of the Dhammasaṅganī. Again, in the Commentarial Chapter of that Text, the analytical units of the Triplets and Couplets, also dealt with in Paṭṭhāna, are given in full. So if there be doubts as to what these units are in the study of Paṭṭhāna, reference must be made to that Chapter as directed in Expositor II, p. 519 : " For the special doctrine which does not come in the three Piṭakas, being defined and determined by the Commentarial Chapter, becomes well determined. It behoves the Abhidhamma student who cannot note the method of procedure in the entire Abhidhamma Piṭaka, the framing of queries, and the numerical series in the Great Book (Paṭṭhāna) to compare or bring them together from the Commentarial Chapter only. "

Dependent Chapter. When the appropriate states are taken for root condition under Dependent Chapter, three answers are obtained, i.e. (i) 1–1, (ii) 2–2, and (iii) 3–3. (1 = faultless state associated with pleasant feeling, 2 = faulty state associated with pleasant feeling, 3 = indeterminate state associated with pleasant feeling.)

Then, from the analytical units, the classified answers are found. And when they are not given in the Text, they can be included with the answers for the Classification Chapters. For example, the analytical units found above are consciousnesses and mental factors which, when classified under the aggregates for Dependent Chapter, are the three mental aggregates, the other aggregate, feeling, being excluded. So the answers for the Classification Chapter with the three answers above are :

(i) Dependent on faultless state associated with pleasant feeling, arises faultless state associated with pleasant feeling by root condition.

Dependent on one faultless aggregate associated with pleasant feeling, arise two aggregates ; dependent on two aggregates, arises one aggregate.

(ii) Dependent on faulty state associated with pleasant feeling, arises faulty state associated with pleasant feeling by root condition.

Dependent on one faulty aggregate associated with pleasant feelinn, arise two . . . (as above).

(iii) Dependent on indeterminate state associated with pleasant feeling, arises indeterminate state associated with pleasant feeling by root condition.

Dependent on one resultant indeterminate or functional indeterminate aggregate associated with pleasant feeling, arise two . . .

At the moment of conception, dependent on one resultant indeterminate aggregate associated with pleasant feeling, arise two . . . . (Synod V, p. 1—the classified answers are not given.)

Similarly, faultless triplet is taken as reference with each of the other two sections of the Feeling Triplet as variants. There are altogether $22 \times 3 \times 21 = 1,386$ sections of this Paṭṭhāna.

6. Couplet–Couplet Paṭṭhāna

Here each of the 100 couplets is taken as reference with each section of the other couplets as variants.

An Example with Root Couplet. The two sections of the root couplet are each taken with the states which have associated roots, the first section of the next couplet. So there are :

(1) states which are roots and associated with roots,
(2) states which are not roots but associated with roots.

Therefore, as with the Couplet Paṭṭhāna, there are three sections, (i) 1, (ii) 2, and (iii) 1, 2 and the same three sub-sections.

The Analytical Units. The analytical units for :

(1) are the six roots excluding delusion from the two delusion-rooted consciousnesses,
(2) are the 71 rooted consciousnesses and 46 mental factors exclusive of the six roots.

Dependent Chapter. When the appropriate states are taken for root condition under Dependent Chapter, 9 answers are obtained, i.e. (i) 1–1, (ii) 1–2, (iii) 1–1, 2, (iv) 2–2, (v) 2–1, (vi) 2–1, 2, (vii) 1, 2–1, (viii) 1, 2–2, and (ix) 1, 2–1, 2, as in the Couplet Paṭṭhāna. The classified answers are also obtained as in that Paṭṭhāna. So the answers for the Classification Chapter are briefly indicated :

(i) Dependent on state which is root and associated with root, arises state which is root and associated with root by root condition.

Dependent on non-greed, arise non-hate and non-delusion ; dependent on non-hate, arise non-greed and non-delusion ; dependent on non-delusion, arise non-greed and non-hate . . . . (Synod V, p. 39—the classified answers are not given.)

Similarly, root couplet is taken as reference with the states which have no associated roots, the second section of the next couplet. There are altogether $100 \times 2 \times 99 = 19,800$ sections of this Paṭṭhāna.

B. Negative Method Division

In this Negative Method Division the six Paṭṭhānas are taken in their negative forms. They are greatly condensed and so are the remaining 12 Paṭṭhānas of the Positive-Negative Method and Negative-Positive Method Divisions. But they can be expanded in the way shown in the Positive Method Division by applying the methods given there. Numerous enumerations are provided in this Division.

1. Triplet Paṭṭhāna

An Example with Not-faultless Triplet. There are seven sections and the same seven sub-sections as in the case of the Faultless Triplet and so, here too, there are 49 questions.

The Analytical Units. The analytical units of (1) not-faultless, (2) not-faulty and (3) not-indeterminate states of the not-faultless triplet are :

States	Analytical units
(1) not-faultless (i.e. faulty and indeterminate).	12 faulty, 36 resultant, and 20 functional consciousnesses, 52 mental factors, 28 matter, Nibbāna.
(2) not-faulty (i.e. faultless and indeterminate).	21 faultless, 36 resultant, and 20 functional consciousnesses, 38 mental factors, 28 matter, Nibbāna.
(3) not-indeterminate (i.e. faultless and faulty).	21 faultless and 12 faulty consciousnesses, 52 mental factors.

Dependent Chapter. When the appropriate states are taken for root condition under Dependent Chapter, 29 answers are obtained, i.e.

(1) With not-faultless as reference, (i) 1–1, (ii) 1–2, (iii) 1–3, (iv) 1–1, 3, (v) 1–1, 2 (5 answers).

(2) With not-faulty as reference, (vi) 2–2, (vii) 2–1, (viii) 2–3, (ix) 2–2, 3, (x) 2–1, 2 (5 answers).

(3) With not-indeterminate as reference, (xi) 3–3, (xii) 3–1, (xiii) 3–2, (xiv) 3–1, 3, (xv) 3–2, 3, (xvi) 3–1, 2 (6 answers).

(4) With not-faultless, not-indeterminate as reference, (xvii) 1, 3–1, (xviii) 1, 3–2, (xix) 1, 3–3, (xx) 1, 3–1, 3, (xxi) 1, 3–1, 2 (5 answers).

(5) With not-faulty, not-indeterminate as reference, (xxii) 2, 3–1, (xxiii) 2, 3–2, (xxiv) 2, 3–3, (xxv) 2, 3–2, 3, (xxvi) 2, 3–1, 2 (5 answers).

(6) With not-faultless, not-faulty as reference, (xxvii) 1, 2–1, (xxviii) 1, 2–2, (xxix) 1, 2–1, 2 (3 answers).

The classified answers can be worked out as shown in the faultless triplet.

Investigation Chapter. For root condition, which belongs to the conascence group of conditions, there are the same 29 answers. The Classification Chapter is given and begins with :

(i) Not-faultless state is related to not-faultless state by root condition.

Not-faultless (i.e. faulty and indeterminate) roots are related to (their) associated aggregates and mind-produced matter by root condition ;

At the moment of conception, not-faultless (i.e. resultant indeterminate) roots are related to (their) associated aggregates and kamma-produced matter by root condition. (Synod V, p. 63.)

This shows how the classified answers are obtained from the answers and the analytical units.

The Other Triplets. The answers for the Classification Chapters and the enumerations under the Seven Chapters have also to be obtained for the Feeling Triplet and the rest of the 22 Triplets.

2. Couplet Paṭṭhāna

Here it is seen that the sections of the couplets are the reverse of those in the Positive Method Division. For example, in

(a) the Positive Method Division, the order of the sections of the root couplet is (1) root states and (2) not-root states, and in

(b) this Negative Method Division, it is (1) not-root states and (2) not not-root states, i.e. root states. The second there becomes the first, and the first, the second. Here also there are three sections, (i) not-root, (2) not not-root, and (3) not-root, not not-root and the same three sub-sections.

Dependent Chapter. With the root couplet for root condition under Dependent Chapter there are also 9 answers as in the Positive Method Division. The Classification Chapter begins with :

(i) Dependent on not-root state, arises not-root state by root condition.

Introduction lxxxiii

Dependent on one not-root aggregate, arise three aggregates and mind-produced matter; dependent on three aggregates, arise one aggregate and mind-produced matter; dependent on two aggregates, arise two aggregates and mind-produced matter;

At the moment of conception, dependent on one not-root aggregate, arise three aggregates and kamma-produced matter. ...

Dependent on one great primary, arise three great primaries.... (Synod V, p. 75—classified answers are given.)

3. Couplet–Triplet Paṭṭhāna

Analytical Units. The analytical units of the states of the first couplet–triplet Paṭṭhāna are:

States	Analytical units
(1) not-root and not-faultless.	12 faulty, 36 resultant, and 20 functional consciousnesses, 46 mental factors exclusive of the 6 roots, 28 matter, Nibbāna.
(2) not-root and not-faulty.	21 faultless, 36 resultant, and 20 functional consciousnesses, 35 mental factors exclusive of 3 faultless roots, 28 matter, Nibbāna.
(3) not-root and not-indeterminate.	21 faultless and 12 faulty consciousnesses, 46 mental factors exclusive of the 6 roots.

Dependent Chapter. For root condition under Dependent Chapter there are 9 answers in the order given in the Positive Method Division. The Classification Chapter begins with:

(i) Dependent on not-root and not-faultless state, arises not-root and not-faultless state by root condition.

Dependent on one not-root and not-faultless (i.e. faulty and indeterminate) aggregate, arise three aggregates and mind-produced matter; dependent on three aggregates, arise one aggregate and mind-produced matter ; dependent on two aggregates, arise two aggregates and mind-produced matter. (Synod V, p. 107—classified answers are given.)

4. Triplet–Couplet Paṭṭhāna

The states of the first triplet–couplet Paṭṭhāna are (1) not-faultless and not-root, (2) not-faulty and not-root, and (3) not-indeterminate and not-root. As in the case of the triplets, there are seven sections, but only the first six can be taken as references.

The Analytical Units. The analytical units of the six sections are :

Sections	Analytical units
(1) Not-faultless and not-root.	12 faulty, 36 resultant, and 20 functional consciousnesses, 46 mental factors exclusive of the 6 roots, 28 matter, Nibbāna.
(2) Not-faulty and not-root.	21 faultless, 36 resultant, and 20 functional consciousnesses, 35 mental factors exclusive of the 3 faultless roots, 28 matter, Nibbāna.
(3) Not-indeterminate and not-root.	21 faultless and 12 faulty consciousnesses, 46 mental factors exclusive of the 6 roots.
(4) Not-faultless and not-root, not-indeterminate and not-root (1 and 3).	12 faulty consciousnesses, 24 mental factors exclusive of the 3 faulty roots.
(5) Not-faulty and not-root, not-indeterminate and not-root (2 and 3).	21 faultless consciousnesses, 35 mental factors exclusive of the 3 faultless roots.
(6) Not-faultless and not-root, not-faulty and not-root (1 and 2).	36 resultant and 20 functional consciousnesses, 35 mental factors exclusive of the 3 indeterminate roots, 28 matter, Nibbāna.

These analytical units have to be found first so that the appropriate ones can be selected for the various chapters and to obtain the enumerations. So Paṭṭhāna cannot be understood if these analytical units are not known.

Dependent Chapter. For root condition under Dependent Chapter, there are 29 answers which are in the same order as those with the example given in the Triplet Paṭṭhāna of this Division. The classified answers are not given but an example with the first answer for the Classification Chapter is :

(i) Dependent on not-faultless and not-root state, arises not-faultless and not-root state by root condition.

Dependent on one not-faultless and not-root aggregate (i.e. faulty, resultant and functional as shown above), arise three aggregates and mind-produced matter ; dependent on three aggregates, arise one aggregate and mind-produced matter ; dependent on two aggregates, arise two aggregates and mind-produced matter ;

At the moment of conception, dependent on one not-faultless and not-root aggregate (i.e. resultant), arise three aggregates and kamma-produced matter . . . dependent on two aggregates, arise two aggregates and kamma-produced matter ; dependent on aggregates, arises (heart-) base ; dependent on (heart-) base, arise aggregates ;

Dependent on one great primary, arise three great primaries ; dependent on three great primaries, arises one great primary ; dependent on two great primaries, arise two great primaries ; dependent on great primaries, arise mind-produced and kamma-produced derived matter. (Synod V, p. 127—classified answers are not given.)

It will be found that these classified answers are the same as those for root condition in the Faultless Triplet of the Triplet Paṭṭhāna in the Positive Method Division.

5. Triplet–Triplet Paṭṭhāna

The states of the first triplet–triplet Paṭṭhāna are (1) not-faultless and not associated with pleasant feeling, (2) not-faulty and not-associated with pleasant feeling, and (3) not-indeterminate and not associated with pleasant feeling. Here also, as in the previous Paṭṭhāna, only six out of the seven sections can be taken as references.

The Analytical Units. The analytical units of the six sections are :

Sections	Analytical units
(1) Not-faultless and not associated with pleasant feeling.	3 cons. accompanied by pain, 6 faulty, 25 resultant, and 11 functional cons. accompanied by neither painful nor pleasant feeling, 51 mental factors exclusive of rapture, 28 matter, Nibbāna.
(2) Not-faulty and not associated with pleasant feeling.	body-cons. accompanied by pain, 13 faultless, 25 resultant and 11 functional cons. accompanied by neither painful nor pleasant feeling, 37 mental factors exclusive of rapture, 28 matter, Nibbāna.
(3) Not-indeterminate and not associated with pleasant feeling.	2 hate-rooted cons., 13 faultless and 6 faulty cons. accompanied by neither painful nor pleasant feeling, 51 mental factors exclusive of rapture.
(4) Not-faultless and not associated with pleasant feeling, not-indeterminate and not associated with pleasant feeling (1 and 3).	2 hate-rooted cons., 6 faulty cons. accompanied by neither painful nor pleasant feeling, 26 mental factors exclusive of rapture.
(5) Not-faulty and not associated with pleasant feeling, not-indeterminate and not associated with pleasant feeling (2 and 3).	13 faultless cons. accompanied by neither painful nor pleasant feeling, 37 mental factors exclusive of rapture.
(6) Not-faultless and not associated with pleasant feeling, not-faulty and not associated with pleasant feeling (1 and 2).	body-cons. accompanied by pain, 25 resultant and 11 functional cons. accompanied by neither painful nor pleasant feeling, 37 mental factors exclusive of rapture, 28 matter, Nibbāna.

Dependent Chapter. For root condition under Dependent Chapter, there are 29 answers in the order usual for them above. There are no classified answers in the Text but an example with the first answer for the Classification Chapter is :

(i) Dependent on not-faultless state not associated with pleasant feeling, arises not-faultless state not associated with pleasant feeling by root condition.

Dependent on one not-faultless aggregate not associated with pleasant feeling, arise three aggregates and mind-produced matter ... dependent on two aggregates, arise two aggregates and mind-produced matter;

At the moment of conception, dependent on one not-faultless (i.e. resultant) aggregate, arise three aggregates and kamma-produced matter ... (Synod V, p. 147—the classified answers are not given.)

6. Couplet–Couplet Paṭṭhāna

The Analytical Units. The analytical units of the states of the first couplet-couplet Paṭṭhāna are:

States	Analytical units
(1) Not-root states which have no associated roots.	18 rootless cons., 12 mental factors, 28 matter, Nibbāna.
(2) Not not-root states which have no associated roots.	delusion of the 2 delusion-rooted cons.

Dependent Chapter. For root condition there are three answers (i) 1–1, (ii) 2–1, and (iii) 1, 2–1. An example with the first answer for the Classification Chapter is:

(i) Dependent on not-root state which has no associated root, arises not-root state which has no associated root by root condition.

Dependent on one great primary, arise three great primaries ... dependent on two great primaries, arise two great primaries; dependent on great primaries, arise mind-produced and kamma-produced derived matter. (Synod V, p. 169—there are no classified answers.)

Note.—Since the mental states are 18 rootless consciousnesses, there cannot be classified answers with them for root condition but only with material states.

C. POSITIVE–NEGATIVE METHOD DIVISION

In the Positive and Negative Method Divisions the sections as references and the sub-sections as variants were both positive and both negative respectively. But in this Positive–Negative

Method Division the sections are positive and the sub-sections are negative. This can be clearly seen from the following examples of the questions in their respective Divisions, (1) Positive Method, (2) Negative Method, and (3) Positive–Negative Method:

Dependent on

(1) faultless state, may there arise faultless state by root condition ?
(2) not-faultless state, may there arise not-faultless state by root condition ?
(3) faultless state, may there arise not-faultless state by root condition ?

Triplet Paṭṭhāna

For the Faultless Triplet of this Division the seven sections and sub-sections are:

Sections	Sub-sections
(1) (1P) faultless.	(1N) not-faultless (i.e. faulty and indeterminate.
(2) (2P) faulty.	(2N) not-faulty (i.e. faultless and indeterminate.
(3) (3P) indeterminate.	(3N) not-indeterminate (i.e. faultless and faulty).
(4) (1P, 3P) faultless, indeterminate.	(1N, 3N) not-faultless, not-indeterminate (i.e. faulty).
(5) (2P, 3P) faulty, indeterminate.	(2N, 3N) not-faulty, not-indeterminate (i.e. faultless).
(6) (1P, 2P) faultless, faulty.	(1N, 2N) not-faultless, not-faulty (i.e. indeterminate).
(7) (1P, 2P, 3P) faultless, faulty, indeterminate (i.e. all).	(1N, 2N, 3N) not-faultless, not-faulty, not-indeterminate (i.e. nil).

With each section as reference, questions can be asked with each of the seven sub-sections. Therefore, there are 49 questions.

The Analytical Units. The analytical units of the first three sections and sub-sections are given below and, by knowing them, those for the rest can be found. Although they were dealt with separately in the Faultless Triplet Paṭṭhānas of the Divisions concerned, they are repeated here for ready reference.

Introduction

(1P) Faultless	(1N) Not-faultless
21 faultless cons., 38 assoc. m.f.	12 faulty, 36 resultant, and 20 functional cons., 52 assoc. m.f., 28 matter, Nibbāna.
(2P) Faulty	**(2N) Not-faulty**
12 faulty cons., 27 assoc. m.f.	21 faultless, 36 resultant, and 20 functional cons., 38 assoc. m.f., 28 matter, Nibbāna.
(3P) Indeterminate	**(3N) Not-indeterminate**
36 resultant and 20 functional cons., 38 assoc. m.f., 28 matter, Nibbāna.	21 faultless and 12 faulty cons., 52 assoc. m.f.

Dependent Chapter. For root condition under Dependent Chapter there are 19 answers. These are:

(1) With faultless as reference, (i) 1P–1N, (ii) 1P–2N, (iii) 1P–3N, (iv) 1P–2N, 3N, (v) 1P–1N, 2N (5 answers).

(2) With faulty as reference, (i) 2P–2N, (ii) 2P–1N, (iii) 2P–3N, (iv) 2P–1N, 3N, (v) 2P–1N, 2N (5 answers).

(3) With indeterminate as reference, (i) 3P–1N, (ii) 3P–2N, (iii) 3P–1N, 2N (3 answers).

(4) With faultless, indeterminate as reference, (i) 1P, 3P–1N, (ii) 1P, 3P–2N, (iii) 1P, 3P–1N, 2N (3 answers).

(5) With faulty, indeterminate as reference, (i) 2P, 3P–1N, (ii) 2P, 3P–2N, (iii) 2P, 3P–1N, 2N (3 answers).

The Classification Chapter begins with:

(i) Dependent on faultless state, arises not-faultless state by root condition.

Dependent on faultless aggregates, arises mind-produced matter. (Synod V, p. 187—classified answers are given.)

2. Couplet Paṭṭhāna

For the root couplet of this Division the three sections and sub-sections are:

Sections	Sub-sections
(1) (1P) root.	(1N) not-root.
(2) (2P) not-root.	(2N) not not-root (i.e. root).
(3) (1P, 2P) root, not-root.	(1N, 2N) not-root, not not-root.

With each section as reference, questions can be asked with each of the three sub-sections. Therefore there are 9 questions.

The Analytical Units. The analytical units of the first two sections and sub-sections are:

(1P) Root	(1N) Not-root
6 roots.	89 consciousnesses, 46 mental factors exclusive of the 6 roots, 28 matter, Nibbāna.
(2P) = (1N) above, i.e. not-root.	(2N) = (1P) above, i.e. root.

Dependent Chapter. For root condition there are 9 answers, i.e. all the questions have answers. They are:

(1) With root as reference, (i) 1P–1N, (ii) 1P–2N, (iii) 1P–1N, 2N.

(2) With not-root as reference, (i) 2P–2N, (ii) 2P–1N, (iii) 2P–1N, 2N.

(3) With root, not-root as reference, (i) 1P, 2P–1N, (ii) 1P, 2P–2N, (iii) 1P, 2P–1N, 2N.

The Classification Chapter begins with:

(i) Dependent on root state, arises not-root state by root condition.

Dependent on root state, arise associated aggregates and mind-produced matter;

At the moment of conception, dependent on root state, arise

associated aggregates and kamma-produced matter. (Synod V, p. 211—classified answers are given.)

3. Couplet–Triplet Paṭṭhāna

For the first couplet–triplet, i.e. root-faultless, of this Division, the three sections and sub-sections are :

Sections	Sub-sections
(1) (1P) root-faultless. (2) (2P) not-root–faultless. (3) (1P, 2P) root-faultless, not-root–faultless.	(1N) not-root–not-faultless. (2N) not not-root–not-faultless. (1N, 2N) not-root–not-faultless, not not-root–not-faultless.

Here also there are 9 questions.

The Analytical Units. The analytical units of the first two sections and sub-sections are :

(1P) root-faultless	(1N) not-root–not-faultless
3 faultless roots.	12 faulty, 36 resultant, and 20 functional cons., 46 mental factors exclusive of the 6 roots, 28 matter, Nibbāna.
(2P) not-root–faultless	(2N) not not-root–not-faultless
21 faultless cons., 35 mental factors exclusive of the 3 faultless roots.	3 faulty and 3 indeterminate (i.e. resultant and functional) roots.

Dependent Chapter. For root condition there are three answers, i.e. :

(1) With root-faultless as reference, (i) 1P–1N.
(2) With not-root–faultless as reference, (i) 2P–1N.
(3) With root-faultless, not-root–faultless as reference, (i) 1P, 2P–1N.

An example with the first answer for the Classification Chapter is :

(i) Dependent on root-faultless state, arises not-root–not-faultless state by root condition.

Dependent on root-faultless state, arises mind-produced matter. (Synod V, p. 229—classified answers are not given.)

4. Triplet–Couplet Paṭṭhāna

For the first triplet-couplet Paṭṭhāna there are seven sections and sub-sections as with those of the other Divisions. The first three of them are :

Sections	Sub-sections
(1) (1P) faultless-root.	(1N) not-faultless–not-root.
(2) (2P) faulty-root.	(2N) not-faulty–not-root.
(3) (3P) indeterminate-root.	(3N) not-indeterminate–not-root.

The others are (4) (1P, 3P) and (1N, 3N), (5) (2P, 3P) and (2N, 3N), (6) (1P, 2P) and (1N, 2N), (7) (1P, 2P, 3P) and (1N, 2N, 3N).

The Analytical Units. The analytical units of the above three sections and sub-sections are :

(1P) faultless-root	(1N) not-faultless–not-root
3 faultless roots.	12 faulty, 36 resultant, and 20 functional cons., 46 mental factors exclusive of the 6 roots, 28 matter, Nibbāna.
(2P) faulty-root	(2N) not-faulty–not-root
3 faulty roots.	21 faultless, 36 resultant, and 20 functional cons., 35 mental factors exclusive of the 3 faultless roots, 28 matter, Nibbāna.
(3P) indeterminate-root	(3N) not-indeterminate–not-root
3 resultant and functional roots.	21 faultless and 12 faulty cons., 46 mental factors exclusive of the 6 roots.

Dependent Chapter. For root condition under Dependent Chapter there are 13 answers. These are :

(1) With faultless-root as reference, (i) 1P–1N, (ii) 1P–2N, (iii) 1P–3N, (iv) 1P–2N, 3N, (v) 1P–1N, 2N (5 answers).

Introduction

(2) With faulty-root as reference, (i) 2P–2N, (ii) 2P–1N, (iii) 2P–3N, (iv) 2P–1N, 3N, (v) 2P–1N, 2N (5 answers).

(3) With indeterminate-root as reference, (i) 3P–1N, (ii) 3P–2N, (iii) 3P–1N, 2N (3 answers).

An example with the first answer for the Classification Chapter is :

(i) Dependent on faultless-root state, arises not-faultless– not-root state by root condition.

Dependent on faultless-root state, arises mind-produced matter. (Synod V, p. 261—classified answers are not given.)

5. Triplet–Triplet Paṭṭhāna

The first three sections and sub-sections of the first triplet– triplet Paṭṭhāna are :

Sections	Sub-sections
(1) (1P) faultless associated with pleasant feeling.	(1N) not-faultless not associated with pleasant feeling.
(2) (2P) faulty associated with pleasant feeling.	(2N) not-faulty not associated with pleasant feeling.
(3) (3P) indeterminate associated with pleasant feeling.	(3N) not-indeterminate not associated with pleasant feeling.

The others are (4) (1P, 3P) and (1N, 3N), (5) (2P, 3P) and (2N, 3N), (6) (1P, 2P) and (1N, 2N), (7) (1P, 2P, 3P) and (1N, 2N, 3N).

The Analytical Units. The analytical units of the above three sections and sub-sections are :

(1P) faultless associated with pleasant feeling	(1N) not-faultless not associated with pleasant feeling
24 (expanded) faultless cons. accompanied by pleasant feeling, 37 mental factors exclusive of feeling.	3 cons. accompanied by pain, 6 faulty, 25 resultant, and 11 functional cons. accompanied by neither painful nor pleasant feeling, 51 mental factors exclusive of rapture, 28 matter, Nibbāna.

(2P) faulty associated with pleasant feeling	(2N) not-faulty not associated with pleasant feeling
4 faulty cons. accompanied by pleasant feeling, 21 mental factors exclusive of feeling.	body-cons. accompanied by pain, 13 faultless, 25 resultant, and 11 functional cons. accompanied by neither painful nor pleasant feeling, 37 mental factors exclusive of rapture, 28 matter, Nibbāna.
(3P) indeterminate associated with pleasant feeling	(3N) not-indeterminate not associated with pleasant feeling
35 indeterminate cons. accompanied by pleasant feeling, 37 mental factors exclusive of feeling.	2 hate-rooted cons., 13 faultless, 6 faulty cons. accompanied by neither painful nor pleasant feeling, 51 mental factors exclusive of rapture.

Dependent Chapter. For root condition under Dependent Chapter there are 13 answers which are in the same order as those in the triplet–couplet Paṭṭhāna above. An example with the first answer for the Classification Chapter is :

(i) Dependent on faultless state associated with pleasant feeling, arises not-faultless state not associated with pleasant feeling by root condition.

Dependent on faultless aggregates associated with pleasant feeling, arises mind-produced matter. (Synod V, p. 309—classified answers are not given.)

6. Couplet–Couplet Paṭṭhāna

For the first couplet–couplet Paṭṭhāna the three sections and sub-sections are :

Sections	Sub-sections
(1) (1P) root which has associated root.	(1N) not-root which has no associated root.
(2) (2P) not-root which has associated root.	(2N) not not-root which has no associated root.
(3) (1P, 2P) root which has associated root, not-root which has associated root.	(1N, 2N) not-root which has no associated root, not not-root which has no associated root.

The Analytical Units. The analytical units of the first two sections and sub-sections are :

(1P) root which has associated root	(1N) not-root which has no associated root
6 roots exclusive of delusion from the 2 delusion-rooted cons.	18 rootless cons., 12 mental factors, 28 matter, Nibbāna.
(2P) not-root which has associated root	(2N) not not-root which has no associated root
71 rooted cons., 46 mental factors exclusive of the 6 roots.	delusion from the 2 delusion-rooted cons.

Dependent Chapter. For root condition under Dependent Chapter there are the three answers :

(1) With root which has associated root as reference, (i) 1P–1N.
(2) With not-root which has associated root as reference, (i) 2P–1N.
(3) With root which has associated root, not-root which has associated root as reference, (i) 1P, 2P–1N.

An example with the first answer for the Classification Chapter is :

(i) Dependent on root state which has associated root, arises not-root state which has no associated root by root condition.

Dependent on roots which have rooted aggregates, arises mind-produced matter ;
At the moment of conception, dependent on roots which have rooted aggregates, arises kamma-produced matter. (Synod V, p. 329—classified answers are not given.)

D. NEGATIVE–POSITIVE METHOD DIVISION

The whole of this Negative–Positive Method Division is the reverse of the preceding Positive–Negative Method Division, i.e. the sub-sections, which are negative states denoted by N, are now the sections, and the sections, which are positive states denoted by P, are now the sub-sections. The analytical units under N and P are the same and will not be given here. The answers, of course, are not the same.

1. Triplet Paṭṭhāna

Dependent Chapter. In the faultless triplet, the first triplet, root condition has 18 answers. These are:

(1) With not-faultless (1N) as reference, (i) 1N–2P, (ii) 1N–3P, (iii) 1N–2P, 3P.
(2) With not-faulty (2N) as reference, (i) 2N–1P, (ii) 2N–3P, (iii) 2N–1P, 3P.
(3) With not-indeterminate (3N) as reference, (i) 3N–3P, (ii) 3N–1P, (iii) 3N–2P, (iv) 3N–1P, 3P, (v) 3N–2P, 3P.
(4) With not-faultless, not-indeterminate (1N, 3N) as reference, (i) 1N, 3N–2P, (ii) 1N, 3N–3P, (iii) 1N, 3N–2P, 3P.
(5) With not-faulty, not-indeterminate (2N, 3N) as reference, (i) 2N, 3N–1P, (ii) 2N, 3N–3P, (iii) 2N, 3N–1P, 3P.
(6) With not-faultless, not-faulty (1N, 2N) as reference, (i) 1N, 2N–3P.

An example with the first answer for the Classification Chapter is:

(i) Dependent on not-faultless state, arises faulty state by root condition.

Dependent on one not-faultless (i.e. faulty) aggregate, arise three aggregates; dependent on three aggregates, arises one aggregate; dependent on two aggregates, arise two aggregates. (Synod V, p. 353—classified answers are not given.)

2. Couplet Paṭṭhāna

Dependent Chapter. In the root couplet, the first couplet, root condition has 9 answers. These are:

(1) With not-root (1N) as reference, (i) 1N–1P, (ii) 1N–2P, (iii) 1N–1P, 2P.
(2) With not not-root (2N) as reference, (i) 2N–2P, (ii) 2N–1P, (iii) 2N–1P, 2P.

(3) With not-root, not not-root (1N, 2N) as reference, (i) 1N, 2N–1P, (ii) 1N, 2N–2P, (iii) 1N, 2N–1P, 2P.

An example with the first answer for the Classification Chapter is :

(i) Dependent on not-root state, arises root state by root condition.

Dependent on not-root aggregates, arise roots ;
At the moment of conception, dependent on not-root aggregates, arise (rebirth) roots ; dependent on (heart-)base, arise (three rebirth) roots. (Synod V, p. 365—classified answers are not given.)

3. Couplet–Triplet Paṭṭhāna

Dependent Chapter. In the first couplet–triplet Paṭṭhāna there are no answers for root condition under Dependent Chapter. The reason is that there are no conascent conditioning and conditioned states with which this Chapter deals.

Conditioned Chapter. For root condition under this Chapter there are three answers. These are :

With not-root–not-faultless (1N) as reference, (i) 1N–1P, (ii) 1N–2P, (iii) 1N–1P, 2P.

An example with the first answer for the Classification Chapter is :

(i) Conditioned by not-root–not-faultless state, arises root-faultless state by root condition.

Conditioned by (heart-)base, arise root-faultless aggregates. (Synod V, p. 379—classified answers are not given.)

4. Triplet–Couplet Paṭṭhāna

Dependent Chapter. In the first triplet–couplet Paṭṭhāna, root condition has 9 answers. These are :

(1) With not-faultless–not-root (1N) as reference, (i) 1N–2P, (ii) 1N–3P.
(2) With not-faulty–not-root (2N) as reference, (i) 2N–1P, (ii) 2N–3P.

(3) With not-indeterminate–not-root (3N) as reference, (i) 3N–1P, (ii) 3N–2P.
(4) With not-faultless–not-root, not-indeterminate–not-root (1N, 3N) as reference, (i) 1N, 3N–2P.
(5) With not-faulty–not-root, not-indeterminate–not-root (2N, 3N) as reference, (i) 2N, 3N–1P.
(6) With not-faultless–not-root, not-faulty–not-root (1N, 2N) as reference, (i) 1N, 2N–3P.

The example with the first answer for the Classification Chapter is:

(i) Dependent on not-faultless–not-root state, arises faulty-root state by root condition.

Dependent on not-faultless–not-root (i.e. faulty) aggregates, arise faulty roots. (Synod V, p. 413—classified answers are not given.)

5. Triplet–Triplet Paṭṭhāna

Dependent Chapter. In the first triplet–triplet Paṭṭhāna, root condition has 9 answers. These are:

(1) With not-faultless not associated with pleasant feeling (1N) as reference, (i) 1N–2P, (ii) 1N–3P.
(2) With not-faulty not associated with pleasant feeling (2N) as reference, (i) 2N–1P, (ii) 2N–3P.
(3) With not-indeterminate not associated with pleasant feeling (3N) as reference, (i) 3N–1P, (ii) 3N–2P.
(4) With not-faultless not associated with pleasant feeling, not-indeterminate not associated with pleasant feeling (1N, 3N) as reference, (i) 1N, 3N–2P.
(5) With not-faulty not associated with pleasant feeling, not-indeterminate not associated with pleasant feeling (2N, 3N) as reference, (i) 2N, 3N–1P.
(6) With not-faultless not associated with pleasant feeling, not-faulty not associated with pleasant feeling (1N, 2N) as reference, (i) 1N, 2N–3P.

An example with the first answer for the Classification Chapter is:

(i) Dependent on not-faultless state not associated with

pleasant feeling, arises faulty state associated with pleasant feeling by root condition.

Dependent on one not-faultless (i.e. faulty) aggregate not associated with pleasant feeling, arise three aggregates ; dependent on three aggregates, arises one aggregate ; dependent on two aggregates, arise two aggregates. (Synod V, p. 444—classified answers are not given.)

6. Couplet–Couplet Paṭṭhāna

Dependent Chapter. In the first couplet–couplet Paṭṭhāna, root condition has 4 answers. These are :

(1) With not-root which has no associated root (1N) as reference, (i) 1N–1P, (ii) 1N–2P, (iii) 1N–1P, 2P.

(2) With not not-root which has no associated root (2N) as reference, (i) 2N–2P.

An example with the first answer for the Classification Chapter is :

(i) Dependent on not-root state which has no associated root, arises root state which has associated root by root condition.

At the moment of conception, dependent on (heart-)base, arise (rebirth) roots. (Synod V, p. 469—classified answers are not given.)

It will be seen from the above that Paṭṭhāna deals with all the ultimate realities and all the conditions in all their various combinations. The Text, of course, does not provide all the numbers of answers in the Enumeration Chapters or all the answers and the classifications of the states in those answers in the Classification Chapters. But what is given is sufficient to find out the underlying methods by which these facts and figures are obtained. And once the methods are known, they can be applied to expand the elisions in both of those Chapters. The Burmese Mahātheras of old estimated that if the Paṭṭhāna Text, as expanded, were to be put into print there would be three cartloads of books.

Although some useful information can be gathered from the classified answers in the Text, the reader can only wonder how the numbers of answers to the different sets of questions could be directly given. But Paṭṭhāna is interesting only when the methods for arriving at these answers are known. This is why an idea of some of the methods and their applications is given in this Introduction. But, as mentioned earlier, more details of the various methods, with explanations and illustrations, must be given to enable the reader to work out all the answers and thereby acquire complete understanding of this vast subject. Of course, as has been emphasized, knowledge of the analytical units of the triplets and couplets, which form the table of contents of the seven books of Abhidhamma, is a prerequisite. And the reason why Abhidhamma is still flourishing in Burma is that there are treatises (Akauks) on the analytical units of Dhammasaṅganī, Dhātu-kathā, Yamaka and Paṭṭhāna which were compiled by Burmese Mahātheras of the past. But even though one may be well-versed in these analytical units it will not be possible to work out the answers unless the methods of utilizing them are pointed out. The Buddha had to teach the methods to His chief disciple, the Elder Sāriputta, who was endowed with analytical knowledge and, as stated in the Expositor I, p. 20 : " To the Elder also the doctrine taught by the Blessed One in hundreds and thousands of methods became very clear." And on the next page it is mentioned that " The textual order of the Abhidhamma originated with Sāriputta ; the numerical series in the Great Book (Paṭṭhāna) was also determined by him. In this way the Elder, without spoiling the unique doctrine, laid down the numerical series in order to make it easy to learn, remember, study and teach the Law."

The Ocean of Method

A person looking at the ocean, which has not been measured, will not know its exact measurements, but at least he will be able to form an estimate of its vastness. In the same way the reader who has gone through this Introduction to Paṭṭhāna will be able to form an estimate that Paṭṭhāna consists of innumerable methods ; that it is very expansive and that it is the province of Omniscience.

Of the four oceans (1) the ocean of repeated births, (2) the ocean of waters, (3) the ocean of method, and (4) the ocean of knowledge, the ocean of method is Paṭṭhāna. In the Expositor

I, p. 14, it is stated as follows: "Which is the ocean of method? The three Piṭakas, the word of the Buddha. For in reflecting upon the two Piṭakas, infinite rapturous joy arises in the sons of clansmen who are faithful, abundantly believing and endowed with superior knowledge. Which are the two? The Vinaya and the Abhidhamma. Infinite rapturous joy arises in those bhikkhus who learn the Vinaya text and reflect that it is the province of the Buddhas, and not of others, to lay down the rule for each fault or transgression according to its gravity.

Infinite rapturous joy also arises in the brethren when reflecting on implications of things supernormal, of colours and of good conduct.

Again, the bhikkhus, who study the Abhidhamma, experience infinite rapturous joy in reflecting. As though grouping the multitude of stars in the sky (into constellations), the Teacher taught things mental and material, dividing them into various parts and portions—things subtle and abstruse such as the unique content of aggregates, sense-organs, elements, controlling faculties, powers, factors of wisdom, kamma and its result; and the distinction between mind and matter. Consider this story of such an experience. The Elder Mahagatigamiyatissa crossed over to the opposite shore of India with the intention of paying homage to the Wisdom Tree. Seated on the upper deck of the boat he looked at the great ocean; but neither the thither nor the hither shore appeared to his vision. There appeared only the great ocean, strewn with foam thrown off by the breaking of the billows, and looking like a sheet of silver spread out on a bed of jasmine flowers. He thought to himself: Which is more extraordinary—the heaving of the ocean waves, or the basis of the method of the twenty-four divisions in the Great Book? Then the limits of the great ocean became apparent to him. Indeed, he thought to himself: This ocean is limited, below by the earth, above by the sky, on one side by the mountain encircling the world-system, and on the other by the seashore. But the limits of the universal Paṭṭhāna are not apparent. And abundant rapture arose in him, as he reflected on the subtle and abstruse Law. Arresting his rapture and increasing his insight even while he was seated, he threw off all the corruptions, and being established in the topmost

Fruition which is Arahantship, he exulted in this song of ecstasy :

> He is the true disciple of the Sage
> Who sees, like a bright jewel in his hand,
> Root-causes, from which all becoming is—
> Lore deep and hard to know, which the Great Sage
> Intuited, and all in order taught.

This is the ocean of method."

THE ABHIDHAMMA WAS EXPOUNDED ONLY BY THE BUDDHA

In the Preface to the Discourse on Elements, U Thein Nyun gave reasons to prove that the Abhidhamma was expounded by the Buddha. Here other reasons will be given, together with appropriate quotations, in confirmation of this fact.

When the systematic exposition of Paṭṭhāna, dealt with above, is frankly considered, the only conclusion that will be arrived at, is that this is the province of Omniscience and that no disciple could have attained that knowledge or have the ability to expound it on his own. The Expositor II, p. 519 states this as : " What is known as Abhidhamma is not the province nor the sphere of a disciple ; it is the province, the sphere of the Buddhas (Omniscient Ones)."

Some are of the opinion that the Abhidhamma was compiled from the Suttas. Again, there are some who are of the opinion that the Abhidhamma was compiled from the Suttas. But this cannot be so. For the subject matter of the Dhammasaṅganī is not to be found in any of the Suttas. In the case of the Suttanta couplets given there, they were expounded by Sāriputta and not by the Buddha. This is stated in the Expositor I, p. 11 : " Thence whence arose the other forty-two (Suttanta) couplets ? By whom were they laid down and taught ? They originated with Sāriputta, Generalissimo of the Law, having been laid down and taught by him. But he did not lay them down through his own self-evolved knowledge. They have been gathered from the Eka-Nipāta and Duka–Nipāta of the Aṅguttara–Nikāya, the Saṅgīti and Dasuttarasuttantas of the Dīgha–Nikāya, in order to help students of the Abhidhamma in their references to the Suttantas."

The Suttanta Classification of Vibhaṅga and the Puggalapaññati were expounded for the deliverance of those devas and brahmas who were not intelligent enough to understand the abstruse Abhidhamma. But the Abhidhamma Classification and Catechism of Vibhaṅga are not to be found in their completeness in any of the Suttas. Besides, the subjects dealt with in Dhātu-kathā, Yamaka and Paṭṭhāna are not to be found in the Suttas. Thus the opinion that the Abhidhamma was compiled from the Suttas does not hold water.

To dispel the views (1) that the Abhidhamma was not expounded by The Buddha, (2) that it was a later addition, and (3) that it was non-existent during The Buddha's time.

(1) Some hold the view that the Abhidhamma was not expounded by The Buddha. It is quite true that the Abhidhamma was not expounded by The Buddha in the human world. The reason for this, already explained in the Discourse on Elements, is that the audience would not be able to remain in the same posture during the whole period that the Abhidhamma was expounded, since a discourse is always completed by The Buddha at one sitting. But Sāriputta preached Abhidhamma to five hundred bhikkhus, his own pupils, when the method was taught to him by The Buddha.

(2) As for the view that the Abhidhamma was added later, one should ask, " By whom was this done ? " If there were any person capable of compiling this profound and abstruse Piṭaka, then his name would still be famous today. But because this Piṭaka cannot be ascribed to any such person it has been assumed that it came into existence after the Third Council. This, however, is an entirely false view.

(3) The Abhidhamma was in existence during The Buddha's time. This can be proved from the following passages in the *Book of the Discipline*, Vol. III :

(*a*) p. 415. " Not given leave means : without asking (for permission). Should ask a question means : if, having asked for leave in regard to Suttanta, she asks about Discipline or about Abhidhamma, there is an offence of expiation. If, having asked for leave in regard to Abhidhamma, she asks about Suttanta or about Discipline, there is an offence of expiation."

(*b*) p. 42. " There is no offence if, not desiring to disparage, he speaks, saying : ' Look here, do you master suttantas or verses or what is extra to dhamma (i.e. Abhidhamma)[1] and afterwards you will master discipline ' ; if he is mad, if he is the first wrong-doer."

These passages clearly show that Abhidhamma was in existence during The Buddha's time because rules about it were laid down by Him.

Also in *Middle Length Sayings I*, p. 270, Sāriputta told The Buddha about the question he put to Moggallāna and the reply he received, which are " . . . ' by what type of monk, reverend Moggallāna, would the Gosiṅga sal-wood be illumined ? ' When I had spoken thus, Lord, the venerable Moggallāna the Great spoke thus to me : ' In this connection, reverend Sāriputta, two monks are talking on Further dhamma[2] ; they ask one another questions ; in answering one another's questions they respond and do not fail, and their talk on dhamma is one that goes forward. By a monk of such a type, reverend Sāriputta, would the Gosiṅga sal-wood be illumined.' " To this The Buddha said, " It is good, Sāriputta, it is good. It is so that Moggallāna, in answering you properly, should answer. For Sāriputta, Moggallāna is a talker on dhamma."[3] Again, at the time The Buddha returned to Saṅkassanagara from Tāvatiṁsā, the realm of 33 gods, Sāriputta, in Sāriputta Sutta, uttered the following in praise of The Buddha :

" Erst have I never seen
Nor heard of one with voice
So sweet as his who came
From Tusitā to teach."

[1,2] It is Abhidhamma and it is specifically stated in the Burmese Editions. In the Translator's Introduction, p. xi, to *The Book of the Discipline*, Vol. III, it is stated, " Abhi- prefixed to a noun has in general an intensive meaning of higher, super, additional ; and it can also mean ' concerning ', ' pertaining to '. Thus for the compound abhidhamma, we get some such phrase as ' the higher doctrine ', ' further, extra doctrine ', or ' what pertains to the doctrine '. It is possible that the cleavage between these two is not very great."

[3] " Moggallāna is called chief of those of psychic power, A.i.23. MA.ii.256 explains that ' abhidhamma-men, having come to knowledge of subtle points, having increased their vision, can achieve a supermundane state '. Non-abhidhamma-men get muddled between ' own doctrine ' (sakavāda) and ' other doctrine ' (paravāda)."

(Suttanipāta verse No. 955 translated by E. M. Hare, p. 139).
The Harvard Oriental Series, p. 229, gives this translation :

> " I ne'er have seen nor ever yet heard tell
> Of such a sweet-tongued Master coming down
> From Tusitā on high to teach the world."

This verse is also found in Mahāniddesa (Sixth Synod, p. 386), where there is a detailed commentary on it. The following is the commentary on the first line : " At the time The Buddha, after having resided for the period of Lent on the Paṇḍukambala Stone at the foot of the Coral tree in Tāvatiṁsā, came down to Saṅkassanagara by the middle pearl stairway surrounded by devas, I, Sāriputta, had never before, with my own eyes and body, seen The Buddha with such a splendid countenance."

When Sāriputta, based on the methods given by The Buddha, preached Abhidhamma to his pupils, The Buddha not only stated that He had expounded the Abhidhamma in Tāvatiṁsā but also narrated this Sāriputta Sutta to be left behind as evidence of having done so for the later generations. The Mahāniddesa was included in the Three Councils.

The next verse No. 956 of Suttanipāta, which is also found on p. 386 of Mahāniddesa is :

> " Devas and men to lead
> Lo! he as seer appears :
> The one who routing gloom
> Outright in rapture dwelt."

Harvard Oriental Series has this translation :

> " Of gods and men—as stands reveal'd in Him,
> Th'all-seeing Lord, who swept all mists away
> And compassed bliss, unaided and alone."

The meaning is : The Buddha with Exalted Eye and the Unrivalled One, after driving away the darkness so that men and devas were able to see one another, abided in bliss. The Mahāniddesa adds : " The Buddha was seen by men just as devas did while He was sitting on the Paṇḍukambala Stone at the foot of the Coral tree and preaching."

These two verses tell us what Sāriputta stated (to The

Buddha) regarding the return of The Buddha to Saṅkassanagara after He expounded the Abhidhamma at Tāvatiṁsā. As further testimony there still exists the pagoda and marble inscriptions erected by King Thiri Dhammāsoka as monuments at the site in Saṅkassanagara where The Buddha returned from Tāvatiṁsā.

Besides, Peta-vatthu (Sixth Synod Edn., p. 159) states :

(1) " At the time The Buddha, the Exalted One, was residing on the Paṇḍukambala Stone at the foot of the Coral tree in Tāvatiṁsā (for expounding the Abhidhamma).

(2) At that time the devas and brahmas of the 10,000 worlds held a meeting and approached The Buddha who resided at the top of Mount Meru (where Tāvatiṁsā is situated).

(3) At that time no deva or brahma could excel in radiance and splendour that of The Buddha."

Moreover, in the Buddhavaṁsa it is stated in :—

(1) Dīpankarā Buddhavaṁsa : " At the time when Dīpankarā Buddha expounded the Dhamma in Tāvatiṁsā, 90,000 crores of devas and brahmas realised the Four Noble Truths by Path-knowledge on three occasions."

(2) Maṅgala Buddhavaṁsa : " At the time when Maṅgala Buddha expounded the Dhamma in Tāvatiṁsā, the abode of Sekya, the Lord of devas, 1,000 crores of devas and brahmas realised the Four Noble Truths by Path-knowledge on two occasions."

(3) Sobhita Buddhavaṁsa : " (Sobhita Buddha), having made the devas and brahmas realise the Four Noble Truths for the first time, then expounded the Dhamma at the second assembly and 9,000 crores realised the Four Noble Truths by Path-knowledge on two occasions."

(4) Dhammadassī Buddhavaṁsa : " At the time when Dhammadassī Buddha returned to the human world after expounding the Dhamma in Tāvatiṁsā, 100 crores of devas and brahmas assembled for the second time."

(5) Kassapa Buddhavaṁsa : " At the time when Kassapa Buddha expounded the Dhamma in detail at the festival of the Sudhamma devas held in the pleasant abode of Tāvatiṁsā, 3,000 crores of devas and brahmas came to know it."

The Abhidhamma, which deals with realities, is the province of Omniscience, but for those who are of the opinion that it was not expounded by The Buddha and yet cannot ascribe it to anyone else, the above extracts are given to prove definitely that it was expounded by The Buddha. This should clear up all doubts about the matter. (According to the Commentary, the word ' dhamma ' in the above extracts denotes Abhidhamma—Dhammanti Abhidhamma—as there is no other teaching besides Abhidhamma that could be expounded.)

Conclusion

Although Abhidhamma has been flourishing in Burma for a long time, very few were interested in the study of Paṭṭhāna because there were no easy methods available for its understanding. In fact, Paṭṭhāna was about to be lost in oblivion. But the Translator painstakingly searched for the methods contained therein and, having succeeded, devised a series of charts by which Paṭṭhāna is now being easily learnt and understood.

When Professor G. P. Malalasekera was in Burma in 1956 he requested the Translator to translate Paṭṭhāna into English for the benefit of those persons in other countries who are studying Buddhism and those who are keenly desirous of understanding Paṭṭhāna. But for one reason or another it was put off. However, when the Pāli Text Society made the same request later, Dhātu-kathā was translated and now Paṭṭhāna. So instead of simply arguing whether Paṭṭhāna, which is part of Abhidhamma, was expounded by The Buddha or not, this translated Text should be studied and understood. Then the facts should be tested as Paṭṭhāna deals with all the causes and effects that arise and cease in the continuity of beings at every instant of the day. Only then will one be in a position to make a personal decision as to whether The Buddha expounded Paṭṭhāna or not.

In particular, may all readers, after having made a proper study of Paṭṭhāna, overcome greed, hate and delusion ; acquire deep knowledge of the causes and effects of things so as to realize Path and Fruition ; attain True Bliss of Nibbāna.

The translation was made from the Sixth Synod Edition of Paṭṭhāna, Volume I. Commentarial and other explanations are not given as footnotes as they will be included in the Guide to Paṭṭhāna which the Translator proposes to compile. Here again, as in the Discourse on Elements, an index is not supplied because it would be so complicated and because the topics, which are given similar treatment, can be easily found from the Table of Contents. Moreover, the P.T.S. agreed there was no necessity.

My thanks are due to Miss I. B. Horner, President of the Pali Text Society, for giving whole-hearted support and encouragement to undertake this translation and for her valuable advice and suggestions. Thanks are also due to Dr. Thein Maung and U Sein Ban for assistance in the draft typing; Daw Khin Khin Hlaing for typing the charts; The Abhidhamma Propagating Society and U San Tin for the supply of stationery.

U Nārada,
Mūla Paṭṭhāna Sayadaw.

---

* In the *Discourse on Elements*, " kusala " was translated as " wholesome " but here in Paṭṭhāna, " faultless " is used. Both these words are appropriate. For the *Expositor* (Vol. I, p. 48) gives the different meanings of " kusala "and states that these words are suitable in this case : " First of all, the word ' kusala ' (moral) means ' of good health ', ' faultless ', ' skilful ', ' productive of happy sentient results ', etc. In such passages as, ' Is your reverence kusala ? ' ' Is your reverence free from ailment ? '—kusala has the meaning of ' good health '. In such passages as, ' Which, sir, is kusala behaviour? ' ' Great king, it is conduct that is blameless ' ; and again in, ' Sir, as the Blessed One has taught the Law verily incomparable with respect to kusala states '—kusala means ' faultless '. In such passages as, ' You are kusala at the different parts of a chariot ' ; ' Graceful women who have been trained and are kusala in singing and dancing,' etc.—kusala means ' skilful '. In such passages as, ' Bhikkhus, (merit flows from) the cause that has built up kusala states,' and ' (Visual cognition springs into existence) because it has been performed and accumulated by a kamma which is kusala '—kusala means ' productive of happy results '. Now here, in the phrase ' moral states ', either ' wholesome ', or ' faultless ', or ' productive of happy results ' is a suitable meaning."

From the above it will be seen that :—

(1) " wholesome " pertains not only to bodily health and material food but also to mental health, since the mind is in a healthy state when the mental corruptions are absent. Thus, " freed from the pain of mental corruptions " is a suitable meaning. For whenever moral consciousnesses arise in one's continuity, the corruptions which are likened to sores and diseases are absent. All the moral states have the property of eliminating the corruptions and this elimination takes place for the moment when they belong to the sensuous type,

for a long period when they belong to the lofty type and for all time when they belong to the Path type.

(2) "faultless" means "free from the fault of corruptions". For when a moral consciousness arises, whether it be sensuous, lofty or Path, it is free from the fault of corruptions. If otherwise, it is no longer moral. Thus this meaning applies to all other moral states which are lofty or supramundane and not only sensuous.

(3) "skilful". If this meaning is considered in the examples given above, it cannot apply to moral states, not even to the sensuous, leave alone the lofty and supramundane. The Commentary states that "skilful" is not a suitable meaning.

(4) "productive of happy results." Moral states function as impulsions, all of which are volitional and therefore produce results. Here the impulsion is moral and therefore it must produce happy results.

The meaning of "kusala" is also given in the Commentaries on the Suttas:—

	Faultless.	Whole-some.	Productive of happy results	Commen-tary page.
Sīlakkhandha	Anavajja	—	—	189
Mūlapaṇṇāsa	,,	—	—	120
Majjhimapaṇṇāsa	,,	—	—	302
Saṁyutta Vol. I	,,	—	—	86
Saṁyutta Vol. III	,,	—	Sukha vipāka	178
Aṅguttara Vol. III	,,	—	—	307
Aṅguttara Vol. III	,,	Arogya	—	385
Paṭisambhidāmagga Vol. I	,,	,,	Sukha vipāka	120
Paṭisambhidāmagga Vol. I	,,	,,	,,	189
Paṭisambhidāmagga Vol. I	,,	,,	—	250
Paṭisambhidāmagga Vol. II	—	,,	—	177
Udāna	Anavajja	—	—	212
Vimāna Vatthu	,,	Arogya	—	119
Suttanipāta	,,	,,	Sukha vipāka	220

Since "faultless" (anavajja) is the meaning generally given in the Commentaries and is a simple and convenient word, "faultless" is used for "kusala" (moral) in this Paṭṭhāna translation.

CONTENTS OF CONDITIONAL RELATIONS

	PAGE
I. ENUMERATION OF THE CONDITIONS	1
II. ANALYTICAL EXPOSITION OF THE CONDITIONS	2
III. QUESTION CHAPTER	

1. CONDITIONS: POSITIVE

By Ones

Root Condition
1. Faultless Section 13
2. Faulty Section 13
3. Indeterminate Section 14
4. Faultless and Indeterminate Section 14
5. Faulty and Indeterminate Section 14
6. Faultless and Faulty Section 15
7. Faultless, Faulty and Indeterminate Section 15

Object Condition, etc. 16

By Twos, etc.

Root Condition 17
Object Condition, etc. 18

2. CONDITIONS: NEGATIVE

Not-root conditions, etc. 18

3. CONDITIONS: POSITIVE–NEGATIVE

Root Condition 19
Object Condition, etc. 20

4. CONDITIONS: NEGATIVE–POSITIVE

Not-root Condition 21
Not-object Condition, etc. 21

IV. ANSWERS

1. Faultless Triplet   I. " DEPENDENT " CHAPTER

1. CONDITIONS: POSITIVE   (i) CLASSIFICATION CHAPTER

Root	9	. . . .	22
Object	3	. . . .	23
Predominance . .	9	. . . .	24
Proximity 3, Contiguity .	3	. . . .	25
Conascence . . .	9	. . . .	26
Mutuality . . .	3	. . . .	28
Dependence . . .	9	. . . .	29
Strong-dependence . .	3	. . . .	29
Prenascence . . .	3	. . . .	29
Repetition . . .	3	. . . .	29
Kamma . . .	9	. . . .	30
Resultant . . .	1	. . . .	31
Nutriment . . .	9	. . . .	31
Faculty . . .	9	. . . .	32

		PAGE
Jhāna 9, Path . . 9		32
Association . . . 3		32
Dissociation . . . 9		32
Presence . . . 9		34
Absence 3, Disappearance 3		35
Non-disappearance . 9		35

1. CONDITIONS : POSITIVE   (ii) ENUMERATION CHAPTER
Numbers (of Answers)

Root Condition as Reference	By Ones	35
	By Twos, By Threes, etc. . . .	35
Object, etc. . . .	By Twos	37
Repetition . . .	,, ...	37
Kamma . . .	,, ...	37
Resultant . . .	,, ...	37
Nutriment, etc. . .	,, ...	38
Non-disappearance .	,, ...	38

2. CONDITIONS : NEGATIVE   (i) CLASSIFICATION CHAPTER

Not-root 2	38
Not-object 5	39
Not-predominance . . . 9	40
Not-proximity 5, Not-contiguity 5	42
Not-mutuality . . . 5	42
Not-strong-dependence . . 5	43
Not-prenascence . . . 7	43
Not-postnascence 9, Not-repetition 9	44
Not-kamma 3	45
Not-resultant . . . 9	45
Not-nutriment . . . 1	46
Not-faculty 1	46
Not-jhāna 1	46
Not-path 1	47
Not-association . . . 5	47
Not-dissociation . . . 3	47
Not-absence 5, Not-disappearance 5	48

2. CONDITIONS : NEGATIVE   (ii) ENUMERATION CHAPTER
Numbers (of Answers)

By Ones		. . . . .	48
Not-root	By Twos, etc.	. . .	49
Not-object	,,	. . .	49
Not-predominance . . .	,,	. . .	50
Not-proximity, etc. . .	,,	. . .	50
Not-prenascence . . .	,,	. . .	50
Not-postnascence, Not-repetition	,,	. . .	51
Not-kamma	,,	. . .	52
Not-resultant . . .	,,	. . .	52
Not-nutriment, etc. . .	,,	. . .	53
Not-association . . .	,,	. . .	53
Not-dissociation . . .	,,	. . .	53
Not-absence, Not-disappearance	,,	. . .	54

3. CONDITIONS: POSITIVE–NEGATIVE

Root	By Twos, etc.	54
Object	,,	55
Predominance	,,	55
Proximity, Contiguity	,,	56
Conascence	,,	56
Mutuality	,,	57
Dependence, Strong-dependence	,,	57
Prenascence	,,	57
Repetition	,,	58
Kamma	,,	58
Resultant	,,	58
Nutriment	,,	59
Faculty	,,	60
Jhāna	,,	61
Path	,,	61
Association	,,	62
Dissociation	,,	62
Presence	,,	63
Absence, Disappearance	,,	64
Non-disappearance	,,	64

4. CONDITIONS: NEGATIVE–POSITIVE

Not-root	By Twos, etc.	65
Not-object	,,	66
Not-predominance	,,	66
Not-proximity, etc.	,,	67
Not-prenascence	,,	67
Not-postnascence	,,	68
Not-repetition	,,	68
Not-kamma	,,	69
Not-resultant	,,	69
Not-nutriment	,,	70
Not-faculty	,,	70
Not-jhāna	,,	70
Not-path	By Threes, etc.	71
Not-association	By Twos, etc.	71
Not-dissociation	,,	71
Not-absence, Not-disappearance	,,	72

1. Faultless Triplet

II. "CONASCENT" CHAPTER

1. CONDITIONS: POSITIVE   (i) CLASSIFICATION CHAPTER

Root 9 73

1. CONDITIONS: POSITIVE   (ii) ENUMERATION CHAPTER

By Ones 74

2. CONDITIONS: NEGATIVE   (i) CLASSIFICATION CHAPTER

Not-root 2 75

2. CONDITIONS: NEGATIVE   (ii) ENUMERATION CHAPTER

By Ones 76

		PAGE
3. CONDITIONS: POSITIVE–NEGATIVE		
Root . By Twos		76
4. CONDITIONS: NEGATIVE–POSITIVE		
Not-root . By Twos		76

1. Faultless Triplet   III. "Conditioned" Chapter

1. CONDITIONS: POSITIVE   (i) CLASSIFICATION CHAPTER

Root . . . 17		77
Object . . . 7		79
Predominance . 17		81
Proximity 7, Contiguity 7		81
Conascence . . 17		81
Mutuality . . 7		82
Dependence . . 17		83
Strong-dependence 7		83
Prenascence . . 7		83
Repetition . . 7		84
Kamma . . 17		85
Resultant . . 1		86
Nutriment . . 17		86
Faculty . . 17		87
Jhāna 17, Path . 17		87
Association . . 3		87
Dissociation . . 17		87
Presence Condition, etc.		91

1. CONDITIONS: POSITIVE   (ii) ENUMERATION CHAPTER

By Ones	91
Root . By Twos, etc.	91
Object, etc. By Twos	92

2. CONDITIONS: NEGATIVE   (i) CLASSIFICATION CHAPTER

Not-root . . 4	93
Not-object . . 5	94
Not-predominance . 17	94
Not-proximity, etc.	95
Not-postnascence, etc.	95
Not-kamma . . 7	95
Not-resultant . 17	96
Not-nutriment, etc.	97
Not-association, etc.	97

2. CONDITIONS: NEGATIVE   (ii) ENUMERATION CHAPTER

By Ones	97
Not-root . By Twos, etc.	98
Not-object, etc. ,, ...	98

3. CONDITIONS: POSITIVE–NEGATIVE

Root . . By Twos, etc.	102
Object, etc. . ,, ...	103

Contents

	PAGE
4. CONDITIONS : NEGATIVE–POSITIVE	
Not-root . By Twos, etc.	109
Not-object, etc. ,, ...	110

1. Faultless Triplet — IV. " Supported " Chapter

1. CONDITIONS : POSITIVE (i) CLASSIFICATION CHAPTER
Positive Root   17   115

1. CONDITIONS : POSITIVE (ii) ENUMERATION CHAPTER
By Ones 118

2. CONDITIONS : NEGATIVE (i) CLASSIFICATION CHAPTER
Not-root   4   118

2. CONDITIONS : NEGATIVE (ii) ENUMERATION CHAPTER
By Ones 119

3. CONDITIONS : POSITIVE–NEGATIVE
Root   By Twos 120

4. CONDITIONS : NEGATIVE–POSITIVE
Not-root   By Twos 120

1. Faultless Triplet — V. " Conjoined " Chapter

1. CONDITIONS : POSITIVE (i) CLASSIFICATION CHAPTER
Root .   3   120
Object, etc.   3   121

1. CONDITIONS : POSITIVE (ii) ENUMERATION CHAPTER
By Ones 123
Root, etc.   By Twos, etc. 123

2. CONDITIONS : NEGATIVE (i) CLASSIFICATION CHAPTER
Not-root . .   2   124
Not-predominance, etc.   3   124

2. CONDITIONS : NEGATIVE (ii) ENUMERATION CHAPTER
By Ones 126
Not-root, etc.   By Twos, etc. 126

3. CONDITIONS : POSITIVE–NEGATIVE
Root .   By Twos, etc. 129
Object, etc.   ,, ... 130

4. CONDITIONS : NEGATIVE–POSITIVE
Not-root . .   By Twos, etc. 134
Not-predominance, etc.   ,, ... 135

			PAGE
1. Faultless Triplet	VI. " Associated " Chapter		
1. CONDITIONS : POSITIVE	(i) CLASSIFICATION CHAPTER		
Root . 3			138

1. CONDITIONS : POSITIVE	(ii) ENUMERATION CHAPTER	
By Ones		139

2. CONDITIONS : NEGATIVE	(i) CLASSIFICATION CHAPTER	
Not-root 2		139

2. CONDITIONS : NEGATIVE	(ii) ENUMERATION CHAPTER	
By Ones		140

3. CONDITIONS : POSITIVE–NEGATIVE		
Root . By Twos		140

4. CONDITIONS : NEGATIVE–POSITIVE		
Not-root By Twos		140

1. Faultless Triplet   VII. " Investigation " Chapter
1. CONDITIONS : POSITIVE   (i) CLASSIFICATION CHAPTER

Root . . .	7	141
Object . . .	9	142
Predominance .	10	146
Proximity . .	7	148
Contiguity . .	7	149
Conascence . .	9	150
Mutuality . .	3	153
Dependence . .	13	154
Strong-dependence .	9	156
Prenascence . .	3	166
Postnascence . .	3	167
Repetition . .	3	167
Kamma . .	7	168
Resultant . .	1	169
Nutriment . .	7	169
Faculty . .	7	170
Jhāna . . .	7	171
Path . . .	7	172
Association . .	3	173
Dissociation . .	5	174
Presence . .	13	175
Absence . .	7	179
Disappearance .	7	179
Non-disappearance	13	179

Contents

	PAGE
1. CONDITIONS : POSITIVE (ii) ENUMERATION CHAPTER	

By Ones 180

Root
   Common 11 180
   Conascence Combinations 24
      Ordinary . . . . 9 . . . 180
      With faculty and path . . . 9 . . . 181
      With predominance, faculty and path 6 . . . 181

Object
   Common 7 182
   (Miscellaneous) Combinations 5 182

Predominance
   Common 15 183
   Combinations 30
      Mixed . . 3 183
      Miscellaneous 3 183
      Conascence . 24
         Predominant desire . . . 6 . . . 183
         With nutriment and faculty . . 6 . . . 184
         With faculty and path . . . 6 . . . 184
         With root, faculty and path . . 6 . . . 185

Proximity
   Common 6 185
   (Miscellaneous) Combinations 3 186

Contiguity
   Common 6 186
   Miscellaneous Combinations 3 186

Conascence
   Common 14 186
   Combinations 10 186

Mutuality
   Common 14 187
   Conascence Combinations 6 187

Dependence
   Common 17 188
   Combinations 20
      Mixed . . 6 188
      Miscellaneous 4 188
      Conascence . 10 189

Strong-dependence
   Common 13 189
   (Miscellaneous) Combinations 7 190

Prenascence
   Common 8 190
   (Miscellaneous) Combinations 7 190

	PAGE
Postnascence	
Common 3	191
(Miscellaneous) Combination 1	191
Repetition	
Common 5	191
(Miscellaneous) Combination 1	191
Kamma	
Common 14	191
Combinations 11	
Miscellaneous 2	191
Conascence 9	192
Resultant	
Common 14	192
(Conascence) Combinations 5	192
Nutriment	
Common 11	193
Combinations 34	
Mixed 1	193
Conascence 33	
Ordinary 9	193
With kamma 9	194
With faculty 9	194
With predominance and faculty 6	195
Faculty	
Common 14	196
Combinations 76	
Mixed 3	196
Miscellaneous 1	196
Conascence 72	
Ordinary 9	196
With path 9	197
With jhāna 9	198
With jhāna and path 9	198
With nutriment 9	199
With predominance and nutriment 6	200
With predominance and path 6	200
With root and path 9	201
With root, predominance and path 6	201
Jhāna	
Common 10	202
Conascence Combinations 36	
Ordinary 9	202
With faculty 9	203
With path 9	203
With faculty and path 9	204

		PAGE
Path		
Common 12		205
Conascence Combinations 57		
Ordinary	9 . . .	205
With faculty	9 . . .	206
With jhāna	9 . . .	206
With faculty and jhāna . . .	9 . . .	207
With predominance and faculty .	6 . . .	208
With root and faculty . . .	9 . . .	208
With root, predominance and faculty	6 . . .	209
Association		
Common 13		209
Conascence Combinations 2		210
Dissociation		
Common 17		210
Combinations 13		
Mixed . .	4	210
Miscellaneous	5	210
Conascence .	4	211
Presence		
Common 18		211
Combinations 29		
Mixed . .	11	211
Miscellaneous	8	212
Conascence .	10	212
Absence		
Common 6		213
(Miscellaneous) Combinations 3		213
Disappearance		
Common 6		214
(Miscellaneous) Combinations 3		214
Non-disappearance		
Common 18		214
Combinations 29		
Mixed . .	11	214
Miscellaneous	8	215
Conascence .	10	215

        2. SELECTION OF THE CONDITIONS FOR NEGATIVE   216

    2. CONDITIONS : NEGATIVE   (ii) ENUMERATION CHAPTER

By Ones	217
Not-root . . By Twos, etc.	217
Not-object . . ,, ...	220
Not-predominance, etc. ,, ...	221
Not-conascence . ,, ...	221
Not-mutuality . ,, ...	222
Not-dependence . ,, ...	223

		PAGE
Not-strong-dependence	By Twos, etc.	223
Not-prenascence	,,	225
Not-postnascence	,,	226
Not-repetition	,,	227
Not-kamma	,,	227
Not-resultant	,,	228
Not-nutriment	,,	228
Not-faculty	,,	230
Not-jhāna, Not-path	,,	231
Not-association	,,	231
Not-dissociation	,,	231
Not-presence	,,	232
Not-absence	,,	234
Not-disappearance	,,	234
Not-non-disappearance	,,	234

3. CONDITIONS : POSITIVE–NEGATIVE

Root
  By Twos 234
  Conascence Combinations 24
    Ordinary . . . . . 9 . . . 235
    With faculty and path . . . 9 . . . 237
    With predominance, faculty and path 6 . . . 238

Object
  By Twos 240
  (Miscellaneous) Combinations 5 240

Predominance
  By Twos 241
  Combinations 30
    Mixed . . 3 241
    Miscellaneous . 3 242
    Conascence . 24
      Predominant desire . . . 6 . . . 243
      With nutriment and faculty . . 6 . . . 244
      With faculty and path . . . 6 . . . 245
      With root, faculty and path . . 6 . . . 247

Proximity
  By Twos 248
  (Miscellaneous) Combinations 3 248

Contiguity
  By Twos 249
  (Miscellaneous) Combinations 3 249

Conascence
  By Twos 250
  Conascence Combinations 10 250

Mutuality
  By Twos 252
  (Conascence) Combinations 6 252

		PAGE
Dependence		
By Twos		253
Combinations 20		
Mixed	6	254
Miscellaneous	4	255
Conascence	10	256
Strong-dependence		
By Twos		258
(Miscellaneous) Combinations 7		258
Prenascence		
By Twos		259
(Miscellaneous) Combinations 7		260
Postnascence		
By Twos		261
(Miscellaneous) Combination 1		261
Repetition		
By Twos		262
(Miscellaneous) Combination 1		262
Kamma		
By Twos		262
Combinations 11		
Miscellaneous	2	262
Conascence (with nutriment)	9	263
Resultant		
By Twos		265
(Conascence) Combinations 5		265
Nutriment		
By Twos		266
Combinations 34		
Mixed	1	266
Conascence 33		
Ordinary	9	267
With kamma	9	268
With faculty	9	270
With predominance and faculty	6	272
Faculty		
By Twos		273
Combinations 76		
Mixed	3	274
Miscellaneous	1	274
Conascence 72		
Ordinary	9	275
With path	9	276
With jhāna	9	277
With jhāna and path	9	278
With nutriment	9	279
With predominance and nutriment	6	280
With predominance and path	6	281
With root and path	9	282
With root, predominance and path	6	282

	PAGE
Jhāna	
By Twos	284
Conascence Combinations 36	
Ordinary . . . . . 9 . . .	284
With faculty . . . . . 9 . . .	285
With path . . . . . 9 . . .	286
With faculty and path . . . 9 . . .	287
Path	
By Twos	288
Conascence Combinations 57	
Ordinary . . . . . 9 . . .	288
With faculty . . . . . 9 . . .	289
With jhāna . . . . . 9 . . .	290
With faculty and jhāna . . . 9 . . .	291
With predominance and faculty . 6 . . .	292
With root and faculty . . . 9 . . .	292
With root, predominance and faculty 6 . . .	293
Association	
By Twos	294
Conascence Combinations 2	294
Dissociation	
By Twos	295
Combinations 13	
Mixed . . 4	295
Miscellaneous . 5	296
Conascence . 4	297
Presence	
By Twos	298
Combinations 29	
Mixed . . 11	298
Miscellaneous . 8	300
Conascence . 10	302
Absence, Disappearance	
By Twos	304
Non-disappearance	
By Twos	304

4. CONDITIONS : NEGATIVE–POSITIVE

Not-root . By Twos, etc.	304
Not-object, etc. ,, ...	306

2. Feeling Triplet   I. " Dependent " Chapter

1. CONDITIONS : POSITIVE   (i) CLASSIFICATION CHAPTER

Root . 3	318
Object, etc.	318

Contents

cxxiii

		PAGE
1. CONDITIONS: POSITIVE	(ii) ENUMERATION CHAPTER	
By Ones		320
Root, etc. By Twos, etc.		321
2. CONDITIONS: NEGATIVE	(i) CLASSIFICATION CHAPTER	
Not-root . 3		321
Not-predominance 3, etc.		322
2. CONDITIONS: NEGATIVE	(ii) ENUMERATION CHAPTER	
By Ones		325
Not-root, etc. By Twos, etc.		325
3. CONDITIONS: POSITIVE–NEGATIVE		
Root . . By Twos, etc.		327
4. CONDITIONS: NEGATIVE–POSITIVE		
Not-root . . By Twos, etc.		328
Not-predominance, etc. ,, ...		329
II. "CONASCENT" CHAPTER . . .		330
III. "CONDITIONED" CHAPTER . . .		330
IV. "SUPPORTED" CHAPTER . . .		331
V. "CONJOINED" CHAPTER . . .		331
VI. "ASSOCIATED" CHAPTER . . .		331

2. Feeling Triplet

VII. "INVESTIGATION" CHAPTER

1. CONDITIONS: POSITIVE		(i) CLASSIFICATION CHAPTER	
Root	3	. . . . . .	331
Object	9	. . . . . .	332
Predominance . .	5	. . . . . .	336
Proximity . . .	7	. . . . . .	338
Contiguity . . .	7	. . . . . .	340
Conascence . . .	3	. . . . . .	340
Mutuality 3, Dependence	3	. . . . . .	341
Strong-dependence .	9	. . . . . .	341
Repetition . . .	3	. . . . . .	347
Kamma	8	. . . . . .	347
Resultant . . .	3	. . . . . .	349
Nutriment, etc.			349

1. CONDITIONS: POSITIVE	(ii) ENUMERATION CHAPTER	
By Ones		350

Root
   Common 10 350
   Combinations 6
      Ordinary Combinations . . 2 350
      With faculty and path . . 2 350
      With predominance, faculty and path 2 350

Object
    Common 2 351
    Combination 1 351

Predominance
    Common 13 351
    Combinations 9 351

Proximity, Contiguity
    Common 6 352
    Combinations 3 352

Conascence, etc.
    Common 13 352
    Combinations 2 352

Strong-dependence
    Common 8 352
    Combinations 5 353

Repetition
    Common 5 353
    Combination 1 353

Kamma
    Common 13 353
    Combinations 4 353

Resultant
    Common 13 353
    Combination 1 354

Nutriment
    Common 10 354
    Combinations 8 354

Faculty
    Common 12 354
    Combinations 16 355

Jhāna
    Common 9 356
    Combinations 6 356

Path
    Common 11 356
    Combinations 14 356

Association
    Common 13 357
    Combinations 2 357

Presence, etc. 357

"Investigation" Chapter

	PAGE
SELECTION OF THE CONDITIONS FOR NEGATIVE	358

2. CONDITIONS: NEGATIVE   (ii) ENUMERATION CHAPTER

| By Ones | . | . | . | . | . | . | . | . | . | 358 |
| Not-root | . | By Twos, etc. | . | . | . | . | . | . | 359 |

3. CONDITIONS: POSITIVE–NEGATIVE

| Root | . | . | By Twos | . | . | . | . | . | . | 359 |
| Ordinary Combination | . | . | . | . | . | . | 360 |

4. CONDITIONS: NEGATIVE–POSITIVE

| Not-root | . | By Twos, etc. | . | . | . | . | . | . | 360 |
| Not-object, etc. | . | ,, | . | . | . | . | . | . | 361 |

3. Resultant Triplet   I. "Dependent" Chapter

1. CONDITIONS: POSITIVE   (i) CLASSIFICATION CHAPTER

Root	.	.	.	13	.	.	.	.	.	.	362
Object	.	.	.	5	.	.	.	.	.	.	364
Predominance	.	9	.	.	.	.	.	.	365
Proximity, etc.	.	.	.	.	.	.	.	.	366

1. CONDITIONS: POSITIVE   (ii) ENUMERATION CHAPTER

| By Ones | . | . | . | . | . | . | . | . | . | 369 |
| Root, etc. | . | . | By Twos, etc. | . | . | . | . | . | 369 |

2. CONDITIONS: NEGATIVE   (i) CLASSIFICATION CHAPTER

Not-root	.	.	10	.	.	.	.	.	.	370
Not-object	.	.	5	.	.	.	.	.	.	372
Not-predominance	.	13	.	.	.	.	.	.	373
Not-proximity, etc.	.	.	.	.	.	.	.	.	373

2. CONDITIONS: NEGATIVE   (ii) ENUMERATION CHAPTER

| By Ones | . | . | . | . | . | . | . | . | . | 380 |
| Not-root | . | . | By Twos, etc. | . | . | . | . | . | 380 |

3. CONDITIONS: POSITIVE–NEGATIVE

| Root | . | . | . | By Twos, etc. | . | . | . | . | . | 381 |

4. CONDITIONS: NEGATIVE–POSITIVE

| Not-root | . | . | . | By Twos, etc. | . | . | . | . | . | 381 |

3. Resultant Triplet   II. "Conascent" Chapter

1. CONDITIONS: POSITIVE (i) CLASSIFICATION CHAPTER	.	382
1. CONDITIONS: POSITIVE (ii) ENUMERATION CHAPTER	.	382
2. CONDITIONS: NEGATIVE	.	.	.	382
3. CONDITIONS: POSITIVE–NEGATIVE	.	.	.	383
4. CONDITIONS: NEGATIVE–POSITIVE	.	.	.	383

cxxvi   *Conditional Relations*

PAGE

3. Resultant Triplet   III. " Conditioned " Chapter

     1. conditions : positive   (i) classification chapter

Root	17	383
Object	7	386
Predominance	17	388
Proximity 7, etc.		390

     1. conditions : positive   (ii) enumeration chapter

By Ones 394
Root . . . By Twos 394

     2. conditions : negative   (i) classification chapter

Not-root . . 12 394
Not-object . . 5 395

     2. conditions : negative   (ii) enumeration chapter

By Ones 396
Not-root . . By Twos 396

     3. conditions : positive–negative

Root . . . By Twos 396

     4. conditions : negative–positive

Not-root . . By Twos, etc. 396

3. Resultant Triplet   IV. " Supported " Chapter

     1–4. conditions : set of four . . . 397

3. Resultant Triplet   V. " Conjoined " Chapter

     1. conditions : positive   (i) classification chapter

Root . . . 3 397

     1. conditions : positive   (ii) enumeration chapter

By Ones 397

     2. conditions : negative   (i) classification chapter . 398
     2. conditions : negative   (ii) enumeration chapter . 398
     3. conditions : positive–negative . . . 398
     4. conditions : negative–positive . . . 398

3. Resultant Triplet   VI. " Associated " Chapter

     1–4. conditions : set of four . . . 399

3. Resultant Triplet VII. "Investigation" Chapter

1. CONDITIONS: POSITIVE (i) CLASSIFICATION CHAPTER

Root	7	399
Object	9	400
Predominance	10	404
Proximity	7	406
Contiguity	7	408
Conascence	11	408
Mutuality	7	409
Dependence	13	410
Strong-dependence	9	411
Prenascence	3	414
Postnascence	3	415
Repetition	2	416
Kamma	9	416
Resultant	3	417
Nutriment	7	418
Faculty	9	418
Jhāna	7	419
Path	7	419
Association	3	420
Dissociation	5	420
Presence	13	421
Absence 7, Disappearance	7	425
Non-disappearance	13	425

1. CONDITIONS: POSITIVE (ii) ENUMERATION CHAPTER

By Ones 425
Root
 Common 11 425

2. SELECTION OF THE CONDITIONS FOR NEGATIVE . . 426

2. CONDITIONS: NEGATIVE (ii) ENUMERATION CHAPTER

By Ones 427
Not-root   By Twos 427

3. CONDITIONS: POSITIVE–NEGATIVE

Root
 By Twos 428
 Combination 428

4. CONDITIONS: NEGATIVE–POSITIVE

Not-root   By Twos, etc. 428

4. Clinging Triplet I. "Dependent" Chapter

1. CONDITIONS: POSITIVE (i) CLASSIFICATION CHAPTER

Root	9	429
Object	3	431
Predominance	5	431
Proximity, etc.		431
Mutuality 3, etc.		432

				PAGE
1. CONDITIONS: POSITIVE	(ii) ENUMERATION CHAPTER			
By Ones				434
By Twos				434
2. CONDITIONS: NEGATIVE	(i) CLASSIFICATION CHAPTER			
Not-root	5			435
Not-object	6			436
Not-predominance	6			437
Not-proximity, etc.				438
Not-kamma 2, etc.				438
2. CONDITIONS: NEGATIVE	(ii) ENUMERATION CHAPTER			
By Ones				441
Not-root	By Twos			441
3. CONDITIONS: POSITIVE–NEGATIVE				
Root	By Twos			442
4. CONDITIONS: NEGATIVE–POSITIVE				
Not-root	By Twos			442

4. Clinging Triplet   II. "CONASCENT" CHAPTER

1–4. CONDITIONS: THE SET OF FOUR				442

4. Clinging Triplet   III. "CONDITIONED" CHAPTER

1. CONDITIONS: POSITIVE	(i) CLASSIFICATION CHAPTER			
Root	11			443
Object	7			444
Predominance	9			446
Proximity				447
1. CONDITIONS: POSITIVE	(ii) ENUMERATION CHAPTER			
By Ones				447
Root	By Twos			447
2. CONDITIONS: NEGATIVE	(i) CLASSIFICATION CHAPTER			
Not-root	5			447
Not-object	6			449
Not-predominance	8			449
Not-proximity, etc.				450
Not-kamma 6, etc.				450
2. CONDITIONS: NEGATIVE	(ii) ENUMERATION CHAPTER			453
3. CONDITIONS: POSITIVE–NEGATIVE				453
4. CONDITIONS: NEGATIVE–POSITIVE				453

4. Clinging Triplet   IV. "SUPPORTED" CHAPTER   453

Contents

4. Clinging Triplet	V. "Conjoined" Chapter		
1. conditions: positive			
Root	3		453
Enumeration Chapter			454
2. conditions: negative			
Not-root	2		454
4. Clinging Triplet	VI. "Associated" Chapter		455
4. Clinging Triplet	VII. "Investigation" Chapter		
1. conditions: positive	(i) classification chapter		
Root	7		455
Object	6		457
Predominance	5		459
Proximity	7		461
Contiguity	7		462
Conascence	9		463
Mutuality	3		465
Dependence	11		465
Strong-dependence	9		467
Prenascence	7		470
Postnascence	9		473
Repetition	2		475
Kamma	8		475
Resultant	6		477
Nutriment	12		478
Faculty	7		481
Jhāna	7		482
Path	7		483
Association	3		484
Dissociation	10		485
Presence	23		488
Absence	7		497
Disappearance	7		497
Non-disappearance	23		497
1. conditions: positive	(ii) enumeration chapter		
By Ones			497
Common			497
2. selection of the conditions for negative			498
2. conditions: negative	(ii) enumeration chapter		
By Ones			501
Not-root	By Twos		501
3. conditions: positive–negative			
Root			
By Twos			501
Combination			501

				PAGE
	4. CONDITIONS: NEGATIVE–POSITIVE			
Not-root	. .	By Twos	. . . .	502

5. Corrupt Triplet   I. "Dependent" Chapter

	1. CONDITIONS: POSITIVE	(i) CLASSIFICATION CHAPTER	
Root	. . . 9	. . . .	502

	1. CONDITIONS: POSITIVE	(ii) ENUMERATION CHAPTER	
By Ones	. . . .	. . . .	504

	2. CONDITIONS: NEGATIVE		
Not-root	. . 2	. . . .	504
By Ones	. . . .	. . . . . .	504

	3. CONDITIONS: POSITIVE–NEGATIVE		
Root	. . .	By Twos	505

	4. CONDITIONS: NEGATIVE–POSITIVE		
Not-root	. .	By Twos	505

5. Corrupt Triplet   VII. "Investigation" Chapter

	1. CONDITIONS: POSITIVE	(i) CLASSIFICATION CHAPTER	
Root	. . . 7	. . . .	505
Object	. . . 6	. . . .	506
Predominance	. 8	. . . .	508
Proximity	. . 7	. . . .	510
Contiguity, etc.	. .	. . . .	511
Prenascence	. . 3	. . . .	514
Postnascence	. 3	. . . .	515
Repetition	. . 3	. . . .	515
Kamma	. . 7	. . . .	516
Resultant	. . 4	. . . .	517
Nutriment	. . 7	. . . .	518
Faculty	. . 7	. . . .	518
Jhāna, etc.	. .	. . . .	518
Dissociation	. . 5	. . . .	518
Presence	. . 13	. . . .	519
Absence	. . 7	. . . .	522
Disappearance	. 7	. . . .	522
Non-disappearance	13	. . . .	522

	1. CONDITIONS: POSITIVE	(ii) ENUMERATION CHAPTER	
By Ones	. . . .	. . . .	522
Root			
Common 11	. . .	. . . .	523
Combinations 9	.	. . . .	523

Contents

		PAGE
2. SELECTION OF THE CONDITIONS FOR NEGATIVE	.	. 524

CONDITIONS: NEGATIVE

By Ones	. . . .	. 525
By Twos	. . . .	. 525

3. CONDITIONS: POSITIVE–NEGATIVE

Root

By Twos	. . . .	. 525
Combinations	. . . .	. 526

4. CONDITIONS: NEGATIVE–POSITIVE

Not-root . . By Twos, By Threes 526

CONDITIONAL RELATIONS
States: Positive
Conditional Relations of Triplets

Veneration to that Exalted One, the Arahat, the Enlightened Buddha

I. Enumeration of the Conditions

1. Root	Condition	(Hetu	Paccayo)	
2. Object	,,	(Ārammana	,,	)
3. Predominance	,,	(Adhipati	,,	)
4. Proximity	,,	(Anantara	,,	)
5. Contiguity	,,	(Samanantara	,,	)
6. Conascence	,,	(Sahajāta	,,	)
7. Mutuality	,,	(Aññamañña	,,	)
8. Dependence	,,	(Nissaya	,,	)
9. Strong-Dependence	,,	(Upanissaya	,,	)
10. Prenascence	,,	(Purejāta	,,	)
11. Postnascence	,,	(Pacchājāta	,,	)
12. Repetition	,,	(Āsevana	,,	)
13. Kamma	,,	(Kamma	,,	)
14. Resultant	,,	(Vipāka	,,	)
15. Nutriment	,,	(Āhāra	,,	)
16. Faculty	,,	(Indriya	,,	)
17. Jhāna	,,	(Jhāna	,,	)
18. Path	,,	(Magga	,,	)
19. Association	,,	(Sampayutta	,,	)
20. Dissociation	,,	(Vippayutta	,,	)
21. Presence	,,	(Atthi	,,	)
22. Absence	,,	(Natthi	,,	)
23. Disappearance	,,	(Vigata	,,	)
24. Non-disappearance	,,	(Avigata	,,	)

End of the Enumeration.

II. ANALYTICAL EXPOSITION OF THE CONDITIONS

1. ROOT CONDITION

The roots are related to the states which are associated with roots, and the matter produced thereby, by root condition.

2. OBJECT CONDITION

(i) Visible object-base is related to eye-consciousness element and its associated states by object condition.

(ii) Sound-base is related to ear-consciousness element and its associated states by object condition.

(iii) Odour-base is related to nose-consciousness element and its associated states by object condition.

(iv) Taste-base is related to tongue-consciousness element and its associated states by object condition.

(v) Tangible object-base is related to body-consciousness element and its associated states by object condition.

(vi) Visible object-base, sound-base, odour-base, taste-base, tangible object-base is related to mind-element and its associated states by object condition.

(vii) All states are related to mind-consciousness element and its associated states by object condition.

(viii) Taking any state as object, these states, consciousness and mental factors, arise; those (former) states are related to those (latter) states by object condition.

3. PREDOMINANCE CONDITION

(i) Predominant desire is related to the states associated with desire, and the matter produced thereby, by predominance condition.

(ii) Predominant effort is related to the states associated with effort, and the matter produced thereby, by predominance condition.

(iii) Predominant consciousness is related to the states associated with consciousness, and the matter produced thereby, by predominance condition.

(iv) Predominant investigating-wisdom is related to the

states associated with investigating-wisdom, and the matter produced thereby, by predominance condition.

(v) Taking any state as estimable object, these states, consciousness and mental factors, arise ; those (former) states are related to those (latter) states by predominance condition.

4. PROXIMITY CONDITION

(i) Eye-consciousness element and its associated states are related to mind-element and its associated states by proximity condition ; mind-element and its associated states are related to mind-consciousness element and its associated states by proximity condition.

(ii) Ear-consciousness element and its associated states are related to mind-element and its associated states by proximity condition ; mind-element and its associated states are related to mind-consciousness element and its associated states by proximity condition.

(iii) Nose-consciousness element and its associated states are related to mind-element and its associated states by proximity condition ; mind-element and its associated states are related to mind-consciousness element and its associated states by proximity condition.

(iv) Tongue-consciousness element and its associated states are related to mind-element and its associated states by proximity condition ; mind-element and its associated states are related to mind-consciousness element and its associated states by proximity condition.

(v) Body-consciousness element and its associated states are related to mind-element and its associated states by proximity condition ; mind-element and its associated states are related to mind-consciousness element and its associated states by proximity condition.

(vi) Preceding faultless states are related to subsequent faultless states by proximity condition.

(vii) Preceding faultless states are related to subsequent indeterminate states by proximity condition.

(viii) Preceding faulty states are related to subsequent faulty states by proximity condition.

(ix) Preceding faulty states are related to subsequent indeterminate states by proximity condition.

(x) Preceding indeterminate states are related to subsequent indeterminate states by proximity condition.

(xi) Preceding indeterminate states are related to subsequent faultless states by proximity condition.

(xii) Preceding indeterminate states are related to subsequent faulty states by proximity condition.

(xiii) In proximity to these states, these (other) states, consciousness and mental factors, arise ; those (former) states are related to those (latter) states by proximity condition.

5. CONTIGUITY CONDITION

(i) Eye-consciousness element and its associated states are related to mind-element and its associated states by contiguity condition ; mind-element and its associated states are related to mind-consciousness element and its associated states by contiguity condition.

(ii) Ear-consciousness element and its associated states are related to mind-element and its associated states by contiguity condition ; mind-element and its associated states are related to mind-consciousness element and its associated states by contiguity condition.

(iii) Nose-consciousness element and its associated states are related to mind-element and its associated states by contiguity condition ; mind-element and its associated states are related to mind-consciousness element and its associated states by contiguity condition.

(iv) Tongue-consciousness element and its associated states are related to mind-element and its associated states by contiguity condition ; mind-element and its associated states are related to mind-consciousness element and its associated states by contiguity condition.

(v) Body-consciousness element and its associated states are related to mind-element and its associated states by contiguity condition ; mind-element and its associated states are related to mind-consciousness element and its associated states by contiguity condition.

(vi) Preceding faultless states are related to subsequent faultless states by contiguity condition.

(vii) Preceding faultless states are related to subsequent indeterminate states by contiguity condition.

(viii) Preceding faulty states are related to subsequent faulty states by contiguity condition.

(ix) Preceding faulty states are related to subsequent indeterminate states by contiguity condition.

(x) Preceding indeterminate states are related to subsequent indeterminate states by contiguity condition.

(xi) Preceding indeterminate states are related to subsequent faultless states by contiguity condition.

(xii) Preceding indeterminate states are related to subsequent faulty states by contiguity condition.

(xiii) In contiguity with these states, these (other) states, consciousness and mental factors, arise ; those (former) states are related to those (latter) states by contiguity condition.

6. CONASCENCE CONDITION

(i) The four immaterial (i.e. mental) aggregates are mutually related to one another by conascence condition.

(ii) The four great primaries are mutually related to one another by conascence condition.

(iii) At the moment of conception, mentality and materiality are mutually related to one another by conascence condition.

(iv) States, consciousness and mental factors, are related to mind-produced matter by conascence condition.

(v) The great primaries are related to derived matter by conascence condition.

(vi) The material states are sometimes related to the immaterial states by conascence condition and are sometimes not related by conascence condition.

7. MUTUALITY CONDITION

(i) The four immaterial aggregates are related to one another by mutuality condition.

(ii) The four great primaries are related to one another by mutuality condition.

(iii) At the moment of conception, mentality and materiality are related to one another by mutuality condition.

8. DEPENDENCE CONDITION

(i) The four immaterial aggregates are mutually related to one another by dependence condition.

(ii) The four great primaries are mutually related to one another by dependence condition.

(iii) At the moment of conception, mentality and materiality are mutually related to one another by dependence condition.

(iv) States, consciousness and mental factors, are related to mind-produced matter by dependence condition.

(v) The great primaries are related to derived matter by dependence condition.

(vi) Eye-base is related to eye-consciousness element and its associated states by dependence condition.

(vii) Ear-base is related to ear-consciousness element and its associated states by dependence condition.

(viii) Nose-base is related to nose-consciousness element and its associated states by dependence condition.

(ix) Tongue-base is related to tongue-consciousness element and its associated states by dependence condition.

(x) Body-base is related to body-consciousness element and its associated states by dependence condition.

(xi) Depending on this matter (i.e. heart-base), mind-element and mind-consciousness element arise; that matter is related to mind-element and mind-consciousness element and their associated states by dependence condition.

9. STRONG-DEPENDENCE CONDITION

(i) Preceding faultless states are related to subsequent faultless states by strong-dependence condition.

(ii) Preceding faultless states are related to some subsequent faulty states by strong-dependence condition.

(iii) Preceding faultless states are related to subsequent indeterminate states by strong-dependence condition.

(iv) Preceding faulty states are related to subsequent faulty states by strong-dependence condition.

(v) Preceding faulty states are related to some subsequent faultless states by strong-dependence condition.

(vi) Preceding faulty states are related to subsequent indeterminate states by strong-dependence condition.

(vii) Preceding indeterminate states are related to subsequent indeterminate states by strong-dependence condition.

(viii) Preceding indeterminate states are related to subsequent faultless states by strong-dependence condition.

(ix) Preceding indeterminate states are related to subsequent faulty states by strong-dependence condition.

(x) Also, weather and food are related by strong-dependence condition; a person is related by strong-dependence condition; a lodging-place is related by strong-dependence condition.

10. PRENASCENCE CONDITION

(i) Eye-base is related to eye-consciousness element and its associated states by prenascence condition.

(ii) Ear-base is related to ear-consciousness element and its associated states by prenascence condition.

(iii) Nose-base is related to nose-consciousness element and its associated states by prenascence condition.

(iv) Tongue-base is related to tongue-consciousness element and its associated states by prenascence condition.

(v) Body-base is related to body-consciousness element and its associated states by prenascence condition.

(vi) Visible object-base is related to eye-consciousness element and its associated states by prenascence condition.

(vii) Sound-base is related to ear-consciousness element and its associated states by prenascence condition.

(viii) Odour-base is related to nose-consciousness element and its associated states by prenascence condition.

(ix) Taste-base is related to tongue-consciousness element and its associated states by prenascence condition.

(x) Tangible object-base is related to body-consciousness element and its associated states by prenascence condition.

(xi) Visible object-base, sound-base, odour-base, taste-base, tangible object-base is related to mind-element and its associated states by prenascence condition.

(xii) Depending on this matter, mind-element and mind-consciousness element arise ; that matter is related to mind-element and its associated states by prenascence condition ; is sometimes related to mind-consciousness element and its associated states by prenascence condition, and is sometimes not related by prenascence condition.

11. POSTNASCENCE CONDITION

The states, postnascent consciousness and mental factors, are related to this prenascent body by postnascence condition.

12. REPETITION CONDITION

(i) Preceding faultless states are related to subsequent faultless states by repetition condition.

(ii) Preceding faulty states are related to subsequent faulty states by repetition condition.

(iii) Preceding functional indeterminate states are related to subsequent functional indeterminate states by repetition condition.

13. KAMMA CONDITION

(i) Faultless and faulty kamma is related to resultant aggregates and kamma-produced matter by kamma condition.

(ii) Volition is related to its associated states, and the matter produced thereby, by kamma condition.

14. RESULTANT CONDITION

The four immaterial resultant aggregates are mutually related to one another by resultant condition.

15. NUTRIMENT CONDITION

(i) Edible food is related to this body by nutriment condition.

(ii) The immaterial nutriments are related to their associated states, and the matter produced thereby, by nutriment condition.

16. FACULTY CONDITION

(i) Eye-faculty is related to eye-consciousness element and its associated states by faculty condition.

(ii) Ear-faculty is related to ear-consciousness element and its associated states by faculty condition.

(iii) Nose-faculty is related to nose-consciousness element and its associated states by faculty condition.

(iv) Tongue-faculty is related to tongue-consciousness element and its associated states by faculty condition.

(v) Body-faculty is related to body-consciousness element and its associated states by faculty condition.

(vi) Physical life-faculty is related to kamma-produced matter by faculty condition

(vii) The immaterial faculties are related to their associated states, and the matter produced thereby, by faculty condition.

17. JHĀNA CONDITION

The jhāna factors are related to their associated states, and the matter produced thereby, by jhāna condition.

18. PATH CONDITION

The path factors are related to their associated states, and the matter produced thereby, by path condition.

19. ASSOCIATION CONDITION

The four immaterial aggregates are mutually related to one another by association condition.

20. DISSOCIATION CONDITION

(i) The material states are related to the immaterial states by dissociation condition.

(ii) The immaterial states are related to the material states by dissociation condition.

21. PRESENCE CONDITION

(i) The four immaterial aggregates are mutually related to one another by presence condition.

(ii) The four great primaries are mutually related to one another by presence condition.

(iii) At the moment of conception, mentality and materiality are mutually related to one another by presence condition.

(iv) States, consciousness and mental factors, are related to mind-produced matter by presence condition.

(v) The great primaries are related to derived matter by presence condition.

(vi) Eye-base is related to eye-consciousness element and its associated states by presence condition.

(vii) Ear-base is related to ear-consciousness element and its associated states by presence condition.

(viii) Nose-base is related to nose-consciousness element and its associated states by presence condition.

(ix) Tongue-base is related to tongue-consciousness element and its associated states by presence condition.

(x) Body-base is related to body-consciousness element and its associated states by presence condition.

(xi) Visible object-base is related to eye-consciousness element and its associated states by presence condition.

(xii) Sound-base is related to ear-consciousness element and its associated states by presence condition.

(xiii) Odour-base is related to nose-consciousness element and its associated states by presence condition.

(xiv) Taste-base is related to tongue-consciousness element and its associated states by presence condition.

(xv) Tangible object-base is related to body-consciousness element and its associated states by presence condition.

(xvi) Visible object-base, sound-base, odour-base, taste-base, tangible object-base is related to mind-element and its associated states by presence condition.

(xvii) Depending on this matter, mind-element and mind-consciousness element arise ; that matter is related to mind-element and mind-consciousness element and their associated states by presence condition.

22. ABSENCE CONDITION

States, consciousness and mental factors, which have just ceased in contiguity, are related to the present states, consciousness and mental factors, by absence condition.

23. DISAPPEARANCE CONDITION

States, consciousness and mental factors, which have just disappeared in contiguity, are related to the present states, consciousness and mental factors, by disappearance condition.

24. NON-DISAPPEARANCE CONDITION

(i) The four immaterial aggregates are mutually related to one another by non-disappearance condition.

(ii) The four great primaries are mutually related to one another by non-disappearance condition.

(iii) At the moment of conception, mentality and materiality are mutually related to one another by non-disappearance condition.

(iv) States, consciousness and mental factors, are related to mind-produced matter by non-disappearance condition.

(v) The great primaries are related to derived matter by non-disappearance condition.

(vi) Eye-base is related to eye-consciousness element and its associated states by non-disappearance condition.

(vii) Ear-base is related to ear-consciousness element and its associated states by non-disappearance condition.

(viii) Nose-base is related to nose-consciousness element and its associated states by non-disappearance condition.

(ix) Tongue-base is related to tongue-consciousness element and its associated states by non-disappearance condition.

(x) Body-base is related to body-consciousness element and its associated states by non-disappearance condition.

(xi) Visible object-base is related to eye-consciousness element and its associated states by non-disappearance condition.

(xii) Sound-base is related to ear-consciousness element and its associated states by non-disappearance condition.

(xiii) Odour-base is related to nose-consciousness element and its associated states by non-disappearance condition.

(xiv) Taste-base is related to tongue-consciousness element and its associated states by non-disappearance condition.

(xv) Tangible object-base is related to body-consciousness element and its associated states by non-disappearance condition.

(xvi) Visible object-base, sound-base, odour-base, taste-base, tangible object-base is related to mind-element and its associated states by non-disappearance condition.

(xvii) Depending on this matter, mind-element and mind-consciousness element arise; that matter is related to mind-element and mind-consciousness element and their associated states by non-disappearance condition.

End of Analytical Exposition of the Conditions.

QUESTION CHAPTER

I. CONDITIONS : POSITIVE

By Ones

1. FAULTLESS SECTION

(Root Condition)

25. (i) Dependent on faultless state, may there arise faultless state by root condition ?

(ii) Dependent on faultless state, may there arise faulty state by root condition ?

(iii) Dependent on faultless state, may there arise indeterminate state by root condition ?

(iv) Dependent on faultless state, may there arise faultless and indeterminate states by root condition ?

(v) Dependent on faultless state, may there arise faulty and indeterminate states by root condition ?

(vi) Dependent on faultless state, may there arise faultless and faulty states by root condition ?

(vii) Dependent on faultless state, may there arise faultless, faulty and indeterminate states by root condition ?

2. FAULTY SECTION

26. (i) Dependent on faulty state, may there arise faulty state by root condition ?

(ii) Dependent on faulty state, may there arise faultless state by root condition ?

(iii) Dependent on faulty state, may there arise indeterminate state by root condition ?

(iv) Dependent on faulty state, may there arise faultless and indeterminate states by root condition ?

(v) Dependent on faulty state, may there arise faulty and indeterminate states by root condition ?

(vi) Dependent on faulty state, may there arise faultless and faulty states by root condition ?

(vii) Dependent on faulty state, may there arise faultless, faulty and indeterminate states by root condition ?

3. INDETERMINATE SECTION

27. (i) Dependent on indeterminate state, may there arise indeterminate state by root condition ?

(ii) Dependent on indeterminate state, may there arise faultless state by root condition ?

(iii) Dependent on indeterminate state, may there arise faulty state by root condition ?

(iv) Dependent on indeterminate state, may there arise faultless and indeterminate states by root condition ?

(v) Dependent on indeterminate state, may there arise faulty and indeterminate states by root condition ?

(vi) Dependent on indeterminate state, may there arise faultless and faulty states by root condition ?

(vii) Dependent on indeterminate state, may there arise faultless, faulty and indeterminate states by root condition ?

4. FAULTLESS AND INDETERMINATE SECTION

28. (i) Dependent on faultless (state)[1] and indeterminate state, may there arise faultless state by root condition ?

(ii) Dependent on faultless and indeterminate state, may there arise faulty state by root condition ?

(iii) Dependent on faultless and indeterminate state, may there arise indeterminate state by root condition ?

(iv) Dependent on faultless and indeterminate state, may there arise faultless and indeterminate states by root condition ?

(v) Dependent on faultless and indeterminate state, may there arise faulty and indeterminate states by root condition ?

(vi) Dependent on faultless and indeterminate state, may there arise faultless and faulty states by root condition ?

(vii) Dependent on faultless and indeterminate state, may there arise faultless, faulty and indeterminate states by root condition ?

5. FAULTY AND INDETERMINATE SECTION

29. (i) Dependent on faulty (state)[1] and indeterminate state, may there arise faultless state by root condition ?

---

[1] To show that these are two different states. This is to be understood in all such cases. In the Pali the singular is used for both of them. But a state can never be both.

(ii) Dependent on faulty and indeterminate state, may there arise faulty state by root condition ?

(iii) Dependent on faulty and indeterminate state, may there arise indeterminate state by root condition ?

(iv) Dependent on faulty and indeterminate state, may there arise faultless and indeterminate states by root condition ?

(v) Dependent on faulty and indeterminate state, may there arise faulty and indeterminate states by root condition ?

(vi) Dependent on faulty and indeterminate state, may there arise faultless and faulty states by root condition ?

(vii) Dependent on faulty and indeterminate state, may there arise faultless, faulty and indeterminate states by root condition ?

6. FAULTLESS AND FAULTY SECTION

30. (i) Dependent on faultless (state)[1] and faulty state, may there arise faultless state by root condition ?

(ii) Dependent on faultless and faulty state, may there arise faulty state by root condition ?

(iii) Dependent on faultless and faulty state, may there arise indeterminate state by root condition ?

(iv) Dependent on faultless and faulty state, may there arise faultless and indeterminate states by root condition ?

(v) Dependent on faultless and faulty state, may there arise faulty and indeterminate states by root condition ?

(vi) Dependent on faultless and faulty state, may there arise faultless and faulty states by root condition ?

(vii) Dependent on faultless and faulty state, may there arise faultless, faulty and indeterminate states by root condition ?

7. FAULTLESS, FAULTY AND INDETERMINATE SECTION

31. (i) Dependent on faultless (state),[1] faulty (state)[1] and indeterminate state, may there arise faultless state by root condition ?

(ii) Dependent on faultless, faulty and indeterminate state, may there arise faulty state by root condition ?

---

[1] A state is either faultless, faulty or indeterminate.

(iii) Dependent on faultless, faulty and indeterminate state, may there arise indeterminate state by root condition?

(iv) Dependent on faultless, faulty and indeterminate state, may there arise faultless and indeterminate states by root condition?

(v) Dependent on faultless, faulty and indeterminate state, may there arise faulty and indeterminate states by root condition?

(vi) Dependent on faultless, faulty and indeterminate state, may there arise faultless and faulty states by root condition?

(vii) Dependent on faultless, faulty and indeterminate state, may there arise faultless, faulty and indeterminate states by root condition?

End of Root Condition.

Object Condition, etc.

32. Dependent on faultless state, may there arise faultless state by object condition?

(Root condition has been fully expanded. Object condition should be done likewise by way of recitation.)

33. Dependent on faultless state, may there arise faultless state by predominance condition?... proximity condition?... contiguity condition?... conascence condition?... mutuality condition?... dependence condition?... strong-dependence condition?... prenascence condition?... postnascence condition?... repetition condition?... kamma condition?... resultant condition?... nutriment condition?... faculty condition?... jhāna condition?... path condition?... association condition?... dissociation condition?... presence condition?... absence condition?... disappearance condition?

34. Dependent on faultless state, may there arise faultless state by non-disappearance condition?... Dependent on faulty state.... Dependent on indeterminate state... Dependent on faultless and indeterminate state... Dependent on faulty and indeterminate state... Dependent on faultless and faulty state....

Dependent on faultless, faulty and indeterminate state, may

there arise faultless state ... arise faulty state ... arise indeterminate state ... arise faultless and indeterminate states ... arise faulty and indeterminate states ... arise faultless and faulty states ... may there arise faultless, faulty and indeterminate states by non-disappearance condition ?

(Root condition has been fully expanded. Non-disappearance condition should be done likewise by way of recitation.)

End of By Ones

By Twos

Root Condition

35. Dependent on faultless state, may there arise faultless state by root and object conditions[1].... Dependent on faultless, faulty and indeterminate state may there arise faultless, faulty and indeterminate states by root and object conditions ?
36. Dependent on faultless state, may there arise faultless state by root and predominance conditions ? ... root and proximity conditions ? ... root and contiguity conditions ? ... root and non-disappearance conditions ?

By Threes

37. Dependent on faultless state, may there arise faultless state by root, object and predominance conditions ? ... root, object and proximity conditions ? ... root, object and non-disappearance conditions ?

By Fours

38. Dependent on faultless state, may there arise faultless state by root, object, predominance and proximity conditions ? ... root, object, predominance and non-disappearance conditions ?

(" By Fives " and so on are abbreviated. " By Ones ", " By Twos ", " By Threes ", " By Fours ", " By Fives " ... " By All Conditions " should be expanded without confusion.)

End of Root Condition.

---

[1] " root condition and object condition " is abbreviated as such in all cases.

Object Condition, etc.

By Twos

39. Dependent on faultless state, may there arise faultless state by object and root conditions ? ... object and predominance conditions ? ... object and non-disappearance conditions ?

Dependent on faultless state, may there arise faultless state by predominance ... proximity ... contiguity ... conascence ... mutuality ... non-disappearance and root conditions ? ... non-disappearance and object conditions ? ... non-disappearance and predominance conditions ? ... non-disappearance and disappearance conditions ?

(By Threes)

40. Dependent on faultless state, may there arise faultless state by non-disappearance, root and object conditions ? ... non-disappearance, root and predominance conditions ? ... non-disappearance, root and proximity conditions ? ... non-disappearance, root and disappearance conditions ?

(By Fours)

41. Dependent on faultless state, may there arise faultless state by non-disappearance, root, object and predominance conditions ? ... non-disappearance, root, object and proximity conditions ? ... disappearance conditions ?

(This should be fully expanded in each section as " By Ones ", " By Twos ", " By Threes ", " By Fours ", " By Fives " ... " By All Conditions " without confusion.)

(*a*) Excellent and supreme are the Paṭṭhāna triplets, couplets,
Couplets-triplets, triplets-couplets,
Triplets-triplets, couplets-couplets,
These six divisions in the Positive Method are profound.

2. CONDITIONS : NEGATIVE

Not-root condition, etc.

42. Dependent on faultless state, may there arise faultless state by not-root condition ?

(In the Positive, root condition has been expanded. In the Negative, not-root condition should be similarly expanded.)

43. Dependent on faultless state, may there arise faultless state by not-object condition ? . . . not-predominance condition ? . . . not-proximity condition ? . . . not-contiguity condition ? . . . not-conascence condition ? . . . not-mutuality condition ? . . . not-dependence condition ? . . . not-strong-dependence condition ? . . . not-prenascence condition ? . . . not-postnascence condition ? . . . not-repetition condition ? . . . not-kamma condition ? . . . not-resultant condition ? . . . not-nutriment condition ? . . . not-faculty condition ? . . . not-jhāna condition ? . . . not-path condition ? . . . not-association condition ? . . . not-dissociation condition ? . . . not-presence condition ? . . . not-absence condition ? . . . not-disappearance condition ? . . . not-non-disappearance condition ?

44. Dependent on faultless state, may there arise faultless state by not-root and not-object conditions ?

(In the Positive, each section is fully expanded as " By Ones ", " By Twos ", " By Threes ", " By Fours " up to " By Twenty-threes ". In the Negative also, it must be expanded similarly.)

(b) Excellent and supreme are the Paṭṭhāna triplets, couplets,
Couplets-triplets, triplets-couplets,
Triplets-triplets, couplets-couplets,
These six divisions in the Negative Method are profound.

3. CONDITIONS : POSITIVE-NEGATIVE

(Root Condition)

45. Dependent on faultless state, may there arise faultless state by root condition, not-object condition ? Dependent on faultless state, may there arise faulty state by root condition, not-object condition ?

(In the Positive, root condition has been fully expanded. In the Positive-Negative, the sections should be expanded similarly.)

46. Dependent on faultless state, may there arise faultless state by root condition, not-predominance condition ? . . . root condition, not-proximity condition ? . . . root condition, not-non-disappearance condition ?

47. Dependent on faultless state, may there arise faultless state by root and object conditions, not-predominance condition ? ... root and object conditions, not-proximity condition ? ... root and object conditions, not-non-disappearance condition ?

By root, object and predominance conditions, not-proximity condition ? ... root, object and predominance conditions, not-non-disappearance condition ?

By root, object, predominance and proximity conditions, not-contiguity condition ? ... root, object, predominance and proximity conditions, not-non-disappearance condition ? ...

By root, object, predominance, proximity, contiguity, conascence, mutuality, dependence, strong-dependence, prenascence, postnascence, repetition, kamma, resultant, nutriment, faculty, jhāna, path, association, dissociation, presence, absence and disappearance conditions, not-non-disappearance condition ?

(Object Condition, etc.)

48. Dependent on faultless state, may there arise faultless state by object condition ... predominance condition ... proximity condition ... non-disappearance condition, not-root condition ? ... non-disappearance condition, not-object condition ? ... non-disappearance condition, not-disappearance condition ?

By non-disappearance and root conditions, not-object condition ? ... non-disappearance and root conditions, not-disappearance condition ?

By non-disappearance, root and object conditions, not-predominance condition ? ... non-disappearance, root and object conditions, not-disappearance condition ?

By non-disappearance, root, object, predominance, proximity, contiguity, conascence conditions ... not-disappearance condition ?

   (c) Excellent and supreme are the Paṭṭhāna triplets, couplets,
   Couplets-triplets, triplets-couplets,
   Triplets-triplets, couplets-couplets,
   These six divisions in the Positive-Negative Method are profound.

4. CONDITIONS : NEGATIVE-POSITIVE

(Not-root Condition)

49. Dependent on faultless state, may there arise faultless state by not-root condition, object condition ?

Dependent on faultless state, may there arise faultless state by not-root condition, predominance condition ? . . . not-root condition, non-disappearance condition ?

50. Dependent on faultless state, may there arise faultless state by not-root and not-object conditions, predominance condition ? . . . . non-disappearance condition ?

By not-root, not-object and not-predominance conditions . . . non-disappearance condition ?

By not-root, not-object, not-predominance, not-proximity, not-contiguity . . . not-presence, not-absence and not-disappearance conditions, non-disappearance condition ?

(Not-object Condition, etc.)

51. Dependent on faultless state, may there arise faultless state by not-object condition, root condition ?

52. Dependent on faultless state, may there arise faultless state by not-object condition, predominance condition ? . . . not-object condition, non-disappearance condition ? . . . not-non-disappearance condition, root condition ? . . . not-non-disappearance condition, object condition ? . . . not-non-disappearance condition, disappearance condition ?

By not-non-disappearance and not-root conditions, object condition ? . . . not-non-disappearance and not-root conditions, disappearance condition ?

By not-non-disappearance, not-root, not-object, not-predominance . . . not-presence and not-absence conditions, disappearance condition ?

> (d) Excellent and supreme are the Paṭṭhāna triplets, couplets,
> Couplets-triplets, triplets-couplets,
> Triplets-triplets, couplets-couplets,
> These six divisions in the Negative-Positive Method are profound.

(ANSWERS)

I. FAULTLESS TRIPLET I. 'DEPENDENT' CHAPTER
I. CONDITIONS: POSITIVE (i) CLASSIFICATION CHAPTER

Positive Root 9

53. (i) Dependent on faultless state, arises faultless state by root condition.

Dependent on one faultless aggregate, arise[1] three (faultless) aggregates; dependent on three (faultless) aggregates, arises[1] one (faultless) aggregate; dependent on two (faultless) aggregates, arise[1] two (faultless) aggregates.

(ii) Dependent on faultless state, arises indeterminate state by root condition.

Dependent on faultless aggregates, arises mind-produced matter.

(iii) Dependent on faultless state, arise faultless and indeterminate states by root condition.

Dependent on one faultless aggregate, arise three aggregates and mind-produced matter; dependent on three aggregates, arise one aggregate and mind-produced matter; dependent on two aggregates, arise two aggregates and mind-produced matter. (3)

(iv) Dependent on faulty state, arises faulty state by root condition.

Dependent on one faulty aggregate, arise three aggregates; dependent on three faulty aggregates, arises one aggregate; dependent on two aggregates, arise two aggregates.

(v) Dependent on faulty state, arises indeterminate state by root condition.

Dependent on faulty aggregates, arises mind-produced matter.

(vi) Dependent on faulty state, arise faulty and indeterminate states by root condition.

Dependent on one faulty aggregate, arise three aggregates

---

[1] The verb is left out in all the classifications of the states, but is here included as in the answers.

and mind-produced matter; dependent on three aggregates, arise one aggregate and mind-produced matter; dependent on two aggregates, arise two aggregates and mind-produced matter. (3)

(vii) Dependent on indeterminate state, arises indeterminate state by root condition.

(*a*) Dependent on one resultant indeterminate or functional indeterminate aggregate, arise three aggregates and mind-produced matter; dependent on three aggregates, arise one aggregate and mind-produced matter; dependent on two aggregates, arise two aggregates and mind-produced matter;

(*b*) At the moment of conception, dependent on one resultant indeterminate aggregate, arise three aggregates and kamma-produced matter; dependent on three aggregates, arise one aggregate and kamma-produced matter; dependent on two aggregates, arise two aggregates and kamma-produced matter; dependent on aggregates, arises (heart-)base; dependent on (heart-)base, arise aggregates;

(*c*) Dependent on one great primary, arise three great primaries; dependent on three great primaries, arises one great primary; dependent on two great primaries, arise two great primaries; dependent on (four) great primaries, arise mind-produced and kamma-produced derived matter. (1)

(viii) Dependent on faultless and indeterminate state, arises indeterminate state by root condition.

Dependent on faultless aggregates and great primaries, arises mind-produced matter. (1)

(ix) Dependent on faulty and indeterminate state, arises indeterminate state by root condition.

Dependent on faulty aggregates and great primaries, arises mind-produced matter. (1)

Object 3

54. (i) Dependent on faultless state, arises faultless state by object condition.

Dependent on one faultless aggregate, arise three aggregates; dependent on three aggregates, arises one aggregate; dependent on two aggregates, arise two aggregates.

(ii) Dependent on faulty state, arises faulty state by object condition.

Dependent on one faulty aggregate, arise three aggregates ; dependent on three aggregates, arises one aggregate ; dependent on two aggregates, arise two aggregates.

(iii) Dependent on indeterminate state, arises indeterminate state by object condition.

(*a*) Dependent on one resultant indeterminate or functional indeterminate aggregate, arise three aggregates ; dependent on three aggregates, arises one aggregate ; dependent on two aggregates, arise two aggregates ;

(*b*) At the moment of conception, dependent on one resultant indeterminate aggregate, arise three aggregates ; dependent on three aggregates, arises one aggregate ; dependent on two aggregates, arise two aggregates ; dependent on (heart-)base, arise aggregates.

Predominance 9

55. (i) Dependent on faultless state, arises faultless state by predominance condition.

Dependent on one faultless aggregate, arise three aggregates ; dependent on three aggregates, arises one aggregate ; dependent on two aggregates, arise two aggregates.

(ii) Dependent on faultless state, arises indeterminate state by predominance condition.

Dependent on faultless aggregates, arises mind-produced matter.

(iii) Dependent on faultless state, arise faultless and indeterminate states by predominance condition.

Dependent on one faultless aggregate, arise three aggregates and mind-produced matter ; dependent on three aggregates, arise one aggregate and mind-produced matter ; dependent on two aggregates, arise two aggregates and mind-produced matter. (3)

(iv) Dependent on faulty state, arises faulty state by predominance condition.

Dependent on one faulty aggregate, arise three aggregates ; dependent on three aggregates, arises one aggregate ; dependent on two aggregates, arise two aggregates.

(v) Dependent on faulty state, arises indeterminate state by predominance condition.

Dependent on faulty aggregates, arises mind-produced matter.

(vi) Dependent on faulty state, arise faulty and indeterminate states by predominance condition.

Dependent on one faulty aggregate, arise three aggregates and mind-produced matter; dependent on three aggregates, arise one aggregate and mind-produced matter; dependent on two aggregates, arise two aggregates and mind-produced matter. (3)

(vii) Dependent on indeterminate state, arises indeterminate state by predominance condition.

(*a*) Dependent on one resultant indeterminate or functional indeterminate aggregate, arise three aggregates and mind-produced matter; dependent on three aggregates, arise one aggregate and mind-produced matter; dependent on two aggregates, arise two aggregates and mind-produced matter;

(*b*) Dependent on one great primary, arise three great primaries; dependent on three great primaries, arises one great primary; dependent on two great primaries, arise two great primaries; dependent on great primaries, arises mind-produced derived matter. (1)

(viii) Dependent on faultless and indeterminate state, arises indeterminate state by predominance condition.

Dependent on faultless aggregates and great primaries, arises mind-produced matter. (1)

(ix) Dependent on faulty and indeterminate state, arises indeterminate state by predominance condition.

Dependent on faulty aggregates and great primaries, arises mind-produced matter. (1)

Proximity 3, Contiguity 3

56. Dependent on faultless state, arises faultless state by proximity condition ... by contiguity condition.

Dependent on one faultless aggregate, arise three aggregates. ... (Proximity and contiguity are the same as object condition.)

Conascence 9

57. (i) Dependent on faultless state, arises faultless state by conascence condition.

Dependent on one faultless aggregate, arise three aggregates ; dependent on three aggregates, arises one aggregate ; dependent on two aggregates, arise two aggregates.

(ii) Dependent on faultless state, arises indeterminate state by conascence condition.

Dependent on faultless aggregates, arises mind-produced matter.

(iii) Dependent on faultless state, arise faultless and indeterminate states by conascence condition.

Dependent on one faultless aggregate, arise three aggregates and mind-produced matter ; dependent on three aggregates, arise one aggregate and mind-produced matter ; dependent on two aggregates, arise two aggregates and mind-produced matter. (3)

(iv) Dependent on faulty state, arises faulty state by conascence condition.

Dependent on one faulty aggregate, arise three aggregates ; dependent on three aggregates, arises one aggregate ; dependent on two aggregates, arise two aggregates.

(v) Dependent on faulty state, arises indeterminate state by conascence condition.

Dependent on faulty aggregates, arises mind-produced matter.

(vi) Dependent on faulty state, arise faulty and indeterminate states by conascence condition.

Dependent on one faulty aggregate, arise three aggregates and mind-produced matter ; dependent on three aggregates, arise one aggregate and mind-produced matter ; dependent on two aggregates, arise two aggregates and mind-produced matter. (3)

(vii) Dependent on indeterminate state, arises indeterminate state by conascence condition.

(*a*) Dependent on one resultant indeterminate or functional indeterminate aggregate, arise three aggregates and mind-produced matter ; dependent on three aggregates, arise one aggregate and mind-produced matter ; dependent on two aggregates, arise two aggregates and mind-produced matter;

(b) At the moment of conception, dependent on one resultant indeterminate aggregate, arise three aggregates and kamma-produced matter; dependent on three aggregates, arise one aggregate and kamma-produced matter; dependent on two aggregates, arise two aggregates and kamma-produced matter; dependent on aggregates, arises (heart-)base; dependent on (heart-)base, arise aggregates;

(c) Dependent on one great primary, arises three great primaries; dependent on three great primaries, arises one great primary; dependent on two great primaries, arise two great primaries; dependent on great primaries, arise mind-produced and kamma-produced derived matter;

(d) Dependent on one external great primary, arise three great primaries; dependent on three great primaries, arises one great primary; dependent on two great primaries, arise two great primaries; dependent on great primaries, arises derived matter;

(e) Dependent on one nutriment-produced great primary, arise three great primaries; dependent on three great primaries, arises one great primary; dependent on two great primaries, arise two great primaries; dependent on great primaries, arises derived matter;

(f) Dependent on one temperature-produced great primary, arise three great primaries; dependent on three great primaries, arises one great primary; dependent on two great primaries, arise two great primaries; dependent on great primaries, arises derived matter;

(g) Dependent on one great primary of non-percipient beings, arise three great primaries; dependent on three great primaries, arises one great primary; dependent on two great primaries, arise two great primaries; dependent on great primaries, arises kamma-produced derived matter. (1)

(viii) Dependent on faultless and indeterminate state, arises indeterminate state by conascence condition.

Dependent on faultless aggregates and great primaries, arises mind-produced matter. (1)

(ix) Dependent on faulty and indeterminate state, arises indeterminate state by conascence condition.

Dependent on faulty aggregates and great primaries, arises mind-produced matter. (1)

Mutuality 3

58. (i) Dependent on faultless state, arises faultless state by mutuality condition.

Dependent on one faultless aggregate, arise three aggregates; dependent on three aggregates, arises one aggregate; dependent on two aggregates, arise two aggregates. (1)[1]

(ii) Dependent on faulty state, arises faulty state by mutuality condition.

Dependent on one faulty aggregate, arise three aggregates; dependent on three aggregates, arises one aggregate; dependent on two aggregates, arise two aggregates. (1)[1]

(iii) Dependent on indeterminate state, arises indeterminate state by mutuality condition.

(*a*) Dependent on one resultant indeterminate or functional indeterminate aggregate, arise three aggregates; dependent on three aggregates, arises one aggregate; dependent on two aggregates, arise two aggregates;

(*b*) At the moment of conception, dependent on one resultant indeterminate aggregate, arise three aggregates and (heart-)base; dependent on three aggregates, arise one aggregate and (heart-)base; dependent on two aggregates, arise two aggregates and (heart-)base; dependent on aggregates, arises (heart-)base; dependent on (heart-)base, arise aggregates;

(*c*) Dependent on one great primary, arise three great primaries; dependent on three great primaries, arises one great primary; dependent on two great primaries, arise two great primaries;

(*d*)–(*g*)[2] External ... nutriment-produced ... temperature-produced ... dependent on one great primary of non-percipient beings, arise three great primaries; dependent on three great primaries, arises one great primary; dependent on two great primaries, arise two great primaries. (1)[3]

---

[1] Given as (3) in the Text.
[2] Given in full in 57(*d*), (*e*), (*f*) and (*g*). It is similarly abridged in the rest of the Text. The difference here is that " derived matter " is excluded.
[3] Left out in the Text.

Dependence 9

59. Dependent on faultless state, arises faultless state by dependence condition.

Dependent on one faultless aggregate. . . . (Dependence condition is the same as conascence condition.)

Strong-dependence 3

60. Dependent on faultless state, arises faultless state by strong-dependence condition.

Dependent on one faultless aggregate . . . (Strong-dependence condition is the same as object condition.)

Prenascence 3

61. (i) Dependent on faultless state, arises faultless state by prenascence condition.

Dependent on one faultless aggregate, arise three aggregates; dependent on three aggregates, arises one aggregate; dependent on two aggregates, arise two aggregates; (dependent on heart-)base, (arise faultless aggregates) by prenascence condition.

(ii) Dependent on faulty state, arises faulty state by prenascence condition.

Dependent on one faulty aggregate, arise three aggregates; dependent on three aggregates, arises one aggregate; dependent on two aggregates, arise two aggregates; (dependent on heart-)base, (arise faulty aggregates) by prenascence condition.

(iii) Dependent on indeterminate state, arises indeterminate state by prenascence condition.

Dependent on one resultant indeterminate or functional indeterminate aggregate, arise three aggregates; dependent on three aggregates, arises one aggregate; dependent on two aggregates, arise two aggregates; (dependent on six) bases, (arise resultant indeterminate or functional indeterminate aggregates) by prenascence condition.

Repetition 3

62. (i) Dependent on faultless state, arises faultless state by repetition condition.

Dependent on one faultless aggregate, arise three aggregates; dependent on three aggregates, arises one aggregate; dependent on two aggregates, arise two aggregates.

(ii) Dependent on faulty state, arises faulty state by repetition condition.

Dependent on one faulty aggregate, arise three aggregates; dependent on three aggregates, arises one aggregate; dependent on two aggregates, arise two aggregates.

(iii) Dependent on indeterminate state, arises indeterminate state by repetition condition.

Dependent on one functional indeterminate aggregate, arise three aggregates; dependent on three aggregates, arises one aggregate; dependent on two aggregates, arise two aggregates.

Kamma 9

63. (i)–(iii) Dependent on faultless state, arises faultless state by kamma condition.

Dependent on one faultless aggregate ... three.

(iv)–(vi) Dependent on faulty state ... three.

(vii) Dependent on indeterminate state, arises indeterminate state by kamma condition.

(a) Dependent on one resultant indeterminate or functional indeterminate aggregate ...

(b) At the moment of conception ...

(c) Dependent on one great primary, arise three great primaries ... dependent on great primaries, arise mind-produced and kamma-produced derived matter;

(d) Dependent on one great primary of non-percipient beings, arise three great primaries ... dependent on great primaries, arises kamma-produced derived matter.

(viii) Dependent on faultless and indeterminate state, arises indeterminate state by kamma condition.

Dependent on faultless aggregates and great primaries, arises mind-produced matter.

(ix) Dependent on faulty and indeterminate state, arises indeterminate state by kamma condition.

Dependent on faulty aggregates and great primaries, arises mind-produced matter.

Resultant 1

64. Dependent on indeterminate state, arises indeterminate state by resultant condition.

(*a*) Dependent on one resultant indeterminate aggregate, arise three aggregates and mind-produced matter; dependent on three aggregates, arise one aggregate and mind-produced matter; dependent on two aggregates, arise two aggregates and mind-produced matter;

(*b*) At the moment of conception, dependent on one resultant indeterminate aggregate, arise three aggregates and kamma-produced matter; dependent on three aggregates, arise one aggregate and kamma-produced matter; dependent on two aggregates, arise two aggregates and kamma-produced matter; dependent on aggregates, arises (heart-)base; dependent on (heart-)base, arise aggregates;

(*c*) Dependent on one great primary, arise three great primaries; dependent on three great primaries, arises one great primary; dependent on two great primaries, arise two great primaries; dependent on great primaries, arise mind-produced and kamma-produced derived matter.

Nutriment 9

65. (i)–(iii) Dependent on faultless state, arises faultless state by nutriment condition.

Dependent on one faultless aggregate ... three.

(iv)–(vi) Dependent on faulty state, arises faulty state by nutriment condition.

Dependent on one faulty aggregate ... three.

(vii) Dependent on indeterminate state, arises indeterminate state by nutriment condition.

(*a*) Dependent on one resultant indeterminate or functional indeterminate aggregate ...

(*b*) At the moment of conception ...

(*c*) Dependent on one great primary, arise three great primaries ... dependent on great primaries, arise mind-produced and kamma-produced derived matter;

(*d*) Dependent on one nutriment-produced great primary ... dependent on great primaries, arises derived matter.

(viii) Dependent on faultless and indeterminate state . . .

(ix) Dependent on faulty and indeterminate state, arises indeterminate state by nutriment condition.

Dependent on faulty aggregates and great primaries, arises mind-produced matter.

Faculty 9

66. (i)–(iii) Dependent on faultless state, arises faultless state by faculty condition.

Dependent on one faultless aggregate . . . three.

(iv)–(vi) Dependent on faulty state . . . three.

(vii)–(ix) Dependent on indeterminate state . . . Dependent on one great primary of non-percipient beings . . . (Faculty condition is the same as kamma condition.)

Jhāna 9, Path 9

67. Dependent on faultless state, arises faultless state by jhāna condition . . . by path condition. (Jhāna and path conditions are the same as root condition.)

Association 3

68. Dependent on faultless state, arises faultless state by association condition.

Dependent on one faultless aggregate . . . (Association condition is also the same as object condition.)

Dissociation 9

69. (i) Dependent on faultless state, arises faultless state by dissociation condition.

Dependent on one faultless aggregate, arise three aggregates; dependent on three aggregates, arises one aggregate; dependent on two aggregates, arise two aggregates; (dependent on heart-)-base, (arise faultless aggregates) by dissociation condition.

(ii) Dependent on faultless state, arises indeterminate state by dissociation condition.

Dependent on faultless aggregates, arises mind-produced matter; (dependent on) aggregates, (arises mind-produced matter) by dissociation condition.

(iii) Dependent on faultless state, arise faultless and indeterminate states by dissociation condition.

Dependent on one faultless aggregate, arise three aggregates and mind-produced matter; dependent on three aggregates, arise one aggregate and mind-produced matter; dependent on two aggregates, arise two aggregates and mind-produced matter; (dependent on heart-)base, (arise) aggregates by dissociation condition; (dependent on) aggregates, (arises) mind-produced matter by dissociation condition. (3)

(iv) Dependent on faulty state, arises faulty state by dissociation condition.

Dependent on one faulty aggregate, arise three aggregates; dependent on three aggregates, arises one aggregate; dependent on two aggregates, arise two aggregates; (dependent on heart-)base, (arise faulty aggregates) by dissociation condition.

(v) Dependent on faulty state, arises indeterminate state by dissociation condition.

Dependent on faulty aggregates, arises mind-produced matter; (dependent on) aggregates, (arises mind-produced matter) by dissociation condition.

(vi) Dependent on faulty state, arise faulty and indeterminate states by dissociation condition.

Dependent on one faulty aggregate, arise three aggregates and mind-produced matter; dependent on three aggregates, arise one aggregate and mind-produced matter; dependent on two aggregates, arise two aggregates and mind-produced matter; (dependent on heart-)base, (arise) aggregates by dissociation condition; (dependent on) aggregates, (arises) mind-produced matter by dissociation condition. (3)

(vii) Dependent on indeterminate state, arises indeterminate state by dissociation condition.

(*a*) Dependent on one resultant indeterminate or functional indeterminate aggregate, arise three aggregates and mind-produced matter; dependent on three aggregates, arise one aggregate and mind-produced matter; dependent on two aggregates, arise two aggregates and mind-produced matter; (dependent on six) bases, (arise) aggregates by dissociation condition; (dependent on) aggregates, (arises) mind-produced matter by dissociation condition;

(b) At the moment of conception, dependent on one resultant indeterminate aggregate, arise three aggregates and kamma-produced matter; dependent on three aggregates, arise one aggregate and kamma-produced matter; dependent on two aggregates, arise two aggregates and kamma-produced matter; (dependent on heart-)base, (arise) aggregates by dissociation condition; (dependent on) aggregates, (arises) kamma-produced matter by dissociation condition; dependent on aggregates, (arises heart-)base; dependent on (heart-)base, (arise) aggregates; (dependent on heart-)base, (arise) aggregates by dissociation condition; (dependent on) aggregates, (arises heart-)base by dissociation condition;

(c) Dependent on one great primary, arise three great primaries; dependent on three great primaries, arises one great primary; dependent on two great primaries, arise two great primaries; dependent on great primaries, arise mind-produced and kamma-produced derived matter; (dependent on) aggregates, (arise mind-produced and kamma-produced matter) by dissociation condition. (1)

(viii) Dependent on faultless and indeterminate state, arises indeterminate state by dissociation condition.

Dependent on faultless aggregates and great primaries, arises mind-produced matter; (dependent on) aggregates, (arises mind-produced matter) by dissociation condition. (1)

(ix) Dependent on faulty and indeterminate state, arises indeterminate state by dissociation condition.

Dependent on faulty aggregates and great primaries, arises mind-produced matter; (dependent on) aggregates, (arises mind-produced matter) by dissociation condition. (1)

Presence 9

70. Dependent on faultless state, arises faultless state by presence condition.

Dependent on one faultless aggregate, arise three aggregates. . . .

(Abbreviated.) (Presence condition is the same as conascence condition.)

Absence 3, Disappearance 3

71. Dependent on faultless state, arises faultless state by absence condition ... by disappearance condition. ... (Absence and disappearance conditions are the same as object condition.)

Non-disappearance 9

72. Dependent on faultless state, arises faultless state by non-disappearance condition.

Dependent on one faultless aggregate, arise three aggregates. ... (Non-disappearance condition is the same as conascence condition.)

(These twenty-three conditions should be expanded for recitation.)

I. CONDITIONS : POSITIVE   (ii) ENUMERATION CHAPTER

NUMBERS (OF ANSWERS)

Root Condition as Reference

By Ones

73. With root (there are) 9 (answers), with object (there are) 3 (answers), predominance 9, proximity 3, contiguity 3, conascence 9, mutuality 3, dependence 9, strong-dependence 3, prenascence 3, repetition 3, kamma 9, resultant 1, nutriment 9, faculty 9, jhāna 9, path 9, association 3, dissociation 9, presence 9, absence 3, disappearance 3, (with) non-disappearance (there are) 9 (answers).[1]

By Twos

74. With root condition and object (there are) 3 (answers), (with root condition and) predominance (there are) 9 (answers), proximity 3, contiguity 3, conascence 9, mutuality 3, dependence 9, strong-dependence 3, prenascence 3, repetition 3, kamma 9, resultant 1, nutriment 9, faculty 9, jhāna 9, path 9, association 3, dissociation 9, presence 9, absence 3, disappearance 3, non-disappearance 9.

[1] The answers are given above.

By Threes

75. With root, object conditions and predominance (there are) 3 (answers), proximity 3, contiguity 3, conascence 3, mutuality 3, dependence 3, strong-dependence 3, prenascence 3, repetition 3, kamma 3, resultant 1, nutriment 3, faculty 3, jhāna 3, path 3, association 3, dissociation 3, presence 3, absence 3, disappearance 3, non-disappearance 3. ...

By Twelves
With Repetition Condition[1]

76. With root, object, predominance, proximity, contiguity, conascence, mutuality, dependence, strong-dependence, prenascence, repetition conditions and kamma (there are) 3 (answers), nutriment 3, faculty 3, jhāna 3, path 3, association 3, dissociation 3, presence 3, absence 3, disappearance 3, non-disappearance 3. ...

By Twenty-two

77. With root, object ... repetition, kamma, nutriment, faculty, jhāna, path, association, dissociation, presence, absence, disappearance conditions and non-disappearance (there are) 3 (answers).

By Thirteens
With Resultant Condition[1]

78. With root, object ... prenascence, kamma, resultant conditions and nutriment (there is) 1 (answer), faculty 1, jhāna 1, path 1, association 1, dissociation 1, presence 1, absence 1, disappearance 1, non-disappearance 1. ...

By Twenty-two

79. With root, object ... prenascence, kamma, resultant, nutriment, faculty, jhāna, path, association, dissociation, presence, absence, disappearance conditions and non-disappearance (there is) 1 (answer).

End of Numbers (of Answers) with Root Condition as Reference.

---

[1] Not mentioned in the Text.

Object, etc.

By Twos

(All[1] those that include object have 3 (answers to the) questions.)

80. With object condition and root (there are) 3 (answers), predominance 3 ... non-disappearance 3. ...

With predominance condition and root (there are) 9 (answers). object 3 ... non-disappearance 9. ...

With proximity, contiguity conditions and root (there are) 3 (answers) ... non-disappearance 3. ...

With conascence condition and root 9. ...

With mutuality condition and root 3. ...

With dependence condition and root 9. ...

With strong-dependence condition and root 3. ...

With prenascence condition and root 3. ...

Repetition

By Twos

81. With repetition condition and root (there are) 3 (answers), object 3, predominance 3, proximity 3, contiguity 3, conascence 3, mutuality 3, dependence 3, strong-dependence 3, prenascence 3, kamma 3, nutriment 3, faculty 3, jhāna 3, path 3, association 3, dissociation 3, presence 3, absence 3, disappearance 3, non-disappearance 3. (With repetition condition and resultant nil.)

Kamma

By Twos

82. With kamma condition and root (there are) 9 (answers). ...

Resultant

By Twos

83. With resultant condition and root (there is) 1 (answer), object 1, predominance 1, proximity 1, contiguity 1, conascence 1, mutuality 1, dependence 1, strong-dependence 1, prenascence 1, kamma 1, nutriment 1, faculty 1, jhāna 1, path 1,

[1] There is one exception (i.e. With object condition and resultant) where the answer is 1.

association 1, dissociation 1, presence 1, absence 1, disappearance 1, non-disappearance 1. (With resultant condition and repetition nil.)

Nutriment, etc.

By Twos

84. With nutriment condition and root (there are) 9 (answers). . . .

With faculty condition and root (there are) 9 (answers). . . .
With jhāna condition and root (there are) 9 (answers). . . .
With path condition and root (there are) 9 (answers). . . .
With association condition and root (there are) 3 (answers). . . .
With dissociation condition and root (there are) 9 (answers). . . .
With presence condition and root (there are) 9 (answers). . . .
With absence condition and root (there are) 3 (answers). . . .
With disappearance condition and root (there are) 3 (answers). . . .

Non-disappearance

By Twos

85. With non-disappearance condition and root (there are) 9 (answers), object 3, predominance 9 . . . absence 3, disappearance 3.

(Taking each condition as reference, the enumeration of the rest should be done for recitation.)

End of Positive.

2. CONDITIONS : NEGATIVE   (i) CLASSIFICATION CHAPTER

Negative Not-root 2

86. (i) Dependent on faulty state, arises faulty state by not-root condition.

Dependent on doubt-accompanied or restlessness-accompanied aggregates, arises doubt-accompanied or restlessness-accompanied delusion.

(ii) Dependent on indeterminate state, arises indeterminate state by not-root condition.

(*a*) Dependent on one rootless resultant indeterminate or functional indeterminate aggregate, arise three aggregates and mind-produced matter; dependent on three aggregates, arise one aggregate and mind-produced matter; dependent on two aggregates, arise two aggregates and mind-produced matter;

(*b*) At the moment of rootless conception, dependent on one resultant indeterminate aggregate, arise three aggregates and kamma-produced matter; dependent on three aggregates, arise one aggregate and kamma-produced matter; dependent on two aggregates, arise two aggregates and kamma-produced matter; dependent on aggregates, arises (heart-)base; dependent on (heart-)base, arise aggregates;

(*c*) Dependent on one great primary, arise three great primaries; dependent on three great primaries, arises one great primary; dependent on two great primaries, arise two great primaries; dependent on great primaries, arise mind-produced and kamma-produced derived matter;

(*d*) External ... nutriment-produced ... temperature-produced ... dependent on one great primary of non-percipient beings, arise three great primaries; dependent on three great primaries, arises one great primary; dependent on two great primaries, arise two great primaries; dependent on great primaries, arises kamma-produced derived matter.

Not-object 5

87. (i) Dependent on faultless state, arises indeterminate state by not-object condition.

Dependent on faultless aggregates, arises mind-produced matter.

(ii) Dependent on faulty state, arises indeterminate state by not-object condition.

Dependent on faulty aggregates, arises mind-produced matter.

(iii) Dependent on indeterminate state, arises indeterminate state by not-object condition.

(*a*) Dependent on resultant indeterminate or functional indeterminate aggregates, arises mind-produced matter;

(*b*) At the moment of conception, dependent on resultant indeterminate aggregates, arises kamma-produced matter; dependent on aggregates, arises (heart-)base;

(c) Dependent on one great primary, arise three great primaries; dependent on three great primaries, arises one great primary; dependent on two great primaries, arise two great primaries; dependent on great primaries, arise mind-produced and kamma-produced derived matter;

(d) External ... nutriment-produced ... temperature-produced ... dependent on one great primary of non-percipient beings, arise three great primaries; dependent on three great primaries, arises one great primary; dependent on two great primaries, arise two great primaries; dependent on great primaries, arises kamma-produced derived matter.

(iv) Dependent on faultless and indeterminate state, arises indeterminate state by not-object condition.

Dependent on faultless aggregates and great primaries, arises mind-produced matter.

(v) Dependent on faulty and indeterminate state, arises indeterminate state by not-object condition.

Dependent on faulty aggregates and great primaries, arises mind-produced matter.

Not-predominance 9

88. (i) Dependent on faultless state, arises faultless state by not-predominance condition.

Dependent on one faultless aggregate, arise three aggregates; dependent on three aggregates, arises one aggregate; dependent on two aggregates, arise two aggregates.

(ii) Dependent on faultless state, arises indeterminate state by not-predominance condition.

Dependent on faultless aggregates, arises mind-produced matter.

(iii) Dependent on faultless state, arise faultless and indeterminate states by not-predominance condition.

Dependent on one faultless aggregate, arise three aggregates and mind-produced matter; dependent on three aggregates, arise one aggregate and mind-produced matter; dependent on two aggregates, arise two aggregates and mind-produced matter. (3)

(iv) Dependent on faulty state, arises faulty state by not-predominance condition.

Dependent on one faulty aggregate, arise three aggregates; dependent on three aggregates, arises one aggregate; dependent on two aggregates, arise two aggregates.

(v) Dependent on faulty state, arises indeterminate state by not-predominance condition.

Dependent on faulty aggregates, arises mind-produced matter.

(vi) Dependent on faulty state, arise faulty and indeterminate states by not-predominance condition.

Dependent on one faulty aggregate, arise three aggregates and mind-produced matter; dependent on three aggregates, arise one aggregate and mind-produced matter; dependent on two aggregates, arise two aggregates and mind-produced matter. (3)

(vii) Dependent on indeterminate state, arises indeterminate state by not-predominance condition.

(a) Dependent on one resultant indeterminate or functional indeterminate aggregate, arise three aggregates and mind-produced matter; dependent on three aggregates, arise one aggregate and mind-produced matter; dependent on two aggregates, arise two aggregates and mind-produced matter;

(b) At the moment of conception, dependent on one resultant indeterminate aggregate, arise three aggregates and kamma-produced matter; dependent on three aggregates, arise one aggregate and kamma-produced matter; dependent on two aggregates, arise two aggregates and kamma-produced matter; dependent on aggregates, arises (heart-)base; dependent on (heart-)base, arise aggregates;

(c) Dependent on one great primary, arise three great primaries; dependent on three great primaries, arises one great primary; dependent on two great primaries, arise two great primaries; dependent on great primaries, arise mind-produced and kamma-produced derived matter;

(d) External ... nutriment-produced ... temperature-produced ... dependent on one great primary of non-percipient beings, arise three great primaries; dependent on three great primaries, arises one great primary; dependent on two great primaries, arise two great primaries; dependent on great primaries, arises kamma-produced derived matter. (1)

(viii) Dependent on faultless and indeterminate state, arises indeterminate state by not-predominance condition.

Dependent on faultless aggregates and great primaries, arises mind-produced matter. (1)

(ix) Dependent on faulty and indeterminate state, arises indeterminate state by not-predominance condition.

Dependent on faulty aggregates and great primaries, arises mind-produced matter. (1)

Not-proximity 5, Not-contiguity 5

89. Dependent on faultless state, arises indeterminate state by not-proximity condition . . . by not-contiguity condition.

Dependent on faultless aggregates, arises mind-produced matter. . . . (Not-proximity and not-contiguity conditions are also the same as not-object condition.)

Not-mutuality 5

90. (i) Dependent on faultless state, arises indeterminate state by not-mutuality condition.

Dependent on faultless aggregates, arises mind-produced matter.

(ii) Dependent on faulty state, arises indeterminate state by not-mutuality condition.

Dependent on faulty aggregates, arises mind-produced matter.

(iii) Dependent on indeterminate state, arises indeterminate state by not-mutuality condition.

(*a*) Dependent on resultant indeterminate or functional indeterminate aggregates, arises mind-produced matter ;

(*b*) At the moment of conception, dependent on resultant indeterminate aggregates, arises kamma-produced matter ;

(*c*) Dependent on great primaries, arise mind-produced and kamma-produced derived matter ;

(*d*) Dependent on external great primaries, arises derived matter ; dependent on nutriment-produced great primaries, arises derived matter ; dependent on temperature-produced great primaries, arises derived matter ; dependent on great primaries of non-percipient beings, arises kamma-produced derived matter.

(iv) Dependent on faultless and indeterminate state, arises indeterminate state by not-mutuality condition.

Dependent on faultless aggregates and great primaries, arises mind-produced matter.

(v) Dependent on faulty and indeterminate state, arises indeterminate state by not-mutuality condition.

Dependent on faulty aggregates and great primaries, arises mind-produced matter.

Not-strong-dependence 5

91. Dependent on faultless state, arises indeterminate state by not-strong-dependence condition.

Dependent on faultless aggregates, arises mind-produced matter. . . . (Not-strong-dependence condition is the same as not-object condition.)

Not-prenascence 7

92. (i) Dependent on faultless state, arises faultless state by not-prenascence condition.

In the immaterial plane, dependent on one faultless aggregate, arise three aggregates; dependent on three aggregates, arises one aggregate; dependent on two aggregates, arise two aggregates.

(ii) Dependent on faultless state, arises indeterminate state by not-prenascence condition.

Dependent on faultless aggregates, arises mind-produced matter. (2)

(iii) Dependent on faulty state, arises faulty state by not-prenascence condition.

In the immaterial plane, dependent on one faulty aggregate, arise three aggregates; dependent on three aggregates, arises one aggregate; dependent on two aggregates, arise two aggregates.

(iv) Dependent on faulty state, arises indeterminate state by not-prenascence condition.

Dependent on faulty aggregates, arises mind-produced matter. (2)

(v) Dependent on indeterminate state, arises indeterminate state by not-prenascence condition.

(a) In the immaterial plane, dependent on one resultant indeterminate or functional indeterminate aggregate, arise three aggregates ; dependent on three aggregates, arises one aggregate ; dependent on two aggregates, arise two aggregates ; dependent on resultant indeterminate or functional indeterminate aggregates, arises mind-produced matter ;

(b) At the moment of conception, dependent on one resultant indeterminate aggregate, arise three aggregates and kamma-produced matter ; dependent on three aggregates, arise one aggregate and kamma-produced matter ; dependent on two aggregates, arise two aggregates and kamma-produced matter ; dependent on aggregates, arises (heart-)base ; dependent on (heart-)base, arise aggregates ;

(c) Dependent on one great primary, arise three great primaries ; dependent on three great primaries, arises one great primary ; dependent on two great primaries, arise two great primaries ; dependent on great primaries, arise mind-produced and kamma-produced derived matter ;

(d) External ... nutriment-produced ... temperature-produced ... dependent on one great primary of non-percipient beings, arise three great primaries ; dependent on three great primaries, arises one great primary ; dependent on two great primaries, arise two great primaries ; dependent on great primaries, arises kamma-produced derived matter. (1)

(vi) Dependent on faultless and indeterminate state, arises indeterminate state by not-prenascence condition.

Dependent on faultless aggregates and great primaries, arises mind-produced matter.

(vii) Dependent on faulty and indeterminate state, arises indeterminate state by not-prenascence condition.

Dependent on faulty aggregates and great primaries, arises mind-produced matter.

Not-postnascence 9, Not-repetition 9

93. Dependent on faultless state, arises faultless state by not-postnascence condition.

Dependent on one faultless aggregate. . . .

Dependent on faultless state, arises faultless state by not-repetition condition.

Dependent on one faultless aggregate. ... (Not-postnascence and not-repetition conditions are also the same as not-predominance condition.)

Not-kamma 3

94. (i) Dependent on faultless state, arises faultless state by not-kamma condition.
Dependent on faultless aggregates, arises faultless volition.

(ii) Dependent on faulty state, arises faulty state by not-kamma condition.
Dependent on faulty aggregates, arises faulty volition.

(iii) Dependent on indeterminate state, arises indeterminate state by not-kamma condition.

(*a*) Dependent on functional indeterminate aggregates, arises functional indeterminate volition;

(*b*) External ... nutriment-produced ... dependent on one temperature-produced great primary, arise three great primaries; dependent on three great primaries, arises one great primary; dependent on two great primaries, arise two great primaries; dependent on great primaries, arises derived matter.

Not-resultant 9

95. (i)–(iii) Dependent on faultless state, arises faultless state by not-resultant condition.
Dependent on one faultless aggregate ... three.

(iv)–(vi) Dependent on faulty state, arises faulty state by not-resultant condition ... three.

(vii) Dependent on indeterminate state, arises indeterminate state by not-resultant condition.

(*a*) Dependent on one functional indeterminate aggregate, arise three aggregates and mind-produced matter; dependent on three aggregates, arise one aggregate and mind-produced matter; dependent on two aggregates, arise two aggregates and mind-produced matter;

(*b*) Dependent on one great primary, arise three great primaries ... dependent on great primaries, arises mind-produced derived matter;

(c) External ... nutriment-produced ... temperature-produced ... dependent on one great primary of non-percipient beings, arise three great primaries ... dependent on great primaries, arises kamma-produced derived matter.

(viii) Dependent on faultless and indeterminate state, arises indeterminate state by not-resultant condition.

Dependent on faultless aggregates and great primaries, arises mind-produced matter.

(ix) Dependent on faulty and indeterminate state, arises indeterminate state by not-resultant condition.

Dependent on faulty aggregates and great primaries, arises mind-produced matter.

Not-nutriment 1

96. Dependent on indeterminate state, arises indeterminate state by not-nutriment condition.

External ... temperature-produced ... dependent on one great primary of non-percipient beings, arise three great primaries ... dependent on great primaries, arises kamma-produced derived matter.

Not-faculty 1

97. Dependent on indeterminate state, arises indeterminate state by not-faculty condition.

External ... nutriment-produced ... dependent on one temperature-produced great primary, arise three great primaries ... dependent on great primaries, arises derived matter; dependent on great primaries of non-percipient beings, arises physical life-faculty.

Not-jhāna 1

98. Dependent on indeterminate state, arises indeterminate state by not-jhāna condition.

(a) Dependent on one five-consciousness-accompanied aggregate, arise three aggregates; dependent on three aggregates, arises one aggregate; dependent on two aggregates, arise two aggregates;

(*b*) External ... nutriment-produced ... temperature-produced ... dependent on one great primary of non-percipient beings, arise three great primaries ... dependent on great primaries, arises kamma-produced derived matter.

Not-path 1

99. Dependent on indeterminate state, arises indeterminate state by not-path condition.

(*a*) Dependent on one rootless resultant indeterminate or functional indeterminate aggregate, arise three aggregates and mind-produced matter; dependent on three aggregates, arise one aggregate and mind-produced matter; dependent on two aggregates, arise two aggregates and mind-produced matter;

(*b*) At the moment of rootless conception, dependent on one resultant indeterminate aggregate, arise three aggregates and kamma-produced matter; dependent on three aggregates, arise one aggregate and kamma-produced matter; dependent on two aggregates, arise two aggregates and kamma-produced matter; dependent on aggregates, arises (heart-)base; dependent on (heart-)base, arise aggregates;

(*c*) Dependent on one great primary, arise three great primaries; dependent on three great primaries, arises one great primary; dependent on two great primaries, arise two great primaries; dependent on great primaries, arise mind-produced and kamma-produced derived matter;

(*d*) External ... nutriment-produced ... temperature-produced ... dependent on one great primary of non-percipient beings, arise three great primaries ... dependent on great primaries, arises kamma-produced derived matter.

Not-association 5

100. Dependent on faultless state, arises indeterminate state by not-association condition.

Dependent on faultless aggregates, arises mind-produced matter. ... (The same as not-object condition.)

Not-dissociation 3

101. (i) Dependent on faultless state, arises faultless state by not-dissociation condition.

In the immaterial plane, dependent on one faultless aggregate, arise three aggregates ; dependent on three aggregates, arises one aggregate ; dependent on two aggregates, arise two aggregates.

(ii) Dependent on faulty state, arises faulty state by not-dissociation condition.

In the immaterial plane, dependent on one faulty aggregate, arise three aggregates ; dependent on three aggregates, arises one aggregate ; dependent on two aggregates, arise two aggregates.

(iii) Dependent on indeterminate state, arises indeterminate state by not-dissociation condition.

(*a*) In the immaterial plane, dependent on one resultant indeterminate or functional indeterminate aggregate, arise three aggregates ; dependent on three aggregates, arises one aggregate ; dependent on two aggregates, arise two aggregates ;

(*b*) External ... nutriment-produced ... temperature-produced ... dependent on one great primary of non-percipient beings, arise three great primaries ... dependent on great primaries, arises kamma-produced derived matter.

Not-absence 5, Not-disappearance 5

102. Dependent on faultless state, arises indeterminate state by not-absence condition ... by not-disappearance condition.

Dependent on faultless aggregates, arises mind-produced matter. ... (Same as not-object condition.)

2. CONDITIONS : NEGATIVE   (ii) ENUMERATION CHAPTER

Numbers (*of Answers*)

By Ones

103. With not-root (there are) 2 (answers), with not-object (there are) 5 (answers), not-predominance 9, not-proximity 5, not-contiguity 5, not-mutuality 5, not-strong-dependence 5, not-prenascence 7, not-postnascence 9, not-repetition 9, not-kamma 3, not-resultant 9, not-nutriment 1, not-faculty 1, not-jhāna 1, not-path 1, not-association 5, not-dissociation 3, not-absence 5, not-disappearance 5.

Not-root

By Twos

104. With not-root condition and not-object (there is) 1 (answer), not-predominance 2, not-proximity 1, not-contiguity 1, not-mutuality 1, not-strong-dependence 1, not-prenascence 2, not-postnascence 2, not-repetition 2, not-kamma 1, not-resultant 2, not-nutriment 1, not-faculty 1, not-jhāna 1, not-path 1, not-association 1, not-dissociation 2, not-absence 1, not-disappearance 1.

By Threes

105. With not-root, not-object conditions and not-predominance (there is) 1 (answer), not-proximity 1, not-contiguity 1, not-mutuality 1, not-strong-dependence 1, not-prenascence 1, not-postnascence 1, not-repetition 1, not-kamma 1, not-resultant 1, not-nutriment 1, not-faculty 1, not-jhāna 1, not-path 1, not-association 1, not-dissociation 1, not-absence 1, not-disappearance 1. ...

By Twenty

106. With not-root, not-object, not-predominance, not-proximity, not-contiguity, not-mutuality, not-strong-dependence, not-prenascence, not-postnascence, not-repetition, not-kamma, not-resultant, not-nutriment, not-faculty, not-jhāna, not-path, not-association, not-dissociation, not-absence conditions and not-disappearance (there is) 1 (answer).

Not-object

By Twos

107. With not-object condition and not-root (there is) 1 (answer), not-predominance 5, not-proximity 5, not-contiguity 5, not-mutuality 5, not-strong-dependence 5, not-prenascence 5, not-postnascence 5, not-repetition 5, not-kamma 1, not-resultant 5, not-nutriment 1, not-faculty 1, not-jhāna 1, not-path 1, not-association 5, not-dissociation 1, not-absence 5, not-disappearance 5. ...

By Fours

108. With not-object, not-root, not-predominance conditions

and not-proximity (there is) 1 (answer) ... not-absence 1, not-disappearance 1. ...

Not-predominance

By Twos

109. With not-predominance condition and not-root (there are) 2 (answers), not-object 5, not-proximity 5, not-contiguity 5, not-mutuality 5, not-strong-dependence 5, not-prenascence 7, not-postnascence 9, not-repetition 9, not-kamma 3, not-resultant 9, not-nutriment 1, not-faculty 1, not-jhāna 1, not-path 1, not-association 5, not-dissociation 3, not-absence 5, not-disappearance 5.

By Threes

110. With not-predominance, not-root conditions and not-object (there is) 1 (answer), not-proximity 1, not-contiguity 1, not-mutuality 1, not-strong-dependence 1, not-prenascence 2, not-postnascence 2, not-repetition 2, not-kamma 1, not-resultant 2, not-nutriment 1, not-faculty 1, not-jhāna 1, not-path 1, not-association 1, not-dissociation 2, not-absence 1, not-disappearance 1.

By Fours

111. With not-predominance, not-root, not object conditions and not-proximity (there is) 1 (answer) ... (All are 1) ... not-dissociation 1, not-absence 1, not-disappearance 1. ...

Not-proximity, etc.

112. With not-proximity condition ... with not-contiguity condition ... with not-mutuality condition ... with not-strong-dependence condition.... (Same as not-object condition.)

Not-prenascence

By Twos

113. With not-prenascence condition and not-root (there are) 2 (answers), not-object 5, not-predominance 7, not-proximity 5, not-contiguity 5, not-mutuality 5, not-strong-dependence 5, not-postnascence 7, not-repetition 7, not-kamma 3, not-resultant 7, not-nutriment 1, not-faculty 1, not-jhāna 1, not-path 1,

not-association 5, not-dissociation 3, not-absence 5, not-disappearance 5.

By Threes

114. With not-prenascence, not-root conditions and not-object (there is) 1 (answer), not-predominance 2, not-proximity 1, not-contiguity 1, not-mutuality 1, not-strong-dependence 1, not-postnascence 2, not-repetition 2, not-kamma 1, not-resultant 2, not-nutriment 1, not-faculty 1, not-jhāna 1, not-path 1, not-association 1, not-dissociation 2, not-absence 1, not-disappearance 1.

By Fours

115. With not-prenascence, not-root, not-object conditions and not-predominance (there is) 1 (answer), not-proximity 1 . . . (All are 1) . . . not-absence 1, not-disappearance 1. . . .

Not-postnascence, Not-repetition

By Twos

116. With not-postnascence condition . . . with not-repetition condition and not-root (there are) 2 (answers), not-object 5, not-predominance 9, not-proximity 5, not-contiguity 5, not-mutuality 5, not-strong-dependence 5, not-prenascence 7, not-postnascence 9, not-kamma 3, not-resultant 9, not-nutriment 1, not-faculty 1, not-jhāna 1, not-path 1, not-association 5, not-dissociation 3, not-absence 5, not-disappearance 5.

By Threes

117. With not-repetition, not-root conditions and not-object (there is) 1 (answer), not-predominance 2, not-proximity 1, not-contiguity 1, not-mutuality 1, not-strong-dependence 1, not-prenascence 2, not-postnascence 2, not-kamma 1, not-resultant 2, not-nutriment 1, not-faculty 1, not-jhāna 1, not-path 1, not-association 1, not-dissociation 2, not-absence 1, not-disappearance 1.

By Fours

118. With not-repetition, not-root, not-object conditions and not-predominance (there is) 1 (answer), not-proximity 1 . . . (All are 1) . . . not-absence 1, not-disappearance 1. . . .

Not-kamma

By Twos

119. With not-kamma condition and not-root (there is) 1 (answer), not-object 1, not-predominance 3, not-proximity 1, not-contiguity 1, not-mutuality 1, not-strong-dependence 1, not-prenascence 3, not-postnascence 3, not-repetition 3, not-resultant 3, not-nutriment 1, not-faculty 1, not-jhāna 1, not-path 1, not-association 1, not-dissociation 3, not-absence 1, not-disappearance 1.

By Threes

120. With not-kamma, not-root conditions and not-object (there is) 1 (answer), not-predominance 1 . . . (All are 1) . . . not-absence 1, not-disappearance 1. . . .

Not-resultant

By Twos

121. With not-resultant condition and not-root (there are) 2 (answers), not-object 5, not-predominance 9, not-proximity 5, not-contiguity 5, not-mutuality 5, not-strong-dependence 5, not-prenascence 7, not-postnascence 9, not-repetition 9, not-kamma 3, not-nutriment 1, not-faculty 1, not-jhāna 1, not-path 1, not-association 5, not-dissociation 3, not-absence 5, not-disappearance 5.

By Threes

122. With not-resultant, not-root conditions and not-object (there is) 1 (answer), not-predominance 2, not-proximity 1, not-contiguity 1, not-mutuality 1, not-strong-dependence 1, not-prenascence 2, not-postnascence 2, not-repetition 2, not-kamma 1, not-nutriment 1, not-faculty 1, not-jhāna 1, not-path 1, not-association 1, not-dissociation 2, not-absence 1, not-disappearance 1.

By Fours

123. With not-resultant, not-root, not-object conditions and not-predominance (there is) 1 (answer) . . . (All are 1) . . . not-absence 1, not-disappearance 1. . . .

Not-nutriment, etc.

By Twos

124. With not-nutriment condition ... with not-faculty condition ... with not-jhāna condition ... with not-path condition and not-root (there is) 1 (answer) ... (All are 1) ... not-absence 1, not-disappearance 1. ...

Not-association

By Twos

125. With not-association condition and not-root (there is) 1 (answer), not-object 5 ... (same as not-object condition) ... not-disappearance 5.

Not-dissociation

By Twos

126. With not-dissociation condition and not-root (there are) 2 (answers), not-object 1, not-predominance 3, not-proximity 1, not-contiguity 1, not-mutuality 1, not-strong-dependence 1, not-prenascence 3, not-postnascence 3, not-repetition 3, not-kamma 3, not-resultant 3, not-nutriment 1, not-faculty 1, not-jhāna 1, not-path 1, not-association 1, not-absence 1, not-disappearance 1.

By Threes

127. With not-dissociation, not-root conditions and not-object (there is) 1 (answer), not-predominance 2, not-proximity 1, not-contiguity 1, not-mutuality 1, not-strong-dependence 1, not-prenascence 2, not-postnascence 2, not-repetition 2, not-kamma 1, not-resultant 2, not-nutriment 1, not-faculty 1, not-jhāna 1, not-path 1, not-association 1, not-absence 1, not-disappearance 1.

By Fours

128. With not-dissociation, not-root, not-object conditions and not-predominance (there is) 1 (answer), not-proximity 1 ... (All are 1) ... not-absence 1, not-disappearance 1. ...

Not-absence, Not-disappearance

By Twos

129. With not-absence condition ... with not-disappearance condition and not-root (there is) 1 (answer), not-object 5, not-predominance 5, not-proximity 5, not-contiguity 5, not-mutuality 5, not-strong-dependence 5, not-prenascence 5, not-postnascence 5, not-repetition 5, not-kamma 1, not-resultant 5, not-nutriment 1, not-faculty 1, not-jhāna 1, not-path 1, not-association 5, not-dissociation 1, not-absence 5.

By Threes

130. With not-disappearance, not-root conditions and not-object (there is) 1 (answer), not-predominance 1 ... (All are 1) ... not-dissociation 1, not-absence 1. ... (All are the same as not-object condition.)

End of Negative.

3. CONDITIONS : POSITIVE-NEGATIVE

Root

By Twos

131. With root condition, not-object (there are) 5 (answers), (with root condition,) not-predominance 9, not-proximity 5, not-contiguity 5, not-mutuality 5, not-strong-dependence 5, not-prenascence 7, not-postnascence 9, not-repetition 9, not-kamma 3, not-resultant 9, not-association 5, not-dissociation 3, not-absence 5, not-disappearance 5.

By Threes

132. With root and object conditions, not-predominance 3 (answers), not-prenascence 3, not-postnascence 3, not-repetition 3, not-kamma 3, not-resultant 3, not-dissociation 3.

By Fours

133. With root, object and predominance conditions, not-prenascence 3 (answers), not-postnascence 3, not-repetition 3, not-kamma 3, not-resultant 3, not-dissociation 3. ...

By Elevens

134. With root, object, predominance, proximity, contiguity, conascence, mutuality, dependence, strong-dependence and

prenascence conditions, not-postnascence 3 (answers), not-repetition 3, not-kamma 3, not-resultant 3.

By Twelves (with repetition)

135. With root, object ... prenascence and repetition conditions, not-postnascence 3 (answers), not-kamma 3, not-resultant 3. ...

By Twenty-threes

136. With root, object ... prenascence, repetition, kamma, nutriment, faculty, jhāna, path, association, dissociation, presence, absence, disappearance and non-disappearance conditions, not-postnascence 3 (answers), not-resultant 3.

By Thirteens (with resultant)

137. With root, object ... prenascence, kamma and resultant conditions, not-postnascence 1 (answer), not-repetition 1. ...

By Twenty-threes

138. With root, object ... prenascence, kamma, resultant, nutriment, faculty, jhāna, path, association, dissociation, presence, absence, disappearance and non-disappearance conditions, not-postnascence 1 (answer), not-repetition 1.

Object

By Twos

139. With object condition, not-root 2 (answers), not-predominance 3, not-prenascence 3, not-postnascence 3, not-repetition 3, not-kamma 3, not-resultant 3, not-jhāna 1, not-path 1, not-dissociation 3.

By Threes

140. With object and root conditions, not-predominance 3 (answers), not-prenascence 3, not-postnascence 3, not-repetition 3, not-kamma 3, not-resultant 3, not-dissociation 3.

(Expand in the same way as root condition.)

Predominance

By Twos

141. With predominance condition, not-object 5, not-proximity 5, not-contiguity 5, not-mutuality 5, not-strong-dependence 5,

not-prenascence 7, not-postnascence 9, not-repetition 9, not-kamma 3, not-resultant 9, not-association 5, not-dissociation 3, not-absence 5, not-disappearance 5. ...

By Fours

142. With predominance, root and object conditions, not-prenascence 3, not-postnascence 3, not-repetition 3, not-kamma 3, not-resultant 3, not-dissociation 3. ...

Proximity, Contiguity

By Twos

(Proximity and contiguity conditions should be expanded in the same way as object condition.)

Conascence

By Twos

143. With conascence condition, not-root 2, not-object 5, not-predominance 9, not-proximity 5, not-contiguity 5, not-mutuality 5, not-strong-dependence 5, not-prenascence 7, not-postnascence 9, not-repetition 9, not-kamma 3, not-resultant 9, not-nutriment 1, not-faculty 1, not-jhāna 1, not-path 1, not-association 5, not-dissociation 3, not-absence 5, not-disappearance 5.

By Threes

144. With conascence and root conditions, not-object 5, not-predominance 9, not-proximity 5, not-contiguity 5, not-mutuality 5, not-strong-dependence 5, not-prenascence 7, not-postnascence 9, not-repetition 9, not-kamma 3, not-resultant 9, not-association 5, not-dissociation 3, not-absence 5, not-disappearance 5.

By Fours

145. With conascence, root and object conditions, not-predominance 3, not-prenascence 3, not-postnascence 3, not-repetition 3, not-kamma 3, not-resultant 3, not-dissociation 3.

(Expand in the same way as root condition.)

Mutuality

By Twos

146. With mutuality condition, not-root 2, not-object 1, not-predominance 3, not-proximity 1, not-contiguity 1, not-strong-dependence 1, not-prenascence 3, not-postnascence 3, not-repetition 3, not-kamma 3, not-resultant 3, not-nutriment 1, not-faculty 1, not-jhāna 1, not-path 1, not-association 1, not-dissociation 3, not-absence 1, not-disappearance 1.

By Threes

147. With mutuality and root conditions, not-object 1, not-predominance 3, not-proximity 1, not-contiguity 1, not-strong-dependence 1, not-prenascence 3, not-postnascence 3, not-repetition 3, not-kamma 3, not-resultant 3, not-association 1, not-dissociation 3, not-absence 1, not-disappearance 1.

By Fours

148. With mutuality, root and object conditions, not-predominance 3, not-prenascence 3, not-postnascence 3, not-repetition 3, not-kamma 3, not-resultant 3, not-dissociation 3.

(Expand in the same way as root condition.)

Dependence, Strong-dependence

By Twos

149. With dependence condition, not-root 2, not-object 5. ...
(Dependence condition is the same as conascence. Strong-dependence condition is the same as object.)

Prenascence

By Twos

150. With prenascence condition, not-root 2, not-predominance 3, not-postnascence 3, not-repetition 3, not-kamma 3, not-resultant 3, not-jhāna 1, not-path 1.

By Threes

151. With prenascence and root conditions, not-predominance 3, not-postnascence 3, not-repetition 3, not-kamma 3, not-resultant 3. ...

(Expand in the same way as root condition.)

Repetition

By Twos

152. With repetition condition, not-root 2, not-predominance 3, not-prenascence 3, not-postnascence 3, not-kamma 3, not-resultant 3, not-path 1, not-dissociation 3.

By Threes

153. With repetition and root conditions, not-predominance 3, not-prenascence 3, not-postnascence 3, not-kamma 3, not-resultant 3, not-dissociation 3. . . .

(Expand in the same way as root condition.)

Kamma

By Twos

154. With kamma condition, not-root 2, not-object 5, not-predominance 9, not-proximity 5, not-contiguity 5, not-mutuality 5, not-strong-dependence 5, not-prenascence 7, not-postnascence 9, not-repetition 9, not-resultant 9, not-nutriment 1, not-faculty 1, not-jhāna 1, not-path 1, not-association 5, not-dissociation 3, not-absence 5, not-disappearance 5.

By Threes

155. With kamma and root conditions, not-object 5, not-predominance 9, not-proximity 5, not-contiguity 5, not-mutuality 5, not-strong-dependence 5, not-prenascence 7, not-postnascence 9, not-repetition 9, not-resultant 9, not-association 5, not-dissociation 3, not-absence 5, not-disappearance 5.

By Fours

156. With kamma, root and object conditions, not-predominance 3, not-prenascence 3, not-postnascence 3, not-repetition 3, not-resultant 3, not-dissociation 3. . . .

(Expand in the same way as root condition.)

Resultant

By Twos

157. With resultant condition, not-root 1, not-object 1, not-predominance 1, not-proximity 1, not-contiguity 1, not-

mutuality 1, not-strong-dependence 1, not-prenascence 1, not-postnascence 1, not-repetition 1, not-jhāna 1, not-path 1, not-association 1, not-dissociation 1, not-absence 1, not-disappearance 1.

By Threes

158. With resultant and root conditions, not-object 1, not-predominance 1, not-proximity 1, not-contiguity 1, not-mutuality 1, not-strong-dependence 1, not-prenascence 1, not-postnascence 1, not-repetition 1, not-association 1, not-dissociation 1, not-absence 1, not-disappearance 1.

By Fours

159. With resultant, root and object conditions, not-predominance 1, not-prenascence 1, not-postnascence 1, not-repetition 1, not-dissociation 1.

By Fives

160. With resultant, root, object and predominance conditions, not-prenascence 1, not-postnascence 1, not-repetition 1, not-dissociation 1. ...

By Twenty-threes

161. With resultant, root, object, predominance, proximity, contiguity, conascence, mutuality, dependence, strong-dependence, prenascence, kamma, nutriment, faculty, jhāna, path, association, dissociation, presence, absence, disappearance and non-disappearance conditions, not-postnascence 1, not-repetition 1.

Nutriment

By Twos

162. With nutriment condition, not-root 2, not-object 5, not-predominance 9, not-proximity 5, not-contiguity 5, not-mutuality 5, not-strong-dependence 5, not-prenascence 7, not-postnascence 9, not-repetition 9, not-kamma 3, not-resultant 9, not-faculty 1, not-jhāna 1, not-path 1, not-association 5, not-dissociation 3, not-absence 5, not-disappearance 5.

By Threes

163. With nutriment and root conditions, not-object 5, not-predominance 9, not-proximity 5, not-contiguity 5, not-mutuality 5, not-strong-dependence 5, not-prenascence 7, not-postnascence 9, not-repetition 9, not-kamma 3, not-resultant 9, not-association 5, not-dissociation 3, not-absence 5, not-disappearance 5.

By Fours

164. With nutriment, root and object conditions, not-predominance 3, not-prenascence 3, not-postnascence 3, not-repetition 3, not-kamma 3, not-resultant 3, not-dissociation 3. . . .

(Expand in the same way as root condition.)

Faculty

By Twos

165. With faculty condition, not-root 2, not-object 5, not-predominance 9, not-proximity 5, not-contiguity 5, not-mutuality 5, not-strong-dependence 5, not-prenascence 7, not-postnascence 9, not-repetition 9, not-kamma 3, not-resultant 9, not-nutriment 1, not-jhāna 1, not-path 1, not-association 5, not-dissociation 3, not-absence 5, not-disappearance 5.

By Threes

166. With faculty and root conditions, not-object 5, not-predominance 9, not-proximity 5, not-contiguity 5, not-mutuality 5, not-strong-dependence 5, not-prenascence 7, not-postnascence 9, not-repetition 9, not-kamma 3, not-resultant 9, not-association 5, not-dissociation 3, not-absence 5, not-disappearance 5.

By Fours

167. With faculty, root and object conditions, not-predominance 3, not-prenascence 3, not-postnascence 3, not-repetition 3, not-kamma 3, not-resultant 3, not-dissociation 3. . . .

(Expand in the same way as root condition.)

Jhāna

By Twos

168. With jhāna condition, not-root 2, not-object 5, not-predominance 9, not-proximity 5, not-contiguity 5, not-mutuality 5, not-strong-dependence 5, not-prenascence 7, not-postnascence 9, not-repetition 9, not-kamma 3, not-resultant 9, not-path 1, not-association 5, not-dissociation 3, not-absence 5, not-disappearance 5.

By Threes

169. With jhāna and root conditions, not-object 5, not-predominance 9, not-proximity 5, not-contiguity 5, not-mutuality 5, not-strong-dependence 5, not-prenascence 7, not-postnascence 9, not-repetition 9, not-kamma 3, not-resultant 9, not-association 5, not-dissociation 3, not-absence 5, not-disappearance 5.

By Fours

170. With jhāna, root and object conditions, not-predominance 3, not-prenascence 3, not-postnascence 3, not-repetition 3, not-kamma 3, not-resultant 3, not-dissociation 3. ...

(Expand in the same way as root condition.)

Path

By Twos

171. With path condition, not-root 1, not-object 5, not-predominance 9, not-proximity 5, not-contiguity 5, not-mutuality 5, not-strong-dependence 5, not-prenascence 7, not-postnascence 9, not-repetition 9, not-kamma 3, not-resultant 9, not-association 5, not-dissociation 3, not-absence 5, not-disappearance 5.

By Threes

172. With path and root conditions, not-object 5, not-predominance 9, not-proximity 5, not-contiguity 5, not-mutuality 5, not-strong-dependence 5, not-prenascence 7, not-postnascence 9, not-repetition 9, not-kamma 3, not-resultant 9, not-association 5, not-dissociation 3, not-absence 5, not-disappearance 5.

By Fours

173. With path, root and object conditions, not-predominance

3, not-prenascence 3, not-postnascence 3, not-repetition 3, not-kamma 3, not-resultant 3, not-dissociation 3. ...

(Expand in the same way as root condition.)

Association

By Twos

174. With association condition, not-root 2, not-predominance 3, not-prenascence 3, not-postnascence 3, not-repetition 3, not-kamma 3, not-resultant 3, not-jhāna 1, not-path 1, not-dissociation 3.

By Threes

175. With association and root conditions, not-predominance 3, not-prenascence 3, not-postnascence 3, not-repetition 3, not-kamma 3, not-resultant 3, not-dissociation 3. ...

(Expand in the same way as root condition.)

Dissociation

By Twos

176. With dissociation condition, not-root 2, not-object 5, not-predominance 9, not-proximity 5, not-contiguity 5, not-mutuality 5, not-strong-dependence 5, not-prenascence 5, not-postnascence 9, not-repetition 9, not-kamma 3, not-resultant 9, not-jhāna 1, not-path 1, not-association 5, not-absence 5, not-disappearance 5.

By Threes

177. With dissociation and root conditions, not-object 5, not-predominance 9, not-proximity 5, not-contiguity 5, not-mutuality 5, not-strong-dependence 5, not-prenascence 5, not-postnascence 9, not-repetition 9, not-kamma 3, not-resultant 9, not-association 5, not-absence 5, not-disappearance 5.

By Fours

178. With dissociation, root and object conditions, not-predominance 3, not-prenascence 1, not-postnascence 3, not-repetition 3, not-kamma 3, not-resultant 3.

By Fives

179. With dissociation, root, object and predominance conditions, not-postnascence 3, not-repetition 3, not-kamma 3, not-resultant 3. ...

By Twelves

180. With dissociation, root, object, predominance, proximity, contiguity, conascence, mutuality, dependence, strong-dependence and prenascence conditions, not-postnascence 3, not-repetition 3, not-kamma 3, not-resultant 3. ...

By Twenty-threes (*with repetition*)

181. With dissociation, root . . . prenascence, repetition, kamma, nutriment . . . and non-disappearance conditions, not-postnascence 3, not-resultant 3.

By Fourteens (*with resultant*)

182. With dissociation, root . . . prenascence, kamma and resultant conditions, not-postnascence 1, not-repetition 1. ...

By Twenty-threes

183. With dissociation, root . . . prenascence, kamma, resultant, nutriment . . . and non-disappearance conditions, not-postnascence 1, not-repetition 1.

Presence

By Twos

184. With presence condition, not-root 2, not-object 5, not-predominance 9, not-proximity 5, not-contiguity 5, not-mutuality 5, not-strong-dependence 5, not-prenascence 7, not-postnascence 9, not-repetition 9, not-kamma 3, not-resultant 9, not-nutriment 1, not-faculty 1, not-jhāna 1, not-path 1, not-association 5, not-dissociation 3, not-absence 5, not-disappearance 5.

By Threes

185. With presence and root conditions, not-object 5, not-predominance 9, not-proximity 5, not-contiguity 5, not-mutuality 5, not-strong-dependence 5, not-prenascence 7,

not-postnascence 9, not-repetition 9, not-kamma 3, not-resultant 9, not-association 5, not-dissociation 3, not-absence 5, not-disappearance 5.

By Fours

186. With presence, root and object conditions, not-predominance 3, not-prenascence 3, not-postnascence 3, not-repetition 3, not-kamma 3, not-resultant 3, not-dissociation 3. ...

(Expand in the same way as root condition.)

Absence, Disappearance

By Twos

187. With absence condition ... with disappearance condition, not-root 2, not-predominance 3, not-prenascence 3, not-postnascence 3, not-repetition 3, not-kamma 3, not-resultant 3, not-jhāna 1, not-path 1, not-dissociation 3. ...

(Expand in the same way as object condition.)

Non-disappearance

By Twos

188. With non-disappearance condition, not-root 2, not-object 5, not-predominance 9, not-proximity 5, not-contiguity 5, not-mutuality 5, not-strong-dependence 5, not-prenascence 7, not-postnascence 9, not-repetition 9, not-kamma 3, not-resultant 9, not-nutriment 1, not-faculty 1, not-jhāna 1, not-path 1, not-association 5, not-dissociation 3, not-absence 5, not-disappearance 5.

By Threes

189. With non-disappearance and root conditions, not-object 5, not-predominance 9, not-proximity 5, not-contiguity 5, not-mutuality 5, not-strong-dependence 5, not-prenascence 7, not-postnascence 9, not-repetition 9, not-kamma 3, not-resultant 9, not-association 5, not-dissociation 3, not-absence 5, not-disappearance 5. ...

(Expand in the same way as root condition.)

End of Positive–Negative Enumeration.

4. CONDITIONS : NEGATIVE–POSITIVE

Not-root

By Twos

190. With not-root condition, object 2, proximity 2, contiguity 2, conascence 2, mutuality 2, dependence 2, strong-dependence 2, prenascence 2, repetition 2, kamma 2, resultant 1, nutriment 2, faculty 2, jhāna 2, path 1, association 2, dissociation 2, presence 2, absence 2, disappearance 2, non-disappearance 2.

By Threes

191. With not-root and not-object conditions, conascence 1, mutuality 1, dependence 1, kamma 1, resultant 1, nutriment 1, faculty 1, jhāna 1, dissociation 1, presence 1, non-disappearance 1. ...

By Sevens

192. With not-root, not-object, not-predominance, not-proximity, not-contiguity and not-mutuality conditions, conascence 1, dependence 1, kamma 1, resultant 1, nutriment 1, faculty 1, jhāna 1, dissociation 1, presence 1, non-disappearance 1 (All are 1). ...

By Tens

193. With not-root, not-object, not-predominance, not-proximity, not-contiguity, not-mutuality, not-strong-dependence, not-prenascence, not-postnascence, not-repetition. (Up to repetition all are the same. When not-kamma is considered, there are five questions.)

With not-root, not-object ... not-repetition and not-kamma conditions, conascence 1, dependence 1, nutriment 1, presence 1, non-disappearance 1. ...

By Fourteens

194. With not-root, not-object, not-predominance, not-proximity, not-contiguity, not-mutuality, not-strong-dependence, not-prenascence, not-postnascence, not-repetition, not-kamma, not-resultant and not-nutriment conditions, conascence 1, dependence 1, presence 1, non-disappearance 1. ...

By Twenty-ones
195. With not-root, not-object, not-predominance, not-proximity, not-contiguity, not-mutuality, not-strong-dependence, not-prenascence, not-postnascence, not-repetition, not-kamma, not-resultant, not-nutriment, not-faculty, not-jhāna, not-path, not-association, not-dissociation, not-absence and not-disappearance conditions, conascence 1, dependence 1, presence 1, non-disappearance 1.

Not-object
By Twos
196. With not-object condition, root 5, predominance 5, conascence 5, mutuality 1, dependence 5, kamma 5, resultant 1, nutriment 5, faculty 5, jhāna 5, path 5, dissociation 5, presence 5, non-disappearance 5.

By Threes
197. With not-object and not-root conditions, conascence 1, mutuality 1, dependence 1, kamma 1, resultant 1, nutriment 1, faculty 1, jhāna 1, dissociation 1, presence 1, non-disappearance 1. . . .

(Expand in the same way as not-root condition.)

Not-predominance
By Twos
198. With not-predominance condition, root 9, object 3, proximity 3, contiguity 3, conascence 9, mutuality 3, dependence 9, strong-dependence 3, prenascence 3, repetition 3, kamma 9, resultant 1, nutriment 9, faculty 9, jhāna 9, path 9, association 3, dissociation 9, presence 9, absence 3, disappearance 3, non-disappearance 9.

By Threes
199. With not-predominance and not-root conditions, object 2, proximity 2, contiguity 2, conascence 2, mutuality 2, dependence 2, strong-dependence 2, prenascence 2, repetition 2, kamma 2, resultant 1, nutriment 2, faculty 2, jhāna 2, path 1, association 2, dissociation 2, presence 2, absence 2, disappearance 2, non-disappearance 2.

Faultless Triplet

By Fours

200. With not-predominance, not-root and not-object conditions, conascence 1, mutuality 1, dependence 1, kamma 1, resultant 1, nutriment 1, faculty 1, jhāna 1, dissociation 1, presence 1, non-disappearance 1. ... (Abbreviated.)

Not-proximity, etc.

By Twos

201. With not-proximity condition ... with not-contiguity condition ... with not-mutuality condition ... with not-strong-dependence condition, root 5, predominance 5, conascence 5, mutuality 1, dependence 5, kamma 5, resultant 1, nutriment 5, faculty 5, jhāna 5, path 5, dissociation 5, presence 5, non-disappearance 5.

By Threes

202. With not-strong-dependence and not-root conditions, conascence 1, mutuality 1, dependence 1, kamma 1, resultant 1, nutriment 1, faculty 1, jhāna 1, dissociation 1, presence 1, non-disappearance 1. ... (Abbreviated.)

Not-prenascence

By Twos

203. With not-prenascence condition, root 7, object 3, predominance 7, proximity 3, contiguity 3, conascence 7, mutuality 3, dependence 7, strong-dependence 3, repetition 3, kamma 7, resultant 1, nutriment 7, faculty 7, jhāna 7, path 7, association 3, dissociation 5, presence 7, absence 3, disappearance 3, non-disappearance 7.

By Threes

204. With not-prenascence and not-root conditions, object 2, proximity 2, contiguity 2, conascence 2, mutuality 2, dependence 2, strong-dependence 2, repetition 1, kamma 2, resultant 1, nutriment 2, faculty 2, jhāna 2, path 1, association 2, dissociation 1, presence 2, absence 2, disappearance 2, non-disappearance 2.

By Fours

205. With not-prenascence, not-root and not-object conditions, conascence 1, mutuality 1, dependence 1, kamma 1, resultant 1, nutriment 1, faculty 1, jhāna 1, dissociation 1, presence 1, non-disappearance 1. ... (Abbreviated.)

Not-postnascence

By Twos

206. With not-postnascence condition, root 9, object 3, predominance 9, proximity 3, contiguity 3, conascence 9, mutuality 3, dependence 9, strong-dependence 3, prenascence 3, repetition 3, kamma 9, resultant 1, nutriment 9, faculty 9, jhāna 9, path 9, association 3, dissociation 9, presence 9, absence 3, disappearance 3, non-disappearance 9.

By Threes

207. With not-postnascence and not-root conditions, object 2, proximity 2, contiguity 2, conascence 2, mutuality 2, dependence 2, strong-dependence 2, prenascence 2, repetition 2, kamma 2, resultant 1, nutriment 2, faculty 2, jhāna 2, path 1, association 2, dissociation 2, presence 2, absence 2, disappearance 2, non-disappearance 2.

By Fours

208. With not-postnascence, not-root and not-object conditions, conascence 1, mutuality 1, dependence 1, kamma 1, resultant 1, nutriment 1, faculty 1, jhāna 1, dissociation 1, presence 1, non-disappearance 1. ... (Abbreviated.)

Not-repetition

By Twos

209. With not-repetition condition, root 9, object 3, predominance 9, proximity 3, contiguity 3, conascence 9, mutuality 3, dependence 9, strong-dependence 3, prenascence 3, kamma 9, resultant 1, nutriment 9, faculty 9, jhāna 9, path 9, association 3, dissociation 9, presence 9, absence 3, disappearance 3, non-disappearance 9.

By Threes

210. With not-repetition and not-root conditions, object 2, proximity 2, contiguity 2, conascence 2, mutuality 2, dependence 2, strong-dependence 2, prenascence 2, kamma 2, resultant 1, nutriment 2, faculty 2, jhāna 2, path 1, association 2, dissociation 2, presence 2, absence 2, disappearance 2, non-disappearance 2.

By Fours

211. With not-repetition, not-root and not-object conditions, conascence 1, mutuality 1, dependence 1, kamma 1, resultant 1, nutriment 1, faculty 1, jhāna 1, dissociation 1, presence 1, non-disappearance 1. ... (Abbreviated.)

Not-kamma

By Twos

212. With not-kamma condition, root 3, object 3, predominance 3, proximity 3, contiguity 3, conascence 3, mutuality 3, dependence 3, strong-dependence 3, prenascence 3, repetition 3, nutriment 3, faculty 3, jhāna 3, path 3, association 3, dissociation 3, presence 3, absence 3, disappearance 3, non-disappearance 3.

By Threes

213. With not-kamma and not-root conditions, object 1, proximity 1, contiguity 1, conascence 1, mutuality 1, dependence 1, strong-dependence 1, prenascence 1, repetition 1, nutriment 1, faculty 1, jhāna 1, association 1, dissociation 1, presence 1, absence 1, disappearance 1, non-disappearance 1.

By Fours

214. With not-kamma, not-root and not-object conditions, conascence 1, mutuality 1, dependence 1, nutriment 1, presence 1, non-disappearance 1. ... (Abbreviated.)

Not-resultant

By Twos

215. With not-resultant condition, root 9, object 3, predominance 9, proximity 3, contiguity 3, conascence 9, mutuality 3,

dependence 9, strong-dependence 3, prenascence 3, repetition 3, kamma 9, nutriment 9, faculty 9, jhāna 9, path 9, association 3, dissociation 9, presence 9, absence 3, disappearance 3, non-disappearance 9.

By Threes

216. With not-resultant and not-root conditions, object 2, proximity 2, contiguity 2, conascence 2, mutuality 2, dependence 2, strong-dependence 2, prenascence 2, repetition 2, kamma 2, nutriment 2, faculty 2, jhāna 2, path 1, association 2, dissociation 2, presence 2, absence 2, disappearance 2, non-disappearance 2.

By Fours

217. With not-resultant, not-root and not-object conditions, conascence 1, mutuality 1, dependence 1, kamma 1, nutriment 1, faculty 1, jhāna 1, dissociation 1, presence 1, non-disappearance 1. ... (Abbreviated.)

Not-nutriment

By Twos

218. With not-nutriment condition, conascence 1, mutuality 1, dependence 1, kamma 1, faculty 1, presence 1, non-disappearance 1. ... (Abbreviated.)

Not-faculty

By Twos

219. With not-faculty condition, conascence 1, mutuality 1, dependence 1, kamma 1, nutriment 1, presence 1, non-disappearance 1. ... (Abbreviated.)

Not-jhāna

By Twos

220. With not-jhāna condition, object 1, proximity 1, contiguity 1, conascence 1, mutuality 1, dependence 1, strong-dependence 1, prenascence 1, kamma 1, resultant 1, nutriment 1, faculty 1, association 1, dissociation 1, presence 1, absence 1, disappearance 1, non-disappearance 1. ... (Abbreviated.)

Not-path
By Threes
221. With not-path and not-root conditions, object 1, proximity 1, contiguity 1, conascence 1, mutuality 1, dependence 1, strong-dependence 1, prenascence 1, repetition 1, kamma 1, resultant 1, nutriment 1, faculty 1, jhāna 1, association 1, dissociation 1, presence 1, absence 1, disappearance 1, non-disappearance 1.

By Fours
222. With not-path, not-root and not-object conditions, conascence 1, mutuality 1, dependence 1, kamma 1, resultant 1, nutriment 1, faculty 1, jhāna 1, dissociation 1, presence 1, non-disappearance 1. ... (Abbreviated.)

Not-association
By Twos
223. With not-association condition, root 5, predominance 5, conascence 5, mutuality 1, dependence 5, kamma 5, resultant 1, nutriment 5, faculty 5, jhāna 5, path 5, dissociation 5, presence 5, non-disappearance 5.

By Threes
224. With not-association and not-root conditions, conascence 1, mutuality 1, dependence 1, kamma 1, resultant 1, nutriment 1, faculty 1, jhāna 1, dissociation 1, presence 1, non-disappearance 1. ... (Abbreviated.)

Not-dissociation
By Twos
225. With not-dissociation condition, root 3, object 3, predominance 3, proximity 3, contiguity 3, conascence 3, mutuality 3, dependence 3, strong-dependence 3, repetition 3, kamma 3, resultant 1, nutriment 3, faculty 3, jhāna 3, path 3, association 3, presence 3, absence 3, disappearance 3, non-disappearance 3.

By Threes
226. With not-dissociation and not-root conditions, object 2, proximity 2, contiguity 2, conascence 2, mutuality 2, dependence 2, strong-dependence 2, repetition 1, kamma 2, nutriment

2, faculty 2, jhāna 2, path 1, association 2, presence 2, absence 2, disappearance 2, non-disappearance 2.

By Fours

227. With not-dissociation, not-root and not-object conditions, conascence 1, mutuality 1, dependence 1, kamma 1, nutriment 1, faculty 1, presence 1, non-disappearance 1. ... (Abbreviated.)

Not-absence, Not-disappearance

By Twos

228. With not-absence condition ... with not-disappearance condition, root 5, predominance 5, conascence 5, mutuality 1, dependence 5, kamma 5, resultant 1, nutriment 5, faculty 5, jhāna 5, path 5, dissociation 5, presence 5, non-disappearance 5.

By Threes

229. With not-disappearance and not-root conditions, conascence 1, mutuality 1, dependence 1, kamma 1, resultant 1, nutriment 1, faculty 1, jhāna 1, dissociation 1, presence 1, non-disappearance 1. ...

By Eights

230. With not-disappearance, not-root, not-object, not-predominance, not-proximity, not-contiguity and not-mutuality conditions, conascence 1, dependence 1, kamma 1, resultant 1, nutriment 1, faculty 1, jhāna 1, dissociation 1, presence 1, non-disappearance 1. ...

By Thirteens

231. With not-disappearance, not-root ... and not-kamma conditions, conascence 1, dependence 1, nutriment 1, presence 1, non-disappearance 1. ...

By Fifteens

232. With not-disappearance, not-root ... not-kamma, not-resultant and not-nutriment conditions, conascence 1, dependence 1, presence 1, non-disappearance 1. ...

By Twenty-ones

233. With not-disappearance, not-root ... not-kamma, not-resultant, not-nutriment, not-faculty, not-jhāna, not-path,

not-association, not-dissociation and not-absence conditions, conascence 1, dependence 1, presence 1, non-disappearance 1.

End of Negative–Positive.

End of " DEPENDENT " CHAPTER.

I. FAULTLESS TRIPLET   II. " CONASCENT " CHAPTER

1. CONDITIONS : POSITIVE   (i). CLASSIFICATION CHAPTER

Root 9

234. (i) Conascent with faultless state, arises faultless state by root condition.

Conascent with one faultless aggregate, arise three aggregates ; conascent with three aggregates, arises one aggregate ; conascent with two aggregates, arise two aggregates.

(ii) Conascent with faultless state, arises indeterminate state by root condition.

Conascent with faultless aggregates, arises mind-produced matter.

(iii) Conascent with faultless state, arise faultless and indeterminate states by root condition.

Conascent with one faultless aggregate, arise three aggregates and mind-produced matter ; conascent with three aggregates, arise one aggregate and mind-produced matter ; conascent with two aggregates, arise two aggregates and mind-produced matter. (3)

235. (iv) Conascent with faulty state, arises faulty state by root condition.

Conascent with one faulty aggregate, arise three aggregates ; conascent with three aggregates, arises one aggregate ; conascent with two aggregates, arise two aggregates.

(v) Conascent with faulty state, arises indeterminate state by root condition.

Conascent with faulty aggregates, arises mind-produced matter.

(vi) Conascent with faulty state, arise faulty and indeterminate states by root condition.

Conascent with one faulty aggregate, arise three aggregates

and mind-produced matter; conascent with three aggregates, arise one aggregate and mind-produced matter; conascent with two aggregates, arise two aggregates and mind-produced matter. (3)

236. (vii) Conascent with indeterminate state, arises indeterminate state by root condition.

(*a*) Conascent with one resultant indeterminate or functional indeterminate aggregate, arise three aggregates and mind-produced matter; conascent with three aggregates, arise one aggregate and mind-produced matter; conascent with two aggregates, arise two aggregates and mind-produced matter;

(*b*) At the moment of conception, conascent with one resultant indeterminate aggregate, arise three aggregates and kamma-produced matter; conascent with three aggregates, arise one aggregate and kamma-produced matter; conascent with two aggregates, arise two aggregates and kamma-produced matter; conascent with aggregates, arises (heart-)base; conascent with (heart-)base, arise aggregates;

(*c*) Conascent with one great primary, arise three great primaries; conascent with three great primaries, arises one great primary; conascent with two great primaries, arise two great primaries; conascent with great primaries, arise mind-produced and kamma-produced derived matter. (1)

237. (viii) Conascent with faultless and indeterminate state, arises indeterminate state by root condition.

Conascent with faultless aggregates and great primaries, arises mind-produced matter. (1)

(ix) Conascent with faulty and indeterminate state, arises indeterminate state by root condition.

Conascent with faulty aggregates and great primaries, arises mind-produced matter. (1)

(Expand in the same way as " Dependent " Chapter.)

I. CONDITIONS : POSITIVE   (ii) ENUMERATION CHAPTER

By Ones

238. With root 9, object 3, predominance 9, proximity 3, contiguity 3, conascence 9, mutuality 3, dependence 9, strong-dependence 3, prenascence 3, repetition 3, kamma 9, resultant

1, nutriment 9, faculty 9, jhāna 9, path 9, association 3, dissociation 9, presence 9, absence 3, disappearance 3, non-disappearance 9.

(Enumerate in the same way as enumerated in
" Dependent " Chapter.)
End of Positive.

2. CONDITIONS : NEGATIVE   (i) CLASSIFICATION CHAPTER

Not-root 2

239. (i) Conascent with faulty state, arises faulty state by not-root condition.

Conascent with doubt-accompanied or restlessness-accompanied aggregates, arises doubt-accompanied or restlessness-accompanied delusion.

(ii) Conascent with indeterminate state, arises indeterminate state by not-root condition.

(*a*) Conascent with one rootless resultant indeterminate or functional indeterminate aggregate, arise three aggregates and mind-produced matter ; conascent with three aggregates, arise one aggregate and mind-produced matter ; conascent with two aggregates, arise two aggregates and mind-produced matter ;

(*b*) At the moment of rootless conception, conascent with one resultant indeterminate aggregate, arise three aggregates and kamma-produced matter ; conascent with three aggregates, arise one aggregate and kamma-produced matter ; conascent with two aggregates, arise two aggregates and kamma-produced matter ; conascent with aggregates, arises (heart-)base ; conascent with (heart-)base, arise aggregates ;

(*c*) Conascent with one great primary, arise three great primaries ; conascent with three great primaries, arises one great primary ; conascent with two great primaries, arise two great primaries ; conascent with great primaries, arise mind-produced and kamma-produced derived matter ;

(*d*) External ... nutriment-produced ... temperature-produced ... conascent with one great primary of non-percipient beings, arise three great primaries ... conascent with great primaries, arises kamma-produced derived matter.

(Expand in the same way as " Dependent " Chapter.)

2. CONDITIONS : NEGATIVE   (ii) ENUMERATION CHAPTER

By Ones

240. With not-root 2, not-object 5, not-predominance 9, not proximity 5, not-contiguity 5, not-mutuality 5, not-strong-dependence 5, not-prenascence 7, not-postnascence 9, not-repetition 9, not-kamma 3, not-resultant 9, not-nutriment 1, not-faculty 1, not-jhāna 1, not-path 1, not-association 5, not-dissociation 3, not-absence 5, not-disappearance 5. ...

End of Negative

3. CONDITIONS : POSITIVE–NEGATIVE

Root

By Twos

241. With root condition, not-object 5, not-predominance 9, not-proximity 5, not-contiguity 5, not-mutuality 5, not-strong-dependence 5, not-prenascence 7, not-postnascence 9, not-repetition 9, not-kamma 3, not-resultant 9, not-association 5, not-dissociation 3, not-absence 5, not-disappearance 5. ...

End of Positive–Negative

4. CONDITIONS : NEGATIVE–POSITIVE

Not-root

By Twos

242. With not-root condition, object 2, proximity 2, contiguity 2, conascence 2, mutuality 2, dependence 2, strong-dependence 2, prenascence 2, repetition 2, kamma 2, resultant 1, nutriment 2, faculty 2, jhāna 2, path 1, association 2, dissociation 2, presence 2, absence 2, disappearance 2, non-disappearance 2. ...

End of Negative–Positive

End of " CONASCENT " CHAPTER

(The term " Dependent " is the same as " Conascent ". The term " Conascent " is the same as " Dependent ".)

1. Faultless Triplet   III. "Conditioned" Chapter
1. conditions: positive   (i) classification chapter

Root 17

243. (i) Conditioned by faultless state, arises faultless state by root condition.

Conditioned by one faultless aggregate, arise three aggregates; conditioned by three aggregates, arises one aggregate; conditioned by two aggregates, arise two aggregates.

(ii) Conditioned by faultless state, arises indeterminate state by root condition.

Conditioned by faultless aggregates, arises mind-produced matter.

(iii) Conditioned by faultless state, arise faultless and indeterminate states by root condition.

Conditioned by one faultless aggregate, arise three aggregates and mind-produced matter; conditioned by three aggregates, arise one aggregate and mind-produced matter; conditioned by two aggregates, arise two aggregates and mind-produced matter. (3)

244. (iv) Conditioned by faulty state, arises faulty state by root condition.

Conditioned by one faulty aggregate, arise three aggregates; conditioned by three aggregates, arises one aggregate; conditioned by two aggregates, arise two aggregates.

(v) Conditioned by faulty state, arises indeterminate state by root condition.

Conditioned by faulty aggregates, arises mind-produced matter.

(vi) Conditioned by faulty state, arise faulty and indeterminate states by root condition.

Conditioned by one faulty aggregate, arise three aggregates and mind-produced matter; conditioned by three aggregates, arise one aggregate and mind-produced matter; conditioned by two aggregates, arise two aggregates and mind-produced matter. (3)

245. (vii) Conditioned by indeterminate state, arises indeterminate state by root condition.

(*a*) Conditioned by one resultant indeterminate or functional indeterminate aggregate, arise three aggregates and mind-produced matter; conditioned by three aggregates, arise one aggregate and mind-produced matter; conditioned by two aggregates, arise two aggregates and mind-produced matter;

(*b*) At the moment of conception, conditioned by one resultant indeterminate aggregate, arise three aggregates and kamma-produced matter; conditioned by three aggregates, arise one aggregate and kamma-produced matter; conditioned by two aggregates, arise two aggregates and kamma-produced matter; conditioned by aggregates, arises (heart-)base; conditioned by (heart-)base, arise aggregates;

(*c*) Conditioned by one great primary, arise three great primaries; conditioned by three great primaries, arises one great primary; conditioned by two great primaries, arise two great primaries; conditioned by great primaries, arise mind-produced and kamma-produced derived matter;

(*d*) Conditioned by (heart-)base, arise resultant indeterminate or functional indeterminate aggregates.

(viii) Conditioned by indeterminate state, arises faultless state by root condition.

Conditioned by (heart-)base, arise faultless aggregates.

(ix) Conditioned by indeterminate state, arises faulty state by root condition.

Conditioned by (heart-)base, arise faulty aggregates.

(x) Conditioned by indeterminate state, arise faultless and indeterminate states by root condition.

Conditioned by (heart-)base, arise faultless aggregates; conditioned by great primaries, arises mind-produced matter.

(xi) Conditioned by indeterminate state, arise faulty and indeterminate states by root condition.

Conditioned by (heart-)base, arise faulty aggregates; conditioned by great primaries, arises mind-produced matter. (5)

246. (xii) Conditioned by faultless and indeterminate state, arises faultless state by root condition.

Conditioned by one faultless aggregate and (heart-)base, arise three aggregates; conditioned by three aggregates and (heart-)-base, arises one aggregate ; conditioned by two aggregates and (heart-)base, arise two aggregates.

(xiii) Conditioned by faultless and indeterminate state, arises indeterminate state by root condition.

Conditioned by faultless aggregates and great primaries, arises mind-produced matter.

(xiv) Conditioned by faultless and indeterminate state, arise faultless and indeterminate states by root condition.

Conditioned by one faultless aggregate and (heart-)base, arise three aggregates ; conditioned by three aggregates and (heart-)base, arises one aggregate ; conditioned by two aggregates and (heart-)base, arise two aggregates ; conditioned by faultless aggregates and great primaries, arises mind-produced matter. (3)

247. (xv) Conditioned by faulty and indeterminate state, arises faulty state by root condition.

Conditioned by one faulty aggregate and (heart-)base, arise three aggregates ; conditioned by three aggregates and (heart-)base, arises one aggregate ; conditioned by two aggregates and (heart-)base, arise two aggregates.

(xvi) Conditioned by faulty and indeterminate state, arises indeterminate state by root condition.

Conditioned by faulty aggregates and great primaries, arises mind-produced matter.

(xvii) Conditioned by faulty and indeterminate state, arise faulty and indeterminate states by root condition.

Conditioned by one faulty aggregate and (heart-)base, arise three aggregates ; conditioned by three aggregates and (heart-)base, arises one aggregate ; conditioned by two aggregates and (heart-)base, arise two aggregates ; conditioned by faulty aggregates and great primaries, arises mind-produced matter. (3)

Object 7

248. (i) Conditioned by faultless state, arises faultless state by object condition.

Conditioned by one faultless aggregate, arise three aggregates ; conditioned by three aggregates, arises one aggregate ; conditioned by two aggregates, arise two aggregates. (1)

249. (ii) Conditioned by faulty state, arises faulty state by object condition.

Conditioned by one faulty aggregate, arise three aggregates; conditioned by three aggregates, arises one aggregate; conditioned by two aggregates, arise two aggregates. (1)

250. (iii) Conditioned by indeterminate state, arises indeterminate state by object condition.

(*a*) Conditioned by one resultant indeterminate or functional indeterminate aggregate, arise three aggregates; conditioned by three aggregates, arises one aggregate; conditioned by two aggregates, arise two aggregates;

(*b*) At the moment of conception, conditioned by one resultant indeterminate aggregate, arise three aggregates; conditioned by three aggregates, arises one aggregate; conditioned by two aggregates, arise two aggregates; conditioned by (heart-)base, arise aggregates;

(*c*) Conditioned by eye-base, arises eye-consciousness; conditioned by ear-base, arises ear-consciousness; conditioned by nose-base, arises nose-consciousness; conditioned by tongue-base, arises tongue-consciousness; conditioned by body-base, arises body-consciousness; conditioned by (heart-)base, arise resultant indeterminate or functional indeterminate aggregates.

(iv) Conditioned by indeterminate state, arises faultless state by object condition.

Conditioned by (heart-)base, arise faultless aggregates.

(v) Conditioned by indeterminate state, arises faulty state by object condition.

Conditioned by (heart-)base, arise faulty aggregates. (3)

251. (vi) Conditioned by faultless and indeterminate state, arises faultless state by object condition.

Conditioned by one faultless aggregate and (heart-)base, arise three aggregates ... conditioned by two aggregates and (heart-)base, arise two aggregates. (1)

252. (vii) Conditioned by faulty and indeterminate state, arises faulty state by object condition.

Conditioned by one faulty aggregate and (heart-)base, arise three aggregates ... conditioned by two aggregates and (heart-)base, arise two aggregates. (1)

Predominance 17

253. (i)–(iii) Conditioned by faultless state, arises faultless state by predominance condition.
   Conditioned by one faultless aggregate ... three.
   (iv)–(vi) Conditioned by faulty state, arises faulty state by predominance condition.
   Conditioned by one faulty aggregate ... three.
      (vii) Conditioned by indeterminate state, arises indeterminate state by predominance condition.
   (a) Conditioned by one resultant indeterminate or functional indeterminate aggregate, arise three aggregates and mind-produced matter....
   (b) Conditioned by one great primary, arise three great primaries ... conditioned by great primaries, arises mind-produced derived matter;
   (c) Conditioned by (heart-)base, arise resultant indeterminate or functional indeterminate aggregates.
      (viii) Conditioned by indeterminate state, arises faultless state by predominance condition.
   Conditioned by (heart-)base, arise faultless aggregates. ...

   (Expand in the same way as root condition.)

Proximity 7, Contiguity 7

254. Conditioned by faultless state, arises faultless state by proximity condition ... by contiguity condition. ...

   (Expand in the same way as object condition.)

Conascence 17

255. (i)–(iii) Conditioned by faultless state, arises faultless state by conascence condition.
   Conditioned by one faultless aggregate ... three.
      (iv)–(vi) Conditioned by faulty state ... three.
         (vii) Conditioned by indeterminate state, arises indeterminate state by conascence condition.
      (a) Conditioned by one resultant indeterminate or functional

indeterminate aggregate, arise three aggregates and mind-produced matter. ...

(b) At the moment of conception. ...

(c) Conditioned by one great primary. ...

(d) External ... nutriment-produced ... temperature-produced ... conditioned by one great primary of non-percipient beings ... conditioned by great primaries, arises kamma-produced derived matter;

(e) Conditioned by eye-base, arises eye-consciousness ... conditioned by body-base, arises body-consciousness; conditioned by (heart-)base, arise resultant indeterminate or functional indeterminate aggregates.

(viii) Conditioned by indeterminate state, arises faultless state by conascence condition.

Conditioned by (heart-)base, arise faultless aggregates. ...

(Expand in the same way as root condition.)

Mutuality 7

256. (i) Conditioned by faultless state, arises faultless state by mutuality condition ... one.

(ii) Conditioned by faulty state, arises faulty state by mutuality condition. ... one.

(iii) Conditioned by indeterminate state, arises indeterminate state by mutuality condition.

(a) Conditioned by one resultant indeterminate or functional indeterminate aggregate, arise three aggregates ... conditioned by two aggregates, arise two aggregates;

(b) At the moment of conception, conditioned by one resultant indeterminate aggregate, arise three aggregates and (heart-)base ... conditioned by two aggregates, arise two aggregates and (heart-)base; conditioned by aggregates, arises (heart-)base; conditioned by (heart-)base, arise aggregates;

(c) Conditioned by one great primary, arise three great primaries ... conditioned by two great primaries, arise two great primaries;

(d) External ... nutriment-produced ... temperature-produced ... conditioned by one great primary of non-percipient beings, arise three great primaries ... conditioned by two great primaries, arise two great primaries;

(e) Conditioned by eye-base, arises eye-consciousness . . . conditioned by body-base, arises body-consciousness; conditioned by (heart-)base, arise resultant indeterminate or functional indeterminate aggregates.

(iv) Conditioned by indeterminate state, arises faultless state by mutuality condition.

Conditioned by (heart-)base, arise faultless aggregates. . . .

(Expand in the same way as object condition.)

Dependence 17

257. Conditioned by faultless state, arises faultless state by dependence condition.

Conditioned by one faultless aggregate, arise three aggregates. . . .

(Expand in the same way as conascence condition.)

Strong-dependence 7

258. Conditioned by faultless state, arises faultless state by strong-dependence condition.

Conditioned by one faultless aggregate. . . . (Same as object condition.)

Prenascence 7

259. (i) Conditioned by faultless state, arises faultless state by prenascence condition.

Conditioned by one faultless aggregate, arise three aggregates . . . conditioned by two aggregates, arise two aggregates; (conditioned by heart-)base, (arise faultless aggregates) by prenascence condition. (1)

(ii) Conditioned by faulty state, arises faulty state by prenascence condition.

Conditioned by one faulty aggregate, arise three aggregates . . . conditioned by two aggregates, arise two aggregates; (conditioned by heart-)base, (arise faulty aggregates) by prenascence condition. (1)

(iii) Conditioned by indeterminate state, arises indeterminate state by prenascence condition.

(a) Conditioned by one resultant indeterminate or functional indeterminate aggregate, arise three aggregates ... conditioned by two aggregates, arise two aggregates; (conditioned by heart-)base, (arise resultant indeterminate or functional indeterminate aggregates) by prenascence condition;

(b) Conditioned by eye-base, arises eye-consciousness ... conditioned by body-base, arises body-consciousness; conditioned by (heart-)base, arise resultant indeterminate or functional indeterminate aggregates; (conditioned by six) bases, (arise aggregates) by prenascence condition.

(iv) Conditioned by indeterminate state, arises faultless state by prenascence condition.

Conditioned by (heart-)base, arise faultless aggregates; (conditioned by heart-)base, (arise aggregates) by prenascence condition.

(v) Conditioned by indeterminate state, arises faulty state by prenascence condition.

Conditioned by (heart-)base, arise faulty aggregates; (conditioned by heart-)base, (arise aggregates) by prenascence condition. (3)

(vi) Conditioned by faultless and indeterminate state, arises faultless state by prenascence condition.

Conditioned by one faultless aggregate and (heart-)base, arise three aggregates ... conditioned by two aggregates and (heart-)base, arise two aggregates; (conditioned by heart-)base, (arise faultless aggregates) by prenascence condition. (1)

(vii) Conditioned by faulty and indeterminate state, arises faulty state by prenascence condition.

Conditioned by one faulty aggregate and (heart-)base, arise three aggregates ... conditioned by two aggregates and (heart-)base, arise two aggregates; (conditioned by heart-)base, (arise faulty aggregates) by prenascence condition. (1)

Repetition 7

260. (i) Conditioned by faultless state, arises faultless state by repetition condition.

Conditioned by one faultless aggregate....

(ii) Conditioned by faulty state, arises faulty state by repetition condition.

Conditioned by one faulty aggregate....

(iii) Conditioned by indeterminate state, arises indeterminate state by repetition condition.

Conditioned by one functional indeterminate aggregate, arise three aggregates ; conditioned by three aggregates, arises one aggregate ; conditioned by two aggregates, arise two aggregates ; conditioned by (heart-)base, arise functional indeterminate aggregates.

(iv) Conditioned by indeterminate state, arises faultless state by repetition condition.

Conditioned by (heart-)base, arise faultless aggregates.

(v) Conditioned by indeterminate state, arises faulty state by repetition condition.

Conditioned by (heart-)base, arise faulty aggregates.

(vi) Conditioned by faultless and indeterminate state. . . .

(vii) Conditioned by faulty and indeterminate state, arises faulty state by repetition condition.

Conditioned by one faulty aggregate and (heart-)base, arise three aggregates. . . .

Kamma 17

261. (i)–(iii) Conditioned by faultless state, arises faultless state by kamma condition.

Conditioned by one faultless aggregate . . . three.

(iv)–(vi) Conditioned by faulty state, arises faulty state by kamma condition . . . three.

(vii) Conditioned by indeterminate state, arises indeterminate state by kamma condition.

(a) Conditioned by one resultant indeterminate or functional indeterminate aggregate. . . .

(b) At the moment of conception. . . .

(c) Conditioned by one great primary. . . .

(d) Conditioned by one great primary of non-percipient beings . . . conditioned by great primaries, arises kamma-produced derived matter ;

(e) Conditioned by eye-base, arises eye-consciousness . . . conditioned by body-base, arises body-consciousness ; conditioned by (heart-)base, arise resultant indeterminate or functional indeterminate aggregates.

(viii) Conditioned by indeterminate state, arises faultless state by kamma condition.

Conditioned by (heart-)base, arise faultless aggregates.

(ix)–(xi) Conditioned by indeterminate state, arises faulty state by kamma condition.

Conditioned by (heart-)base, arise faulty aggregates. . . . (5).

(xii)–(xiv) Conditioned by faultless and indeterminate state, arises faultless state . . . indeterminate state . . . faultless and indeterminate states by kamma condition. . . .

(xv)–(xvii) Conditioned by faulty and indeterminate state, arises faulty state . . . indeterminate state . . . faulty and indeterminate states by kamma condition.

Conditioned by one faulty aggregate and (heart-)base . . . conditioned by faulty aggregates and great primaries, arises mind-produced matter.

Resultant 1

262. Conditioned by indeterminate state, arises indeterminate state by resultant condition.

(a) Conditioned by one resultant indeterminate aggregate. . . .

(b) At the moment of conception. . . .

(c) Conditioned by one great primary. . . .

(d) Conditioned by eye-base, arises eye-consciousness . . . conditioned by body-base, arises body-consciousness; conditioned by (heart-)base, arise resultant indeterminate aggregates.

Nutriment 17

263. (i)–(iii) Conditioned by faultless state, arises faultless state by nutriment condition.

Conditioned by one faultless aggregate . . . three.

(iv)–(vi) Conditioned by faulty state . . . three.

(vii)–(xvii) Conditioned by indeterminate state, arises indeterminate state by nutriment condition. . . .

(b) At the moment of conception. . . .

(c) Conditioned by one nutriment-produced great primary. . . .

(d) Conditioned by eye-base, arises eye-consciousness . . . conditioned by body-base, arises body-consciousness; conditioned by (heart-)base, arise resultant indeterminate or functional indeterminate aggregates ... (complete).

Faculty 17

264. Conditioned by faultless state, arises faultless state by faculty condition. ...

Conditioned by one great primary of non-percipient beings. ...

Conditioned by eye-base, arises eye-consciousness ... conditioned by body-base, arises body-consciousness; conditioned by (heart-)base, arise resultant indeterminate or functional indeterminate aggregates. ...

(Expand faculty condition in the same way as
kamma condition.)

Jhāna 17, Path 17

265. Conditioned by faultless state, arises faultless state by jhāna condition ... by path condition. ...

(Expand jhāna and path conditions in the
same way as root condition.)

Association 7

266. Conditioned by faultless state, arises faultless state by association condition ... (same as object condition).

Dissociation 17

267. (i) Conditioned by faultless state, arises faultless state by dissociation condition.

Conditioned by one faultless aggregate, arise three aggregates ... conditioned by two aggregates, arise two aggregates; (conditioned by heart-)base, (arise faultless aggregates) by dissociation condition.

(ii) Conditioned by faultless state, arises indeterminate state by dissociation condition.

Conditioned by faultless aggregates, arises mind-produced matter; (conditioned by) aggregates, (arises mind-produced matter) by dissociation condition.

(iii) Conditioned by faultless state, arise faultless and indeterminate states by dissociation condition.

Conditioned by one faultless aggregate, arise three aggregates and mind-produced matter ... conditioned by two aggregates, arise two aggregates and mind-produced matter ; (conditioned by heart-)base, arise aggregates by dissociation condition ; (conditioned by) aggregates, arises mind-produced matter by dissociation condition. (3)

(iv) Conditioned by faulty state, arises faulty state by dissociation condition.

Conditioned by one faulty aggregate, arise three aggregates ... conditioned by two aggregates, arise two aggregates ; (conditioned by heart-)base, (arise faulty aggregates) by dissociation condition.

(v) Conditioned by faulty state, arises indeterminate state by dissociation condition.

Conditioned by faulty aggregates, arises mind-produced matter ; (conditioned by) aggregates, (arises mind-produced matter) by dissociation condition.

(vi) Conditioned by faulty state, arise faulty and indeterminate states by dissociation condition.

Conditioned by one faulty aggregate, arise three aggregates and mind-produced matter ... conditioned by two aggregates, arise two aggregates and mind-produced matter ; (conditioned by heart-)base, arise aggregates by dissociation condition ; (conditioned by) aggregates, arises mind-produced matter by dissociation condition. (3)

(vii) Conditioned by indeterminate state, arises indeterminate state by dissociation condition.

(a) Conditioned by one resultant indeterminate or functional indeterminate aggregate, arise three aggregates and mind-produced matter ... conditioned by two aggregates, arise two aggregates and mind-produced matter ; (conditioned by six) bases, arise aggregates by dissociation condition ; (conditioned by) aggregates, arises mind-produced matter by dissociation condition ;

(b) At the moment of conception, conditioned by one resultant indeterminate aggregate, arise three aggregates and kamma-produced matter ... conditioned by two aggregates, arise two aggregates and kamma-produced matter; (conditioned by heart-)base, arise aggregates by dissociation condition; (conditioned by) aggregates, arises kamma-produced matter by dissociation condition; conditioned by aggregates, arises (heart-)base; conditioned by (heart-)base, arise aggregates; (conditioned by heart-)base, arise aggregates by dissociation condition; (conditioned by) aggregates, arises (heart-)base by dissociation condition;

(c) Conditioned by one great primary... conditioned by great primaries, arise mind-produced and kamma-produced derived matter; (conditioned by faultless, faulty, resultant indeterminate or functional indeterminate) aggregates, (arises mind-produced or kamma-produced matter) by dissociation condition;

(d) Conditioned by eye-base, arises eye-consciousness... conditioned by body-base, arises body-consciousness; conditioned by (heart-)base, arise resultant indeterminate or functional indeterminate aggregates; (conditioned by six) bases, (arise aggregates) by dissociation condition.

(viii) Conditioned by indeterminate state, arises faultless state by dissociation condition.

Conditioned by (heart-)base, arise faultless aggregates; (conditioned by heart-)base, (arise faultless aggregates) by dissociation condition.

(ix) Conditioned by indeterminate state, arises faulty state by dissociation condition.

Conditioned by (heart-)base, arise faulty aggregates; (conditioned by heart-)base, (arise faulty aggregates) by dissociation condition.

(x) Conditioned by indeterminate state, arise faultless and indeterminate states by dissociation condition.

Conditioned by (heart-)base, arise faultless aggregates; conditioned by great primaries, arises mind-produced matter; (conditioned by heart-)base, (arise aggregates) by dissociation condition; (conditioned by) aggregates, (arises mind-produced matter) by dissociation condition.

(xi) Conditioned by indeterminate state, arise faulty and indeterminate states by dissociation condition.

Conditioned by (heart-)base, arise faulty aggregates; conditioned by great primaries, arises mind-produced matter;

(conditioned by heart-)base, (arise aggregates) by dissociation condition ; (conditioned by) aggregates, (arises mind-produced matter) by dissociation condition. (5)

(xii) Conditioned by faultless and indeterminate state, arises faultless state by dissociation condition.

Conditioned by one faultless aggregate and (heart-)base, arise three aggregates ; conditioned by three aggregates and (heart-)base, arises one aggregate ; conditioned by two aggregates and (heart-)base, arise two aggregates ; (conditioned by heart-)base, (arise faultless aggregates) by dissociation condition.

(xiii) Conditioned by faultless and indeterminate state, arises indeterminate state by dissociation condition.

Conditioned by faultless aggregates and great primaries, arises mind-produced matter ; (conditioned by) aggregates, (arises mind-produced matter) by dissociation condition.

(xiv) Conditioned by faultless and indeterminate state, arise faultless and indeterminate states by dissociation condition.

Conditioned by one faultless aggregate and (heart-)base, arise three aggregates ; conditioned by three aggregates and (heart-)base, arises one aggregate ; conditioned by two aggregates and (heart-)base, arise two aggregates ; conditioned by faultless aggregates and great primaries, arises mind-produced matter ; (conditioned by heart-)base, arise aggregates by dissociation condition ; (conditioned by) aggregates, arises mind-produced matter by dissociation condition. (3)

(xv) Conditioned by faulty and indeterminate state, arises faulty state by dissociation condition.

Conditioned by one faulty aggregate and (heart-)base, arise three aggregates . . . conditioned by two aggregates and (heart-)base, arise two aggregates ; (conditioned by heart-)base, (arise faulty aggregates) by dissociation condition.

(xvi) Conditioned by faulty and indeterminate state, arises indeterminate state by dissociation condition.

Conditioned by faulty aggregates and great primaries, arises mind-produced matter ; (conditioned by) aggregates, (arises mind-produced matter) by dissociation condition.

(xvii) Conditioned by faulty and indeterminate state, arise faulty and indeterminate states by dissociation condition.

Conditioned by one faulty aggregate and (heart-)base, arise three aggregates ... two aggregates; conditioned by faulty aggregates and great primaries, arises mind-produced matter; (conditioned by heart-)base, arise aggregates by dissociation condition; (conditioned by) aggregates, arises mind-produced matter by dissociation condition. (3)

Presence condition, etc.

268. Conditioned by faultless state, arises faultless state by presence condition ... (Do presence condition the same as conascence condition; absence and disappearance conditions are the same as object condition; non-disappearance condition is the same as conascence condition.)

I. CONDITIONS: POSITIVE   (ii) ENUMERATION CHAPTER

By Ones

269. With root (there are) 17 (answers), object 7, predominance 17, proximity 7, contiguity 7, conascence 17, mutuality 7, dependence 17, strong-dependence 7, prenascence 7, repetition 7, kamma 17, resultant 1, nutriment 17, faculty 17, jhāna 17, path 17, association 7, dissociation 17, presence 17, absence 7, disappearance 7, non-disappearance 17.

Root

By Twos

270. With root condition and object 7, predominance 17, proximity 7, contiguity 7, conascence 17 ... non-disappearance 17.

By Threes

With root, object conditions and predominance 7 ... (All are 7), resultant 1 ... non-disappearance 7. ...

By Twelves (with repetition)

With root, object, predominance, proximity, contiguity, conascence, mutuality, dependence, strong-dependence, prenascence, repetition conditions and kamma 7, nutriment 7 ... non-disappearance 7. ...

By Twenty-two

With root, object ... prenascence, repetition, kamma, nutriment ... disappearance conditions and non-disappearance 7.

By Thirteens (with resultant)

With root, object ... prenascence, kamma, resultant conditions and nutriment 1 ... non-disappearance 1. ...

By Twenty-two (with resultant)

With root, object ... prenascence, kamma, resultant, nutriment ... disappearance conditions and non-disappearance 1.

End of Root

Object

By Twos

271. With object condition and root 7, predominance 7. ...

(Expand object condition in the same way as root condition.)

Predominance

By Twos

272. With predominance condition and root 17, ...

Proximity, Contiguity

By Twos

273. With proximity condition ... with contiguity condition and root 7. ...

Conascence, etc.

By Twos

274. With conascence condition ... with mutuality condition ... with dependence condition ... with strong-dependence condition ... with prenascence condition. ...

With repetition condition and root 7, object 7, predominance 7, proximity 7, contiguity 7, conascence 7, mutuality 7, dependence 7, strong-dependence 7, prenascence 7, kamma 7, nutriment 7, faculty 7, jhāna 7, path 7, association 7, dissociation 7, presence 7, absence 7, disappearance 7, non-disappearance 7. ...

Kamma, Resultant

By Twos

275. With kamma condition ... with resultant condition and root 1, object 1, predominance 1, proximity 1, contiguity 1, conascence 1, mutuality 1, dependence 1, strong-dependence 1, prenascence 1, kamma 1, nutriment 1, faculty 1, jhāna 1, path 1, association 1, dissociation 1, presence 1, absence 1, disappearance 1, non-disappearance 1. ...

Nutriment, etc.

By Twos

276. With nutriment condition ... with faculty condition ... with jhāna condition ... with path condition ... with association condition ... with dissociation condition ... with presence condition ... with absence condition ... with disappearance condition. ...

With non-disappearance condition and root 17, object 7 ... disappearance 7. ...

End of Positive " Conditioned " Chapter.

2. CONDITIONS : NEGATIVE (i) CLASSIFICATION CHAPTER

Not-root 4

277. (i) Conditioned by faulty state, arises faulty state by not-root condition.

Conditioned by doubt-accompanied or restlessness-accompanied aggregates, arises doubt-accompanied or restlessness-accompanied delusion. (1)

(ii) Conditioned by indeterminate state, arises indeterminate state by not-root condition.

(a) Conditioned by one rootless resultant indeterminate or functional indeterminate aggregate, arise three aggregates and mind-produced matter ... conditioned by two aggregates, arise two aggregates and mind-produced matter ;

(b) At the moment of rootless conception, conditioned by one resultant indeterminate aggregate, arise three aggregates and kamma-produced matter ... conditioned by two aggregates, arise two aggregates and kamma-produced matter; conditioned by aggregates, arises (heart-)base; conditioned by (heart-)base, arise aggregates;

(c) Conditioned by one great primary, arise three great primaries ... conditioned by great primaries, arise mind-produced and kamma-produced derived matter;

(d) External ... nutriment-produced ... temperature-produced ... conditioned by one great primary of non-percipient beings, arise three great primaries ... conditioned by great primaries, arises kamma-produced derived matter;

(e) Conditioned by eye-base, arises eye-consciousness ... conditioned by body-base, arises body-consciousness; conditioned by (heart-)base, arise rootless resultant indeterminate or functional indeterminate aggregates.

(iii) Conditioned by indeterminate state, arises faulty state by not-root condition.

Conditioned by (heart-)base, arises doubt-accompanied or restlessness-accompanied delusion. (2)

(iv) Conditioned by faulty and indeterminate state, arises faulty state by not-root condition.

Conditioned by doubt-accompanied or restlessness-accompanied aggregates and (heart-)base, arises doubt-accompanied or restlessness-accompanied delusion.

Not-object 5

278. Conditioned by faultless state, arises indeterminate state by not-object condition.

Conditioned by faultless aggregates, arises mind-produced matter. ...

(Expand in the same way as not-object condition in " Dependent " Chapter.)

Not-predominance 17

279. (i)–(iii) Conditioned by faultless state, arises faultless state by not-predominance condition.

Conditioned by one faultless aggregate ... three.

(iv)–(vi) Conditioned by faulty state ... three.

(vii) (a) Conditioned by indeterminate state. ...

Faultless Triplet

(b) At the moment of conception. ... (Complete indeterminate.)

(c) External ... nutriment-produced ... temperature-produced ... conditioned by one great primary of non-percipient beings. ...

(d) Conditioned by eye-base, arises eye-consciousness ... conditioned by body-base, arises body-consciousness; conditioned by (heart-)base, arise resultant indeterminate or functional indeterminate aggregates.

(viii)–(xvii) Conditioned by indeterminate state, arises faultless state by not-predominance condition.

Conditioned by (heart-)base, arise faultless aggregates. ...

(Expand in the same way as conascence condition in the Positive.)

Not-proximity, etc.

280. Conditioned by faultless state, arises indeterminate state by not-proximity condition ... by not-contiguity condition ... by not-mutuality condition ... by not-strong-dependence condition ... by not-prenascence condition. ...

(Expand in the same way as in " Dependent " Chapter.)

Not-postnascence, etc.

281. Conditioned by faultless state, arises faultless state by not-postnascence condition ... by not-repetition condition ... conditioned by eye-base. ... (Complete not-postnascence and not-repetition conditions, 17.)

(Expand in the same way as conascence condition in the Positive.)

Not-kamma 7

282. (i) Conditioned by faultless state, arises faultless state by not-kamma condition.

Conditioned by faultless aggregates, arises faultless volition.

(ii) Conditioned by faulty state, arises faulty state by not-kamma condition.

Conditioned by faulty aggregates, arises faulty volition.

(iii) Conditioned by indeterminate state, arises indeterminate state by not-kamma condition.

(*a*) Conditioned by functional indeterminate aggregates, arises functional indeterminate volition ;

(*b*) External ... nutriment-produced ... conditioned by one temperature-produced great primary ... derived matter ;

(*c*) Conditioned by (heart-)base, arises functional indeterminate volition.

(iv) Conditioned by indeterminate state, arises faultless state by not-kamma condition.

Conditioned by (heart-)base, arises faultless volition.

(v) Conditioned by indeterminate state, arises faulty state by not-kamma condition.

Conditioned by (heart-)base, arises faulty volition.

(vi) Conditioned by faultless and indeterminate state, arises faultless state by not-kamma condition.

Conditioned by faultless aggregates and (heart-)base, arises faultless volition.

(vii) Conditioned by faulty and indeterminate state, arises faulty state by not-kamma condition.

Conditioned by faulty aggregates and (heart-)base, arises faulty volition.

Not-resultant 17

283. (i)–(iii) Conditioned by faultless state, arises faultless state by not-resultant condition.

Conditioned by one faultless aggregate ... three.

(iv)–(vi) Conditioned by faulty state ... three.

(vii) Conditioned by indeterminate state, arises indeterminate state by not-resultant condition.

(*a*) Conditioned by one functional indeterminate aggregate, arise three aggregates and mind-produced matter ... conditioned by two aggregates, arise two aggregates and mind-produced matter ;

(*b*) Conditioned by one great primary, arise three great primaries ... conditioned by great primaries, arises mind-produced derived matter ;

(*c*) External ... nutriment-produced ... temperature-produced ... conditioned by one great primary of non-percipient beings, arise three great primaries ... conditioned by great primaries, arises kamma-produced derived matter ;

(*d*) Conditioned by (heart-)base, arise functional indeterminate aggregates.

(viii)–(xvii) Conditioned by indeterminate state, arises faultless state by not-resultant condition.

Conditioned by (heart-)base, arise faultless aggregates. . . .

[Expand all excluding resultant (indeterminate).]

Not-nutriment, etc.

284. Conditioned by indeterminate state, arises indeterminate state by not-nutriment condition . . . by not-faculty condition . . . by not-jhāna condition. . . .

Conditioned by eye-base, arises eye-consciousness . . . conditioned by body-base, arises body-consciousness. (This is the difference in not-jhāna.)

By not-path condition . . . conditioned by eye-base, arises eye-consciousness . . . conditioned by body-base, arises body-consciousness ; conditioned by (heart-)base, arise rootless resultant indeterminate or functional indeterminate aggregates. (This is the difference in not-path.) . . .

(Expand the rest in the same way as the Negative of " Dependent " Chapter.)

Not-association, etc.

285. Not-association condition . . . not-dissociation condition . . . not-absence condition . . .

Conditioned by faultless state, arises indeterminate state by not-disappearance condition.

Conditioned by faultless aggregates, arises mind-produced matter. . . .

(Expand in the same way as in " Dependent " Chapter.)

2. CONDITIONS : NEGATIVE   (ii) ENUMERATION CHAPTER

By Ones

286. With not-root (there are) 4 (answers), not-object 5, not-predominance 17, not-proximity 5, not-contiguity 5, not-mutuality 5, not-strong-dependence 5, not-prenascence 7,

not-postnascence 17, not-repetition 17, not-kamma 7, not-resultant 17, not-nutriment 1, not-faculty 1, not-jhāna 1, not-path 1, not-association 5, not-dissociation 3, not-absence 5, not-disappearance 5.

Not-root
By Twos

287. With not-root condition and not-object 1, not-predominance 4, not-proximity 1, not-contiguity 1, not-mutuality 1, not-strong-dependence 1, not-prenascence 2, not-postnascence 4, not-repetition 4, not-kamma 1, not-resultant 4, not-nutriment 1, not-faculty 1, not-jhāna 1, not-path 1, not-association 1, not-dissociation 2, not-absence 1, not-disappearance 1.

By Threes

With not-root, not-object conditions and not-predominance 1, not-proximity 1, not-contiguity 1 . . . (All are 1) . . . not-absence 1, not-disappearance 1. . . .

Not-object
By Twos

288. With not-object condition and not-root 1, not-predominance 5, not-proximity 5, not-contiguity 5, not-mutuality 5, not-strong-dependence 5, not-prenascence 5, not-postnascence 5, not-repetition 5, not-kamma 1, not-resultant 5, not-nutriment 1, not-faculty 1, not-jhāna 1, not-path 1, not-association 5, not-dissociation 1, not-absence 5, not-disappearance 5.

By Threes

With not-object, not-root conditions and not-predominance 1 . . . not-disappearance 1. . . .

Not-predominance
By Twos

289. With not-predominance condition and not-root 4, not-object 5, not-proximity 5, not-contiguity 5, not-mutuality 5, not-strong-dependence 5, not-prenascence 7, not-postnascence 17, not-repetition 17, not-kamma 7, not-resultant 17, not-nutriment 1, not-faculty 1, not-jhāna 1, not-path 1, not-association 5, not-dissociation 3, not-absence 5, not-disappearance 5.

By Threes

With not-predominance, not-root conditions and not-object 1, not-proximity 1, not-contiguity 1, not-mutuality 1, not-strong-dependence 1, not-prenascence 2, not-postnascence 4, not-repetition 4, not-kamma 1, not-resultant 4, not-nutriment 1, not-faculty 1, not-jhāna 1, not-path 1, not-association 1, not-dissociation 2, not-absence 1, not-disappearance 1.

By Fours

With not-predominance, not-root, not-object conditions and not-proximity 1 ... (All are 1). ...

Not-proximity, etc.

290. With not-proximity condition ... with not-contiguity condition ... with not-mutuality condition ... with not-strong-dependence condition ... (same as not-object condition).

Not-prenascence

By Twos

291. With not-prenascence condition and not-root 2, not-object 5, not-predominance 7, not-proximity 5, not-contiguity 5, not-mutuality 5, not-strong-dependence 5, not-postnascence 7, not-repetition 7, not-kamma 3, not-resultant 7, not-nutriment 1, not-faculty 1, not-jhāna 1, not-path 1, not-association 5, not-dissociation 3, not-absence 5, not-disappearance 5.

By Threes

With not-prenascence, not-root conditions and not-object 1, not-predominance 2, not-proximity 1, not-contiguity 1, not-mutuality 1, not-strong-dependence 1, not-postnascence 2, not-repetition 2, not-kamma 1, not-resultant 2, not-nutriment 1, not-faculty 1, not-jhāna 1, not-path 1, not-association 1, not-dissociation 2, not-absence 1, not-disappearance 1.

By Fours

With not-prenascence, not-root, not-object conditions and not-predominance 1 ... (All are 1) ... not-disappearance 1. ...

Not-postnascence, Not-repetition

By Twos

292. With not-postnascence condition ... with not-repetition condition and not-root 4, not-object 5, not-predominance 17, not-proximity 5, not-contiguity 5, not-mutuality 5, not-strong-dependence 5, not-prenascence 7, not-postnascence 17, not kamma 7, not-resultant 17, not-nutriment 1, not-faculty 1, not-jhāna 1, not-path 1, not-association 5, not-dissociation 3, not-absence 5, not-disappearance 5.

By Threes

With not-repetition, not-root conditions and not-object 1, not-predominance 4, not-proximity 1, not-contiguity 1, not-mutuality 1, not-strong-dependence 1, not-prenascence 2, not-postnascence 4, not-kamma 1, not-resultant 4, not-nutriment 1, not-faculty 1, not-jhāna 1, not-path 1, not-association 1, not-dissociation 2, not-absence 1, not-disappearance 1.

By Fours

With not-repetition, not-root, not-object conditions and not-predominance 1 ... (All are 1) ... not-disappearance 1. ...

Not-kamma

By Twos

293. With not-kamma condition and not-root 1, not-object 1, not-predominance 7, not-proximity 1, not-contiguity 1, not-mutuality 1, not-strong-dependence 1, not-prenascence 3, not-postnascence 7, not-repetition 7, not-resultant 7, not-nutriment 1, not-faculty 1, not-jhāna 1, not-path 1, not-association 1, not-dissociation 3, not-absence 1, not-disappearance 1.

By Threes

With not-kamma, not-root conditions and not-object 1 ... (All are 1) ... not-disappearance 1. ...

Not-resultant

By Twos

294. With not-resultant condition and not-root 4, not-object 5, not-predominance 17, not-proximity 5, not-contiguity 5,

not-mutuality 5, not-strong-dependence 5, not-prenascence 7, not-postnascence 17, not-repetition 17, not-kamma 7, not-nutriment 1, not-faculty 1, not-jhāna 1, not-path 1, not-association 5, not-dissociation 3, not-absence 5, not-disappearance 5.

By Threes
With not-resultant, not-root conditions and not-object 1, not-predominance 4, not-proximity 1, not-contiguity 1, not-mutuality 1, not-strong-dependence 1, not-prenascence 2, not-postnascence 4, not-repetition 4, not-kamma 1, not-nutriment 1, not-faculty 1, not-jhāna 1, not-path 1, not-association 1, not-dissociation 2, not-absence 1, not-disappearance 1.

By Fours
With not-resultant, not-root, not-object conditions and not-predominance 1 ... (All are 1) ... not-disappearance 1. ...

Not-nutriment, etc.

By Twos
295. With not-nutriment condition and not-root 1 ... (All are 1) ... not-disappearance 1. ...
  With not-faculty condition and not-root 1 ... (All are 1). ...
  With not-jhāna condition and not-root 1 ... (All are 1). ...
  With not-path condition and not-root 1 ... (All are 1). ...
  With not-association condition ... (same as not-object condition).

Not-dissociation

By Twos
296. With not-dissociation condition and not-root 2, not-object 1, not-predominance 3, not-proximity 1, not-contiguity 1, not-mutuality 1, not-strong-dependence 1, not-prenascence 3, not-postnascence 3, not-repetition 3, not-kamma 3, not-resultant 3, not-nutriment 1, not-faculty 1, not-jhāna 1, not-path 1, not-association 1, not-absence 1, not-disappearance 1.

By Threes
With not-dissociation, not-root conditions and not-object 1, not-predominance 2, not-proximity 1, not-contiguity 1, not-mutuality 1, not-strong-dependence 1, not-prenascence 2,

not-postnascence 2, not-repetition 2, not-kamma 1, not-resultant 2, not-nutriment 1, not-faculty 1, not-jhāna 1, not-path 1, not-association 1, not-absence 1, not-disappearance 1.

By Fours

With not-dissociation, not-root, not-object conditions and not-predominance 1, ... (All are 1). ...

With not-absence condition ... with not-disappearance condition ... (same as not-object condition).

End of Negative " Conditioned " Chapter.

3. CONDITIONS : POSITIVE–NEGATIVE

Root

By Twos

297. With root condition, not-object 5, not-predominance 17, not-proximity 5, not-contiguity 5, not-mutuality 5, not-strong-dependence 5, not-prenascence 7, not-postnascence 17, not-repetition 17, not-kamma 7, not-resultant 17, not-association 5, not-dissociation 3, not-absence 5, not-disappearance 5.

By Threes

With root and object conditions, not-predominance 7, not-prenascence 3, not-postnascence 7, not-repetition 7, not-kamma 7, not-resultant 7, not-dissociation 3. ...

By Elevens

With root, object, predominance, proximity, contiguity, conascence, mutuality, dependence, strong-dependence and prenascence conditions, not-postnascence 7, not-repetition 7, not-kamma 7, not-resultant 7.

By Twelves (with repetition)

With root, object ... prenascence and repetition conditions, not-postnascence 7, not-kamma 7, not-resultant 7. ...

By Twenty-threes

With root, object ... prenascence, repetition, kamma, nutriment, faculty, jhāna, path, association, dissociation, presence, absence, disappearance and non-disappearance conditions, not-postnascence 7, not-resultant 7.

By Thirteens (with resultant)
With root, object ... prenascence, kamma and resultant conditions, not-postnascence 1, not-repetition 1. ...

By Twenty-threes (with resultant)
With root, object ... prenascence, kamma, resultant, nutriment ... and non-disappearance conditions, not-postnascence 1, not-repetition 1.

Object

By Twos
298. With object condition, not-root 4, not-predominance 7, not-prenascence 3, not-postnascence 7, not-repetition 7, not-kamma 7, not-resultant 7, not-jhāna 1, not-path 1, not-dissociation 3.

By Threes
With object and root conditions, not-predominance 7, not-prenascence 3, not-postnascence 7, not-repetition 7, not-kamma 7, not-resultant 7, not-dissociation 3. ...

(Enumerate in the same way as root condition.)

Predominance

By Twos
299. With predominance condition, not-object 5, not-proximity 5, not-contiguity 5, not-mutuality 5, not-strong-dependence 5, not-prenascence 7, not-postnascence 17, not-repetition 17, not-kamma 7, not-resultant 17, not-association 5, not-dissociation 3, not-absence 5, not-disappearance 5.

With predominance and root conditions ... (Abbreviated.)

Proximity, Contiguity

With proximity condition ... with contiguity condition ...

(Expand in the same way as object condition.)

Conascence

By Twos

300. With conascence condition, not-root 4, not-object 5, not-predominance 17, not-proximity 5, not-contiguity 5, not-mutuality 5, not-strong-dependence 5, not-prenascence 7, not-postnascence 17, not-repetition 17, not-kamma 7, not-resultant 17, not-nutriment 1, not-faculty 1, not-jhāna 1, not-path 1, not-association 5, not-dissociation 3, not-absence 5, not-disappearance 5.

By Threes

With conascence and root conditions, not-object 5 ... (Abbreviated) ... not-resultant 17, not-association 5, not-dissociation 3, not-absence 5, not-disappearance 5.

With conascence, root and object conditions ... (Abbreviated.)

Mutuality

By Twos

301. With mutuality condition, not-root 4, not-object 1, not-predominance 7, not-proximity 1, not-contiguity 1, not-strong-dependence 1, not-prenascence 3, not-postnascence 7, not-repetition 7, not-kamma 7, not-resultant 7, not-nutriment 1, not-faculty 1, not-jhāna 1, not-path 1, not-association 1, not-dissociation 3, not-absence 1, not-disappearance 1.

By Threes

With mutuality and root conditions, not-object 1, not-predominance 7, not-proximity 1, not-contiguity 1, not-strong-dependence 1, not-prenascence 3, not-postnascence 7, not-repetition 7, not-kamma 7, not-resultant 7, not-association 1, not-dissociation 3, not-absence 1, not-disappearance 1.

By Fours

With mutuality, root and object conditions, not-predominance 7. ... (Abbreviated.)

Dependence

By Twos

302. With dependence condition, not-root 4 (Dependence condition is the same as conascence condition).

Strong-dependence

By Twos

303. With strong-dependence condition, not-root 4 (Strong-dependence condition is the same as object condition).

Prenascence

By Twos

304. With prenascence condition, not-root 4, not-predominance 7, not-postnascence 7, not-repetition 7, not-kamma 7, not-resultant 7, not-jhāna 1, not-path 1.

With prenascence and root conditions . . .

Repetition

By Twos

305. With repetition condition, not-root 4, not-predominance 7, not-prenascence 3, not-postnascence 7, not-kamma 7, not-resultant 7, not-path 1, not-dissociation 3.

By Threes

With repetition and root conditions, not-predominance 7, not-prenascence 3, not-postnascence 7, not-kamma 7, not-resultant 7, not-dissociation 3.

By Fours

306. With repetition, root and object conditions, not-predominance 7. . . . (Abbreviated.)

By Twenty-threes[1]

With repetition, root . . . prenascence, kamma, nutriment . . . and non-disappearance conditions, not-postnascence 7, not-resultant 7.

Kamma

By Twos

307. With kamma condition, not-root 4, not-object 5, not-predominance 17, not-proximity 5, not-contiguity 5, not-mutuality 5, not-strong-dependence 5, not-prenascence 7,

---

[1] Not mentioned in the Text.

not-postnascence 17, not-repetition 17, not-resultant 17, not-nutriment 1, not-faculty 1, not-jhāna 1, not-path 1, not-association 5, not-dissociation 3, not-absence 5, not-disappearance 5.

By Threes

With kamma and root conditions, not-object 5 . . . not-resultant 17, not-association 5, not-dissociation 3, not-absence 5, not-disappearance 5. . . . (Abbreviated.)

Resultant

By Twos

308. With resultant condition, not-root 1, not-object 1, not-predominance 1, not-proximity 1, not-contiguity 1, not-mutuality 1, not-strong-dependence 1, not-prenascence 1, not-postnascence 1, not-repetition 1, not-jhāna 1, not-path 1, not-association 1, not-dissociation 1, not-absence 1, not-disappearance 1.

By Threes

With resultant and root conditions, not-object 1, not-predominance 1, not-proximity 1, not-contiguity 1, not-mutuality 1, not-strong-dependence 1, not-prenascence 1, not-postnascence 1, not-repetition 1, not-association 1, not-dissociation 1, not-absence 1, not-disappearance 1. . . .

By Twelves

With resultant, root, object . . . and prenascence conditions, not-postnascence 1, not-repetition 1. . . .

By Twenty-threes

With resultant, root . . . prenascence, kamma, nutriment . . . and non-disappearance conditions, not-postnascence 1, not-repetition 1. (Abbreviated.)

Nutriment

By Twos

309. With nutriment condition, not-root 4, not-object 5, not-predominance 17, not-proximity 5, not-contiguity 5, not-mutuality 5, not-strong-dependence 5, not-prenascence 7,

not-postnascence 17, not-repetition 17, not-kamma 7, not-resultant 17, not-faculty 1, not-jhāna 1, not-path 1, not-association 5, not-dissociation 3, not-absence 5, not-disappearance 5.

By Threes
With nutriment and root conditions, not-object 5 ... not-resultant 17, not-association 5, not-dissociation 3, not-absence 5, not-disappearance 5. ... (Abbreviated.)

Faculty
By Twos
310. With faculty condition, not-root 4, not-object 5 ... not-resultant 17, not-nutriment 1, not-jhāna 1, not-path 1, not-association 5, not-dissociation 3, not-absence 5, not-disappearance 5.

With faculty and root conditions. ... (Abbreviated.)

Jhāna
By Twos
311. With jhāna condition, not-root 4, not-object 5 ... not-resultant 17, not-path 1, not-association 5, not-dissociation 3, not-absence 5, not-disappearance 5.

With jhana and root conditions. ... (Abbreviated.)

Path
By Twos
312. With path condition, not-root 3, not-object 5 ... not-resultant 17, not-association 5, not-dissociation 3, not-absence 5, not-disappearance 5.

With path and root conditions, not-object 5. ... (Abbreviated.)

Association
With association condition ... (same as object condition).

Dissociation
By Twos
313. With dissociation condition, not-root 4, not-object 5, not-predominance 17, not-proximity 5, not-contiguity 5,

not-mutuality 5, not-strong-dependence 5, not-prenascence 5, not-postnascence 17, not-repetition 17, not-kamma 7, not-resultant 17, not-jhāna 1, not-path 1, not-association 5, not-absence 5, not-disappearance 5.

By Threes
With dissociation and root conditions, not-object 5, not-predominance 17, not-proximity 5, not-contiguity 5, not-mutuality 5, not-strong-dependence 5, not-prenascence 5, not-postnascence 17, not-repetition 17, not-kamma 7, not-resultant 17, not-association 5, not-absence 5, not-disappearance 5.

By Fours
With dissociation, root and object conditions, not-predominance 7, not-prenascence 1, not-postnascence 7, not-repetition 7, not-kamma 7, not-resultant 7.

By Fives
With dissociation, root, object and predominance conditions, not-postnascence 7, not-repetition 7, not-kamma 7, not-resultant 7. ...

By Thirteens (with repetition)
With dissociation, root, object, predominance ... prenascence and repetition conditions, not-postnascence 7, not-kamma 7, not-resultant 7. ...

By Twenty-threes
With dissociation, root ... repetition, kamma, nutriment ... and non-disappearance conditions, not-postnascence 7, not-resultant 7.

By Fourteens (with resultant)
With dissociation, root, object ... (Abbreviated) ... prenascence, kamma and resultant conditions, not-postnascence 1, not-repetition 1. ...

By Twenty-threes
With dissociation, root ... prenascence, kamma, resultant, nutriment ... (Abbreviated) ... and non-disappearance conditions, not-postnascence 1, not-repetition 1.

With presence condition ... (same as conascence condition).
With absence condition ... with disappearance condition ... (same as object condition).
With non-disappearance condition ... (same as conascence condition).

End of Positive–Negative in " Conditioned " Chapter.

4. CONDITIONS : NEGATIVE–POSITIVE

Not-root

By Twos

314. With not-root condition, object 4, proximity 4, contiguity 4, conascence 4, mutuality 4, dependence 4, strong-dependence 4, prenascence 4, repetition 4, kamma 4, resultant 1, nutriment 4, faculty 4, jhāna 4, path 3, association 4, dissociation 4, presence 4, absence 4, disappearance 4, non-disappearance 4.

By Threes

With not-root, not-object conditions, conascence 1, mutuality 1, dependence 1, kamma 1, resultant 1, nutriment 1, faculty 1, jhāna 1, dissociation 1, presence 1, non-disappearance 1. ...

By Sevens

With not-root, not-object, not-predominance, not-proximity, not-contiguity, not-mutuality conditions, conascence 1, dependence 1, kamma 1, resultant 1, nutriment 1, faculty 1, jhāna 1, dissociation 1, presence 1, non-disappearance 1. ...

By Twelves

With not-root, not-object, not-predominance, not-proximity, not-contiguity, not-mutuality, not-strong-dependence, not-prenascence, not-postnascence, not-repetition, not-kamma conditions, conascence 1, dependence 1, nutriment 1, presence 1, non-disappearance 1. ...

By Fourteens

With not-root, not-object ... not-kamma, not-resultant, not-nutriment conditions, conascence 1, dependence 1, presence 1, non-disappearance 1. ...

By Twenty-ones

With not-root, not-object ... not-kamma, not-resultant, not-nutriment, not-faculty ... not-disappearance conditions, conascence 1, dependence 1, presence 1, non-disappearance 1. (Abbreviated.)

Not-object

By Twos

315. With not-object condition, root 5, predominance 5, conascence 5, mutuality 1, dependence 5, kamma 5, resultant 1, nutriment 5, faculty 5, jhāna 5, path 5, dissociation 5, presence 5, non-disappearance 5.

By Threes

With not-object, not-root conditions, conascence 1, mutuality 1, dependence 1, kamma 1, resultant 1, nutriment 1, faculty 1, jhāna 1, dissociation 1, presence 1, non-disappearance 1. ... (Abbreviated.)

Not-predominance

By Twos

316. With not-predominance condition, root 17, object 7, proximity 7, contiguity 7, conascence 17, mutuality 7, dependence 17, strong-dependence 7, prenascence 7, repetition 7, kamma 17, resultant 1, nutriment 17, faculty 17, jhāna 17, path 17, association 7, dissociation 17, presence 17, absence 7, disappearance 7, non-disappearance 17.

By Threes

With not-predominance, not-root conditions, object 4, proximity 4, contiguity 4, conascence 4, mutuality 4, dependence 4, strong-dependence 4, prenascence 4, repetition 4, kamma 4, resultant 1, nutriment 4, faculty 4, jhāna 4, path 3, association 4, dissociation 4, presence 4, absence 4, disappearance 4, non-disappearance 4.

By Fours

With not-predominance, not-root, not-object conditions, conascence 1 ... non-disappearance 1. ... (Abbreviated.)

Not-proximity, etc.

By Twos

317. With not-proximity condition ... with not-contiguity condition ... with not-mutuality condition ... with not-strong-dependence condition ... (same as not-object condition).

Not-prenascence

By Twos

318. With not-prenascence condition, root 7, object 3, predominance 7, proximity 3, contiguity 3, conascence 7, mutuality 3, dependence 7, strong-dependence 3, repetition 3, kamma 7, resultant 1, nutriment 7, faculty 7, jhāna 7, path 7, association 3, dissociation 5, presence 7, absence 3, disappearance 3, non-disappearance 7.

By Threes

With not-prenascence, not-root conditions, object 2, proximity 2, contiguity 2, conascence 2, mutuality 2, dependence 2, strong-dependence 2, repetition 1, kamma 2, resultant 1, nutriment 2, faculty 2, jhāna 2, path 1, association 2, dissociation 1, presence 2, absence 2, disappearance 2, non-disappearance 2.

By Fours

With not-prenascence, not-root, not-object conditions, conascence 1 ... non-disappearance 1. ... (Abbreviated.)

Not-postnascence

By Twos

319. With not-postnascence condition, root 17, object 7, predominance 17, proximity 7, contiguity 7, conascence 17, mutuality 7, dependence 17, strong-dependence 7, prenascence 7, repetition 7, kamma 17, resultant 1, nutriment 17, faculty 17, jhāna 17, path 17, association 7, dissociation 17, presence 17, absence 7, disappearance 7, non-disappearance 17.

By Threes

With not-postnascence, not-root conditions, object 4, proximity 4, contiguity 4, conascence 4, mutuality 4, dependence 4, strong-dependence 4, prenascence 4, repetition 4, kamma 4, resultant

1, nutriment 4, faculty 4, jhāna 4, path 3, association 4, dissociation 4, presence 4, absence 4, disappearance 4, non-disappearance 4.

By Fours
With not-postnascence, not-root, not-object conditions, conascence 1 ... non-disappearance 1. ... (Abbreviated.)

Not-repetition
By Twos
320. With not-repetition condition, root 17, object 7, predominance 17, proximity 7, contiguity 7, conascence 17, mutuality 7, dependence 17, strong-dependence 7, prenascence 7, kamma 17, resultant 1, nutriment 17, faculty 17, jhāna 17, path 17, association 7, dissociation 17, presence 17, absence 7, disappearance 7, non-disappearance 17.

By Threes
With not-repetition, not-root conditions, object 4, proximity 4, contiguity 4, conascence 4, mutuality 4, dependence 4, strong-dependence 4, prenascence 4, kamma 4, resultant 1, nutriment 4, faculty 4, jhāna 4, path 3, association 4, dissociation 4, presence 4, absence 4, disappearance 4, non-disappearance 4.

By Fours
With not-repetition, not-root, not-object conditions, conascence 1 ... non-disappearance 1. ... (Abbreviated.)

Not-kamma
By Twos
321. With not-kamma condition, root 7, object 7, predominance 7, proximity 7, contiguity 7, conascence 7, mutuality 7, dependence 7, strong-dependence 7, prenascence 7, repetition 7, nutriment 7, faculty 7, jhāna 7, path 7, association 7, dissociation 7, presence 7, absence 7, disappearance 7, non-disappearance 7.

By Threes
With not-kamma, not-root conditions, object 1, proximity 1, contiguity 1, conascence 1, mutuality 1, dependence 1,

Faultless Triplet

strong-dependence 1, prenascence 1, repetition 1, nutriment 1, faculty 1, jhāna 1, association 1, dissociation 1, presence 1, absence 1, disappearance 1, non-disappearance 1.

By Fours

With not-kamma, not-root, not-object conditions, conascence 1, mutuality 1, dependence 1, nutriment 1, presence 1, non-disappearance 1. ... (Abbreviated.)

By Twos   *Not-resultant*

322. With not-resultant condition, root 17, object 7, predominance 17, proximity 7, contiguity 7, conascence 17, mutuality 7, dependence 17, strong-dependence 7, prenascence 7, repetition 7, kamma 17, nutriment 17, faculty 17, jhāna 17, path 17, association 7, dissociation 17, presence 17, absence 7, disappearance 7, non-disappearance 17.

By Threes

With not-resultant, not-root conditions, object 4, proximity 4, contiguity 4, conascence 4, mutuality 4, dependence 4, strong-dependence 4, prenascence 4, repetition 4, kamma 4, nutriment 4, faculty 4, jhāna 4, path 3, association 4, dissociation 4, presence 4, absence 4, disappearance 4, non-disappearance 4.

By Fours

With not-resultant, not-root, not-object conditions, conascence 1, mutuality 1, dependence 1, kamma 1, nutriment 1, faculty 1, jhāna 1, dissociation 1, presence 1, non-disappearance 1. ... (Abbreviated.)

By Twos   *Not-nutriment*

323. With not-nutriment condition, conascence 1, mutuality 1, dependence 1, kamma 1, faculty 1, presence 1, non-disappearance 1. ... (Abbreviated.)

By Twos   *Not-faculty*

324. With not-faculty condition, conascence 1, mutuality 1, dependence 1, kamma 1, nutriment 1, presence 1, non-disappearance 1. ... (Abbreviated.)

Not-jhāna
By Twos

325. With not-jhāna condition, object 1, proximity 1, contiguity 1, conascence 1, mutuality 1, dependence 1, strong-dependence 1, prenascence 1, kamma 1, resultant 1, nutriment 1, faculty 1, association 1, dissociation 1, presence 1, absence 1, disappearance 1, non-disappearance 1. ...

By Fours

With not-jhāna, not-root, not-object conditions, conascence 1, mutuality 1, dependence 1, kamma 1, nutriment 1, faculty 1, presence 1, non-disappearance 1. ... (Abbreviated.)

Not-path
By Twos

326. With not-path condition, object 1, proximity 1, contiguity 1, conascence 1, mutuality 1, dependence 1, strong-dependence 1, prenascence 1, repetition 1, kamma 1, resultant 1, nutriment 1, faculty 1, jhāna 1, association 1, dissociation 1, presence 1, absence 1, disappearance 1, non-disappearance 1. ...

By Fours

With not-path, not-root, not-object conditions, conascence 1, mutuality 1, dependence 1, kamma 1, resultant 1, nutriment 1, faculty 1, jhāna 1, dissociation 1, presence 1, non-disappearance 1. ... (Abbreviated.)

Not-association
By Twos

327. With not-association condition, root 5, predominance 5, mutuality 1, dependence 5, kamma 5, resultant 1, nutriment 5, faculty 5, jhāna 5, path 5, dissociation 5, presence 5, non-disappearance 5.

By Threes

With not-association, not-root conditions, conascence 1 ... non-disappearance 1. ... (Abbreviated.)

Not-dissociation

By Twos

328. With not-dissociation condition, root 3, object 3, predominance 3, proximity 3, contiguity 3, conascence 3, mutuality 3, dependence 3, strong-dependence 3, repetition 3, kamma 3, resultant 1, nutriment 3, faculty 3, jhāna 3, path 3, association 3, presence 3, absence 3, disappearance 3, non-disappearance 3.

By Threes

With not-dissociation, not-root conditions, object 2, proximity 2, contiguity 2, conascence 2, mutuality 2, dependence 2, strong-dependence 2, repetition 1, kamma 2, nutriment 2, faculty 2, jhāna 2, path 1, association 2, presence 2, absence 2, disappearance 2, non-disappearance 2.

By Fours

With not-dissociation, not-root, not-object conditions, conascence 1, mutuality 1, dependence 1, kamma 1, nutriment 1, faculty 1, presence 1, non-disappearance 1. ... (Abbreviated.)

Not-absence, Not-disappearance

With not-absence condition ... with not-disappearance condition ... (same as not-object condition).

End of Negative–Positive in "Conditioned" Chapter.

End of "CONDITIONED" CHAPTER.

1. FAULTLESS TRIPLET   IV. "SUPPORTED" CHAPTER
1. CONDITIONS: POSITIVE   (i) CLASSIFICATION CHAPTER

Positive Root 17

329. (i) Supported by faultless state, arises faultless state by root condition.

Supported by one faultless aggregate, arise three aggregates; supported by three aggregates, arises one aggregate; supported by two aggregates, arise two aggregates.

(ii) Supported by faultless state, arises indeterminate state by root condition.

Supported by faultless aggregates, arises mind-produced matter.

(iii) Supported by faultless state, arise faultless and indeterminate states by root condition.

Supported by one faultless aggregate, arise three aggregates and mind-produced matter; supported by three aggregates, arise one aggregate and mind-produced matter; supported by two aggregates, arise two aggregates and mind-produced matter. (3)

330. (iv) Supported by faulty state, arises faulty state by root condition.

Supported by one faulty aggregate, arise three aggregates ... supported by two aggregates, arise two aggregates.

(v) Supported by faulty state, arises indeterminate state by root condition.

Supported by faulty aggregates, arises mind-produced matter.

(vi) Supported by faulty state, arise faulty and indeterminate states by root condition.

Supported by one faulty aggregate, arise three aggregates and mind-produced matter ... supported by two aggregates, arise two aggregates and mind-produced matter. (3)

331. (vii) Supported by indeterminate state, arises indeterminate state by root condition.

(*a*) Supported by one resultant indeterminate or functional indeterminate aggregate, arise three aggregates and mind-produced matter; supported by three aggregates, arise one aggregate and mind-produced matter; supported by two aggregates, arise two aggregates and mind-produced matter;

(*b*) At the moment of conception, supported by one resultant indeterminate aggregate, arise three aggregates and kamma-produced matter; supported by three aggregates, arise one aggregate and kamma-produced matter; supported by two aggregates, arise two aggregates and kamma-produced matter; supported by aggregates, arises (heart-)base; supported by (heart-)base, arise aggregates;

(*c*) Supported by one great primary, arise three great primaries; supported by three great primaries, arises one great primary; supported by two great primaries, arise two great primaries; supported by great primaries, arise mind-produced and kamma-produced derived matter;

(d) Supported by (heart-)base, arise resultant indeterminate or functional indeterminate aggregates.

(viii) Supported by indeterminate state, arises faultless state by root condition.

Supported by (heart-)base, arise faultless aggregates.

(ix) Supported by indeterminate state, arises faulty state by root condition.

Supported by (heart-)base, arise faulty aggregates.

(x) Supported by indeterminate state, arise faultless and indeterminate states by root condition.

Supported by (heart-)base, arise faultless aggregates; supported by great primaries, arises mind-produced matter.

(xi) Supported by indeterminate state, arise faulty and indeterminate states by root condition.

Supported by (heart-)base, arise faulty aggregates; supported by great primaries, arises mind-produced matter. (5)

332. (xii) Supported by faultless and indeterminate state, arises faultless state by root condition.

Supported by one faultless aggregate and (heart-)base, arise three aggregates ... supported by two aggregates and (heart-)base, arise two aggregates.

(xiii) Supported by faultless and indeterminate state, arises indeterminate state by root condition.

Supported by faultless aggregates and great primaries, arises mind-produced matter.

(xiv) Supported by faultless and indeterminate state, arise faultless and indeterminate states by root condition.

Supported by one faultless aggregate and (heart-)base, arise three aggregates ... supported by two aggregates and (heart-)base, arise two aggregates; supported by faultless aggregates and great primaries, arises mind-produced matter. (3)

(xv) Supported by faulty and indeterminate state, arises faulty state by root condition.

Supported by one faulty aggregate and (heart-)base, arise three aggregates ... supported by two aggregates and (heart-)base, arise two aggregates.

(xvi) Supported by faulty and indeterminate state, arises indeterminate state by root condition.

Supported by faulty aggregates and great primaries, arises mind-produced matter.

(xvii) Supported by faulty and indeterminate state, arise faulty and indeterminate states by root condition.

Supported by one faulty aggregate and (heart-)base, arise three aggregates ... supported by two aggregates and (heart-)base, arise two aggregates ; supported by faulty aggregates and great primaries, arises mind-produced matter. (3)

(Expand in the same way as " Conditioned " Chapter.)

1. CONDITIONS : POSITIVE   (ii) ENUMERATION CHAPTER

By Ones

333. With root (there are) 17 (answers), object 7, predominance 17, proximity 7, contiguity 7, conascence 17, mutuality 7, dependence 17, strong-dependence 7, prenascence 7, repetition 7, kamma 17, resultant 1, nutriment 17, faculty 17, jhāna 17, path 17, association 7, dissociation 17, presence 17, absence 7, disappearance 7, non-disappearance 17.

(Expand in the same way as " Conditioned " Chapter.)
End of Positive in " Supported " Chapter.

2. CONDITIONS : NEGATIVE   (i) CLASSIFICATION CHAPTER

Not-root 4

334. (i) Supported by faulty state, arises faulty state by not-root condition.

Supported by doubt-accompanied or restlessness-accompanied aggregates, arises doubt-accompanied or restlessness-accompanied delusion. (1)

(ii) Supported by indeterminate state, arises indeterminate state by not-root condition.

(a) Supported by one rootless resultant indeterminate or functional indeterminate aggregate, arise three aggregates and mind-produced matter ; supported by three aggregates, arise one aggregate and mind-produced matter ; supported by two aggregates, arise two aggregates and mind-produced matter ;

(b) At the moment of rootless conception, supported by one resultant indeterminate aggregate, arise three aggregates and kamma-produced matter . . . supported by two aggregates, arise two aggregates and kamma-produced matter ; supported by aggregates, arises (heart-)base ; supported by (heart-)base, arise aggregates ;

(c) Supported by one great primary, arise three great primaries . . . supported by great primaries, arise mind-produced and kamma-produced derived matter ;

(d) External . . . nutriment-produced . . . temperature-produced . . . supported by one great primary of non-percipient beings, arise three great primaries . . . supported by great primaries, arises kamma-produced derived matter ;

(e) Supported by eye-base, arises eye-consciousness . . . supported by body-base, arises body-consciousness ; supported by (heart-)base, arise rootless resultant indeterminate or functional indeterminate aggregates.

(iii) Supported by indeterminate state, arises faulty state by not-root condition.

Supported by (heart-)base, arises doubt-accompanied or restlessness-accompanied delusion. (2)

(iv) Supported by faulty and indeterminate state, arises faulty state by not-root condition.

Supported by doubt-accompanied or restlessness-accompanied aggregates and (heart-)base, arises doubt-accompanied or restlessness-accompanied delusion. (1)

(Expand in the same way as " Conditioned " Chapter.)

2. CONDITIONS : NEGATIVE   (ii) ENUMERATION CHAPTER

By Ones

335. With not-root 4, not-object 5, not-predominance 17, not-proximity 5, not-contiguity 5, not-mutuality 5, not-strong-dependence 5, not-prenascence 7, not-postnascence 17, not-repetition 17, not-kamma 7, not-resultant 17, not-nutriment 1, not-faculty 1, not-jhāna 1, not-path 1, not-association 5, not-dissociation 3, not-absence 5, not-disappearance 5. . . .

End of Negative in " Supported " Chapter.

3. CONDITIONS : POSITIVE–NEGATIVE

Root

By Twos

336. With root condition, not-object 5, not-predominance 17, not-proximity 5, not-contiguity 5, not-mutuality 5, not-strong-dependence 5, not-prenascence 7, not-postnascence 17, not-repetition 17, not-kamma 7, not-resultant 17, not-association 5, not-dissociation 3, not-absence 5, not-disappearance 5. ... (Abbreviated.)

End of Positive–Negative in " Supported " Chapter.

4. CONDITIONS : NEGATIVE–POSITIVE

Not-root

By Twos

337. With not-root condition, object 4, proximity 4, contiguity 4, conascence 4, mutuality 4, dependence 4, strong-dependence 4, prenascence 4, repetition 4, kamma 4, resultant 1, nutriment 4, faculty 4, jhāna 4, path 3, association 4, dissociation 4, presence 4, absence 4, disappearance 4, non-disappearance 4. ... (Abbreviated.)

End of Negative–Positive in " Supported " Chapter.
(The term " Conditioned " is the same as " Supported ". The term " Supported " is the same as " Conditioned ".)

End of " SUPPORTED " CHAPTER.

I. Faultless Triplet   V. " Conjoined " Chapter

1. CONDITIONS : POSITIVE   (i) CLASSIFICATION CHAPTER

Root 3

338. (i) Conjoined with faultless state, arises faultless state by root condition.

Conjoined with one faultless aggregate, arise three aggregates ; conjoined with three aggregates, arises one aggregate ; conjoined with two aggregates, arise two aggregates. (1)

Faultless Triplet

(ii) Conjoined with faulty state, arises faulty state by root condition.

Conjoined with one faulty aggregate, arise three aggregates; conjoined with three aggregates, arises one aggregate; conjoined with two aggregates, arise two aggregates. (1)

(iii) Conjoined with indeterminate state, arises indeterminate state by root condition.

(a) Conjoined with one resultant indeterminate or functional indeterminate aggregate, arise three aggregates; conjoined with three aggregates, arises one aggregate; conjoined with two aggregates, arise two aggregates;

(b) At the moment of conception, conjoined with one resultant indeterminate aggregate, arise three aggregates; conjoined with three aggregates, arises one aggregate; conjoined with two aggregates, arise two aggregates. (1)

Object, etc., 3

339. Conjoined with faultless state, arises faultless state by object condition ... by predominance condition (there is no "At the moment of conception" in predominance) ... by proximity condition ... by contiguity condition ... by conascence condition ... by mutuality condition ... by dependence condition ... by strong-dependence condition.... (All sections are the same as root condition.)

Prenascence 3

340. (i) Conjoined with faultless state, arises faultless state by prenascence condition.

Conjoined with one faultless aggregate, arise three aggregates; conjoined with three aggregates, arises one aggregate; conjoined with two aggregates, arise two aggregates; (conjoined with heart-)base, (arise faultless aggregates) by prenascence condition.

(ii) Conjoined with faulty state, arises faulty state by prenascence condition.

Conjoined with one faulty aggregate, arise three aggregates; conjoined with three aggregates, arises one aggregate; conjoined with two aggregates, arise two aggregates; (conjoined with heart-)base, (arise faulty aggregates) by prenascence condition.

(iii) Conjoined with indeterminate state, arises indeterminate state by prenascence condition.

Conjoined with one resultant indeterminate or functional indeterminate aggregate, arise three aggregates; conjoined with three aggregates, arises one aggregate; conjoined with two aggregates, arise two aggregates; (conjoined with six) bases, (arise resultant indeterminate or functional indeterminate aggregates) by prenascence condition.

Repetition 3

341. Conjoined with faultless state . . . faulty state . . .

Conjoined with indeterminate state, arises indeterminate state by repetition condition.

Conjoined with one functional indeterminate aggregate. . . .

Kamma 3

342. Conjoined with faultless state, arises faultless state by kamma condition. . . .

Conjoined with faulty state . . .

Conjoined with indeterminate state . . .

Resultant 1

343. Conjoined with indeterminate state, arises indeterminate state by resultant condition.

(Conjoined with one) resultant indeterminate. . . .

Nutriment, etc., 3

344. Conjoined with faultless state, arises faultless state by nutriment condition . . . by faculty condition . . . by jhāna condition . . . by path condition . . . by association condition. . . .

(All these sections are the same as root condition.)

Dissociation 3

345. (i) Conjoined with faultless state, arises faultless state by dissociation condition.

Conjoined with one faultless aggregate, arise three aggregates ... conjoined with two aggregates, arise two aggregates; (conjoined with heart-)base, (arise faultless aggregates) by dissociation condition.

(ii) ... faulty state ... (conjoined with heart-)base, (arise faulty aggregates) by dissociation condition.

(iii) ... indeterminate state ... (conjoined with six) bases, (arise resultant indeterminate or functional indeterminate aggregates) by dissociation condition.

Presence, etc., 3

346. Conjoined with faultless state, arises faultless state by presence condition ... by absence condition ... by disappearance condition ... by non-disappearance condition ... (Same as root condition.)

I. CONDITIONS : POSITIVE   (ii) ENUMERATION CHAPTER

By Ones

347. With root 3, object 3, predominance 3, proximity 3, contiguity 3, conascence 3, mutuality 3, dependence 3, strong-dependence 3, prenascence 3, repetition 3, kamma 3, resultant 1, nutriment 3, faculty 3, jhāna 3, path 3, association 3, dissociation 3, presence 3, absence 3, disappearance 3, non-disappearance 3.

Root

By Twos

348. With root condition and object 3. (Expand root condition.) ...

Repetition

By Twos

349. With repetition condition and root 3, object 3, predominance 3, proximity 3, contiguity 3, conascence 3, mutuality 3, dependence 3, strong-dependence 3, prenascence 3, kamma 3, nutriment 3, faculty 3, jhāna 3, path 3, association 3, dissociation 3, presence 3, absence 3, disappearance 3, non-disappearance 3. (Abbreviated.)

Resultant

By Twos

350. With resultant condition and root 1, object 1, predominance 1, proximity 1, contiguity 1, conascence 1, mutuality 1, dependence 1, strong-dependence 1, prenascence 1, kamma 1, nutriment 1, faculty 1, jhāna 1, path 1, association 1, dissociation 1, presence 1, absence 1, disappearance 1, non-disappearance 1. ...

End of Positive in " Conjoined " Chapter.

2. CONDITIONS : NEGATIVE   (i) CLASSIFICATION CHAPTER

Not-root 2

351. (i) Conjoined with faulty state, arises faulty state by not-root condition.

Conjoined with doubt-accompanied or restlessness-accompanied aggregates, arises doubt-accompanied or restlessness-accompanied delusion.

(ii) Conjoined with indeterminate state, arises indeterminate state by not-root condition.

(*a*) Conjoined with one rootless resultant indeterminate or functional indeterminate aggregate, arise three aggregates ; conjoined with three aggregates, arises one aggregate ; conjoined with two aggregates, arise two aggregates ;

(*b*) At the moment of rootless conception, conjoined with one resultant indeterminate aggregate, arise three aggregates ; conjoined with three aggregates, arises one aggregate ; conjoined with two aggregates, arise two aggregates.

Not-predominance, etc., 3

352. Conjoined with faultless state, arises faultless state by not-predominance condition . . . by not-prenascence condition.

In the immaterial plane, conjoined with one faultless aggregate, arise three aggregates . . . conjoined with two aggregates, arise two aggregates. . . .

(. . . faulty state . . . indeterminate state . . .)[1]

---

[1] Misplaced under 353.

Not-postnascence 3, Not-repetiton 3

353. Conjoined with faultless state, arises faultless state by not-postnascence condition . . . three . . . by not-repetition condition . . . three.

Not-kamma 3

354. (i) Conjoined with faultless state, arises faultless state by not-kamma condition.
Conjoined with faultless aggregates, arises faultless volition.
  (ii) Conjoined with faulty state, arises faulty state by not-kamma condition.
Conjoined with faulty aggregates, arises faulty volition.
  (iii) Conjoined with indeterminate state, arises indeterminate state by not-kamma condition.
Conjoined with functional indeterminate aggregates, arises functional indeterminate volition.

Not-resultant 3

355. Conjoined with faultless state . . . faulty state . . .
Conjoined with indeterminate state, arises indeterminate state by not-resultant condition.
Conjoined with one functional indeterminate aggregate. . . .
(In the classification of the Negative in " Conjoined " Chapter, there is no " conception " for not-kamma and not-resultant, but there are for all the rest.)

Not-jhāna 1

356. Conjoined with indeterminate state, arises indeterminate state by not-jhāna condition.
Conjoined with one five-fold consciousness-accompanied aggregate, arise three aggregates . . . conjoined with two aggregates, arise two aggregates.

Not-path 1

357. Conjoined with indeterminate state, arises indeterminate state by not-path condition.
  (a) Conjoined with one rootless resultant indeterminate or

functional indeterminate aggregate, arise three aggregates ... conjoined with two aggregates, arise two aggregates ;

(b) At the moment of rootless conception. ...

Not-dissociation 3

358. (i) Conjoined with faultless state, arises faultless state by not-dissociation condition.

In the immaterial plane, conjoined with one faultless aggregate, arise three aggregates ... conjoined with two aggregates, arise two aggregates.

(ii) Conjoined with faulty state, arises faulty state by not-dissociation condition.

In the immaterial plane, conjoined with one faulty aggregate, arise three aggregates ... conjoined with two aggregates, arise two aggregates.

(iii) Conjoined with indeterminate state, arises indeterminate state by not-dissociation condition.

In the immaterial plane, conjoined with one resultant indeterminate or functional indeterminate aggregate, arise three aggregates ... conjoined with two aggregates, arise two aggregates. (There is no " conception " in not-dissociation.)

2. CONDITIONS : NEGATIVE   (ii) ENUMERATION CHAPTER

By Ones

359. With not-root 2, not-predominance 3, not-prenascence 3, not-postnascence 3, not-repetition 3, not-kamma 3, not-resultant 3, not-jhāna 1, not-path 1, not-dissociation 3.

Not-root

By Twos

360. With not-root condition and not-predominance 2, not-prenascence 2, not-postnascence 2, not-repetition 2, not-kamma 1, not-resultant 2, not-jhāna 1, not-path 1, not-dissociation 2.

By Threes

With not-root, not-predominance conditions and not-prenascence 2, not-postnascence 2, not-repetition 2, not-kamma 1, not-resultant 2, not-jhāna 1, not-path 1, not-dissociation 2.

By Fours
With not-root, not-predominance, not-prenascence conditions and not-postnascence 2, not-repetition 2, not-kamma 1, not-resultant 2, not-path 1, not-dissociation 2. ...

By Sixes
With not-root, not-predominance, not-prenascence, not-postnascence, not-repetition conditions and not-kamma 1, not-resultant 2, not-path 1, not-dissociation 2.

By Sevens
With not-root, not-predominance, not-prenascence, not-postnascence, not-repetition, not-kamma conditions and not-resultant 1, not-path 1, not-dissociation 1. ...

By Nine
With not-root, not-predominance... not-kamma, not-resultant, not-path conditions and not-dissociation 1.

Not-predominance
By Twos
361. With not-predominance condition and not-root 2, not-prenascence 3, not-postnascence 3, not-repetition 3, not-kamma 3, not-resultant 3, not-jhāna 1, not-path 1, not-dissociation 3.

By Threes
With not-predominance, not-root conditions and not-prenascence 2, not-postnascence 2, not-repetition 2, not-kamma 1, not-resultant 2, not-jhāna 1, not-path 1, not-dissociation 2. ...
(Abbreviated.)

Not-prenascence
By Twos
362. With not-prenascence condition and not-root 2, not-predominance 3, not-postnascence 3, not-repetition 3, not-kamma 3, not-resultant 3, not-path 1, not-dissociation 3.

By Threes
With not-prenascence, not-root conditions and not-predominance 2, not-postnascence 2, not-repetition 2, not-kamma 1,

not-resultant 2, not-path 1, not-dissociation 2. ... (Abbreviated.)

Not-postnascence, Not-repetition

By Twos

363. With not-postnascence condition ... with not-repetition condition and not-root 2, not-predominance 3, not-prenascence 3, not-postnascence 3, not-kamma 3, not-resultant 3, not-jhāna 1, not-path 1, not-dissociation 3.

By Threes

With not-repetition, not-root conditions and not-predominance 2, not-prenascence 2, not-postnascence 2, not-kamma 1, not-resultant 2, not-jhāna 1, not-path 1, not-dissociation 2. ... (Abbreviated.)

Not-kamma

By Twos

364. With not-kamma condition and not-root 1, not-predominance 3, not-prenascence 3, not-postnascence 3, not-repetition 3, not-resultant 3, not-path 1, not-dissociation 3.

By Threes

With not-kamma, not-root conditions and not-predominance 1, not-prenascence 1, not-postnascence 1, not-repetition 1, not-resultant 1, not-path 1, not-dissociation 1. ... (Abbreviated.)

Not-resultant

By Twos

365. With not-resultant condition and not-root 2, not-predominance 3, not-prenascence 3, not-postnascence 3, not-repetition 3, not-kamma 3, not-path 1, not-dissociation 3. ...

By Sevens

With not-resultant, not-root, not-predominance, not-prenascence, not-postnascence, not-repetition conditions and not-kamma 1, not-path 1, not-dissociation 2. ... (Abbreviated.)

Not-jhāna

By Twos

366. With not-jhāna condition and not-root 1, not-predominance 1, not-postnascence 1, not-repetition 1, not-path 1. ...

By Six

With not-jhāna, not-root, not-predominance, not-postnascence, not-repetition conditions and not-path 1.

Not-path

By Twos

367. With not-path condition and not-root 1, not-predominance 1, not-prenascence 1, not-postnascence 1, not-repetition 1, not-kamma 1, not-resultant 1, not-jhāna 1, not-dissociation 1. ... (Abbreviated.)

Not-dissociation

By Twos

368. With not-dissociation condition and not-root 2, not-predominance 3, not-prenascence 3, not-postnascence 3, not-repetition 3, not-kamma 3, not-resultant 3, not-path 1.

By Threes

With not-dissociation, not-root conditions and not-predominance 2, not-prenascence 2, not-postnascence 2, not-repetition 2, not-kamma 1, not-resultant 2, not-path 1. ...

By Nine

With not-dissociation, not-root, not-predominance, not-prenascence, not-postnascence, not-repetition, not-kamma, not resultant conditions and not-path 1.

End of Negative

3. CONDITIONS : POSITIVE–NEGATIVE

Root

By Twos

369. With root condition, not-predominance 3, not-prenascence 3, not-postnascence 3, not-repetition 3, not-kamma 3, not-resultant 3, not-dissociation 3.

By Threes
With root and object conditions, not-predominance 3, not-prenascence 3, not-postnascence 3, not-repetition 3, not-kamma 3, not-resultant 3, not-dissociation 3.

By Fours
With root, object and predominance conditions, not-prenascence 3, not-postnascence 3, not-repetition 3, not-kamma 3, not-resultant 3, not-dissociation 3. ...

By Elevens
With root, object, predominance, proximity, contiguity, conascence, mutuality, dependence, strong-dependence and prenascence conditions, not-postnascence 3, not-repetition 3, not-kamma 3, not-resultant 3.

By Twelves (*with repetition*)
With root, object ... prenascence and repetition conditions, not-postnascence 3, not-kamma 3, not-resultant 3. ...

By Twenty-threes (*with repetition*)
With root, object ... prenascence, repetition, kamma, nutriment ... and non-disappearance conditions, not-postnascence 3, not-resultant 3.

By Thirteens (*with resultant*)
With root, object ... prenascence, kamma and resultant conditions, not-postnascence 1, not-repetition 1. ...

By Twenty-threes (*with resultant*)
With root, object ... prenascence, kamma, resultant, nutriment ... and non-disappearance conditions, not-postnascence 1, not-repetition 1.

Object

By Twos
370. With object condition, not-root 2, not-predominance 3, not-prenascence 3, not-postnascence 3, not-repetition 3, not-kamma 3, not-resultant 3, not-jhāna 1, not-path 1, not-dissociation 3.

By Threes
With object and root conditions, not-predominance 3. ... (Abbreviated.)

Predominance
By Twos
371. With predominance condition, not-prenascence 3, not-postnascence 3, not-repetition 3, not-kamma 3, not-resultant 3, not-dissociation 3.

By Threes, etc.
With predominance and root conditions ... (Abbreviated.)

Proximity, etc.
372. With proximity condition ... with contiguity condition ... with conascence condition ... with mutuality condition ... with dependence condition ... with strong-dependence condition ...

(Expand in the same way as object condition.)

Prenascence
By Twos
373. With prenascence condition, not-root 2, not-predominance 3, not-postnascence 3, not-repetition 3, not-kamma 3, not-resultant 3, not-jhāna 1, not-path 1.

By Threes
With prenascence and root conditions, not-predominance 3, not-postnascence 3, not-repetition 3, not-kamma 3, not-resultant 3. ... (Abbreviated.)

Repetition
By Twos
374. With repetition condition, not-root 2, not-predominance 3, not-prenascence 3, not-postnascence 3, not-kamma 3, not-resultant 3, not-path 1, not-dissociation 3.

By Threes
With repetition and root conditions, not-predominance 3, not-prenascence 3, not-postnascence 3, not-kamma 3, not-resultant 3, not-dissociation 3. ... (Abbreviated.)

Kamma

By Twos

375. With kamma condition, not-root 2, not-predominance 3, not-prenascence 3, not-postnascence 3, not-repetition 3, not-resultant 3, not-jhāna 1, not-path 1, not-dissociation 3.

By Threes

With kamma and root conditions, not-predominance 3. ...
(Abbreviated.)

Resultant

By Twos

376. With resultant condition, not-root 1, not-predominance 1, not-prenascence 1, not-postnascence 1, not-repetition 1, not-jhāna 1, not-path 1, not-dissociation 1.

By Threes

With resultant and root conditions, not-predominance 1. ...
(Abbreviated.)

Nutriment

By Twos

377. With nutriment condition, not-root 2, not-predominance 3, not-prenascence 3, not-postnascence 3, not-repetition 3, not-kamma 3, not-resultant 3, not-jhāna 1, not-path 1, not-dissociation 3.

By Threes

With nutriment and root conditions, not-predominance 3. ...
(Abbreviated.)

Faculty

By Twos

378. With faculty condition, not-root 2, not-predominance 3, not-prenascence 3, not-postnascence 3, not-repetition 3, not-kamma 3, not-resultant 3, not-jhāna 1, not-path 1, not-dissociation 3.

By Threes

With faculty and root conditions, not-predominance 3. ...
(Abbreviated).

Jhāna

By Twos

379. With jhāna condition, not-root 2, not-predominance 3, not-prenascence 3, not-postnascence 3, not-repetition 3, not-kamma 3, not-resultant 3, not-path 1, not-dissociation 3.

By Threes

With jhāna and root conditions, not-predominance 3. ... (Abbreviated.)

Path

By Twos

380. With path condition, not-root 1, not-predominance 3, not-prenascence 3, not-postnascence 3, not-repetition 3, not-kamma 3, not-resultant 3, not-dissociation 3.

By Threes

With path and root conditions, not-predominance 3. ... (Abbreviated.)

Association

By Twos

381. With association condition, not-root 2, not-predominance 3, not-prenascence 3, not-postnascence 3, not-repetition 3, not-kamma 3, not-resultant 3, not-jhāna 1, not-path 1, not-dissociation 3.

By Threes

With association and root conditions, not-predominance 3. ... (Abbreviated.)

Dissociation

By Twos

382. With dissociation condition, not-root 2, not-predominance 3, not-prenascence 1, not-postnascence 3, not-repetition 3, not-kamma 3, not-resultant 3, not-jhāna 1, not-path 1.

By Threes

With dissociation and root conditions, not-predominance 3, not-prenascence 1, not-postnascence 3, not-repetition 3, not-kamma 3, not-resultant 3.

By Fours

With dissociation, root and object conditions, not-predominance 3, not-prenascence 1, not-postnascence 3, not-repetition 3, not-kamma 3, not-resultant 3. ...

By Twelves

With dissociation, root, object ... and prenascence conditions, not-postnascence 3, not-repetition 3, not-kamma 3, not-resultant 3. ...

By Twenty-threes (*with repetition*)

With dissociation, root ... prenascence, repetition, kamma, nutriment ... and non-disappearance conditions, not-postnascence 3, not-resultant 3.

By Twenty-threes (*with resultant*)

With dissociation, root ... prenascence, kamma, resultant, nutriment ... and non-disappearance conditions, not-postnascence 1, not-repetition 1.

Presence, etc.

383. With presence condition ... with absence condition ... with disappearance condition ... with non-disappearance condition ...

(Expand in the same way as object condition.)

End of Positive–Negative.

4. CONDITIONS : NEGATIVE–POSITIVE

Not-root

By Twos

384. With not-root condition, object 2, proximity 2, contiguity 2, conascence 2, mutuality 2, dependence 2, strong-dependence 2, prenascence 2, repetition 2, kamma 2, resultant 1, nutriment 2, faculty 2, jhāna 2, path 1, association 2, dissociation 2, presence 2, absence 2, disappearance 2, non-disappearance 2.

By Threes
With not-root and not-predominance conditions, object 2 ... non-disappearance 2 (All are 2).[1]

By Fours
With not-root, not-predominance and not-prenascence conditions, object 2, proximity 2, contiguity 2, conascence 2, mutuality 2, dependence 2, strong-dependence 2, repetition 1, kamma 2, resultant 1, nutriment 2, faculty 2, jhāna 2, path 1, association 2, dissociation 1, presence 2, absence 2, disappearance 2, non-disappearance 2. ...

By Sevens
With not-root, not-predominance, not-prenascence, not-postnascence, not-repetition and not-kamma conditions, object 1, proximity 1, contiguity 1, conascence 1, mutuality 1, dependence 1, strong-dependence 1, nutriment 1, faculty 1, jhāna 1, association 1, presence 1, absence 1, disappearance 1, non-disappearance 1. (All are 1). ...

By Tens
With not-root, not-predominance, not-prenascence, not-postnascence, not-repetition, not-kamma, not-resultant, not-path and not-dissociation conditions, object 1, proximity 1, contiguity 1, conascence 1, mutuality 1, dependence 1, strong-dependence 1, nutriment 1, faculty 1, jhāna 1, association 1, presence 1, absence 1, disappearance 1, non-disappearance 1. (Not-resultant, not-path, not-dissociation and not-kamma conditions are the same.)

By Twos   *Not-predominance*
385. With not-predominance condition, root 3, object 3 ... non-disappearance 3.

By Threes
With not-predominance and not-root conditions, object 2 ... non-disappearance 2.

(When not-root is taken with not-predominance, make it the same as not-root condition.)

---
[1] Except resultant and path which are 1.

Not-prenascence

By Twos

386. With not-prenascence condition, root 3, object 3 ... repetition 3, kamma 3, resultant 1.

(Expand all sections. There are three questions in those sections which are left out. When not-root is taken with not-prenascence, there is only one question with repetition and path. The rest are the same as not-root condition. Not-prenascence condition is completed in the same way as not-predominance condition.)

Not-kamma

By Twos

387. With not-kamma condition, root 3, object 3, predominance 3, proximity 3, contiguity 3, conascence 3, mutuality 3, dependence 3, strong-dependence 3, prenascence 3, repetition 3, nutriment 3, faculty 3, jhāna 3, path 3, association 3, dissociation 3, presence 3, absence 3, disappearance 3, non-disappearance 3.

By Threes

With not-kamma and not-root conditions, object 1, proximity 1, contiguity 1, conascence 1, mutuality 1, dependence 1, strong-dependence 1, prenascence 1, repetition 1, nutriment 1, faculty 1, jhāna 1, association 1, dissociation 1, presence 1, absence 1, disappearance 1, non-disappearance 1. ...

By Fives

With not-kamma, not-root, not-predominance and not-prenascence conditions, object 1, proximity 1, contiguity 1, conascence 1, mutuality 1, dependence 1, strong-dependence 1, nutriment 1, faculty 1, jhāna 1, association 1, presence 1, absence 1, disappearance 1, non-disappearance 1.

(Expand all the remaining sections in this way. Abbreviated.)

Not-resultant

By Twos

388. With not-resultant condition, root 3 (Abbreviated. Complete) ... non-disappearance 3. ...

Faulltless Triplet

By Fives

With not-resultant, not-root, not-predominance and not-prenascence conditions, object 2, proximity 2, contiguity 2, conascence 2, mutuality 2, dependence 2, strong-dependence 2, repetition 1, kamma 2, nutriment 2, faculty 2, jhāna 2, path 1, association 2, presence 2, absence 2, disappearance 2, non-disappearance 2.

(It is different only with not-resultant condition. All the rest are the same as not-root condition.)

Not-jhāna

By Twos

389. With not-jhāna condition, object 1, proximity 1, contiguity 1, conascence 1, mutuality 1, dependence 1, strong-dependence 1, prenascence 1, kamma 1, resultant 1, nutriment 1, faculty 1, association 1, dissociation 1, presence 1, absence 1, disappearance 1, non-disappearance 1. ...

By Sevens

With not-jhāna, not-root, not-predominance, not-postnascence, not-repetition and not-path conditions, object 1, proximity 1, contiguity 1, conascence 1, mutuality 1, dependence 1, strong-dependence 1, prenascence 1, kamma 1, resultant 1, nutriment 1, faculty 1, association 1, dissociation 1, presence 1, absence 1, disappearance 1, non-disappearance 1.

Not-path

By Twos

390. With not-path condition, object 1, proximity 1, contiguity 1, conascence 1, mutuality 1, dependence 1, strong-dependence 1, prenascence 1, repetition 1, kamma 1, resultant 1, nutriment 1, faculty 1, jhāna 1, association 1, dissociation 1, presence 1, absence 1, disappearance 1, non-disappearance 1. ...

By Fives

With not-path, not-root, not-predominance and not-prenascence conditions, object 1, proximity 1, contiguity 1, conascence 1, mutuality 1, dependence 1, strong-dependence 1, kamma 1, resultant 1, nutriment 1, faculty 1, jhāna 1, association 1, dissociation 1, presence 1, absence 1, disappearance 1, non-disappearance 1.

By Sixes, etc.
   With not-path, not-root . . . (Abbreviated.)

By Twos   *Not-dissociation*

391. With not-dissociation condition, root 3, object 3, predominance 3, proximity 3, contiguity 3, conascence 3, mutuality 3, dependence 3, strong-dependence 3, repetition 3, kamma 3, resultant 1, nutriment 3, faculty 3, jhāna 3, path 3, association 3, presence 3, absence 3, disappearance 3, non-disappearance 3.

By Threes
With not-dissociation and not-root conditions, object 2, proximity 2, contiguity 2, conascence 2, mutuality 2, dependence 2, strong-dependence 2, repetition 1, kamma 2, nutriment 2, faculty 2, jhāna 2, path 1, association 2, presence 2, absence 2, disappearance 2, non-disappearance 2. . . .

By Nines
With not-dissociation, not-root, not-predominance, not-prenascence, not-postnascence (Not-repetition condition is also the same as not-root), not-kamma, not-resultant and not-path conditions (These three conditions are the same), object 1, proximity 1, contiguity 1, conascence 1, mutuality 1, dependence 1, strong-dependence 1, nutriment 1, faculty 1, jhāna 1, association 1, presence 1, absence 1, disappearance 1, non-disappearance 1.

End of Negative–Positive
End of " CONJOINED " CHAPTER.

I. FAULTLESS TRIPLET   VI. " ASSOCIATED " CHAPTER
I. CONDITIONS : POSITIVE   (i) CLASSIFICATION CHAPTER

Root 3

392. (i) Associated with faultless state, arises faultless state by root condition.

Associated with one faultless aggregate, arise three aggregates; associated with three aggregates, arises one aggregate; associated with two aggregates, arise two aggregates.

393. (ii) Associated with faulty state, arises faulty state by root condition.

Associated with one faulty aggregate, arise three aggregates; associated with three aggregates, arises one aggregate; associated with two aggregates, arise two aggregates.

394. (iii) Associated with indeterminate state, arises indeterminate state by root condition.

(*a*) Associated with one resultant indeterminate or functional indeterminate aggregate, arise three aggregates; associated with three aggregates, arises one aggregate; associated with two aggregates, arise two aggregates;

(*b*) At the moment of conception, associated with one resultant indeterminate aggregate, arise three aggregates; associated with three aggregates, arises one aggregate; associated with two aggregates, arise two aggregates.... (Abbreviated.)

1. CONDITIONS: POSITIVE   (ii) ENUMERATION CHAPTER

By Ones

395. With root 3, object 3, predominance 3, proximity 3, contiguity 3, conascence 3, mutuality 3, dependence 3, strong-dependence 3, prenascence 3, repetition 3, kamma 3, resultant 1, nutriment 3, faculty 3, jhāna 3, path 3, association 3, dissociation 3, presence 3, absence 3, disappearance 3, non-disappearance 3. ...

End of Positive

2. CONDITIONS: NEGATIVE   (i) CLASSIFICATION CHAPTER

Not-root 2

396. (i) Associated with faulty state, arises faulty state by not-root condition.

Associated with doubt-accompanied or restlessness-accompanied aggregates, arises doubt-accompanied or restlessness-accompanied delusion.

397. (ii) Associated with indeterminate state, arises indeterminate state by not-root condition.

(*a*) Associated with one rootless resultant indeterminate or functional indeterminate aggregate, arise three aggregates; associated with three aggregates, arises one aggregate; associated with two aggregates, arise two aggregates;

(*b*) At the moment of rootless conception, associated with one resultant indeterminate aggregate, arise three aggregates; associated with three aggregates, arises one aggregate; associated with two aggregates, arise two aggregates. ... (Abbreviated.)

2. CONDITIONS : NEGATIVE   (ii) ENUMERATION CHAPTER

By Ones

398. With not-root 2, not-predominance 3, not-prenascence 3, not-postnascence 3, not-repetition 3, not-kamma 3, not-resultant 3, not-jhāna 1, not-path 1, not-dissociation 3. ... (Abbreviated.)

End of Negative

3. CONDITIONS : POSITIVE–NEGATIVE

Root

By Twos

399. With root condition, not-predominance 3, not-prenascence 3, not-postnascence 3, not-repetition 3, not-kamma 3, not-resultant 3, not-dissociation 3. ... (Abbreviated.)

End of Positive–Negative

4. CONDITIONS : NEGATIVE–POSITIVE

Not-root

By Twos

400. With not-root condition, object 2, proximity 2, contiguity 2, conascence 2, mutuality 2, dependence 2, strong-dependence 2, prenascence 2, repetition 2, kamma 2, resultant 1, nutriment

2, faculty 2, jhāna 1, path 1, association 2, dissociation 2, presence 2, absence 2, disappearance 2, non-disappearance 2. . . . (Abbreviated.)

End of Negative–Positive
End of " ASSOCIATED " CHAPTER.

(The term " Conjoined " is the same as " Associated ". The term " Associated " is the same as " Conjoined ".)

1. FAULTLESS TRIPLET   VII. " INVESTIGATION " CHAPTER

1. CONDITIONS: POSITIVE   (i) CLASSIFICATION CHAPTER

Root 7

401. (i) Faultless state is related to faultless state by root condition.

Faultless roots are related to (their) associated aggregates by root condition.

(ii) Faultless state is related to indeterminate state by root condition.

Faultless roots are related to mind-produced matter by root condition.

(iii) Faultless state is related to faultless (state) and indeterminate state by root condition.

Faultless roots are related to (their) associated aggregates and mind-produced matter by root condition. (3)

402. (iv) Faulty state is related to faulty state by root condition.

Faulty roots are related to (their) associated aggregates by root condition.

(v) Faulty state is related to indeterminate state by root condition.

Faulty roots are related to mind-produced matter by root condition.

(vi) Faulty state is related to faulty and indeterminate state by root condition.

Faulty roots are related to (their) associated aggregates and mind-produced matter by root condition. (3)

s

403. (vii) Indeterminate state is related to indeterminate state by root condition.

(*a*) Resultant indeterminate or functional indeterminate roots are related to (their) associated aggregates and mind-produced matter by root condition ;

(*b*) At the moment of conception, resultant indeterminate roots are related to (their) associated aggregates and kamma-produced matter by root condition. (1)

Object 9

404. (i) Faultless state is related to faultless state by object condition.

After having offered the offering, having undertaken the precept, having fulfilled the duty of observance, (one) reviews it. (One) reviews (such acts) formerly well done. Having emerged from jhāna, (one) reviews the jhāna. Learners review change-of-lineage. (They) review purification. Learners, having emerged from Path, review the Path. Learners or common worldlings practise insight into the impermanency, suffering and impersonality of the faultless (state). By the knowledge of penetration into others' minds (they) know the faultless mind of the other being.

Faultless " infinity of space " is related to faultless " infinity of consciousness " by object condition. Faultless " nothingness " is related to faultless " neither-perception-nor-non-perception " by object condition.

Faultless aggregates are related to knowledge of supernormal power, knowledge of penetration into others' minds, knowledge of remembrance of past existences, knowledge of rebirths according to one's kamma, knowledge of future existences by object condition.

405. (ii) Faultless state is related to faulty state by object condition.

After having offered the offering, having undertaken the precept, having fulfilled the duty of observance, (one) enjoys and delights in it. Taking it as object, arises lust, arises wrong views, arises doubt, arises restlessness, arises grief. (One) enjoys and delights in (such acts) formerly well done. Taking it as object, arises lust, arises wrong views, arises doubt, arises restlessness, arises grief.

Having emerged from jhāna, (one) enjoys and delights in the jhāna. Taking it (jhāna) as object, arises lust, arises wrong views, arises doubt, arises restlessness. When jhāna has disappeared, (one) regrets it and thereby arises grief.

406. (iii) Faultless state is related to indeterminate state by object condition.

Having emerged from (Arahatta) Path, the Arahat reviews the Path. (He) reviews (the faultless acts) formerly well done. (He) practises insight into the impermanency, suffering and impersonality of the faultless (state). By the knowledge of penetration into others' minds (he) knows the faultless mind of the other being.

Learners or common worldlings practise insight into the impermanency, suffering and impersonality of the faultless (state). When faultless (state) has ceased, the resultant (state) arises as registering (consciousness).

(Learners or common worldlings) enjoy and delight in the faultless (state). Taking it as object, arises lust, arises wrong views, arises doubt, arises restlessness, arises grief. When faulty (state) has ceased, the resultant arises as registering.

Faultless "infinity of space" is related to resultant or functional "infinity of consciousness" by object condition. Faultless "nothingness" is related to resultant or functional "neither-perception-nor-non-perception" by object condition.

Faultless aggregates are related to knowledge of penetration into others' minds, knowledge of remembrance of past existences, knowledge of rebirths according to one's kamma, knowledge of future existences, (mind-door) advertence by object condition. (3)

407. (iv) Faulty state is related to faulty state by object condition.

(One) enjoys and delights in lust. Taking it as object, arises lust, arises wrong views, arises doubt, arises restlessness, arises grief. (One) enjoys and delights in wrong views. Taking it as object, arises lust, arises wrong views, arises doubt, arises restlessness, arises grief.

Taking doubt as object, arises doubt, arises wrong views,

arises restlessness, arises grief. Taking restlessness as object, arises restlessness, arises wrong views, arises doubt, arises grief. Taking grief as object, arises grief, arises wrong views, arises doubt, arises restlessness.

408. (v) Faulty state is related to faultless state by object condition.

Learners review the eradicated defilements. (They) review the uneradicated defilements. (They) know the defilements addicted to before.

Learners or common worldlings practise insight into the impermanency, suffering and impersonality of the faulty (state). By the knowledge of penetration into others' minds, (they) know the faulty mind of the other being.

Faulty aggregates are related to knowledge of penetration into others' minds, knowledge of remembrance of past existences, knowledge of rebirths according to one's kamma, knowledge of future existences by object condition.

409. (vi) Faulty state is related to indeterminate state by object condition.

The Arahat reviews the eradicated defilements. (He) knows the defilements addicted to before. (He) practises insight into the impermanency, suffering and impersonality of the faulty (state). By the knowledge of penetration into others' minds, (he) knows the faulty mind of the other being.

Learners or common worldlings practise insight into the impermanency, suffering and impersonality of the faulty (state). When faultless (state) has ceased, the resultant arises as registering.

(One) enjoys and delights in the faulty (state). Taking it as object, arises lust, arises wrong views, arises doubt, arises restlessness, arises grief. When faulty (state) has ceased, the resultant arises as registering.

Faulty aggregates are related to knowledge of penetration into others' minds, knowledge of remembrance of past existences, knowledge of rebirths according to one's kamma, knowledge of future existences, advertence by object condition. (3)

410. (vii) Indeterminate state is related to indeterminate state by object condition.

The Arahat reviews (Arahatta) Fruition. (He) reviews

Nibbāna. Nibbāna is related to Fruition, (mind-door) advertence by object condition.

The Arahat practises insight into the impermanency, suffering and impersonality of the eye (base) ; ... ear (base) ... nose ... tongue ... body ... visible object ... sound ... smell ... taste ... tangible object ... (heart-)base ; (he) practises insight into the impermanency, suffering and impersonality of the resultant indeterminate or functional indeterminate aggregates.

By the power of divine-eye, (The Arahat) sees the visible object. By the power of divine-ear element, hears the sound. By the knowledge of penetration into others' minds (he) knows the resultant indeterminate or functional indeterminate mind of the other being.

Functional " infinity of space " is related to functional " infinity of consciousness " by object condition. Functional " nothingness " is related to functional " neither-perception-nor-non-perception " by object condition.

Visible object-base is related to eye-consciousness by object condition ; sound-base to ear-consciousness ; smell-base to nose-consciousness ; taste-base to tongue-consciousness ; tangible object-base is related to body-consciousness by object condition.

Indeterminate aggregates are related to knowledge of supernormal power, knowledge of penetration into others' minds, knowledge of remembrance of past existences, knowledge of future existences, advertence by object condition.

411. (viii) Indeterminate state is related to faultless state by object condition.

Learners review (lower) Fruition. (They) review Nibbāna. Nibbāna is related to change-of-lineage, purification, Path by object condition.

Learners or common worldlings practise insight into the impermanency, suffering and impersonality of the eye ; ... ear ... nose ... tongue ... body ... visible object ... sound ... smell ... taste ... tangible object ... (heart-)base ; (they) practise insight into the impermanency, suffering and impersonality of the resultant indeterminate or functional indeterminate aggregates.

By the power of divine-eye, (they) see the visible object. By the power of divine-ear element, hear the sound. By the knowledge of penetration into others' minds, (they) know the resultant indeterminate or functional indeterminate mind of the other being.

Indeterminate aggregates are related to knowledge of supernormal power, knowledge of penetration into others' minds, knowledge of remembrance of past existences, knowledge of future existences by object condition.

412. (ix) Indeterminate state is related to faulty state by object condition.

(One) enjoys and delights in the eye. Taking it as object, arises lust, arises wrong views, arises doubt, arises restlessness, arises grief. ... ear ... nose ... tongue ... body ... visible object ... sound ... smell ... taste ... tangible object ... (heart-)base. ... (One) enjoys and delights in the resultant indeterminate or functional indeterminate aggregates. Taking it as object, arises lust, arises wrong views, arises doubt, arises restlessness, arises grief. (3)

Predominance 10

413. (i) Faultless state is related to faultless state by predominance condition.

(It is of two kinds, namely :) (*a*) object-predominance, (*b*) conascence-predominance.

(*a*) *Object-predominance* : After having offered the offering, having undertaken the precept, having fulfilled the duty of observance, (one) esteems and reviews it. (One) esteems and reviews (such acts) formerly well done. Having emerged from jhāna, (one) esteems and reviews the jhāna. Learners esteem and review change-of-lineage. (They) esteem and review purification. Learners, having emerged from Path, esteem and review the Path.

(*b*) *Conascence-predominance* : Faultless predominance is related to (its) associated aggregates by predominance condition.

414. (ii) Faultless state is related to faulty state by predominance condition.

(*a*) *Object-predominance* : After having offered the offering, having undertaken the precept, having fulfilled the duty of observance, (one) esteems, enjoys and delights in it. Taking it as estimable object, arises lust, arises wrong views. (One) esteems, enjoys and delights in (faultless acts) formerly well done. Taking it as estimable object, arises lust, arises wrong views.

Having emerged from jhāna, (one) esteems, enjoys and delights in the jhāna. Taking it as estimable object, arises lust, arises wrong views.

(iii) Faultless state is related to indeterminate state by predominance condition.

(It is of two kinds, namely :) (*a*) object-predominance, (*b*) conascence-predominance.

(*a*) *Object-predominance* : Having emerged from (Arahatta) Path, the Arahat esteems and reviews the Path.

(*b*) *Conascence-predominance* : Faultless predominance is related to mind-produced matter by predominance condition.

(iv) Faultless state is related to faultless and indeterminate state by predominance condition.

Conascence-predominance : Faultless predominance is related to (its) associated aggregates and mind-produced matter by predominance condition. (4).

415. (v) Faulty state is related to faulty state by predominance condition.

(It is of two kinds, namely :) (*a*) object-predominance, (*b*) conascence-predominance.

(*a*) *Object-predominance* : (One) esteems, enjoys and delights in lust. Taking it as estimable object, arises lust, arises wrong views. (One) esteems, enjoys and delights in wrong views. Taking it as estimable object, arises lust, arises wrong views.

(*b*) *Conascence-predominance* : Faulty predominance is related to (its) associated aggregates by predominance condition.

(vi) Faulty state is related to indeterminate state by predominance condition.

Conascence-predominance : Faulty predominance is related to mind-produced matter by predominance condition.

(vii) Faulty state is related to faulty and indeterminate state by predominance condition.

Conascence-predominance : Faulty predominance is related

to (its) associated aggregates and mind-produced matter by predominance condition. (3)

416. (viii) Indeterminate state is related to indeterminate state by predominance condition.

(It is of two kinds, namely :) (*a*) object-predominance, (*b*) conascence-predominance.

(*a*) *Object-predominance* : The Arahat esteems and reviews (Arahatta) Fruition. He esteems and reviews Nibbāna. Nibbāna is related to Fruition by predominance condition.

(*b*) *Conascence-predominance* : Resultant indeterminate or functional indeterminate predominance is related to (its) associated aggregates and mind-produced matter by predominance condition.

(ix) Indeterminate state is related to faultless state by predominance condition.

Object-predominance : Learners esteem and review (lower) Fruition. (They) esteem and review Nibbāna. Nibbāna is related to change-of-lineage, purification, Path by predominance condition.

(x) Indeterminate state is related to faulty state by predominance condition.

Object-predominance : (One) esteems, enjoys and delights in the eye. Taking it as estimable object, arises lust, arises wrong views. ... ear ... nose ... tongue ... body ... visible object ... sound ... smell ... taste ... tangible object ... (heart-)base. ... (One) esteems, enjoys and delights in the resultant indeterminate or functional indeterminate aggregates. Taking it as estimable object, arises lust, arises wrong views. (3)

Proximity 7

417. (i) Faultless state is related to faultless state by proximity condition.

Preceding faultless aggregates are related to subsequent faultless aggregates by proximity condition. Adaptation to change-of-lineage ; adaptation to purification ; change-of-lineage to Path ; purification is related to Path by proximity condition.

(ii) Faultless state is related to indeterminate state by proximity condition.

Faultless (state) to emergence ; Path to Fruition ; adaptation to attainment of Fruition of Learners ; having emerged from the attainment of Extinction, faultless neither-perception-nor-non-perception is related to the attainment of Fruition by proximity condition. (2)

(iii) Faulty state is related to faulty state by proximity condition.

Preceding faulty aggregates are related to subsequent faulty aggregates by proximity condition.

(iv) Faulty state is related to indeterminate state by proximity condition.

Faulty (state) is related to emergence by proximity condition. (2)

(v) Indeterminate state is related to indeterminate state by proximity condition.

Preceding resultant indeterminate or functional indeterminate aggregates are related to subsequent resultant indeterminate or functional indeterminate aggregates by proximity condition. Life-continuum to advertence ; functional to emergence ; adaptation of the Arahat to attainment of Fruition (of the Arahat) ; having emerged from the attainment of Extinction, functional neither-perception-nor-non-perception is related to the attainment of Fruition by proximity condition.

(vi) Indeterminate state is related to faultless state by proximity condition.

Advertence is related to faultless aggregates by proximity condition.

(vii) Indeterminate state is related to faulty state by proximity condition.

Advertence is related to faulty aggregates by proximity condition. (3)

Contiguity 7

418. (i) Faultless state is related to faultless state by contiguity condition.

Preceding faultless aggregates are related to subsequent faultless aggregates by contiguity condition. Adaptation to change-of-lineage ; adaptation to purification ; change-of-lineage to Path ; purification is related to Path by contiguity condition.

(ii) Faultless state is related to indeterminate state by contiguity condition.

Faultless (state) to emergence ; Path to Fruition ; adaptation to attainment of Fruition of Learners ; having emerged from the attainment of Extinction, faultless neither-perception-nor-non-perception is related to the attainment of Fruition by contiguity condition. (2)

(iii) Faulty state is related to faulty state by contiguity condition.

Preceding faulty aggregates are related to subsequent faulty aggregates by contiguity condition.

(iv) Faulty state is related to indeterminate state by contiguity condition.

Faulty (state) is related to emergence by contiguity condition. (2)

(v) Indeterminate state is related to indeterminate state by contiguity condition.

Preceding resultant indeterminate or functional indeterminate aggregates are related to subsequent resultant indeterminate or functional indeterminate aggregates by contiguity condition. Life-continuum to advertence ; functional to emergence ; adaptation of the Arahat to attainment of Fruition (of the Arahat) ; having emerged from the attainment of Extinction, functional neither-perception-nor-non-perception is related to the attainment of Fruition by contiguity condition.

(vi) Indeterminate state is related to faultless state by contiguity condition.

Advertence is related to faultless aggregates by contiguity condition.

(vii) Indeterminate state is related to faulty state by contiguity condition.

Advertence is related to faulty aggregates by contiguity condition. (3)

Conascence 9

419. (i) Faultless state is related to faultless state by conascence condition.

One faultless aggregate is related to three (faultless) aggregates by conascence condition ; three aggregates are related to one aggregate by conascence condition ; two aggregates are related to two aggregates by conascence condition.

(ii) Faultless state is related to indeterminate state by conascence condition.

Faultless aggregates are related to mind-produced matter by conascence condition.

(iii) Faultless state is related to faultless and indeterminate state by conascence condition.

One faultless aggregate is related to three aggregates and mind-produced matter by conascence condition ; three aggregates are related to one aggregate and mind-produced matter by conascence condition ; two aggregates are related to two aggregates and mind-produced matter by conascence condition. (3)

(iv) Faulty state is related to faulty state by conascence condition.

One faulty aggregate is related to three aggregates by conascence condition ; three aggregates are related to one aggregate by conascence condition ; two aggregates are related to two aggregates by conascence condition.

(v) Faulty state is related to indeterminate state by conascence condition.

Faulty aggregates are related to mind-produced matter by conascence condition.

(vi) Faulty state is related to faulty and indeterminate state by conascence condition.

One faulty aggregate is related to three aggregates and mind-produced matter by conascence condition ; three aggregates are related to one aggregate and mind-produced matter by conascence condition ; two aggregates are related to two aggregates and mind-produced matter by conascence condition. (3)

(vii) Indeterminate state is related to indeterminate state by conascence condition.

(*a*) One resultant indeterminate or functional indeterminate aggregate is related to three aggregates and mind-produced matter by conascence condition ; three aggregates are related to one aggregate and mind-produced matter by conascence condition ; two aggregates are related to two aggregates and mind-produced matter by conascence condition ;

(*b*) At the moment of conception, one resultant indeterminate aggregate is related to three aggregates and kamma-produced matter by conascence condition; three aggregates are related to one aggregate and kamma-produced matter by conascence condition; two aggregates are related to two aggregates and kamma-produced matter by conascence condition; aggregates are related to (heart-)base by conascence condition; (heart-)base is related to aggregates by conascence condition;

(c) One great primary is related to three great primaries by conascence condition; three great primaries are related to one great primary by conascence condition; two great primaries are related to two great primaries by conascence condition; great primaries are related to mind-produced and kamma-produced derived matter by conascence condition;

(d) One external great primary is related to three great primaries by conascence condition; three great primaries are related to one great primary by conascence condition; two great primaries are related to two great primaries by conascence condition; great primaries are related to derived matter by conascence condition;

One nutriment-produced great primary is related to three great primaries by conascence condition; three great primaries are related to one great primary by conascence condition; two great primaries are related to two great primaries by conascence condition; great primaries are related to derived matter by conascence condition;

One temperature-produced great primary is related to three great primaries by conascence condition; three great primaries are related to one great primary by conascence condition; two great primaries are related to two great primaries by conascence condition; great primaries are related to derived matter by conascence condition;

(e) One great primary of non-percipient beings is related to three great primaries by conascence condition; three great primaries are related to one great primary by conascence condition; two great primaries are related to two great primaries by conascence condition; great primaries are related to kamma-produced derived matter by conascence condition. (1)

(viii) Faultless and indeterminate states are related to indeterminate state by conascence condition.

Faultless aggregates and great primaries are related to mind-produced matter by conascence condition. (1)

(ix) Faulty and indeterminate states are related to indeterminate state by conascence condition.

Faulty aggregates and great primaries are related to mind-produced matter by conascence condition. (1)

Mutuality 3

420. (i) Faultless state is related to faultless state by mutuality condition.

One faultless aggregate is related to three aggregates by mutuality condition ; three aggregates are related to one aggregate by mutuality condition ; two aggregates are related to two aggregates by mutuality condition. (1)

(ii) Faulty state is related to faulty state by mutuality condition.

One faulty aggregate is related to three aggregates by mutuality condition ; three aggregates are related to one aggregate by mutuality condition ; two aggregates are related to two aggregates by mutuality condition. (1)

(iii) Indeterminate state is related to indeterminate state by mutuality condition.

(*a*) One resultant indeterminate or functional indeterminate aggregate is related to three aggregates by mutuality condition ; three aggregates are related to one aggregate by mutuality condition ; two aggregates are related to two aggregates by mutuality condition ;

(*b*) At the moment of conception, one resultant indeterminate aggregate is related to three aggregates and (heart-)base by mutuality condition ; three aggregates are related to one aggregate and (heart-)base by mutuality condition ; two aggregates are related to two aggregates and (heart-)base by mutuality condition ; aggregates are related to (heart-)base by mutuality condition ; (heart-)base is related to aggregates by mutuality condition ;

(*c*) One great primary is related to three great primaries by mutuality condition ; three great primaries are related to one great primary by mutuality condition ; two great primaries are related to two great primaries by mutuality condition.

(d) [1]External . . . nutriment-produced . . . temperature-produced . . . one great primary of non-percipient beings is related to three great primaries by mutuality condition ; three great primaries are related to one great primary by mutuality condition ; two great primaries are related to two great primaries by mutuality condition. (1)

Dependence 13

421. (i) Faultless state is related to faultless state by dependence condition.

One faultless aggregate is related to three aggregates by dependence condition ; three aggregates are related to one aggregate by dependence condition ; two aggregates are related to two aggregates by dependence condition.

(ii) Faultless state is related to indeterminate state by dependence condition.

Faultless aggregates are related to mind-produced matter by dependence condition.

(iii) Faultless state is related to faultless and indeterminate state by dependence condition.

One faultless aggregate is related to three aggregates and mind-produced matter by dependence condition ; three aggregates are related to one aggregate and mind-produced matter by dependence condition ; two aggregates are related to two aggregates and mind-produced matter by dependence condition. (3)

(iv) Faulty state is related to faulty state by dependence condition.

One faulty aggregate is related to three aggregates by dependence condition ; three aggregates are related to one aggregate by dependence condition ; two aggregates are related to two aggregates by dependence condition.

(v) Faulty state is related to indeterminate state by dependence condition.

Faulty aggregates are related to mind-produced matter by dependence condition.

---

[1] See No. 419 (vii) (d) where it is given in full. From now on they are elided. Here, in mutuality condition, there is no relation between great primaries and derived-matter.

(vi) Faulty state is related to faulty and indeterminate state by dependence condition.

One faulty aggregate is related to three aggregates and mind-produced matter by dependence condition ; three aggregates are related to one aggregate and mind-produced matter by dependence condition ; two aggregates are related to two aggregates and mind-produced matter by dependence condition. (3)

(vii) Indeterminate state is related to indeterminate state by dependence condition.

(*a*) One resultant indeterminate or functional indeterminate aggregate is related to three aggregates and mind-produced matter by dependence condition ; three aggregates are related to one aggregate and mind-produced matter by dependence condition ; two aggregates are related to two aggregates and mind-produced matter by dependence condition ;

(*b*) At the moment of conception, one resultant indeterminate aggregate is related to three aggregates and kamma-produced matter by dependence condition ; three aggregates are related to one aggregate and kamma-produced matter by dependence condition ; two aggregates are related to two aggregates and kamma-produced matter by dependence condition ; aggregates are related to (heart-)base by dependence condition ; (heart-)base is related to aggregates by dependence condition ;

(*c*) One great primary is related to three great primaries by dependence condition ; three great primaries are related to one great primary by dependence condition ; two great primaries are related to two great primaries by dependence condition ; great primaries are related to mind-produced and kamma-produced derived matter by dependence condition ;

(*d*) External . . . nutriment-produced . . . temperature-produced . . . one great primary of non-percipient beings is related to three great primaries by dependence condition ; three great primaries are related to one great primary by dependence condition ; two great primaries are related to two great primaries by ·dependence condition ; great primaries are related to kamma-produced derived matter by dependence condition ;

(*e*) Eye-base is related to eye-consciousness by dependence condition ; ear-base . . . nose-base . . . tongue-base . . . body-base is related to body-consciousness by dependence condition ; (heart-)base is related to resultant indeterminate or functional indeterminate aggregates by dependence condition.

(viii) Indeterminate state is related to faultless state by dependence condition.

(Heart-)base is related to faultless aggregates by dependence condition.

(ix) Indeterminate state is related to faulty state by dependence condition.

(Heart-)base is related to faulty aggregates by dependence condition. (3)

422. (x) Faultless and indeterminate states are related to faultless state by dependence condition.

One faultless aggregate and (heart-)base are related to three aggregates by dependence condition ; three aggregates and (heart-)base are related to one aggregate by dependence condition ; two aggregates and (heart-)base are related to two aggregates by dependence condition.

(xi) Faultless and indeterminate states are related to indeterminate state by dependence condition.

Faultless aggregates and great primaries are related to mind-produced matter by dependence condition. (2)

(xii) Faulty and indeterminate states are related to faulty state by dependence condition.

One faulty aggregate and (heart-)base are related to three aggregates by dependence condition ; three aggregates and (heart-)base are related to one aggregate by dependence condition ; two aggregates and (heart-)base are related to two aggregates by dependence condition.

(xiii) Faulty and indeterminate states are related to indeterminate state by dependence condition.

Faulty aggregates and great primaries are related to mind-produced matter by dependence condition. (2)

Strong-dependence 9

423. (i) Faultless state is related to faultless state by strong-dependence condition.

(It is of three kinds, namely :) (*a*) object-strong-dependence,

(b) proximity-strong-dependence, (c) natural strong-dependence.

(a) *Object-strong-dependence* : After having offered the offering, having undertaken the precept, having fulfilled the duty of observance, (one) esteems and reviews it. (One) esteems and reviews (such acts) formerly well done. Having emerged from jhāna, (one) esteems and reviews the jhāna. Learners esteem and review change-of-lineage. They esteem and review purification. Learners, having emerged from Path, esteem and review the Path.

(b) *Proximity-strong-dependence* : Preceding faultless aggregates are related to subsequent faultless aggregates by strong-dependence condition. Adaptation to change-of-lineage ; adaptation to purification ; change-of-lineage to Path ; purification is related to Path by strong-dependence condition.

(c) *Natural strong-dependence* : By the strong-dependence of confidence, (one) offers the offering, undertakes the precept, fulfils the duty of observance, develops jhāna, develops insight, develops Path, develops superknowledge, develops attainment. ... precept ... learning ... generosity. ... By the strong-dependence of wisdom, (one) offers the offering, undertakes the precept, fulfils the duty of observance, develops jhāna, develops insight, develops Path, develops superknowledge, develops attainment. Confidence, precept, learning, generosity, wisdom is related to confidence, precept, learning, generosity, wisdom by strong-dependence condition.

The preparation for first jhāna is related to first jhāna by strong-dependence condition ; the preparation for second jhāna is related to second jhāna by strong-dependence condition ; the preparation for third jhāna is related to third jhāna by strong-dependence condition ; the preparation for fourth jhāna is related to fourth jhāna by strong-dependence condition ; the preparation for infinity of space is related to infinity of space by strong-dependence condition ; the preparation for infinity of consciousness is related to infinity of consciousness by strong-dependence condition ; the preparation for nothingness is related to nothingness by strong-dependence condition ; the preparation for neither-perception-nor-non-perception is related to neither-perception-nor-non-perception by strong-dependence condition.

First jhāna is related to second jhāna by strong-dependence condition ; second jhāna is related to third jhāna by strong-dependence condition ; third jhāna is related to fourth jhāna by strong-dependence condition ; fourth jhāna is related to infinity of space by strong-dependence condition ; infinity of space is related to infinity of consciousness by strong-dependence condition ; infinity of consciousness is related to nothingness by strong-dependence condition ; nothingness is related to neither-perception-nor-non-perception by strong-dependence condition.

The preparation for divine-eye is related to divine-eye by strong-dependence condition ; the preparation for divine-ear element is related to divine-ear element by strong-dependence condition ; the preparation for knowledge of supernormal power is related to knowledge of supernormal power by strong-dependence condition ; the preparation for knowledge of penetration into others' minds is related to knowledge of penetration into others' minds by strong-dependence condition ; the preparation for knowledge of remembrance of past existences is related to knowledge of remembrance of past existences by strong-dependence condition ; the preparation for knowledge of rebirths according to one's kamma is related to knowledge of rebirths according to one's kamma by strong-dependence condition ; the preparation for knowledge of future existences is related to knowledge of future existences by strong-dependence condition.

Divine-eye is related to divine-ear element by strong dependence condition ; divine-ear element is related to knowledge of supernormal power by strong-dependence condition ; knowledge of supernormal power is related to knowledge of penetration into others' minds by strong-dependence condition ; knowledge of penetration into others' minds is related to knowledge of remembrance of past existences by strong-dependence condition ; knowledge of remembrance of past existences is related to knowledge of rebirths according to one's kamma by strong-dependence condition ; knowledge of rebirths according to one's kamma is related to knowledge of future existences by strong-dependence condition.

The preparation for first Path is related to first Path by

strong-dependence condition ; the preparation for second Path is related to second Path by strong-dependence condition ; the preparation for third Path is related to third Path by strong-dependence condition ; the preparation for fourth Path is related to fourth Path by strong-dependence condition.

First Path is related to second Path by strong-dependence condition ; second Path is related to third Path by strong-dependence condition ; third Path is related to fourth Path by strong-dependence condition.

Learners, by the strong-dependence of the Path, generate the attainments which have not yet arisen. (They) enter the attainments which have arisen. (They) practise insight into the impermanency, suffering and impersonality of the formations. The (lower) Path is related to the Learner's analytical knowledge of meaning, analytical knowledge of the Dhamma, analytical knowledge of language, analytical knowledge of the above three, knowledge of correct and faulty conclusion by strong-dependence condition.

(ii) Faultless state is related to faulty state by strong-dependence condition.

(It is of two kinds, namely :) (*a*) object-strong-dependence, (*b*) natural strong-dependence.

(*a*) *Object-strong-dependence* : After having offered the offering, having undertaken the precept, having fulfilled the duty of observance, (one) esteems, enjoys and delights in it. Taking it as estimable object, arises lust, arises wrong views. (One) esteems, enjoys and delights in (the faultless acts) formerly well done. Taking it as estimable object, arises lust, arises wrong views. Having emerged from jhāna, (one) esteems, enjoys and delights in the jhāna. Taking it as estimable object, arises lust, arises wrong views.

(*b*) *Natural strong-dependence* : By the strong-dependence of confidence, (one) arouses conceit, adopts wrong views. . . . precept . . . learning . . . generosity. . . . By the strong-dependence of wisdom, (one) arouses conceit, adopts wrong views. Confidence, precept, learning, generosity, wisdom is related to lust, hate, delusion, conceit, wrong views, wish by strong-dependence condition.

(iii) Faultless state is related to indeterminate state by strong-dependence condition.

(It is of three kinds, namely :) (*a*) object-strong-dependence, (*b*) proximity-strong-dependence, (*c*) natural strong-dependence.

(*a*) *Object-strong-dependence* : Having emerged from (Arahatta) Path, the Arahat esteems and reviews the Path.

(*b*) *Proximity-strong-dependence* : Faultless (impulsion) to emergence ; Path to Fruition ; adaptation to attainment of Fruition of the Learners ; having emerged from the attainment of Extinction, faultless neither-perception-nor-non-perception is related to the attainment of Fruition by strong-dependence condition.

(*c*) *Natural strong-dependence* : By the strong-dependence of confidence, (one) tortures oneself, tortures oneself fully, experiences the suffering caused by searching. . . . precept . . . learning . . . generosity. . . . By the strong-dependence of wisdom, (one) tortures oneself, tortures oneself fully, experiences the suffering caused by searching. Confidence, precept, learning, generosity, wisdom is related to bodily happiness, bodily pain, attainment of Fruition by strong-dependence condition. Faultless kamma is related to (its) resultant by strong-dependence condition.

The Arahat, by the strong-dependence of the Path, generates the functional attainment which has not yet arisen. (He) enters (the functional attainment) which has arisen. (He) practises insight into the impermanency, suffering and impersonality of the formations. The (Arahatta) Path is related to the Arahat's analytical knowledge of meaning, analytical knowledge of the Dhamma, analytical knowledge of language, analytical knowledge of the above three, knowledge of correct and faulty conclusion by strong-dependence condition. Path is related to the attainment of Fruition by strong-dependence condition. (3)

(iv) Faulty state is related to faulty state by strong-dependence condition.

(It is of three kinds, namely :) (*a*) object-strong-dependence, (*b*) proximity-strong-dependence, (*c*) natural strong-dependence.

(*a*) *Object-strong-dependence* : (One) esteems, enjoys and delights in lust. Taking it as estimable object, arises lust, arises wrong views. (One) esteems, enjoys and delights in wrong views. Taking it as estimable object, arises lust, arises wrong views.

(b) *Proximity-strong-dependence*: Preceding faulty aggregates are related to subsequent faulty aggregates by strong-dependence condition.

(c) *Natural strong-dependence*: By the strong-dependence of lust, (one) kills a living being, takes the property of others which has not been given to one, speaks untruth, slanders, uses rude speech, babbles foolishly, breaks into a house, plunders the property of others, leaves behind only one house, stands at the junction of highways, goes to other men's wives, plunders villages, plunders market-towns, commits matricide, commits patricide, kills an Arahat, draws blood from the body of a Buddha with evil intent, causes schism in the Saṅgha.

By the strong-dependence of hate . . . By the strong-dependence of delusion . . . By the strong-dependence of conceit . . . By the strong-dependence of wrong views . . . By the strong-dependence of wish, (one) kills a living being . . . causes schism in the Saṅgha. Lust, hate, delusion, conceit, wrong views, wish is related to lust, hate, delusion, conceit, wrong views, wish by strong-dependence condition.

Killing is related to killing by strong-dependence condition. Killing (is related) to stealing . . . unlawful intercourse with the other sex . . . lying . . . slander . . . rude speech .. . foolish babble . . . avarice . . . ill-will . . . (killing) is related to wrong views by strong-dependence condition.

Stealing (is related) to stealing . . . unlawful intercourse with the other sex . . . lying (Abbreviated.) wrong views . . . (stealing) is related to killing by strong-dependence condition. (Bind the cycle.) Unlawful intercourse with the other sex . . . Lying . . . Slander . . . Rude speech . . . Foolish babble . . . Avarice . . . Ill-will . . . Wrong views is related to wrong views by strong-dependence condition. Wrong views to killing . . . stealing . . . unlawful intercourse with the other sex . . . lying . . . slander . . . rude speech . . . foolish babble . . . avarice . . . (wrong views) is related to ill-will by strong-dependence condition.

Matricide is related to matricide by strong-dependence condition. Matricide to patricide by strong-dependence . . . killing an Arahat . . . wounding a Buddha . . . causing schism in the Saṅgha . . . (matricide) is related to wrong views with fixed destiny by strong-dependence condition.

Patricide to patricide . . . killing an Arahat . . . wounding a Buddha . . . causing schism in the Saṅgha . . . wrong views with fixed destiny . . . (patricide) is related to matricide by strong-dependence condition.

Killing an Arahat to killing an Arahat . . . wounding a Buddha . . .

Wounding a Buddha to wounding a Buddha . . .

Causing schism in the Saṅgha to causing schism in the Sangha . . .

Wrong views with fixed destiny is related to wrong views with fixed destiny by strong-dependence condition. Wrong views with fixed destiny to matricide by strong-dependence . . . killing an Arahat . . . wounding a Buddha . . . is related to causing schism in the Saṅgha by strong-dependence condition. (Perform the cycle.)

(v) Faulty state is related to faultless state by strong-dependence condition.

Natural strong-dependence : By the strong-dependence of lust, (one) offers the offering, undertakes the precept, fulfils the duty of observance, develops jhāna, develops insight, develops Path, develops superknowledge, develops attainment. . . . hate . . . delusion . . . conceit . . . wrong views. . . . By the strong-dependence of wish, (one) offers the offering, undertakes the precept, fulfils the duty of observance, develops jhāna, develops insight, develops Path, develops superknowledge, develops attainment. Lust, hate, delusion, conceit, wrong views, wish is related to confidence, precept, learning, generosity, wisdom by strong-dependence condition.

After having killed, (one) offers the offering, undertakes the precept, fulfils the duty of observance, develops jhāna, develops insight, develops Path, develops superknowledge, develops attainment, to counteract it.

After having stolen . . . lied . . . slandered . . . used rude speech . . . babbled foolishly . . . broken into a house . . . plundered the property of others . . . left behind only one house . . . stood at the junction of highways . . . gone to other men's wives . . . plundered villages. . . . After having plundered market-towns, (one) offers the offering, undertakes the precept, fulfils the duty of observance, develops jhāna, develops insight, develops Path, develops superknowledge, develops attainment, to counteract it.

After having committed matricide, (one) offers the offering, undertakes the precept, fulfils the duty of observance, to counteract it. After having committed patricide . . . killed an Arahat . . . drawn blood from the body of a Buddha with evil intent. . . . After having caused schism in the Saṅgha, (one) offers the offering, undertakes the precept, fulfils the duty of observance, to counteract it.

(vi) Faulty state is related to indeterminate state by strong-dependence condition.

(It is of two kinds, namely :) (*a*) proximity-strong-dependence, (*b*) natural strong-dependence.

(*a*) *Proximity-strong-dependence* : Faulty (impulsion) is related to emergence by strong-dependence condition.

(*b*) *Natural strong-dependence* : By the strong-dependence of lust, (one) tortures oneself, tortures oneself fully, experiences the suffering caused by searching. . . . hate . . . delusion . . . conceit . . . wrong views. . . . By the strong-dependence of wish, (one) tortures oneself, tortures oneself fully, experiences the suffering caused by searching. Lust, hate, delusion, conceit, wrong views, wish is related to bodily happiness, bodily pain, attainment of Fruition by strong-dependence condition. Faulty kamma is related to (its) resultant by strong-dependence condition. (3)

(vii) Indeterminate state is related to indeterminate state by strong-dependence condition.

(It is of three kinds, namely :) (*a*) object-strong-dependence, (*b*) proximity-strong-dependence, (*c*) natural strong-dependence.

(*a*) *Object-strong-dependence* : The Arahat esteems and reviews (Arahatta) Fruition. (He) esteems and reviews Nibbāna. Nibbāna is related to Fruition by strong-dependence condition.

(*b*) *Proximity-strong-dependence* : Preceding resultant indeterminate or functional indeterminate aggregates are related to subsequent resultant indeterminate or functional indeterminate aggregates by strong-dependence condition. Life-continuum to advertence ; functional (impulsion) to emergence ; adaptation of the Arahat to attainment of Fruition (of the Arahat); having emerged from the attainment of Extinction, functional neither-perception-nor-non-perception is related to the attainment of the Fruition by strong-dependence condition.

(c) *Natural strong-dependence*: Bodily happiness is related to bodily happiness, bodily pain, attainment of Fruition by strong-dependence condition. Bodily pain is related to bodily happiness, bodily pain, attainment of Fruition by strong-dependence condition. Temperature is related to bodily happiness, bodily pain, attainment of Fruition by strong-dependence condition. Food is related to bodily happiness, bodily pain, attainment of Fruition by strong-dependence condition. Lodging-place is related to bodily happiness, bodily pain, attainment of Fruition by strong-dependence condition. Bodily happiness, bodily pain, temperature, food, lodging-place is related to bodily happiness, bodily pain, attainment of Fruition by strong-dependence condition. Attainment of Fruition is related to bodily happiness by strong-dependence condition.

The Arahat, by the strong-dependence of bodily happiness, generates the functional attainment which has not yet arisen, (He) enters the (functional) attainment which has arisen, (He) practises insight into the impermanency, suffering and impersonality of the formations. ... bodily pain ... temperature ... food ... by the strong-dependence of lodging-place, generates the functional attainment which has not yet arisen, enters the (functional) attainment which has arisen, practises insight into the impermanency, suffering and impersonality of the formations.

(viii) Indeterminate state is related to faultless state by strong-dependence condition.

(It is of three kinds, namely :) (a) object-strong-dependence, (b) proximity-strong-dependence, (c) natural strong-dependence.

(a) *Object-strong-dependence*: Learners esteem and review ((lower) Fruition. (They) esteem and review Nibbāna. Nibbāna is related to change-of-lineage, purification, Path by strong-dependence condition.

(b) *Proximity-strong-dependence*: Advertence is related to faultless aggregates by strong-dependence condition.

(c) *Natural strong-dependence* : By the strong-dependence of bodily happiness, (one) offers the offering, undertakes the precept, fulfils the duty of observance, develops jhāna, develops insight, develops Path, develops superknowledge, develops attainment. ... bodily pain ... temperature ... food. ... By the strong-dependence of lodging-place, (one) offers the offering, undertakes the precept, fulfils the duty of observance, develops jhāna, develops insight, develops Path, develops superknowledge, develops attainment. Bodily happiness, bodily pain, temperature, food, lodging-place is related to confidence, precept, learning, generosity, wisdom by strong-dependence condition.

(ix) Indeterminate state is related to faulty state by strong-dependence condition.

(It is of three kinds, namely :) (*a*) object-strong-dependence, (*b*) proximity-strong-dependence, (*c*) natural strong-dependence.

(*a*) *Object-strong-dependence* : (One) esteems, enjoys and delights in the eye. Taking it as estimable object, arises lust, arises wrong views. ... ear ... nose ... tongue ... body ... visible object ... sound ... smell ... taste ... tangible object ... (heart-)base. ... (One) esteems, enjoys and delights in the resultant indeterminate or functional indeterminate aggregates. Taking it as estimable object, arises lust, arises wrong views.

(*b*) *Proximity-strong-dependence* : Advertence is related to faulty aggregates by strong-dependence condition.

(*c*) *Natural strong-dependence* : By the strong-dependence of bodily happiness, (one) kills a living being, takes the property of others which has not been given to one, speaks untruth, slanders, uses rude speech, babbles foolishly, breaks into a house, plunders the property of others, leaves behind only one house, stands at the junction of highways, goes to other men's wives, plunders villages, plunders market-towns, commits matricide, commits patricide, kills an Arahat, draws blood from the body of a Buddha with evil intent, causes schism in the Saṅgha.

... bodily pain ... temperature ... food. ... By the strong-dependence of lodging-place, (one) kills a living being ... (Abbreviated.) ... causes schism in the Saṅgha. Bodily happiness, bodily pain, temperature, food, lodging-place is related to lust, hate, delusion, conceit, wrong views, wish by strong-dependence condition. (3)

Prenascence 3

424. (i) Indeterminate state is related to indeterminate state by prenascence condition.

(It is of two kinds, namely :) (*a*) object-prenascence, (*b*) base-prenascence.

(*a*) *Object-prenascence* : The Arahat practises insight into the impermanency, suffering and impersonality of the eye. . . . ear . . . nose . . . tongue . . . body . . . visible object . . . sound . . . smell . . . taste . . . tangible object. . . . (He) practises insight into the impermanency, suffering and impersonality of the (heart-)base. (The Arahat), by the power of divine-eye, sees the visible object. By the power of divine-ear element, hears the sound.

Visible object-base is related to eye-consciousness by prenascence condition ; sound-base to ear-consciousness . . . smell-base to nose-consciousness . . . taste-base to tongue-consciousness . . . tangible object-base is related to body-consciousness by prenascence condition.

(*b*) *Base-prenascence* : Eye-base is related to eye-consciousness by prenascence condition ; ear-base to ear-consciousness . . . nose-base to nose-consciousness . . . tongue-base to tongue-consciousness . . . body-base is related to body-consciousness by prenascence condition ; (heart-)base is related to resultant indeterminate or functional indeterminate aggregates by prenascence condition.

(ii) Indeterminate state is related to faultless state by prenascence condition.

(It is of two kinds, namely :) (*a*) object-prenascence, (*b*) base-prenascence.

(*a*) *Object-prenascence* : Learners or common worldlings practise insight into the impermanency, suffering and impersonality of the eye. . . . ear . . . nose . . . tongue . . . body . . . visible object . . . sound . . . smell . . . taste . . . tangible object . . . (they) practise insight into the impermanency, suffering and impersonality of the (heart-)base. (Learners or common worldlings), by the power of divine-eye, see the visible object. By the power of divine-ear element, hear the sound.

(b) *Base-prenascence*: (Heart-)base is related to faultless aggregates by prenascence condition.

(iii) Indeterminate state is related to faulty state by prenascence condition.

(It is of two kinds, namely :) (a) object-prenascence, (b) base-prenascence.

(a) *Object-prenascence*: (One) enjoys and delights in the eye. Taking it as object, arises lust, arises wrong views, arises doubt, arises restlessness, arises grief. ... ear ... nose ... tongue ... body ... visible object ... sound ... smell ... taste ... tangible object. ... (One) enjoys and delights in the (heart-)base. Taking it as object, arises lust ... arises grief.

(b) *Base-prenascence*: (Heart-)base is related to faulty aggregates by prenascence condition. (3)

Postnascence 3

425. (i) Faultless state is related to indeterminate state by postnascence condition.

Postnascent faultless aggregates are related to this prenascent body by postnascence condition.

(ii) Faulty state is related to indeterminate state by postnascence condition.

Postnascent faulty aggregates are related to this prenascent body by postnascence condition.

(iii) Indeterminate state is related to indeterminate state by postnascence condition.

Postnascent resultant indeterminate or functional indeterminate aggregates are related to this prenascent body by postnascence condition.

Repetition 3

426. (i) Faultless state is related to faultless state by repetition condition.

Preceding faultless aggregates are related to subsequent

faultless aggregates by repetition condition. Adaptation to change-of-lineage ; adaptation to purification ; change-of-lineage to Path ; purification is related to Path by repetition condition. (1)

(ii) Faulty state is related to faulty state by repetition condition.

Preceding faulty aggregates are related to subsequent faulty aggregates by repetition condition. (1)

(iii) Indeterminate state is related to indeterminate state by repetition condition.

Preceding functional indeterminate aggregates are related to subsequent functional indeterminate aggregates by repetition condition. (1)

Kamma 7

427. (i) Faultless state is related to faultless state by kamma condition.

Faultless volition is related to (its) associated aggregates by kamma condition.

(ii) Faultless state is related to indeterminate state by kamma condition.

(It is of two kinds, namely :) (*a*) conascence(-kamma), (*b*) asynchronous (kamma).

(*a*) Conascent faultless volition is related to mind-produced matter by kamma condition.

(*b*) Asynchronous faultless volition is related to (its) resultant aggregates and kamma-produced matter by kamma condition.

(iii) Faultless state is related to faultless and indeterminate state by kamma condition.

Faultless volition is related to (its) associated aggregates and mind-produced matter by kamma condition. (3)

(iv) Faulty state is related to faulty state by kamma condition.

Faulty volition is related to (its) associated aggregates by kamma condition.

(v) Faulty state is related to indeterminate state by kamma condition.

(It is of two kinds, namely :) (*a*) conascence(-kamma), (*b*) asynchronous (kamma).

(*a*) Conascent faulty volition is related to mind-produced matter by kamma condition.

(*b*) Asynchronous faulty volition is related to (its) resultant aggregates and kamma-produced matter by kamma condition.

(vi) Faulty state is related to faulty and indeterminate state by kamma condition.

Faulty volition is related to (its) associated aggregates and mind-produced matter by kamma condition. (3)

(vii) Indeterminate state is related to indeterminate state by kamma condition.

(*a*) Resultant indeterminate or functional indeterminate volition is related to (its) associated aggregates and mind-produced matter by kamma condition;

(*b*) At the moment of conception, resultant indeterminate volition is related to (its) associated aggregates and kamma-produced matter by kamma condition; volition is related to (heart-)base by kamma condition. (1)

Resultant 1

428. Indeterminate state is related to indeterminate state by resultant condition.

(*a*) One resultant indeterminate aggregate is related to three aggregates and mind-produced matter by resultant condition; three aggregates are related to one aggregate and mind-produced matter by resultant condition; two aggregates are related to two aggregates and mind-produced matter by resultant condition.

(*b*) At the moment of conception, one resultant indeterminate aggregate is related to three aggregates and kamma-produced matter by resultant condition; three aggregates are related to one aggregate and kamma-produced matter by resultant condition; two aggregates are related to two aggregates and kamma-produced matter by resultant condition; aggregates are related to (heart-)base by resultant condition. (1)

Nutriment 7

429. (i) Faultless state is related to faultless state by nutriment condition.

Faultless nutriments are related to (their) associated aggregates by nutriment condition.

(ii) Faultless state is related to indeterminate state by nutriment condition.

Faultless nutriments are related to mind-produced matter by nutriment condition.

(iii) Faultless state is related to faultless and indeterminate state by nutriment condition.

Faultless nutriments are related to (their) associated aggregates and mind-produced matter by nutriment condition. (3)

(iv) Faulty state is related to faulty state by nutriment condition.

Faulty nutriments are related to (their) associated aggregates by nutriment condition.

(v) Faulty state is related to indeterminate state by nutriment condition.

Faulty nutriments are related to mind-produced matter by nutriment condition.

(vi) Faulty state is related to faulty and indeterminate state by nutriment condition.

Faulty nutriments are related to (their) associated aggregates and mind-produced matter by nutriment condition. (3)

(vii) Indeterminate state is related to indeterminate state by nutriment condition.

(*a*) Resultant indeterminate or functional indeterminate nutriments are related to (their) associated aggregates and mind-produced matter by nutriment condition;

(*b*) At the moment of conception, resultant indeterminate nutriments are related to (their) associated aggregates and kamma-produced matter by nutriment condition;

(*c*) Edible food is related to this body by nutriment condition. (1)

Faculty 7

430. (i) Faultless state is related to faultless state by faculty condition.

Faultless faculties are related to (their) associated aggregates by faculty condition.

(ii) Faultless state is related to indeterminate state by faculty condition.
Faultless faculties are related to mind-produced matter by faculty condition.
   (iii) Faultless state is related to faultless and indeterminate state by faculty condition.
Faultless faculties are related to (their) associated aggregates and mind-produced matter by faculty condition. (3)
   (iv) Faulty state is related to faulty state by faculty condition.
Faulty faculties are related to (their) associated aggregates by faculty condition.
   (v) Faulty state is related to indeterminate state by faculty condition.
Faulty faculties are related to mind-produced matter by faculty condition.
   (vi) Faulty state is related to faulty and indeterminate state by faculty condition.
Faulty faculties are related to (their) associated aggregates and mind-produced matter by faculty condition. (3)
   (vii) Indeterminate state is related to indeterminate state by faculty condition.
(a) Resultant indeterminate or functional indeterminate faculties are related to (their) associated aggregates and mind-produced matter by faculty condition ;
(b) At the moment of conception, resultant indeterminate faculties are related to (their) associated aggregates and kamma-produced matter by faculty condition ;
(c) Eye-faculty is related to eye-consciousness by faculty condition ; ear-faculty to ear-consciousness ... nose-faculty to nose-consciousness ... tongue-faculty to tongue-consciousness ... body-faculty is related to body-consciousness by faculty condition ;
(d) Physical life-faculty is related to kamma-produced matter by faculty condition. (1)

Jhāna 7

431. (i) Faultless state is related to faultless state by jhāna condition.

Faultless jhāna factors are related to (their) associated aggregates by jhāna condition.

(ii) Faultless state is related to indeterminate state by jhāna condition.

Faultless jhāna factors are related to mind-produced matter by jhāna condition.

(iii) Faultless state is related to faultless and indeterminate state by jhāna condition.

Faultless jhāna factors are related to (their) associated aggregates and mind-produced matter by jhāna condition. (3)

(iv) Faulty state is related to faulty state by jhāna condition.

Faulty jhāna factors are related to (their) associated aggregates by jhāna condition.

(v) Faulty state is related to indeterminate state by jhāna condition.

Faulty jhāna factors are related to mind-produced matter by jhāna condition.

(vi) Faulty state is related to faulty and indeterminate state by jhāna condition.

Faulty jhāna factors are related to (their) associated aggregates and mind-produced matter by jhāna condition. (3)

(vii) Indeterminate state is related to indeterminate state by jhāna condition.

(*a*) Resultant indeterminate or functional indeterminate jhāna factors are related to (their) associated aggregates and mind-produced matter by jhāna condition ;

(*b*) At the moment of conception, resultant indeterminate jhāna factors are related to (their) associated aggregates and kamma-produced matter by jhāna condition. (1)

Path 7

432. (i) Faultless state is related to faultless state by path condition.

Faultless path factors are related to (their) associated aggregates by path condition.

(ii) Faultless state is related to indeterminate state by path condition.

Faultless path factors are related to mind-produced matter by path condition.

(iii) Faultless state is related to faultless and indeterminate state by path condition.

Faultless path factors are related to (their) associated aggregates and mind-produced matter by path condition. (3)

(iv) Faulty state is related to faulty state by path condition.

Faulty path factors are related to (their) associated aggregates by path condition.

(v) Faulty state is related to indeterminate state by path condition.

Faulty path factors are related to mind-produced matter by path condition.

(vi) Faulty state is related to faulty and indeterminate state by path condition.

Faulty path factors are related to (their) associated aggregates and mind-produced matter by path condition. (3)

(vii) Indeterminate state is related to indeterminate state by path condition.

(*a*) Resultant indeterminate or functional indeterminate path factors are related to (their) associated aggregates and mind-produced matter by path condition ;

(*b*) At the moment of conception, resultant indeterminate path factors are related to (their) associated aggregates and kamma-produced matter by path condition. (1)

Association 3

433. (i) Faultless state is related to faultless state by association condition.

One faultless aggregate is related to three aggregates by association condition ; three aggregates are related to one aggregate by association condition ; two aggregates are related to two aggregates by association condition.

(ii) Faulty state is related to faulty state by association condition.

One faulty aggregate is related to three aggregates by association condition ; three aggregates are related to one aggregate by association condition ; two aggregates are related to two aggregates by association condition.

(iii) Indeterminate state is related to indeterminate state by association condition.

(a) One resultant indeterminate or functional indeterminate aggregate is related to three aggregates by association condition ; three aggregates are related to one aggregate by association condition ; two aggregates are related to two aggregates by association condition ;

(b) At the moment of conception, one resultant indeterminate aggregate is related to three aggregates by association condition ; three aggregates are related to one aggregate by association condition ; two aggregates are related to two aggregates by association condition.

Dissociation 5

434. (i) Faultless state is related to indeterminate state by dissociation condition.

(It is of two kinds, namely :) (a) conascence, (b) postnascence.

(a) Conascent faultless aggregates are related to mind-produced matter by dissociation condition.

(b) Postnascent faultless aggregates are related to this prenascent body by dissociation condition. (1)

(ii) Faulty state is related to indeterminate state by dissociation condition.

(It is of two kinds, namely :) (a) conascence, (b) postnascence.

(a) Conascent faulty aggregates are related to mind-produced matter by dissociation condition.

(b) Postnascent faulty aggregates are related to this prenascent body by dissociation condition. (1)

(iii) Indeterminate state is related to indeterminate state by dissociation condition.

(It is of three kinds, namely :) (a) conascence, (b) prenascence, (c) postnascence.

(a) Conascent resultant indeterminate or functional indeterminate aggregates are related to mind-produced matter by dissociation condition ;

At the moment of conception, resultant indeterminate aggregates are related to kamma-produced matter by dissociation condition ; aggregates are related to (heart-)base by dissociation condition ; (heart-)base is related to aggregates by dissociation condition.

(b) Prenascent eye-base is related to eye-consciousness by dissociation condition ; ear-base is related to ear-consciousness by dissociation condition ; nose-base is related to nose-consciousness by dissociation condition ; tongue-base is related to tongue-consciousness by dissociation condition ; body-base is related to body-consciousness by dissociation condition ; (heart-)base is related to resultant indeterminate or functional indeterminate aggregates by dissociation condition.

(c) Postnascent resultant indeterminate or functional indeterminate aggregates are related to this prenascent body by dissociation condition.

(iv) Indeterminate state is related to faultless state by dissociation condition.

Prenascent (heart-)base is related to faultless aggregates by dissociation condition.

(v) Indeterminate state is related to faulty state by dissociation condition.

Prenascent (heart-)base is related to faulty aggregates by dissociation condition. (3)

Presence 13

435. (i) Faultless state is related to faultless state by presence condition.

One faultless aggregate is related to three aggregates by presence condition ; three aggregates are related to one aggregate by presence condition ; two aggregates are related to two aggregates by presence condition.

(ii) Faultless state is related to indeterminate state by presence condition.

(It is of two kinds, namely :) (a) conascence, (b) postnascence.

(a) Conascent faultless aggregates are related to mind-produced matter by presence condition.

(b) Postnascent faultless aggregates are related to this prenascent body by presence condition.

(iii) Faultless state is related to faultless and indeterminate state by presence condition.

One faultless aggregate is related to three aggregates and

mind-produced matter by presence condition ; three aggregates are related to one aggregate and mind-produced matter by presence condition ; two aggregates are related to two aggregates and mind-produced matter by presence condition. (3)

(iv) Faulty state is related to faulty state by presence condition.

One faulty aggregate is related to three aggregates by presence condition ; three aggregates are related to one aggregate by presence condition ; two aggregates are related to two aggregates by presence condition.

(v) Faulty state is related to indeterminate state by presence condition.

(It is of two kinds, namely :) (*a*) conascence, (*b*) postnascence.

(*a*) Conascent faulty aggregates are related to mind-produced matter by presence condition.

(*b*) Postnascent faulty aggregates are related to this prenascent body by presence condition.

(vi) Faulty state is related to faulty and indeterminate state by presence condition.

One faulty aggregate is related to three aggregates and mind-produced matter by presence condition ; three aggregates are related to one aggregate and mind-produced matter by presence condition ; two aggregates are related to two aggregates and mind-produced matter by presence condition. (3)

(vii) Indeterminate state is related to indeterminate state by presence condition.

(It is of five kinds, namely :) (*a*) conascence, (*b*) prenascence, (*c*) postnascence, (*d*) nutriment, (*e*) faculty.

(*a*) (1) One conascent resultant indeterminate or functional indeterminate aggregate is related to three aggregates and mind-produced matter by presence condition ; three aggregates are related to one aggregate and mind-produced matter by presence condition ; two aggregates are related to two aggregates and mind-produced matter by presence condition ;

(2) At the moment of conception, one resultant indeterminate aggregate is related to three aggregates and kamma-produced matter by presence condition ; three aggregates are related to one aggregate and kamma-produced matter by presence condition ; two aggregates are related to two

aggregates and kamma-produced matter by presence condition; aggregates are related to (heart-)base by presence condition; (heart-)base is related to aggregates by presence condition;

(3) One great primary is related to three great primaries by presence condition; three great primaries are related to one great primary by presence condition; two great primaries are related to two great primaries by presence condition; great primaries are related to mind-produced and kamma-produced derived matter by presence condition;

External . . . nutriment-produced . . . temperature-produced . . . one great primary of non-percipient beings is related to three great primaries by presence condition; three great primaries are related to one great primary by presence condition; two great primaries are related to two great primaries by presence condition; great primaries are related to kamma-produced derived matter by presence condition.

(b) (*Object-*)*prenascence*: The Arahat practises insight into the impermanency, suffering and impersonality of the eye. . . . ear . . . nose . . . tongue . . . body . . . visible object . . . sound . . . smell . . . taste . . . tangible object. . . . (He) practises insight into the impermanency, suffering and impersonality of the (heart-)base. (The Arahat), by the power of divine-eye, sees the visible object. By the power of divine-ear element, hears the sound.

Visible object-base is related to eye-consciousness by presence condition; sound . . . tangible object-base is related to body-consciousness by presence condition.

(*Base-*)*prenascence*: Eye-base is related to eye-consciousness by presence condition; ear-base to ear-consciousness . . . nose-base to nose-consciousness . . . tongue-base to tongue-consciousness . . . body-base is related to body-consciousness by presence condition; (heart-)base is related to resultant indeterminate or functional indeterminate aggregates by presence condition.

(c) Postnascent resultant indeterminate or functional indeterminate aggregates are related to this prenascent body by presence condition.

(d) Edible food is related to this body by presence condition.

(e) Physical life-faculty is related to kamma-produced matter by presence condition.

(viii) Indeterminate state is related to faultless state by presence condition.

(*Object-*)*prenascence* : Learners or common worldlings practise insight into the impermanency, suffering and impersonality of the eye. ... ear ... nose ... tongue ... body ... visible object ... sound ... smell ... taste ... tangible object. ... (They) practise insight into the impermanency, suffering and impersonality of the (heart-)base. (Learners or common worldlings), by the power of divine-eye, see the visible object. By the power of divine-ear element, hear the sound.

(*Base-*)*prenascence* : (Heart-)base is related to faultless aggregates by presence condition.

(ix) Indeterminate state is related to faulty state by presence condition.

(*Object-*)*prenascence* : (One) enjoys and delights in the eye. Taking it as object, arises lust, arises wrong views, arises doubt, arises restlessness, arises grief. ... ear ... nose ... tongue ... body ... visible object ... sound ... smell ... taste ... tangible object. ... (One) enjoys and delights in the (heart-)base. Taking it as object, arises lust ... arises grief.

(*Base-*)*prenascence* :) (Heart-)base is related to faulty aggregates by presence condition. (3)

(x) Faultless and indeterminate states are related to faultless state by presence condition.

Conascence—prenascence : One conascent faultless aggregate and (heart-)base are related to three aggregates by presence condition ... two aggregates and (heart-)base are related to two aggregates by presence condition.

(xi) Faultless and indeterminate states are related to indeterminate state by presence condition.

(It is of three kinds, namely :) (*a*) conascence, (*b*) postnascence-nutriment, (*c*) (postnascence-)faculty.

(*a*) Conascent faultless aggregates and great primaries are related to mind-produced matter by presence condition.

(*b*) Postnascent faultless aggregates and edible food are related to this body by presence condition.

(*c*) Postnascent faultless aggregates and physical life-faculty are related to kamma-produced matter by presence condition. (2)

(xii) Faulty and indeterminate states are related to faulty state by presence condition.

Conascence—prenascence: One conascent faulty aggregate and (heart-)base are related to three aggregates by presence condition ; three aggregates and (heart-)base are related to one aggregate by presence condition ; two aggregates and (heart-)base are related to two aggregates by presence condition.

(xiii) Faulty and indeterminate states are related to indeterminate state by presence condition.

(It is of three kinds, namely :) (*a*) conascence, (*b*) postnascence-nutriment, (*c*) (postnascence-)faculty.

(*a*) Conascent faulty aggregates and great primaries are related to mind-produced matter by presence condition.

(*b*) Postnascent faulty aggregates and edible food are related to this body by presence condition.

(*c*) Postnascent faulty aggregates and physical life-faculty are related to kamma-produced matter by presence condition. (2)

Absence 7

436. Faultless state is related to faultless state by absence condition.

Preceding faultless aggregates are related to subsequent faultless aggregates by absence condition . . . (Abbreviated.)

(Expand in the same way as proximity condition.)

Disappearance 7

437. Faultless state is related to faultless state by disappearance condition.

Preceding faultless aggregates are related to subsequent faultless aggregates by disappearance condition . . . (Abbreviated.)

(Expand in the same way as proximity condition.)

Non-disappearance 13

438. Faultless state is related to faultless state by non-disappearance condition.

One faultless aggregate is related to three aggregates by non-disappearance condition ; three aggregates are related to one aggregate by non-disappearance condition ; two aggregates are related to two aggregates by non-disappearance condition . . . (Abbreviated.)

(Expand in the same way as presence condition.)

End of Classification of " Investigation " Chapter.

I. CONDITIONS : POSITIVE   (ii) ENUMERATION CHAPTER

By Ones

439. With root (there are) 7 (answers), object 9, predominance 10, proximity 7, contiguity 7, conascence 9, mutuality 3, dependence 13, strong-dependence 9, prenascence 3, postnascence 3, repetition 3, kamma 7, resultant 1, nutriment 7, faculty 7, jhāna 7, path 7, association 3, dissociation 5, presence 13, absence 7, disappearance 7, non-disappearance 13.

Root

Common 11

440. With root condition and predominance (there are) 4 (answers), conascence 7, mutuality 3, dependence 7, resultant 1, faculty 4, path 4, association 3, dissociation 3, presence 7, non-disappearance 7. (11)

Conascence Combinations 24

Ordinary 9

Without resultant 4

441. 1. Combination of root, conascence, dependence, presence and non-disappearance (has) 7 (answers) ;

2. Of root, conascence, mutuality, dependence, presence and non-disappearance 3 ;

3. Of root, conascence, mutuality, dependence, association, presence and non-disappearance 3 ;

4. Of root, conascence, dependence, dissociation, presence and non-disappearance 3.

With resultant 5

5. Combination of root, conascence, dependence, resultant, presence and non-disappearance 1;

6. Of root, conascence, mutuality, dependence, resultant, presence and non-disappearance 1;

7. Of root, conascence, mutuality, dependence, resultant, association, presence and non-disappearance 1;

8. Of root, conascence, dependence, resultant, dissociation, presence and non-disappearance 1;

9. Of root, conascence, mutuality, dependence, resultant, dissociation, presence and non-disappearance 1.

With faculty and path 9
Without resultant 4

442. 10. Combination of root, conascence, dependence, faculty, path, presence and non-disappearance 4;

11. Of root, conascence, mutuality, dependence, faculty, path, presence and non-disappearance 2;

12. Of root, conascence, mutuality, dependence, faculty, path, association, presence and non-disappearance 2;

13. Of root, conascence, dependence, faculty, path, dissociation, presence and non-disappearance 2.

With resultant 5

14. Combination of root, conascence, dependence, resultant, faculty, path, presence and non-disappearance 1;

15. Of root, conascence, mutuality, dependence, resultant, faculty, path, presence and non-disappearance 1;

16. Of root, conascence, mutuality, dependence, resultant, faculty, path, association, presence and non-disappearance 1;

17. Of root, conascence, dependence, resultant, faculty, path, dissociation, presence and non-disappearance 1;

18. Of root, conascence, mutuality, dependence, resultant, faculty, path, dissociation, presence and non-disappearance 1.

With predominance, faculty and path 6
Without resultant 3

443. 19. Combination of root, predominance, conascence, dependence, faculty, path, presence and non-disappearance 4;

20. Of root, predominance, conascence, mutuality, dependence, faculty, path, association, presence and non-disappearance 2 ;

21. Of root, predominance, conascence, dependence, faculty, path, dissociation, presence and non-disappearance 2.

With resultant 3

22. Combination of root, predominance, conascence, dependence, resultant, faculty, path, presence and non-disappearance 1 ;

23. Of root, predominance, conascence, mutuality, dependence, resultant, faculty, path, association, presence and non-disappearance 1 ;

24. Of root, predominance, conascence, dependence, resultant, faculty, path, dissociation, presence and non-disappearance 1.

End of Root

Object

Common 7

444. With object condition and predominance (there are) 7 (answers), dependence 3, strong-dependence 7, prenascence 3, dissociation 3, presence 3, non-disappearance 3. (7)

(Miscellaneous) Combinations 5

445. 1. Combination of object, predominance and strong-dependence 7 ;

2. Of object, prenascence, presence and non-disappearance 3 ;

3. Of object, dependence, prenascence, dissociation, presence and non-disappearance 3 ;

4. Of object, predominance, strong-dependence, prenascence, presence and non-disappearance 1 ;

5. Of object, predominance, dependence, strong-dependence, prenascence, dissociation, presence and non-disappearance 1.

End of Object

Faultless Triplet

Predominance

Common 15

446. With predominance condition and root (there are) 4 (answers), object 7, conascence 7, mutuality 3, dependence 8, strong-dependence 7, prenascence 1, resultant 1, nutriment 7, faculty 7, path 7, association 3, dissociation 4, presence 8, non-disappearance 8. (15)

Combinations 30

Mixed 3

447. 1. Combination of predominance, presence and non-disappearance (has) 8 (answers) ;

2. Of predominance, dependence, presence and non-disappearance 8 ;

3. Of predominance, dependence, dissociation, presence and non-disappearance 4.

Miscellaneous 3

448. 4. Combination of predominance, object and strong-dependence 7 ;

5. Of predominance, object, strong-dependence, prenascence, presence and non-disappearance 1 ;

6. Of predominance, object, dependence, strong-dependence, prenascence, dissociation, presence and non-disappearance 1.

Conascence 24

Predominant desire 6

Without resultant 3

449. 7. Combination of predominance, conascence, dependence, presence and non-disappearance 7 ;

8. Of predominance, conascence, mutuality, dependence, association, presence and non-disappearance 3 ;

9. Of predominance, conascence, dependence, dissociation, presence and non-disappearance 3.

With resultant 3

10. Combination of predominance, conascence, dependence, resultant, presence and non-disappearance 1 ;

11. Of predominance, conascence, mutuality, dependence, resultant, association, presence and non-disappearance 1 ;

12. Of predominance, conascence, dependence, resultant, dissociation, presence and non-disappearance 1.

With nutriment and faculty 6

Without resultant 3

450. 13. Combination of predominance, conascence, dependence, nutriment, faculty, presence and non-disappearance 7 ;

14. Of predominance, conascence, mutuality, dependence, nutriment, faculty, association, presence and non-disappearance 3 ;

15. Of predominance, conascence, dependence, nutriment, faculty, dissociation, presence and non-disappearance 3.

With resultant 3

16. Combination of predominance, conascence, dependence, resultant, nutriment, faculty, presence and non-disappearance 1 ;

17. Of predominance, conascence, mutuality, dependence, resultant, nutriment, faculty, association, presence and non-disappearance 1 ;

18. Of predominance, conascence, dependence, resultant, nutriment, faculty, dissociation, presence and non-disappearance 1.

With faculty and path 6

Without resultant 3

451. 19. Combination of predominance, conascence, dependence, faculty, path, presence and non-disappearance 7 ;

20. Of predominance, conascence, mutuality, dependence, faculty, path, association, presence and non-disappearance 3 ;

21. Of predominance, conascence, dependence, faculty, path, dissociation, presence and non-disappearance 3.

With resultant 3

22. Combination of predominance, conascence, dependence, resultant, faculty, path, presence and non-disappearance 1;

23. Of predominance, conascence, mutuality, dependence, resultant, faculty, path, association, presence and non-disappearance 1;

24. Of predominance, conascence, dependence, resultant, faculty, path, dissociation, presence and non-disappearance 1.

With root, faculty and path 6

Without resultant 3

452. 25. Combination of predominance, root, conascence, dependence, faculty, path, presence and non-disappearance 4;

26. Of predominance, root, conascence, mutuality, dependence, faculty, path, association, presence and non-disappearance 2;

27. Of predominance, root, conascence, dependence, faculty, path, dissociation, presence and non-disappearance 2.

With resultant 3

28. Combination of predominance, root, conascence, dependence, resultant, faculty, path, presence and non-disappearance 1;

29. Of predominance, root, conascence, mutuality, dependence, resultant, faculty, path, association, presence and non-disappearance 1;

30. Of predominance, root, conascence, dependence, resultant, faculty, path, dissociation, presence and non-disappearance 1.

End of Predominance

Proximity

Common 6

453. With proximity condition and contiguity (there are) 7 (answers), strong-dependence 7, repetition 3, kamma 1, absence 7, disappearance 7. (6)

(*Miscellaneous*) *Combinations 3*

454. 1. Combination of proximity, contiguity, strong-dependence, absence and disappearance 7 ;

2. Of proximity, contiguity, strong-dependence, repetition, absence and disappearance 3 ;

3. Of proximity, contiguity, strong-dependence, kamma, absence and disappearance 1.

End of Proximity

Contiguity

Common 6

455. With contiguity condition and proximity (there are) 7 (answers), strong-dependence 7, repetition 3, kamma 1, absence 7, disappearance 7. (6)

Miscellaneous Combinations 3

456. 1. Combination of contiguity, proximity, strong-dependence, absence and disappearance 7 ;

2. Of contiguity, proximity, strong-dependence, repetition, absence and disappearance 3 ;

3. Of contiguity, proximity, strong-dependence, kamma, absence and disappearance 1.

End of Contiguity

Conascence

Common 14

457. With conascence condition and root 7, predominance 7, mutuality 3, dependence 9, kamma 7, resultant 1, nutriment 7, faculty 7, jhāna 7, path 7, association 3, dissociation 3, presence 9, non-disappearance 9. (14)

Combinations 10

Without resultant 5

458. 1. Combination of conascence, dependence, presence and non-disappearance 9 ;

2. Of conascence, mutuality, dependence, presence and non-disappearance 3 ;

3. Of conascence, mutuality, dependence, association, presence and non-disappearance 3 ;

4. Of conascence, dependence, dissociation, presence and non-disappearance 3 ;

5. Of conascence, mutuality, dependence, dissociation, presence and non-disappearance 1.

With resultant 5

6. Combination of conascence, dependence, resultant, presence and non-disappearance 1 ;

7. Of conascence, mutuality, dependence, resultant, presence and non-disappearance 1 ;

8. Of conascence, mutuality, dependence, resultant, association, presence and non-disappearance 1 ;

9. Of conascence, dependence, resultant, dissociation, presence and non-disappearance 1 ;

10. Of conascence, mutuality, dependence, resultant, dissociation, presence and non-disappearance 1.

End of Conascence

Mutuality

Common 14

459. With mutuality condition and root 3, predominance 3, conascence 3, dependence 3, kamma 3, resultant 1, nutriment 3, faculty 3, jhāna 3, path 3, association 3, dissociation 1, presence 3, non-disappearance 3. (14)

Conascence Combinations 6

Without resultant 3

460. 1. Combination of mutuality, conascence, dependence, presence and non-disappearance 3 ;

2. Of mutuality, conascence, dependence, association, presence and non-disappearance 3 ;

3. Of mutuality, conascence, dependence, dissociation, presence and non-disappearance 1.

With resultant 3

4. Combination of mutuality, conascence, dependence, resultant, presence and non-disappearance 1 ;

5. Of mutuality, conascence, dependence, resultant, association, presence and non-disappearance 1 ;

6. Of mutuality, conascence, dependence, resultant, dissociation, presence and non-disappearance 1.

End of Mutuality

Dependence

Common 17

461. With dependence condition and root 7, object 3, predominance 8, conascence 9, mutuality 3, strong-dependence 1, prenascence 3, kamma 7, resultant 1, nutriment 7, faculty 7, jhāna 7, path 7, association 3, dissociation 5, presence 13, non-disappearance 13. (17)

Combinations 20

Mixed 6

462. 1. Combination of dependence, presence and non-disappearance 13 ;

2. Of dependence, predominance, presence and non-disappearance 8 ;

3. Of dependence, faculty, presence and non-disappearance 7 ;

4. Of dependence, dissociation, presence and non-disappearance 5 ;

5. Of dependence, predominance, dissociation, presence and non-disappearance 4 ;

6. Of dependence, faculty, dissociation, presence and non-disappearance 3.

Miscellaneous 4

463. 7. Combination of dependence, prenascence, dissociation, presence and non-disappearance 3 ;

8. Of dependence, object, prenascence, dissociation, presence and non-disappearance 3 ;

9. Of dependence, object, predominance, strong-dependence, prenascence, dissociation, presence and non-disappearance 1 ;

10. Of dependence, prenascence, faculty, dissociation, presence and non-disappearance 1.

Conascence 10
Without resultant 5

464. 11. Combination of dependence, conascence, presence and non-disappearance 9 ;

12. Of dependence, conascence, mutuality, presence and non-disappearance 3 ;

13. Of dependence, conascence, mutuality, association, presence and non-disappearance 3 ;

14. Of dependence, conascence, dissociation, presence and non-disappearance 3 ;

15. Of dependence, conascence, mutuality, dissociation, presence and non-disappearance 1.

With resultant 5

16. Combination of dependence, conascence, resultant, presence and non-disappearance 1 ;

17. Of dependence, conascence, mutuality, resultant, presence and non-disappearance 1 ;

18. Of dependence, conascence, mutuality, resultant, association, presence and non-disappearance 1 ;

19. Of dependence, conascence, resultant, dissociation, presence and non-disappearance 1 ;

20. Of dependence, conascence, mutuality, resultant, dissociation, presence and non-disappearance 1.

End of Dependence

Strong-dependence
Common 13

465. With strong-dependence condition and object 7, predominance 7, proximity 7, contiguity 7, dependence 1, prenascence 1, repetition 3, kamma 2, dissociation 1, presence 1, absence 7, disappearance 7, non-disappearance 1. (13)

(*Miscellaneous*) *Combinations* 7

466. 1. Combination of strong-dependence, object and predominance 7 ;

2. Of strong-dependence, object, predominance, prenascence, presence and non-disappearance 1 ;

3. Of strong-dependence, object, predominance, dependence, prenascence, dissociation, presence and non-disappearance 1 ;

4. Of strong-dependence, proximity, contiguity, absence and disappearance 7 ;

5. Of strong-dependence, proximity, contiguity, repetition, absence and disappearance 3 ;

6. Of strong-dependence and kamma 2 ;

7. Of strong-dependence, proximity, contiguity, kamma, absence and disappearance 1.

End of Strong-dependence

Prenascence

Common 8

467. With prenascence condition and object 3, predominance 1, dependence 3, strong-dependence 1, faculty 1, dissociation 3, presence 3, non-disappearance 3. (8)

(*Miscellaneous*) *Combinations* 7

468. 1. Combination of prenascence, presence and non-disappearance 3 ;

2. Of prenascence, dependence, dissociation, presence and non-disappearance 3 ;

3 Of prenascence, object, presence and non-disappearance 3 ;

4. Of prenascence, object, dependence, dissociation, presence and non-disappearance 3 ;

5. Of prenascence, object, predominance, strong-dependence, presence and non-disappearance 1 ;

6. Of prenascence, object, predominance, dependence, strong-dependence, dissociation, presence and non-disappearance 1 ;

7. Of prenascence, dependence, faculty, dissociation, presence and non-disappearance 1.

End of Prenascence

Postnascence

Common 3

469. With postnascence condition and dissociation 3, presence 3, non-disappearance 3. (3)

(*Miscellaneous*) *Combination 1*

470. Combination of postnascence, dissociation, presence and non-disappearance 3.

End of Postnascence

Repetition

Common 5

471. With repetition condition and proximity 3, contiguity 3, strong-dependence 3, absence 3, disappearance 3. (5)

(*Miscellaneous*) *Combination 1*

472. Combination of repetition, proximity, contiguity, strong-dependence, absence and disappearance 3.

End of Repetition

Kamma

Common 14

473. With kamma condition and proximity 1, contiguity 1, conascence 7, mutuality 3, dependence 7, strong-dependence 2, resultant 1, nutriment 7, association 3, dissociation 3, presence 7, absence 1, disappearance 1, non-disappearance 7. (14)

Combinations 11

Miscellaneous 2

474. 1. Combination of kamma and strong-dependence 2 ;
   2. Of kamma, proximity, contiguity, strong-dependence, absence and disappearance 1.

Conascence 9

With nutriment 9

Without resultant 4 [1]

475. 3. Combination of kamma, conascence, dependence, nutriment, presence and non-disappearance 7;

4. Of kamma, conascence, mutuality, dependence, nutriment, presence and non-disappearance 3;

5. Of kamma, conascence, mutuality, dependence, nutriment, association, presence and non-disappearance 3;

6. Of kamma, conascence, dependence, nutriment, dissociation, presence and non-disappearance 3.

With resultant 5 [1]

7. Combination of kamma, conascence, dependence, resultant, nutriment, presence and non-disappearance 1;

8. Of kamma, conascence, mutuality, dependence, resultant, nutriment, presence and non-disappearance 1;

9. Of kamma, conascence, mutuality, dependence, resultant, nutriment, association, presence and non-disappearance 1;

10. Of kamma, conascence, dependence, resultant, nutriment, dissociation, presence and non-disappearance 1;

11. Of kamma, conascence, mutuality, dependence, resultant, nutriment, dissociation, presence and non-disappearance 1.

End of Kamma

Resultant

Common 14

476. With resultant condition and root 1, predominance 1, conascence 1, mutuality 1, dependence 1, kamma 1, nutriment 1, faculty 1, jhāna 1, path 1, association 1, dissociation 1, presence 1, non-disappearance 1. (14)

(Conascence) Combinations 5

477. 1. Combination of resultant, conascence, dependence, presence and non-disappearance 1;

[1] Not " 3 " as in the Text.

2. Of resultant, conascence, mutuality, dependence, presence and non-disappearance 1;

3. Of resultant, conascence, mutuality, dependence, association, presence and non-disappearance 1;

4. Of resultant, conascence, dependence, dissociation, presence and non-disappearance 1;

5. Of resultant, conascence, mutuality, dependence, dissociation, presence and non-disappearance 1.

End of Resultant

Nutriment

Common 11

478. With nutriment condition and predominance 7, conascence 7, mutuality 3, dependence 7, kamma 7, resultant 1, faculty 7, association 3, dissociation 3, presence 7, non-disappearance 7. (11)

Combinations 34

Mixed 1

479. 1. Combination of nutriment, presence and non-disappearance 7.

Conascence 33

Ordinary 9

Without resultant 4

480. 2. Combination of nutriment, conascence, dependence, presence and non-disappearance 7;

3. Of nutriment, conascence, mutuality, dependence, presence and non-disappearance 3;

4. Of nutriment, conascence, mutuality, dependence, association, presence and non-disappearance 3;

5. Of nutriment, conascence, dependence, dissociation, presence and non-disappearance 3.

With resultant 5

6. Combination of nutriment, conascence, dependence, resultant, presence and non-disappearance 1;

7. Of nutriment, conascence, mutuality, dependence, resultant, presence and non-disappearance 1 ;

8. Of nutriment, conascence, mutuality, dependence, resultant, association, presence and non-disappearance 1 ;

9. Of nutriment, conascence, dependence, resultant, dissociation, presence and non-disappearance 1 ;

10. Of nutriment, conascence, mutuality, dependence, resultant, dissociation, presence and non-disappearance 1.

With kamma 9

Without resultant 4

481. 11. Combination of nutriment, conascence, dependence, kamma, presence and non-disappearance 7 ;

12. Of nutriment, conascence, mutuality, dependence, kamma, presence and non-disappearance 3 ;

13. Of nutriment, conascence, mutuality, dependence, kamma, association, presence and non-disappearance 3 ;

14. Of nutriment, conascence, dependence, kamma, dissociation, presence and non-disappearance 3.

With resultant 5

15. Combination of nutriment, conascence, dependence, kamma, resultant, presence and non-disappearance 1 ;

16. Of nutriment, conascence, mutuality, dependence, kamma, resultant, presence and non-disappearance 1 ;

17. Of nutriment, conascence, mutuality, dependence, kamma, resultant, association, presence and non-disappearance 1 ;

18. Of nutriment, conascence, dependence, kamma, resultant, dissociation, presence and non-disappearance 1 ;

19. Of nutriment, conascence, mutuality, dependence, kamma, resultant, dissociation, presence and non-disappearance 1.

With faculty 9

Without resultant 4

482. 20. Combination of nutriment, conascence, dependence, faculty, presence and non-disappearance 7 ;

21. Of nutriment, conascence, mutuality, dependence, faculty, presence and non-disappearance 3 ;

22. Of nutriment, conascence, mutuality, dependence, faculty, association, presence and non-disappearance 3 ;

23. Of nutriment, conascence, dependence, faculty, dissociation, presence and non-disappearance 3.

With resultant 5

24. Combination of nutriment, conascence, dependence, resultant, faculty, presence and non-disappearance 1 ;

25. Of nutriment, conascence, mutuality, dependence, resultant, faculty, presence and non-disappearance 1 ;

26. Of nutriment, conascence, mutuality, dependence, resultant, faculty, association, presence and non-disappearance 1 ;

27. Of nutriment, conascence, dependence, resultant, faculty, dissociation, presence and non-disappearance 1 ;

28. Of nutriment, conascence, mutuality, dependence, resultant, faculty, dissociation, presence and non-disappearance 1.

With predominance and faculty 6

Without resultant 3

483. 29. Combination of nutriment, predominance, conascence, dependence, faculty, presence and non-disappearance 7 ;

30. Of nutriment, predominance, conascence, mutuality, dependence, faculty, association, presence and non-disappearance 3 ;

31. Of nutriment, predominance, conascence, dependence, faculty, dissociation, presence and non-disappearance 3.

With resultant 3

32. Combination of nutriment, predominance, conascence, dependence, resultant, faculty, presence and non-disappearance 1 ;

33. Of nutriment, predominance, conascence, mutuality, dependence, resultant, faculty, association, presence and non-disappearance 1 ;

34. Of nutriment, predominance, conascence, dependence, resultant, faculty, dissociation, presence and non-disappearance 1.

End of Nutriment

Faculty

Common 14

484. With faculty condition and root 4, predominance 7, conascence 7, mutuality 3, dependence 7, prenascence 1, resultant 1, nutriment 7, jhāna 7, path 7, association 3, dissociation 3, presence 7, non-disappearance 7. (14)

Combinations 76

Mixed 3

485. 1. Combination of faculty, presence and non-disappearance 7;

2. Of faculty, dependence, presence and non-disappearance 7;

3. Of faculty, dependence, dissociation, presence and non-disappearance 3.

Miscellaneous 1

486. 4. Combination of faculty, dependence, prenascence, dissociation, presence and non-disappearance 1.

Conascence 72

Ordinary [1] 9

Without resultant 4

487. 5. Combination of faculty, conascence, dependence, presence and non-disappearance 7;

6. Of faculty, conascence, mutuality, dependence, presence and non-disappearance 3;

7. Of faculty, conascence, mutuality, dependence, association, presence and non-disappearance 3;

---

[1] Not " mutuality " as in the Text.

8. Of faculty, conascence, dependence, dissociation, presence and non-disappearance 3.

With resultant 5

9. Combination of faculty, conascence, dependence, resultant, presence and non-disappearance 1 ;

10. Of faculty, conascence, mutuality, dependence, resultant, presence and non-disappearance 1 ;

11. Of faculty, conascence, mutuality, dependence, resultant, association, presence and non-disappearance 1 ;

12. Of faculty, conascence, dependence, resultant, dissociation, presence and non-disappearance 1 ;

13. Of faculty, conascence, mutuality, dependence, resultant, dissociation, presence and non-disappearance 1.

With path 9

Without resultant 4

488. 14. Combination of faculty, conascence, dependence, path, presence and non-disappearance 7 ;

15. Of faculty, conascence, mutuality, dependence, path, presence and non-disappearance 3 ;

16. Of faculty, conascence, mutuality, dependence, path, association, presence and non-disappearance 3 ;

17. Of faculty, conascence, dependence, path, dissociation, presence and non-disappearance 3.

With resultant 5

18. Combination of faculty, conascence, dependence, resultant, path, presence and non-disappearance 1 ;

19. Of faculty, conascence, mutuality, dependence, resultant, path, presence and non-disappearance 1 ;

20. Of faculty, conascence, mutuality, dependence, resultant, path, association, presence and non-disappearance 1 ;

21. Of faculty, conascence, dependence, resultant, path, dissociation, presence and non-disappearance 1 ;

22. Of faculty, conascence, mutuality, dependence, resultant, path, dissociation, presence and non-disappearance 1.

With jhāna 9
Without resultant 4

489. 23. Combination of faculty, conascence, dependence, jhāna, presence and non-disappearance 7 ;

24. Of faculty, conascence, mutuality, dependence, jhāna, presence and non-disappearance 3 ;

25. Of faculty, conascence, mutuality, dependence, jhāna, association, presence and non-disappearance 3 ;

26. Of faculty, conascence, dependence, jhāna, dissociation, presence and non-disappearance 3.

With resultant 5

27. Combination of faculty, conascence, dependence, resultant, jhāna, presence and non-disappearance 1 ;

28. Of faculty, conascence, mutuality, dependence, resultant, jhāna, presence and non-disappearance 1 ;

29. Of faculty, conascence, mutuality, dependence, resultant, jhāna, association, presence and non-disappearance 1 ;

30. Of faculty, conascence, dependence, resultant, jhāna, dissociation, presence and non-disappearance 1 ;

31. Of faculty, conascence, mutuality, dependence, resultant, jhāna, dissociation, presence and non-disappearance 1.

With jhāna and path 9
Without resultant 4

490. 32. Combination of faculty, conascence, dependence, jhāna, path, presence and non-disappearance 7 ;

33. Of faculty, conascence, mutuality, dependence, jhāna, path, presence and non-disappearance 3 ;

34. Of faculty, conascence, mutuality, dependence, jhāna, path, association, presence and non-disappearance 3 ;

35. Of faculty, conascence, dependence, jhāna, path, dissociation, presence and non-disappearance 3.

With resultant 5

36. Combination of faculty, conascence, dependence, resultant, jhāna, path, presence and non-disappearance 1 ;

37. Of faculty, conascence, mutuality, dependence, resultant, jhāna, path, presence and non-disappearance 1;

38. Of faculty, conascence, mutuality, dependence, resultant, jhāna, path, association, presence and non-disappearance 1;

39. Of faculty, conascence, dependence, resultant, jhāna, path, dissociation, presence and non-disappearance 1;

40. Of faculty, conascence, mutuality, dependence, resultant, jhāna, path, dissociation, presence and non-disappearance 1.

With nutriment 9

Without resultant 4

491. 41. Combination of faculty, conascence, dependence, nutriment, presence and non-disappearance 7;

42. Of faculty, conascence, mutuality, dependence, nutriment, presence and non-disappearance 3;

43. Of faculty, conascence, mutuality, dependence, nutriment, association, presence and non-disappearance 3;

44. Of faculty, conascence, dependence, nutriment, dissociation, presence and non-disappearance 3.

With resultant 5

45. Combination of faculty, conascence, dependence, resultant, nutriment, presence and non-disappearance 1;

46. Of faculty, conascence, mutuality, dependence, resultant, nutriment, presence and non-disappearance 1;

47. Of faculty, conascence, mutuality, dependence, resultant, nutriment, association, presence and non-disappearance 1;

48. Of faculty, conascence, dependence, resultant, nutriment, dissociation, presence and non-disappearance 1;

49. Of faculty, conascence, mutuality, dependence, resultant, nutriment, dissociation, presence and non-disappearance 1.

With predominance and nutriment 6

Without resultant 3

492. 50. Combination of faculty, predominance, conascence, dependence, nutriment, presence and non-disappearance 7 ;

51. Of faculty, predominance, conascence, mutuality, dependence, nutriment, association, presence and non-disappearance 3 ;

52. Of faculty, predominance, conascence, dependence, nutriment, dissociation, presence and non-disappearance 3.

With resultant 3

53. Combination of faculty, predominance, conascence, dependence, resultant, nutriment, presence and non-disappearance 1 ;

54. Of faculty, predominance, conascence, mutuality, dependence, resultant, nutriment, association, presence and non-disappearance 1 ;

55. Of faculty, predominance, conascence, dependence, resultant, nutriment, dissociation, presence and non-disappearance 1.

With predominance and path 6

Without resultant 3

493. 56. Combination of faculty, predominance, conascence, dependence, path, presence and non-disappearance 7 ;

57. Of faculty, predominance, conascence, mutuality, dependence, path, association, presence and non-disappearance 3 ;

58. Of faculty, predominance, conascence, dependence, path, dissociation, presence and non-disappearance 3.

With resultant 3

59. Combination of faculty, predominance, conascence, dependence, resultant, path, presence and non-disappearance 1 ;

60. Of faculty, predominance, conascence, mutuality, dependence, resultant, path, association, presence and non-disappearance 1 ;

61. Of faculty, predominance, conascence, dependence, resultant, path, dissociation, presence and non-disappearance 1.

With root and path 9

Without resultant 4

494. 62. Combination of faculty, root, conascence, dependence, path, presence and non-disappearance 4 ;

63. Of faculty, root, conascence, mutuality, dependence, path, presence and non-disappearance 2 ;

64. Of faculty, root, conascence, mutuality, dependence, path, association, presence and non-disappearance 2 ;

65. Of faculty, root, conascence, dependence, path, dissociation, presence and non-disappearance 2.

With resultant 5

66. Combination of faculty, root, conascence, dependence, resultant, path, presence and non-disappearance 1 ;

67. Of faculty, root, conascence, mutuality, dependence, resultant, path, presence and non-disappearance 1 ;

68. Of faculty, root, conascence, mutuality, dependence, resultant, path, association, presence and non-disappearance 1 ;

69. Of faculty, root, conascence, dependence, resultant, path, dissociation, presence and non-disappearance 1 ;

70. Of faculty, root, conascence, mutuality, dependence, resultant, path, dissociation, presence and non-disappearance 1.

With root, predominance and path 6

Without resultant 3

495. 71. Combination of faculty, root, predominance, conascence, dependence, path, presence and non-disappearance 4 ;

72. Of faculty, root, predominance, conascence, mutuality, dependence, path, association, presence and non-disappearance 2 ;

73. Of faculty, root, predominance, conascence, dependence, path, dissociation, presence and non-disappearance 2.

With resultant 3

74. Combination of faculty, root, predominance, conascence, dependence, resultant, path, presence and non-disappearance 1 ;

75. Of faculty, root, predominance, conascence, mutuality, dependence, resultant, path, association, presence and non-disappearance 1 ;

76. Of faculty, root, predominance, conascence, dependence, resultant, path, dissociation, presence and non-disappearance 1.

End of Faculty

Jhāna

Common 10

496. With jhāna condition and conascence 7, mutuality 3, dependence 7, resultant 1, faculty 7, path 7, association 3, dissociation 3, presence 7, non-disappearance 7. (10)

Conascence Combinations 36

Ordinary 9

Without resultant 4

497. 1. Combination of jhāna, conascence, dependence, presence and non-disappearance 7 ;

2. Of jhāna, conascence, mutuality, dependence, presence and non-disappearance 3 ;

3. Of jhāna, conascence, mutuality, dependence, association, presence and non-disappearance 3 ;

4. Of jhāna, conascence, dependence, dissociation, presence and non-disappearance 3.

With resultant 5

5. Combination of jhāna, conascence, dependence, resultant, presence and non-disappearance 1 ;

6. Of jhāna, conascence, mutuality, dependence, resultant, presence and non-disappearance 1 ;

7. Of jhāna, conascence, mutuality, dependence, resultant, association, presence and non-disappearance 1 ;
8. Of jhāna, conascence, dependence, resultant, dissociation, presence and non-disappearance 1 ;
9. Of jhāna, conascence, mutuality, dependence, resultant, dissociation, presence and non-disappearance 1.

With faculty 9

Without resultant 4

498. 10. Combination of jhāna, conascence, dependence, faculty, presence and non-disappearance 7 ;
11. Of jhāna, conascence, mutuality, dependence, faculty, presence and non-disappearance 3 ;
12. Of jhāna, conascence, mutuality, dependence, faculty, association, presence and non-disappearance 3 ;
13. Of jhāna, conascence, dependence, faculty, dissociation, presence and non-disappearance 3.

With resultant 5

14. Combination of jhāna, conascence, dependence, resultant, faculty, presence and non-disappearance 1 ;
15. Of jhāna, conascence, mutuality, dependence, resultant, faculty, presence and non-disappearance 1 ;
16. Of jhāna, conascence, mutuality, dependence, resultant, faculty, association, presence and non-disappearance 1 ;
17. Of jhāna, conascence, dependence, resultant, faculty, dissociation, presence and non-disappearance 1 ;
18. Of jhāna, conascence, mutuality, dependence, resultant, faculty, dissociation, presence and non-disappearance 1.

With path 9

Without resultant 4

499. 19. Combination of jhāna, conascence, dependence, path, presence and non-disappearance 7 ;
20. Of jhāna, conascence, mutuality, dependence, path, presence and non-disappearance 3 ;

21. Of jhāna, conascence, mutuality, dependence, path, association, presence and non-disappearance 3 ;

22. Of jhāna, conascence, dependence, path, dissociation, presence and non-disappearance 3.

With resultant 5

23. Combination of jhāna, conascence, dependence, resultant, path, presence and non-disappearance 1 ;

24. Of jhāna, conascence, mutuality, dependence, resultant, path, presence and non-disappearance 1 ;

25. Of jhāna, conascence, mutuality, dependence, resultant, path, association, presence and non-disappearance 1 ;

26. Of jhāna, conascence, dependence, resultant, path, dissociation, presence and non-disappearance 1 ;

27. Of jhāna, conascence, mutuality, dependence, resultant, path, dissociation, presence and non-disappearance 1.

With faculty and path 9

Without resultant 4

500. 28. Combination of jhāna, conascence, dependence, faculty, path, presence and non-disappearance 7 ;

29. Of jhāna, conascence, mutuality, dependence, faculty, path, presence and non-disappearance 3 ;

30. Of jhāna, conascence, mutuality, dependence, faculty, path, association, presence and non-disappearance 3 ;

31. Of jhāna, conascence, dependence, faculty, path, dissociation, presence and non-disappearance 3.

With resultant 5

32. Combination of jhāna, conascence, dependence, resultant, faculty, path, presence and non-disappearance 1 ;

33. Of jhāna, conascence, mutuality, dependence, resultant, faculty, path, presence and non-disappearance 1 ;

34. Of jhāna, conascence, mutuality, dependence, resultant, faculty, path, association, presence and non-disappearance 1 ;

35. Of jhāna, conascence, dependence, resultant, faculty, path, dissociation, presence and non-disappearance 1 ;

36. Of jhāna, conascence, mutuality, dependence, resultant, faculty, path, dissociation, presence and non-disappearance 1.

End of Jhāna

Path

Common 12 [1]

501. With path condition and root 4, predominance 7, conascence 7, mutuality 3, dependence 7, resultant 1, faculty 7, jhāna 7, association 3, dissociation 3, presence 7, non-disappearance 7. (12)

Conascence Combinations 57

Ordinary 9

Without resultant 4

502. 1. Combination of path, conascence, dependence, presence and non-disappearance 7 ;

2. Of path, conascence, mutuality, dependence, presence and non-disappearance 3 ;

3. Of path, conascence, mutuality, dependence, association, presence and non-disappearance 3 ;

4. Of path, conascence, dependence, dissociation, presence and non-disappearance 3.

With resultant 5

5. Combination of path, conascence, dependence, resultant, presence and non-disappearance 1 ;

6. Of path, conascence, mutuality, dependence, resultant, presence and non-disappearance 1 ;

7. Of path, conascence, mutuality, dependence, resultant, association, presence and non-disappearance 1 ;

8. Of path, conascence, dependence, resultant, dissociation, presence and non-disappearance 1 ;

---

[1] Not " 10 " as in the Text.

9. Of path, conascence, mutuality, dependence, resultant, dissociation, presence and non-disappearance 1.

With faculty 9

Without resultant 4

503. 10. Combination of path, conascence, dependence, faculty, presence and non-disappearance 7 ;
11. Of path, conascence, mutuality, dependence, faculty, presence and non-disappearance 3 ;
12. Of path, conascence, mutuality, dependence, faculty, association, presence and non-disappearance 3 ;
13. [1] Of path, conascence, dependence, faculty, dissociation, presence and non-disappearance 3.

With resultant 5

14. Combination of path, conascence, dependence, resultant, faculty, presence and non-disappearance 1 ;
15. Of path, conascence, mutuality, dependence, resultant, faculty, presence and non-disappearance 1 ;
16. Of path, conascence, mutuality, dependence, resultant, faculty, association, presence and non-disappearance 1 ;
17. Of path, conascence, dependence, resultant, faculty, dissociation, presence and non-disappearance 1 ;
18. Of path, conascence, mutuality, dependence, resultant, faculty, dissociation, presence and non-disappearance 1.

With jhāna 9

Without resultant 4

504. 19. Combination of path, conascence, dependence, jhāna, presence and non-disappearance 7 ;
20. Of path, conascence, mutuality, dependence, jhāna, presence and non-disappearance 3 ;
21. Of path, conascence, mutuality, dependence, jhāna, association, presence and non-disappearance 3 ;
22. Of path, conascence, dependence, jhāna, dissociation, presence and non-disappearance 3.

---

[1] Misplaced under " With resultant ".

With resultant 5

23. Combination of path, conascence, dependence, resultant, jhāna, presence and non-disappearance 1;

24. Of path, conascence, mutuality, dependence, resultant, jhāna, presence and non-disappearance 1;

25. Of path, conascence, mutuality, dependence, resultant, jhāna, association, presence and non-disappearance 1;

26. Of path, conascence, dependence, resultant, jhāna, dissociation, presence and non-disappearance 1;

27. Of path, conascence, mutuality, dependence, resultant, jhāna, dissociation, presence and non-disappearance 1.

With faculty and jhāna 9

Without resultant 4

505. 28. Combination of path, conascence, dependence, faculty, jhāna, presence and non-disappearance 7;

29. Of path, conascence, mutuality, dependence, faculty, jhāna, presence and non-disappearance 3;

30. Of path, conascence, mutuality, dependence, faculty, jhāna, association, presence and non-disappearance 3;

31. Of path, conascence, dependence, faculty, jhāna, dissociation, presence and non-disappearance 3.

With resultant 5

32. Combination of path, conascence, dependence, resultant, faculty, jhāna, presence and non-disappearance 1;

33. Of path, conascence, mutuality, dependence, resultant, faculty, jhāna, presence and non-disappearance 1;

34. Of path, conascence, mutuality, dependence, resultant, faculty, jhāna, association, presence and non-disappearance 1;

35. Of path, conascence, dependence, resultant, faculty, jhāna, dissociation, presence and non-disappearance 1;

36. Of path, conascence, mutuality, dependence, resultant, faculty, jhāna, dissociation, presence and non-disappearance 1.

With predominance and faculty 6

Without resultant 3

506. 37. Combination of path, predominance, conascence, dependence, faculty, presence and non-disappearance 7 ;

38. Of path, predominance, conascence, mutuality, dependence, faculty, association, presence and non-disappearance 3 ;

39. Of path, predominance, conascence, dependence, faculty, dissociation, presence and non-disappearance 3.

With resultant 3

40. Combination of path, predominance, conascence, dependence, resultant, faculty, presence and non-disappearance 1 ;

41. Of path, predominance, conascence, mutuality, dependence, resultant, faculty, association, presence and non-disappearance 1 ;

42. Of path, predominance, conascence, dependence, resultant, faculty, dissociation, presence and non-disappearance 1.

With root and faculty 9

Without resultant 4

507. 43. Combination of path, root, conascence, dependence, faculty, presence and non-disappearance 4 ;

44. Of path, root, conascence, mutuality, dependence, faculty, presence and non-disappearance 2 ;

45. Of path, root, conascence, mutuality, dependence, faculty, association, presence and non-disappearance 2 ;

46. Of path, root, conascence, dependence, faculty, dissociation, presence and non-disappearance 2.

With resultant 5

47. Combination of path, root, conascence, dependence, resultant, faculty, presence and non-disappearance 1 ;

48. Of path, root, conascence, mutuality, dependence, resultant, faculty, presence and non-disappearance 1;

49. Of path, root, conascence, mutuality, dependence, resultant, faculty, association, presence and non-disappearance 1;

50. Of path, root, conascence, dependence, resultant, faculty, dissociation, presence and non-disappearance 1;

51. Of path, root, conascence, mutuality, dependence, resultant, faculty, dissociation, presence and non-disappearance 1.

With root, predominance and faculty 6

Without resultant 3

508. 52. Combination of path, root, predominance, conascence, dependence, faculty, presence and non-disappearance 4;

53. Of path, root, predominance, conascence, mutuality, dependence, faculty, association, presence and non-disappearance 2;

54. Of path, root, predominance, conascence, dependence, faculty, dissociation, presence and non-disappearance 2.

With resultant 3

55. Combination of path, root, predominance, conascence, dependence, resultant, faculty, presence and non-disappearance 1;

56. Of path, root, predominance, conascence, mutuality, dependence, resultant, faculty, association, presence and non-disappearance 1;

57. Of path, root, predominance, conascence, dependence, resultant, faculty, dissociation, presence and non-disappearance 1.

End of Path

Association

Common 13

509. With association condition and root 3, predominance 3, conascence 3, mutuality 3, dependence 3, kamma 3, resultant 1, nutriment 3, faculty 3, jhāna 3, path 3, presence 3, non-disappearance 3. (13)

Conascence Combinations 2

Without resultant 1

510. 1. Combination of association, conascence, mutuality, dependence, presence and non-disappearance 3.

With resultant 1

2. Combination of association, conascence, mutuality, dependence, resultant, presence and non-disappearance 1.

End of Association

Dissociation

Common 17

511. With dissociation condition and root 3, object 3, predominance 4, conascence 3, mutuality 1, dependence 5, strong-dependence 1, prenascence 3, postnascence 3, kamma 3, resultant 1, nutriment 3, faculty 3, jhāna 3, path 3, presence 5, non-disappearance 5. (17)

Combinations 13

Mixed 4

512. 1. Combination of dissociation, presence and non-disappearance 5 ;

2. Of dissociation, dependence, presence and non-disappearance 5 ;

3. Of dissociation, predominance, dependence, presence and non-disappearance 4 ;

4. Of dissociation, dependence, faculty, presence and non-disappearance 3.

Miscellaneous 5

513. 5. Combination of dissociation, postnascence, presence and non-disappearance 3 ;

6. Of dissociation, dependence, prenascence, presence and non-disappearance 3 ;

7. Of dissociation, object, dependence, prenascence, presence and non-disappearance 3 ;

8. Of dissociation, object, predominance, dependence, strong-dependence, prenascence, presence and non-disappearance 1 ;

9. Of dissociation, dependence, prenascence, faculty, presence and non-disappearance 1.

Conascence 4

Without resultant 2

514. 10. Combination of dissociation, conascence, dependence, presence and non-disappearance 3 ;

11. Of dissociation, conascence, mutuality, dependence, presence and non-disappearance 1.

With resultant 2

12. Combination of dissociation, conascence, dependence, resultant, presence and non-disappearance 1 ;

13. Of dissociation, conascence, mutuality, dependence, resultant, presence and non-disappearance 1.

End of Dissociation

Presence

Common 18

515. With presence condition and root 7, object 3, predominance 8, conascence 9, mutuality 3, dependence 13, strong-dependence 1, prenascence 3, postnascence 3, kamma 7, resultant 1, nutriment 7, faculty 7, jhāna 7, path 7, association 3, dissociation 5, non-disappearance 13. (18).

Combinations 29

Mixed 11

516. 1. Combination of presence and non-disappearance 13 ;
  2. Of presence, dependence and non-disappearance 13 ;
  3. Of presence, predominance and non-disappearance 8 ;

4. Of presence, predominance, dependence and non-disappearance 8 ;
5. Of presence, nutriment and non-disappearance 7 ;
6. Of presence, faculty and non-disappearance 7 ;
7. Of presence, dependence, faculty and non-disappearance 7 ;
8. Of presence, dissociation and non-disappearance 5 ;
9. Of presence, dependence, dissociation and non-disappearance 5 ;
10. Of presence, predominance, dependence, dissociation and non-disappearance 4 ;
11. Of presence, dependence, faculty,[1] dissociation and non-disappearance 3.

Miscellaneous 8

517. 12. Combination of presence, postnascence, dissociation and non-disappearance 3 ;
13. Of presence, prenascence and non-disappearance 3 ;
14. Of presence, dependence, prenascence, dissociation and non-disappearance 3 ;
15. Of presence, object, prenascence and non-disappearance 3 ;
16. Of presence, object, dependence, prenascence, dissociation and non-disappearance 3 ;
17. Of presence, object, predominance, strong-dependence, prenascence and non-disappearance 1 ;
18. Of presence, object, predominance, dependence, strong-dependence, prenascence, dissociation and non-disappearance 1 ;
19. Of presence, dependence, prenascence, faculty, dissociation and non-disappearance 1.

Conascence 10

Without resultant 5

518. 20. Combination of presence, conascence, dependence and non-disappearance 9 ;

---

[1] Left out in the Text.

21. Of presence, conascence, mutuality, dependence and non-disappearance 3 ;
22. Of presence, conascence, mutuality, dependence, association and non-disappearance 3 ;
23. Of presence, conascence, dependence, dissociation and non-disappearance 3 ;
24. Of presence, conascence, mutuality, dependence, dissociation and non-disappearance 1.

With resultant 5

25. Combination of presence, conascence, dependence, resultant and non-disappearance 1 ;
26. Of presence, conascence, mutuality, dependence, resultant and non-disappearance 1 ;
27. Of presence, conascence, mutuality, dependence, resultant, association and non-disappearance 1 ;
28. Of presence, conascence, dependence, resultant, dissociation and non-disappearance 1 ;
29. Of presence, conascence, mutuality, dependence, resultant, dissociation and non-disappearance 1.

End of Presence

Absence

Common 6

519. With absence condition and proximity 7, contiguity 7, strong-dependence 7, repetition 3, kamma 1, disappearance 7. (6)

(*Miscellaneous*) *Combinations* 3

520. 1. Combination of absence, proximity, contiguity, strong-dependence and disappearance 7 ;
2. Of absence, proximity, contiguity, strong-dependence, repetition and disappearance 3 ;
3. Of absence, proximity, contiguity, strong-dependence, kamma and disappearance 1.

End of Absence

Disappearance

Common 6

521. With disappearance condition and proximity 7, contiguity 7, strong-dependence 7, repetition 3, kamma 1, absence 7. (6)

(Miscellaneous) Combinations 3

522. 1. Combination of disappearance, proximity, contiguity, strong-dependence and absence 7 ;

2. Of disappearance, proximity, contiguity, strong-dependence, repetition and absence 3 ;

3. Of disappearance, proximity, contiguity, strong-dependence, kamma and absence 1.

End of Disappearance

Non-Disappearance

Common 18

523. With non-disappearance condition and root 7, object 3, predominance 8, conascence 9, mutuality 3, dependence 13, strong-dependence 1, prenascence 3, postnascence 3, kamma 7, resultant 1, nutriment 7, faculty 7, jhāna 7, path 7, association 3, dissociation 5, presence 13. (18)

Combinations 29

Mixed 11

524. 1. Combination of non-disappearance and presence 13 ;

2. Of non-disappearance, dependence and presence 13 ;

3. Of non-disappearance, predominance and presence 8 ;

4. Of non-disappearance, predominance, dependence and presence 8 ;

5. Of non-disappearance, nutriment and presence 7 ;

6. Of non-disappearance, faculty and presence 7 ;

7. Of non-disappearance, dependence, faculty and presence 7 ;

8. Of non-disappearance, dissociation and presence 5 ;

9. Of non-disappearance, dependence, dissociation and presence 5 ;

10. Of non-disappearance, predominance, dependence, dissociation and presence 4 ;

11. Of non-disappearance, dependence, faculty, dissociation and presence 3.

Miscellaneous 8

525. 12. Combination of non-disappearance, postnascence, dissociation and presence 3 ;
 13. Of non-disappearance, prenascence and presence 3 ;
 14. Of non-disappearance, dependence, prenascence, dissociation and presence 3 ;
 15. Of non-disappearance, object, prenascence and presence 3 ;
 16. Of non-disappearance, object, dependence, prenascence, dissociation and presence 3 ;
 17. Of non-disappearance, object, predominance, strong-dependence, prenascence and presence 1 ;
 18. Of non-disappearance, object, predominance, dependence, strong-dependence, prenascence, dissociation and presence 1 ;
 19. Of non-disappearance, dependence, prenascence, faculty, dissociation and presence 1.

Conascence 10

Without resultant 5

526. 20. Combination of non-disappearance, conascence, dependence and presence 9 ;
 21. Of non-disappearance, conascence, mutuality, dependence and presence 3 ;
 22. Of non-disappearance, conascence, mutuality, dependence, association and presence 3 ;
 23. Of non-disappearance, conascence, dependence, dissociation and presence 3 ;
 24. Of non-disappearance, conascence, mutuality, dependence, dissociation and presence 1.

With resultant 5

 25. Combination of non-disappearance, conascence, dependence, resultant and presence 1 ;

26. Of non-disappearance, conascence, mutuality, dependence, resultant and presence 1 ;

27. Of non-disappearance, conascence, mutuality, dependence, resultant, association and presence 1 ;

28. Of non-disappearance, conascence, dependence, resultant, dissociation and presence 1 ;

29. Of non-disappearance, conascence, mutuality, dependence, resultant, dissociation and presence 1.

End of Non-disappearance

End of Positive Enumeration in " Investigation " Chapter.

2. SELECTION OF THE CONDITIONS FOR NEGATIVE

527. (i) Faultless state is related to faultless state by object condition, conascence condition, strong-dependence condition.

(ii) Faultless state is related to faulty state by object condition, strong-dependence condition.

(iii) Faultless state is related to indeterminate state by object condition, conascence condition, strong-dependence condition, postnascence condition, kamma condition.

(iv) Faultless state is related to faultless and indeterminate state by conascence condition. (4)

528. (v) Faulty state is related to faulty state by object condition, conascence condition, strong-dependence condition.

(vi) Faulty state is related to faultless state by object condition, strong-dependence condition.

(vii) Faulty state is related to indeterminate state by object condition, conascence condition, strong-dependence condition, postnascence condition, kamma condition.

(viii) Faulty state is related to faulty and indeterminate state by conascence condition. (4)

529. (ix) Indeterminate state is related to indeterminate state by object condition, conascence condition, strong-dependence condition, prenascence condition, postnascence condition, nutriment condition, faculty condition.

(x) Indeterminate state is related to faultless state by object condition, strong-dependence condition, prenascence condition.

(xi) Indeterminate state is related to faulty state by object condition, strong-dependence condition, prenascence condition. (3)

530. (xii) Faultless and indeterminate states are related to faultless state by conascence-prenascence.

(xiii) Faultless and indeterminate states are related to indeterminate state by conascence, postnascence-nutriment-faculty. (2)

531. (xiv) Faulty and indeterminate states are related to faulty state by conascence-prenascence.

(xv) Faulty and indeterminate states are related to indeterminate state by conascence, postnascence-nutriment-faculty. (2)

End of Selection of the Conditions for Negative in
" Investigation " Chapter.

2. CONDITIONS : NEGATIVE   (ii) ENUMERATION CHAPTER

By Ones

532. With not-root (condition, there are) 15 (answers), not-object 15, not-predominance 15, not-proximity 15, not-contiguity 15, not-conascence 11, not-mutuality 11, not-dependence 11, not-strong-dependence 15, not-prenascence 13, not-postnascence 15, not-repetition 15, not-kamma 15, not-resultant 15, not-nutriment 15, not-faculty 15, not-jhāna 15, not-path 15, not-association 11, not-dissociation 9, not-presence 9, not-absence 15, not-disappearance 15, not-non-disappearance 9.

Not-root

By Twos

533. With not-root condition and not-object (condition, there are) 15 (answers), not-predominance 15, not-proximity 15, not-contiguity 15, not-conascence 11, not-mutuality 11, not-dependence 11, not-strong-dependence 15, not-prenascence 13, not-postnascence 15, not-repetition 15, not-kamma 15, not-resultant 15, not-nutriment 15, not-faculty 15, not-jhāna 15,

not-path 15, not-association 11, not-dissociation 9, not-presence 9, not-absence 15, not-disappearance 15, not-non-disappearance 9.

By Threes

With not-root, not-object conditions and not-predominance 15, not-proximity 15, not-contiguity 15, not-conascence 11, not-mutuality 11, not-dependence 11, not-strong-dependence 13, not-prenascence 13, not-postnascence 15, not-repetition 15, not-kamma 15, not-resultant 15, not-nutriment 15, not-faculty 15, not-jhāna 15, not-path 15, not-association 11, not-dissociation 9, not-presence 9, not-absence 15, not-disappearance 15, not-non-disappearance 9. ...

By Sixes

With not-root, not-object, not-predominance, not-proximity, not-contiguity conditions and not-conascence 11, not-mutuality 11, not-dependence 11, not-strong-dependence 13, not-prenascence 13, not postnascence 15, not-repetition 15, not-kamma 15, not-resultant 15, not-nutriment 15, not-faculty 15, not-jhāna 15, not-path 15, not-association 11, not-dissociation 9, not-presence 9, not-absence 15, not-disappearance 15, not-non-disappearance 9.

By Sevens

With not-root, not-object, not-predominance, not-proximity, not-contiguity, not-conascence conditions and not-mutuality 11, not-dependence 11, not-strong-dependence 7, not-prenascence 11, not-postnascence 9, not-repetition 11, not-kamma 11, not-resultant 11, not-nutriment 11, not-faculty 11, not-jhāna 11, not-path 11, not-association 11, not-dissociation 9, not-presence 9, not-absence 11, not-disappearance 11, not-non-disappearance 9.

By Eights

With not-root, not-object, not-predominance, not-proximity, not-contiguity, not-conascence, not-mutuality conditions and not-dependence 11, not-strong-dependence 7, not-prenascence 11, not-postnascence 9, not-repetition 11, not-kamma 11, not-resultant 11, not-nutriment 11, not-faculty 11, not-jhāna 11, not-path 11, not-association 11, not-dissociation 9, not-presence 9, not-absence 11, not-disappearance 11, not-non-disappearance 9.

By Nines

With not-root, not-object, not-predominance, not-proximity, not-contiguity, not-conascence, not-mutuality, not-dependence conditions and not-strong-dependence 5, not-prenascence 11, not-postnascence 9, not-repetition 11, not-kamma 11, not-resultant 11, not-nutriment 11, not-faculty 11, not-jhāna 11, not-path 11, not-association 11, not-dissociation 9, not-presence 9, not-absence 11, not-disappearance 11, not-non-disappearance 9.

By Tens

With not-root, not-object, not-predominance, not-proximity, not-contiguity, not-conascence, not-mutuality, not-dependence, not-strong-dependence conditions and not-prenascence 5, not-postnascence 3, not-repetition 5, not-kamma 5, not-resultant 5, not-nutriment 5, not-faculty 5, not-jhāna 5, not-path 5, not-association 5, not-dissociation 3, not-presence 2, not-absence 5, not-disappearance 5, not-non-disappearance 2.

By Elevens

With not-root, not-object, not-predominance, not-proximity, not-contiguity, not-conascence, not-mutuality, not-dependence, not-strong-dependence, not-prenascence conditions and not-postnascence 3, not-repetition 5, not-kamma 5, not-resultant 5, not-nutriment 5, not-faculty 5, not-jhāna 5, not-path 5, not-association 5, not-dissociation 3, not-presence 2, not-absence 5, not-disappearance 5, not-non-disappearance 2.

By Twelves

With not-root, not-object, not-predominance, not-proximity, not-contiguity . . . not-prenascence, not-postnascence conditions and not-repetition 3, not-kamma 1, not-resultant 3, not-nutriment 3, not-faculty 3, not-jhāna 3, not-path 3, not-association 3, not-dissociation 3, not-presence 2, not-absence 3, not-disappearance 3, not-non-disappearance 2. . . .

By Fourteens

With not-root, not-object . . . not-postnascence, not-repetition, not-kamma conditions and not-resultant 1, not-nutriment 1, not-faculty 1, not-jhāna 1, not-path 1, not-association 1, not-dissociation 1, not-absence 1, not-disappearance 1. . . .

[1] By Sixteens (with nutriment)

With not-root, not-object . . . not-kamma, not-resultant, not-nutriment conditions and not-jhāna 1, not-path 1, not-association 1, not-dissociation 1, not-absence 1, not-disappearance 1.[1]

By Seventeens

With not-root, not-object . . . not-kamma, not-resultant, not-nutriment, not-jhāna conditions and not-path 1, not-association 1, not-dissociation 1, not-absence 1, not-disappearance 1. . . .

By Twenty-one

With not-root, not-object . . . not-nutriment, not-jhāna, not-path, not-association, not-dissociation, not-absence conditions and not-disappearance 1.

By Sixteens (with faculty)

With not-root, not-object . . . not-kamma, not-resultant, not-faculty conditions and not-jhāna 1, not-path 1, not-association 1, not-dissociation 1, not-absence 1, not-disappearance 1. . . .

Again—By Twenty-one

With not-root, not-object . . . not-kamma, not-resultant, not-faculty, not-jhāna, not-path, not-association, not-dissociation, not-absence conditions and not-disappearance 1.

End of Not-root

Not-object

By Twos

534. With not-object condition and not-root 15, not-predominance 15, not-proximity 15, not-contiguity 15, not-conascence 11, not-mutuality 11, not-dependence 11, not-strong-dependence 13, not-prenascence 13, not-postnascence 15,

---

[1] This portion is not mentioned in the Text.

not-repetition 15, not-kamma 15, not-resultant 15, not-nutriment 15, not-faculty 15, not-jhāna 15, not-path 15, not-association 11, not-dissociation 9, not-presence 9, not-absence 15, not-disappearance 15, not-non-disappearance 9. ...

By Sevens

With not-object, not-root, not-predominance, not-proximity, not-contiguity, not-conascence conditions and not-mutuality 11, not-dependence 11, not-strong-dependence 7, not-prenascence 11, not-postnascence 9, not-repetition 11, not-kamma 11, not-resultant 11, not-nutriment 11, not-faculty 11, not-jhāna 11, not-path 11, not-association 11, not-dissociation 9, not-presence 9, not-absence 11, not-disappearance 11, not-non-disappearance 9. ...

(Expand in the same way as not-root condition.)

End of Not-object

Not-predominance, etc.

535. With not-predominance condition . . . with not-proximity condition . . . with not-contiguity condition . . . (Expand in the same way as not-root condition.)

Not-conascence

By Twos

536. With not-conascence condition and not-root 11, not-object 11, not-predominance 11, not-proximity 11, not-contiguity 11, not-mutuality 11, not-dependence 11, not-strong-dependence 11, not-prenascence 11, not-postnascence 9, not-repetition 11, not-kamma 11, not-resultant 11, not-nutriment 11, not-faculty 11, not-jhāna 11, not-path 11, not-association 11, not-dissociation 9, not-presence 9, not-absence 11, not-disappearance 11, not-non-disappearance 9. ...

By Fours

With not-conascence, not-root, not-object conditions and not-predominance 11, not-proximity 11, not-contiguity 11, not-mutuality 11, not-dependence 11, not-strong-dependence 7, not-prenascence 11, not-postnascence 9, not-repetition 11, not-kamma 11, not-resultant 11, not-nutriment 11, not-faculty 11, not-jhāna 11, not-path 11, not-association 11, not-dissociation 9, not-presence 9, not-absence 11, not-disappearance 11, not-non-disappearance 9.

With not-conascence, not-root . . . (Abbreviated.)

End of Not-conascence

Not-mutuality

By Twos

537. With not-mutuality condition and not-root 11, not-object 11, not-predominance 11, not-proximity 11, not-contiguity 11, not-conascence 11, not-dependence 11, not-strong-dependence 11, not-prenascence 11, not-postnascence 11, not-repetition 11, not-kamma 11, not-resultant 11, not-nutriment 11, not-faculty 11, not-jhāna 11, not-path 11, not-association 11, not-dissociation 9, not-presence 9, not-absence 11, not-disappearance 11, not-non-disappearance 9. . . .

By Fours

With not-mutuality, not-root, not-object conditions and not-predominance 11, not-proximity 11, not-contiguity 11, not-conascence 11, not-dependence 11, not-strong-dependence 7, not-prenascence 11, not-postnascence 11, not-repetition 11, not-kamma 11, not-resultant 11, not-nutriment 11, not-faculty 11, not-jhāna 11, not-path 11, not-association 11, not-dissociation 9, not-presence 9, not-absence 11, not-disappearance 11, not-non-disappearance 9. . . .

By Eights

With not-mutuality, not-root, not-object, not-predominance, not-proximity, not-contiguity, not-conascence conditions and not-dependence 11, not-strong-dependence 7, not-prenascence 11, not-postnascence 9, not-repetition 11, not-kamma 11, not-resultant 11, not-nutriment 11, not-faculty 11, not-jhāna 11, not-path 11, not-association 11, not-dissociation 9, not-presence 9, not-absence 11, not-disappearance 11, not-non-disappearance 9. . . . (Abbreviated.)

End of Not-mutuality

Not-dependence

By Twos

538. With not-dependence condition and not-root 11, not-object 11, not-predominance 11, not-proximity 11, not-contiguity 11, not-conascence 11, not-mutuality 11, not-strong-dependence 11, not-prenascence 11, not-postnascence 9, not-repetition 11, not-kamma 11, not-resultant 11, not-nutriment 11, not-faculty 11, not-jhāna 11, not-path 11, not-association 11, not-dissociation 9, not-presence 9, not-absence 11, not-disappearance 11, not-non-disappearance 9. . . .

By Fours

With not-dependence, not-root, not-object conditions and not-predominance 11, not-proximity 11, not-contiguity 11, not-conascence 11, not-mutuality 11, not-strong-dependence 5, not-prenascence 11, not-postnascence 9, not-repetition 11, not-kamma 11, not-resultant 11, not-nutriment 11, not-faculty 11, not-jhāna 11, not-path 11, not-association 11, not-dissociation 9, not-presence 9, not-absence 11, not-disappearance 11, not-non-disappearance 9. . . .

By Tens

With not-dependence, not-root, not-object, not-predominance, not-proximity, not-contiguity, not-conascence, not-mutuality, not-strong-dependence conditions and not-prenascence 5, not-postnascence 3, not-repetition 5, not-kamma 5, not-resultant 5, not-nutriment 5, not-faculty 5, not-jhāna 5, not-path 5, not-association 5, not-dissociation 3, not-presence 2, not-absence 5, not-disappearance 5, not-non-disappearance 2. . . . (Abbreviated.)

End of Not-dependence

Not-strong-dependence

By Twos

539. With not-strong-dependence condition and not-root 15, not-object 13, not-predominance 15, not-proximity 15, not-contiguity 15, not-conascence 11, not-mutuality 11, not-dependence 11, not-prenascence 13, not-postnascence 15, not-repetition 15, not-kamma 15, not-resultant 15, not-nutriment

15, not-faculty 15, not-jhāna 15, not-path 15, not-association 11, not-dissociation 9, not-presence 9, not-absence 15, not-disappearance 15, not-non-disappearance 9. ...

By Fours

With not-strong-dependence, not-root, not-object conditions and not-predominance 13, not-proximity 13, not-contiguity 13, not-conascence 7, not-mutuality 7, not-dependence 5, not-prenascence 9, not-postnascence 13, not-repetition 13, not-kamma 13, not-resultant 13, not-nutriment 13, not-faculty 13, not-jhāna 13, not-path 13, not-association 7, not-dissociation 5, not-presence 2, not-absence 13, not-disappearance 13, not-non-disappearance 2. ...

By Eights

With not-strong-dependence, not-root, not-object, not-predominance, not-proximity, not-contiguity, not-conascence conditions and not-mutuality 7, not-dependence 5, not-prenascence 5, not-postnascence 5, not-repetition 7, not-kamma 7, not-resultant 7, not-nutriment 7, not-faculty 7, not-jhāna 7, not-path 7, not-association 7, not-dissociation 3, not-presence 2, not-absence 7, not-disappearance 7, not-non-disappearance 2.

By Nines

With not-strong-dependence, not-root, not-object, not-predominance, not-proximity, not-contiguity, not-conascence, not-mutuality conditions and not-dependence 5, not-prenascence 5, not-postnascence 5, not-repetition 7, not-kamma 7, not-resultant 7, not-nutriment 7, not-faculty 7, not-jhāna 7, not-path 7, not-association 7, not-dissociation 3, not-presence 2, not-absence 7, not-disappearance 7, not-non-disappearance 2.

By Tens

With not-strong-dependence, not-root, not-object, not-predominance, not-proximity, not-contiguity, not-conascence, not-mutuality, not-dependence conditions and not-prenascence 5, not-postnascence 3, not-repetition 5, not-kamma 5, not-resultant 5, not-nutriment 5, not-faculty 5, not-jhāna 5, not-path 5, not-association 5, not-dissociation 3, not-presence 2, not-absence 5, not-disappearance 5, not-non-disappearance 2. ... (Abbreviated.)

End of Not-strong-dependence

Not-prenascence

By Twos

540. With not-prenascence condition and not-root 13, not-object 13, not-predominance 13, not-proximity 13, not-contiguity 13, not-conascence 11, not-mutuality 11, not-dependence 11, not-strong-dependence 13, not-postnascence 13, not-repetition 13, not-kamma 13, not-resultant 13, not-nutriment 13, not-faculty 13, not-jhāna 13, not-path 3, not-association 11, not-dissociation 9, not-presence 9, not-absence 13, not-disappearance 13, not-non-disappearance 9. ...

By Fours

With not-prenascence, not-root, not-object conditions and not-predominance 13, not-proximity 13, not-contiguity 13, not-conascence 11, not-mutuality 11, not-dependence 11, not-strong-dependence 9, not-postnascence 13, not-repetition 13, not-kamma 13, not-resultant 13, not-nutriment 13, not-faculty 13, not-jhāna 13, not-path 13, not-association 11, not-dissociation 9, not-presence 9, not-absence 13, not-disappearance 13, not-non-disappearance 9. ... .

By Eights

With not-prenascence, not-root, not-object, not-predominance, not-proximity, not-contiguity, not-conascence conditions and not-mutuality 11, not-dependence 11, not-strong-dependence 5, not-postnascence 9, not-repetition 11, not-kamma 11, not-resultant 11, not-nutriment 11, not-faculty 11, not-jhāna 11, not-path 11, not-association 11, not-dissociation 9, not-presence 9, not-absence 11, not-disappearance 11, not-non-disappearance 9. ...

By Tens

With not-prenascence, not-root, not-object, not-predominance, not-proximity, not-contiguity, not-conascence, not-mutuality, not-dependence conditions and not-strong-dependence 5, not-postnascence 9, not-repetition 11, not-kamma

11, not-resultant 11, not-nutriment 11, not-faculty 11, not-jhāna 11, not-path 11, not-association 11, not-dissociation 9, not-presence 9, not-absence 11, not-disappearance 11, not-non-disappearance 9.

By Elevens

With not-prenascence, not-root, not-object . . . not-dependence, not-strong-dependence conditions and not-postnascence 3, not-repetition 5, not-kamma 5, not-resultant 5, not-nutriment 5, not-faculty 5, not-jhāna 5, not-path 5, not-association 5, not-dissociation 3, not-presence 2, not-absence 5, not-disappearance 5, not-non-disappearance 2. . . . (Abbreviated.)

End of Not-prenascence

Not-postnascence

By Twos

541. With not-postnascence condition and not-root 15, not-object 15, not-predominance 15, not-proximity 15, not-contiguity 15, not-conascence 9, not-mutuality 11, not-dependence 9, not-strong-dependence 15, not-prenascence 13, not-repetition 15, not-kamma 15, not-resultant 15, not-nutriment 15, not-faculty 15, not-jhāna 15, not-path 15, not-association 11, not-dissociation 9, not-presence 9, not-absence 15, not-disappearance 15, not-non-disappearance 9. . . .

By Fours

With not-postnascence, not-root, not-object conditions and not-predominance 15, not-proximity 15, not-contiguity 15, not-conascence 9, not-mutuality 11, not-dependence 9, not-strong-dependence 13, not-prenascence 13, not-repetition 15, not-kamma 15, not-resultant 15, not-nutriment 15, not-faculty 15, not-jhāna 15, not-path 15, not-association 11, not-dissociation 9, not-presence 9, not-absence 15, not-disappearance 15, not-non-disappearance 9. . . .

By Eights

With not-postnascence, not-root, not-object, not-predominance, not-proximity, not-contiguity, not-conascence conditions and not-mutuality 9, not-dependence 9, not-strong-dependence 5, not-prenascence 9, not-repetition 9, not-kamma 9, not-resultant 9, not-nutriment 9, not-faculty 9, not-jhāna 9, not-path 9, not-association 9, not-dissociation 9, not-presence 9, not-absence 9, not-disappearance 9, not-non-disappearance 9. ...

By Tens

With not-postnascence, not-root, not-object, not-predominance, not-proximity, not-contiguity, not-conascence, not-mutuality, not-dependence conditions and not-strong-dependence 3, not-prenascence 9, not-repetition 9, not-kamma 9, not-resultant 9, not-nutriment 9, not-faculty 9, not-jhāna 9, not-path 9, not-association 9, not-dissociation 9, not-presence 9, not-absence 9, not-disappearance 9, not-non-disappearance 9.

By Elevens

With not-postnascence, not-root . . . not-dependence, not-strong-dependence conditions and not-prenascence 3, not-repetition 3, not-kamma 1, not-resultant 3, not-nutriment 3, not-faculty 3, not-jhāna 3, not-path 3, not-association 3, not-dissociation 3, not-presence 2, not-absence 3, not-disappearance 3, not-non-disappearance 2. . . . (Abbreviated.)

End of Not-postnascence

With not-repetition condition . . . (Expand in the same way as not-root condition.)

Not-kamma

By Twos

542. With not-kamma condition and not-root 15, not-object 15, not-predominance 15, not-proximity 15, not-contiguity 15, not-conascence 11, not-mutuality 11, not-dependence 11, not-strong-dependence 15, not-prenascence 13, not-postnascence 15, not-repetition 15, not-resultant 15, not-nutriment 15, not-faculty 15, not-jhāna 15, not-path 15, not-association 11, not-dissociation 9, not-presence 9, not-absence 15, not-disappearance 15, not-non-disappearance 9. ...

By Fours

With not-kamma, not-root, not-object conditions and not-predominance 15 . . . not-strong-dependence 13, not-prenascence 13, not-postnascence 15 . . . not-non-disappearance 9. . . .

By Tens

With not-kamma, not-root, not-object . . . not-dependence conditions and not-strong-dependence 5, not-prenascence 11, not-postnascence 9, not-repetition 11 . . . not-non-disappearance 9.

By Elevens

With not-kamma, not-root . . . not-strong-dependence conditions and not-prenascence 5, not-postnascence 1, not-repetition 5, not-resultant 5, not-nutriment 5, not-faculty 5, not-jhāna 5, not-path 5, not-association 5, not-dissociation 1, not-absence 5, not-disappearance 5. . . .

By Thirteens

With not-kamma, not-root . . . not-prenascence, not-postnascence conditions and not-repetition 1, not-resultant 1, not-nutriment 1, not-faculty 1, not-jhāna 1, not-path 1, not-association 1, not-dissociation 1, not-absence 1, not-disappearance 1. . . . (Abbreviated.)

End of Not-kamma

Not-resultant

With not-resultant condition . . .

(Expand in the same way as not-root condition.)

Not-nutriment

By Twos

543. With not-nutriment condition and not-root 15, not-object 15, not-predominance 15, not-proximity 15, not-contiguity 15, not-conascence 11, not-mutuality 11, not-dependence 11, not-strong-dependence 15, not-prenascence 13 . . . not-non-disappearance 9. . . .

By Fours

With not-nutriment, not-root, not-object conditions and not-predominance 15 . . . not-strong-dependence 13 . . . not-non-disappearance 9. . . .

By Eights

With not-nutriment, not root . . . not-conascence conditions and not-mutuality 11, not-dependence 11, not-strong-dependence 7, not-prenascence 11, not-postnascence 9, not-repetition 11, not-kamma 11, not-resultant 11, not-faculty 9, not-jhāna 11, not-path 11, not-association 11, not-dissociation 9, not-presence 9, not-absence 11, not-disappearance 11, not-non-disappearance 9. . . .

By Tens

With not-nutriment, not-root . . . not-dependence conditions and not-strong-dependence 5, not-prenascence 11, not-postnascence 9, not-repetition 11, not-kamma 11, not-resultant 11, not-faculty 9, not-jhāna 11, not-path 11, not-association 11, not-dissociation 9, not-presence 9, not-absence 11, not-disappearance 11, not-non-disappearance 9.

By Elevens

With not-nutriment, not-root . . . not-strong-dependence conditions and not-prenascence 5, not-postnascence 3, not-repetition 5, not-kamma 5, not-resultant 5, not-faculty 3, not-jhāna 5, not-path 5, not-association 5, not-dissociation 3, not-presence 2, not-absence 5, not-disappearance 5, not-non-disappearance 2. . . .

By Thirteens

With not-nutriment, not-root . . . not-prenascence, not-postnascence conditions and not-repetition 3, not-kamma 1, not-resultant 3, not-faculty 2, not-jhāna 3, not-path 3, not-association 3, not-dissociation 3, not-presence 2, not-absence 3, not-disappearance 3, not-non-disappearance 2. . . .

By Fifteens

With not-nutriment, not-root . . . not-postnascence, not-repetition, not-kamma conditions and not-resultant 1, not-jhāna 1, not-path 1, not-association 1, not-dissociation 1, not-absence 1, not-disappearance 1. ...

By Eighteens

With not-nutriment, not-root ... not-kamma, not-resultant, not-jhāna, not-path conditions and not-association 1, not-dissociation 1, not-absence 1, not-disappearance 1. ... (Abbreviated.)

Not-faculty

By Twos

544. With not-faculty condition and not-root 15, not-object 15 ... not-non-disappearance 9. ...

By Fours

With not-faculty, not-root, not-object conditions and not-predominance 15 ... not-strong-dependence 13 ... not-non-disappearance 9. ...

By Eights

With not-faculty, not-root ... not-conascence conditions and not-mutuality 11, not-dependence 11, not-strong-dependence 7, not-prenascence 11, not-postnascence 9, not-repetition 11, not-kamma 11, not-resultant 11, not-nutriment 9, not-jhāna 11, not-path 11, not-association 11, not-dissociation 9, not-presence 9, not-absence 11, not-disappearance 11, not-non-disappearance 9. ...

By Tens

With not-faculty, not-root ... not-dependence conditions and not-strong-dependence 5, not-prenascence 11, not-postnascence 9, not-repetition 11, not-kamma 11, not-resultant 11, not-nutriment 9, not-jhāna 11, not-path 11, not-association 11, not-dissociation 9, not-presence 9, not-absence 11, not-disappearance 11, not-non-disappearance 9.

By Elevens

With not-faculty, not-root ... not-strong-dependence conditions and not-prenascence 5, not-postnascence 3, not-repetition 5, not-kamma 5, not-resultant 5, not-nutriment 3. ... (Continue.)

By Thirteens

With not-faculty, not-root . . . not-prenascence, not-postnascence conditions and not-repetition 3, not-kamma 1, not-resultant 3, not-nutriment 2, not-jhāna 3, not-path 3, not-association 3, not-dissociation 3, not-presence 2, not-absence 3, not-disappearance 3, not-non-disappearance 2. . . .

By Fifteens

With not-faculty, not-root . . . not-kamma conditions and not-resultant 1, not-jhāna 1, not-path 1, not-association 1, not-dissociation 1, not-absence 1, not-disappearance 1. . . .

By Twenty-one

With not-faculty, not-root . . . not-kamma, not-resultant, not-jhāna, not-path, not-association, not-dissociation, not-absence conditions and not-disappearance 1. (Abbreviated.)

Not-jhāna, Not-path

With not-jhāna condition . . . with not-path condition . . .

(Expand in the same way as not-root condition.)

Not-association

With not-association condition . . .

(Expand in the same way as not-mutuality condition.)

Not-dissociation

By Twos

545. With not-dissociation condition and not-root 9, not-object 9, not-predominance 9, not-proximity 9, not-contiguity 9, not-conascence 9, not-mutuality 9, not-dependence 9, not-strong-dependence 9, not-prenascence 9, not-postnascence 9, not-repetition 9, not-kamma 9, not-resultant 9, not-nutriment 9, not-faculty 9, not-jhāna 9, not-path 9, not-association 9, not-presence 9, not-absence 9, not-disappearance 9, not-non-disappearance 9. . . .

By Fours

With not-dissociation, not-root, not-object conditions and not-predominance 9, not-proximity 9, not-contiguity 9, not-conascence 9, not-mutuality 9, not-dependence 9, not-strong-dependence 5, not-prenascence 9, not-postnascence 9, not-repetition 9, not-kamma 9, not-resultant 9, not-nutriment 9, not-faculty 9, not-jhāna 9, not-path 9, not-association 9, not-presence 9, not-absence 9, not-disappearance 9, not-non-disappearance 9. ...

By Tens

With not-dissociation, not-root, not-object, not-predominance, not-proximity, not-contiguity, not-conascence, not-mutuality, not-dependence conditions and not-strong-dependence 3, not-prenascence 9 ... not-non-disappearance 9.

By Elevens

With not-dissociation, not-root, not-object (Conditions abbreviated), not-dependence, not-strong-dependence conditions and not-prenascence 3, not-postnascence 3, not-repetition 3, not-kamma 1, not-resultant 3, not-nutriment 3, not-faculty 3, not-jhāna 3, not-path 3, not-association 3, not-presence 2, not-absence 3, not-disappearance 3, not-non-disappearance 2. ...

By Eighteens (with faculty) [1]

With not-dissociation, not-root, not-object (Conditions abbreviated), not-kamma, not-resultant, not-faculty conditions and not-jhāna 1 ... not-disappearance 1. ... (Abbreviated.)

Not-presence

By Twos

546. With not-presence condition and not-root 9, not-object 9, not-predominance 9, not-proximity 9, not-contiguity 9, not-conascence 9, not-mutuality 9, not-dependence 9, not-strong-dependence 9, not-prenascence 9, not-postnascence 9, not-repetition 9, not-kamma 9, not-resultant 9, not-nutriment 9, not-faculty 9, not-jhāna 9, not-path 9, not-association 9, not-dissociation 9, not-absence 9, not-disappearance 9, not-non-disappearance 9. ...

[1] Not mentioned in the Text.

By Fours
With not-presence, not-root, not-object conditions and not-predominance 9 . . . not-dependence 9, not-strong-dependence 2 . . .

By Tens
With not-presence, not-root, not-object, not-predominance, not-proximity, not-contiguity, not-conascence, not-mutuality, not-dependence conditions and not-strong-dependence 2, not-prenascence 9 . . . not-non-disappearance 9.

By Elevens (with strong-dependence) [1]
With not-presence, not-root, not-object (Conditions abbreviated), not-strong-dependence conditions and not-prenascence 2, not-postnascence 2, not-repetition 2, not-resultant 2, not-nutriment 2, not-faculty 2, not-jhāna 2, not-path 2, not-association 2, not-dissociation 2, not-absence 2, not-disappearance 2, not-non-disappearance 2. . . .

By Seventeens
With not-presence, not-root, not-object (Conditions abbreviated), not-repetition, not-resultant, not-nutriment, not-faculty conditions and not-jhāna 2 . . . not-non-disappearance 2. . . .

By Twenty-ones
With not-presence, not-root . . . not-strong-dependence, not-prenascence, not-postnascence, not-repetition, not-resultant, not-nutriment, not-faculty . . . not-dissociation conditions and not-absence 2, not-disappearance 2, not-non-disappearance 2. . . .

By Twenty-three (with strong-dependence)
With not-presence, not-root . . . not-disappearance conditions and not-non-disappearance 2.

[2] By Fourteens (with kamma)
With not-presence, not-root . . . not-dependence, not-prenascence, not-postnascence, not-repetition, not-kamma conditions and not-resultant 9, not-nutriment 9, not-faculty 9,

---

[1] Not mentioned in the Text.
[2] This portion is not included in the Text.

not-jhāna 9, not-path 9, not-association 9, not-dissociation 9, not-absence 9, not-disappearance 9, not-non-disappearance 9. ...[1]

By Twenty-three (with kamma)

With not-presence, not-root (Conditions abbreviated), not-dependence, not-prenascence (Conditions abbreviated), not-kamma ... not-disappearance conditions and not-non-disappearance 9.

Not-absence

By Twos

547. With not-absence condition and not-root 15 ... (Abbreviated).

With not-absence and not-disappearance (the same as not-root condition).

Not-disappearance

By Twos

548. With not-disappearance condition and not-root 15 ... (Abbreviated).

Not-non-disappearance

By Twos

549. With not-non-disappearance condition and not-root 9, not-object 9, not-predominance 9 ... not-disappearance 9.

Not-non-disappearance condition (the same as not-presence condition).

End of Negative Enumeration of " Investigation " Chapter.

3. CONDITIONS : POSITIVE-NEGATIVE

Root

By Twos

550. With root condition, not-object (condition) 7, not-predominance 7, not-proximity 7, not-contiguity 7, not-

---

[1] This portion is not included in the Text.

mutuality 3, not-strong-dependence 7, not-prenascence 7, not-postnascence 7, not-repetition 7, not-kamma 7, not-resultant 7, not-nutriment 7, not-faculty 7, not-jhāna 7, not-path 7, not-association 3, not-dissociation 3, not-absence 7, not-disappearance 7.

Conascence Combinations 24

Ordinary 9

Without resultant 4

551. 1. Combinations of root, conascence, dependence, presence and non-disappearance conditions, not-object (condition) 7, not-predominance 7, not-proximity 7, not-contiguity 7, not-mutuality 3, not-strong-dependence 7, not-prenascence 7, not-postnascence 7, not-repetition 7, not-kamma 7, not-resultant 7, not-nutriment 7, not-faculty 7, not-jhāna 7, not-path 7, not-association 3, not-dissociation 3, not-absence 7, not-disappearance 7 ;

2. Of root, conascence, mutuality, dependence, presence and non-disappearance conditions, not-object 3, not-predominance 3, not-proximity 3, not-contiguity 3, not-strong-dependence 3, not-prenascence 3, not-postnascence 3, not-repetition 3, not-kamma 3, not-resultant 3, not-nutriment 3, not-faculty 3, not-jhāna 3, not-path 3, not-association 1, not-dissociation 3, not-absence 3, not-disappearance 3 ;

3. Of root, conascence, mutuality, dependence, association, presence and non-disappearance conditions, not-object 3, not-predominance 3, not-proximity 3, not-contiguity 3, not-strong-dependence 3, not-prenascence 3, not-postnascence 3, not-repetition 3, not-kamma 3, not-resultant 3, not-nutriment 3, not-faculty 3, not-jhāna 3, not-path 3, not-dissociation 3, not-absence 3, not-disappearance 3 ;

4. Of root, conascence, dependence, dissociation, presence and non-disappearance conditions, not-object 3, not-predominance 3, not-proximity 3, not-contiguity 3, not-mutuality 3, not-strong-dependence 3, not-prenascence 3, not-postnascence 3, not-repetition 3, not-kamma 3, not-resultant 3,

not-nutriment 3, not-faculty 3, not-jhāna 3, not-path 3, not-association 3, not-absence 3, not-disappearance 3.

With resultant 5

5. Combinations of root, conascence, dependence, resultant, presence and non-disappearance conditions, not-object (condition) 1, not-predominance 1, not-proximity 1, not-contiguity 1, not-mutuality 1, not-strong-dependence 1, not-prenascence 1, not-postnascence 1, not-repetition 1, not-kamma 1, not-nutriment 1, not-faculty 1, not-jhāna 1, not-path 1, not-association 1, not-dissociation 1, not-absence 1, not-disappearance 1 ;

6. Of root, conascence, mutuality, dependence, resultant, presence and non-disappearance conditions, not-object 1, not-predominance 1, not-proximity 1, not-contiguity 1, not-strong-dependence 1, not-prenascence 1, not-postnascence 1, not-repetition 1, not-kamma 1, not-nutriment 1, not-faculty 1, not-jhāna 1, not-path 1, not-association 1, not-dissociation 1, not-absence 1, not-disappearance 1 ;

7. Of root, conascence, mutuality, dependence, resultant, association, presence and non-disappearance conditions, not-object 1, not-predominance 1, not-proximity 1, not-contiguity 1, not-strong-dependence 1, not-prenascence 1, not-postnascence 1, not-repetition 1, not-kamma 1, not-nutriment 1, not-faculty 1, not-jhāna 1, not-path 1, not-dissociation 1, not-absence 1, not-disappearance 1 ;

8. Of root, conascence, dependence, resultant, dissociation, presence and non-disappearance conditions, not-object 1, not-predominance 1, not-proximity 1, not-contiguity 1, not-mutuality 1, not-strong-dependence 1, not-prenascence 1, not-postnascence 1, not-repetition 1, not-kamma 1, not-nutriment 1, not-faculty 1, not-jhāna 1, not-path 1, not-association 1, not-absence 1, not-disappearance 1 ;

9. Of root, conascence, mutuality, dependence, resultant, dissociation, presence and non-disappearance conditions, not-object 1, not-predominance 1, not-proximity 1, not-contiguity 1, not-strong-dependence 1, not-prenascence 1, not-postnascence 1, not-repetition 1, not-kamma 1, not-nutriment 1,

not-faculty 1, not-jhāna 1, not-path 1, not-association 1, not-absence 1, not-disappearance 1.

With faculty and path 9

Without resultant 4

552. 10. Combinations of root, conascence, dependence, faculty, path, presence and non-disappearance conditions, not-object 4, not-predominance 4, not-proximity 4, not-contiguity 4, not-mutuality 2, not-strong-dependence 4, not-prenascence 4, not-postnascence 4, not-repetition 4, not-kamma 4, not-resultant 4, not-nutriment 4, not-jhāna 4, not-association 2, not-dissociation 2, not-absence 4, not-disappearance 4 ;

11. Of root, conascence, mutuality, dependence, faculty, path, presence and non-disappearance conditions, not-object 2, not-predominance 2, not-proximity 2, not-contiguity 2, not-strong-dependence 2, not-prenascence 2, not-postnascence 2, not-repetition 2, not-kamma 2, not-resultant 2, not-nutriment 2, not-jhāna 2, not-association 1, not-dissociation 2, not-absence 2, not-disappearance 2 ;

12. Of root, conascence, mutuality, dependence, faculty, path, association, presence and non-disappearance conditions, not-object 2, not-predominance 2, not-proximity 2, not-contiguity 2, not-strong-dependence 2, not-prenascence 2, not-postnascence 2, not-repetition 2, not-kamma 2, not-resultant 2, not-nutriment 2, not-jhāna 2, not-dissociation 2, not-absence 2, not-disappearance 2 ;

13. Of root, conascence, dependence, faculty, path, dissociation, presence and non-disappearance conditions, not-object 2, not-predominance 2, not-proximity 2, not-contiguity 2, not-mutuality 2, not-strong-dependence 2, not-prenascence 2, not-postnascence 2, not-repetition 2, not-kamma 2, not-resultant 2, not-nutriment 2, not-jhāna 2, not-association 2, not-absence 2, not-disappearance 2.

With resultant 5

14. Combinations of root, conascence, dependence, resultant, faculty, path, presence and non-disappearance conditions, not-object 1, not-predominance 1, not-proximity 1,

not-contiguity 1, not-mutuality 1, not-strong-dependence 1, not-prenascence 1, not-postnascence 1, not-repetition 1, not-kamma 1, not-nutriment 1, not-jhāna 1, not-association 1, not-dissociation 1, not-absence 1, not-disappearance 1 ;

15. Of root, conascence, mutuality, dependence, resultant, faculty, path, presence and non-disappearance conditions, not-object 1, not-predominance 1, not-proximity 1, not-contiguity 1, not-strong-dependence 1, not-prenascence 1, not-postnascence 1, not-repetition 1, not-kamma 1, not-nutriment 1, not-jhāna 1, not-association 1, not-dissociation 1, not-absence 1, not-disappearance 1 ;

16. Of root, conascence, mutuality, dependence, resultant, faculty, path, association, presence and non-disappearance conditions, not-object 1, not-predominance 1, not-proximity 1, not-contiguity 1, not-strong-dependence 1, not-prenascence 1, not-postnascence 1, not-repetition 1, not-kamma 1, not-nutriment 1, not-jhāna 1, not-dissociation 1, not-absence 1, not-disappearance 1 ;

17. Of root, conascence, dependence, resultant, faculty, path, dissociation, presence and non-disappearance conditions, not-object 1, not-predominance 1, not-proximity 1, not-contiguity 1, not-mutuality 1, not-strong-dependence 1, not-prenascence 1, not-postnascence 1, not-repetition 1, not-kamma 1, not-nutriment 1, not-jhāna 1, not-association 1, not-absence 1, not-disappearance 1 ;

18. Of root, conascence, mutuality, dependence, resultant, faculty, path, dissociation, presence and non-disappearance conditions, not-object 1, not-predominance 1, not-proximity 1, not-contiguity 1, not-strong-dependence 1, not-prenascence 1, not-postnascence 1, not-repetition 1, not-kamma 1, not-nutriment 1, not-jhāna 1, not-association 1, not-absence 1, not-disappearance 1.

With predominance, faculty and path 6

Without resultant 3

553. 19. Combinations of root, predominance, conascence, dependence, faculty, path, presence and non-disappearance

conditions, not-object 4, not-proximity 4, not-contiguity 4, not-mutuality 2, not-strong-dependence 4, not-prenascence 4, not-postnascence 4, not-repetition 4, not-kamma 4, not-resultant 4, not-nutriment 4, not-jhāna 4, not-association 2, not-dissociation 2, not-absence 4, not-disappearance 4 ;

20. Of root, predominance, conascence, mutuality, dependence, faculty, path, association, presence and non-disappearance conditions, not-object 2, not-proximity 2, not-contiguity 2, not-strong-dependence 2, not-prenascence 2, not-postnascence 2, not-repetition 2, not-kamma 2, not-resultant 2, not-nutriment 2, not-jhāna 2, not-dissociation 2, not-absence 2, not-disappearance 2 ;

21. Of root, predominance, conascence, dependence, faculty, path, dissociation, presence and non-disappearance conditions, not-object 2, not-proximity 2, not-contiguity 2, not-mutuality 2, not-strong-dependence 2, not-prenascence 2, not-postnascence 2, not-repetition 2, not-kamma 2, not-resultant 2, not-nutriment 2, not-jhāna 2, not-association 2, not-absence 2, not-disappearance 2.

With resultant 3

22. Combinations of root, predominance, conascence, dependence, resultant, faculty, path, presence and non-disappearance conditions, not-object 1, not-proximity 1, not-contiguity 1, not-mutuality 1, not-strong-dependence 1, not-prenascence 1, not-postnascence 1, not-repetition 1, not-kamma 1, not-nutriment 1, not-jhāna 1, not-association 1, not-dissociation 1, not-absence 1, not-disappearance 1 ;

23. Of root, predominance, conascence, mutuality, dependence, resultant, faculty, path, association, presence and non-disappearance conditions, not-object 1, not-proximity 1, not-contiguity 1, not-strong-dependence 1, not-prenascence 1, not-postnascence 1, not-repetition 1, not-kamma 1, not-nutriment 1, not-jhāna 1, not-dissociation 1, not-absence 1, not-disappearance 1 ;

24. Of root, predominance, conascence, dependence, resultant, faculty, path, dissociation, presence and non-disappearance conditions, not-object 1, not-proximity 1,

not-contiguity 1, not-mutuality 1, not-strong-dependence 1, not-prenascence 1, not-postnascence 1, not-repetition 1, not-kamma 1, not-nutriment 1, not-jhāna 1, not-association 1, not-absence 1, not-disappearance 1.

End of Root

Object

By Twos

554. With object condition, not-root 9, not-predominance 9, not-proximity 9, not-contiguity 9, not-conascence 9, not-mutuality 9, not-dependence 9, not-strong-dependence 9, not-prenascence 9, not-postnascence 9, not-repetition 9, not-kamma 9, not-resultant 9, not-nutriment 9, not-faculty 9, not-jhāna 9, not-path 9, not-association 9, not-dissociation 9, not-presence 9, not-absence 9, not-disappearance 9, not-non-disappearance 9.

(Miscellaneous) Combinations 5

555. 1. Combinations of object, predominance and strong-dependence conditions, not-root 7, not-proximity 7, not-contiguity 7, not-conascence 7, not-mutuality 7, not-dependence 7, not-prenascence 7, not-postnascence 7, not-repetition 7, not-kamma 7, not-resultant 7, not-nutriment 7, not-faculty 7, not-jhāna 7, not-path 7, not-association 7, not-dissociation 7, not-presence 7, not-absence 7, not-disappearance 7, not-non-disappearance 7 ;

2. Of object, prenascence, presence and non-disappearance conditions, not-root 3, not-predominance 3, not-proximity 3, not-contiguity 3, not-conascence 3, not-mutuality 3, not-dependence 3, not-strong-dependence 3, not-postnascence 3, not-repetition 3, not-kamma 3, not-resultant 3, not-nutriment 3, not-faculty 3, not-jhāna 3, not-path 3, not-association 3, not-dissociation 3, not-absence 3, not-disappearance 3 ;

3. Of object, dependence, prenascence, dissociation, presence and non-disappearance conditions, not-root 3, not-predominance 3, not-proximity 3, not-contiguity 3, not-conascence 3, not-mutuality 3, not-strong-dependence 3, not-postnascence 3, not-repetition 3, not-kamma 3, not-resultant 3, not-nutriment 3, not-faculty 3, not-jhāna 3, not-path 3, not-association 3, not-absence 3, not-disappearance 3 ;

4. Of object, predominance, strong-dependence, prenascence, presence and non-disappearance conditions, not-root 1, not-proximity 1, not-contiguity 1, not-conascence 1, not-mutuality 1, not-dependence 1, not-postnascence 1, not-repetition 1, not-kamma 1, not-resultant 1, not-nutriment 1, not-faculty 1, not-jhāna 1, not-path 1, not-association 1, not-dissociation 1, not-absence 1, not-disappearance 1 ;

5. Of object, predominance, dependence, strong-dependence, prenascence, dissociation, presence and non-disappearance conditions, not-root 1, not-proximity 1, not-contiguity 1, not-conascence 1, not-mutuality 1, not-postnascence 1, not-repetition 1, not-kamma 1, not-resultant 1, not-nutriment 1, not-faculty 1, not-jhāna 1, not-path 1, not-association 1, not-absence 1, not-disappearance 1.

End of Object

Predominance

By Twos

556. With predominance condition, not-root 10, not-object 7, not-proximity 10, not-contiguity 10, not-conascence 7, not-mutuality 8, not-dependence 7, not-strong-dependence 7, not-prenascence 10, not-postnascence 10, not-repetition 10, not-kamma 10, not-resultant 10, not-nutriment 10, not-faculty 10, not-jhāna 10, not-path 10, not-association 8, not-dissociation 7, not-presence 7, not-absence 10, not-disappearance 10, not-non-disappearance 7.

Combinations 30

Mixed 3

557. 1. Combinations of predominance, presence and non-disappearance conditions, not-root 8, not-object 7, not-proximity 8, not-contiguity 8, not-conascence 1, not-mutuality 4, not-dependence 1, not-strong-dependence 7, not-prenascence 7, not-postnascence 8, not-repetition 8, not-kamma 8, not-resultant 8, not-nutriment 8, not-faculty 8, not-jhāna 8, not-path 8, not-association 4, not-dissociation 4, not-absence 8, not-disappearance 8 ;

2. Of predominance, dependence, presence and non-disappearance conditions, not-root 8, not-object 7, not-proximity 8, not-contiguity 8, not-conascence 1, not-mutuality 4, not-strong-dependence 7, not-prenascence 7, not-postnascence 8, not-repetition 8, not-kamma 8, not-resultant 8, not-nutriment 8, not-faculty 8, not-jhāna 8, not-path 8, not-association 4, not-dissociation 3, not-absence 8, not-disappearance 8 ;

3. Of predominance, dependence, dissociation, presence and non-disappearance conditions, not-root 4, not-object 3, not-proximity 4, not-contiguity 4, not-conascence 1, not-mutuality 4, not-strong-dependence 3, not-prenascence 3, not-postnascence 4, not-repetition 4, not-kamma 4, not-resultant 4, not-nutriment 4, not-faculty 4, not-jhāna 4, not-path 4, not-association 4, not-absence 4, not-disappearance 4.

Miscellaneous 3

558. 4. Combinations of predominance, object and strong-dependence conditions, not-root 7, not-proximity 7, not-contiguity 7, not-conascence 7, not-mutuality 7, not-dependence 7, not-prenascence 7, not-postnascence 7, not-repetition 7, not-kamma 7, not-resultant 7, not-nutriment 7, not-faculty 7, not-jhāna 7, not-path 7, not-association 7, not-dissociation 7, not-presence 7, not-absence 7, not-disappearance 7, not-non-disappearance 7 ;

5. Of predominance, object, strong-dependence, prenascence, presence and non-disappearance conditions, not-root 1, not-proximity 1, not-contiguity 1, not-conascence 1, not-mutuality 1, not-dependence 1, not-postnascence 1, not-repetition 1, not-kamma 1, not-resultant 1, not-nutriment 1, not-faculty 1, not-jhāna 1, not-path 1, not-association 1, not-dissociation 1, not-absence 1, not-disappearance 1 ;

6. Of predominance, object, dependence, strong-dependence, prenascence, dissociation, presence and non-disappearance conditions, not-root 1, not-proximity 1, not-contiguity 1, not-conascence 1, not-mutuality 1, not-postnascence 1, not-repetition 1, not-kamma 1, not-resultant 1, not-nutriment 1, not-faculty 1, not-jhāna 1, not-path 1, not-association 1, not-absence 1, not-disappearance 1.

Conascence 24

Predominant desire 6

Without resultant 3

559. 7. Combinations of predominance, conascence, dependence, presence and non-disappearance conditions, not-root 7, not-object 7, not-proximity 7, not-contiguity 7, not-mutuality 3, not-strong-dependence 7, not-prenascence 7, not-postnascence 7, not-repetition 7, not-kamma 7, not-resultant 7, not-nutriment 7, not-faculty 7, not-jhāna 7, not-path 7, not-association 3, not-dissociation 3, not-absence 7, not-disappearance 7 ;

8. Of predominance, conascence, mutuality, dependence, association, presence and non-disappearance conditions, not-root 3, not-object 3, not-proximity 3, not-contiguity 3, not-strong-dependence 3, not-prenascence 3, not-postnascence 3, not-repetition 3, not-kamma 3, not-resultant 3, not-nutriment 3, not-faculty 3, not-jhāna 3, not-path 3, not-dissociation 3, not-absence 3, not-disappearance 3 ;

9. Of predominance, conascence, dependence, dissociation, presence and non-disappearance conditions, not-root 3, not-object 3, not-proximity 3, not-contiguity 3, not-mutuality 3, not-strong-dependence 3, not-prenascence 3, not-postnascence 3, not-repetition 3, not-kamma 3, not-resultant 3, not-nutriment 3, not-faculty 3, not-jhāna 3, not-path 3, not-association 3, not-absence 3, not-disappearance 3.

With resultant 3

10. Combinations of predominance, conascence, dependence, resultant, presence and non-disappearance conditions, not-root 1, not-object 1, not-proximity 1, not-contiguity 1, not-mutuality 1, not-strong-dependence 1, not-prenascence 1, not-postnascence 1, not-repetition 1, not-kamma 1, not-nutriment 1, not-faculty 1, not-jhāna 1, not-path 1, not-association 1, not-dissociation 1, not-absence 1, not-disappearance 1 ;

11. Of predominance, conascence, mutuality, dependence, resultant, association, presence and non-disappearance conditions, not-root 1, not-object 1, not-proximity 1, not-contiguity 1, not-strong-dependence 1, not-prenascence 1, not-postnascence 1, not-repetition 1, not-kamma 1, not-nutriment 1, not-faculty 1, not-jhāna 1, not-path 1, not-dissociation 1, not-absence 1, not-disappearance 1 ;

12. Of predominance, conascence, dependence, resultant, dissociation, presence and non-disappearance conditions, not-root 1, not-object 1, not-proximity 1, not-contiguity 1, not-mutuality 1, not-strong-dependence 1, not-prenascence 1, not-postnascence 1, not-repetition 1, not-kamma 1, not-nutriment 1, not-faculty 1, not-jhāna 1, not-path 1, not-association 1, not-absence 1, not-disappearance 1.

[1] With nutriment and faculty 6

Without resultant 3

560. 13. Combinations of predominance, conascence, dependence, nutriment, faculty, presence and non-disappearance conditions, not-root 7, not-object 7, not-proximity 7, not-contiguity 7, not-mutuality 3, not-strong-dependence 7, not-prenascence 7, not-postnascence 7, not-repetition 7, not-kamma 7, not-resultant 7, not-jhāna 7, not-path 7, not-association 3, not-dissociation 3, not-absence 7, not-disappearance 7 ;

14. Of predominance, conascence, mutuality, dependence, nutriment, faculty, association, presence and non-disappearance conditions, not-root 3, not-object 3, not-proximity 3, not-contiguity 3, not-strong-dependence 3, not-prenascence 3, not-postnascence 3, not-repetition 3, not-kamma 3, not-resultant 3, not-jhāna 3, not-path 3, not-dissociation 3, not-absence 3, not-disappearance 3 ;

15. Of predominance, conascence, dependence, nutriment, faculty, dissociation, presence and non-disappearance conditions, not-root 3, not-object 3, not-proximity 3, not-contiguity 3, not-mutuality 3, not-strong-dependence 3, not-prenascence 3,

[1] Not as in the Text.

not-postnascence 3, not-repetition 3, not-kamma 3, not-resultant 3, not-jhāna 3, not-path 3, not-association 3, not-absence 3, not-disappearance 3.

With resultant 3

16. Combinations of predominance, conascence, dependence, resultant, nutriment, faculty, presence and non-disappearance conditions, not-root 1, not-object 1, not-proximity 1, not-contiguity 1, not-mutuality 1, not-strong-dependence 1, not-prenascence 1, not-postnascence 1, not-repetition 1, not-kamma 1, not-jhāna 1, not-path 1, not-association 1, not-dissociation 1, not-absence 1, not-disappearance 1;

17. Of predominance, conascence, mutuality, dependence, resultant, nutriment, faculty, association, presence and non-disappearance conditions, not-root 1, not-object 1, not-proximity 1, not-contiguity 1, not-strong-dependence 1, not-prenascence 1, not-postnascence 1, not-repetition 1, not-kamma 1, not-jhāna 1, not-path 1, not-dissociation 1, not-absence 1, not-disappearance 1;

18. Of predominance, conascence, dependence, resultant, nutriment, faculty, dissociation, presence and non-disappearance conditions, not-root 1, not-object 1, not-proximity 1, not-contiguity 1, not-mutuality 1, not-strong-dependence 1, not-prenascence 1, not-postnascence 1, not-repetition 1, not-kamma 1, not-jhāna 1, not-path 1, not-association 1, not-absence 1, not-disappearance 1.

[1] With faculty and path 6

Without resultant 3

561. 19. Combinations of predominance, conascence, dependence, faculty, path, presence and non-disappearance conditions, not-root 7, not-object 7, not-proximity 7, not-contiguity 7, not-mutuality 3, not-strong-dependence 7, not-prenascence 7, not-postnascence 7, not-repetition 7, not-kamma 7, not-resultant 7, not-nutriment 7, not-jhāna 7, not-association 3, not-dissociation 3, not-absence 7, not-disappearance 7;

[1] Not as in the Text.

20. Of predominance, conascence, mutuality, dependence, faculty, path, association, presence and non-disappearance conditions, not-root 3, not-object 3, not-proximity 3, not-contiguity 3, not-strong-dependence 3, not-prenascence 3, not-postnascence 3, not-repetition 3, not-kamma 3, not-resultant 3, not-nutriment 3, not-jhāna 3, not-dissociation 3, not-absence 3, not-disappearance 3 ;

21. Of predominance, conascence, dependence, faculty, path, dissociation, presence and non-disappearance conditions, not-root 3, not-object 3, not-proximity 3, not-contiguity 3, not-mutuality 3, not-strong-dependence 3, not-prenascence 3, not-postnascence 3, not-repetition 3, not-kamma 3, not-resultant 3, not-nutriment 3, not-jhāna 3, not-association 3, not-absence 3, not-disappearance 3.

With resultant 3

22. Combinations of predominance, conascence, dependence, resultant, faculty, path, presence and non-disappearance conditions, not-root 1, not-object 1, not-proximity 1, not-contiguity 1, not-mutuality 1, not-strong-dependence 1, not-prenascence 1, not-postnascence 1, not-repetition 1, not-kamma 1, not-nutriment 1, not-jhāna 1, not-association 1, not-dissociation 1, not-absence 1, not-disappearance 1 ;

23. Of predominance, conascence, mutuality, dependence, resultant, faculty, path, association, presence and non-disappearance conditions, not-root 1, not-object 1, not-proximity 1, not-contiguity 1, not-strong-dependence 1, not-prenascence 1, not-postnascence 1, not-repetition 1, not-kamma 1, not-nutriment 1, not-jhāna 1, not-dissociation 1, not-absence 1, not-disappearance 1 ;

24. Of predominance, conascence, dependence, resultant, faculty, path, dissociation, presence and non-disappearance conditions, not-root 1, not-object 1, not-proximity 1, not-contiguity 1, not-mutuality 1, not-strong-dependence 1, not-prenascence 1, not-postnascence 1, not-repetition 1, not-kamma 1, not-nutriment 1, not-jhāna 1, not-association 1, not-absence 1, not-disappearance 1.

[1] With root, faculty and path 6

Without resultant 3

562. 25. Combinations of predominance, root, conascence, dependence, faculty, path, presence and non-disappearance conditions, not-object 4, not-proximity 4, not-contiguity 4, not-mutuality 2, not-strong-dependence 4, not-prenascence 4, not-postnascence 4, not-repetition 4, not-kamma 4, not-resultant 4, not-nutriment 4, not-jhāna 4, not-association 2, not-dissociation 2, not-absence 4, not-disappearance 4 ;

26. Of predominance, root, conascence, mutuality, dependence, faculty, path, association, presence and non-disappearance conditions, not-object 2, not-proximity 2, not-contiguity 2, not-strong-dependence 2, not-prenascence 2, not-postnascence 2, not-repetition 2, not-kamma 2, not-resultant 2, not-nutriment 2, not-jhāna 2, not-dissociation 2, not-absence 2, not-disappearance 2 ;

27. Of predominance, root, conascence, dependence, faculty, path, dissociation, presence and non-disappearance conditions, not-object 2, not-proximity 2, not-contiguity 2, not-mutuality 2, not-strong-dependence 2, not-prenascence 2, not-postnascence 2, not-repetition 2, not-kamma 2, not-resultant 2, not-nutriment 2, not-jhāna 2, not-association 2, not-absence 2, not-disappearance 2.

With resultant 3

28. Combinations of predominance, root, conascence, dependence, resultant, faculty, path, presence and non-disappearance conditions, not-object 1, not-proximity 1, not-contiguity 1, not-mutuality 1, not-strong-dependence 1, not-prenascence 1, not-postnascence 1, not-repetition 1, not-kamma 1, not-nutriment 1, not-jhāna 1, not-association 1, not-dissociation 1, not-absence 1, not-disappearance 1 ;

29. Of predominance, root, conascence, mutuality, dependence, resultant, faculty, path, association, presence and non-disappearance conditions, not-object 1, not-proximity 1, not-contiguity 1, not-strong-dependence 1, not-prenascence 1,

[1] Not as in the Text.

not-postnascence 1, not-repetition 1, not-kamma 1, not-nutriment 1, not-jhāna 1, not-dissociation 1, not-absence 1, not-disappearance 1 ;

30. Of predominance, root, conascence, dependence, resultant, faculty, path, dissociation, presence and non-disappearance conditions, not-object 1, not-proximity 1, not-contiguity 1, not-mutuality 1, not-strong-dependence 1, not-prenascence 1, not-postnascence 1, not-repetition 1, not-kamma 1, not-nutriment 1, not-jhāna 1, not-association 1, not-absence 1, not-disappearance 1.

End of Predominance

Proximity

By Twos

563. With proximity condition, not-root 7, not-object 7, not-predominance 7, not-conascence 7, not-mutuality 7, not-dependence 7, not-prenascence 7, not-postnascence 7, not-repetition 5, not-kamma 7, not-resultant 7, not-nutriment 7, not-faculty 7, not-jhāna 7, not-path 7, not-association 7, not-dissociation 7, not-presence 7, not-non-disappearance 7.

(Miscellaneous) Combinations 3

564.1. Combinations of proximity, contiguity, strong-dependence, absence and disappearance conditions, not-root 7, not-object 7, not-predominance 7, not-conascence 7, not-mutuality 7, not-dependence 7, not-prenascence 7, not-postnascence 7, not-repetition 5, not-kamma 7, not-resultant 7, not-nutriment 7, not-faculty 7, not-jhāna 7, not-path 7, not-association 7, not-dissociation 7, not-presence 7, not-non-disappearance 7 ;

2. Of proximity, contiguity, strong-dependence, repetition, absence and disappearance conditions, not-root 3, not-object 3, not-predominance 3, not-conascence 3, not-mutuality 3, not-dependence 3, not-prenascence 3, not-postnascence 3, not-kamma 3, not-resultant 3, not-nutriment 3, not-faculty 3, not-jhāna 3, not-path 3, not-association 3, not-dissociation 3, not-presence 3, not-non-disappearance 3 ;

3. Of proximity, contiguity, strong-dependence, kamma, absence and disappearance conditions, not-root 1, not-object 1,

not-predominance 1, not-conascence 1, not-mutuality 1, not-dependence 1, not-prenascence 1, not-postnascence 1, not-repetition 1, not-resultant 1, not-nutriment 1, not-faculty 1, not-jhāna 1, not-path 1, not-association 1, not-dissociation 1, not-presence 1, not-non-disappearance 1.

End of Proximity

By Twos *Contiguity*

565. With contiguity condition, not-root 7, not-object 7, not-predominance 7, not-conascence 7, not-mutuality 7, not-dependence 7, not-prenascence 7, not-postnascence 7, not-repetition 5, not-kamma 7, not-resultant 7, not-nutriment 7, not-faculty 7, not-jhāna 7, not-path 7, not-association 7, not-dissociation 7, not-presence 7, not-non-disappearance 7.

(Miscellaneous) Combinations 3

566. 1. Combinations of contiguity, proximity, strong-dependence, absence and disappearance conditions, not-root 7, not-object 7, not-predominance 7, not-conascence 7, not-mutuality 7, not-dependence 7, not-prenascence 7, not-postnascence 7, not-repetition 5, not-kamma 7, not-resultant 7, not-nutriment 7, not-faculty 7, not-jhāna 7, not-path 7, not-association 7, not-dissociation 7, not-presence 7, not-non-disappearance 7 ;

2. Of contiguity, proximity, strong-dependence, repetition, absence and disappearance conditions, not-root 3, not-object 3, not-predominance 3, not-conascence 3, not-mutuality 3, not-dependence 3, not-prenascence 3, not-postnascence 3, not-kamma 3, not-resultant 3, not-nutriment 3, not-faculty 3, not-jhāna 3, not-path 3, not-association 3, not-dissociation 3, not-presence 3, not-non-disappearance 3 ;

3. Of contiguity, proximity, strong-dependence, kamma, absence and disappearance conditions, not-root 1, not-object 1, not-predominance 1, not-conascence 1, not-mutuality 1, not-dependence 1, not-prenascence 1, not-postnascence 1, not-repetition 1, not-resultant 1, not-nutriment 1, not-faculty 1, not-jhāna 1, not-path 1, not-association 1, not-dissociation 1, not-presence 1, not-non-disappearance 1.

End of Contiguity

Conascence

By Twos

567. With conascence condition, not-root 9, not-object 9, not-predominance 9, not-proximity 9, not-contiguity 9, not-mutuality 5, not-strong-dependence 9, not-prenascence 9, not-postnascence 9, not-repetition 9, not-kamma 9, not-resultant 9, not-nutriment 9, not-faculty 9, not-jhāna 9, not-path 9, not-association 5, not-dissociation 3, not-absence 9, not-disappearance 9.

Conascence Combinations 10

Without resultant 5

568. 1. Combinations of conascence, dependence, presence and non-disappearance conditions, not-root 9, not-object 9, not-predominance 9, not-proximity 9, not-contiguity 9, not-mutuality 5, not-strong-dependence 9 . . . not-path 9, not-association 5, not-dissociation 3, not-absence 9, not-disappearance 9 ;

2. Of conascence, mutuality, dependence, presence and non-disappearance conditions, not-root 3, not-object 3, not-predominance 3, not-proximity 3, not-contiguity 3, not-strong-dependence 3, not-prenascence 3, not-postnascence 3, not-repetition 3, not-kamma 3, not-resultant 3, not-nutriment 3, not-faculty 3, not-jhāna 3, not-path 3, not-association 1, not-dissociation 3, not-absence 3, not-disappearance 3 ;

3. Of conascence, mutuality, dependence, association, presence and non-disappearance conditions, not-root 3, not-object 3, not-predominance 3, not-proximity 3, not-contiguity 3, not-strong-dependence 3, not-prenascence 3, not-postnascence 3, not-repetition 3, not-kamma 3, not-resultant 3, not-nutriment 3, not-faculty 3, not-jhāna 3, not-path 3, not-dissociation 3, not-absence 3, not-disappearance 3 ;

4. Of conascence, dependence, dissociation, presence and non-disappearance conditions, not-root 3, not-object 3, not-predominance 3, not-proximity 3, not-contiguity 3, not-mutuality 3, not-strong-dependence 3, not-prenascence 3, not-postnascence 3, not-repetition 3, not-kamma 3, not-resultant 3,

Faultless Triplet

not-nutriment 3, not-faculty 3, not-jhāna 3, not-path 3, not-association 3, not-absence 3, not-disappearance 3 ;

5. Of conascence, mutuality, dependence, dissociation, presence and non-disappearance conditions, not-root 1, not-object 1, not-predominance 1, not-proximity 1, not-contiguity 1, not-strong-dependence 1, not-prenascence 1, not-postnascence 1, not-repetition 1, not-kamma 1, not-resultant 1, not-nutriment 1, not-faculty 1, not-jhāna 1, not-path 1, not-association 1, not-absence 1, not-disappearance 1.

With resultant 5

6. Combinations of conascence, dependence, resultant, presence and non-disappearance conditions, not-root 1, not-object 1, not-predominance 1, not-proximity 1, not-contiguity 1, not-mutuality 1, not-strong-dependence 1, not-prenascence 1, not-postnascence 1, not-repetition 1, not-kamma 1, not-nutriment 1, not-faculty 1, not-jhāna 1, not-path 1, not-association 1, not-dissociation 1, not-absence 1, not-disappearance 1 ;

7. Of conascence, mutuality, dependence, resultant, presence and non-disappearance conditions, not-root 1, not-object 1, not-predominance 1, not-proximity 1, not-contiguity 1, not-strong-dependence 1, not-prenascence 1, not-postnascence 1, not-repetition 1, not-kamma 1, not-nutriment 1, not-faculty 1, not-jhāna 1, not-path 1, not-association 1, not-dissociation 1, not-absence 1, not-disappearance 1 ;

8. Of conascence, mutuality, dependence, resultant, association, presence and non-disappearance conditions, not-root 1, not-object 1, not-predominance 1, not-proximity 1, not-contiguity 1, not-strong-dependence 1, not-prenascence 1, not-postnascence 1, not-repetition 1, not-kamma 1, not-nutriment 1, not-faculty 1, not-jhāna 1, not-path 1, not-dissociation 1, not-absence 1, not-disappearance 1 ;

9. Of conascence, dependence, resultant, dissociation, presence and non-disappearance conditions, not-root 1, not-object 1, not-predominance 1, not-proximity 1, not-contiguity 1, not-mutuality 1, not-strong-dependence 1, not-prenascence 1, not-postnascence 1, not-repetition 1, not-kamma 1,

not-nutriment 1, not-faculty 1, not-jhāna 1, not-path 1, not-association 1, not-absence 1, not-disappearance 1 ;

10. Of conascence, mutuality, dependence, resultant, dissociation, presence and non-disappearance conditions, not-root 1, not-object 1, not-predominance 1, not-proximity 1, not-contiguity 1, not-strong-dependence 1, not-prenascence 1, not-postnascence 1, not-repetition 1, not-kamma 1, not-nutriment 1, not-faculty 1, not-jhāna 1, not-path 1, not-association 1, not-absence 1, not-disappearance 1.

End of Conascence

Mutuality

By Twos

569. With mutuality condition, not-root 3, not-object 3, not-predominance 3, not-proximity 3, not-contiguity 3, not-strong-dependence 3, not-prenascence 3, not-postnascence 3, not-repetition 3, not-kamma 3, not-resultant 3, not-nutriment 3, not-faculty 3, not-jhāna 3, not-path 3, not-association 1, not-dissociation 3, not-absence 3, not-disappearance 3.

(Conascence) Combinations 6

Without resultant 3

570. 1. Combinations of mutuality, conascence, dependence, presence and non-disappearance conditions, not-root 3, not-object 3, not-predominance 3, not-proximity 3, not-contiguity 3, not-strong-dependence 3, not-prenascence 3, not-postnascence 3, not-repetition 3, not-kamma 3, not-resultant 3, not-nutriment 3, not-faculty 3, not-jhāna 3, not-path 3, not-association 1, not-dissociation 3, not-absence 3, not-disappearance 3 ;

2. Of mutuality, conascence, dependence, association, presence and non-disappearance conditions, not-root 3, not-object 3, not-predominance 3, not-proximity 3, not-contiguity 3, not-strong-dependence 3, not-prenascence 3, not-postnascence 3, not-repetition 3, not-kamma 3, not-resultant 3, not-nutriment 3, not-faculty 3, not-jhāna 3, not-path 3, not-dissociation 3, not-absence 3, not-disappearance 3 ;

3. Of mutuality, conascence, dependence, dissociation, presence and non-disappearance conditions, not-root 1, not-object 1, not-predominance 1, not-proximity 1, not-contiguity 1, not-strong-dependence 1, not-prenascence 1, not-postnascence 1, not-repetition 1, not-kamma 1, not-resultant 1, not-nutriment 1, not-faculty 1, not-jhāna 1, not-path 1, not-association 1, not-absence 1, not-disappearance 1.

With resultant 3

4. Combinations of mutuality, conascence, dependence, resultant, presence and non-disappearance conditions, not-root 1, not-object 1, not-predominance 1, not-proximity 1, not-contiguity 1, not-strong-dependence 1, not-prenascence 1, not-postnascence 1, not-repetition 1, not-kamma 1, not-nutriment 1, not-faculty 1, not-jhāna 1, not-path 1, not-association 1, not-dissociation 1, not-absence 1, not-disappearance 1 ;

5. Of mutuality, conascence, dependence, resultant, association, presence and non-disappearance conditions, not-root 1, not-object 1, not-predominance 1, not-proximity 1, not-contiguity 1, not-strong-dependence 1, not-prenascence 1, not-postnascence 1, not-repetition 1, not-kamma 1, not-nutriment 1, not-faculty 1, not-jhāna 1, not-path 1, not-dissociation 1, not-absence 1, not-disappearance 1 ;

6. Of mutuality, conascence, dependence, resultant, dissociation presence and non-disappearance conditions, not-root 1, not-object 1, not-predominance 1, not-proximity 1, not-contiguity 1, not-strong-dependence 1, not-prenascence 1, not-postnascence 1, not-repetition 1, not-kamma 1, not-nutriment 1, not-faculty 1, not-jhāna 1, not-path 1, not-association 1, not-absence 1, not-disappearance 1.

End of Mutuality

Dependence

By Twos

571. With dependence condition, not-root 13, not-object 13, not-predominance 13, not-proximity 13, not-contiguity 13, not-conascence 3, not-mutuality 7, not-strong-dependence 13,

not-prenascence 9, not-postnascence 13, not-repetition 13, not-kamma 13, not-resultant 13, not-nutriment 13, not-faculty 13, not-jhāna 13, not-path 13, not-association 7, not-dissociation 3, not-absence 13, not-disappearance 13.

Combinations 20

Mixed 6

572. 1. Combinations of dependence, presence and non-disappearance conditions, not-root 13, not-object 13, not-predominance 13, not-proximity 13, not-contiguity 13, not-conascence 3, not-mutuality 7, not-strong-dependence 13, not-prenascence 9, not-postnascence 13, not-repetition 13, not-kamma 13, not-resultant 13, not-nutriment 13, not-faculty 13, not-jhāna 13, not-path 13, not-association 7, not-dissociation 3, not-absence 13, not-disappearance 13 ;

2. Of dependence, predominance, presence and non-disappearance conditions, not-root 8, not-object 7, not-proximity 8, not-contiguity 8, not-conascence 1, not-mutuality 4, not-strong-dependence 7, not-prenascence 7, not-postnascence 8, not-repetition 8, not-kamma 8, not-resultant 8, not-nutriment 8, not-faculty 8, not-jhāna 8, not-path 8, not-association 4, not-dissociation 3, not-absence 8, not-disappearance 8 ;

3. Of dependence, faculty, presence and non-disappearance conditions, not-root 7, not-object 7, not-predominance 7, not-proximity 7, not-contiguity 7, not-conascence 1, not-mutuality 3, not-strong-dependence 7, not-prenascence 7, not-postnascence 7, not-repetition 7, not-kamma 7, not-resultant 7, not-nutriment 7, not-jhāna 7, not-path 7, not-association 3, not-dissociation 3, not-absence 7, not-disappearance 7 ;

4. Of dependence, dissociation, presence and non-disappearance conditions, not-root 5, not-object 5, not-predominance 5, not-proximity 5, not-contiguity 5, not-conascence 3, not-mutuality 5, not-strong-dependence 5, not-prenascence 3, not-postnascence 5, not-repetition 5, not-kamma 5, not-resultant 5, not-nutriment 5, not-faculty 5, not-jhāna 5, not-path 5, not-association 5, not-absence 5, not-disappearance 5 ;

5. Of dependence, predominance, dissociation, presence and non-disappearance conditions, not-root 4, not-object 3, not-proximity 4, not-contiguity 4, not-conascence 1, not-mutuality 4, not-strong-dependence 3, not-prenascence 3, not-postnascence 4, not-repetition 4, not-kamma 4, not-resultant 4, not-nutriment 4, not-faculty 4, not-jhāna 4, not-path 4, not-association 4, not-absence 4, not-disappearance 4 ;

6. Of dependence, faculty, dissociation, presence and non-disappearance conditions, not-root 3, not-object 3, not-predominance 3, not-proximity 3, not-contiguity 3, not-conascence 1, not-mutuality 3, not-strong-dependence 3, not-prenascence 3, not-postnascence 3, not-repetition 3, not-kamma 3, not-resultant 3, not-nutriment 3, not-jhāna 3, not-path 3, not-association 3, not-absence 3, not-disappearance 3.

Miscellaneous 4

573. 7. Combinations of dependence, prenascence, dissociation, presence and non-disappearance conditions, not-root 3, not-object 3, not-predominance 3, not-proximity 3, not-contiguity 3, not-conascence 3, not-mutuality 3, not-strong-dependence 3, not-postnascence 3, not-repetition 3, not-kamma 3, not-resultant 3, not-nutriment 3, not-faculty 3, not-jhāna 3, not-path 3, not-association 3, not-absence 3, not-disappearance 3 ;

8. Of dependence, object, prenascence, dissociation, presence and non-disappearance conditions, not-root 3, not-predominance 3, not-proximity 3, not-contiguity 3, not-conascence 3, not-mutuality 3, not-strong-dependence 3, not-postnascence 3, not-repetition 3, not-kamma 3, not-resultant 3, not-nutriment 3, not-faculty 3, not-jhāna 3, not-path 3, not-association 3, not-absence 3, not-disappearance 3 ;

9. Of dependence, object, predominance, strong-dependence, prenascence, dissociation, presence and non-disappearance conditions, not-root 1, not-proximity 1, not-contiguity 1, not-conascence 1, not-mutuality 1, not-postnascence 1, not-repetition 1, not-kamma 1, not-resultant 1, not-nutriment 1, not-faculty 1, not-jhāna 1, not-path 1, not-association 1, not-absence 1, not-disappearance 1 ;

10. Of dependence, prenascence, faculty, dissociation,

presence and non-disappearance conditions, not-root 1, not-object 1, not-predominance 1, not-proximity 1, not-contiguity 1, not-conascence 1, not-mutuality 1, not-strong-dependence 1, not-postnascence 1, not-repetition 1, not-kamma 1, not-resultant 1, not-nutriment 1, not-jhāna 1, not-path 1, not-association 1, not-absence 1, not-disappearance 1.

Conascence 10

Without resultant 5

574. 11. Combinations of dependence, conascence, presence and non-disappearance conditions, not-root 9, not-object 9, not-predominance 9, not-proximity 9, not-contiguity, 9, not-mutuality 5, not-strong-dependence 9, not-prenascence 9, not-postnascence 9, not-repetition 9, not-kamma 9, not-resultant 9, not-nutriment 9, not-faculty 9, not-jhāna 9, not-path 9, not-association 5, not-dissociation 3, not-absence 9, not-disappearance 9;

12. Of dependence, conascence, mutuality, presence and non-disappearance conditions, not-root 3, not-object 3, not-predominance 3, not-proximity 3, not-contiguity 3, not-strong-dependence 3, not-prenascence 3, not-postnascence 3, not-repetition 3, not-kamma 3, not-resultant 3, not-nutriment 3, not-faculty 3, not-jhāna 3, not-path 3, not-association 1, not-dissociation 3, not-absence 3, not-disappearance 3;

13. Of dependence, conascence, mutuality, association, presence and non-disappearance conditions, not-root 3, not-object 3, not-predominance 3, not-proximity 3, not-contiguity 3, not-strong-dependence 3, not-prenascence 3, not-postnascence 3, not-repetition 3, not-kamma 3, not-resultant 3, not-nutriment 3, not-faculty 3, not-jhāna 3, not-path 3, not-dissociation 3, not-absence 3, not-disappearance 3;

14. Of dependence, conascence, dissociation, presence and non-disappearance conditions, not-root 3, not-object 3, not-predominance 3, not-proximity 3, not-contiguity 3, not-mutuality 3, not-strong-dependence 3, not-prenascence 3, not-postnascence 3, not-repetition 3, not-kamma 3, not-resultant 3, not-nutriment 3, not-faculty 3, not-jhāna 3, not-path 3, not-association 3, not-absence 3, not-disappearance 3;

15. Of dependence, conascence, mutuality, dissociation, presence and non-disappearance conditions, not-root 1, not-object 1, not-predominance 1, not-proximity 1, not-contiguity 1, not-strong-dependence 1, not-prenascence 1, not-postnascence 1, not-repetition 1, not-kamma 1, not-resultant 1, not-nutriment 1, not-faculty 1, not-jhāna 1, not-path 1, not-association 1, not-absence 1, not-disappearance 1.

With resultant 5

16. Combinations of dependence, conascence, resultant, presence and non-disappearance conditions, not-root 1, not-object 1, not-predominance 1, not-proximity 1, not-contiguity 1, not-mutuality 1, not-strong-dependence 1, not-prenascence 1, not-postnascence 1, not-repetition 1, not-kamma 1, not-nutriment 1, not-faculty 1, not-jhāna 1, not-path 1, not-association 1, not-dissociation 1, not-absence 1, not-disappearance 1 ;

17. Of dependence, conascence, mutuality, resultant, presence and non-disappearance conditions, not-root 1, not-object 1, not-predominance 1, not-proximity 1, not-contiguity 1, not-strong-dependence 1, not-prenascence 1, not-postnascence 1, not-repetition 1, not-kamma 1, not-nutriment 1, not-faculty 1, not-jhāna 1, not-path 1, not-association 1, not-dissociation 1, not-absence 1, not-disappearance 1 ;

18. Of dependence, conascence, mutuality, resultant, association, presence and non-disappearance conditions, not-root 1, not-object 1, not-predominance 1, not-proximity 1, not-contiguity 1, not-strong-dependence 1, not-prenascence 1, not-postnascence 1, not-repetition 1, not-kamma 1, not-nutriment 1, not-faculty 1, not-jhāna 1, not-path 1, not-dissociation 1, not-absence 1, not-disappearance 1 ;

19. Of dependence, conascence, resultant, dissociation, presence and non-disappearance conditions, not-root 1, not-object 1, not-predominance 1, not-proximity 1, not-contiguity 1, not-mutuality 1, not-strong-dependence 1, not-prenascence 1, not-postnascence 1, not-repetition 1, not-kamma 1, not-nutriment 1, not-faculty 1, not-jhāna 1, not-path 1, not-association 1, not-absence 1, not-disappearance 1 ;

20. Of dependence, conascence, mutuality, resultant, dissociation, presence and non-disappearance conditions, not-root 1, not-object 1, not-predominance 1, not-proximity 1, not-contiguity 1, not-strong-dependence 1, not-prenascence 1, not-postnascence 1, not-repetition 1, not-kamma 1, not-nutriment 1, not-faculty 1, not-jhāna 1, not-path 1, not-association 1, not-absence 1, not-disappearance 1.

End of Dependence

Strong-dependence

By Twos

575. With strong-dependence condition, not-root 9, not-object 9, not-predominance 9, not-proximity 9, not-contiguity 9, not-conascence 9, not-mutuality 9, not-dependence 9, not-prenascence 9, not-postnascence 9, not-repetition 9, not-kamma 9, not-resultant 9, not-nutriment 9, not-faculty 9, not-jhāna 9, not-path 9, not-association 9, not-dissociation 9, not-presence 9, not-absence 9, not-disappearance 9, not-non-disappearance 9.

(Miscellaneous) Combinations 7

576. 1. Combinations of strong-dependence, object and predominance conditions, not-root 7, not-proximity 7, not-contiguity 7, not-conascence 7, not-mutuality 7, not-dependence 7, not-prenascence 7, not-postnascence 7, not-repetition 7, not-kamma 7, not-resultant 7, not-nutriment 7, not-faculty 7, not-jhāna 7, not-path 7, not-association 7, not-dissociation 7, not-presence 7, not-absence 7, not-disappearance 7, not-non-disappearance 7;

2. Of strong-dependence, object, predominance, prenascence, presence and non-disappearance conditions, not-root 1, not-proximity 1, not-contiguity 1, not-conascence 1, not-mutuality 1, not-dependence 1, not-postnascence 1, not-repetition 1, not-kamma 1, not-resultant 1, not-nutriment 1, not-faculty 1, not-jhāna 1, not-path 1, not-association 1, not-dissociation 1, not-absence 1, not-disappearance 1;

3. Of strong-dependence, object, predominance, dependence, prenascence, dissociation, presence and non-disappearance conditions, not-root 1, not-proximity 1, not-contiguity

1, not-conascence 1, not-mutuality 1, not-postnascence 1, not-repetition 1, not-kamma 1, not-resultant 1, not-nutriment 1, not-faculty 1, not-jhāna 1, not-path 1, not-association 1, not-absence 1, not-disappearance 1 ;

4. Of strong-dependence, proximity, contiguity, absence and disappearance conditions, not-root 7, not-object 7, not-predominance 7, not-conascence 7, not-mutuality 7, not-dependence 7, not-prenascence 7, not-postnascence 7, not-repetition 5, not-kamma 7, not-resultant 7, not-nutriment 7, not-faculty 7, not-jhāna 7, not-path 7, not-association 7, not-dissociation 7, not-presence 7, not-non-disappearance 7 ;

5. Of strong-dependence, proximity, contiguity, repetition, absence and disappearance conditions, not-root 3, not-object 3, not-predominance 3, not-conascence 3, not-mutuality 3, not-dependence 3, not-prenascence 3, not-postnascence 3, not-kamma 3, not-resultant 3, not-nutriment 3, not-faculty 3, not-jhāna 3, not-path 3, not-association 3, not-dissociation 3, not-presence 3, not-non-disappearance 3 ;

6. Of strong-dependence and kamma conditions, not-root 2, not-object 2, not-predominance 2, not-proximity 2, not-contiguity 2, not-conascence 2, not-mutuality 2, not-dependence 2, not-prenascence 2, not-postnascence 2, not-repetition 2, not-resultant 2, not-nutriment 2, not-faculty 2, not-jhāna 2, not-path 2, not-association 2, not-dissociation 2, not-presence 2, not-absence 2, not-disappearance 2, not-non-disappearance 2 ;

7. Of strong-dependence, proximity, contiguity, kamma, absence and disappearance conditions, not-root 1, not-object 1, not-predominance 1, not-conascence 1, not-mutuality 1, not-dependence 1, not-prenascence 1, not-postnascence 1, not-repetition 1, not-resultant 1, not-nutriment 1, not-faculty 1, not-jhāna 1, not-path 1, not-association 1, not-dissociation 1, not-presence 1, not-non-disappearance 1.

End of Strong-dependence

Prenascence

By Twos

577. With prenascence condition, not-root 3, not-object 3, not-predominance 3, not-proximity 3, not-contiguity 3, not-

conascence 3, not-mutuality 3, not-dependence 3, not-strong-dependence 3, not-postnascence 3, not-repetition 3, not-kamma 3, not-resultant 3, not-nutriment 3, not-faculty 3, not-jhāna 3, not-path 3, not-association 3, not-dissociation 3, not-absence 3, not-disappearance 3.

(Miscellaneous) Combinations 7

578. 1. Combinations of prenascence, presence and non-disappearance conditions, not-root 3, not-object 3, not-predominance 3, not-proximity 3, not-contiguity 3, not-conascence 3, not-mutuality 3, not-dependence 3, not-strong-dependence 3, not-postnascence 3, not-repetition 3, not-kamma 3, not-resultant 3, not-nutriment 3, not-faculty 3, not-jhāna 3, not-path 3, not-association 3, not-dissociation 3, not-absence 3, not-disappearance 3 ;

2. Of prenascence, dependence, dissociation, presence and non-disappearance conditions, not-root 3, not-object 3, not-predominance 3, not-proximity 3, not-contiguity 3, not-conascence 3, not-mutuality 3, not-strong-dependence 3, not-postnascence 3, not-repetition 3, not-kamma 3, not-resultant 3, not-nutriment 3, not-faculty 3, not-jhāna 3, not-path 3, not-association 3, not-absence 3, not-disappearance 3 ;

3. Of prenascence, object, presence and non-disappearance conditions, not-root 3, not-predominance 3, not-proximity 3, not-contiguity 3, not-conascence 3, not-mutuality 3, not-dependence 3, not-strong-dependence 3, not-postnascence 3, not-repetition 3, not-kamma 3, not-resultant 3, not-nutriment 3, not-faculty 3, not-jhāna 3, not-path 3, not-association 3, not-dissociation 3, not-absence 3, not-disappearance 3 ;

4. Of prenascence, object, dependence, dissociation, presence and non-disappearance conditions, not-root 3, not-predominance 3, not-proximity 3, not-contiguity 3, not-conascence 3, not-mutuality 3, not-strong-dependence 3, not-postnascence 3, not-repetition 3, not-kamma 3, not-resultant 3, not-nutriment 3, not-faculty 3, not-jhāna 3, not-path 3, not-association 3, not-absence 3, not-disappearance 3 ;

5. Of prenascence, object, predominance, strong-dependence, presence and non-disappearance conditions, not-root 1, not-proximity 1, not-contiguity 1, not-conascence 1,

not-mutuality 1, not-dependence 1, not-postnascence 1, not-repetition 1, not-kamma 1, not-resultant 1, not-nutriment 1, not-faculty 1, not-jhāna 1, not-path 1, not-association 1, not-dissociation 1, not-absence 1, not-disappearance 1 ;

6. Of prenascence, object, predominance, dependence, strong-dependence, dissociation, presence and non-disappearance conditions, not-root 1, not-proximity 1, not-contiguity 1, not-conascence 1, not-mutuality 1, not-postnascence 1, not-repetition 1, not-kamma 1, not-resultant 1, not-nutriment 1, not-faculty 1, not-jhāna 1, not-path 1, not-association 1, not-absence 1, not-disappearance 1 ;

7. Of prenascence, dependence, faculty, dissociation, presence and non-disappearance conditions, not-root 1, not-object 1, not-predominance 1, not-proximity 1, not-contiguity 1, not-conascence 1, not-mutuality 1, not-strong-dependence 1, not-postnascence 1, not-repetition 1, not-kamma 1, not-resultant 1, not-nutriment 1, not-jhāna 1, not-path 1, not-association 1, not-absence 1, not-disappearance 1.

End of Prenascence

Postnascence

By Twos

579. With postnascence condition, not-root 3, not-object 3, not-predominance 3, not-proximity 3, not-contiguity 3, not-conascence 3, not-mutuality 3, not-dependence 3, not-strong-dependence 3, not-prenascence 3, not-repetition 3, not-kamma 3, not-resultant 3, not-nutriment 3, not-faculty 3, not-jhāna 3, not-path 3, not-association 3, not-absence 3, not-disappearance 3.

(Miscellaneous) Combination 1

580. Combinations of postnascence, dissociation, presence and non-disappearance conditions, not-root 3, not-object 3, not-predominance 3, not-proximity 3, not-contiguity 3, not-conascence 3, not-mutuality 3, not-dependence 3, not-strong-dependence 3, not-prenascence 3, not-repetition 3, not-kamma 3, not-resultant 3, not-nutriment 3, not-faculty 3, not-jhāna 3,

not-path 3, not-association 3, not-absence 3, not-disappearance 3.

End of Postnascence

Repetition

By Twos

581. With repetition condition, not-root 3, not-object 3, not-predominance 3, not-conascence 3, not-mutuality 3, not-dependence 3, not-prenascence 3, not-postnascence 3, not-kamma 3, not-resultant 3, not-nutriment 3, not-faculty 3, not-jhāna 3, not-path 3, not-association 3, not-dissociation 3, not-presence 3, not-non-disappearance 3.

(Miscellaneous) Combination 1

582. Combinations of repetition, proximity, contiguity, strong-dependence, absence and disappearance conditions, not-root 3, not-object 3, not-predominance 3, not-conascence 3, not-mutuality 3, not-dependence 3, not-prenascence 3, not-postnascence 3, not-kamma 3, not-resultant 3, not-nutriment 3, not-faculty 3, not-jhāna 3, not-path 3, not-association 3, not-dissociation 3, not-presence 3, not-non-disappearance 3.

End of Repetition

Kamma

By Twos

583. With kamma condition, not-root 7, not-object 7, not-predominance 7, not-proximity 7, not-contiguity 7, not-conascence 2, not-mutuality 3, not-dependence 2, not-strong-dependence 7, not-prenascence 7, not-postnascence 7, not-repetition 7, not-resultant 7, not-nutriment 2, not-faculty 7, not-jhāna 7, not-path 7, not-association 3, not-dissociation 5, not-presence 2, not-absence 7, not-disappearance 7, not-non-disappearance 2.

Combinations 11

Miscellaneous 2

584. 1. Combinations of kamma and strong-dependence conditions, not-root 2, not-object 2, not-predominance 2, not-proximity 2, not-contiguity 2, not-conascence 2, not-mutuality

2, not-dependence 2, not-prenascence 2, not postnascence 2, not-repetition 2, not-resultant 2, not-nutriment 2, not-faculty 2, not-jhāna 2, not-path 2, not-association 2, not-dissociation 2, not-presence 2, not-absence 2, not-disappearance 2, not-non-disappearance 2 ;

2. Of kamma, proximity, contiguity, strong-dependence, absence and disappearance conditions, not-root 1, not-object 1, not-predominance 1, not-conascence 1, not-mutuality 1, not-dependence 1, not-prenascence 1, not-postnascence 1, not-repetition 1, not-resultant 1, not-nutriment 1, not-faculty 1, not-jhāna 1, not-path 1, not-association 1, not-dissociation 1, not-presence 1, not-non-disappearance 1.

Conascence (with nutriment) 9

Without resultant 4

585. 3. Combinations of kamma, conascence, dependence, nutriment, presence and non-disappearance conditions, not-root 7, not-object 7, not-predominance 7, not-proximity 7, not-contiguity 7, not-mutuality 3, not-strong-dependence 7, not-prenascence 7, not-postnascence 7, not-repetition 7, not-resultant 7, not-faculty 7, not-jhāna 7, not-path 7, not-association 3, not-dissociation 3, not- absence 7, not-disappearance 7 ;

4. Of kamma, conascence, mutuality, dependence, nutriment, presence and non-disappearance conditions, not-root 3, not-object 3, not-predominance 3, not-proximity 3, not-contiguity 3, not-strong-dependence 3, not-prenascence 3, not-postnascence 3, not-repetition 3, not-resultant 3, not-faculty 3, not-jhāna 3, not-path 3, not-association 1, not-dissociation 3, not-absence 3, not-disappearance 3 ;

5. Of kamma, conascence, mutuality, dependence, nutriment, association, presence and non-disappearance conditions, not-root 3, not-object 3, not-predominance 3, not-proximity 3, not-contiguity 3, not-strong-dependence 3, not-prenascence 3, not-postnascence 3, not-repetition 3, not-resultant 3, not-faculty 3, not-jhāna 3, not-path 3, not-dissociation 3, not-absence 3, not-disappearance 3 ;

6. Of kamma, conascence, dependence, nutriment, dissociation, presence and non-disappearance conditions, not-root

3, not-object 3, not-predominance 3, not-proximity 3, not-contiguity 3, not-mutuality 3, not-strong-dependence 3, not-prenascence 3, not-postnascence 3, not-repetition 3, not-resultant 3, not-faculty 3, not-jhāna 3, not-path 3, not-association 3, not-absence 3, not-disappearance 3.

With resultant 5

7. Combinations of kamma, conascence, dependence, resultant, nutriment, presence and non-disappearance conditions, not-root 1, not-object 1, not-predominance 1, not-proximity 1, not-contiguity 1, not-mutuality 1, not-strong-dependence 1, not-prenascence 1, not-postnascence 1, not-repetition 1, not-faculty 1, not-jhāna 1, not-path 1, not-association 1, not-dissociation 1, not-absence 1, not-disappearance 1;

8. Of kamma, conascence, mutuality, dependence, resultant, nutriment, presence and non-disappearance conditions, not-root 1, not-object 1, not-predominance 1, not-proximity 1, not-contiguity 1, not-strong-dependence 1, not-prenascence 1, not-postnascence 1, not-repetition 1, not-faculty 1, not-jhāna 1, not-path 1, not-association 1, not-dissociation 1, not-absence 1, not-disappearance 1;

9. Of kamma, conascence, mutuality, dependence, resultant, nutriment, association, presence and non-disappearance conditions, not-root 1, not-object 1, not-predominance 1, not-proximity 1, not-contiguity 1, not-strong-dependence 1, not-prenascence 1, not-postnascence 1, not-repetition 1, not-faculty 1, not-jhāna 1, not-path 1, not-dissociation 1, not-absence 1, not-disappearance 1;

10. Of kamma, conascence, dependence, resultant, nutriment, dissociation, presence and non-disappearance conditions, not-root 1, not-object 1, not-predominance 1, not-proximity 1, not-contiguity 1, not-mutuality 1, not-strong-dependence 1, not-prenascence 1, not-postnascence 1, not-repetition 1, not-faculty 1, not-jhāna 1, not-path 1, not-association 1, not-absence 1, not-disappearance 1;

11. Of kamma, conascence, mutuality, dependence, resultant, nutriment, dissociation, presence and non-disap-

pearance conditions, not-root 1, not-object 1, not-predominance 1, not-proximity 1, not-contiguity 1, not-strong-dependence 1, not-prenascence 1, not-postnascence 1, not-repetition 1, not-faculty 1, not-jhāna 1, not-path 1, not-association 1, not-absence 1, not-disappearance 1.

End of Kamma

Resultant

By Twos

586. With resultant condition, not-root 1, not-object 1, not-predominance 1, not-proximity 1, not-contiguity 1, not-mutuality 1, not-strong-dependence 1, not-prenascence 1, not-postnascence 1, not-repetition 1, not-kamma 1, not-nutriment 1, not-faculty 1, not-jhāna 1, not-path 1, not-association 1, not-dissociation 1, not-absence 1, not-disappearance 1.

(Conascence) Combinations 5

587. 1. Combinations of resultant, conascence, dependence, presence and non-disappearance conditions, not-root 1, not-object 1, not-predominance 1, not-proximity 1, not-contiguity 1, not-mutuality 1, not-strong-dependence 1, not-prenascence 1, not-postnascence 1, not-repetition 1, not-kamma 1, not-nutriment 1, not-faculty 1, not-jhāna 1, not-path 1, not-association 1, not-dissociation 1, not-absence 1, not-disappearance 1 ;

2. Of resultant, conascence, mutuality, dependence, presence and non-disappearance conditions, not-root 1, not-object 1, not-predominance 1, not-proximity 1, not-contiguity 1, not-strong-dependence 1, not-prenascence 1, not-postnascence 1, not-repetition 1, not-kamma 1, not-nutriment 1, not-faculty 1, not-jhāna 1, not-path 1, not-association 1, not-dissociation 1, not-absence 1, not-disappearance 1 ;

3. Of resultant, conascence, mutuality, dependence, association, presence and non-disappearance conditions, not-root 1, not-object 1, not-predominance 1, not-proximity 1, not-contiguity 1, not-strong-dependence 1, not-prenascence 1, not-postnascence 1, not-repetition 1, not-kamma 1, not-nutriment 1, not-faculty 1, not-jhāna 1, not-path 1, not-dissociation 1, not-absence 1, not-disappearance 1 ;

4. Of resultant, conascence, dependence, dissociation, presence and non-disappearance conditions, not-root 1, not-object 1, not-predominance 1, not-proximity 1, not-contiguity 1, not-mutuality 1, not-strong-dependence 1, not-prenascence 1, not-postnascence 1, not-repetition 1, not-kamma 1, not-nutriment 1, not-faculty 1, not-jhāna 1, not-path 1, not-association 1, not-absence 1, not-disappearance 1;

5. Of resultant, conascence, mutuality, dependence, dissociation, presence and non-disappearance conditions, not-root 1, not-object 1, not-predominance 1, not-proximity 1, not-contiguity 1, not-strong-dependence 1, not-prenascence 1, not-postnascence 1, not-repetition 1, not-kamma 1, not-nutriment 1, not-faculty 1, not-jhāna 1, not-path 1, not-association 1, not-absence 1, not-disappearance 1.

End of Resultant

Nutriment

By Twos

588. With nutriment condition, not-root 7, not-object 7, not-predominance 7, not-proximity 7, not-contiguity 7, not-conascence 1, not-mutuality 3, not-dependence 1, not-strong-dependence 7, not-prenascence 7, not-postnascence 7, not-repetition 7, not-kamma 7, not-resultant 7, not-faculty 7, not-jhāna 7, not-path 7, not-association 3, not-dissociation 3, not-absence 7, not-disappearance 7.

Combinations 34

Mixed 1

589. 1. Combinations of nutriment, presence and non-disappearance conditions, not-root 7, not-object 7, not-predominance 7, not-proximity 7, not-contiguity 7, not-conascence 1, not-mutuality 3, not-dependence 1, not-strong-dependence 7, not-prenascence 7, not-postnascence 7, not-repetition 7, not-kamma 7, not-resultant 7, not-faculty 7, not-jhāna 7, not-path 7, not-association 3, not-dissociation 3, not-absence 7, not-disappearance 7.

Conascence 33

Ordinary 9

Without resultant 4

590. 2. Combinations of nutriment, conascence, dependence, presence and non-disappearance conditions, not-root 7, not-object 7, not-predominance 7, not-proximity 7, not-contiguity 7, not-mutuality 3, not-strong-dependence 7, not-prenascence 7, not-postnascence 7, not-repetition 7, not-kamma 7, not-resultant 7, not-faculty 7, not-jhāna 7, not-path 7, not-association 3, not-dissociation 3, not-absence 7, not-disappearance 7 ;

3. Of nutriment, conascence, mutuality, dependence, presence and non-disappearance conditions, not-root 3, not-object 3, not-predominance 3, not-proximity 3, not-contiguity 3, not-strong-dependence 3, not-prenascence 3, not-postnascence 3, not-repetition 3, not-kamma 3, not-resultant 3, not-faculty 3, not-jhāna 3, not-path 3, not-association 1, not-dissociation 3, not-absence 3, not-disappearance 3 ;

4. Of nutriment, conascence, mutuality, dependence, association, presence and non-disappearance conditions, not-root 3, not-object 3, not-predominance 3, not-proximity 3, not-contiguity 3, not-strong-dependence 3, not-prenascence 3, not-postnascence 3, not-repetition 3, not-kamma 3, not-resultant 3, not-faculty 3, not-jhāna 3, not-path 3, not-dissociation 3, not-absence 3, not-disappearance 3 ;

5. Of nutriment, conascence, dependence, dissociation, presence and non-disappearance conditions, not-root 3, not-object 3, not-predominance 3, not-proximity 3, not-contiguity 3, not-mutuality 3, not-strong-dependence 3, not-prenascence 3, not-postnascence 3, not-repetition 3, not-kamma 3, not-resultant 3, not-faculty 3, not-jhāna 3, not-path 3, not-association 3, not-absence 3, not-disappearance 3.

With resultant 5

6. Combinations of nutriment, conascence, dependence, resultant, presence and non-disappearance conditions, not-root 1, not-object 1, not-predominance 1, not-proximity 1, not-contiguity 1, not-mutuality 1, not-strong-dependence 1, not-prenascence 1, not-postnascence 1, not-repetition 1, not-kamma

1, not-faculty 1, not-jhāna 1, not-path 1, not-association 1, not-dissociation 1, not-absence 1, not-disappearance 1;

7. Of nutriment, conascence, mutuality, dependence, resultant, presence and non-disappearance conditions, not-root 1, not-object 1, not-predominance 1, not-proximity 1, not-contiguity 1, not-strong-dependence 1, not-prenascence 1, not-postnascence 1, not-repetition 1, not-kamma 1, not-faculty 1, not-jhāna 1, not-path 1, not-association 1, not-dissociation 1, not-absence 1, not-disappearance 1;

8. Of nutriment, conascence, mutuality, dependence, resultant, association, presence and non-disappearance conditions, not-root 1, not-object 1, not-predominance 1, not-proximity 1, not-contiguity 1, not-strong-dependence 1, not-prenascence 1, not-postnascence 1, not-repetition 1, not-kamma 1, not-faculty 1, not-jhāna 1, not-path 1, not-dissociation 1, not-absence 1, not-disappearance 1;

9. Of nutriment, conascence, dependence, resultant, dissociation, presence and non-disappearance conditions, not-root 1, not-object 1, not-predominance 1, not-proximity 1, not-contiguity 1, not-mutuality 1, not-strong-dependence 1, not-prenascence 1, not-postnascence 1, not-repetition 1, not-kamma 1, not-faculty 1, not-jhāna 1, not-path 1, not-association 1, not-absence 1, not-disappearance 1;

10. Of nutriment, conascence, mutuality, dependence, resultant, dissociation, presence and non-disappearance conditions, not-root 1, not-object 1, not-predominance 1, not-proximity 1, not-contiguity 1, not-strong-dependence 1, not-prenascence 1, not-postnascence 1, not-repetition 1, not-kamma 1, not-faculty 1, not-jhāna 1, not-path 1, not-association 1, not-absence 1, not-disappearance 1.

With kamma 9

Without resultant 4

591. 11. Combinations of nutriment, conascence, dependence, kamma, presence and non-disappearance conditions, not-root 7, not-object 7, not-predominance 7, not-proximity 7, not-contiguity 7, not-mutuality 3, not-strong-dependence 7, not-prenascence 7, not-postnascence 7, not-repetition 7, not-

resultant 7, not-faculty 7, not-jhāna 7, not-path 7, not-association 3, not-dissociation 3, not-absence 7, not-disappearance 7 ;

12. Of nutriment, conascence, mutuality, dependence, kamma, presence and non-disappearance conditions, not-root 3, not-object 3, not-predominance 3, not-proximity 3, not-contiguity 3, not-strong-dependence 3, not-prenascence 3, not-postnascence 3, not-repetition 3, not-resultant 3, not-faculty 3, not-jhāna 3, not-path 3, not-association 1, not-dissociation 3, not-absence 3, not-disappearance 3 ;

13. Of nutriment, conascence, mutuality, dependence, kamma, association, presence and non-disappearance conditions, not-root 3, not-object 3, not-predominance 3, not-proximity 3, not-contiguity 3, not-strong-dependence 3, not-prenascence 3, not-postnascence 3, not-repetition 3, not-resultant 3, not-faculty 3, not-jhāna 3, not-path 3, not-dissociation 3, not-absence 3, not-disappearance 3 ;

14. Of nutriment, conascence, dependence, kamma, dissociation, presence and non-disappearance conditions, not-root 3, not-object 3, not-predominance 3, not-proximity 3, not-contiguity 3, not-mutuality 3, not-strong-dependence 3, not-prenascence 3, not-postnascence 3, not-repetition 3, not-resultant 3, not-faculty 3, not-jhāna 3, not-path 3, not-association 3, not-absence 3, not-disappearance 3.

With resultant 5

15. Combinations of nutriment, conascence, dependence, kamma, resultant, presence and non-disappearance conditions, not-root 1, not-object 1, not-predominance 1, not-proximity 1, not-contiguity 1, not-mutuality 1, not-strong-dependence 1, not-prenascence 1, not-postnascence 1, not-repetition 1, not-faculty 1, not-jhāna 1, not-path 1, not-association 1, not-dissociation 1, not-absence 1, not-disappearance 1 ;

16. Of nutriment, conascence, mutuality, dependence, kamma, resultant, presence and non-disappearance conditions, not-root 1, not-object 1, not-predominance 1, not-proximity 1, not-contiguity 1, not-strong-dependence 1, not-prenascence 1, not-postnascence 1, not-repetition 1, not-faculty 1, not-jhāna 1,

not-path 1, not-association 1, not-dissociation 1, not-absence 1, not-disappearance 1 ;

17. Of nutriment, conascence, mutuality, dependence, kamma, resultant, association, presence and non-disappearance conditions, not-root 1, not-object 1, not-predominance 1, not-proximity 1, not-contiguity 1, not-strong-dependence 1, not-prenascence 1, not-postnascence 1, not-repetition 1, not-faculty 1, not-jhāna 1, not-path 1, not-dissociation 1, not-absence 1, not-disappearance 1 ;

18. Of nutriment, conascence, dependence, kamma, resultant, dissociation, presence and non-disappearance conditions, not-root 1, not-object 1, not-predominance 1, not-proximity 1, not-contiguity 1, not-mutuality 1 ,[1] not-strong-dependence 1, not-prenascence 1, not-postnascence 1, not-repetition 1, not-faculty 1, not-jhāna 1, not-path 1, not-association 1, not-absence 1, not-disappearance 1 ;

19. Of nutriment, conascence, mutuality, dependence, kamma, resultant, dissociation, presence and non-disappearance conditions, not-root 1, not-object 1, not-predominance 1, not-proximity 1, not-contiguity 1, not-strong-dependence 1, not-prenascence 1, not-postnascence 1, not-repetition 1, not-faculty 1, not-jhāna 1, not-path 1, not-association 1, not-absence 1, not-disappearance 1.

With faculty 9

Without resultant 4

592. 20. Combinations of nutriment, conascence, dependence, faculty, presence and non-disappearance conditions, not-root 7, not-object 7, not-predominance 7, not-proximity 7, not-contiguity 7, not-mutuality 3, not-strong-dependence 7, not-prenascence 7, not-postnascence 7, not-repetition 7, not-kamma 7, not-resultant 7, not-jhāna 7, not-path 7, not-association 3, not-dissociation 3, not-absence 7, not-disappearance 7 ;

21. Of nutriment, conascence, mutuality, dependence, faculty, presence and non-disappearance conditions, not-root 3,

---

[1] Left out in the Text.

not-object 3, not-predominance 3, not-proximity 3, not-contiguity 3, not-strong-dependence 3, not-prenascence 3, not-postnascence 3, not-repetition 3, not-kamma 3, not-resultant 3, not-jhāna 3, not-path 3, not-association 1, not-dissociation 3, not-absence 3, not-disappearance 3 ;

22. Of nutriment, conascence, mutuality, dependence, faculty, association, presence and non-disappearance conditions, not-root 3, not-object 3, not-predominance 3, not-proximity 3, not-contiguity 3, not-strong-dependence 3, not-prenascence 3, not-postnascence 3, not-repetition 3, not-kamma 3, not-resultant 3, not-jhāna 3, not-path 3, not-dissociation 3, not-absence 3, not-disappearance 3 ;

23. Of nutriment, conascence, dependence, faculty, dissociation, presence and non-disappearance conditions, not-root 3, not-object 3, not-predominance 3, not-proximity 3, not-contiguity 3, not-mutuality 3, not-strong-dependence 3, not-prenascence 3, not-postnascence 3, not-repetition 3, not-kamma 3, not-resultant 3, not-jhāna 3, not-path 3, not-association 3, not-absence 3, not-disappearance 3.

With resultant 5

24. Combinations of nutriment, conascence, dependence, resultant, faculty, presence and non-disappearance conditions, not-root 1, not-object 1, not-predominance 1, not-proximity 1, not-contiguity 1, not-mutuality 1, not-strong-dependence 1, not-prenascence 1, not-postnascence 1, not-repetition 1, not-kamma 1, not-jhāna 1, not-path 1, not-association 1, not-dissociation 1, not-absence 1, not-disappearance 1 ;

25. Of nutriment, conascence, mutuality, dependence, resultant, faculty, presence and non-disappearance conditions, not-root 1, not-object 1, not-predominance 1, not-proximity 1, not-contiguity 1, not-strong-dependence 1, not-prenascence 1, not-postnascence 1, not-repetition 1, not-kamma 1, not-jhāna 1, not-path 1, not-association 1, not-dissociation 1, not-absence 1, not-disappearance 1 ;

26. Of nutriment, conascence, mutuality, dependence, resultant, faculty, association, presence and non-disappearance conditions, not-root 1, not-object 1, not-predominance 1,

not-proximity 1, not-contiguity 1, not-strong-dependence 1, not-prenascence 1, not-postnascence 1, not-repetition 1, not-kamma 1, not-jhāna 1, not-path 1, not-dissociation 1, not-absence 1, not-disappearance 1 ;

27. Of nutriment, conascence, dependence, resultant, faculty, dissociation, presence and non-disappearance conditions, not-root 1, not-object 1, not-predominance 1, not-proximity 1, not-contiguity 1, not-mutuality 1, not-strong-dependence 1, not-prenascence 1, not-postnascence 1, not-repetition 1, not-kamma 1, not-jhāna 1, not-path 1, not-association 1, not-absence 1, not-disappearance 1 ;

28. Of nutriment, conascence, mutuality, dependence, resultant, faculty, dissociation, presence and non-disappearance conditions, not-root 1, not-object 1, not-predominance 1, not-proximity 1, not-contiguity 1, not-strong-dependence 1, not-prenascence 1, not-postnascence 1, not-repetition 1, not-kamma 1, not-jhāna 1, not-path 1, not-association 1, not-absence 1, not-disappearance 1.

With predominance and faculty 6

Without resultant 3

593. 29. Combinations of nutriment, predominance, conascence, dependence, faculty, presence and non-disappearance conditions, not-root 7, not-object 7, not-proximity 7, not-contiguity 7, not-mutuality 3, not-strong-dependence 7, not-prenascence 7, not-postnascence 7, not-repetition 7, not-kamma 7, not-resultant 7, not-jhāna 7, not-path 7, not-association 3, not-dissociation 3, not-absence 7, not-disappearance 7 ;

30. Of nutriment, predominance, conascence, mutuality, dependence, faculty, association, presence and non-disappearance conditions, not-root 3, not-object 3, not-proximity 3, not-contiguity 3, not-strong-dependence 3, not-prenascence 3, not-postnascence 3, not-repetition 3, not-kamma 3, not-resultant 3, not-jhāna 3, not-path 3, not-dissociation 3, not-absence 3, not-disappearance 3 ;

31. Of nutriment, predominance, conascence, dependence, faculty, dissociation, presence and non-disappearance conditions, not-root 3, not-object 3, not-proximity 3, not-contiguity

Faultless Triplet

3, not-mutuality 3, not-strong-dependence 3, not-prenascence 3, not-postnascence 3, not-repetition 3, not-kamma 3, not-resultant 3, not-jhāna 3, not-path 3, not-association 3, not-absence 3, not-disappearance 3.

With resultant 3

32. Combinations of nutriment, predominance, conascence, dependence, resultant, faculty, presence and non-disappearance conditions, not-root 1, not-object 1, not-proximity 1, not-contiguity 1, not-mutuality 1, not-strong-dependence 1, not-prenascence 1, not-postnascence 1, not-repetition 1, not-kamma 1, not-jhāna 1, not-path 1, not-association 1, not-dissociation 1, not-absence 1, not-disappearance 1;

33. Of nutriment, predominance, conascence, mutuality, dependence, resultant, faculty, association, presence and non-disappearance conditions, not-root 1, not-object 1, not-proximity 1, not-contiguity 1, not-strong-dependence 1, not-prenascence 1, not-postnascence 1, not-repetition 1, not-kamma 1, not-jhāna 1, not-path 1, not-dissociation 1, not-absence 1, not-disappearance 1;

34. Of nutriment, predominance, conascence, dependence, resultant, faculty, dissociation, presence and non-disappearance conditions, not-root 1, not-object 1, not-proximity 1, not-contiguity 1, not-mutuality 1, not-strong-dependence 1, not-prenascence 1, not-postnascence 1, not-repetition 1, not-kamma 1, not-jhāna 1, not-path 1, not-association 1, not-absence 1, not-disappearance 1.

End of Nutriment

Faculty

By Twos

594. With faculty condition, not-root 7, not-object 7, not-predominance 7, not-proximity 7, not-contiguity 7, not-conascence 1, not-mutuality 3, not-dependence 1, not-strong-dependence 7, not-prenascence 7, not-postnascence 7, not-repetition 7, not-kamma 7, not-resultant 7, not-nutriment 7,

not-jhāna 7, not-path 7, not-association 3, not-dissociation 3, not-absence 7, not-disappearance 7.

Combinations 76

Mixed 3

595. 1. Combinations of faculty, presence and non-disappearance conditions, not-root 7, not-object 7, not-predominance 7, not-proximity 7, not-contiguity 7, not-conascence 1, not-mutuality 3, not-dependence 1, not-strong-dependence 7, not-prenascence 7, not-postnascence 7, not-repetition 7, not-kamma 7, not-resultant 7, not-nutriment 7, not-jhāna 7, not-path 7, not-association 3, not-dissociation 3, not-absence 7, not-disappearance 7 ;

2. Of faculty, dependence, presence and non-disappearance conditions, not-root 7, not-object 7, not-predominance 7, not-proximity 7, not-contiguity 7, not-conascence 1, not-mutuality 3, not-strong-dependence 7, not-prenascence 7, not-postnascence 7, not-repetition 7, not-kamma 7, not-resultant 7, not-nutriment 7, not-jhāna 7, not-path 7, not-association 3, not-dissociation 3, not-absence 7, not-disappearance 7 ;

3. Of faculty, dependence, dissociation, presence and non-disappearance conditions, not-root 3, not-object 3, not-predominance 3, not-proximity 3, not-contiguity 3, not-conascence 1, not-mutuality 3, not-strong-dependence 3, not-prenascence 3, not-postnascence 3, not-repetition 3, not-kamma 3, not-resultant 3, not-nutriment 3, not-jhāna 3, not-path 3, not-association 3, not-absence 3, not-disappearance 3.

Miscellaneous 1

596. 4. Combinations of faculty, dependence, prenascence, dissociation, presence and non-disappearance conditions, not-root 1, not-object 1, not-predominance 1, not-proximity 1, not-contiguity 1, not-conascence 1, not-mutuality 1, not-strong-dependence 1, not-postnascence 1, not-repetition 1, not-kamma 1, not-resultant 1, not-nutriment 1, not-jhāna 1, not-path 1, not-association 1, not-absence 1, not-disappearance 1.

Conascence 72

Ordinary 9

Without resultant 4

597. 5. Combinations of faculty, conascence, dependence, presence and non-disappearance conditions, not-root 7, not-object 7, not-predominance 7, not-proximity 7, not-contiguity 7, not-mutuality 3, not-strong-dependence 7, not-prenascence 7, not-postnascence 7, not-repetition 7, not-kamma 7, not-resultant 7, not-nutriment 7, not-jhāna 7, not-path 7, not-association 3, not-dissociation 3, not-absence 7, not-disappearance 7 ;

6. Of faculty, conascence, mutuality, dependence, presence and non-disappearance conditions, not-root 3, not-object 3, not-predominance 3, not-proximity 3, not-contiguity 3, not-strong-dependence 3, not-prenascence 3, not-postnascence 3, not-repetition 3, not-kamma 3, not-resultant 3, not-nutriment 3, not-jhāna 3, not-path 3, not-association 1, not-dissociation 3, not-absence 3, not-disappearance 3 ;

7. Of faculty, conascence, mutuality, dependence, association, presence and non-disappearance conditions, not-root 3, not-object 3, not-predominance 3, not-proximity 3, not-contiguity 3, not-strong-dependence 3, not-prenascence 3, not-postnascence 3, not-repetition 3, not-kamma 3, not-resultant 3, not-nutriment 3, not-jhāna 3, not-path 3, not-dissociation 3, not-absence 3, not-disappearance 3 ;

8. Of faculty, conascence, dependence, dissociation, presence and non-disappearance conditions, not-root 3, not-object 3, not-predominance 3, not-proximity 3, not-contiguity 3, not-mutuality 3, not-strong-dependence 3, not-prenascence 3, not-postnascence 3, not-repetition 3, not-kamma 3, not-resultant 3, not-nutriment 3, not-jhāna 3, not-path 3, not-association 3, not-absence 3, not-disappearance 3.

With resultant 5

9. Combinations of faculty, conascence, dependence, resultant, presence and non-disappearance conditions, not-root 1, not-object 1, not-predominance 1, not-proximity 1,

not-contiguity 1, not-mutuality 1, not-strong-dependence 1, not-prenascence 1, not-postnascence 1, not-repetition 1, not-kamma 1, not-nutriment 1, not-jhāna 1, not-path 1, not-association 1, not-dissociation 1, not-absence 1, not-disappearance 1 ;

10. Of faculty, conascence, mutuality, dependence, resultant, presence and non-disappearance conditions, not-root 1, not-object 1, not-predominance 1, not-proximity 1, not-contiguity 1, not-strong-dependence 1, not-prenascence 1, not-postnascence 1, not-repetition 1, not-kamma 1, not-nutriment 1, not-jhāna 1, not-path 1, not-association 1, not-dissociation 1, not-absence 1, not-disappearance 1 ;

11. Of faculty, conascence, mutuality, dependence, resultant, association, presence and non-disappearance conditions, not-root 1, not-object 1, not-predominance 1, not-proximity 1, not-contiguity 1, not-strong-dependence 1, not-prenascence 1, not-postnascence 1, not-repetition 1, not-kamma 1, not-nutriment 1, not-jhāna 1, not-path 1, not-dissociation 1, not-absence 1, not-disappearance 1 ;

12. Of faculty, conascence, dependence, resultant, dissociation, presence and non-disappearance conditions, not-root 1, not-object 1, not-predominance 1, not-proximity 1, not-contiguity 1, not-mutuality 1, not-strong-dependence 1, not-prenascence 1, not-postnascence 1, not-repetition 1, not-kamma 1, not-nutriment 1, not-jhāna 1, not-path 1, not-association 1, not-absence 1, not-disappearance 1 ;

13. Of faculty, conascence, mutuality, dependence, resultant, dissociation, presence and non-disappearance conditions, not-root 1, not-object 1, not-predominance 1, not-proximity 1, not-contiguity 1, not-strong-dependence 1, not-prenascence 1, not-postnascence 1, not-repetition 1, not-kamma 1, not-nutriment 1, not-jhāna 1, not-path 1, not-association 1, not-absence 1, not-disappearance 1.

With path 9

Without resultant 4

598. 14. Combinations of faculty, conascence, dependence, path, presence and non-disappearance conditions, not-root 7,

not-object 7 ... not-mutuality 3, not-strong-dependence 7 ... not-association 3, not-dissociation 3, not-absence 7, not-disappearance 7;

15. Of faculty, conascence, mutuality, dependence, path, presence and non-disappearance conditions, not-root 3 ... not-association 1, not-dissociation 3, not-absence 3, not-disappearance 3;

16. Of faculty, conascence, mutuality, dependence, path, association, presence and non-disappearance conditions, not-root 3 ... not-disappearance 3;

17. Of faculty, conascence, dependence, path, dissociation, presence and non-disappearance conditions, not-root 3 ... not-disappearance 3.

With resultant 5

18. Combinations of faculty, conascence, dependence, resultant, path, presence and non-disappearance conditions, not-root 1 ... not-disappearance 1;

19. Of faculty, conascence, mutuality, dependence, resultant, path, presence and non-disappearance conditions, not-root 1 ... not-disappearance 1;

20. Of faculty, conascence, mutuality, dependence, resultant, path, association, presence and non-disappearance conditions, not-root 1 ... not-disappearance 1;

21. Of faculty, conascence, dependence, resultant, path, dissociation, presence and non-disappearance conditions, not-root 1 ... not-disappearance 1;

22. Of faculty, conascence, mutuality, dependence, resultant, path, dissociation, presence and non-disappearance conditions, not-root 1 ... not-disappearance 1.

With jhāna 9

Without resultant 4

599. 23. Combinations of faculty, conascence, dependence, jhāna, presence and non-disappearance conditions, not-root 7 ... not-mutuality 3, not-strong-dependence 7 ... not-association 3, not-dissociation 3, not-absence 7, not-disappearance 7;

24. Of faculty, conascence, mutuality, dependence, jhāna, presence and non-disappearance conditions, not-root 3 . . . not-association 1, not-dissociation 3, not-absence 3, not-disappearance 3 ;

25. Of faculty, conascence, mutuality, dependence, jhāna, association, presence and non-disappearance conditions, not-root 3 . . . not-disappearance 3 ;

26. Of faculty, conascence, dependence, jhāna, dissociation, presence and non-disappearance conditions, not-root 3 . . . not-disappearance 3.

With resultant 5

27. Combinations of faculty, conascence, dependence, resultant, jhāna, presence and non-disappearance conditions, not-root 1 . . . not-disappearance 1 ;

28. Of faculty, conascence, mutuality, dependence, resultant, jhāna, presence and non-disappearance conditions, not-root 1 . . . not-disappearance 1 ;

29. Of faculty, conascence, mutuality, dependence, resultant, jhāna, association, presence and non-disappearance conditions, not-root 1 . . . not-disappearance 1 ;

30. Of faculty, conascence, dependence, resultant, jhāna, dissociation, presence and non-disappearance conditions, not-root 1 . . . not-disappearance 1 ;

31. Of faculty, conascence, mutuality, dependence, resultant, jhāna, dissociation, presence and non-disappearance conditions, not-root 1 . . . not-disappearance 1.

With jhāna and path 9

Without resultant 4

600. 32. Combinations of faculty, conascence, dependence, jhāna, path, presence and non-disappearance conditions, not-root 7 . . . not-mutuality 3, not-strong-dependence 7 . . . not-association 3, not-dissociation 3, not-absence 7, not-disappearance 7 ;

33. Of faculty, conascence, mutuality, dependence, jhāna, path, presence and non-disappearance conditions, not-root

3 . . . not-strong-dependence 3 . . . not-association 1, not-dissociation 3, not-absence 3, not-disappearance 3 ;

34. Of faculty, conascence, mutuality, dependence, jhāna, path, association, presence and non-disappearance conditions, not-root 3 . . . not-disappearance 3 ;

35. Of faculty, conascence, dependence, jhāna, path, dissociation, presence and non-disappearance conditions, not-root 3 . . . not-disappearance 3.

With resultant 5

36. Combinations of faculty, conascence, dependence, resultant, jhāna, path, presence and non-disappearance conditions, not-root 1 . . . not-disappearance 1 ;

37. Of faculty, conascence, mutuality, dependence, resultant, jhāna, path, presence and non-disappearance conditions, not-root 1 . . . not-disappearance 1 ;

38. Of faculty, conascence, mutuality, dependence, resultant, jhāna, path, association, presence and non-disappearance conditions, not-root 1 . . . not-disappearance 1 ;

39. Of faculty, conascence, dependence, resultant, jhāna, path, dissociation, presence and non-disappearance conditions, not-root 1 . . . not-disappearance 1 ;

40. Of faculty, conascence, mutuality, dependence, resultant, jhāna, path, dissociation, presence and non-disappearance conditions, not-root 1 . . . not-disappearance 1.

With nutriment 9

Without resultant 4

601. 41. Combinations of faculty, conascence, dependence, nutriment, presence and non-disappearance conditions, not root 7 . . . not-mutuality 3, not-strong-dependence 7 . . . not-association 3, not-dissociation 3, not-absence 7, not-disappearance 7 ;

42. Of faculty, conascence, mutuality, dependence, nutriment, presence and non-disappearance conditions, not-root 3 . . . not-association 1, not-dissociation 3, not-absence 3, not-disappearance 3 ;

43. Of faculty, conascence, mutuality, dependence, nutriment, association, presence and non-disappearance conditions, not-root 3 . . . not-disappearance 3 ;

44. Of faculty, conascence, dependence, nutriment, dissociation, presence and non-disappearance conditions, not-root 3 . . . not-disappearance 3.

With resultant 5

45. Combinations of faculty, conascence, dependence, resultant, nutriment, presence and non-disappearance conditions, not-root 1 . . . not-disappearance 1 ;

46. Of faculty, conascence, mutuality, dependence, resultant, nutriment, presence and non-disappearance conditions, not-root 1 . . . not-disappearance 1 ;

47. Of faculty, conascence, mutuality, dependence, resultant, nutriment, association, presence and non-disappearance conditions, not-root 1 . . . not-disappearance 1 ;

48. Of faculty, conascence, dependence, resultant, nutriment, dissociation, presence and non-disappearance conditions, not-root 1 . . . not-disappearance 1 ;

49. Of faculty, conascence, mutuality, dependence, resultant, nutriment, dissociation, presence and non-disappearance conditions, not-root 1 . . . not-disappearance 1.

With predominance and nutriment 6

Without resultant 3

602. 50. Combinations of faculty, predominance, conascence, dependence, nutriment, presence and non-disappearance conditions, not-root 7 . . . not-mutuality 3, not-strong-dependence 7 . . . not-association 3, not-dissociation 3, not-absence 7, not-disappearance 7 ;

51. Of faculty, predominance, conascence, mutuality, dependence, nutriment, association, presence and non-disappearance conditions, not-root 3 . . . not-disappearance 3 ;

52. Of faculty, predominance, conascence, dependence, nutriment, dissociation, presence and non-disappearance conditions, not-root 3 . . . not-disappearance 3.

With resultant 3

53. Combinations of faculty, predominance, conascence, dependence, resultant, nutriment, presence and non-disappearance conditions, not-root 1 ... not-disappearance 1;

54. Of faculty, predominance, conascence, mutuality, dependence, resultant, nutriment, association, presence and non-disappearance conditions, not-root 1 ... not-disappearance 1;

55. Of faculty, predominance, conascence, dependence, resultant, nutriment, dissociation, presence and non-disappearance conditions, not-root 1 ... not-disappearance 1.

With predominance and path 6
Without resultant 3

603. 56. Combinations of faculty, predominance, conascence, dependence, path, presence and non-disappearance conditions, not-root 7 ... not-mutuality 3, not-strong-dependence 7 ... not-association 3, not-dissociation 3, not-absence 7, not-disappearance 7;

57. Of faculty, predominance, conascence, mutuality, dependence, path, association, presence and non-disappearance conditions, not-root 3 ... not-disappearance 3;

58. Of faculty, predominance, conascence, dependence, path, dissociation, presence and non-disappearance conditions, not-root 3 ... not-disappearance 3.

With resultant 3

59. Combinations of faculty, predominance, conascence, dependence, resultant, path, presence and non-disappearance conditions, not-root 1 ... not-disappearance 1;

60. Of faculty, predominance, conascence, mutuality, dependence, resultant, path, association, presence and non-disappearance conditions, not-root 1 ... not-disappearance 1;

61. Of faculty, predominance, conascence, dependence, resultant, path, dissociation, presence and non-disappearance conditions, not-root 1 ... not-disappearance 1.

With root and path 9
Without resultant 4

604. 62. Combinations of faculty, root, conascence, dependence, path, presence and non-disappearance conditions, not-object 4 ... not-mutuality 2, not-strong-dependence 4 ... not-association 2, not-dissociation 2, not-absence 4, not-disappearance 4 ;

63. Of faculty, root, conascence, mutuality, dependence, path, presence and non-disappearance conditions, not-object 2 ... not-association 1, not-dissociation 2, not-absence 2, not-disappearance 2 ;

64. Of faculty, root, conascence, mutuality, dependence, path, association, presence and non-disappearance conditions, not-object 2 ... not-disappearance 2 ;

65. Of faculty, root, conascence, dependence, path, dissociation, presence and non-disappearance conditions, not-object 2 ... not-disappearance 2.

With resultant 5

66. Combinations of faculty, root, conascence, dependence, resultant, path, presence and non-disappearance conditions, not-object 1 ... not-disappearance 1 ;

67. Of faculty, root, conascence, mutuality, dependence, resultant, path, presence and non-disappearance conditions, not-object 1 ... not-disappearance 1 ;

68. Of faculty, root, conascence, mutuality, dependence, resultant, path, association, presence and non-disappearance conditions, not-object 1 ... not-disappearance 1 ;

69. Of faculty, root, conascence, dependence, resultant, path, dissociation, presence and non-disappearance conditions, not-object 1 ... not-disappearance 1 ;

70. Of faculty, root, conascence, mutuality, dependence, resultant, path, dissociation, presence and non-disappearance conditions, not-object 1 ... not-disappearance 1.

With root, predominance and path 6
Without resultant 3

605. 71. Combinations of faculty, root, predominance, conascence, dependence, path, presence and non-disappearance

conditions, not-object 4, not-proximity 4, not-contiguity 4, not mutuality 2, not-strong-dependence 4, not-prenascence 4, not-postnascence 4, not-repetition 4, not-kamma 4, not-resultant 4, not-nutriment 4, not-jhāna 4, not-association 2, not-dissociation 2, not-absence 4, not-disappearance 4 ;

72. Of faculty, root, predominance, conascence, mutuality, dependence, path, association, presence and non-disappearance conditions, not-object 2, not-proximity 2, not-contiguity 2, not-strong-dependence 2, not-prenascence 2, not-postnascence 2, not-repetition 2, not-kamma 2, not-resultant 2, not-nutriment 2, not-jhāna 2, not-dissociation 2, not-absence 2, not-disappearance 2 ;

73. Of faculty, root, predominance, conascence, dependence, path, dissociation, presence and non-disappearance conditions, not-object 2, not-proximity 2, not-contiguity 2, not-mutuality 2, not-strong-dependence 2, not-prenascence 2, not-postnascence 2, not-repetition 2, not-kamma 2, not-resultant 2, not-nutriment 2, not-jhāna 2, not-association 2, not-absence 2, not-disappearance 2.

With resultant 3

74. Combinations of faculty, root, predominance, conascence, dependence, resultant, path, presence and non-disappearance conditions, not-object 1, not-proximity 1, not-contiguity 1, not-mutuality 1, not-strong-dependence 1, not-prenascence 1, not-postnascence 1, not-repetition 1, not-kamma 1, not-nutriment 1, not-jhāna 1, not-association 1, not-dissociation 1, not-absence 1, not-disappearance 1 ;

75. Of faculty, root, predominance, conascence, mutuality, dependence, resultant, path, association, presence and non-disappearance conditions, not-object 1, not-proximity 1, not-contiguity 1, not-strong-dependence 1, not-prenascence 1, not-postnascence 1, not-repetition 1, not-kamma 1, not-nutriment 1, not-jhāna 1, not-dissociation 1, not-absence 1, not-disappearance 1 ;

76. Of faculty, root, predominance, conascence, dependence, resultant, path, dissociation, presence and non-disappearance conditions, not-object 1, not-proximity 1, not-contiguity 1, not-mutuality 1, not-strong-dependence 1,

not-prenascence 1, not-postnascence 1, not-repetition 1, not-kamma 1, not-nutriment 1, not-jhāna 1, not-association 1, not-absence 1, not-disappearance 1.

End of Faculty

Jhāna

By Twos

606. With jhāna condition, not-root 7, not-object 7, not-predominance 7, not-proximity 7, not-contiguity 7, not-mutuality 3, not-strong-dependence 7, not-prenascence 7, not-postnascence 7, not-repetition 7, not-kamma 7, not-resultant 7, not-nutriment 7, not-faculty 7, not-path 7, not-association 3, not-dissociation 3, not-absence 7, not-disappearance 7.

Conascence Combinations 36

Ordinary 9

Without resultant 4

607. 1. Combinations of jhāna, conascence, dependence, presence and non-disappearance conditions, not-root 7 . . . not-mutuality 3, not-strong-dependence 7 . . . not-association 3, not-dissociation 3, not-absence 7, not-disappearance 7 ;

2. Of jhāna, conascence, mutuality, dependence, presence and non-disappearance conditions, not-root 3 . . . not-association 1, not-dissociation 3, not-absence 3, not-disappearance 3 ;

3. Of jhāna, conascence, mutuality, dependence, association, presence and non-disappearance conditions, not-root 3 . . . not-disappearance 3 ;

4. Of jhāna, conascence, dependence, dissociation, presence and non-disappearance conditions, not-root 3 . . . not-disappearance 3.

With resultant 5

5. Combinations of jhāna, conascence, dependence, resultant, presence and non-disappearance conditions, not-root 1 . . . not-disappearance 1 ;

6. Of jhāna, conascence, mutuality, dependence, resultant, presence and non-disappearance conditions, not-root 1 ... not-disappearance 1;

7. Of jhāna, conascence, mutuality, dependence, resultant, association, presence and non-disappearance conditions, not-root 1 ... not-disappearance 1;

8. Of jhāna, conascence, dependence, resultant, dissociation, presence and non-disappearance conditions, not-root 1 ... not-disappearance 1;

9. Of jhāna, conascence, mutuality, dependence, resultant, dissociation, presence and non-disappearance conditions, not-root 1 ... not-disappearance 1.

With faculty 9

Without resultant 4

608. 10. Combinations of jhāna, conascence, dependence, faculty, presence and non-disappearance conditions, not-root 7 ... not-mutuality 3, not-strong-dependence 7 ... not-association 3, not-dissociation 3, not-absence 7, not-disappearance 7;

11. Of jhāna, conascence, mutuality, dependence, faculty, presence and non-disappearance conditions, not-root 3 ... not-association 1, not-dissociation 3, not-absence 3, not-disappearance 3;

12. Of jhāna, conascence, mutuality, dependence, faculty, association, presence and non-disappearance conditions, not-root 3 ... not-disappearance 3;

13. Of jhāna, conascence, dependence, faculty, dissociation, presence and non-disappearance conditions, not-root 3 ... not-disappearance 3.

With resultant 5

14. Combinations of jhāna, conascence, dependence, resultant, faculty, presence and non-disappearance conditions, not-root 1 ... not-disappearance 1;

15. Of jhāna, conascence, mutuality, dependence, resultant, faculty, presence and non-disappearance conditions, not-root 1 ... not-disappearance 1;

16. Of jhāna, conascence, mutuality, dependence, resultant, faculty, association, presence and non-disappearance conditions, not-root 1 . . . not-disappearance 1 ;

17. Of jhāna, conascence, dependence, resultant, faculty, dissociation, presence and non-disappearance conditions, not-root . . . not-disappearance 1 ;

18. Of jhāna, conascence, mutuality, dependence, resultant, faculty, dissociation, presence and non-disappearance conditions, not-root 1 . . . not-disappearance 1.

With path 9

Without resultant 4

609. 19. Combinations of jhāna, conascence, dependence, path, presence and non-disappearance conditions, not-root 7 . . . not-mutuality 3, not-strong-dependence 7 . . . not-association 3, not-dissociation 3,[1] not-absence 7, not-disappearance 7 ;

20. Of jhāna, conascence, mutuality, dependence, path, presence and non-disappearance conditions, not-root 3 . . . not-association 1, not-dissociation 3, not-absence 3, not-disappearance 3 ;

21. Of jhāna, conascence, mutuality, dependence, path, association, presence and non-disappearance conditions, not-root 3 . . . not-disappearance 3 ;

22. Of jhāna, conascence, dependence, path, dissociation, presence and non-disappearance conditions, not-root 3 . . . not-disappearance 3.

With resultant 5

23. Combinations of jhāna, conascence, dependence, resultant, path, presence and non-disappearance conditions, not-root 1 . . . not-disappearance 1 ;

24. Of jhāna, conascence, mutuality, dependence, resultant, path, presence and non-disappearance conditions, not-root 1 . . . not-disappearance 1 ;

25. Of jhāna, conascence, mutuality, dependence, resultant, path, association, presence and non-disappearance conditions, not-root 1 . . . not-disappearance 1 ;

[1] Left out in the Text.

26. Of jhāna, conascence, dependence, resultant, path, dissociation, presence and non-disappearance conditions, not-root 1 . . . not-disappearance 1 ;

27. Of jhāna, conascence, mutuality, dependence, resultant, path, dissociation, presence and non-disappearance conditions, not-root 1 . . . not-disappearance 1.

With faculty and path 9

Without resultant 4

610. 28. Combinations of jhāna, conascence, dependence, faculty, path, presence and non-disappearance conditions, not-root 7 . . . not-mutuality 3, not-strong-dependence 7 . . . not-association 3, not-dissociation 3,[1] not-absence 7, not-disappearance 7 ;

29. Of jhāna, conascence, mutuality, dependence, faculty, path, presence and non-disappearance conditions, not-root 3 . . . not-association 1, not-dissociation 3, not-absence 3, not-disappearance 3 ;

30. Of jhāna, conascence, mutuality, dependence, faculty, path, association, presence and non-disappearance conditions, not-root 3 . . . not-disappearance 3 ;

31. Of jhāna, conascence, dependence, faculty, path, dissociation, presence and non-disappearance conditions, not-root 3 . . . not-disappearance 3.

With resultant 5

32. Combinations of jhāna, conascence, dependence, resultant, faculty, path, presence and non-disappearance conditions, not-root 1 . . . not-disappearance 1 ;

33. Of jhāna, conascence, mutuality, dependence, resultant, faculty, path, presence and non-disappearance conditions, not-root 1 . . . not-disappearance 1 ;

34. Of jhāna, conascence, mutuality, dependence, resultant, faculty, path, association, presence and non-disappearance conditions, not-root 1 . . . not-disappearance 1 ;

35. Of jhāna, conascence, dependence, resultant, faculty,

---

[1] Left out in the Text.

path, dissociation, presence and non-disappearance conditions, not-root 1 ... not-disappearance 1 ;

36. Of jhāna, conascence, mutuality, dependence, resultant, faculty, path, dissociation, presence and non-disappearance conditions, not-root 1 ... not-disappearance 1.

End of Jhāna

Path

By Twos

611. With path condition, not-root 7, not-object 7, not-predominance 7, not-proximity 7, not-contiguity 7, not-mutuality 3, not-strong-dependence 7, not-prenascence 7, not-postnascence 7, not-repetition 7, not-kamma 7, not-resultant 7, not-nutriment 7, not-faculty 7, not-jhāna 7, not-association 3, not-dissociation 3, not-absence 7, not-disappearance 7.

Conascence Combinations 57

Ordinary 9

Without resultant 4

612. 1. Combinations of path, conascence, dependence, presence and non-disappearance conditions, not-root 7 ... not-mutuality 3, not-strong-dependence 7 ... not-association 3, not-dissociation 3, not-absence 7, not-disappearance 7 ;

2. Of path, conascence, mutuality, dependence, presence and non-disappearance conditions, not-root 3 ... not-association 1, not-dissociation 3, not-absence 3, not-disappearance 3 ;

3. Of path, conascence, mutuality, dependence, association, presence and non-disappearance conditions, not-root 3 ... not-disappearance 3 ;

4. Of path, conascence, dependence, dissociation, presence and non-disappearance conditions, not-root 3 ... not-disappearance 3.

With resultant 5

5. Combinations of path, conascence, dependence, resultant, presence and non-disappearance conditions, not-root 1 ... not-disappearance 1 ;

6. Of path, conascence, mutuality, dependence, resultant, presence and non-disappearance conditions, not-root 1 . . . not-disappearance 1 ;

7. Of path, conascence, mutuality, dependence, resultant, association, presence and non-disappearance conditions, not-root 1 . . . not-disappearance 1 ;

8. Of path, conascence, dependence, resultant, dissociation, presence and non-disappearance conditions, not-root 1 . . . not-disappearance 1 ;

9. Of path, conascence, mutuality, dependence, resultant, dissociation, presence and non-disappearance conditions, not-root 1 . . . not-disappearance 1.

With faculty 9

Without resultant 4

613. 10. Combinations of path, conascence, dependence, faculty, presence and non-disappearance conditions, not-root 7 . . . not-mutuality 3, not-strong-dependence 7 . . . not-association 3, not-dissociation 3, not-absence 7, not-disappearance 7 ;

11. Of path, conascence, mutuality, dependence, faculty, presence and non-disappearance conditions, not-root 3 . . . not-association 1, not-dissociation 3, not-absence 3, not-disappearance 3 ;

12. Of path, conascence, mutuality, dependence, faculty, association, presence and non-disappearance conditions, not-root 3 . . . not-disappearance 3 ;

13. Of path, conascence, dependence, faculty, dissociation, presence and non-disappearance conditions, not-root 3 . . . not-disappearance 3.

With resultant 5

14. Combinations of path, conascence, dependence, resultant, faculty, presence and non-disappearance conditions, not-root 1 . . . not-disappearance 1 ;

15. Of path, conascence, mutuality, dependence, resultant, faculty, presence and non-disappearance conditions, not-root 1 . . . not-disappearance 1 ;

16. Of path, conascence, mutuality, dependence, resultant, faculty, association, presence and non-disappearance conditions, not-root 1 . . . not-disappearance 1 ;

17. Of path, conascence, dependence, resultant, faculty, dissociation, presence and non-disappearance conditions, not-root 1 . . . not-disappearance 1 ;

18. Of path, conascence, mutuality, dependence, resultant, faculty, dissociation, presence and non-disappearance conditions, not-root 1 . . . not-disappearance 1.

With jhāna 9

Without resultant 4

614. 19. Combinations of path, conascence, dependence, jhāna, presence and non-disappearance conditions, not-root 7 . . . not-mutuality 3, not-strong-dependence 7 . . . not-association 3, not-dissociation 3, not-absence 7, not-disappearance 7 ;

20. Of path, conascence, mutuality, dependence, jhāna, presence and non-disappearance conditions, not-root 3 . . . not-association 1, not-dissociation 3, not-absence 3, not-disappearance 3 ;

21. Of path, conascence, mutuality, dependence, jhāna, association, presence and non-disappearance conditions, not-root 3 . . . not-disappearance 3 ;

22. Of path, conascence, dependence, jhāna, dissociation, presence and non-disappearance conditions, not-root 3 . . . not-disappearance 3.

With resultant 5

23. Combinations of path, conascence, dependence, resultant, jhāna, presence and non-disappearance conditions, not-root 1 . . . not-disappearance 1 ;

24. Of path, conascence, mutuality, dependence, resultant, jhāna, presence and non-disappearance conditions, not-root 1 . . . not-disappearance 1 ;

25. Of path, conascence, mutuality, dependence, resultant, jhāna, association, presence and non-disappearance conditions, not-root 1 . . . not-disappearance 1 ;

26. Of path, conascence, dependence, resultant, jhāna, dissociation, presence and non-disappearance conditions, not-root 1 ... not-disappearance 1;

27. Of path, conascence, mutuality, dependence, resultant, jhāna, dissociation, presence and non-disappearance conditions, not-root 1 ... not-disappearance 1.

With faculty and jhāna 9
Without resultant 4

615. 28. Combinations of path, conascence, dependence, faculty, jhāna, presence and non-disappearance conditions, not-root 7 ... not-mutuality 3, not-strong-dependence 7 ... not-association 3, not-dissociation 3, not-absence 7, not-disappearance 7;

29. Of path, conascence, mutuality, dependence, faculty, jhāna, presence and non-disappearance conditions, not-root 3 ... not-association 1, not-dissociation 3, not-absence 3, not-disappearance 3;

30. Of path, conascence, mutuality, dependence, faculty, jhāna, association, presence and non-disappearance conditions, not-root 3 ... not-disappearance 3;

31. Of path, conascence, dependence, faculty, jhāna, dissociation, presence and non-disappearance conditions, not-root 3 ... not-disappearance 3.

With resultant 5

32. Combinations of path, conascence, dependence, resultant, faculty, jhāna, presence and non-disappearance conditions, not-root 1 ... not-disappearance 1;

33. Of path, conascence, mutuality, dependence, resultant, faculty, jhāna, presence and non-disappearance conditions, not-root 1 ... not-disappearance 1;

34. Of path, conascence, mutuality, dependence, resultant, faculty, jhāna, association, presence and non-disappearance conditions, not-root 1 ... not-disappearance 1;

35. Of path, conascence, dependence, resultant, faculty, jhāna, dissociation, presence and non-disappearance conditions, not-root 1 ... not-disappearance 1;

36. Of path, conascence, mutuality, dependence, resultant, faculty, jhāna, dissociation, presence and non-disappearance conditions, not-root 1 ... not-disappearance 1.

With predominance and faculty 6

Without resultant 3

616. 37. Combinations of path, predominance, conascence, dependence, faculty, presence and non-disappearance conditions, not-root 7 ... not-mutuality 3, not-strong-dependence 7 ... not-association 3, not-dissociation 3, not-absence 7, not-disappearance 7 ;

38. Of path, predominance, conascence, mutuality, dependence, faculty, association, presence and non-disappearance conditions, not-root 3 ... not-disappearance 3 ;

39. Of path, predominance, conascence, dependence, faculty, dissociation, presence and non-disappearance conditions, not-root 3 ... not-disappearance 3.

With resultant 3

40. Combinations of path, predominance, conascence, dependence, resultant, faculty, presence and non-disappearance conditions, not-root 1 ... not-disappearance 1 ;

41. Of path, predominance, conascence, mutuality, dependence, resultant, faculty, association, presence and non-disappearance conditions, not-root 1 ... not-disappearance 1 ;

42. Of path, predominance, conascence, dependence, resultant, faculty, dissociation, presence and non-disappearance conditions, not-root 1 ... not-disappearance 1.

With root and faculty 9

Without resultant 4

617. 43. Combinations of path, root, conascence, dependence, faculty, presence and non-disappearance conditions, not-object 4 ... not-mutuality 2, not-strong-dependence 4 ... not-association 2, not-dissociation 2, not-absence 4, not-disappearance 4 ;

44. Of path, root, conascence, mutuality, dependence, faculty, presence and non-disappearance conditions, not-object 2 . . . not-association 1, not-dissociation 2, not-absence 2, not-disappearance 2 ;

45. Of path, root, conascence, mutuality, dependence, faculty, association, presence and non-disappearance conditions, not-object 2 . . . not-disappearance 2 ;

46. Of path, root, conascence, dependence, faculty, dissociation, presence and non-disappearance conditions, not-object 2 . . . not-disappearance 2.

With resultant 5

47. Combinations of path, root, conascence, dependence, resultant, faculty, presence and non-disappearance conditions, not-object 1 . . . not-disappearance 1 ;

48. Of path, root, conascence, mutuality, dependence, resultant, faculty, presence and non-disappearance conditions, not-object 1 . . . not-disappearance 1 ;

49. Of path, root, conascence, mutuality, dependence, resultant, faculty, association, presence and non-disappearance conditions, not-object 1 . . . not-disappearance 1 ;

50. Of path, root, conascence, dependence, resultant, faculty, dissociation, presence and non-disappearance conditions, not-object 1 . . . not-disappearance 1 ;

51. Of path, root, conascence, mutuality, dependence, resultant, faculty, dissociation, presence and non-disappearance conditions, not-object 1 . . . not-disappearance 1.

With root, predominance and faculty 6

Without resultant 3

618. 52. Combinations of path, root, predominance, conascence, dependence, faculty, presence and non-disappearance conditions, not-object 4 . . . not-mutuality 2, not-strong-dependence 4 . . . not-association 2, not-dissociation 2, not-absence 4, not-disappearance 4 ;

53. Of path, root, predominance, conascence, mutuality, dependence, faculty, association, presence and non-disappearance conditions, not-object 2 . . . not-disappearance 2 ;

54. Of path, root, predominance, conascence, dependence, faculty, dissociation, presence and non-disappearance conditions, not-object 2 . . . not-disappearance 2.

With resultant 3

55. Combinations of path, root, predominance, conascence, dependence, resultant, faculty, presence and non-disappearance conditions, not-object 1 . . . not-disappearance 1 ;

56. Of path, root, predominance, conascence, mutuality, dependence, resultant, faculty, association, presence and non-disappearance conditions, not-object 1 . . . not-disappearance 1 ;

57. Of path, root, predominance, conascence, dependence, resultant, faculty, dissociation, presence and non-disappearance conditions, not-object 1 . . . not-disappearance 1.

End of Path

Association

By Twos

619. With association condition, not-root 3, not-object 3, not-predominance 3, not-proximity 3, not-contiguity 3, not-strong-dependence 3, not-prenascence 3, not-postnascence 3, not-repetition 3, not-kamma 3, not-resultant 3, not-nutriment 3, not-faculty 3, not-jhāna 3, not-path 3, not-dissociation 3, not-absence 3, not-disappearance 3.

Conascence Combinations 2

Without resultant 1

620. Combinations of association, conascence, mutuality, dependence, presence and non-disappearance conditions not-root 3 . . . not-disappearance 3.

With resultant 1

Combinations of association, conascence, mutuality, dependence, resultant, presence and non-disappearance conditions, not-root 1 . . . not-disappearance 1.

End of Association

Dissociation

By Twos

621. With dissociation condition, not-root 5, not-object 5, not-predominance 5, not-proximity 5, not-contiguity 5, not-conascence 5, not-mutuality 5, not-dependence 3, not-strong-dependence 5, not-prenascence 3, not-postnascence 5, not-repetition 5, not-kamma 5, not-resultant 5, not-nutriment 5, not-faculty 5, not-jhāna 5, not-path 5, not-association 5, not-absence 5, not-disappearance 5.

Combinations 13

Mixed 4

622. 1. Combinations of dissociation, presence and non-disappearance conditions, not-root 5, not-object 5, not-predominance 5, not-proximity 5, not-contiguity 5, not-conascence 5, not-mutuality 5, not-dependence 3, not-strong-dependence 5, not-prenascence 3, not-postnascence 5, not-repetition 5, not-kamma 5, not-resultant 5, not-nutriment 5, not-faculty 5, not-jhāna 5, not-path 5, not-association 5, not-absence 5, not-disappearance 5 ;

2. Of dissociation, dependence, presence and non-disappearance conditions, not-root 5, not-object 5, not-predominance 5, not-proximity 5, not-contiguity 5, not-conascence 3, not-mutuality 5, not-strong-dependence 5, not-prenascence 3, not-postnascence 5, not-repetition 5, not-kamma 5, not-resultant 5, not-nutriment 5, not-faculty 5, not-jhāna 5, not-path 5, not-association 5, not-absence 5, not-disappearance 5 ;

3. Of dissociation, predominance, dependence, presence and non-disappearance conditions, not-root 4, not-object 3, not-proximity 4, not-contiguity 4, not-conascence 1, not-mutuality 4, not-strong-dependence 3, not-prenascence 3, not-postnascence 4, not-repetition 4, not-kamma 4, not-resultant 4, not-nutriment 4, not-faculty 4, not-jhāna 4, not-path 4, not-association 4, not-absence 4, not-disappearance 4 ;

4. Of dissociation, dependence, faculty, presence and non-disappearance conditions, not-root 3, not-object 3, not-predominance 3, not-proximity 3, not-contiguity 3, not-conascence 1, not-mutuality 3, not-strong-dependence 3, not-

prenascence 3, not-postnascence 3, not-repetition 3, not-kamma 3, not-resultant 3, not-nutriment 3, not-jhāna 3, not-path 3, not-association 3, not-absence 3, not-disappearance 3.

Miscellaneous 5

623. 5. Combinations of dissociation, postnascence, presence and non-disappearance conditions, not-root 3, not-object 3, not-predominance 3, not-proximity 3, not-contiguity 3, not-conascence 3, not-mutuality 3, not-dependence 3, not-strong-dependence 3, not-prenascence 3, not-repetition 3, not-kamma 3, not-resultant 3, not-nutriment 3, not-faculty 3, not-jhāna 3, not-path 3, not-association 3, not-absence 3, not-disappearance 3 ;

6. Of dissociation, dependence, prenascence, presence and non-disappearance conditions, not-root 3, not-object 3, not-predominance 3, not-proximity 3, not-contiguity 3, not-conascence 3, not-mutuality 3, not-strong-dependence 3, not-postnascence 3, not-repetition 3, not-kamma 3, not-resultant 3, not-nutriment 3, not-faculty 3, not-jhāna 3, not-path 3, not-association 3, not-absence 3, not-disappearance 3 ;

7. Of dissociation, object, dependence, prenascence, presence and non-disappearance conditions, not-root 3, not-predominance 3, not-proximity 3, not-contiguity 3, not-conascence 3, not-mutuality 3, not-strong-dependence 3, not-postnascence 3, not-repetition 3, not-kamma 3, not-resultant 3, not-nutriment 3, not-faculty 3, not-jhāna 3, not-path 3, not-association 3, not-absence 3, not-disappearance 3 ;

8. Of dissociation, object, predominance, dependence, strong-dependence, prenascence, presence and non-disappearance conditions, not-root 1, not-proximity 1, not-contiguity 1, not-conascence 1, not-mutuality 1, not-postnascence 1, not-repetition 1, not-kamma 1, not-resultant 1, not-nutriment 1, not-faculty 1, not-jhāna 1, not-path 1, not-association 1, not-absence 1, not-disappearance 1 ;

9. Of dissociation, dependence, prenascence, faculty, presence and non-disappearance conditions, not-root 1, not-object 1, not-predominance 1, not-proximity 1, not-contiguity 1, not-conascence 1, not-mutuality 1, not-strong-dependence 1,

not-postnascence 1, not-repetition 1, not-kamma 1, not-resultant 1, not-nutriment 1, not-jhāna 1, not-path 1, not-association 1, not-absence 1, not-disappearance 1.

Conascence 4

Without resultant 2

624. 10. Combinations of dissociation, conascence, dependence, presence and non-disappearance conditions, not-root 3, not-object 3, not-predominance 3, not-proximity 3, not-contiguity 3, not-mutuality 3, not-strong-dependence 3, not-prenascence 3, not-postnascence 3, not-repetition 3, not-kamma 3, not-resultant 3, not-nutriment 3, not-faculty 3, not-jhāna 3, not-path 3, not-association 3, not-absence 3, not-disappearance 3 ;

11. Of dissociation, conascence, mutuality, dependence, presence and non-disappearance conditions, not-root 1, not-object 1, not-predominance 1, not-proximity 1, not-contiguity 1, not-strong-dependence 1, not-prenascence 1, not-postnascence 1, not-repetition 1, not-kamma 1, not-resultant 1, not-nutriment 1, not-faculty 1, not-jhāna 1, not-path 1, not-association 1, not-absence 1, not-disappearance 1.

With resultant 2

12. Combinations of dissociation, conascence, dependence, resultant, presence and non-disappearance conditions, not-root 1, not-object 1, not-predominance 1, not-proximity 1, not-contiguity 1, not-mutuality 1, not-strong-dependence 1, not-prenascence 1, not-postnascence 1, not-repetition 1, not-kamma 1, not-nutriment 1, not-faculty 1, not-jhāna 1, not-path 1, not-association 1, not-absence 1, not-disappearance 1 ;

13. Of dissociation, conascence, mutuality, dependence, resultant, presence and non-disappearance conditions, not-root 1, not-object 1, not-predominance 1, not-proximity 1, not-contiguity 1, not-strong-dependence 1, not-prenascence 1, not-postnascence 1, not-repetition 1, not-kamma 1, not-nutriment 1, not-faculty 1, not-jhāna 1, not-path 1, not-association 1, not-absence 1, not-disappearance 1.

End of Dissociation

Presence

By Twos

625. With presence condition, not-root 13, not-object 13, not-predominance 13, not-proximity 13, not-contiguity 13, not-conascence 7, not-mutuality 7, not-dependence 7, not-strong-dependence 13, not-prenascence 9, not-postnascence 13, not-repetition 13, not-kamma 13, not-resultant 13, not-nutriment 13, not-faculty 13, not-jhāna 13, not-path 13, not-association 7, not-dissociation 5, not-absence 13, not-disappearance 13.

Combinations 29

Mixed 11

626. 1. Combinations of presence and non-disappearance conditions, not-root 13, not-object 13, not-predominance 13, not-proximity 13, not-contiguity 13, not-conascence 7, not-mutuality 7, not-dependence 7, not-strong-dependence 13, not-prenascence 9, not-postnascence 13, not-repetition 13, not-kamma 13, not-resultant 13, not-nutriment 13, not-faculty 13, not-jhāna 13, not-path 13, not-association 7, not-dissociation 5, not-absence 13, not-disappearance 13 ;

2. Of presence, dependence and non-disappearance conditions, not-root 13, not-object 13, not-predominance 13, not-proximity 13, not-contiguity 13, not-conascence 3, not-mutuality 7, not-strong-dependence 13, not-prenascence 9, not-postnascence 13, not-repetition 13, not-kamma 13, not-resultant 13, not-nutriment 13, not-faculty 13, not-jhāna 13, not-path 13, not-association 7, not-dissociation 3, not-absence 13, not-disappearance 13 ;

3. Of presence, predominance and non-disappearance conditions, not-root 8, not-object 7, not-proximity 8, not-contiguity 8, not-conascence 1, not-mutuality 4, not-dependence 1, not-strong-dependence 7, not-prenascence 7, not-postnascence 8, not-repetition 8, not-kamma 8, not-resultant 8, not-nutriment 8, not-faculty 8, not-jhāna 8, not-path 8, not-association 4, not-dissociation 4, not-absence 8, not-disappearance 8 ;

4. Of presence, predominance, dependence and non-disappearance conditions, not-root 8, not-object 7, not-

proximity 8, not-contiguity 8, not-conascence 1, not-mutuality 4, not-strong-dependence 7, not-prenascence 7, not-postnascence 8, not-repetition 8, not-kamma 8, not-resultant 8, not-nutriment 8, not-faculty 8, not-jhāna 8, not-path 8, not-association 4, not-dissociation 3, not-absence 8, not-disappearance 8 ;

5. Of presence, nutriment and non-disappearance conditions, not-root 7, not-object 7, not-predominance 7, not-proximity 7, not-contiguity 7, not-conascence 1, not-mutuality 3, not-dependence 1, not-strong-dependence 7, not-prenascence 7, not-postnascence 7, not-repetition 7, not-kamma 7, not-resultant 7, not-faculty 7, not-jhāna 7, not-path 7, not-association 3, not-dissociation 3, not-absence 7, not-disappearance 7 ;

6. Of presence, faculty and non-disappearance conditions, not-root 7, not-object 7, not-predominance 7, not-proximity 7, not-contiguity 7, not-conascence 1, not-mutuality 3, not-dependence 1, not-strong-dependence 7, not-prenascence 7, not-postnascence 7, not-repetition 7, not-kamma 7, not-resultant 7, not-nutriment 7, not-jhāna 7, not-path 7, not-association 3, not-dissociation 3, not-absence 7, not-disappearance 7 ;

7. Of presence, dependence, faculty and non-disappearance conditions, not-root 7, not-object 7, not-predominance 7, not-proximity 7, not-contiguity 7, not-conascence 1, not-mutuality 3, not-strong-dependence 7, not-prenascence 7, not-postnascence 7, not-repetition 7, not-kamma 7, not-resultant 7, not-nutriment 7, not-jhāna 7, not-path 7, not-association 3, not-dissociation 3, not-absence 7, not-disappearance 7 ;

8. Of presence, dissociation and non-disappearance conditions, not-root 5, not-object 5, not-predominance 5, not-proximity 5, not-contiguity 5, not-conascence 5, not-mutuality 5, not-dependence 3, not-strong-dependence 5, not-prenascence 3, not-postnascence 5, not-repetition 5, not-kamma 5, not-resultant 5, not-nutriment 5, not-faculty 5, not-jhāna 5, not-path 5, not-association 5, not-absence 5, not-disappearance 5 ;

9. Of presence, dependence, dissociation and non-disappearance conditions, not-root 5, not-object 5, not-predominance 5, not-proximity 5, not-contiguity 5, not-conascence 3, not-mutuality 5, not-strong-dependence 5, not-prenascence 3, not-

postnascence 5, not-repetition 5, not-kamma 5, not-resultant 5, not-nutriment 5, not-faculty 5, not-jhāna 5, not-path 5, not-association 5, not-absence 5, not-disappearance 5 ;

10. Of presence, predominance, dependence, dissociation and non-disappearance conditions, not-root 4, not-object 3, not-proximity 4, not-contiguity 4, not-conascence 1, not-mutuality 4, not-strong-dependence 3, not-prenascence 3, not-postnascence 4, not-repetition 4, not-kamma 4, not-resultant 4, not-nutriment 4, not-faculty 4, not-jhāna 4, not-path 4, not-association 4, not-absence 4, not-disappearance 4 ;

11. Of presence, dependence, faculty, dissociation and non-disappearance conditions, not-root 3, not-object 3, not-predominance 3, not-proximity 3, not-contiguity 3, not-conascence 1, not-mutuality 3, not-strong-dependence 3, not-prenascence 3, not-postnascence 3, not-repetition 3, not-kamma 3, not-resultant 3, not-nutriment 3, not-jhāna 3, not-path 3, not-association 3, not-absence 3, not-disappearance 3.

Miscellaneous 8

627. 12. Combinations of presence, postnascence, dissociation and non-disappearance conditions, not-root 3, not-object 3, not-predominance 3, not-proximity 3, not-contiguity 3, not-conascence 3, not-mutuality 3, not-dependence 3, not-strong-dependence 3, not-prenascence 3, not-repetition 3, not-kamma 3, not-resultant 3, not-nutriment 3, not-faculty 3, not-jhāna 3, not-path 3, not-association 3, not-absence 3, not-disappearance 3 ;

13. Of presence, prenascence and non-disappearance conditions, not-root 3, not-object 3, not-predominance 3, not-proximity 3, not-contiguity 3, not-conascence 3, not-mutuality 3, not-dependence 3, not-strong-dependence 3, not-postnascence 3, not-repetition 3, not-kamma 3, not-resultant 3, not-nutriment 3, not-faculty 3, not-jhāna 3, not-path 3, not-association 3, not-dissociation 3, not-absence 3, not-disappearance 3 ;

14. Of presence, dependence, prenascence, dissociation and non-disappearance conditions, not-root 3, not-object 3, not-predominance 3, not-proximity 3, not-contiguity 3, not-conascence 3, not-mutuality 3, not-strong-dependence 3,

not-postnascence 3, not-repetition 3, not-kamma 3, not-resultant 3, not-nutriment 3, not-faculty 3, not-jhāna 3, not-path 3, not-association 3, not-absence 3, not-disappearance 3 ;

15. Of presence, object, prenascence and non-disappearance conditions, not-root 3, not-predominance 3, not-proximity 3, not-contiguity 3, not-conascence 3, not-mutuality 3, not-dependence 3, not-strong-dependence 3, not-postnascence 3, not-repetition 3, not-kamma 3, not-resultant 3, not-nutriment 3, not-faculty 3, not-jhāna 3, not-path 3, not-association 3, not-dissociation 3, not-absence 3, not-disappearance 3 ;

16. Of presence, object, dependence, prenascence, dissociation and non-disappearance conditions, not-root 3, not-predominance 3, not-proximity 3, not-contiguity 3, not-conascence 3, not-mutuality 3, not-strong-dependence 3, not-postnascence 3, not-repetition 3, not-kamma 3, not-resultant 3, not-nutriment 3, not-faculty 3, not-jhāna 3, not-path 3, not-association 3, not-absence 3, not-disappearance 3 ;

17. Of presence, object, predominance, strong-dependence, prenascence and non-disappearance conditions, not-root 1, not-proximity 1, not-contiguity 1, not-conascence 1, not-mutuality 1, not-dependence 1, not-postnascence 1, not-repetition 1, not-kamma 1, not-resultant 1, not-nutriment 1, not-faculty 1, not-jhāna 1, not-path 1, not-association 1, not-dissociation 1, not-absence 1, not-disappearance 1 ;

18. Of presence, object, predominance, dependence, strong-dependence, prenascence, dissociation and non-disappearance conditions, not-root 1, not-proximity 1, not-contiguity 1, not-conascence 1, not-mutuality 1, not-postnascence 1, not-repetition 1, not-kamma 1, not-resultant 1, not-nutriment 1, not-faculty 1, not-jhāna 1, not-path 1, not-association 1, not-absence 1, not-disappearance 1 ;

19. Of presence, dependence, prenascence, faculty, dissociation and non-disappearance conditions, not-root 1, not-object 1, not-predominance 1, not-proximity 1, not-contiguity 1, not-conascence 1, not-mutuality 1, not-strong-dependence 1, not-postnascence 1, not-repetition 1, not-kamma 1, not-resultant 1, not-nutriment 1, not-jhāna 1, not-path 1, not-association 1, not-absence 1, not-disappearance 1.

Conascence 10

Without resultant 5

628. 20. Combinations of presence, conascence, dependence and non-disappearance conditions, not-root 9, not-object 9, not-predominance 9, not-proximity 9, not-contiguity 9, not-mutuality 5, not-strong-dependence 9, not-prenascence 9, not-postnascence 9, not-repetition 9, not-kamma 9, not-resultant 9, not-nutriment 9, not-faculty 9, not-jhāna 9, not-path 9, not-association 5, not-dissociation 3, not-absence 9, not-disappearance 9;

21. Of presence, conascence, mutuality, dependence and non-disappearance conditions, not-root 3, not-object 3, not-predominance 3, not-proximity 3, not-contiguity 3, not-strong-dependence 3, not-prenascence 3, not-postnascence 3, not-repetition 3, not-kamma 3, not-resultant 3, not-nutriment 3, not-faculty 3, not-jhāna 3, not-path 3, not-association 1, not-dissociation 3, not-absence 3, not-disappearance 3;

22. Of presence, conascence, mutuality, dependence, association and non-disappearance conditions, not-root 3, not-object 3, not-predominance 3, not-proximity 3, not-contiguity 3, not-strong-dependence 3, not-prenascence 3, not-postnascence 3, not-repetition 3, not-kamma 3, not-resultant 3, not-nutriment 3, not-faculty 3, not-jhāna 3, not-path 3, not-dissociation 3, not-absence 3, not-disappearance 3;

23. Of presence, conascence, dependence, dissociation and non-disappearance conditions, not-root 3, not-object 3, not-predominance 3, not-proximity 3, not-contiguity 3, not-mutuality 3, not-strong-dependence 3, not-prenascence 3, not-postnascence 3, not-repetition 3, not-kamma 3, not-resultant 3, not-nutriment 3, not-faculty 3, not-jhāna 3, not-path 3, not-association 3, not-absence 3, not-disappearance 3;

24. Of presence, conascence, mutuality, dependence, dissociation and non-disappearance conditions, not-root 1, not-object 1, not-predominance 1, not-proximity 1, not-contiguity 1, not-strong-dependence 1, not-prenascence 1, not-postnascence 1, not-repetition 1, not-kamma 1, not-resultant 1, not-nutriment 1, not-faculty 1, not-jhāna 1, not-path 1, not-association 1, not-absence 1, not-disappearance 1.

With resultant 5

25. Combinations of presence, conascence, dependence, resultant and non-disappearance conditions, not-root 1, not-object 1, not-predominance 1, not-proximity 1, not-contiguity 1, not-mutuality 1, not-strong-dependence 1, not-prenascence 1, not-postnascence 1, not-repetition 1, not-kamma 1, not-nutriment 1, not-faculty 1, not-jhāna 1, not-path 1, not-association 1, not-dissociation 1, not-absence 1, not-disappearance 1;

26. Of presence, conascence, mutuality, dependence, resultant and non-disappearance conditions, not-root 1, not-object 1, not-predominance 1, not-proximity 1, not-contiguity 1, not-strong-dependence 1, not-prenascence 1, not-postnascence 1, not-repetition 1, not-kamma 1, not-nutriment 1, not-faculty 1, not-jhāna 1, not-path 1, not-association 1, not-dissociation 1, not-absence 1, not-disappearance 1;

27. Of presence, conascence, mutuality, dependence, resultant, association and non-disappearance conditions, not-root 1, not-object 1, not-predominance 1, not-proximity 1, not-contiguity 1, not-strong-dependence 1, not-prenascence 1, not-postnascence 1, not-repetition 1, not-kamma 1, not-nutriment 1, not-faculty 1, not-jhāna 1, not-path 1, not-dissociation 1, not-absence 1, not-disappearance 1;

28. Of presence, conascence, dependence, resultant, dissociation and non-disappearance conditions, not-root 1, not-object 1, not-predominance 1, not-proximity 1, not-contiguity 1, not-mutuality 1, not-strong-dependence 1, not-prenascence 1, not-postnascence 1, not-repetition 1, not-kamma 1, not-nutriment 1, not-faculty 1, not-jhāna 1, not-path 1, not-association 1, not-absence 1, not-disappearance 1;

29. Of presence, conascence, mutuality, dependence, resultant, dissociation and non-disappearance conditions, not-root 1, not-object 1, not-predominance 1, not-proximity 1, not-contiguity 1, not-strong-dependence 1, not-prenascence 1, not-postnascence 1, not-repetition 1, not-kamma 1, not-nutriment 1, not-faculty 1, not-jhāna 1, not-path 1, not-association 1, not-absence 1, not-disappearance 1.

End of Presence

Absence, Disappearance

By Twos

629. With absence condition, not-root 7 ... with disappearance condition, not-root 7 ... (Absence and disappearance conditions are also the same as proximity condition.)

Non-disappearance

By Twos

630. With non-disappearance condition, not-root 13 ... (Non-disappearance condition should be expanded in the same way as presence condition.)

End of Positive-Negative of " Investigation " Chapter

4. CONDITIONS : NEGATIVE-POSITIVE

Not-root

By Twos

631. With not-root condition, object (condition) 9, predominance 10, proximity 7, contiguity 7, conascence 9, mutuality 3, dependence 13, strong-dependence 9, prenascence 3, postnascence 3, repetition 3, kamma 7, resultant 1, nutriment 7, faculty 7, jhāna 7, path 7, association 3, dissociation 5, presence 13, absence 7, disappearance 7, non-disappearance 13.

By Threes

With not-root and not-object conditions, predominance 7, proximity 7, contiguity 7, conascence 9, mutuality 3, dependence 13, strong-dependence 9, prenascence 3, postnascence 3, repetition 3, kamma 7, resultant 1, nutriment 7, faculty 7, jhāna 7, path 7, association 3, dissociation 5, presence 13, absence 7, disappearance 7, non-disappearance 13.

By Fours

With not-root, not-object and not-predominance conditions, proximity 7, contiguity 7, conascence 9, mutuality 3, dependence 13, strong-dependence 9, prenascence 3, postnascence 3, repetition 3, kamma 7, resultant 1, nutriment 7, faculty 7, jhāna 7, path 7, association 3, dissociation 5, presence 13, absence 7, disappearance 7, non-disappearance 13. ...

By Sixes

With not-root, not-object, not-predominance, not-proximity, and not-contiguity conditions, conascence 9, mutuality 3, dependence 13, strong-dependence 9, prenascence 3, postnascence 3, kamma 7, resultant 1, nutriment 7, faculty 7, jhāna 7, path 7, association 3, dissociation 5, presence 13, non-disappearance 13.

By Sevens

With not-root, not-object, not-predominance, not-proximity, not-contiguity and not-conascence conditions, dependence 3, strong-dependence 9, prenascence 3, postnascence 3, kamma 2, nutriment 1, faculty 1, dissociation 5, presence 7, non-disappearance 7.

By Eights

With not-root, not-object, not-predominance, not-proximity, not-contiguity, not-conascence and not-mutuality conditions, dependence 3, strong-dependence 9, prenascence 3, postnascence 3, kamma 2, nutriment 1, faculty 1, dissociation 5, presence 7, non-disappearance 7.

By Nines

With not-root, not-object . . . not-mutuality and not-dependence conditions, strong-dependence 9, postnascence 3, kamma 2, nutriment 1, faculty 1, dissociation 3, presence 5, non-disappearance 5. . . .

By Elevens

With not-root, not-object (Conditions abbreviated), not-dependence, not-strong-dependence and not-prenascence conditions, postnascence 3, kamma 2, nutriment 1, faculty 1, dissociation 3, presence 5, non-disappearance 5.

By Twelves

With not-root, not-object (Conditions abbreviated), not-strong-dependence, not-prenascence and not-postnascence conditions, kamma 2, nutriment 1, faculty 1, presence 1, non-disappearance 1. . . .

By Sixteens (with nutriment)

With not-root, not-object (Conditions abbreviated), not-postnascence, not-repetition, not-kamma, not-resultant and not-nutriment conditions, faculty 1, presence 1, non-disappearance 1. ...

By Twenty-twos

With not-root, not-object (Conditions abbreviated), not-nutriment, not-jhāna, not-path, not-association, not-dissociation, not-absence and not-disappearance conditions, faculty 1, presence 1, non-disappearance 1.

By Sixteens (with faculty)

With not-root, not-object (Conditions abbreviated), not-resultant and not-faculty conditions, nutriment 1, presence 1, non-disappearance 1. ...

By Twenty-twos (with faculty)

With not-root, not-object (Conditions abbreviated), not-faculty, not-jhāna, not-path, not-association, not-dissociation, not-absence and not-disappearance conditions, nutriment 1, presence 1, non-disappearance 1.

End of Not-root

Not-object

By Twos

632. With not-object condition, root 7, predominance 7, proximity 7, contiguity 7, conascence 9, mutuality 3, dependence 13, strong-dependence 9, prenascence 3, postnascence 3, repetition 3, kamma 7, resultant 1, nutriment 7, faculty 7, jhāna 7, path 7, association 3, dissociation 5, presence 13, absence 7, disappearance 7, non-disappearance 13. ...

By Eights

With not-object, not-root, not-predominance, not-proximity, not-contiguity, not-conascence and not-mutuality conditions, dependence 3, strong-dependence 9, prenascence 3, postnascence 3, kamma 2, nutriment 1, faculty 1, dissociation 5, presence 7, non-disappearance 7. ...

End of Not-object

Not-predominance

By Twos

633. With not-predominance condition, root 7, object 9 . . .

(Expand in the same way as not-root condition.)

End of Not-predominance

Not-proximity, Not-contiguity

By Twos

634. With not-proximity condition . . . with not-contiguity condition, root 7, object 9, predominance 10, conascence 9, mutuality 3, dependence 13, strong-dependence 9, prenascence 3, postnascence 3, kamma 7, resultant 1, nutriment 7, faculty 7, jhāna 7, path 7, association 3, dissociation 5, presence 13, non-disappearance 13. . . .

By Eights

With not-contiguity, not-root, not-object, not-predominance, not-proximity, not-conascence and not-mutuality conditions, dependence 3, strong-dependence 9, prenascence 3, postnascence 3, kamma 2, nutriment 1, faculty 1, dissociation 5, presence 7, non-disappearance 7. . . . (Abbreviated.)

End of Not-contiguity

Not-conascence

By Twos

635. With not-conascence condition, object 9, predominance 7, proximity 7, contiguity 7, dependence 3, strong-dependence 9, prenascence 3, postnascence 3, repetition 3, kamma 2, nutriment 1, faculty 1, dissociation 5, presence 7, absence 7, disappearance 7, non-disappearance 7. . . .

By Fives

With not-conascence, not-root, not-object and not-predominance conditions, proximity 7, contiguity 7, dependence 3, strong-dependence 9, prenascence 3, postnascence 3, repetition 3, kamma 2, nutriment 1, faculty 1, dissociation 5, presence 7, absence 7, disappearance 7, non-disappearance 7. . . .

By Nines

With not-conascence, not-root, not-object, not-predominance, not-proximity, not-contiguity, not-mutuality and not-dependence conditions, strong-dependence 9, postnascence 3, kamma 2, nutriment 1, faculty 1, dissociation 3, presence 5, non-disappearance 5. ... (Abbreviated.)

End of Not-conascence

Not-mutuality

By Twos

636. With not-mutuality condition, root 3, object 9, predominance 8, proximity 7, contiguity 7, conascence 5, dependence 7, strong-dependence 9, prenascence 3, postnascence 3, repetition 3, kamma 3, resultant 1, nutriment 3, faculty 3, jhāna 3, path 3, dissociation 5, presence 7, absence 7, disappearance 7, non-disappearance 7. ...

By Fours

With not-mutuality, not-root and not-object conditions, predominance 3, proximity 7, contiguity 7, conascence 5, dependence 7, strong-dependence 9, prenascence 3, postnascence 3, repetition 3, kamma 3, resultant 1, nutriment 3, faculty 3, jhāna 3, path 3, dissociation 5, presence 7, absence 7, disappearance 7, non-disappearance 7. ...

By Eights

With not-mutuality, not-root, not-object, not-predominance, not-proximity, not-contiguity and not-conascence conditions, dependence 3, strong-dependence 9, prenascence 3, postnascence 3, kamma 2, nutriment 1, faculty 1, dissociation 5, presence 7, non-disappearance 7. ... (Abbreviated.)

End of Not-mutuality

Not-dependence

By Twos

637. With not-dependence condition, object 9, predominance 7, proximity 7, contiguity 7, strong-dependence 9, prenascence 3,

postnascence 3, repetition 3, kamma 2, nutriment 1, faculty 1, dissociation 3, presence 7, absence 7, disappearance 7, non-disappearance 7. ...

By Fives

With not-dependence, not-root, not-object and not-predominance conditions, proximity 7, contiguity 7, strong-dependence 9, postnascence 3, repetition 3, kamma 2, nutriment 1, faculty 1, dissociation 3, presence 5, absence 7, disappearance 7, non-disappearance 5. ...

By Nines

With not-dependence, not-root, not-object, not-predominance, not-proximity, not-contiguity, not-conascence and not-mutuality conditions, strong-dependence 9, postnascence 3, kamma 2, nutriment 1, faculty 1, dissociation 3, presence 5, non-disappearance 5. ... (Abbreviated.)

End of Not-dependence

Not-strong-dependence

By Twos

638. With not-strong-dependence condition, root 7, object 9, predominance 7, conascence 9, mutuality 3, dependence 13, prenascence 3, postnascence 3, kamma 7, resultant 1, nutriment 7, faculty 7, jhāna 7, path 7, association 3, dissociation 5, presence 13, non-disappearance 13. ...

By Eights

With not-strong-dependence, not-root, not-object, not-predominance, not-proximity, not-contiguity and not-conascence conditions, dependence 3, prenascence 3, postnascence 3, kamma 2, nutriment 1, faculty 1, dissociation 5, presence 7, non-disappearance 7. ... (Abbreviated.)

End of Not-strong-dependence

Not-prenascence

By Twos

639. With not-prenascence condition, root 7, object 9, predominance 10, proximity 7, contiguity 7, conascence 9, mutuality 3, dependence 9, strong-dependence 9, postnascence 3,

repetition 3, kamma 7, resultant 1, nutriment 7, faculty 7, jhāna 7, path 7, association 3, dissociation 3, presence 9, absence 7, disappearance 7, non-disappearance 9. ...

By Fours

With not-prenascence, not-root and not-object conditions, predominance 7, proximity 7, contiguity 7, conascence 9, mutuality 3, dependence 9, strong-dependence 9, postnascence 3, repetition 3, kamma 7, resultant 1, nutriment 7, faculty 7, jhāna 7, path 7, association 3, dissociation 3, presence 9, absence 7, disappearance 7, non-disappearance 9. ...

By Nines

With not-prenascence, not-root, not-object, not-predominance, not-proximity, not-contiguity, not-conascence and not-mutuality conditions, strong-dependence 9, postnascence 3, kamma 2, nutriment 1, faculty 1, dissociation 3, presence 5, non-disappearance 5. ... (Abbreviated.)

End of Not-prenascence

Not-postnascence

By Twos

640. With not-postnascence condition, root 7, object 9, predominance 10, proximity 7, contiguity 7, conascence 9, mutuality 3, dependence 13, strong-dependence 9, prenascence 3, repetition 3, kamma 7, resultant 1, nutriment 7, faculty 7, jhāna 7, path 7, association 3, dissociation 5, presence 13, absence 7, disappearance 7, non-disappearance 13. ...

By Nines

With not-postnascence, not-root, not-object, not-predominance, not-proximity, not-contiguity, not-conascence and not-mutuality conditions, dependence 3, strong-dependence 9, prenascence 3, kamma 2, nutriment 1, faculty 1, dissociation 3, presence 3, non-disappearance 3.

By Tens

With not-postnascence, not-root, not-object, not-predominance, not-proximity, not-contiguity, not-conascence, not-mutuality and not-dependence conditions, strong-dependence 9, kamma 2, nutriment 1, faculty 1, presence 1, non-disappearance 1. ... (Abbreviated.)

End of Not-postnascence

Not-repetition

By Twos

641. With not-repetition condition, root 7, object 9, predominance 10, proximity 5, contiguity 5, conascence 9, mutuality 3, dependence 13, strong-dependence 9, prenascence 3, postnascence 3, kamma 7, resultant 1, nutriment 7, faculty 7, jhāna 7, path 7, association 3, dissociation 5, presence 13, absence 5, disappearance 5, non-disappearance 13. ...

By Nines

With not-repetition, not-root, not-object, not-predominance, not-proximity, not-contiguity, not-conascence and not-mutuality conditions, dependence 3, strong-dependence 9, prenascence 3, postnascence 3, kamma 2, nutriment 1, faculty 1, dissociation 5, presence 7, non-disappearance 7. ... (Abbreviated.)

End of Not-repetition

Not-kamma

By Twos

642. With not-kamma condition, root 7, object 9, predominance 10, proximity 7, contiguity 7, conascence 9, mutuality 3, dependence 13, strong-dependence 9, prenascence 3, postnascence 3, repetition 3, resultant 1, nutriment 7, faculty 7, jhāna 7, path 7, association 3, dissociation 5, presence 13, absence 7, disappearance 7, non-disappearance 13. ...

By Nines

With not-kamma, not-root, not-object, not-predominance, not-proximity, not-contiguity, not-conascence and not-mutuality conditions, dependence 3, strong-dependence 9, prenascence 3, postnascence 3, nutriment 1, faculty 1, dissociation 5, presence 7, non-disappearance 7. ... (Abbreviated.)

End of Not-kamma

Not-resultant

By Twos

643. With not-resultant condition, root 7 . . . non-disappearance 13.

(Expand in the same way as not-root condition.)

End of Not-resultant

Not-nutriment

By Twos

644. With not-nutriment condition, root 7, object 9, predominance 10, proximity 7, contiguity 7, conascence 9, mutuality 3, dependence 13, strong-dependence 9, prenascence 3, postnascence 3, repetition 3, kamma 2, resultant 1, faculty 7, jhāna 7, path 7, association 3, dissociation 5, presence 13, absence 7, disappearance 7, non-disappearance 13. . . .

By Fours

With not-nutriment, not-root and not-object conditions, predominance 7, proximity 7, contiguity 7, conascence 9, mutuality 3, dependence 13, strong-dependence 9, prenascence 3, postnascence 3, repetition 3, kamma 2, resultant 1, faculty 7, jhāna 7, path 7, association 3, dissociation 5, presence 13, absence 7, disappearance 7, non-disappearance 13. . . .

By Twenty-twos

With not-nutriment, not-root, not-object, not-predominance, not-proximity, not-contiguity . . . not-kamma, not-resultant, not-jhāna, not-path, not-association, not-dissociation, not-absence and not-disappearance conditions, faculty 1, presence 1, non-disappearance 1. (Abbreviated.)

End of Not-nutriment

Not-faculty

By Twos

645. With not-faculty condition, root 7, object 9 . . . non-disappearance 13. . . . (With not-faculty condition, kamma there are seven questions.)

By Twenty-twos

With not-faculty, not-root, not-object (Conditions abbreviated), not-resultant, not-jhāna, not-path, not-association, not-dissociation, not-absence and not-disappearance conditions, nutriment 1, presence 1, non-disappearance 1. (The same as not root condition. Abbreviated.)

End of Not-faculty

Not-jhāna

By Twos

646. With not-jhāna condition, root 7, object 9 . . . non-disappearance 13.

(Expand not-jhāna condition in the same way as not-root condition.)

End of Not-jhāna

Not-path

By Twos

647. With not-path condition, root 7 . . . non-disappearance 13.

(Expand in the same way as not-root condition.)

End of Not-path

Not-association

By Twos

648. With not-association condition, root 3, object 9, predominance 8, proximity 7, contiguity 7, conascence 5, mutuality 1, dependence 7, strong-dependence 9, prenascence 3, postnascence 3, repetition 3, kamma 3, resultant 1, nutriment 3, faculty 3, jhāna 3, path 3, dissociation 5, presence 7, absence 7, disappearance 7, non-disappearance 7. . . .

By Fours

With not-association, not-root and not-object conditions, predominance 3, proximity 7, contiguity 7, conascence 5, mutuality 1, dependence 7, strong-dependence 9, prenascence 3, postnascence 3, repetition 3, kamma 3, resultant 1, nutriment 3, faculty 3, jhāna 3, path 3, dissociation 5, presence 7, absence 7, disappearance 7, non-disappearance 7. ...

By Nines

With not-association, not-root, not-object, not-predominance, not-proximity, not-contiguity, not-conascence and not-mutuality conditions, dependence 3, strong-dependence 9, prenascence 3, postnascence 3, kamma 2, nutriment 1, faculty 1, dissociation 5, presence 7, non-disappearance 7.

By Tens

With not-association, not-root (Conditions abbreviated), not-conascence, not-mutuality and not-dependence conditions, strong-dependence 9, postnascence 3, kamma 2, nutriment 1, faculty 1, dissociation 3, presence 5, non-disappearance 5. ...

By Twelves

With not-association, not-root (Conditions abbreviated), not-dependence, not-strong-dependence and not-prenascence conditions, postnascence 3, kamma 2, nutriment 1, faculty 1, dissociation 3, presence 5, non-disappearance 5. ... (Abbreviated.)

End of Not-association

Not-dissociation

By Twos

649. With not-dissociation condition, root 3, object 9, predominance 7, proximity 7, contiguity 7, conascence 3, mutuality 3, dependence 3, strong-dependence 9, prenascence 3, repetition 3, kamma 5, resultant 1, nutriment 3, faculty 3, jhāna 3, path 3, association 3, presence 5, absence 7, disappearance 7, non-disappearance 5. ...

By Fours

With not-dissociation, not-root and not-object conditions, predominance 3, proximity 7, contiguity 7, conascence 3, mutuality 3, dependence 3, strong-dependence 9, repetition 3, kamma 5, resultant 1, nutriment 3, faculty 3, jhāna 3, path 3, association 3, presence 3, absence 7, disappearance 7, non-disappearance 3. ...

Faultless Triplet

By Sevens

With not-dissociation, not-root, not-object, not-predominance, not-proximity and not-contiguity conditions, conascence 3, mutuality 3, dependence 3, strong-dependence 9, kamma 5, resultant 1, nutriment 3, faculty 3, jhāna 3, path 3, association 3, presence 3, non-disappearance 3. ...

By Nines

With not-dissociation, not-root, not-object, not-predominance, not-proximity, not-contiguity, not-conascence and not-mutuality conditions, strong-dependence 9, kamma 2, nutriment 1, faculty 1, presence 1, non-disappearance 1. ...

By Elevens

With not-dissociation, not-root, not-object, not-predominance, not-proximity, not-contiguity, not-conascence, not-mutuality, not-dependence and not-strong-dependence conditions, kamma 2, nutriment 1, faculty 1, presence 1, non-disappearance 1. ...

By Fifteens

With not-dissociation, not-root (Conditions abbreviated), and not-kamma conditions, nutriment 1, faculty 1, presence 1, non-disappearance 1. ...

By Seventeens (*with nutriment*)

With not-dissociation, not-root ... not-kamma, not-resultant and not-nutriment conditions, faculty 1, presence 1, non-disappearance 1. ...

By Twenty-twos

With not-dissociation, not-root (Conditions abbreviated), not-nutriment, not-jhāna, not-path, not-association, not-absence and not-disappearance conditions, faculty 1, presence 1, non-disappearance 1.

By Seventeens (*with faculty*)

With not-dissociation, not-root (Conditions abbreviated), not-resultant and not-faculty conditions, nutriment 1, presence 1, non-disappearance 1. ...

By Twenty-twos

With not-dissociation, not-root (Conditions abbreviated), not-faculty, not-jhāna, not-path, not-association, not-absence and not-disappearance conditions, nutriment 1, presence 1, non-disappearance 1.

End of Not-dissociation

Not-presence

By Twos

650. With not-presence condition, object 9, predominance 7, proximity 7, contiguity 7, strong-dependence 9, repetition 3, kamma 2, absence 7, disappearance 7. ...

By Fours

With not-presence, not-root and not-object conditions, proximity 7, contiguity 7, strong-dependence 9, repetition 3, kamma 2, absence 7, disappearance 7. ...

By Sevens

With not-presence, not-root, not-object, not-predominance, not-proximity and not-contiguity conditions, strong-dependence 9, kamma 2. ...

[1] *By Eleven (with strong-dependence)*

With not-presence, not-root . . . not-dependence and not-strong-dependence conditions, kamma 2.[1] ...

By Twenty-four (with strong-dependence)

With not-presence, not-root, not-object, not-predominance, not-proximity, not-contiguity, not-conascence, not-mutuality, not-dependence, not-strong-dependence, not-prenascence, not-postnascence, not-repetition, not-resultant, not-nutriment, not-faculty, not-jhāna, not-path, not-association, not-dissociation, not-absence, not-disappearance and not-non-disappearance conditions, kamma 2.

[1] *By Fourteen (with kamma)*

With not-presence, not-root . . . not-dependence, not-prenascence, not-postnascence, not-repetition and not-kamma conditions, strong-dependence 9.[1] ...

---

[1] This portion is not mentioned in the Text.

Faultless Triplet

By Twenty-four (with kamma)

With not-presence, not-root, not-object, not-predominance, not-proximity, not-contiguity, not-conascence, not-mutuality, not-dependence, not-prenascence, not-postnascence, not-repetition, not-kamma, not-resultant, not-nutriment, not-faculty, not-jhāna, not-path, not-association, not-dissociation, not-absence, not-disappearance and not-non-disappearance conditions, strong-dependence 9.

End of Not-presence

Not-absence

By Twos

651. With not-absence condition, root 7 . . . non-disappearance 13.

(Expand in the same way as not-root condition.)

End of Not-absence

Not-disappearance

By Twos

652. With not-disappearance condition, root 7 . . . non-disappearance 13.

(Expand in the same way as not-root condition.)

End of Not-disappearance

Not-non-disappearance

By Twos

653. With not-non-disappearance condition, object 9 . . . absence 7, disappearance 7.

(Expand in the same way as not-presence condition.)

End of Not-non-disappearance

End of Negative-Positive of " Investigation " Chapter

END OF FAULTLESS TRIPLET

2. FEELING TRIPLET [1]   I. " DEPENDENT " CHAPTER
I. CONDITIONS : POSITIVE   (i) CLASSIFICATION CHAPTER

Root 3

1. (i) Dependent on state associated with pleasant feeling, arises state associated with pleasant feeling by root condition.

(*a*) Dependent on one aggregate associated with pleasant feeling, arise two aggregates ; dependent on two aggregates, arises one aggregate ;

(*b*) At the moment of conception, dependent on one aggregate associated with pleasant feeling, arise two aggregates ; dependent on two aggregates, arises one aggregate.

(ii) Dependent on state associated with painful feeling, arises state associated with painful feeling by root condition.

Dependent on one aggregate associated with painful feeling, arise two aggregates ; dependent on two aggregates, arises one aggregate.

(iii) Dependent on state associated with neither painful nor pleasant feeling, arises state associated with neither painful nor pleasant feeling by root condition.

(*a*) Dependent on one aggregate associated with neither painful nor pleasant feeling, arise two aggregates ; dependent on two aggregates, arises one aggregate ;

(*b*) At the moment of conception, dependent on one aggregate associated with neither painful nor pleasant feeling, arise two aggregates ; dependent on two aggregates, arises one aggregate.

Object, etc.

2. Dependent on state associated with pleasant feeling, arises state associated with pleasant feeling by object condition . . . by predominance condition (there is no conception in predominance) . . . by proximity condition . . . by contiguity condition . . . by conascence condition . . . by mutuality condition . . . by dependence condition . . . by strong-dependence condition . . . by prenascence condition.

---

[1] This comprises (1) state associated with pleasant feeling, (2) state associated with painful feeling, (3) state associated with neither painful nor pleasant feeling.

(a) Dependent on one aggregate associated with pleasant feeling, arise two aggregates ; dependent on two aggregates, arises one aggregate ; (Dependent on heart-)base, (arise aggregates associated with pleasant feeling) by prenascence condition. (Abbreviated.)

Repetition, etc.

3. (i) Dependent on state associated with pleasant feeling, arises state associated with pleasant feeling by repetition condition . . . by kamma condition . . . by resultant condition.

(a) Dependent on one aggregate associated with pleasant feeling, arise two aggregates ; dependent on two aggregates, arises one aggregate ;

(b) At the moment of conception, dependent on one aggregate associated with pleasant feeling, arise two aggregates ; dependent on two aggregates, arises one aggregate.

(ii) Dependent on state associated with painful feeling, arises state associated with painful feeling by resultant condition.

Dependent on one aggregate accompanied by pain-accompanied body-consciousness, arise two aggregates ; dependent on two aggregates, arises one aggregate.

(iii) Dependent on state associated with neither painful nor pleasant feeling, arises state associated with neither painful nor pleasant feeling by resultant condition.

(a) Dependent on one aggregate associated with neither painful nor pleasant feeling, arise two aggregates ; dependent on two aggregates, arises one aggregate ;

(b) At the moment of conception, dependent on one aggregate associated with neither painful nor pleasant feeling, arise two aggregates ; dependent on two aggregates, arises one aggregate.

Nutriment, etc.

4. (i) Dependent on state associated with pleasant feeling, arises state associated with pleasant feeling by nutriment condition . . . by faculty condition . . . by jhāna condition . . . by path condition, . . . by association condition . . . by dissociation condition.

(a) Dependent on one aggregate associated with pleasant feeling, arise two aggregates; dependent on two aggregates, arises one aggregate. (Dependent on heart-)base (arise aggregates associated with pleasant feeling) by dissociation condition.

(b) At the moment of conception, dependent on one aggregate associated with pleasant feeling, arise two aggregates; dependent on two aggregates, arises one aggregate. (Dependent on heart-)base, (arise resultant aggregates associated with pleasant feeling) by dissociation condition.

(ii) Dependent on state associated with painful feeling, arises state associated with painful feeling by dissociation condition.

Dependent on one aggregate associated with painful feeling, arise two aggregates; dependent on two aggregates, arises one aggregate. (Dependent on heart-)base, (arise aggregates associated with painful feeling) by dissociation condition.

(iii) Dependent on state associated with neither painful nor pleasant feeling, arises state associated with neither painful nor pleasant feeling by dissociation condition.

(a) Dependent on one aggregate associated with neither painful nor pleasant feeling, arise two aggregates; dependent on two aggregates, arises one aggregate. (Dependent on heart-)base, (arise aggregates associated with neither painful nor pleasant feeling) by dissociation condition;

(b) At the moment of conception, dependent on one aggregate associated with neither painful nor pleasant feeling, arise two aggregates; dependent on two aggregates, arises one aggregate. (Dependent on heart-)base, (arise aggregates associated with neither painful nor pleasant feeling) by dissociation condition. (Abbreviated.)

Presence, etc.

5. By presence condition . . . by absence condition . . . by disappearance condition . . . by non-disappearance condition. . . .

I. CONDITIONS : POSITIVE   (ii) ENUMERATION CHAPTER

By Ones

6. With root (there are) 3 (answers), with object 3 . . . non-disappearance 3.

Feeling Triplet

Root, etc.

By Twos, etc.

7. With root condition and object (there are) 3 (answers) . . . resultant 2 . . . non-disappearance 3. . . .

With object condition . . . with predominance condition and root (there are) 3 (answers) . . . resultant 2 . . . non-disappearance 3. . . .

With repetition condition and root (there are) 3 (answers) . . . kamma 3, nutriment 3 . . . non-disappearance 3. . . .

With resultant condition and root (there are) 2 (answers), object 3, predominance 2 . . . prenascence 3, kamma 3 . . . jhāna 2, path 2 . . . non-disappearance 3. . . .

With jhāna condition and root (there are) 3 (answers) . . . resultant 2 . . . non-disappearance 3. . . .

With path condition and root 3 . . . resultant 2 . . . non-disappearance 3. . . .

With non-disappearance condition and root 3 . . . absence 3, disappearance 3. . . .

(Expand in the same way as the enumeration of conditions in Faultless Triplet.)

2. CONDITIONS : NEGATIVE   (i) CLASSIFICATION CHAPTER

Not-root 3

8. (i) Dependent on state associated with pleasant feeling, arises state associated with pleasant feeling by not-root condition.

Dependent on one rootless aggregate associated with pleasant feeling, arise two aggregates; dependent on two aggregates, arises one aggregate.

(ii) Dependent on state associated with painful feeling, arises state associated with painful feeling by not-root condition.

Dependent on one aggregate accompanied by pain-accompanied body-consciousness, arise two aggregates; dependent on two aggregates, arises one aggregate.

(iii) Dependent on state associated with neither painful nor pleasant feeling, arises state associated with neither painful nor pleasant feeling by not-root condition.

(a) Dependent on one rootless aggregate associated with

neither painful nor pleasant feeling, arise two aggregates; dependent on two aggregates, arises one aggregate;

(b) At the moment of rootless conception, dependent on one aggregate associated with neither painful nor pleasant feeling, arise two aggregates; dependent on two aggregates, arises one aggregate;

(c) Dependent on doubt-accompanied or restlessness-accompanied aggregates, arises doubt-accompanied or restlessness-accompanied delusion.

Not-predominance 3

9. Dependent on state associated with pleasant feeling, arises state associated with pleasant feeling by not-predominance condition. (Conception is to be completed for not-predominance.)

Not-prenascence 2

10. (i) Dependent on state associated with pleasant feeling, arises state associated with pleasant feeling by not-prenascence condition.

(a) In the immaterial plane, dependent on one aggregate associated with pleasant feeling, arise two aggregates; dependent on two aggregates, arises one aggregate;

(b) At the moment of conception, dependent on one aggregate associated with pleasant feeling, arise two aggregates; dependent on two aggregates, arises one aggregate.

(ii) Dependent on state associated with neither painful nor pleasant feeling, arises state associated with neither painful nor pleasant feeling by not-prenascence condition.

(a) In the immaterial plane, dependent on one aggregate associated with neither painful nor pleasant feeling, arise two aggregates; dependent on two aggregates, arises one aggregate;

(b) At the moment of conception, dependent on one aggregate associated with neither painful nor pleasant feeling, arise two aggregates; dependent on two aggregates, arises one aggregate.

Not-postnascence 3, Not-repetition 3

11. Dependent on state associated with pleasant feeling, arises state associated with pleasant feeling by not-postnascence

condition . . . by not-repetition condition. (Conception is to be completed for not-postnascence and not-repetition.)

Not-kamma 3

12. (i) Dependent on state associated with pleasant feeling, arises state associated with pleasant feeling by not-kamma condition.

Dependent on aggregates associated with pleasant feeling, arises volition associated with pleasant feeling.

(ii) Dependent on state associated with painful feeling, arises state associated with painful feeling by not-kamma condition.

Dependent on aggregates associated with painful feeling, arises volition associated with painful feeling.

(iii) Dependent on state associated with neither painful nor pleasant feeling, arises state associated with neither painful nor pleasant feeling by not-kamma condition.

Dependent on aggregates associated with neither painful nor pleasant feeling, arises volition associated with neither painful nor pleasant feeling.

Not-resultant 3, Not-jhāna 3

13. (i) Dependent on state associated with pleasant feeling, arises state associated with pleasant feeling by not-resultant condition . . . by not-jhāna condition.

Dependent on one aggregate accompanied by pleasure-accompanied body-consciousness, arise two aggregates; dependent on two aggregates, arises one aggregate.

(ii) Dependent on state associated with painful feeling, arises state associated with painful feeling by not-jhāna condition.

Dependent on one aggregate accompanied by pain-accompanied body-consciousness, arise two aggregates; dependent on two aggregates, arises one aggregate.

(iii) Dependent on state associated with neither painful nor pleasant feeling, arises state associated with neither painful nor pleasant feeling by not-jhāna condition.

Dependent on one aggregate accompanied by four-fold

consciousnesses, arise two aggregates; dependent on two aggregates, arises one aggregate.

Not-path 3

14. (i) Dependent on state associated with pleasant feeling, arises state associated with pleasant feeling by not-path condition.

Dependent on one rootless aggregate associated with pleasant feeling, arise two aggregates; dependent on two aggregates, arises one aggregate.

(ii) Dependent on state associated with painful feeling, arises state associated with painful feeling by not-path condition.

Dependent on one aggregate accompanied by pain-accompanied body-consciousness, arise two aggregates; dependent on two aggregates, arises one aggregate.

(iii) Dependent on state associated with neither painful nor pleasant feeling, arises state associated with neither painful nor pleasant feeling by not-path condition.

(*a*) Dependent on one rootless aggregate associated with neither painful nor pleasant feeling, arises two aggregates; dependent on two aggregates, arises one aggregate;

(*b*) At the moment of rootless conception, dependent on one aggregate associated with neither painful nor pleasant feeling, arise two aggregates; dependent on two aggregates, arises one aggregate.

Not-dissociation 2

15. (i) Dependent on state associated with pleasant feeling, arises state associated with pleasant feeling by not-dissociation condition.

In the immaterial plane, dependent on one aggregate associated with pleasant feeling, arise two aggregates; dependent on two aggregates, arises one aggregate.

(ii) Dependent on state associated with neither painful nor pleasant feeling, arises state associated with neither painful nor pleasant feeling by not-dissociation condition.

In the immaterial plane, dependent on one aggregate

associated with neither painful nor pleasant feeling, arise two aggregates ; dependent on two aggregates, arises one aggregate.

2. CONDITIONS : NEGATIVE   (ii) ENUMERATION CHAPTER

By Ones

16. With not-root (there are) 3 (answers), not-predominance 3, not-prenascence 2, not-postnascence 3, not-repetition 3, not-kamma 3, not-resultant 3, not-jhāna 3, not-path 3, not-dissociation 2.

Not-root

By Twos

17. With not-root condition and not-predominance (there are) 3 (answers), not-prenascence 1, not-postnascence 3, not-repetition 3, not-kamma 2, not-resultant 2, not-jhāna 3, not-path 3, not-dissociation 1. . . .

By Fours

With not-root, not-predominance, not-prenascence conditions and not-postnascence (there is) 1 (answer), not-repetition 1, not-kamma 1, not-resultant 1, not-path 1, not-dissociation 1. . . .

By Nine

With not-root, not-predominance, not-prenascence, not-postnascence, not-repetition, not-kamma, not-resultant, not-path conditions and not-dissociation (there is) 1 (answer).

Not-predominance

By Twos

18. With not-predominance condition and not-root (there are) 3 (answers), not-prenascence 2, not-postnascence 3, not-repetition 3, not-kamma 3, not-resultant 3, not-jhāna 3, not-path 3, not-dissociation 2. . . . (Abbreviated.)

Not-prenascence

By Twos

19. With not-prenascence condition and not-root 1, not-predominance 2, not-postnascence 2, not-repetition 2, not-kamma 2, not-resultant 2, not-path 1, not-dissociation 2.

By Threes

With not-prenascence, not-root conditions and not-predominance 1, not-postnascence 1, not-repetition 1, not-kamma 1, not-resultant 1, not-path 1, not-dissociation 1. ... (Abbreviated.)

Not-postnascence, etc.

By Twos

20. With not-postnascence condition ... with not-repetition condition ... with not-kamma condition and not-root 2, not-predominance 3, not-prenascence 2, not-postnascence 3, not-repetition 3, not-resultant 3, not-path 2, not-dissociation 2.

By Threes

With not-kamma, not-root conditions and not-predominance 2, not-prenascence 1, not-postnascence 2, not-repetition 2, not-resultant 2, not-path 2, not-dissociation 1. ...

By Fives

With not-kamma, not-root, not-predominance, not-prenascence conditions and not-postnascence 1, not-repetition 1, not-resultant 1, not-path 1, not-dissociation 1. ... (Abbreviated.)

Not-resultant

By Twos

21. With not-resultant condition and not-root 2, not-predominance 3, not-prenascence 2, not-postnascence 3, not-repetition 3, not-kamma 3, not-path 2, not-dissociation 2.

With not-resultant condition ... (the same as not-kamma condition).

Not-jhāna

By Twos

22. With not-jhāna condition and not-root 3, not-predominance 3, not-postnascence 3, not-repetition 3, not-path 3. ...

By Six

With not-jhāna, not-root, not-predominance, not-postnascence, not-repetition conditions and not-path 3. (Abbreviated.)

Not-path

By Twos

23. With not-path condition and not-root 3, not-predominance 3, not-prenascence 1, not-postnascence 3, not-repetition 3, not-kamma 2, not-resultant 2, not-jhāna 3, not-dissociation 1.

By Threes

With not-path, not-root conditions and not-predominance 3, not-prenascence 1, not-postnascence 3, not-repetition 3, not-kamma 2, not-resultant 2, not-jhāna 3, not-dissociation 1. ...

By Fives

With not-path, not-root, not-predominance, not-prenascence conditions and not-postnascence 1, not-repetition 1, not-kamma 1, not-resultant 1, not-dissociation 1. ... (Abbreviated.)

Not-dissociation

By Twos

24. With not-dissociation condition and not-root 1, not-predominance 2, not-prenascence 2, not-postnascence 2, not-repetition 2, not-kamma 2, not-resultant 2, not-path 1.

By Threes

With not-dissociation, not-root conditions and not-predominance 1, not-prenascence 1, not-postnascence 1, not-repetition 1, not-kamma 1, not-resultant 1, not-path 1. ...

By Nine

With not-dissociation, not-root, not-predominance, not-prenascence, not-postnascence, not-repetition, not-kamma, not-resultant conditions and not-path 1. (Abbreviated.)

End of Negative Enumeration

3. CONDITIONS: POSITIVE-NEGATIVE

Root

By Twos

25. With root condition, not-predominance 3, not-prenascence 2, not-postnascence 3, not-repetition 3, not-kamma 3, not-resultant 3, not-dissociation 2.

By Threes

With root and object conditions, not-predominance 3, not-prenascence 2, not-postnascence 3, not-repetition 3, not-kamma 3, not-resultant 3, not-dissociation 2.

(Enumerate in the same way as Faultless Triplet.)

End of Positive-Negative

4. CONDITIONS : NEGATIVE-POSITIVE

Not-root

By Twos

26. With not-root condition, object 3, proximity 3, contiguity 3, conascence 3, mutuality 3, dependence 3, strong-dependence 3, prenascence 3, repetition 2, kamma 3, resultant 3, nutriment 3, faculty 3, jhāna 2, path 1, association 3, dissociation 3, presence 3, absence 3, disappearance 3, non-disappearance 3.

By Threes

With not-root and not-predominance conditions, object 3, proximity 3, contiguity 3, conascence 3, mutuality 3, dependence 3, strong-dependence 3, prenascence 3, repetition 2, kamma 3, resultant 3, nutriment 3, faculty 3, jhāna 2, path 1, association 3, dissociation 3, presence 3, absence 3, disappearance 3, non-disappearance 3.

By Fours

With not-root, not-predominance and not-prenascence conditions, object 1, proximity 1, contiguity 1, conascence 1, mutuality 1, dependence 1, strong-dependence 1, repetition 1, kamma 1, resultant 1, nutriment 1, faculty 1, jhāna 1, path 1, association 1, dissociation 1, presence 1, absence 1, disappearance 1, non-disappearance 1. ...

By Sevens

With not-root, not-predominance, not-prenascence, not-postnascence, not-repetition and not-kamma conditions, object 1, proximity 1, contiguity 1, conascence 1, mutuality 1, dependence 1, strong-dependence 1, nutriment 1, faculty 1, jhāna 1, association 1, presence 1, absence 1, disappearance 1, non-disappearance 1. ...

By Tens

With not-root, not-predominance ... not-kamma, not-resultant, not-path and not-dissociation conditions, object 1, proximity 1, contiguity 1, conascence 1, mutuality 1, dependence 1, strong-dependence 1, nutriment 1, faculty 1, jhāna 1, association 1, presence 1, absence 1, disappearance 1, non-disappearance 1. ... (Abbreviated.)

End of Not-root

Not-predominance

By Twos

27. With not-predominance condition, root 3 ... non-disappearance 3. ... (Abbreviated.)

Not-prenascence

By Twos

28. With not-prenascence condition, root 2 ... non-disappearance 2. ... (Abbreviated.)

Not-postnascence, etc.

By Twos

29. With not-postnascence condition ... with not-repetition condition ... with not-kamma condition ... with not-resultant condition, root 3 ... non-disappearance 3. ... (Abbreviated.)

Not-jhāna

By Twos

30. With not-jhāna condition, object 3, proximity 3, contiguity 3, conascence 3, mutuality 3, dependence 3, strong-dependence 3, prenascence 3, kamma 3, resultant 3, nutriment 3, faculty 3, association 3, dissociation 3, presence 3, absence 3, disappearance 3, non-disappearance 3. ... (Abbreviated.)

Not-path
By Twos

31. With not-path condition, object 3, proximity 3, contiguity 3 ... repetition 1, kamma 3 ... jhāna 2 ... non-disappearance 3. ... (Abbreviated.)

Not-dissociation
By Twos

32. With not-dissociation condition, root 2, object 2, predominance 2, proximity 2, contiguity 2, conascence 2, mutuality 2, dependence 2, strong-dependence 2, repetition 2, kamma 2, resultant 2, nutriment 2, faculty 2, jhāna 2, path 2, association 2, presence 2, absence 2, disappearance 2, non-disappearance 2.

By Threes

With not-dissociation and not-root conditions, object 1, proximity 1, contiguity 1, conascence 1, mutuality 1, dependence 1, strong-dependence 1, repetition 1, kamma 1, nutriment 1, faculty 1, jhāna 1, path 1, association 1, presence 1, absence 1, disappearance 1, non-disappearance 1. ...

By Tens

With not-dissociation, not-root, not-predominance, not-prenascence, not-postnascence, not-repetition, not-kamma, not-resultant and not-path conditions, object 1, proximity 1, contiguity 1, conascence 1, mutuality 1, dependence 1, strong-dependence 1, nutriment 1, faculty 1, jhāna 1, association 1, presence 1, absence 1, disappearance 1, non-disappearance 1.

End of Negative-Positive

End of " DEPENDENT " CHAPTER

II. " Conascent " Chapter

33. Conascent with state associated with pleasant feeling. ...

III. " Conditioned " Chapter

34. Conditioned by state associated with pleasant feeling. ...

IV. " SUPPORTED " CHAPTER

35. Supported by state associated with pleasant feeling. ...

V. " CONJOINED " CHAPTER

36. Conjoined with state associated with pleasant feeling. ...

VI. " ASSOCIATED " CHAPTER

37. Associated with state associated with pleasant feeling, arises state associated with pleasant feeling by root condition.

Associated with one aggregate associated with pleasant feeling, arise two aggregates ; associated with two aggregates, arises one aggregate. ... (Abbreviated.)

End of " ASSOCIATED " CHAPTER

2. FEELING TRIPLET   VII. " INVESTIGATION " CHAPTER

1. CONDITIONS : POSITIVE   (i) CLASSIFICATION CHAPTER

Root 3

38. (i) State associated with pleasant feeling is related to state associated with pleasant feeling by root condition.

(*a*) Roots associated with pleasant feeling are related to (their) associated aggregates by root condition ;

(*b*) At the moment of conception, roots associated with pleasant feeling are related to (their) associated aggregates by root condition. (1)

(ii) State associated with painful feeling is related to state associated with painful feeling by root condition.

Roots associated with painful feeling are related to (their) associated aggregates by root condition. (1)

(iii) State associated with neither painful nor pleasant feeling is related to state associated with neither painful nor pleasant feeling by root condition.

(*a*) Roots associated with neither painful nor pleasant feeling are related to (their) associated aggregates by root condition ;

(*b*) At the moment of conception, roots associated with

neither painful nor pleasant feeling are related to (their) associated aggregates by root condition. (1)

Object 9

39. (i) State associated with pleasant feeling is related to state associated with pleasant feeling by object condition.

After having offered the offering, having undertaken the precept, having fulfilled the duty of observance with the mind associated with pleasant feeling, (one) reviews (it) with the mind associated with pleasant feeling. Having emerged from jhāna, emerged from Path, emerged from Fruition associated with pleasant feeling, (one) reviews (it) with the mind associated with pleasant feeling.

The Noble persons, with the mind associated with pleasant feeling, review the eradicated defilements which were associated with pleasant feeling, review the uneradicated defilements, know the defilements addicted to before.

(One) practises insight into the impermanency, suffering and impersonality of the aggregates associated with pleasant feeling with the mind associated with pleasant feeling; enjoys and delights in (those aggregates). Taking it as object arises lust, arises wrong views associated with pleasant feeling. Taking the aggregates associated with pleasant feeling as object, arise aggregates associated with pleasant feeling. (1)

(ii) State associated with pleasant feeling is related to state associated with painful feeling by object condition.

After having offered the offering, having undertaken the precept, having fulfilled the duty of observance with the mind associated with pleasant feeling, (one) regrets (it) and arises grief. When jhāna associated with pleasant feeling has disappeared, (one) regrets (it) and arises grief. Taking the aggregates associated with pleasant feeling as object, arise aggregates associated with painful feeling. (2)

(iii) State associated with pleasant feeling is related to state associated with neither painful nor pleasant feeling by object condition.

After having offered the offering, having undertaken the precept, having fulfilled the duty of observance with the mind associated with pleasant feeling, (one) reviews (it) with the mind associated with neither painful nor pleasant feeling. Having emerged from jhāna, emerged from Path, emerged from Fruition associated with pleasant feeling, (one) reviews (it) with the mind associated with neither painful nor pleasant feeling.

The Noble persons, with the mind associated with neither painful nor pleasant feeling, review the eradicated defilements which were associated with pleasant feeling, review the uneradicated defilements, know the defilements addicted to before.

(One) practises insight into the impermanency, suffering and impersonality of the aggregates associated with pleasant feeling with the mind associated with neither painful nor pleasant feeling; enjoys and delights in (those aggregates). Taking it as object arises lust, arises wrong views, arises doubt, arises restlessness associated with neither painful nor pleasant feeling.

By the knowledge of penetration into others' minds, (one) knows the other being's mind associated with pleasant feeling. The aggregates associated with pleasant feeling are related to knowledge of penetration into others' minds, knowledge of remembrance of past existences, knowledge of rebirths according to one's kamma, knowledge of future existences, advertence by object condition. Taking the aggregates associated with pleasant feeling as object, arise aggregates associated with neither painful nor pleasant feeling. (3)

40. (iv) State associated with painful feeling is related to state associated with painful feeling by object condition.

Taking hate as object, arises hate, arises delusion. Taking delusion associated with painful feeling as object, arises delusion, arises hate. Taking pain-accompanied body-consciousness as object, arises hate, arises delusion. Taking the aggregates associated with painful feeling as object, arise aggregates associated with painful feeling. (1)

(v) State associated with painful feeling is related to state associated with pleasant feeling by object condition.

The Noble persons, with the mind associated with pleasant feeling, review the eradicated defilements which were associated with painful feeling, review the uneradicated defilements, know the defilements addicted to before.

(One) practises insight into the impermanency, suffering and impersonality of the aggregates associated with painful feeling with the mind associated with pleasant feeling. Taking the aggregates associated with painful feeling as object, arise aggregates associated with pleasant feeling. (2)

(vi) State associated with painful feeling is related to state associated with neither painful nor pleasant feeling by object condition.

The Noble persons, with the mind associated with neither painful nor pleasant feeling, review the eradicated defilements which were associated with painful feeling, review the uneradicated defilements, know the defilements addicted to before.

(One) practises insight into the impermanency, suffering and impersonality of the aggregates associated with painful feeling with the mind associated with neither painful nor pleasant feeling. By the knowledge of penetration into others' minds, (one) knows the other being's mind associated with painful feeling. The aggregates associated with painful feeling are related to knowledge of penetration into others' minds, knowledge of remembrance of past existences, knowledge of rebirths according to one's kamma, knowledge of future existences, advertence by object condition. Taking the aggregates associated with painful feeling as object, arise aggregates associated with neither painful nor pleasant feeling. (3)

41. (vii) State associated with neither painful nor pleasant feeling is related to state associated with neither painful nor pleasant feeling by object condition.

After having offered the offering, having undertaken the precept, having fulfilled the duty of observance with the mind associated with neither painful nor pleasant feeling, (one) reviews (it) with the mind associated with neither painful nor pleasant feeling. Having emerged from jhāna, emerged from Path, emerged from Fruition associated with neither painful nor pleasant feeling, (one) reviews (it) with the mind associated with neither painful nor pleasant feeling.

The Noble persons, with the mind associated with neither painful nor pleasant feeling, review the eradicated defilements which were associated with neither painful nor pleasant feeling, review the uneradicated defilements, know the defilements addicted to before.

(One) practises insight into the impermanency, suffering and impersonality of the aggregates associated with neither painful nor pleasant feeling with the mind associated with neither painful nor pleasant feeling ; enjoys and delights in (those aggregates). Taking it as object arises lust, arises wrong views, arises doubt, arises restlessness associated with neither painful nor pleasant feeling. By the knowledge of penetration into others' minds, (one) knows the other being's mind associated with neither painful nor pleasant feeling.

Infinity of space is related to infinity of consciousness by object condition. Nothingness is related to neither-perception-nor-non-perception by object condition. The aggregates associated with neither painful nor pleasant feeling are related to knowledge of supernormal power, knowledge of penetration into others' minds, knowledge of remembrance of past existences, knowledge of rebirths according to one's kamma, knowledge of future existences, advertence by object condition. Taking the aggregates associated with neither painful nor pleasant feeling as object, arise aggregates associated with neither painful nor pleasant feeling. (1)

(viii) State associated with neither painful nor pleasant feeling is related to state associated with pleasant feeling by object condition.

After having offered the offering, having undertaken the precept, having fulfilled the duty of observance with the mind associated with neither painful nor pleasant feeling, (one) reviews (it) with the mind associated with pleasant feeling. Having emerged from jhāna, emerged from Path, emerged from Fruition associated with neither painful nor pleasant feeling, (one) reviews (it) with the mind associated with pleasant feeling.

The Noble persons, with the mind associated with pleasant feeling, review the eradicated defilements which were associated with neither painful nor pleasant feeling, review the uneradicated defilements, know the defilements addicted to before.

(One) practises insight into the impermanency, suffering and impersonality of the aggregates associated with neither painful nor pleasant feeling with the mind associated with pleasant feeling ; enjoys and delights in (those aggregates). Taking it as object arises lust, arises wrong views associated with pleasant feeling. Taking the aggregates associated with neither painful nor pleasant feeling as object, arise aggregates associated with pleasant feeling. (2)

(ix) State associated with neither painful nor pleasant feeling is related to state associated with painful feeling by object condition.

After having offered the offering, having undertaken the precept, having fulfilled the duty of observance with the mind associated with neither painful nor pleasant feeling, (one) regrets (it) and arises grief. When jhāna associated with neither painful nor pleasant feeling has disappeared, (one) regrets (it) and arises grief. Taking the aggregates associated with neither painful nor pleasant feeling as object, arise aggregates associated with painful feeling. (3)

Predominance 5

42. (i) State associated with pleasant feeling is related to state associated with pleasant feeling by predominance condition.

(It is of two kinds, namely :) (*a*) object-predominance, (*b*) conascence-predominance.

(*a*) *Object-predominance* : After having offered the offering, having undertaken the precept, having fulfilled the duty of observance with the mind associated with pleasant feeling, (one) esteems and reviews it with the mind associated with pleasant feeling. Having emerged from jhāna, emerged from Path, emerged from Fruition associated with pleasant feeling, (one) esteems and reviews it with the mind associated with pleasant feeling. (One) esteems, enjoys and delights in the aggregates associated with pleasant feeling, with the mind associated with pleasant feeling. Taking it as estimable object, arises lust, arises wrong views associated with pleasant feeling.

(*b*) *Conascence-predominance* : Predominance associated with pleasant feeling is related to (its) associated aggregates by predominance condition. (1)

(ii) State associated with pleasant feeling is related to state associated with neither painful nor pleasant feeling by predominance condition.

Object-predominance : After having offered the offering, having undertaken the precept, having fulfilled the duty of observance with the mind associated with pleasant feeling, (one) esteems and reviews it with the mind associated with neither painful nor pleasant feeling. Having emerged from jhāna, emerged from Path, emerged from Fruition associated with pleasant feeling, (one) esteems and reviews it with the mind associated with neither painful nor pleasant feeling. (One) esteems, enjoys and delights in the aggregates associated with pleasant feeling, with the mind associated with neither painful nor pleasant feeling. Taking it as estimable object, arises lust, arises wrong views associated with neither painful nor pleasant feeling. (2)

43. (iii) State associated with painful feeling is related to state associated with painful feeling by predominance condition.

Conascence-predominance : Predominance associated with painful feeling is related to (its) associated aggregates by predominance condition. (1)

44. (iv) State associated with neither painful nor pleasant feeling is related to state associated with neither painful nor pleasant feeling by predominance condition.

(It is of two kinds, namely :) (*a*) object-predominance, (*b*) conascence-predominance.

(*a*) *Object-predominance* : After having offered the offering, having undertaken the precept, having fulfilled the duty of observance with the mind associated with neither painful nor pleasant feeling, (one) esteems and reviews it with the mind associated with neither painful nor pleasant feeling. Having emerged from jhāna, emerged from Path, emerged from Fruition associated with neither painful nor pleasant feeling, (one) esteems and reviews it with the mind associated with neither painful nor pleasant feeling. (One) esteems, enjoys and delights in the aggregates associated with neither painful nor pleasant feeling, with the mind associated with neither painful nor pleasant feeling. Taking it as estimable object, arises lust, arises wrong views associated with neither painful nor pleasant feeling.

(b) *Conascence-predominance* : Predominance associated with neither painful nor pleasant feeling is related to (its) associated aggregates by predominance condition. (1)

(v) State associated with neither painful nor pleasant feeling is related to state associated with pleasant feeling by predominance condition.

Object-predominance : After having offered the offering, having undertaken the precept, having fulfilled the duty of observance with the mind associated with neither painful nor pleasant feeling, (one) esteems and reviews it with the mind associated with pleasant feeling. Having emerged from jhāna, emerged from Path, emerged from Fruition associated with neither painful nor pleasant feeling, (one) esteems and reviews it with the mind associated with pleasant feeling. (One) esteems, enjoys and delights in the aggregates associated with neither painful nor pleasant feeling, with the mind associated with pleasant feeling. Taking it as estimable object, arises lust, arises wrong views associated with pleasant feeling. (2)

Proximity 7

45. (i) State associated with pleasant feeling is related to state associated with pleasant feeling by proximity condition.

Preceding aggregates associated with pleasant feeling are related to subsequent aggregates associated with pleasant feeling by proximity condition. Adaptation associated with pleasant feeling is related to change-of-lineage associated with pleasant feeling by proximity condition ; adaptation to purification ; change-of-lineage to Path ; purification to Path ; Path to Fruition ; Fruition to Fruition ; adaptation is related to attainment of Fruition associated with pleasant feeling by proximity condition. The aggregates associated with pleasant feeling are related to emergence associated with pleasant feeling by proximity condition. (1)

(ii) State associated with pleasant feeling is related to state associated with neither painful nor pleasant feeling by proximity condition.

Death-consciousness associated with pleasant feeling is related to rebirth-consciousness associated with neither painful nor pleasant feeling by proximity condition. Life-continuum associated with pleasant feeling is related to advertence by proximity condition. Body-consciousness accompanied by pleasure is related to resultant mind-element by proximity condition. Resultant mind-consciousness element associated with pleasant feeling is related to functional mind-consciousness element by proximity condition. Life-continuum associated with pleasant feeling is related to life-continuum associated with neither painful nor pleasant feeling by proximity condition. Faultless or faulty associated with pleasant feeling is related to emergence associated with neither painful nor pleasant feeling ; functional to emergence ; Fruition is related to emergence by proximity condition. (2)

46. (iii) State associated with painful feeling is related to state associated with painful feeling by proximity condition.

Preceding aggregates associated with painful feeling are related to subsequent aggregates associated with painful feeling by proximity condition. (1)

(iv) State associated with painful feeling is related to state associated with neither painful nor pleasant feeling by proximity condition.

Body-consciousness accompanied by pain is related to resultant mind-element by proximity condition. The aggregates associated with painful feeling are related to emergence associated with neither painful nor pleasant feeling by proximity condition. (2)

47. (v) State associated with neither painful nor pleasant feeling is related to state associated with neither painful nor pleasant feeling by proximity condition.

Preceding aggregates associated with neither painful nor pleasant feeling are related to subsequent aggregates associated with neither painful nor pleasant feeling by proximity condition. Adaptation associated with neither painful nor pleasant feeling is related to change-of-lineage associated with neither painful nor pleasant feeling by proximity condition ; adaptation to purification ; change-of-lineage to Path ; purification to Path ; Path to Fruition ; Fruition to Fruition ; adaptation to attainment of Fruition [1] (associated with neither painful nor pleasant feeling); having emerged from the attainment of Extinction,

[1] Left out in the Text.

neither-perception-nor-non-perception is related to the attainment of Fruition associated with neither painful nor pleasant feeling by proximity condition. The aggregates associated with neither painful nor pleasant feeling are related to emergence associated with neither painful nor pleasant feeling by proximity condition. (1)

(vi) State associated with neither painful nor pleasant feeling is related to state associated with pleasant feeling by proximity condition.

Death-consciousness associated with neither painful nor pleasant feeling is related to rebirth-consciousness associated with pleasant feeling by proximity condition. Advertence is related to the aggregates associated with pleasant feeling by proximity condition. Resultant mind-element is related to resultant mind-consciousness element associated with pleasant feeling by proximity condition. Life-continuum associated with neither painful nor pleasant feeling is related to life-continuum associated with pleasant feeling by proximity condition. Faultless or faulty associated with neither painful nor pleasant feeling is related to emergence associated with pleasant feeling; functional to emergence; Fruition to emergence; having emerged from the attainment of Extinction, neither-perception-nor-non-perception is related to the attainment of Fruition associated with pleasant feeling by proximity condition. (2)

(vii) State associated with neither painful nor pleasant feeling is related to state associated with painful feeling by proximity condition.

Advertence is related to the aggregates associated with painful feeling by proximity condition. (3)

Contiguity 7

48. State associated with pleasant feeling is related to state associated with pleasant feeling by contiguity condition (the same as proximity condition).

Conascence 3

49. (i) State associated with pleasant feeling is related to state associated with pleasant feeling by conascence condition.

(*a*) One aggregate associated with pleasant feeling is related to two aggregates by conascence condition ; two aggregates are related to one aggregate by conascence condition ;

(*b*) At the moment of conception, one aggregate associated with pleasant feeling is related to two aggregates by conascence condition ; two aggregates are related to one aggregate by conascence condition. (1)

50. (ii) State associated with painful feeling is related to state associated with painful feeling by conascence condition.

One aggregate associated with painful feeling is related to two aggregates by conascence condition ; two aggregates are related to one aggregate by conascence condition. (Conception associated with painful feeling is not obtained.) (1)

51. (iii) State associated with neither painful nor pleasant feeling is related to state associated with neither painful nor pleasant feeling by conascence condition.

(*a*) One aggregate associated with neither painful nor pleasant feeling is related to two aggregates by conascence condition ; two aggregates are related to one aggregate by conascence condition ;

(*b*) At the moment of conception, one aggregate associated with neither painful nor pleasant feeling is related to two aggregates by conascence condition ; two aggregates are related to one aggregate by conascence condition. (1)

Mutuality 3, Dependence 3

52. State associated with pleasant feeling is related to state associated with pleasant feeling by mutuality condition ... by dependence condition. (Mutuality and dependence are also the same as conascence condition.)

Strong-dependence 9

53. (i) State associated with pleasant feeling is related to state associated with pleasant feeling by strong-dependence condition.

(It is of three kinds, namely :) (*a*) object-strong-dependence, (*b*) proximity-strong-dependence, (*c*) natural strong-dependence. ...

(*c*) *Natural strong-dependence* : By the strong-dependence of confidence associated with pleasant feeling, (one), with the mind associated with pleasant feeling, offers the offering, undertakes the precept, fulfils the duty of observance, develops jhāna associated with pleasant feeling, develops insight, develops Path, develops attainment; arouses conceit, adopts wrong views. ... precept associated with pleasant feeling ... learning ... generosity ... wisdom ... lust ... delusion ... conceit ... wrong views ... wish. ... By the strong-dependence of body-consciousness accompanied by pleasure, (one), with the mind associated with pleasant feeling, offers the offering ... develops attainment (In the confidence group of five " arouses conceit, adopts wrong views " are to be done but not for the rest), with the mind associated with pleasant feeling takes the property of others which has not been given to one, speaks untruth, slanders, babbles foolishly, breaks into a house, plunders the property of others, leaves behind only one house, stands at the junction of highways, goes to other men's wives, plunders villages, plunders market-towns. Confidence associated with pleasant feeling, precept ... learning ... generosity ... wisdom ... lust ... delusion ... conceit ... wrong views ... wish ... body-consciousness accompanied by pleasure is related to confidence associated with pleasant feeling, precept ... learning ... generosity ... wisdom ... lust ... delusion ... conceit ... wrong views ... wish ... body-consciousness accompanied by pleasure, the aggregates associated with pleasant feeling by strong-dependence condition. (i)

(ii) State associated with pleasant feeling is related to state associated with painful feeling by strong-dependence condition.

Natural strong-dependence: By the strong-dependence of confidence associated with pleasant feeling, (one) tortures oneself, tortures oneself fully, experiences the suffering caused by searching. ... precept associated with pleasant feeling ... learning ... generosity. ... By the strong-dependence of wisdom ... (one) tortures oneself, tortures oneself fully, experiences the suffering caused by searching. By the strong-dependence of lust associated with pleasant feeling ... delusion ... conceit ... wrong views ... wish. ... By the strong-dependence of body-consciousness accompanied by pleasure, (one) kills a living being, with the mind associated with painful feeling takes the property of others which has not been given to one, speaks untruth, slanders, uses rude speech, babbles foolishly, breaks into a house, plunders the property of others, leaves behind only one house, stands at the junction of highways, goes to other men's wives, plunders villages, plunders market-towns, commits matricide, commits patricide, kills an Arahat, draws blood from the body of a Buddha with evil intent, causes schism in the Saṅgha. Confidence associated with pleasant feeling, precept ... learning ... generosity ... wisdom ... lust ... delusion ... conceit ... wrong views ... wish ... body-consciousness accompanied by pleasure is related to hate, delusion, body-consciousness accompanied by pain, the aggregates associated with painful feeling by strong-dependence condition. (2)

(iii) State associated with pleasant feeling is related to state associated with neither painful nor pleasant feeling by strong-dependence condition.

(It is of three kinds, namely :) (*a*) object-strong-dependence, (*b*) proximity-strong-dependence, (*c*) natural strong-dependence. ...

(*c*) *Natural strong-dependence* : By the strong-dependence of confidence associated with pleasant feeling, (one), with the mind associated with neither painful nor pleasant feeling, offers the offering, undertakes the precept, fulfils the duty of observance, develops jhāna associated with neither painful nor pleasant feeling, develops insight, develops Path, develops superknowledge, develops attainment; arouses conceit, adopts wrong views. ... precept associated with pleasant feeling ... learning ... generosity ... wisdom ... lust ... delusion ... conceit ... wrong views ... wish. ... By the strong-dependence of body-consciousness accompanied by pleasure, (one), with the mind associated with neither painful nor pleasant feeling, offers the offering ... develops attainment, with the mind associated with neither painful nor pleasant feeling takes the property of others which has not been given to one, speaks untruth, slanders, babbles foolishly, breaks into a house, plunders the property of others, leaves behind only one house, stands at the junction of highways, goes to other men's wives, plunders villages, plunders market-towns. Confidence associated with pleasant feeling, precept ... learning ... generosity ... wisdom ... lust ... delusion ... conceit ... wrong views ... wish ... body-consciousness accompanied by pleasure is related to confidence associated with neither painful nor pleasant feeling, precept ... learning ... generosity ... wisdom ... lust ... delusion ... conceit ... wrong views ... wish ... the aggregates associated with neither painful nor pleasant feeling by strong-dependence condition. (3)

54. (iv) State associated with painful feeling is related to state associated with painful feeling by strong-dependence condition.

(It is of two kinds, namely :) (*a*) proximity-strong-dependence, (*b*) natural strong-dependence. ...

(*b*) *Natural strong-dependence* : By the strong-dependence of hate, (one) kills a living being, with the mind associated with painful feeling takes the property of others which has not been given to one ... causes schism in the Saṅgha. ... delusion. ... By the strong-dependence of body-consciousness accompanied by pain, (one) kills a living being, with the mind associated with painful feeling takes the property of others which has not been given to one ... causes schism in the Saṅgha. Hate, delusion, body-consciousness accompanied by pain is related to hate, delusion, body-consciousness accompanied by pain, the aggregates associated with painful feeling by strong-dependence condition. (1)

(v) State associated with painful feeling is related to state associated with pleasant feeling by strong-dependence condition.

Natural strong-dependence : By the strong-dependence of hate, (one), with the mind associated with pleasant feeling, offers the offering ... develops attainment, with the mind associated with pleasant feeling takes the property of others which has not been given to one ... plunders market-towns. ... delusion. ... By the strong-dependence of body-consciousness accompanied by pain, (one), with the mind associated with pleasant feeling, offers the offering ... plunders market-towns. Hate, delusion, body-consciousness accompanied by pain is related to confidence associated with pleasant feeling ...

body-consciousness accompanied by pleasure, the aggregates associated with pleasant feeling by strong-dependence condition. (2)

(vi) State associated with painful feeling is related to state associated with neither painful nor pleasant feeling by strong-dependence condition.

(It is of two kinds, namely :) (*a*) proximity-strong-dependence, (*b*) natural strong-dependence. ...

(*b*) *Natural strong-dependence* : By the strong-dependence of hate, (one), with the mind associated with neither painful nor pleasant feeling, offers the offering ... plunders market-towns. ... delusion. ... By the strong-dependence of body-consciousness accompanied by pain, (one), with the mind associated with neither painful nor pleasant feeling, offers the offering ... plunders market-towns. Hate, delusion, body-consciousness accompanied by pain is related to confidence associated with neither painful nor pleasant feeling ... wish ... the aggregates associated with neither painful nor pleasant feeling by strong-dependence condition. (3)

55. (vii) State associated with neither painful nor pleasant feeling is related to state associated with neither painful nor pleasant feeling by strong-dependence condition.

(It is of three kinds, namely :) (*a*) object-strong-dependence, (*b*) proximity-strong-dependence, (*c*) natural strong-dependence. ...

(*c*) *Natural strong-dependence* : By the strong-dependence of confidence associated with neither painful nor pleasant feeling, (one), with the mind associated with neither painful nor pleasant feeling, offers the offering ... adopts wrong views. ... precept associated with neither painful nor pleasant feeling ... learning ... generosity ... wisdom ... lust ... delusion ... conceit ... wrong views. ... By the strong-dependence of wish associated with neither painful nor pleasant feeling, (one), with the mind associated with neither painful nor pleasant feeling, offers the offering ... develops attainment, with the mind associated with neither painful nor pleasant feeling takes the property of others which has not been given to one ... plunders market-towns. Confidence associated with neither painful nor pleasant feeling, precept ... learning ... generosity ...

wisdom ... lust ... delusion ... conceit ... wrong views ... wish ... is related to confidence associated with neither painful nor pleasant feeling ... wish ... the aggregates associated with neither painful nor pleasant feeling by strong-dependence condition. (1)

(viii) State associated with neither painful nor pleasant feeling is related to state associated with pleasant feeling by strong-dependence condition.

(It is of three kinds, namely:) (*a*) object-strong-dependence, (*b*) proximity-strong-dependence, (*c*) natural strong-dependence. ...

(*c*) *Natural strong-dependence* : By the strong-dependence of confidence associated with neither painful nor pleasant feeling, (one), with the mind associated with pleasant feeling, offers the offering ... adopts wrong views. ... precept associated with neither painful nor pleasant feeling. ... By the strong-dependence of wish associated with neither painful nor pleasant feeling, (one), with the mind associated with pleasant feeling, offers the offering ... develops attainment, with the mind associated with pleasant feeling takes the property of others which has not been given to one ... plunders market-towns. Confidence associated with neither painful nor pleasant feeling ... wish ... is related to confidence associated with pleasant feeling ... wish ... body-consciousness accompanied by pleasure, the aggregates associated with pleasant feeling by strong-dependence condition. (2)

(ix) State associated with neither painful nor pleasant feeling is related to state associated with painful feeling by strong-dependence condition.

(It is of two kinds, namely:) (*a*) proximity-strong-dependence, (*b*) natural strong-dependence. ...

(*b*) *Natural strong-dependence* : By the strong-dependence of confidence associated with neither painful nor pleasant feeling, (one) tortures oneself, tortures oneself fully, experiences the suffering caused by searching. ... precept associated with neither painful nor pleasant feeling. ... By the strong-dependence of wish associated with neither painful nor pleasant feeling, (one) kills a living being, with the mind associated with painful feeling takes the property of others which has not been given to one ... causes schism in the Saṅgha. Confidence associated with neither painful nor pleasant feeling ... wish ... is related to hate, delusion, body-consciousness accompanied by pain, the aggregates associated with painful feeling by strong-dependence condition. (3)

Repetition 3

56. (i) State associated with pleasant feeling is related to state associated with pleasant feeling by repetition condition.

Preceding aggregates associated with pleasant feeling are related to subsequent aggregates associated with pleasant feeling by repetition condition. Adaptation associated with pleasant feeling to change-of-lineage ; adaptation to purification ; change-of-lineage to Path ; purification is related to Path by repetition condition. (1)

(ii) State associated with painful feeling is related to state associated with painful feeling by repetition condition.

Preceding aggregates associated with painful feeling are related to subsequent aggregates associated with painful feeling by repetition condition. (1)

(iii) State associated with neither painful nor pleasant feeling is related to state associated with neither painful nor pleasant feeling by repetition condition.

Preceding aggregates associated with neither painful nor pleasant feeling are related to subsequent aggregates associated with neither painful nor pleasant feeling by repetition condition. Adaptation associated with neither painful nor pleasant feeling to change-of-lineage ; adaptation to purification ; change-of-lineage to Path ; purification is related to Path by repetition condition. (1)

Kamma 8

57. (i) State associated with pleasant feeling is related to state associated with pleasant feeling by kamma condition.

(It is of two kinds, namely :) (*a*) conascence (-kamma), (*b*) asynchronous (kamma).

(*a*) Conascent volition associated with pleasant feeling is related to (its) associated aggregates by kamma condition. At the moment of conception. ...

(b) Asynchronous volition associated with pleasant feeling is related to (its) resultant aggregates associated with pleasant feeling by kamma condition. (1)

(ii) State associated with pleasant feeling is related to state associated with painful feeling by kamma condition.

Asynchronous volition associated with pleasant feeling is related to resultant aggregates associated with painful feeling by kamma condition. (2)

(iii) State associated with pleasant feeling is related to state associated with neither painful nor pleasant feeling by kamma condition.

Asynchronous volition associated with pleasant feeling is related to resultant aggregates associated with neither painful nor pleasant feeling by kamma condition. (3)

58. (iv) State associated with painful feeling is related to state associated with painful feeling by kamma condition.

(It is of two kinds, namely :) (a) conascence(-kamma), (b) asynchronous (kamma).

(a) Conascent volition associated with painful feeling is related to (its) associated aggregates by kamma condition.

(b) Asynchronous volition associated with painful feeling is related to resultant aggregates associated with painful feeling by kamma condition. (1)

(v) State associated with painful feeling is related to state associated with neither painful nor pleasant feeling by kamma condition.

Asynchronous volition associated with painful feeling is related to resultant aggregates associated with neither painful nor pleasant feeling by kamma condition. (2)

59. (vi) State associated with neither painful nor pleasant feeling is related to state associated with neither painful nor pleasant feeling by kamma condition.

(It is of two kinds, namely :) (a) conascence(-kamma), (b) asynchronous (kamma).

(a) Conascent volition associated with neither painful nor pleasant feeling is related to (its) associated aggregates by kamma condition.

(b) Asynchronous volition associated with neither painful nor pleasant feeling is related to resultant aggregates associated with neither painful nor pleasant feeling by kamma condition. (1)

(vii) State associated with neither painful nor pleasant feeling is related to state associated with pleasant feeling by kamma condition.

Asynchronous volition associated with neither painful nor pleasant feeling is related to resultant aggregates associated with pleasant feeling by kamma condition. (2)

(viii) State associated with neither painful nor pleasant feeling is related to state associated with painful feeling by kamma condition.

Asynchronous volition associated with neither painful nor pleasant feeling is related to resultant aggregates associated with painful feeling by kamma condition. (3)

Resultant 3

60. (i) State associated with pleasant feeling is related to state associated with pleasant feeling by resultant condition.

(*a*) One resultant aggregate associated with pleasant feeling is related to two aggregates by resultant condition; two aggregates are related to one aggregate by resultant condition;

(*b*) At the moment of conception, one resultant aggregate associated with pleasant feeling is related to two aggregates by resultant condition; two aggregates are related to one aggregate ... (1)

(ii) State associated with painful feeling is related to state associated with painful feeling by resultant condition.

One resultant aggregate associated with painful feeling is related to two aggregates by resultant condition ... (1)

(iii) (State associated with) neither painful nor pleasant feeling ...

(*a*) One resultant aggregate associated with neither painful nor pleasant feeling is related to two aggregates ...

(*b*) At the moment of conception ... (1)

Nutriment, etc.

61. State associated with pleasant feeling is related to state associated with pleasant feeling by nutriment condition ... by

Hh

faculty condition ... by jhāna condition ... by path condition ... by association condition ... by presence condition ... by absence condition ... by disappearance condition ... by non-disappearance condition. ...

I. CONDITIONS : POSITIVE   (ii) ENUMERATION CHAPTER

By Ones

62. With root (there are) 3 (answers), object 9, predominance 5, proximity 7, contiguity 7, conascence 3, mutuality 3, dependence 3, strong-dependence 9, repetition 3, kamma 8, resultant 3, nutriment 3, faculty 3, jhāna 3, path 3, association 3, presence 3, absence 7, disappearance 7, non-disappearance 3.

Root

Common 10

63. With root condition and predominance (there are) 2 (answers), conascence 3, mutuality 3, dependence 3, resultant 2, faculty 2, path 2, association 3, presence 3, non-disappearance 3.

Combinations (6)

Ordinary combinations (2)

Combination of root, conascence, mutuality, dependence, association, presence and non-disappearance (has) 3 (answers) ;

Of root, conascence, mutuality, dependence, resultant, association, presence and non-disappearance 2.

With faculty and path combinations (2)

64. Combination of root, conascence, mutuality, dependence, faculty, path, association, presence and non-disappearance 2 ;

Of root, conascence, mutuality, dependence, resultant, faculty, path, association, presence and non-disappearance 2.

With predominance, faculty and path combinations (2).

65. Combination of root, predominance, conascence, mutuality, dependence, faculty, path, association, presence and non-disappearance 2 ;

Of root, predominance, conascence, mutuality, dependence,

resultant, faculty, path, association, presence and non-disappearance 2.

Object

Common 2

66. With object condition and predominance 4, strong-dependence 4.

Object combination (1)

67. Combination of object, predominance and strong-dependence 4.

Predominance

Common 13

68. With predominance condition and root 2, object 4, conascence 3, mutuality 3, dependence 3, strong-dependence 4, resultant 2, nutriment 3, faculty 3, path 3, association 3, presence 3, non-disappearance 3.

Predominance combinations (9)

69. Combination of predominance, object and strong-dependence 4.

Combination of predominance, conascence, mutuality, dependence, association, presence and non-disappearance 3 ;

Of predominance, conascence, mutuality, dependence, resultant, association, presence and non-disappearance 2.

Combination of predominance, conascence, mutuality, dependence, nutriment, faculty, association, presence and non-disappearance 3 ;

Of predominance, conascence, mutuality, dependence, resultant, nutriment, faculty, association, presence and non-disappearance 2.

Combination of predominance, conascence, mutuality, dependence, faculty, path, association, presence and non-disappearance 3 ;

Of predominance, conascence, mutuality, dependence, resultant, faculty, path, association, presence and non-disappearance 2.

Combination of predominance, root, conascence, mutuality,

dependence, faculty, path, association, presence and non-disappearance 2 ;

Of predominance, root, conascence, mutuality, dependence, resultant, faculty, path, association, presence and non-disappearance 2.

Proximity

Common 6

70. With proximity condition and contiguity 7, strong-dependence 7, repetition 3, kamma 2, absence 7, disappearance 7.

Combinations (3)

71. Combination of proximity, contiguity, strong-dependence, absence and disappearance 7 ;

Of proximity, contiguity, strong-dependence, repetition, absence and disappearance 3 ;

Of proximity, contiguity, strong-dependence, kamma, absence and disappearance 2.

With contiguity condition (the same as proximity).

Conascence, etc.

Common 13

72. With conascence condition... with mutuality condition... with dependence condition and root 3, predominance 3, conascence 3, mutuality 3, kamma 3, resultant 3, nutriment 3, faculty 3, jhāna 3, path 3, association 3, presence 3, non-disappearance 3.

Combinations (2)

Combination of dependence, conascence, mutuality, association, presence and non-disappearance 3 ;

Of dependence, conascence, mutuality, resultant, association, presence and non-disappearance 3.

Strong-dependence

Common 8

73. With strong-dependence condition and object 4, predominance 4, proximity 7, contiguity 7, repetition 3, kamma 8, absence 7, disappearance 7.

Combinations (5)

74. Combination of strong-dependence, object and predominance 4.

Combination of strong-dependence, proximity, contiguity, absence and disappearance 7 ;

Of strong-dependence, proximity, contiguity, repetition, absence and disappearance 3.

Combination of strong-dependence and kamma 8 ;

Of strong-dependence, proximity, contiguity, kamma, absence and disappearance 2.

Repetition
Common 5

75. With repetition condition and proximity 3, contiguity 3, strong-dependence 3, absence 3, disappearance 3.

Combination (1)

Combination of repetition, proximity, contiguity, strong-dependence, absence and disappearance 3.

Kamma
Common 13

76. With kamma condition and proximity 2, contiguity 2, conascence 3, mutuality 3, dependence 3, strong-dependence 8, resultant 3, nutriment 3, association 3, presence 3, absence 2, disappearance 2, non-disappearance 3.

Combinations (4)

Combination of kamma and strong-dependence 8 ;

Of kamma, proximity, contiguity, strong-dependence, absence and disappearance 2.

Combination of kamma, conascence, mutuality, dependence, nutriment, association, presence and non-disappearance 3 ;

Of kamma, conascence, mutuality, dependence, resultant, nutriment, association, presence and non-disappearance 3.

Resultant
Common 13

77. With resultant condition and root 2, predominance 2, conascence 3 ... jhāna 2, path 2, association 3, presence 3, non-disappearance 3.

Combination (1)

Combination of resultant, conascence, mutuality, dependence, association, presence and non-disappearance 3.

Nutriment

Common 10

78. With nutriment condition and predominance 3, conascence 3, mutuality 3, dependence 3, kamma 3, resultant 3, faculty 3, association 3, presence 3, non-disappearance 3.

Combinations (8)

Combination of nutriment, conascence, mutuality, dependence, association, presence and non-disappearance 3 ;

Of nutriment, conascence, mutuality, dependence, resultant, association, presence and non-disappearance 3.

Combination of nutriment, conascence, mutuality, dependence, kamma, association, presence and non-disappearance 3 ;

Of nutriment, conascence, mutuality, dependence, kamma, resultant, association, presence and non-disappearance 3.

Combination of nutriment, conascence, mutuality, dependence, faculty, association, presence and non-disappearance 3 ;

Of nutriment, conascence, mutuality, dependence, resultant, faculty, association, presence and non-disappearance 3.

Combination of nutriment, predominance, conascence, mutuality, dependence, faculty, association, presence and non-disappearance 3 ;

Of nutriment, predominance, conascence, mutuality, dependence, resultant, faculty, association, presence and non-disappearance 2.

Faculty

Common 12

79. With faculty condition and root 2, predominance 3, conascence 3, mutuality 3, dependence 3, resultant 3, nutriment 3, jhāna 3, path 3, association 3, presence 3, non-disappearance 3.

Combinations (16)

Combination of faculty, conascence, mutuality, dependence, association, presence and non-disappearance 3;

Of faculty, conascence, mutuality, dependence, resultant, association, presence and non-disappearance 3.

Combination of faculty, conascence, mutuality, dependence, path, association, presence and non-disappearance 3;

Of faculty, conascence, mutuality, dependence, resultant, path, association, presence and non-disappearance 2.

Combination of faculty, conascence, mutuality, dependence, jhāna, path, association, presence and non-disappearance 3;

Of faculty, conascence, mutuality, dependence, resultant, jhāna, path, association, presence and non-disappearance 2.

Combination of faculty, conascence, mutuality, dependence, nutriment, association, presence and non-disappearance 3;

Of faculty, conascence, mutuality, dependence, resultant, nutriment, association, presence and non-disappearance 3.

Combination of faculty, predominance, conascence, mutuality, dependence, nutriment, association, presence and non-disappearance 3;

Of faculty, predominance, conascence, mutuality, dependence, resultant, nutriment, association, presence and non-disappearance 2.

Combination of faculty, predominance, conascence, mutuality, dependence, path, association, presence and non-disappearance 3;

Of faculty, predominance, conascence, mutuality, dependence, resultant, path, association, presence and non-disappearance 2.

Combination of faculty, root, conascence, mutuality, dependence, path, association, presence and non-disappearance 2;

Of faculty, root, conascence, mutuality, dependence, resultant, path, association, presence and non-disappearance 2.

Combination of faculty, root, predominance, conascence, mutuality, dependence, path, association, presence and non-disappearance 2;

Of faculty, root, predominance, conascence, mutuality, dependence, resultant, path, association, presence and non-disappearance 2.

Jhāna

Common 9

80. With jhāna condition and conascence 3, mutuality 3, dependence 3, resultant 2, faculty 3, path 3, association 3, presence 3, non-disappearance 3.

Combinations (6)

Combination of jhāna, conascence, mutuality, dependence, association, presence and non-disappearance 3 ;

Of jhāna, conascence, mutuality, dependence, resultant, association, presence and non-disappearance 2.

Combination of jhāna, conascence, mutuality, dependence, path, association, presence and non-disappearance 3 ;

Of jhāna, conascence, mutuality, dependence, resultant, path, association, presence and non-disappearance 2.

Combination of jhāna, conascence, mutuality, dependence, faculty, path, association, presence and non-disappearance 3 ;

Of jhāna, conascence, mutuality, dependence, resultant, faculty, path, association, presence and non-disappearance 2.

Path

Common 11

81. With path condition and root 2, predominance 3, conascence 3, mutuality 3, dependence 3, resultant 3, faculty 3, jhāna 3, association 3, presence 3, non-disappearance 3.

Combinations (14)

Combination of path, conascence, mutuality, dependence, association, presence and non-disappearance 3 ;

Of path, conascence, mutuality, dependence, resultant, association, presence and non-disappearance 2.

Combination of path, conascence, mutuality, dependence, faculty, association, presence and non-disappearance 3 ;

Of path, conascence, mutuality, dependence, resultant, faculty, association, presence and non-disappearance 2.

Combination of path, conascence, mutuality, dependence, jhāna, association, presence and non-disappearance 3 ;

Of path, conascence, mutuality, dependence, resultant, jhāna, association, presence and non-disappearance 2.

Combination of path, conascence, mutuality, dependence, faculty, jhāna, association, presence and non-disappearance 3 ;

Of path, conascence, mutuality, dependence, resultant, faculty, jhāna, association, presence and non-disappearance 2.

Combination of path, predominance, conascence, mutuality, dependence, faculty, association, presence and non-disappearance 3 ;

Of path, predominance, conascence, mutuality, dependence, resultant, faculty, association, presence and non-disappearance 2.

Combination of path, root, conascence, mutuality, dependence, faculty, association, presence and non-disappearance 2 ;

Of path, root, conascence, mutuality, dependence, resultant, faculty, association, presence and non-disappearance 2.

Combination of path, root, predominance, conascence, mutuality, dependence, faculty, association, presence and non-disappearance 2 ;

Of path, root, predominance, conascence, mutuality, dependence, resultant, faculty, association, presence and non-disappearance 2.

Association

Common 13

82. With association condition and root 3, predominance 3, conascence 3, mutuality 3, dependence 3, kamma 3, resultant 3, nutriment 3, faculty 3, jhāna 3, path 3, presence 3, non-disappearance 3.

Combinations (2)

Combination of association, conascence, mutuality, dependence, presence and non-disappearance 3 ;

Of association, conascence, mutuality, dependence, resultant, presence and non-disappearance 3.

(With presence condition . . . with absence condition . . . with disappearance condition . . . with non-disappearance condition . . .)

End of Positive of " Investigation " Chapter

"INVESTIGATION" CHAPTER
SELECTION OF THE CONDITIONS FOR NEGATIVE

83. (i) State associated with pleasant feeling is related to state associated with pleasant feeling by object condition, conascence condition, strong-dependence condition, kamma condition. (1)

(ii) State associated with pleasant feeling is related to state associated with painful feeling by object condition, strong-dependence condition, kamma condition. (2)

(iii) State associated with pleasant feeling is related to state associated with neither painful nor pleasant feeling by object condition, strong-dependence condition, kamma condition. (3)

84. (iv) State associated with painful feeling is related to state associated with painful feeling by object condition, conascence condition, strong-dependence condition, kamma condition. (1)

(v) State associated with painful feeling is related to state associated with pleasant feeling by object condition, strong-dependence condition. (2)

(vi) State associated with painful feeling is related to state associated with neither painful nor pleasant feeling by object condition, strong-dependence condition, kamma condition. (3)

85. (vii) State associated with neither painful nor pleasant feeling is related to state associated with neither painful nor pleasant feeling by object condition, conascence condition, strong-dependence condition, kamma condition. (1)

(viii) State associated with neither painful nor pleasant feeling is related to state associated with pleasant feeling by object condition, strong-dependence condition, kamma condition. (2)

(ix) State associated with neither painful nor pleasant feeling is related to state associated with painful feeling by object condition, strong-dependence condition, kamma condition. (3)

2. CONDITIONS : NEGATIVE   (ii) ENUMERATION CHAPTER
By Ones

86. With not-root (condition there are) 9 (answers), not-object 9, not-predominance 9, not-proximity 9, not-contiguity 9,

not-conascence 9, not-mutuality 9, not-dependence 9, not-strong-dependence 9, not-prenascence 9, not-postnascence 9, not-repetition 9, not-kamma 9, not-resultant 9, not-nutriment 9, not-faculty 9, not-jhāna 9, not-path 9, not-association 9, not-dissociation 9, not-presence 9, not-absence 9, not-disappearance 9, not-non-disappearance 9.

Not-root

By Twos

87. With not-root condition and not-object 9 ... not-non-disappearance 9.

By Threes

With not-root, not-object conditions and not-predominance 9 ... not-strong-dependence 8 ... not-non-disappearance 9. ...

By Twenty-three

With not-root, not-object ... not-strong-dependence, not-prenascence, not-postnascence, not-repetition, not-resultant, not-nutriment ... conditions and not-non-disappearance 8.

End of Not-root

(Also enumerate all the conditions without confusion in the same way as enumerated in the Negative Enumeration of the Faultless Triplet.)

End of Negative

3. CONDITIONS : POSITIVE-NEGATIVE

Root

By Twos [1]

88. With root condition, not-object (there are) 3 (answers), not-predominance 3, not-proximity 3, not-contiguity 3, not-strong-dependence 3, not-prenascence 3, not-postnascence 3, not-repetition 3, not-kamma 3, not-resultant 3, not-nutriment 3, not-faculty 3, not-jhāna 3, not-path 3, not-dissociation 3, not-absence 3, not-disappearance 3.

---

[1] It cannot be " common " as in the Text.

Ordinary combination

89. Combinations of root, conascence, mutuality, dependence, association, presence and non-disappearance conditions, not-object 3 ... not-disappearance 3.

(Also enumerate in the same way as enumerated in the Positive-Negative Enumeration of the Faultless Triplet for recital.)

With kamma condition, not-root 8, not-object 8 ... not-non-disappearance 8. ... (Abbreviated.)

End of Positive-Negative Enumeration

4. CONDITIONS : NEGATIVE-POSITIVE

Not-root

By Twos

90. With not-root condition, object (condition) 9, predominance 5, proximity 7, contiguity 7, conascence 3, mutuality 3, dependence 3, strong-dependence 9, repetition 3, kamma 8, resultant 3, nutriment 3, faculty 3, jhāna 3, path 3, association 3, presence 3, absence 7, disappearance 7, non-disappearance 3.

By Threes

With not-root and not-object conditions, predominance 3, proximity 7 ... non-disappearance 3. ...

By Sixes

With not-root, not-object, not-predominance, not-proximity and not-contiguity conditions, conascence 3, mutuality 3, dependence 3, strong-dependence 9, kamma 8, resultant 3 ... non-disappearance 3. ...

By Nines

With not-root, not-object (conditions abbreviated) and not-dependence conditions, strong-dependence 9, kamma 8. ...

By Twenty-four (with strong-dependence)

With not-root, not-object ... not-strong-dependence, not-prenascence, not-postnascence, not-repetition, not-resultant, not-nutriment, not-faculty, not-jhāna, not-path, not-association, not-dissociation, not-presence, not-absence, not-disappearance and not-non-disappearance conditions, kamma 8.

By Twenty-four (with kamma)

With not-root, not-object ... not-dependence, not-prenascence, not-postnascence, not-repetition, not-kamma ... not-disappearance and not-non-disappearance conditions, strong-dependence 9.

End of Not-root

By Twos — Not-object

91. With not-object condition, root 3 ... kamma 8 ... non-disappearance 3. ...

By Twos — Not-non-disappearance

92. With not-non-disappearance condition, object 9, predominance 4, proximity 7, contiguity 7, strong-dependence 9, repetition 3, kamma 8, absence 7, disappearance 7. ...

By Fours

With not-non-disappearance, not-root and not-object conditions, proximity 7, contiguity 7, strong-dependence 9, repetition 3, kamma 8, absence 7, disappearance 7. ...

By Twenty-four (with strong-dependence)

With not-non-disappearance, not-root, not-object, not-predominance, not-proximity, not-contiguity, not-conascence, not-mutuality, not-dependence, not-strong-dependence, not-prenascence, not-postnascence, not-repetition, not-resultant, not-nutriment, not-faculty, not-jhāna, not-path, not-association, not-dissociation, not-presence, not-absence and not-disappearance conditions, kamma 8.

By Twenty-four (with kamma)

With not-non-disappearance, not-root ... not-dependence, not-prenascence ... not-kamma ... and not-disappearance conditions, strong-dependence 9.

(Enumerate in the same way as enumerated in the Negative-Positive Enumeration of the Faultless Triplet for recital.)

End of Negative-Positive
END OF FEELING TRIPLET

3. RESULTANT TRIPLET [1] I. "DEPENDENT" CHAPTER
   I. CONDITIONS : POSITIVE   (i) CLASSIFICATION CHAPTER

Root 13

1. (i) Dependent on resultant state, arises resultant state by root condition.

(*a*) Dependent on one resultant aggregate, arise three aggregates ... dependent on two aggregates, arise two aggregates ;

(*b*) At the moment of conception, dependent on one resultant aggregate, arise three aggregates ... dependent on two aggregates, arise two aggregates. (1)

(ii) Dependent on resultant state, arises state which is neither resultant nor producing resultant state by root condition.

(*a*) Dependent on resultant aggregates, arises mind-produced matter ;

(*b*) At the moment of conception, dependent on resultant aggregates, arises kamma-produced matter ; dependent on aggregates, arises (heart-)base. (2)

(iii) Dependent on resultant state, arise states, resultant (state) and state which is neither resultant nor producing resultant state, by root condition.

(*a*) Dependent on one resultant aggregate, arise three aggregates and mind-produced matter ... dependent on two aggregates, arise two aggregates and mind-produced matter ;

(*b*) At the moment of conception, dependent on one resultant aggregate, arise three aggregates and kamma-produced matter ... dependent on two aggregates, arise two aggregates and kamma-produced matter. (3)

2. (iv) Dependent on state producing resultant state, arises state producing resultant state by root condition.

Dependent on one aggregate, the state producing resultant state, arise three aggregates ... dependent on two aggregates, arise two aggregates. (1)

(v) Dependent on state producing resultant state, arises

---

[1] This comprises (1) resultant state, (2) state producing resultant state, (3) state which is neither resultant nor producing resultant state.

state which is neither resultant nor producing resultant state by root condition.

Dependent on aggregates, the states producing resultant states, arises mind-produced matter. (2)

(vi) Dependent on state producing resultant state, arise states, state producing resultant state and state which is neither resultant nor producing resultant state, by root condition.

Dependent on one aggregate, the state producing resultant state, arise three aggregates and mind-produced matter ...; dependent on two aggregates, arise two aggregates and mind-produced matter. (3)

3. (vii) Dependent on state which is neither resultant nor producing resultant state, arises state which is neither resultant nor producing resultant state by root condition.

(*a*) Dependent on one aggregate, the state which is neither resultant nor producing resultant state, arise three aggregates and mind-produced matter ... dependent on two aggregates, arise two aggregates and mind-produced matter ;

(*b*) Dependent on one great primary, arise three great primaries ... dependent on two great primaries, arise two great primaries ; dependent on great primaries, arise mind-produced and kamma-produced derived matter. (1)

(viii) Dependent on state which is neither resultant nor producing resultant state, arises resultant state by root condition.

At the moment of conception, dependent on (heart-) base, arise resultant aggregates. (2)

(ix) Dependent on state which is neither resultant nor producing resultant state, arise states, resultant (state) and state which is neither resultant nor producing resultant state, by root condition.

At the moment of conception, dependent on (heart-)base, arise resultant aggregates ; dependent on great primaries, arises kamma-produced matter. (3)

4. (x) Dependent on state, resultant and state which is neither resultant nor producing resultant state, arises resultant state by root condition.

At the moment of conception, dependent on one resultant

aggregate and (heart-)base, arise three aggregates ... dependent on two aggregates and (heart-)base, arise two aggregates. (1)

(xi) Dependent on state, resultant and state which is neither resultant nor producing resultant state, arises state which is neither resultant nor producing resultant state by root condition.

(*a*) Dependent on resultant aggregates and great primaries, arises mind-produced matter ;

(*b*) At the moment of conception, dependent on resultant aggregates and great primaries, arises kamma-produced matter. (2)

(xii) Dependent on state, resultant and state which is neither resultant nor producing resultant state, arise states, resultant and state which is neither resultant nor producing resultant state, by root condition.

At the moment of conception, dependent on one resultant aggregate and (heart-)base, arise three aggregates ... dependent on two aggregates and (heart-)base, arise two aggregates ; dependent on resultant aggregates and great primaries, arises kamma-produced matter. (3)

5. (xiii) Dependent on state, state producing resultant state and state which is neither resultant nor producing resultant state, arises state which is neither resultant nor producing resultant state by root condition.

Dependent on aggregates, the states producing resultant states, and great primaries, arises mind-produced matter. (1)

Object 5

6. (i) Dependent on resultant state, arises resultant state by object condition.

(*a*) Dependent on one resultant aggregate, arise three aggregates ... dependent on two aggregates, arise two aggregates ;

(*b*) At the moment of conception, dependent on one resultant aggregate, arise three aggregates ... dependent on two aggregates, arise two aggregates. (1)

7. (ii) Dependent on state producing resultant state, arises state producing resultant state by object condition.

Dependent on one aggregate, the state producing resultant state, arise three aggregates ... dependent on two aggregates, arise two aggregates. (1)

8. (iii) Dependent on state which is neither resultant nor producing resultant state, arises state which is neither resultant nor producing resultant state by object condition.

Dependent on one aggregate, the state which is neither resultant nor producing resultant state, arise three aggregates ... dependent on two aggregates, arise two aggregates. (1)

(iv) Dependent on state which is neither resultant nor producing resultant state, arises resultant state by object condition.

At the moment of conception, dependent on (heart-)base, arise resultant aggregates. (2)

9. (v) Dependent on state, resultant and state which is neither resultant nor producing resultant state, arises resultant state by object condition.

At the moment of conception, dependent on one resultant aggregate and (heart-)base, arise three aggregates ... dependent on two aggregates and (heart-)base, arise two aggregates. (1)

Predominance 9

10. (i) Dependent on resultant state, arises resultant state by predominance condition.

Dependent on one resultant aggregate, arise three aggregates ... dependent on two aggregates, arise two aggregates. (1)

(ii) Dependent on resultant state, arises state which is neither resultant nor producing resultant state by predominance condition.

Dependent on resultant aggregates, arises mind-produced matter. (2)

(iii) Dependent on resultant state, arise states, resultant and state which is neither resultant nor producing resultant state, by predominance condition.

Dependent on one resultant aggregate, arise three aggregates and mind-produced matter ... dependent on two aggregates, arise two aggregates and mind-produced matter. (3)

(iv)–(vi) Dependent on state producing resultant state ... three.

11. (vii) Dependent on state which is neither resultant nor producing resultant state, arises state which is neither resultant nor producing resultant state by predominance condition.

(*a*) Dependent on one aggregate, the state which is neither resultant nor producing resultant state, arise three aggregates and mind-produced matter ... dependent on two aggregates, arise two aggregates and mind-produced matter ;

(*b*) Dependent on one great primary, arise three great primaries ... dependent on great primaries, arises mind-produced derived matter.

12. (viii) Dependent on state, resultant and state which is neither resultant nor producing resultant state, arises state which is neither resultant nor producing resultant state by predominance condition.

Dependent on resultant aggregates and great primaries, arises mind-produced matter. (1)

(ix) Dependent on state, state producing resultant state and state which is neither resultant nor producing resultant state, arises state which is neither resultant nor producing resultant state by predominance condition.

Dependent on aggregates, the states producing resultant states, and great primaries, arises mind-produced matter. (1)

Proximity, etc.

13. Dependent on resultant state, arises resultant state by proximity condition ... by contiguity condition (the same as object condition) ... by conascence condition (conascence is all the same as root condition).

Dependent on state which is neither resultant nor producing resultant state, arises state which is neither resultant nor producing resultant state by conascence condition. ... External ... nutriment-produced ... temperature-produced ... non-percipient beings ... (this is the difference in conascence condition).

Mutuality 7

14. (i) Dependent on resultant state, arises resultant state by mutuality condition.

(*a*) Dependent on one resultant aggregate, arise three aggregates ... dependent on two aggregates, arise two aggregates ;

(*b*) At the moment of conception, dependent on one resultant aggregate, arise three aggregates ... dependent on two aggregates, arise two aggregates. (1)

(ii) Dependent on resultant state, arises state which is neither resultant nor producing resultant state by mutuality condition.

At the moment of conception, dependent on resultant aggregates, arises (heart-)base. (2)

(iii) Dependent on resultant state, arise states, resultant and state which is neither resultant nor producing resultant state, by mutuality condition.

At the moment of conception, dependent on one resultant aggregate, arise three aggregates and (heart-)base ... dependent on two aggregates, arise two aggregates and (heart-)base. (3)

(iv) Dependent on state producing resultant state, arises state producing resultant state by mutuality condition.

Dependent on one aggregate, the state producing resultant state, arise three aggregates ... dependent on two aggregates, arise two aggregates. (1)

15. (v) Dependent on state which is neither resultant nor producing resultant state, arises state which is neither resultant nor producing resultant state by mutuality condition.

(*a*) Dependent on one aggregate, the state which is neither resultant nor producing resultant state, arise three aggregates. ...

(*b*) One great primary ... External ... nutriment-produced ... temperature-produced ... one great primary of non-percipient beings. ... (1)

(vi) Dependent on state which is neither resultant nor producing resultant state, arises resultant state by mutuality condition.

At the moment of conception, dependent on (heart-)base, arise resultant aggregates. (2)

(vii) Dependent on state, resultant and state which is neither resultant nor producing resultant state, arises resultant state by mutuality condition.

At the moment of conception, dependent on one resultant aggregate and (heart-)base, arise three aggregates . . . dependent on two aggregates and (heart-)base, arise two aggregates.

Dependence, etc.

16. Dependent on resultant state, arises resultant state by dependence condition (Abbreviated) . . . by strong-dependence condition . . . by prenascence condition. . . .

Repetition 2

17. (i) Dependent on state producing resultant state, arises state producing resultant state by repetition condition.

Dependent on one aggregate, the state producing resultant state, arise three aggregates . . . dependent on two aggregates, arise two aggregates.

(ii) Dependent on state which is neither resultant nor producing resultant state, arises state which is neither resultant nor producing resultant state by repetition condition.

Dependent on one aggregate, the state which is neither resultant nor producing resultant state, arise three aggregates . . . dependent on two aggregates, arise two aggregates.

Kamma 13, Resultant 9

18. (i)–(iii) Dependent on resultant state, arises resultant state by kamma condition (Abbreviated) . . . by resultant condition. . . . three.

(iv) Dependent on state which is neither resultant nor producing resultant state, arises state which is neither resultant nor producing resultant state by resultant condition.

Dependent on one great primary, arise three great primaries . . . dependent on great primaries, arise mind-produced and kamma-produced derived matter. (1)

(v) Dependent on state which is neither resultant nor producing resultant state, arises resultant state by resultant condition.

At the moment of conception, dependent on (heart-)base, arise resultant aggregates. (2)

(vi) Dependent on state which is neither resultant nor producing resultant state, arise states, resultant and state which is neither resultant nor producing resultant state, by resultant condition.

At the moment of conception, dependent on (heart-)base, arise resultant aggregates; dependent on great primaries, arises kamma-produced matter. (3)

(vii)–(ix) Dependent on state, resultant and state which is neither resultant nor producing resultant state, arises resultant state by resultant condition ... arises state which is neither resultant nor producing resultant state by resultant condition ... arise states, resultant and state which is neither resultant nor producing resultant state, by resultant condition. ...

Nutriment, etc.

19. Dependent on resultant state, arises resultant state by nutriment condition (Abbreviated) ... by faculty condition ... by jhāna condition ... by path condition ... by association condition ... by dissociation condition ... by presence condition ... by absence condition ... by disappearance condition ... by non-disappearance condition. ...

I. CONDITIONS : POSITIVE   (ii) ENUMERATION CHAPTER

By Ones

20. With root (there are) 13 (answers), object 5, predominance 9, proximity 5, contiguity 5, conascence 13, mutuality 7, dependence 13, strong-dependence 5, prenascence 3, repetition 2, kamma 13, resultant 9, nutriment 13, faculty 13, jhāna 13, path 13, association 5, dissociation 13, presence 13, absence 5, disappearance 5, non-disappearance 13.

Root

By Twos

21. With root condition and object 5 ... non-disappearance 13. ...

(Enumerate in the same way as the Faultless Triplet Enumeration.)

Repetition

By Twos

22. With repetition condition and root 2, object 2, predominance 2, proximity 2, contiguity 2, conascence 2, mutuality 2, dependence 2, strong-dependence 2, prenascence 2, kamma 2, nutriment 2, faculty 2, jhāna 2, path 2, association 2, dissociation 2, presence 2, absence 2, disappearance 2, non-disappearance 2. ...

Resultant

By Twos

23. With resultant condition and root 9, object 3, predominance 5, proximity 3, contiguity 3, conascence 9, mutuality 6, dependence 9, strong-dependence 3, prenascence 1, kamma 9, nutriment 9, faculty 9, jhāna 9, path 9, association 3, dissociation 9, presence 9, absence 3, disappearance 3, non-disappearance 9. ... (Abbreviated.)

End of Positive Enumeration

2. CONDITIONS : NEGATIVE   (i) CLASSIFICATION CHAPTER

Not-root 10

24. (i) Dependent on resultant state, arises resultant state by not-root condition.

(*a*) Dependent on one rootless-resultant aggregate, arise three aggregates ... dependent on two aggregates, arise two aggregates ;

(*b*) At the moment of rootless conception, dependent on one resultant aggregate, arise three aggregates ; dependent on three aggregates, arises one aggregate ; dependent on two aggregates, arise two aggregates. (1)

(ii) Dependent on resultant state, arises state which is neither resultant nor producing resultant state by not-root condition.

(*a*) Dependent on rootless-resultant aggregates, arises mind-produced matter ;

(*b*) At the moment of rootless conception, dependent on resultant aggregates, arises kamma-produced matter ; dependent on aggregates, arises (heart-)base. (2)

(iii) Dependent on resultant state, arise states, resultant and state which is neither resultant nor producing resultant state, by not-root condition.

(*a*) Dependent on one rootless-resultant aggregate, arise three aggregates and mind-produced matter ... dependent on two aggregates, arise two aggregates and mind-produced matter;

(*b*) At the moment of rootless conception, dependent on one resultant aggregate, arise three aggregates and kamma-produced matter ... dependent on two aggregates, arise two aggregates and kamma-produced matter. (3)

25. (iv) Dependent on state producing resultant state, arises state producing resultant state by not-root condition.

Dependent on doubt-accompanied or restlessness-accompanied aggregates, arises doubt-accompanied or restlessness-accompanied delusion. (1)

(v) Dependent on state which is neither resultant nor producing resultant state, arises state which is neither resultant nor producing resultant state by not-root condition.

(*a*) Dependent on one rootless aggregate, the state which is neither resultant nor producing resultant state, arise three aggregates and mind-produced matter ... dependent on two aggregates, arise two aggregates and mind-produced matter;

(*b*) Dependent on one great primary, arise three great primaries ... dependent on two great primaries, arise two great primaries; dependent on great primaries, arise mind-produced and kamma-produced derived matter;

External ... nutriment-produced ... temperature-produced ... dependent on one great primary of non-percipient beings, arise three great primaries ... dependent on great primaries, arises kamma-produced derived matter. (1)

(vi) Dependent on state which is neither resultant nor producing resultant state, arises resultant state by not-root condition.

At the moment of rootless conception, dependent on (heart-)-base, arise resultant aggregates. (2)

(vii) Dependent on state which is neither resultant nor producing resultant state, arise states, resultant and state which is neither resultant nor producing resultant state, by not-root condition.

At the moment of rootless conception, dependent on (heart-)-base, arise resultant aggregates ; dependent on great primaries, arises kamma-produced matter. (3)

26. (viii) Dependent on state, resultant and state which is neither resultant nor producing resultant state, arises resultant state by not-root condition.

At the moment of rootless conception, dependent on one resultant aggregate and (heart-)base, arise three aggregates . . . dependent on two aggregates and (heart-)base, arise two aggregates. (1)

(ix) Dependent on state, resultant and state which is neither resultant nor producing resultant state, arises state which is neither resultant nor producing resultant state by not-root condition.

(*a*) Dependent on rootless-resultant aggregates and great primaries, arises mind-produced matter ;

(*b*) At the moment of rootless conception, dependent on resultant aggregates and great primaries, arises kamma-produced matter. (2)

(x) Dependent on state, resultant and state which is neither resultant nor producing resultant state, arise states, resultant and state which is neither resultant nor producing resultant state, by not-root condition.

At the moment of rootlesss conception, dependent on one resultant aggregate and (heart-)base, arise three aggregates . . . dependent on two aggregates and (heart-)base, arise two aggregates ; dependent on resultant aggregates and great primaries, arises kamma-produced matter. (3)

Not-object 5

27. (i) Dependent on resultant state, arises state which is neither resultant nor producing resultant state by not-object condition.

(*a*) Dependent on resultant aggregates, arises mind-produced matter ;

(*b*) At the moment of conception, dependent on resultant aggregates, arises kamma-produced matter ; dependent on aggregates, arises (heart-)base. (1)

28. (ii) Dependent on state producing resultant state, arises

state which is neither resultant nor producing resultant state by not-object condition.

Dependent on aggregates, the states producing resultant states, arises mind-produced matter. (1)

29. (iii) Dependent on state which is neither resultant nor producing resultant state, arises state which is neither resultant nor producing resultant state by not-object condition.

(a) Dependent on aggregates, the states which are neither resultants nor producing resultant states, arises mind-produced matter ;

(b) Dependent on one great primary, arise three great primaries ... dependent on great primaries, arise mind-produced and kamma-produced derived matter ;

(c) External ... nutriment-produced ... temperature-produced ... dependent on one great primary of non-percipient beings, arise three great primaries ... dependent on great primaries, arises kamma-produced derived matter. (1)

30. (iv) Dependent on state, resultant and state which is neither resultant nor producing resultant state, arises state which is neither resultant nor producing resultant state by not-object condition.

(a) Dependent on resultant aggregates and great primaries, arises mind-produced matter ;

(b) At the moment of conception, dependent on resultant aggregates and great primaries, arises kamma-produced matter. (1)

31. (v) Dependent on state, state producing resultant state and state which is neither resultant nor producing resultant state, arises state which is neither resultant nor producing resultant state by not-object condition.

Dependent on aggregates, the states producing resultant states, and great primaries, arises mind-produced matter. (1)

Not-predominance 13

32. Dependent on resultant state, arises resultant state by not-predominance condition. (Abbreviated.) (The same as Positive conascence.)

Not-proximity, etc.

33. Dependent on resultant state, arises state which is neither

resultant nor producing resultant state by not-proximity condition ... by not-contiguity condition ... by not-mutuality condition ... dependent on great primaries, arise mind-produced and kamma-produced derived matter. External ... nutriment-produced ... temperature-produced ... dependent on great primaries of non-percipient beings, arises kamma-produced derived matter. (This is the difference) ... by not-mutuality condition ... by not-strong-dependence condition. ... (Abbreviated.)

Not-prenascence 12

34. (i) Dependent on resultant state, arises resultant state by not-prenascence condition.

In the immaterial plane, dependent on one resultant aggregate, arise three aggregates ... dependent on two aggregates, arise two aggregates. At the moment of conception, (dependent on) one resultant aggregate ... (Abbreviated.) (1)

(ii) Dependent on resultant state, arises state which is neither resultant nor producing resultant state by not-prenascence condition.

Dependent on resultant aggregates, arises mind-produced matter. At the moment of conception ... (Abbreviated.) (2)

(iii) Dependent on resultant state, arise states, resultant and state which is neither resultant nor producing resultant state, by not-prenascence condition.

At the moment of conception, dependent on one resultant aggregate, arise three aggregates and kamma-produced matter ... dependent on two aggregates, arise two aggregates and kamma-produced matter. (3)

(iv) Dependent on state producing resultant state, arises state producing resultant state by not-prenascence condition.

In the immaterial plane, dependent on one aggregate, the state producing resultant state, arise three aggregates ... dependent on two aggregates, arise two aggregates. (1)

(v) Dependent on state producing resultant state, arises state which is neither resultant nor producing resultant state by not-prenascence condition.

Dependent on aggregates, the states producing resultant states, arises mind-produced matter. (2)

35. (vi) Dependent on state which is neither resultant nor producing resultant state, arises state which is neither resultant nor producing resultant state by not-prenascence condition.

In the immaterial plane, dependent on one aggregate, the state which is neither resultant nor producing resultant state, arise three aggregates ... dependent on two aggregates, arise two aggregates.

Dependent on aggregates, the states which are neither resultants nor producing resultant states, arises mind-produced matter. Dependent on one great primary, arise three great primaries. ... External ... nutriment-produced ... temperature-produced ... dependent on one great primary of non-percipient beings ... (1)

(vii) Dependent on state which is neither resultant nor producing resultant state, arises resultant state by not-prenascence condition.

At the moment of conception, dependent on (heart-)base, arise resultant aggregates. (2)

(viii) Dependent on state which is neither resultant nor producing resultant state, arise states, resultant and state which is neither resultant nor producing resultant state, by not-prenascence condition.

At the moment of conception, dependent on (heart-)base, arise resultant aggregates; dependent on great primaries, arises kamma-produced matter. (3)

36. (ix) Dependent on state, resultant and state which is neither resultant nor producing resultant state, arises resultant state by not-prenascence condition.

At the moment of conception, dependent on one resultant aggregate and (heart-)base, arise three aggregates ... dependent on two aggregates and (heart-)base, arise two aggregates. (1)

(x) Dependent on state, resultant and state which is neither resultant nor producing resultant state, arises state which is neither resultant nor producing resultant state by not-prenascence condition.

Dependent on resultant aggregates and great primaries,

arises mind-produced matter. At the moment of conception, dependent on resultant aggregates and great primaries, arises kamma-produced matter. (2)

(xi) Dependent on state, resultant and state which is neither resultant nor producing resultant state, arise states, resultant and state which is neither resultant nor producing resultant state, by not-prenascence condition.

At the moment of conception, dependent on one resultant aggregate and (heart-)base, arise three aggregates ... dependent on two aggregates and (heart-)base, arise two aggregates; dependent on resultant aggregates and great primaries, arises kamma-produced matter. (3)

37. (xii) Dependent on state, state producing resultant state and state which is neither resultant nor producing resultant state, arises state which is neither resultant nor producing resultant state by not-prenascence condition.

Dependent on aggregates, the states producing resultant states, and great primaries, arises mind-produced matter. (1)

Not-postnascence, etc., 13

38. Dependent on resultant state, arises resultant state by not-postnascence condition ... by not-repetition condition. ... (Abbreviated.)

Not-kamma 2

39. (i) Dependent on state producing resultant state, arises state producing resultant state by not-kamma condition.

Dependent on aggregates, the states producing resultant states, arises volition, the state producing resultant state.

(ii) Dependent on state which is neither resultant nor producing resultant state, arises state which is neither resultant nor producing resultant state by not-kamma condition.

Dependent on aggregates, the states which are neither resultants nor producing resultant states, arises volition, the state which is neither resultant nor producing resultant state. External ... nutriment-produced ... dependent on one temperature-produced great primary, arise three great primaries ... dependent on great primaries, arises derived matter.

Not-resultant 5

40. (i) Dependent on state producing resultant state, arises state producing resultant state by not-resultant condition.

Dependent on one aggregate, the state producing resultant state, arise three aggregates ... dependent on two aggregates, arise two aggregates. (1)

(ii) Dependent on state producing resultant state, arises state which is neither resultant nor producing resultant state by not-resultant condition.

Dependent on aggregates, the states producing resultant states, arises mind-produced matter. (2)

(iii) Dependent on state producing resultant state, arise states, state producing resultant state and state which is neither resultant nor producing resultant state, by not-resultant condition.

Dependent on one aggregate, the state producing resultant state, arise three aggregates and mind-produced matter ... dependent on two aggregates, arise two aggregates and mind-produced matter. (3)

41. (iv) Dependent on state which is neither resultant nor producing resultant state, arises state which is neither resultant nor producing resultant state by not-resultant condition.

Dependent on one aggregate, the state which is neither resultant nor producing resultant state, arise three aggregates and mind-produced matter ... dependent on two aggregates, arise two aggregates and mind-produced matter. Dependent on one great primary, arise three great primaries ... dependent on great primaries, arises mind-produced derived matter. External ... nutriment-produced ... temperature-produced ... dependent on one great primary of non-percipient beings, arise three great primaries ... dependent on great primaries, arises kamma-produced derived matter. (1)

(v) Dependent on state, state producing resultant state and state which is neither resultant nor producing resultant state, arises state which is neither resultant nor producing resultant state by not-resultant condition.

Dependent on aggregates, the states producing resultant states, and great primaries, arises mind-produced matter.

Not-nutriment 1

42. Dependent on state which is neither resultant nor producing resultant state, arises state which is neither resultant nor producing resultant state by not-nutriment condition.

External ... temperature-produced ... dependent on one great primary of non-percipient beings, arise three great primaries ... dependent on great primaries, arises kamma-produced derived matter.

Not-faculty 1

43. Dependent on state which is neither resultant nor producing resultant state, arises state which is neither resultant nor producing resultant state by not-faculty condition.

External ... nutriment-produced ... dependent on one temperature-produced great primary, arise three great primaries ... dependent on great primaries of non-percipient beings, arises physical life-faculty.

Not-jhāna 2

44. (i) Dependent on resultant state, arises resultant state by not-jhāna condition.

Dependent on one fivefold consciousness-accompanied aggregate, arise three aggregates ... dependent on two aggregates, arise two aggregates.

(ii) Dependent on state which is neither resultant nor producing resultant state, arises state which is neither resultant nor producing resultant state by not-jhāna condition.

External ... nutriment-produced ... temperature-produced ... dependent on one great primary of non-percipient beings. ...

Not-path 9

45. (i)–(iii) Dependent on resultant state, arises resultant state by not-path condition.

Dependent on one rootless-resultant aggregate ... three.

(iv)–(vi) Dependent on state which is neither resultant nor producing resultant state, arises state which is neither resultant nor producing resultant state by not-path condition.

Dependent on one rootless aggregate, the state which is neither resultant nor producing resultant state ... three.

(vii)–(ix) Dependent on state, resultant and state which is neither resultant nor producing resultant state, arises resultant state by not-path condition.

At the moment of rootless conception, dependent on one resultant aggregate and (heart-)base ... three.

Not-association 5

46. (i)–(ii) Dependent on resultant state, arises state which is neither resultant nor producing resultant state by not-association condition. ... two.

(iii)–(iv) Dependent on state producing resultant state, arises state which is neither resultant nor producing resultant state by not-association condition. ... two.

(v) Dependent on state which is neither resultant nor producing resultant state ... one.

Not-dissociation 3

47. (i) Dependent on resultant state, arises resultant state by not-dissociation condition.

In the immaterial plane, dependent on one resultant aggregate, arise three aggregates ... dependent on two aggregates, arise two aggregates.

(ii) Dependent on state producing resultant state, arises state producing resultant state by not-dissociation condition.

In the immaterial plane, dependent on one aggregate, the state producing resultant state, arise three aggregates ... dependent on two aggregates, arise two aggregates.

(iii) Dependent on state which is neither resultant nor producing resultant state, arises state which is neither resultant nor producing resultant state by not-dissociation condition.

In the immaterial plane, dependent on one aggregate, the state which is neither resultant nor producing resultant state, arise three aggregates ... dependent on two aggregates, arise two aggregates. External ... nutriment-produced ... temperature-produced ... dependent on one great primary of non-percipient beings, arise three great primaries ... dependent on great primaries, arises kamma-produced derived matter.

Not-absence 5, Not-disappearance 5

48. Dependent on resultant state, arises state which is neither resultant nor producing resultant state by not-absence condition ... by not-disappearance condition. ... (Abbreviated.)

2. CONDITIONS : NEGATIVE   (ii) ENUMERATION CHAPTER

By Ones

49. With not-root (condition there are) 10 (answers), not-object 5, not-predominance 13, not-proximity 5, not-contiguity 5, not-mutuality 5, not-strong-dependence 5, not-prenascence 12, not-postnascence 13, not-repetition 13, not-kamma 2, not-resultant 5, not-nutriment 1, not-faculty 1, not-jhāna 2, not-path 9, not-association 5, not-dissociation 3, not-absence 5, not-disappearance 5.

Not-root

By Twos

50. With not-root condition and not-object 3, not-predominance 10, not-proximity 3, not-contiguity 3, not-mutuality 3, not-strong-dependence 3, not-prenascence 10, not-postnascence 10, not-repetition 10, not-kamma 1, not-resultant 2, not-nutriment 1, not-faculty 1, not-jhāna 2, not-path 9, not-association 3, not-dissociation 2, not-absence 3, not-disappearance 3.

By Threes

With not-root, not-object conditions and not-predominance 3, not-proximity 3, not-contiguity 3 ... not-kamma 1, not-resultant 1, not-nutriment 1, not-faculty 1, not-jhāna 1, not-path 3, not-association 3, not-dissociation 1, not-absence 3, not-disappearance 3. ... (Abbreviated.)

End of Not-root

(Enumerate here also in the same way as the Faultless Triplet which was enumerated for recital.)

End of Negative

3. CONDITIONS: POSITIVE-NEGATIVE
Root

By Twos

51. With root condition, not-object 5, not-predominance 13, not-proximity 5, not-contiguity 5, not-mutuality 5, not-strong-dependence 5, not-prenascence 12, not-postnascence 13, not-repetition 13, not-kamma 2, not-resultant 5, not-association 5, not-dissociation 3, not-absence 5, not-disappearance 5.

By Threes

With root and object conditions, not-predominance 5, not-prenascence 5, not-postnascence 5, not-repetition 5, not-kamma 2, not-resultant 2, not-dissociation 3.

By Fours

With root, object and predominance conditions, not-prenascence 3, not-postnascence 3, not-repetition 3, not-kamma 2, not-resultant 2, not-dissociation 3. ...

By Nines

With root, object, predominance, proximity (Conditions abbreviated), and prenascence conditions, not-postnascence 3, not-repetition 3, not-kamma 2, not-resultant 2. ... (Abbreviated.)

(Enumerate in the same way as enumerated in the Positive-Negative Enumeration of Faultless Triplet.)

End of Positive-Negative

4. CONDITIONS: NEGATIVE-POSITIVE
Not-root

By Twos

52. With not-root condition, object 5, proximity 5, contiguity 5, conascence 10, mutuality 7, dependence 10, strong-dependence 5, prenascence 3, repetition 2, kamma 10, resultant 9, nutriment 10, faculty 10, jhāna 10, path 1, association 5, dissociation 10, presence 10, absence 5, disappearance 5, non-disappearance 10.

By Threes

With not-root and not-object conditions, conascence 3, mutuality 2, dependence 3, kamma 3, resultant 3, nutriment 3, faculty 3, jhāna 3, dissociation 3, presence 3, non-disappearance 3. ...

By Sevens

With not-root, not-object, not-predominance, not-proximity, not-contiguity and not-mutuality conditions, conascence 3, dependence 3, kamma 3, resultant 3, nutriment 3, faculty 3, jhāna 3, dissociation 3, presence 3, non-disappearance 3. ... (Abbreviated.)

(Enumerate in the same way as enumerated in not-root condition of the Faultless Triplet. Expand in the same way as expanded in the Negative-Positive of Faultless Triplet.)

End of Negative-Positive

End of " DEPENDENT " CHAPTER

3. Resultant Triplet   II. " Conascent " Chapter

1. conditions : positive   (i) classification chapter

53. Conascent with resultant state, arises resultant state by root condition.

Conascent with one resultant aggregate, arise three aggregates ; conascent with three aggregates, arises one aggregate ; conascent with two aggregates, arise two aggregates. ... (Abbreviated.)

1. conditions : positive   (ii) enumeration chapter

54. With root 13 ... non-disappearance 13. ...

2. conditions : negative

55. Conascent with resultant state, arises resultant state by not-root condition.

Conascent with one rootless-resultant aggregate, arise three aggregates ; conascent with three aggregates, arises one aggregate; conascent with two aggregates, arise two aggregates. ... (Abbreviated.)

(With not-root 10 ... not-disappearance 5. ...) [1]

3. CONDITIONS : POSITIVE-NEGATIVE

56. With root condition, not-object 5 ... not-dissociation 3. ...

4. CONDITIONS : NEGATIVE-POSITIVE

57. With not-root condition, object 5 ... non-disappearance 10. ...

End of " CONASCENT " CHAPTER

3. RESULTANT TRIPLET   III. " CONDITIONED " CHAPTER

1. CONDITIONS : POSITIVE   (i) CLASSIFICATION CHAPTER

Root 17

58. (i) Conditioned by resultant state, arises resultant state by root condition.

Conditioned by one resultant aggregate, arise three aggregates; conditioned by three aggregates, arises one aggregate; conditioned by two aggregates, arise two aggregates.

At the moment of conception ... (1)

(ii) Conditioned by resultant state, arises state which is neither resultant nor producing resultant state by root condition.

Conditioned by resultant aggregates, arises mind-produced matter.

At the moment of conception, conditioned by resultant aggregates, arises kamma-produced matter. ... (2)

(iii) Conditioned by resultant state, arise states, resultant and state which is neither resultant nor producing resultant state, by root condition.

Conditioned by one resultant aggregate, arise three aggregates

---

[1] Left out in the Text.

and mind-produced matter ... conditioned by two aggregates, arise two aggregates and mind-produced matter.

At the moment of conception ... (3)

(iv) Conditioned by state producing resultant state, arises state producing resultant state by root condition.

Conditioned by one aggregate, the state producing resultant state, arise three aggregates ... conditioned by two aggregates, arise two aggregates. (1)

(v) Conditioned by state producing resultant state, arises state which is neither resultant nor producing resultant state by root condition.

Conditioned by aggregates, the states producing resultant states, arises mind-produced matter. (2)

(vi) Conditioned by state producing resultant state, arise states, state producing resultant state and state which is neither resultant nor producing resultant state, by root condition.

Conditioned by one aggregate, the state producing resultant state, arise three aggregates and mind-produced matter ... conditioned by two aggregates, arise two aggregates and mind-produced matter. (3)

(vii) Conditioned by state which is neither resultant nor producing resultant state, arises state which is neither resultant nor producing resultant state by root condition.

Conditioned by one aggregate, the state which is neither resultant nor producing resultant state, arise three aggregates and mind-produced matter ... conditioned by two aggregates, arise two aggregates and mind-produced matter.

Conditioned by one great primary ... conditioned by great primaries, arise mind-produced and kamma-produced derived matter; conditioned by (heart-)base, arise aggregates, the states which are neither resultants nor producing resultant states. (1)

(viii) Conditioned by state which is neither resultant nor producing resultant state, arises resultant state by root condition.

Conditioned by (heart-)base, arise resultant aggregates.

At the moment of conception, conditioned by (heart-)base, arise resultant aggregates. (2)

(ix) Conditioned by state which is neither resultant nor

producing resultant state, arises state producing resultant state by root condition.

Conditioned by (heart-)base, arise aggregates, the states producing resultant states. (3)

(x) Conditioned by state which is neither resultant nor producing resultant state, arise states, resultant and state which is neither resultant nor producing resultant state, by root condition.

Conditioned by (heart-)base, arise resultant aggregates; conditioned by great primaries, arises mind-produced matter.

At the moment of conception, conditioned by (heart-)base, arise resultant aggregates; conditioned by great primaries, arises kamma-produced matter. (4)

(xi) Conditioned by state which is neither resultant nor producing resultant state, arise states, state producing resultant state and state which is neither resultant nor producing resultant state, by root condition.

Conditioned by (heart-)base, arise aggregates, the states producing resultant states; conditioned by great primaries, arises mind-produced matter. (5)

59. (xii) Conditioned by state, resultant and state which is neither resultant nor producing resultant state, arises resultant state by root condition.

Conditioned by one resultant aggregate and (heart-)base, arise three aggregates ... conditioned by two aggregates and (heart-)base, arise two aggregates.

At the moment of conception, conditioned by one resultant aggregate and (heart-)base, arise three aggregates ... conditioned by two aggregates and (heart-)base, arise two aggregates. (1)

(xiii) Conditioned by state, resultant and state which is neither resultant nor producing resultant state, arises state which is neither resultant nor producing resultant state by root condition.

Conditioned by resultant aggregates and great primaries, arises mind-produced matter.

At the moment of conception, conditioned by resultant aggregates and great primaries, arises kamma-produced matter. (2)

(xiv) Conditioned by state, resultant and state which is neither resultant nor producing resultant state, arise states, resultant and state which is neither resultant nor producing resultant state, by root condition.

Conditioned by one resultant aggregate and (heart-)base, arise three aggregates ... conditioned by two aggregates and (heart-)base, arise two aggregates; conditioned by resultant aggregates and great primaries, arises mind-produced matter.

At the moment of conception, conditioned by one resultant aggregate and (heart-)base, arise three aggregates ... conditioned by two aggregates and (heart-)base, arise two aggregates; conditioned by resultant aggregates and great primaries, arises kamma-produced matter. (3)

60. (xv) Conditioned by state, state producing resultant state and state which is neither resultant nor producing resultant state, arises state producing resultant state by root condition.

Conditioned by one aggregate, the state producing resultant state, and (heart-)base, arise three aggregates ... conditioned by two aggregates and (heart-)base, arise two aggregates. (1)

(xvi) Conditioned by state, state producing resultant state and state which is neither resultant nor producing resultant state, arises state which is neither resultant nor producing resultant state by root condition.

Conditioned by aggregates, the states producing resultant states, and great primaries, arises mind-produced matter. (2)

(xvii) Conditioned by state, state producing resultant state and state which is neither resultant nor producing resultant state, arise states, state producing resultant state and state which is neither resultant nor producing resultant state, by root condition.

Conditioned by one aggregate, the state producing resultant state, and (heart-)base, arise three aggregates ... conditioned by two aggregates and (heart-)base, arise two aggregates; conditioned by aggregates, the states producing resultant states, and great primaries, arises mind-produced matter. (3)

Object 7

61. (i) Conditioned by resultant state, arises resultant state by object condition.

Conditioned by one resultant aggregate, arise three aggregates ... conditioned by two aggregates, arise two aggregates. At the moment of conception. ... (1)

(ii) Conditioned by state producing resultant state, arises state producing resultant state by object condition.

Conditioned by one aggregate, the state producing resultant state, arise three aggregates ... conditioned by two aggregates, arise two aggregates. (1)

(iii) Conditioned by state which is neither resultant nor producing resultant state, arises state which is neither resultant nor producing resultant state by object condition.

Conditioned by one aggregate, the state which is neither resultant nor producing resultant state, arise three aggregates ... conditioned by two aggregates, arise two aggregates ; conditioned by (heart-)base, arise aggregates, the states which are neither resultants nor producing resultant states. (1)

(iv) Conditioned by state which is neither resultant nor producing resultant state, arises resultant state by object condition.

Conditioned by eye-base, arises eye-consciousness ; conditioned by ear-base, arises ear-consciousness ; conditioned by nose-base, arises nose-consciousness ; conditioned by tongue-base, arises tongue-consciousness ; conditioned by body-base, arises body-consciousness ; conditioned by (heart-)base, arise resultant aggregates. At the moment of conception, conditioned by (heart-)base, arise resultant aggregates. (2)

(v) Conditioned by state which is neither resultant nor producing resultant state, arises state producing resultant state by object condition.

Conditioned by (heart-)base, arise aggregates, the states producing resultant states. (3)

(vi) Conditioned by state, resultant and state which is neither resultant nor producing resultant state, arises resultant state by object condition.

Conditioned by one eye-consciousness-accompanied aggregate and eye-base, arise three aggregates ... conditioned by two aggregates and eye-base, arise two aggregates ; ... ear ... nose ... tongue ... body ... ; conditioned by one resultant aggregate and (heart-)base, arise three aggregates ...

conditioned by two aggregates and (heart-)base, arise two aggregates.

At the moment of conception, conditioned by one resultant aggregate and (heart-)base, arise three aggregates ... conditioned by two aggregates and (heart-)base, arise two aggregates. (1)

(vii) Conditioned by state, state producing resultant state and state which is neither resultant nor producing resultant state, arises state producing resultant state by object condition.

Conditioned by one aggregate, the state producing resultant state, and (heart-)base, arise three aggregates ... conditioned by two aggregates and (heart-)base, arise two aggregates. (1)

Predominance 17

62. (i)–(iii) Conditioned by resultant state, arises resultant state by predominance condition.

Conditioned by one resultant aggregate ... three. (There is no " at the moment of conception " in predominance.)

(iv)–(vi) Conditioned by state producing resultant state ... three.

(vii) Conditioned by state which is neither resultant nor producing resultant state, arises state which is neither resultant nor producing resultant state by predominance condition.

Conditioned by one aggregate, the state which is neither resultant nor producing resultant state, arise three aggregates and mind-produced matter ... conditioned by two aggregates, arise two aggregates and mind-produced matter.

Conditioned by one great primary, arise three great primaries ... conditioned by great primaries, arises mind-produced derived matter ; conditioned by (heart-)base, arise aggregates, the states which are neither resultants nor producing resultant states. (1)

(viii) Conditioned by state which is neither resultant nor producing resultant state, arises resultant state by predominance condition.

Conditioned by (heart-)base, arise resultant aggregates. (2)

(ix) Conditioned by state which is neither resultant nor producing resultant state, arises state producing resultant state by predominance condition.

Conditioned by (heart-)base, arise aggregates, the states producing resultant states. (3)

(x) Conditioned by state which is neither resultant nor producing resultant state, arise states, resultant and state which is neither resultant nor producing resultant state, by predominance condition.

Conditioned by (heart-)base, arise resultant aggregates ; conditioned by great primaries, arises mind-produced matter. (4)

(xi) Conditioned by state which is neither resultant nor producing resultant state, arise states, state producing resultant state and state which is neither resultant nor producing resultant state, by predominance condition.

Conditioned by (heart-)base, arise aggregates, the states producing resultant states ; conditioned by great primaries, arises mind-produced matter. (5)

63. (xii) Conditioned by state, resultant and state which is neither resultant nor producing resultant state, arises resultant state by predominance condition.

Conditioned by one resultant aggregate and (heart-)base, arise three aggregates ... conditioned by two aggregates and (heart-)base, arise two aggregates. (1)

(xiii) Conditioned by state, resultant and state which is neither resultant nor producing resultant state, arises state which is neither resultant nor producing resultant state by predominance condition.

Conditioned by resultant aggregates and great primaries, arises mind-produced matter. (2)

(xiv) Conditioned by state, resultant and state which is neither resultant nor producing resultant state, arise states, resultant and state which is neither resultant nor producing resultant state, by predominance condition.

Conditioned by one resultant aggregate and (heart-)base, arise three aggregates ... conditioned by two aggregates and (heart-)base, arise two aggregates ; conditioned by resultant aggregates and great primaries, arises mind-produced matter. (3)

64. (xv) Conditioned by state, state producing resultant state and state which is neither resultant nor producing resultant state, arises state producing resultant state by predominance condition.

Conditioned by one aggregate, the state producing resultant state, and (heart-)base, arise three aggregates ... conditioned by two aggregates and (heart-)base, arise two aggregates. (1)

(xvi) Conditioned by state, state producing resultant state and state which is neither resultant nor producing resultant state, arises state which is neither resultant nor producing resultant state by predominance condition.

Conditioned by aggregates, the states producing resultant states, and great primaries, arises mind-produced matter. (2)

(xvii) Conditioned by state, state producing resultant state and state which is neither resultant nor producing resultant state, arise states, state producing resultant state and state which is neither resultant nor producing resultant state, by predominance condition.

Conditioned by one aggregate, the state producing resultant state, and (heart-)base, arise three aggregates ... conditioned by two aggregates and (heart-)base, arise two aggregates; conditioned by aggregates, the states producing resultant states, and great primaries, arises mind-produced matter. (3)

Proximity 7, Contiguity 7

65. Conditioned by resultant state, arises resultant state by proximity condition ... by contiguity condition ... (the same as object condition).

Mutuality 9

66. (i) By conascence condition ... by mutuality condition.

Conditioned by one resultant aggregate, arise three aggregates ... conditioned by two aggregates, arise two aggregates.

At the moment of conception, conditioned by one resultant aggregate, arise three aggregates ... conditioned by two aggregates, arise two aggregates. (1)

(ii) Conditioned by resultant state, arises state which is neither resultant nor producing resultant state by mutuality condition.

At the moment of conception, conditioned by resultant aggregates, arises (heart-)base. (2)

(iii) Conditioned by resultant state, arise states, resultant and state which is neither resultant nor producing resultant state, by mutuality condition.

At the moment of conception, conditioned by one resultant aggregate, arise three aggregates and (heart-)base . . . conditioned by two aggregates, arise two aggregates and (heart-)-base. (3) 67. (iv) Conditioned by state producing resultant state, arises state producing resultant state by mutuality condition.

Conditioned by one aggregate, the state producing resultant state, arise three aggregates . . . conditioned by two aggregates arise two aggregates. (1)

(v) Conditioned by state which is neither resultant nor producing resultant state, arises state which is neither resultant nor producing resultant state by mutuality condition.

Conditioned by one aggregate, the state which is neither resultant nor producing resultant state, arise three aggregates . . . conditioned by two aggregates, arise two aggregates.

Conditioned by one great primary, arise three great primaries . . . External . . . nutriment-produced . . . temperature-produced . . . conditioned by one great primary of non-percipient beings, arise three great primaries . . . conditioned by two great primaries, arise two great primaries ; conditioned by (heart-)base, arise aggregates, the states which are neither resultants nor producing resultant states. (1)

(vi) Conditioned by state which is neither resultant nor producing resultant state, arises resultant state by mutuality condition.

Conditioned by eye-base, arises eye-consciousness . . . conditioned by body-base, arises body-consciousness ; conditioned by (heart-)base, arise resultant aggregates.

At the moment of conception, conditioned by (heart-)base, arise resultant aggregates. (2)

(vii) Conditioned by state which is neither resultant nor producing resultant state, arises state producing resultant state by mutuality condition.

Conditioned by (heart-)base, arise aggregates, the states producing resultant states. (3)

(viii) Conditioned by state, resultant and state which is neither resultant nor producing resultant state, arises resultant state by mutuality condition.

Conditioned by one eye-consciousness-accompanied aggregate and eye-base, arise three aggregates ... conditioned by two aggregates and eye-base, arise two aggregates; ... ear ... nose ... tongue ... body ... ; conditioned by one resultant aggregate and (heart-)base, arise three aggregates ... conditioned by two aggregates and (heart-)base, arise two aggregates.

At the moment of conception, conditioned by one resultant aggregate and (heart-)base, arise three aggregates ... conditioned by two aggregates and (heart-)base, arise two aggregates. (1)

(ix) Conditioned by state, state producing resultant state and state which is neither resultant nor producing resultant state, arises state producing resultant state by mutuality condition.

Conditioned by one aggregate, the state producing resultant state, and (heart-)base, arise three aggregates ... conditioned by two aggregates and (heart-)base, arise two aggregates. (1)

Dependence 17

68. Conditioned by resultant state, arises resultant state by dependence condition. (The same as conascence.)

Strong-dependence 7, Prenascence 7

69. By strong-dependence condition ... by prenascence condition.

Conditioned by one resultant aggregate, arise three aggregates ... conditioned by two aggregates, arise two aggregates; (conditioned by heart-)base, (arise resultant aggregates) by prenascence condition. (The same as proximity.) (Abbreviated.)

Repetition 4

70. (i) Conditioned by state producing resultant state, arises state producing resultant state by repetition condition.

Conditioned by one aggregate, the state producing resultant state, arise three aggregates ; conditioned by three aggregates, arises one aggregate ; conditioned by two aggregates, arise two aggregates. (1)

(ii) Conditioned by state which is neither resultant nor producing resultant state, arises state which is neither resultant nor producing resultant state by repetition condition.

Conditioned by one aggregate, the state which is neither resultant nor producing resultant state ... conditioned by (heart-)base, arise aggregates, the states which are neither resultants nor producing resultant states. (1)

(iii) Conditioned by state which is neither resultant nor producing resultant state, arises state producing resultant state by repetition condition.

Conditioned by (heart-)base, arise aggregates, the states producing resultant states. (2)

(iv) Conditioned by state, state producing resultant state and state which is neither resultant nor producing resultant state, arises state producing resultant state by repetition condition.

Conditioned by one aggregate, the state producing resultant state, and (heart-)base, arise three aggregates ; conditioned by three aggregates and (heart-)base, arises one aggregate ; conditioned by two aggregates and (heart-)base, arise two aggregates.

Kamma 17

71. Conditioned by resultant state, arises resultant state by kamma condition. ... three. (The same as conascence.)

Resultant 9

72. (i)–(iii) Conditioned by resultant state, arises resultant state by resultant condition. ... three.

(iv)–(vi) Conditioned by state which is neither resultant nor producing resultant state, arises state which is neither resultant nor producing resultant state by resultant condition.

Conditioned by one great primary, arise three great primaries ... conditioned by two great primaries, arise two great primaries ; conditioned by great primaries, arise mind-produced and kamma-produced derived matter ... resultant and both ... three.

(vii)–(ix) Resultant and state which is neither resultant nor producing resultant state ... three.

Nutriment, etc.

By nutriment condition ... by faculty condition ... by jhāna condition ... by path condition ... by association condition ... by dissociation condition ... by presence condition ... by absence condition ... by disappearance condition ... by non-disappearance condition.

1. CONDITIONS : POSITIVE   (ii) ENUMERATION CHAPTER

By Ones

73. With root 17, object 7, predominance 17, proximity 7, contiguity 7, conascence 17, mutuality 9, dependence 17, strong-dependence 7, prenascence 7, repetition 4, kamma 17, resultant 9, nutriment 17, faculty 17, jhāna 17, path 17, association 7, dissociation 17, presence 17, absence 7, disappearance 7, non-disappearance 17.

Root

By Twos

74. With root condition and object 7, predominance 17 ... non-disappearance 17.
(Enumerate in the same way as Faultless Triplet Enumeration.)

End of Positive

2. CONDITIONS : NEGATIVE   (i) CLASSIFICATION CHAPTER

Not-root 12

75. (i)–(iii) Conditioned by resultant state, arises resultant state by not-root condition.
    Conditioned by one rootless-resultant aggregate ... three.
      (iv) Conditioned by state producing resultant state, arises state producing resultant state by not-root condition.
    Conditioned by doubt-accompanied or restlessness-accompanied aggregates, arises doubt-accompanied or restlessness-accompanied delusion.

(v) Conditioned by state which is neither resultant nor producing resultant state, arises state which is neither resultant nor producing resultant state by not-root condition.

Conditioned by one rootless aggregate, the state which is neither resultant nor producing resultant state ... (1)

(vi) Conditioned by state which is neither resultant nor producing resultant state, arises resultant state by not-root condition.

Conditioned by eye-base, arises eye-consciousness. ... (2)

(vii) Conditioned by state which is neither resultant nor producing resultant state, arises state producing resultant state by not-root condition.

Conditioned by (heart-)base, arises doubt-accompanied or restlessness-accompanied delusion. (3)

(viii) Conditioned by state which is neither resultant nor producing resultant state, arise states, resultant and state which is neither resultant nor producing resultant state, by not-root condition.

Conditioned by (heart-)base, arise rootless-resultant aggregates; conditioned by great primaries, arises mind-produced matter. At the moment of rootless conception. ... (4)

76. (ix)–(xi) Conditioned by state, resultant and state which is neither resultant nor producing resultant state, arises resultant state ... arises state which is neither resultant nor producing resultant state ... arise states, resultant and state which is neither resultant nor producing resultant state, by not-root condition. ...

(xii) Conditioned by state, state producing resultant state and state which is neither resultant nor producing resultant state, arises state producing resultant state by not-root condition.

Conditioned by doubt-accompanied or restlessness-accompanied aggregates and (heart-)base, arise doubt-accompanied or restlessness-accompanied delusion.

Not-object 5

77. Conditioned by resultant state, arises state which is neither resultant nor producing resultant state by not-object condition. (Abbreviated. All sections should be expanded.)

2. CONDITIONS : NEGATIVE   (ii) ENUMERATION CHAPTER

By Ones

78. With not-root 12, not-object 5, not-predominance 17, not-proximity 5, not-contiguity 5, not-mutuality 5, not-strong-dependence 5, not-prenascence 12, not-postnascence 17, not-repetition 17, not-kamma 4, not-resultant 9, not-nutriment 1, not-faculty 1, not-jhāna 4, not-path 9, not-association 5, not-dissociation 3, not-absence 5, not-disappearance 5.

Not-root

By Twos

79. With not-root condition and not-object 3, not-predominance 12, not-proximity 3, not-contiguity 3 ... not-kamma 1, not-resultant 4, not-nutriment 1, not-faculty 1, not-jhāna 4, not-path 9, not-association 3, not-dissociation 2, not-absence 3, not-disappearance 3.

(Enumerate in the same way as the Faultless Triplet Negative Enumeration.)

End of Negative

3. CONDITIONS : POSITIVE-NEGATIVE

Root

By Twos

80. With root condition, not-object 5, not-predominance 17 ... not-disappearance 5.

(Enumerate in the same way as the Faultless Triplet Positive-Negative Enumeration.)

End of Positive-Negative

4. CONDITIONS : NEGATIVE-POSITIVE

Not-root

By Twos

81. With not-root condition, object 7, proximity 7, contiguity 7, conascence 12, mutuality 9, dependence 12, strong-dependence 7, prenascence 7, repetition 4, kamma 12, resultant 9, nutriment

12, faculty 12, jhāna 12, path 3, association 7, dissociation 12, presence 12, absence 7, disappearance 7, non-disappearance 12.

By Threes

With not-root and not-object conditions, conascence 3, mutuality 2 ... non-disappearance 3.

(Enumerate in the same way as the Faultless Triplet Negative-Positive Enumeration.)

End of Negative-Positive

End of " CONDITIONED " CHAPTER

3. RESULTANT TRIPLET   IV. " SUPPORTED " CHAPTER

1–4. CONDITIONS : THE SET OF FOUR

82. Supported by resultant state, arises resultant state by root condition.

Supported by one resultant aggregate, arise three aggregates. ...

With root 17. ...

With not-root 12 ... not-disappearance 5.

With root condition, not-object 5 ... not-dissociation 3.

With not-root condition, object 7 ... non-disappearance 12.

End of " SUPPORTED " CHAPTER

3. RESULTANT TRIPLET   V. " CONJOINED " CHAPTER

1. CONDITIONS : POSITIVE   (i) CLASSIFICATION CHAPTER

Root 3

83. Conjoined with resultant state, arises resultant state by root condition.

Conjoined with one resultant aggregate, arise three aggregates ... (Abbreviated. All sections should be expanded.)

1. CONDITIONS : POSITIVE   (ii) ENUMERATION CHAPTER

By Ones

84. With root 3, object 3, predominance 3, proximity 3, contiguity 3, conascence 3, mutuality 3, dependence 3, strong-dependence 3, prenascence 3, repetition 2, kamma 3, resultant 1,

nutriment 3, faculty 3, jhāna 3, path 3, association 3, dissociation 3, presence 3, absence 3, disappearance 3, non-disappearance 3. ... (Abbreviated.)

(Enumerate in the same way as the Faultless Triplet Enumeration.)

End of Positive

2. CONDITIONS : NEGATIVE (i) CLASSIFICATION CHAPTER

85. Conjoined with resultant state, arises resultant state by not-root condition.

Conjoined with one rootless-resultant aggregate, arise three aggregates ... conjoined with two aggregates, arise two aggregates. (All sections should be classified.)

2. CONDITIONS : NEGATIVE (ii) ENUMERATION CHAPTER

86. With not-root 3, not-predominance 3, not-prenascence 3, not-postnascence 3, not-repetition 3, not-kamma 2, not-resultant 2, not-jhāna 1, not-path 2, not-dissociation 3.

(Enumerate in the same way as the Faultless Triplet Negative Enumeration.)

End of Negative

3. CONDITIONS : POSITIVE-NEGATIVE

87. With root condition, not-predominance 3 ... not-dissociation 3.

(Enumerate in the same way as the Faultless Triplet Positive-Negative Enumeration.)

End of Positive-Negative

4. CONDITIONS : NEGATIVE-POSITIVE

88. With not-root condition, object 3 ... path 1 ... non-disappearance 3.

(Enumerate in the same way as the Faultless Triplet Negative-Positive Enumeration.)

End of Negative-Positive

End of " CONJOINED " CHAPTER

3. RESULTANT TRIPLET   VI. "ASSOCIATED" CHAPTER

1–4. CONDITIONS : SET OF FOUR

89. Associated with resultant state, arises resultant state by root condition.

Associated with one resultant aggregate, arise three aggregates. ...

With root 3. ...
With not-root 3. ...
With root condition, not-predominance 3. ...
With not-root condition, object 3. ...

End of "ASSOCIATED" CHAPTER

3. RESULTANT TRIPLET   VII. "INVESTIGATION" CHAPTER

1. CONDITIONS : POSITIVE   (i) CLASSIFICATION CHAPTER

Root 7

90. (i) Resultant state is related to resultant state by root condition.

Resultant roots are related to (their) associated aggregates by root condition.

At the moment of conception, resultant roots are related to (their) associated aggregates by root condition. (1)

(ii) Resultant state is related to state which is neither resultant nor producing resultant state by root condition.

Resultant roots are related to mind-produced matter by root condition.

At the moment of conception, resultant roots are related to kamma-produced matter by root condition. (2)

(iii) Resultant state is related to resultant (state) and state which is neither resultant nor producing resultant state by root condition.

Resultant roots are related to (their) associated aggregates and mind-produced matter by root condition.

At the moment of conception, resultant roots are related to (their) associated aggregates and kamma-produced matter by root condition. (3)

91. (iv) State producing resultant state is related to state producing resultant state by root condition.

Roots, the states producing resultant states, are related to (their) associated aggregates by root condition. (1)

(v) State producing resultant state is related to state which is neither resultant nor producing resultant state by root condition.

Roots, the states producing resultant states, are related to mind-produced matter by root condition. (2)

(vi) State producing resultant state is related to state producing resultant state and state which is neither resultant nor producing resultant state by root condition.

Roots, the states producing resultant states, are related to (their) associated aggregates and mind-produced matter by root condition. (3)

(vii) State which is neither resultant nor producing resultant state is related to state which is neither resultant nor producing resultant state by root condition.

Roots which are neither resultants nor producing resultant states are related to (their) associated aggregates and mind-produced matter by root condition.

Object 9

92. (i) Resultant state is related to resultant state by object condition.

One practises insight into the impermanency, suffering and impersonality of the resultant aggregates; enjoys and delights in (those aggregates). Taking it as object arises lust. arises wrong views, arises doubt, arises restlessness, arises grief. When the faultless or faulty (state) has ceased, the resultant arises as registering (consciousness). (1)

(ii) Resultant state is related to state producing resultant state by object condition.

Learners review (lower) Fruition. (They) practise insight into the impermanency, suffering and impersonality of the resultant aggregates; enjoy and delight in (those aggregates). Taking it as object arises lust . . . arises grief. By the knowledge of penetration into others' minds, (they) know the resultant mind of the other being. Resultant aggregates are related to knowledge of penetration into others' minds, knowledge of remembrance of past existences, knowledge of future existences by object condition. (2)

(iii) Resultant state is related to state which is neither resultant nor producing resultant state by object condition.

The Arahat reviews (Arahatta) Fruition. (He) practises insight into the impermanency, suffering and impersonality of the resultant aggregates. By the knowledge of penetration into others' minds, (he) knows the resultant mind of the other being. Resultant aggregates are related to knowledge of penetration into others' minds, knowledge of remembrance of past existences, knowledge of future existences, advertence by object condition. (3)

93. (iv) State producing resultant state is related to state producing resultant state by object condition.

After having offered the offering, having undertaken the precept, having fulfilled the duty of observance, (one) reviews it. (One) reviews (such acts) formerly well done. Having emerged from jhāna, (one) reviews the jhāna. Learners review change-of-lineage. (They) review purification. Learners, having emerged from Path, review the Path.

Learners review the eradicated defilements. (They) review the uneradicated defilements. (They) know the defilements addicted to before. (They) practise insight into the impermanency, suffering and impersonality of the aggregates which are the states producing resultant states ; enjoy and delight in (those aggregates). Taking it as object arises lust ... arises grief. By the knowledge of penetration into others' minds, (they) know the mind, which is the state producing resultant state, of the other being.

Faultless infinity of space is related to faultless infinity of consciousness by object condition. Faultless nothingness is related to faultless neither-perception-nor-non-perception by object condition. Aggregates, which are the states producing resultant states, are related to knowledge of supernormal power, knowledge of penetration into others' minds, knowledge of remembrance of past existences, knowledge of rebirths according to one's kamma, knowledge of future existences by object condition. (1)

(v) State producing resultant state is related to resultant state by object condition.

(They) practise insight into the impermanency, suffering and impersonality of the aggregates which are the states producing resultant states; enjoy and delight in (those aggregates). Taking it as object arises lust . . . arise grief. When the faultless or faulty (state) has ceased, the resultant arises as registering. Faultless infinity of space is related to resultant infinity of consciousness by object condition. Faultless nothingness is related to resultant neither-perception-nor-non-perception by object condition. (2)

(vi) State producing resultant state is related to state which is neither resultant nor producing resultant state by object condition.

Having emerged from (Arahatta) Path, the Arahat reviews the Path. He reviews the acts formerly well done. The Arahat reviews the eradicated defilements. (He) knows the defilements addicted to before. (He) practises insight into the impermanency, suffering and impersonality of the aggregates which are the states producing resultant states. By the knowledge of penetration into others' minds, (he) knows the mind, which is the state producing resultant state, of the other being. Faultless infinity of space is related to functional infinity of consciousness by object condition. Faultless nothingness is related to functional neither-perception-nor-non-perception by object condition. Aggregates, which are the states producing resultant states, are related to knowledge of penetration into others' minds, knowledge of remembrance of past existences, knowledge of rebirths according to one's kamma, knowledge of future existences, advertence by object condition. (3)

94. (vii) State which is neither resultant nor producing resultant state is related to state which is neither resultant nor producing resultant state by object condition.

The Arahat reviews Nibbāna. Nibbāna is related to advertence by object condition. The Arahat practises insight into the impermanency, suffering and impersonality of the eye-(-base); . . . ear . . . nose . . . tongue . . . body . . . visible objects . . . sounds . . . smells . . . tastes . . . tangible objects . . . (heart-)base; (he) practises insight into the impermanency, suffering and impersonality of the aggregates, the states which are neither resultants nor producing resultant states.

By the power of divine-eye, (the Arahat) sees the visible object. By the power of divine-ear element, hears the sound. By the knowledge of penetration into others' minds, (he) knows the mind, the state which is neither resultant nor producing resultant state, of the other being. Functional infinity of space is related to functional infinity of consciousness by object condition. Functional nothingness is related to functional neither-perception-nor-non-perception by object condition. Aggregates, the states which are neither resultants nor producing resultant states, are related to knowledge of supernormal power, knowledge of penetration into others' minds, knowledge of remembrance of past existences, knowledge of future existences, advertence by object condition. (1)

(viii) State which is neither resultant nor producing resultant state is related to resultant state by object condition.

Nibbāna is related to Fruition by object condition. Learners or common worldlings practise insight into the impermanency, suffering and impersonality of the eye(-base); enjoy and delight in (the eye-base). Taking it as object arises lust ... arises grief. When the faultless or faulty (state) has ceased, the resultant arises as registering. ... ear ... nose ... tongue ... body ... visible objects ... sounds ... smells ... tastes ... tangible objects ... (heart-)base. ... (They) practise insight into the impermanency, suffering and impersonality of the aggregates, the states which are neither resultants nor producing resultant states; enjoy and delight in (those aggregates). Taking it as object arises lust ... arises grief. When the faultless or faulty (state) has ceased, the resultant arises as registering. Visible object-base to eye-consciousness ... tangible object-base is related to body-consciousness by object condition. (2)

(ix) State which is neither resultant nor producing resultant state is related to state producing resultant state by object condition.

Learners review Nibbana. Nibbana is related to change-of-lineage, purification, Path by object condition. Learners or common worldlings practise insight into the impermanency, suffering and impersonality of the eye(-base); enjoy and delight in (the eye-base). Taking it as object arises lust ... arises grief. ... ear. ... (They) practise insight into the impermanency, suffering and impersonality of the aggregates, the states which are neither resultants nor producing resultant states; enjoy and delight in. ...

By the power of divine-eye, (they) see the visible object. By the power of divine-ear element, hear the sound. By the knowledge of penetration into others' minds, (they) know the mind, the state which is neither resultant nor producing resultant state, of the other being. Aggregates, the states which are neither resultants nor producing resultant states, are related to knowledge of supernormal power, knowledge of penetration into others' minds, knowledge of remembrance of past existences, knowledge of future existences by object condition. (3)

Predominance 10

95. (i) Resultant state is related to resultant state by predominance condition.

Conascence-predominance: Resultant predominance is related to (its) associated aggregates by predominance condition. (1)

(ii) Resultant state is related to state producing resultant state by predominance condition.

Object-predominance: Learners esteem and review (lower) Fruition. (They) esteem, enjoy and delight in the resultant aggregates. Taking it as estimable object, arises lust, arises wrong views. (2)

(iii) Resultant state is related to state which is neither resultant nor producing resultant state by predominance condition.

(It is of two kinds, namely :) (*a*) object-predominance, (*b*) conascence-predominance.

(*a*) *Object-predominance*: The Arahat esteems and reviews (Arahatta) Fruition.

(*b*) *Conascence-predominance*: Resultant predominance is related to mind-produced matter by predominance condition. (3)

(iv) Resultant state is related to resultant (state) and state which is neither resultant nor producing resultant state by predominance condition.

Conascence-predominance : Resultant predominance is related to (its) associated aggregates and mind-produced matter by predominance condition. (4)

96. (v) State producing resultant state is related to state producing resultant state by predominance condition.

(It is of two kinds, namely :) (*a*) object-predominance, (*b*) conascence-predominance.

(*a*) *Object-predominance* : After having offered the offering, having undertaken the precept, having fulfilled the duty of observance, (one) esteems and reviews it. (One) esteems and reviews (such acts) formerly well done. Having emerged from jhāna, (one) esteems and reviews the jhāna. Learners esteem and review change-of-lineage. (They) esteem and review purification. Learners, having emerged from Path, esteem and review the Path. (They) esteem, enjoy and delight in the aggregates which are the states producing resultant states. Taking it as estimable object, arises lust, arises wrong views.

(*b*) *Conascence-predominance* : Predominant states producing resultant states are related to (their) associated aggregates by predominance condition. (1)

(vi) State producing resultant state is related to state which is neither resultant nor producing resultant state by predominance condition.

(It is of two kinds, namely :) (*a*) object-predominance, (*b*) conascence-predominance.

(*a*) *Object-predominance* : Having emerged from (Arahatta) Path, the Arahat esteems and reviews the Path.

(*b*) *Conascence-predominance* : Predominant states producing resultant states are related to mind-produced matter by predominance condition. (2)

(vii) State producing resultant state is related to state producing resultant state and state which is neither resultant nor producing resultant state by predominance condition.

Conascence-predominance : Predominant states producing resultant states are related to (their) associated aggregates and mind-produced matter by predominance condition. (3)

(viii) State which is neither resultant nor producing resultant state is related to state which is neither resultant nor producing resultant state by predominance condition.

(It is of two kinds, namely :) (*a*) object-predominance, (*b*) conascence-predominance.

(*a*) *Object-predominance* : The Arahat esteems and reviews Nibbāna.

(*b*) *Conascence-predominance* : Predominant states, which are neither resultants nor producing resultant states, are related to (their) associated aggregates and mind-produced matter by predominance condition. (1)

(ix) State which is neither resultant nor producing resultant state is related to resultant state by predominance condition.

Object-predominance : Nibbāna is related to Fruition by predominance condition. (2)

(x) State which is neither resultant nor producing resultant state is related to state producing resultant state by predominance condition.

Object-predominance : Learners esteem and review Nibbāna. Nibbāna is related to change-of-lineage, purification, Path by predominance condition. (One) esteems, enjoys and delights in the eye. Taking it as estimable object, arises lust, arises wrong views. . . . ear . . . . (One) esteems, enjoys and delights in the aggregates, the states which are neither resultants nor producing resultant states. Taking it as estimable object, arises lust, arises wrong views. (3)

Proximity 7

97. (i) Resultant state is related to resultant state by proximity condition.

Preceding resultant aggregates are related to subsequent resultant aggregates by proximity condition. Five-fold consciousness is related to resultant mind-element by proximity condition. Resultant mind-element is related to resultant mind-consciousness element by proximity condition. (1)

(ii) Resultant state is related to state which is neither resultant nor producing resultant state by proximity condition.

Life-continuum is related to advertence by proximity

condition. Resultant mind-consciousness element is related to functional mind-consciousness element by proximity condition. (2)

(iii) State producing resultant state is related to state producing resultant state by proximity condition.

Preceding aggregates, the states producing resultant states, are related to subsequent aggregates, the states producing resultant states, by proximity condition. Adaptation to change-of-lineage; adaptation to purification; change-of-lineage to Path; purification is related to Path by proximity condition. (1)

(iv) State producing resultant state is related to resultant state by proximity condition.

Aggregates, the states producing resultant states, to emergence; Path to Fruition; Learners' adaptation to attainment of Fruition; having emerged from the attainment of Extinction, faultless neither-perception-nor-non-perception is related to the attainment of Fruition by proximity condition. (2)

(v) State which is neither resultant nor producing resultant state is related to state which is neither resultant nor producing resultant state by proximity condition.

Preceding aggregates, the states which are neither resultants nor producing resultant states, are related to subsequent aggregates, the states which are neither resultants nor producing resultant states, by proximity condition. (1)

(vi) State which is neither resultant nor producing resultant state is related to resultant state by proximity condition.

Advertence is related to five-fold consciousness by proximity condition. Aggregates, which are neither resultants nor producing resultant states, to emergence; the Arahat's adaptation to attainment of Fruition; having emerged from the attainment of Extinction, functional neither-perception-nor-non-perception is related to the attainment of Fruition by proximity condition. (2)

(vii) State which is neither resultant nor producing resultant state is related to state producing resultant state by proximity condition.

Advertence is related to the aggregates which are the states producing resultant states by proximity condition. (3)

Contiguity 7

98. Resultant state is related to resultant state by contiguity condition. (The same as proximity.)

Conascence 11

99. (i)–(iii) Resultant state is related to resultant state by conascence condition.

One resultant aggregate ... three.

(iv)–(vi) State producing resultant state is related to state producing resultant state by conascence condition. ... three.

(vii) State which is neither resultant nor producing resultant state is related to state which is neither resultant nor producing resultant state by conascence condition.

One aggregate, the state which is neither resultant nor producing resultant state. ... One great primary. ... External ... nutriment-produced... temperature-produced ... one great primary of non-percipient beings. ... (1)

(viii) State which is neither resultant nor producing resultant state is related to resultant state by conascence condition.

At the moment of conception, (heart-)base is related to resultant aggregates by conascence condition. (2)

(ix) States, resultant and state which is neither resultant nor producing resultant state, are related to resultant state by conascence condition.

At the moment of conception, one resultant aggregate and (heart-)base are related to three aggregates. ... (1)

(x) States, resultant and state which is neither resultant nor producing resultant state, are related to state which is neither resultant nor producing resultant state by conascence condition.

Resultant aggregates and great primaries are related to mind-produced matter. ... At the moment of conception, resultant aggregates and great primaries are related to kamma-produced matter by conascence condition. (2)

(xi) States, state producing resultant state and state

which is neither resultant nor producing resultant state, are related to state which is neither resultant nor producing resultant state by conascence condition.

Aggregates, the states producing resultant states, and great primaries are related to mind-produced matter by conascence condition. (1)

Mutuality 7

100. (i) Resultant state is related to resultant state by mutuality condition.

One resultant aggregate. ... At the moment of conception. ... (1)

(ii) Resultant state is related to state which is neither resultant nor producing resultant state by mutuality condition.

At the moment of conception, resultant aggregates are related to (heart-)base by mutuality condition. (2)

(iii) Resultant state is related to resultant and state which is neither resultant nor producing resultant state by mutuality condition.

At the moment of conception, one resultant aggregate is related to three aggregates and (heart-)base by mutuality condition. ... (3)

(iv) State producing resultant state is related to state producing resultant state by mutuality condition.

One aggregate, the state producing resultant state, is related to three aggregates ... two aggregates are related to two aggregates. ... (1)

(v) State which is neither resultant nor producing resultant state is related to state which is neither resultant nor producing resultant state by mutuality condition.

One aggregate, the state which is neither resultant nor producing resultant state, is related to three aggregates ... two aggregates are related to two aggregates. ... (1)

(vi) State which is neither resultant nor producing resultant state is related to resultant state by mutuality condition.

At the moment of conception, (heart-)base is related to resultant aggregates. ... (2)

(vii) States, resultant and state which is neither resultant nor producing resultant state, are related to resultant state. . . .

At the moment of conception, one resultant aggregate and (heart-)base . . . (1) (7 questions).

Dependence 13

101. (i)–(iii) Resultant state is related to resultant state by dependence condition. . . . three.

(iv)–(vi) State producing resultant state is related to state producing resultant state . . . three.

(vii) State which is neither resultant nor producing resultant state is related to state which is neither resultant nor producing resultant state. . . . (1)

(viii) State which is neither resultant nor producing resultant state is related to resultant state. . . .

Eye-base is related to eye-consciousness by dependence condition . . . body-base to body-consciousness . . . (heart-)base to resultant aggregates. . . . At the moment of conception, (heart-)base to resultant aggregates. . . . (2)

(ix) State which is neither resultant nor producing resultant state is related to state producing resultant state by dependence condition.

(Heart-)base is related to the aggregates, the states producing resultant states. . . . (3)

(x) States, resultant and state which is neither resultant nor producing resultant state, are related to resultant state by dependence condition.

One eye-consciousness-accompanied aggregate and eye-base . . . one body-consciousness-accompanied aggregate and body-base . . . one resultant aggregate and (heart-)base are related to three aggregates. . . . At the moment of conception, one resultant aggregate and (heart-)base. . . . (1)

(xi) States, resultant and state which is neither resultant nor producing resultant state, are related to state which is neither resultant nor producing resultant state. . . .

Resultant aggregates and great primaries . . . (Abbreviated.) At the moment of conception. . . . (2)

(xii) States, state producing resultant state and state which is neither resultant nor producing resultant state, are related to state producing resultant state by dependence condition.

One aggregate, the state producing resultant state, and (heart-)base. ... (1)

(xiii) States, state producing resultant state and state which is neither resultant nor producing resultant state, are related to state which is neither resultant nor producing resultant state by dependence condition.

The aggregates, the states producing resultant states, and great primaries are related to mind-produced matter. ... (2) (13 questions).

Strong-dependence 9

102. (i) Resultant state is related to resultant state by strong-dependence condition.

(It is of two kinds, namely :) (*a*) proximity-strong-dependence, (*b*) natural strong-dependence. ...

(*b*) *Natural strong-dependence* : Bodily happiness is related to bodily happiness, bodily pain, attainment of Fruition by strong-dependence condition. Bodily pain is related to bodily happiness, bodily pain, attainment of Fruition by strong-dependence condition. Attainment of Fruition is related to bodily happiness by strong-dependence condition. (1)

(ii) Resultant state is related to state producing resultant state by strong-dependence condition.

(It is of two kinds, namely :) (*a*) object-strong-dependence, (*b*) natural strong-dependence. ...

(*b*) *Natural strong-dependence* : By the strong-dependence of bodily happiness, (one) offers the offering, undertakes the precept ... causes schism in the Saṅgha. By the strong-dependence of bodily pain, (one) offers the offering, undertakes the precept ... causes schism in the Saṅgha. Bodily happiness, bodily pain is related to confidence ... wish by strong-dependence condition. (2)

(iii) Resultant state is related to state which is neither resultant nor producing resultant state by strong-dependence condition.

(It is of three kinds, namely :) (*a*) object-strong-dependence,

(*b*) proximity-strong-dependence, (*c*) natural strong-dependence. ...

(*c*) *Natural strong-dependence* : The Arahat, by the strong-dependence of bodily happiness, generates the functional attainment which has not yet arisen, enters the (functional) attainment which has arisen, practises insight into the impermanency, suffering and impersonality of the formations. (The Arahat), by the strong-dependence of bodily pain, generates the functional attainment which has not yet arisen, enters the (functional) attainment which has arisen. ... (3)

103. (iv) State producing resultant state is related to state producing resultant state by strong-dependence condition.

(It is of three kinds, namely :) (*a*) object-strong-dependence, (*b*) proximity-strong-dependence, (*c*) natural strong-dependence. ...

(*c*) *Natural strong-dependence* : By the strong-dependence of confidence, (one) offers the offering . . . ; arouses conceit, adopts wrong views. ... precept ... learning ... generosity. ... By the strong-dependence of wisdom, (one) offers the offering... adopts wrong views. ... lust ... hate ... delusion ... conceit ... wrong views. ... By the strong-dependence of wish, (one) offers the offering ... develops attainment, kills a living being ... causes schism in the Saṅgha. Confidence ... wish is related to confidence, precept ... wish by strong-dependence condition.

The preparation for first jhāna to first ... the preparation for neither-perception-nor-non-perception to neither-perception-nor-non-perception ... first jhāna to second ... nothingness to neither-perception-nor-non-perception. ...

The preparation for first Path to first ... the preparation for fourth Path to fourth ... first Path to second ... third Path is related to fourth Path by strong-dependence condition.

Learners, by the strong-dependence of the Path, generate the faultless attainments which have not yet arisen. ... The Path is related to the Learner's analytical knowledge of meaning ... knowledge of correct and faulty conclusion by strong-dependence condition.

Killing is related to killing ... wrong views by strong-dependence condition. ... Wrong views to wrong views ...

ill-will. . . . Matricide to matricide . . . wrong views with fixed destiny. . . . Wrong views with fixed destiny is related to wrong views with fixed destiny . . . causing schism in the Saṅgha by strong-dependence condition. (1)

(v) State producing resultant state is related to resultant state by strong-dependence condition.

(It is of two kinds, namely :) (*a*) proximity-strong-dependence, (*b*) natural strong-dependence. . . .

(*b*) *Natural strong-dependence* : By the strong-dependence of confidence, (one) tortures oneself, tortures oneself fully, experiences the suffering caused by searching. . . . By the strong-dependence of wish, (one) tortures oneself, tortures oneself fully. . . . Confidence . . . wish is related to bodily happiness, bodily pain, attainment of Fruition by strong-dependence condition. Faultless or faulty kamma is related to resultant by strong-dependence condition. Path is related to the attainment of Fruition by strong-dependence condition. (2)

(vi) State producing resultant state is related to state which is neither resultant nor producing resultant state by strong-dependence condition.

(It is of two kinds, namely :) (*a*) object-strong-dependence, (*b*) natural strong-dependence. . . .

(*b*) *Natural strong-dependence* : The Arahat, by the strong-dependence of the Path, generates the functional attainment which has not yet arisen, enters the (functional) attainment which has arisen, practises insight into the impermanency, suffering and impersonality of the formations. The Path is related to the Arahat's analytical knowledge of meaning . . . knowledge of correct and faulty conclusion by strong-dependence condition. (3)

104. (vii) State which is neither resultant nor producing resultant state is related to state which is neither resultant nor producing resultant state by strong-dependence condition.

(It is of three kinds, namely :) (*a*) object-strong-dependence, (*b*) proximity-strong-dependence, (*c*) natural strong-dependence. . . .

(*c*) *Natural strong-dependence* : The Arahat, by the strong-dependence of temperature . . . food . . . lodging-place, generates the functional attainment which has not yet arisen. . . . (1)

(viii) State which is neither resultant nor producing resultant state is related to resultant state by strong-dependence condition.

(It is of three kinds, namely :) (*a*) object-strong-dependence, (*b*) proximity-strong-dependence, (*c*) natural strong-dependence. ...

(*c*) *Natural strong-dependence*: Temperature, food, lodging-place is related to bodily happiness, bodily pain, attainment of Fruition by strong-dependence condition. (2)

(ix) State which is neither resultant nor producing resultant state is related to state producing resultant state by strong-dependence condition.

(It is of three kinds, namely :) (*a*) object-strong-dependence, (*b*) proximity-strong-dependence, (*c*) natural strong-dependence. ...

(*c*) *Natural strong-dependence*: By the strong-dependence of temperature, (one) offers the offering ... causes schism in the Saṅgha. ... food. ... By the strong-dependence of lodging-place, (one) offers the offering ... causes schism in the Saṅgha. Temperature, food, lodging-place is related to confidence ... wish by strong-dependence condition.

Prenascence 3

105. (i) State which is neither resultant nor producing resultant state is related to state which is neither resultant nor producing resultant state by prenascence condition.

(It is of two kinds, namely :) (*a*) object-prenascence, (*b*) base-prenascence.

(*a*) *Object-prenascence*: The Arahat practises insight into the impermanency ... of the eye ... body ... visible objects ... tangible objects. (He) practises insight into the impermanency ... of the (heart-)base. (The Arahat), by the power of divine-eye, (sees) the visible object. By the power of divine-ear element, (hears) the sound. ...

(*b*) *Base-prenascence*: (Heart-)base is related to the aggregates, the states which are neither resultants nor producing resultant states, by prenascence condition. (1)

(ii) State which is neither resultant nor producing resultant state is related to resultant state by prenascence condition.

(It is of two kinds, namely :) (*a*) object-prenascence, (*b*) base-prenascence.

(*a*) *Object-prenascence* : Learners or common worldlings practise insight into the impermanency, suffering and impersonality of the eye ; enjoy and delight in (the eye). Taking it as object arises lust ... arises grief. When the faultless or faulty has ceased, the resultant arises as registering. ... ear. ... (They) practise insight into the impermanency ... (heart-)base ... arises as registering.

Visible object-base to eye-consciousness by prenascence ... tangible object-base to body-consciousness. ...

(*b*) *Base-prenascence* : Eye-base to eye-consciousness ... body-base to body-consciousness ... (heart-)base is related to resultant aggregates by prenascence condition. (2)

(iii) State which is neither resultant nor producing resultant state is related to state producing resultant state by prenascence condition.

(It is of two kinds, namely :) (*a*) object-prenascence, (*b*) base-prenascence.

(*a*) *Object-prenascence* : Learners or common worldlings ... of the eye. Taking it as object arises lust ... arises grief. ... ear ... practise insight into the impermanency ... (heart-)base ... grief. (They), by the power of divine-eye, (see) the visible object. By the power of divine-ear element, (hear) the sound. ...

(*b*) *Base-prenascence* : (Heart-)base is related to the aggregates, the states producing resultant states, by prenascence condition. (3)

Postnascence 3

106. (i) Resultant state is related to state which is neither resultant nor producing resultant state by postnascence condition.

Postnascent resultant aggregates are related to this prenascent body by postnascence condition. (1)

(ii) State producing resultant state is related to state which is neither resultant nor producing resultant state by postnascence condition. ...

(iii) State which is neither resultant nor producing resultant state is related to state which is neither resultant nor producing resultant state by postnascence condition. ...

Repetition 2

107. (i) State producing resultant state is related to state producing resultant state by repetition condition.

Preceding aggregates, the states producing resultant states, are related to subsequent aggregates, the states producing resultant states. ... Adaptation to change-of-lineage; adaptation to purification; change-of-lineage to Path; purification is related to Path by repetition condition.

(ii) State which is neither resultant nor producing resultant state is related to state which is neither resultant nor producing resultant state by repetition condition.

Preceding ... condition.

Kamma 9

108. (i) Resultant state is related to resultant state by kamma condition.

Resultant volition is related to (its) associated aggregates by kamma condition. At the moment of conception, resultant volition. ... (1)

(ii) Resultant state is related to state which is neither resultant nor producing resultant state by kamma condition.

Resultant volition is related to mind-produced matter by kamma condition. At the moment of conception, resultant volition to kamma-produced matter. ... Volition is related to (heart-)base by kamma condition. (2)

(iii) Resultant state is related to resultant and state which is neither resultant nor producing resultant state by kamma condition.

Resultant volition is related to (its) associated aggregates and mind-produced matter by kamma condition. At the moment of conception, resultant volition is related to (its) associated aggregates and kamma-produced matter by kamma condition. (3)

(iv) State producing resultant state is related to state producing resultant state by kamma condition.

Volition, the state producing resultant state, is related to (its) associated aggregates by kamma condition. (1)

(v) State producing resultant state is related to resultant state by kamma condition.

Asynchronous volition, the state producing resultant state, is related to resultant aggregates by kamma condition. (2)

(vi) State producing resultant state is related to state which is neither resultant nor producing resultant state by kamma condition.

(It is of two kinds, namely :) (*a*) conascence(-kamma), (*b*) asynchronous (kamma).

(*a*) Conascent volition, the state producing resultant state, is related to mind-produced matter by kamma condition.

(*b*) Asynchronous volition, the state producing resultant state, is related to kamma-produced matter by kamma condition. (3)

(vii) State producing resultant state is related to resultant and state which is neither resultant nor producing resultant state by kamma condition.

Asynchronous volition, the state producing resultant state, is related to resultant aggregates and kamma-produced matter by kamma condition. (4)

(viii) State producing resultant state is related to state producing resultant state and state which is neither resultant nor producing resultant state by kamma condition.

Volition, the state producing resultant state, is related to (its) associated aggregates and mind-produced matter by kamma condition. (5)

(ix) State which is neither resultant nor producing resultant state is related to state which is neither resultant nor producing resultant state by kamma condition.

Volition, the state which is neither resultant nor producing resultant state, is related to (its) associated aggregates and mind-produced matter by kamma condition.

Resultant 3

109. (i) Resultant state is related to resultant state by resultant condition.

One resultant aggregate is related to three aggregates by resultant condition. ... At the moment of conception. ... (1)

(ii) Resultant state is related to state which is neither resultant nor producing resultant state by resultant condition.

Resultant aggregates are related to mind-produced matter by resultant condition. At the moment of conception, resultant aggregates are related to kamma-produced matter by resultant condition; aggregates to (heart-)base. ... (2)

(iii) Resultant state is related to resultant and state which is neither resultant nor producing resultant state by resultant condition.

One resultant aggregate is related to three aggregates and mind-produced matter by resultant condition. ... At the moment of conception, one resultant aggregate is related to three aggregates and kamma-produced matter by resultant condition. ... (3)

Nutriment 7

110. (i)–(iii) Resultant state is related to resultant state by nutriment condition.

Resultant nutriments to (their) associated aggregates ... three. (Conception also ought to be done for these three.)

(iv)–(vi) State producing resultant state is related to state producing resultant state by nutriment condition. ... three.

(vii) State which is neither resultant nor producing resultant state is related to state which is neither resultant nor producing resultant state by nutriment condition.

Nutriments, the states which are neither resultants nor producing resultant states, are related to (their) associated aggregates and mind-produced matter by nutriment condition. Edible food is related to this body by nutriment condition.

Faculty 9

111. (i)–(iii) Resultant state is related to resultant state by faculty condition. ... three. (Conception ought to be done.)

(iv)–(vi) State producing resultant state is related to state producing resultant state by faculty condition. ... three.

(vii) State which is neither resultant nor producing

resultant state is related to state which is neither resultant nor producing resultant state by faculty condition.

Faculties, the states which are neither resultants nor producing resultant states, are related to (their) associated aggregates and mind-produced matter by faculty condition. Physical life-faculty is related to kamma-produced matter by faculty condition. (1)

(viii) State which is neither resultant nor producing resultant state is related to resultant state by faculty condition.

Eye-faculty is related to eye-consciousness by faculty condition ... body-faculty ... (2)

(ix) States, resultant and state which is neither resultant nor producing resultant state, are related to resultant state by faculty condition.

Eye-faculty and eye-consciousness are related to eye-consciousness-accompanied aggregates by faculty condition ... body-faculty and body-consciousness are related to body-consciousness-accompanied aggregates by faculty condition.

Jhāna 7

112. (i)–(iii) Resultant state is related to resultant state by jhāna condition. ... three.

(iv)–(vi) State producing resultant state is related to state producing resultant state by jhāna condition. ... three.

(vii) State which is neither resultant nor producing resultant state is related to state which is neither resultant nor producing resultant state by jhāna condition.

Jhāna factors, the states which are neither resultants nor producing resultant states, are related to (their) associated aggregates and mind-produced matter by jhāna condition.

Path 7

113. (i)–(iii) Resultant state is related to resultant state by path condition. ... three

(iv)–(vi) State producing resultant state is related to state producing resultant state by path condition. ... three.

(vii) State which is neither resultant nor producing

resultant state is related to state which is neither resultant nor producing resultant state by path condition.

Path factors, the states which are neither resultants nor producing resultant states, are related to (their) associated aggregates and mind-produced matter by path condition.

Association 3

114. (i) Resultant state is related to resultant state by association condition.

One resultant aggregate to three ... two aggregates to two. ... At the moment of conception. ...

(ii) State producing resultant state is related to state producing resultant state by association condition. ...

(iii) State which is neither resultant nor producing resultant state is related to state which is neither resultant nor producing resultant state by association condition.

... two aggregates are related to two aggregates by association condition.

Dissociation 5

115. (i) Resultant state is related to state which is neither resultant nor producing resultant state by dissociation condition.

(It is of two kinds, namely :) (*a*) conascence, (*b*) postnascence.

(*a*) Conascent resultant aggregates are related to mind-produced matter by dissociation condition. At the moment of conception, resultant aggregates are related to kamma-produced matter by dissociation condition; aggregates are related to (heart-)base by dissociation condition.

(*b*) Postnascent resultant aggregates are related to this prenascent body by dissociation condition. (1)

(ii) State producing resultant state is related to state which is neither resultant nor producing resultant state by dissociation condition.

(It is of two kinds, namely :) (*a*) conascence, (*b*) postnascence.

(*a*) Conascent aggregates, the states producing resultant states, are related to mind-produced matter by dissociation condition.

(*b*) Postnascent aggregates, the states producing resultant states, are related to this prenascent body by dissociation condition. (1)

(iii) State which is neither resultant nor producing resultant state is related to state which is neither resultant nor producing resultant state by dissociation condition.

(It is of three kinds, namely :) (*a*) conascence, (*b*) prenascence, (*c*) postnascence.

(*a*) Conascent aggregates, the states which are neither resultants nor producing resultant states, are related to mind-produced matter by dissociation condition.

(*b*) Prenascent (heart-)base is related to the aggregates, the states which are neither resultants nor producing resultant states, by dissociation condition.

(*c*) Postnascent aggregates, the states which are neither resultants nor producing resultant states, are related to this prenascent body by dissociation condition. (1)

(iv) State which is neither resultant nor producing resultant state is related to resultant state by dissociation condition.

(It is of two kinds, namely :) (*a*) conascence, (*b*) prenascence.

(*a*) At the moment of conception, conascent (heart-)base is related to resultant aggregates by dissociation condition.

(*b*) Prenascent eye-base to eye-consciousness ... body-base to body-consciousness ... (heart-)base is related to resultant aggregates by dissociation condition. (2)

(v) State which is neither resultant nor producing resultant state is related to state producing resultant state by dissociation condition.

Prenascent (heart-)base is related to the aggregates, the states producing resultant states, by dissociation condition. (3)

Presence 13

116. (i) Resultant state is related to resultant state by presence condition.

One resultant aggregate to three. ... At the moment of conception, one resultant aggregate to three. ... (1)

(ii) Resultant state to state which is neither resultant nor producing resultant state. ...

(It is of two kinds, namely :) (*a*) conascence, (*b*) postnascence.

(a) Conascent resultant aggregates are related to mind-produced matter by presence condition. At the moment of conception, resultant aggregates are related to kamma-produced matter by presence condition.

(b) Postnascent resultant aggregates are related to this prenascent body by presence condition. (2)

(iii) Resultant state is related to resultant and state which is neither resultant nor producing resultant state by presence condition.

One resultant aggregate is related to three aggregates and mind-produced matter by presence condition. ... At the moment of conception. ... (3)

117. (iv) State producing resultant state is related to state producing resultant state by presence condition.

... two aggregates are related to two aggregates by presence condition. (1)

(v) State producing resultant state is related to state which is neither resultant nor producing resultant state by presence condition.

(It is of two kinds, namely :) (a) conascence, (b) postnascence.

(a) Conascent aggregates, the states producing resultant states, are related to mind-produced matter by presence condition.

(b) Postnascent aggregates, the states producing resultant states, are related to this prenascent body by presence condition. (2)

(vi) State producing resultant state to state producing resultant state and state which is neither resultant nor producing resultant state. ...

One aggregate, the state producing resultant state, is related to three aggregates and mind-produced matter by presence condition. ... (3)

(vii) State which is neither resultant nor producing resultant state is related to state which is neither resultant nor producing resultant state. ...

(It is of five kinds, namely :) (a) conascence, (b) prenascence, (c) postnascence, (d) nutriment, (e) faculty.

(a) One conascent aggregate, the state which is neither resultant nor producing resultant state, is related to three

aggregates and mind-produced matter by presence condition ...
two aggregates are related to two aggregates and mind-produced matter by presence condition.

One great primary ... great primaries are related to mind-produced and kamma-produced derived matter by presence condition. External ... nutriment-produced ... temperature-produced ... one great primary of non-percipient beings. ...

(b) (*Object-*)*prenascence* : The Arahat ... impermanency ... of the eye. ... ear ... impermanency ... (heart)-base. (The Arahat), by the power of divine-eye, sees the visible object. By the power of divine-ear element, hears the sound.

(*Base-*)*prenascence* : (Heart-)base is related to the aggregates, the states which are neither resultants nor producing resultant states, by presence condition.

(c) Postnascent aggregates, the states which are neither resultants nor producing resultant states, are related to this prenascent body by presence condition.

(d) Edible food is related to this body by presence condition.

(e) Physical life-faculty is related to kamma-produced matter by presence condition. (1)

(viii) State which is neither resultant nor producing resultant state is related to resultant state by presence condition.

(It is of two kinds, namely :) (a) conascence, (b) prenascence.

(a) At the moment of conception, conascent (heart-)base is related to resultant aggregates by presence condition.

(b) (*Object-*)*prenascence* : Learners or common worldlings ... impermanency ... of the eye ; enjoy. ... Taking it as object (arises) lust ... grief. When the faultless or faulty has ceased, the resultant (arises as) registering. ... ear ... (heart-)base ... resultant (arises as) registering. Visible object-base to eye-consciousness ... tangible object-base to body-consciousness. ...

(*Base-*)*prenascence* : Eye-base to eye-consciousness ... body-base to body-consciousness ... (heart-)base is related to resultant aggregates by presence condition. (2)

(ix) State which is neither resultant nor producing resultant state is related to state producing resultant state by presence condition.

(*Object-*)*prenascence* : Learners or common worldlings ... impermanency ... of the eye ; enjoy ... arises grief. ... ear ... impermanency ... of the (heart-)base ... arises grief. (They), by the power of divine-eye. ...

(*Base-*)*prenascence* : (Heart-)base is related to the aggregates, the states producing resultant states, by presence condition. (3)
118. (x) States, resultant and state which is neither resultant nor producing resultant state, are related to resultant state by presence condition.

(*Mixed*) *conascence-prenascence* : One conascent eye-consciousness-accompanied aggregate and eye-base to three ... body-consciousness-accompanied. ... One resultant aggregate and (heart-)base to three aggregates. ... At the moment of conception, one resultant aggregate and (heart-)base to three. ... (1)

(xi) States, resultant and state which is neither resultant nor producing resultant state, are related to state which is neither resultant nor producing resultant state by presence condition.

(It is of three kinds, namely :) (*a*) conascence, (*b*) (mixed) postnascence-nutriment, (*c*) (mixed postnascence-)faculty.

(*a*) Conascent resultant aggregates and great primaries are related to mind-produced matter by presence condition. At the moment of conception, resultant aggregates and great primaries are related to kamma-produced matter by presence condition.

(*b*) (*Mixed postnascence-nutriment* :) Postnascent resultant aggregates and edible food to this body. ...

(*c*) (*Mixed postnascence-faculty* :) Postnascent resultant aggregates and physical life-faculty are related to kamma-produced matter by presence condition. (2)

(xii) States, state producing resultant state and state which is neither resultant nor producing resultant state, to state producing resultant state. ...

(*Mixed*) *conascence-prenascence* : One conascent aggregate, the state producing resultant state, and (heart-)base to three. ... (1)

(xiii) States, state producing resultant state and state which is neither resultant nor producing resultant state, are related to state which is neither resultant nor producing resultant state by presence condition.

(It is of three kinds, namely :) (*a*) conascence, (*b*) (mixed) postnascence-nutriment, (*c*) (mixed postnascence-)faculty.

(*a*) Conascent aggregates, the states producing resultant states, and great primaries are related to mind-produced matter by presence condition.

(*b*) (*Mixed postnascence-nutriment* :) Postnascent aggregates, the states producing resultant states, and edible food are related to this prenascent body by presence condition.

(*c*) (*Mixed postnascence-faculty* :) Postnascent aggregates, the states producing resultant states, and physical life-faculty are related to kamma-produced matter by presence condition. (2)

Absence 7, Disappearance 7 and Non-disappearance 13

119. Resultant state ... (Absence and disappearance are the same as proximity. Non-disappearance is the same as presence.)

I. CONDITIONS : POSITIVE   (ii) ENUMERATION CHAPTER

By Ones

120. With root 7, object 9, predominance 10, proximity 7, contiguity 7, conascence 11, mutuality 7, dependence 13, strong-dependence 9, prenascence 3, postnascence 3, repetition 2, kamma 9, resultant 3, nutriment 7, faculty 9, jhāna 7, path 7, association 3, dissociation 5, presence 13, absence 7, disappearance 7, non-disappearance 13.

Root

Common 11

With root condition and predominance (there are) 7 (answers), conascence 7, mutuality 5, dependence 7, resultant 3, faculty 7, path 7, association 3, dissociation 3, presence 7, non-disappearance 7.

(Expand in the same way as enumerated in the Positive Enumeration of the Faultless Triplet "Investigation" Chapter.)

End of Positive

2. SELECTION OF THE CONDITIONS FOR NEGATIVE

121. (i) Resultant state is related to resultant state by object condition, conascence condition, strong-dependence condition. (1)

(ii) Resultant state is related to state producing resultant state by object condition, strong-dependence condition. (2)

(iii) Resultant state is related to state which is neither resultant nor producing resultant state by object condition, conascence condition, strong-dependence condition, postnascence condition. (3)

(iv) Resultant state is related to resultant and state which is neither resultant nor producing resultant state by conascence condition. (4)

(v) State producing resultant state is related to state producing resultant state by object condition, conascence condition, strong-dependence condition. (1)

(vi) State producing resultant state is related to resultant state by object condition, strong-dependence condition, kamma condition. (2)

(vii) State producing resultant state is related to state which is neither resultant nor producing resultant state by object condition, conascence condition, strong-dependence condition, postnascence condition, kamma condition. (3)

(viii) State producing resultant state is related to resultant and state which is neither resultant nor producing resultant state by kamma condition. (4)

(ix) State producing resultant state is related to state producing resultant state and state which is neither resultant nor producing resultant state by conascence condition. (5)

(x) State which is neither resultant nor producing resultant state is related to state which is neither resultant nor producing resultant state by object condition, conascence condition, strong-dependence condition, prenascence condition, postnascence condition, nutriment condition, faculty condition. (1)

(xi) State which is neither resultant nor producing resultant state is related to resultant state by object condition, conascence condition, strong-dependence condition, prenascence condition. (2)

(xii) State which is neither resultant nor producing resultant state is related to state producing resultant state by object condition, strong-dependence condition, prenascence condition. (3)

(xiii) States, resultant and state which is neither resultant nor producing resultant state, are related to resultant state by conascence-prenascence. (1)

(xiv) States, resultant and state which is neither resultant nor producing resultant state, are related to state which is neither resultant nor producing resultant state by conascence, postnascence-nutriment-faculty. (2)

(xv) States, state producing resultant state and state which is neither resultant nor producing resultant state, are related to state producing resultant state by conascence-prenascence. (1)

(xvi) States, state producing resultant state and state which is neither resultant nor producing resultant state, are related to state which is neither resultant nor producing resultant state by conascence, postnascence-nutriment-faculty. (2)

2. CONDITIONS : NEGATIVE (ii) ENUMERATION CHAPTER

By Ones

122. With not-root 16, not-object 16, not-predominance 16, not-proximity 16, not-contiguity 16, not-conascence 12, not-mutuality 12, not-dependence 12, not-strong-dependence 16, not-prenascence 14, not-postnascence 16, not-repetition 16, not-kamma 15, not-resultant 14, not-nutriment 16, not-faculty 16, not-jhāna 16, not-path 16, not-association 12, not-dissociation 10, not-presence 10, not-absence 16, not-disappearance 16, not-non-disappearance 10.

By Twos

With not-root condition and not-object 16 ... not-non-disappearance 10.

(Expand in the same way as expanded in the Negative Enumeration of Faultless Triplet.)

End of Negative

3. CONDITIONS : POSITIVE-NEGATIVE

Root

By Twos

123. With root condition, not-object 7, not-predominance 7, not-proximity 7, not-contiguity 7, not-mutuality 3, not-strong-dependence 7, not-prenascence 7, not-postnascence 7, not-repetition 7, not-kamma 7, not-resultant 4, not-nutriment 7, not-faculty 7, not-jhāna 7, not-path 7, not-association 3, not-dissociation 3, not-absence 7, not-disappearance 7.

Combinations

Combinations of root, conascence, dependence, presence and non-disappearance, not-object 7 . . . not-mutuality 3 . . . not-resultant 4 . . . not-association 3, not-dissociation 3 . . . not-disappearance 7.

(Expand in the same way as expanded in the Positive-Negative Enumeration of Faultless Triplet. This recital should be done without confusion.)

End of Positive-Negative

4. CONDITIONS : NEGATIVE-POSITIVE

Not-root

By Twos

124. With not-root condition, object 9, predominance 10, proximity 7, contiguity 7, conascence 11, mutuality 7, dependence 13, strong-dependence 9, prenascence 3, postnascence 3, repetition 2, kamma 9, resultant 3, nutriment 7, faculty 9, jhāna 7, path 7, association 3, dissociation 5, presence 13, absence 7, disappearance 7, non-disappearance 13.

By Threes

With not-root and not-object conditions, predominance 7 . . . non-disappearance 13.

(Expand in the same way as expanded in the Negative-Positive Enumeration of Faultless Triplet.)

End of Negative-Positive

END OF RESULTANT TRIPLET

4. CLINGING TRIPLET [1]   I. "DEPENDENT" CHAPTER
I. CONDITIONS: POSITIVE   (i) CLASSIFICATION CHAPTER

Root 9

1. (i) Dependent on state acquired by clinging and favourable to clinging, arises state acquired by clinging and favourable to clinging by root condition.

Dependent on one aggregate acquired by clinging and favourable to clinging, arise three aggregates ... dependent on two aggregates, arise two aggregates. At the moment of conception, dependent on one aggregate acquired by clinging and favourable to clinging, arise three aggregates and kamma-produced matter ... dependent on two aggregates, arise two aggregates and kamma-produced matter; dependent on aggregates, arises (heart-)base; dependent on (heart-)base, arise aggregates.

Dependent on one great primary acquired by clinging and favourable to clinging, arise three great primaries ... dependent on two great primaries, arise two great primaries; dependent on great primaries, arises kamma-produced derived matter. (1)

(ii) Dependent on state acquired by clinging and favourable to clinging, arises state not acquired by clinging but favourable to clinging by root condition.

Dependent on aggregates acquired by clinging and favourable to clinging, arises mind-produced matter. (2)

(iii) Dependent on state acquired by clinging and favourable to clinging, arise states, (state) acquired by clinging and favourable to clinging and (state) not acquired by clinging but favourable to clinging, by root condition.

Dependent on one aggregate acquired by clinging and favourable to clinging, arise three aggregates and mind-produced matter ... dependent on two aggregates, arise two aggregates and mind-produced matter. (3)

(iv) Dependent on state not acquired by clinging but favourable to clinging, arises state not acquired by clinging but favourable to clinging by root condition.

---

[1] Comprises (1) state acquired by clinging and favourable to clinging, (2) state not acquired by clinging but favourable to clinging, (3) state not acquired by clinging and not favourable to clinging.

Dependent on one aggregate not acquired by clinging but favourable to clinging, arise three aggregates and mind-produced matter ... dependent on two aggregates, arise two aggregates and mind-produced matter. Dependent on one great primary not acquired by clinging but favourable to clinging, arise three great primaries ... dependent on great primaries, arises mind-produced derived matter. (1)

(v) Dependent on state not acquired by clinging and not favourable to clinging, arises state not acquired by clinging and not favourable to clinging by root condition.

Dependent on one aggregate not acquired by clinging and not favourable to clinging, arise three aggregates ... dependent on two aggregates, arise two aggregates. (1)

(vi) Dependent on state not acquired by clinging and not favourable to clinging, arises state not acquired by clinging but favourable to clinging by root condition.

Dependent on aggregates not acquired by clinging and not favourable to clinging, arises mind-produced matter. (2)

(vii) Dependent on state not acquired by clinging and not favourable to clinging, arise states, not acquired by clinging but favourable to clinging and not acquired by clinging and not favourable to clinging, by root condition.

Dependent on one aggregate not acquired by clinging and not favourable to clinging, arise three aggregates and mind-produced matter ... dependent on two aggregates, arise two aggregates and mind-produced matter. (3)

((viii) Dependent on state not acquired by clinging but favourable to clinging and (state) not acquired by clinging and not favourable to clinging, arises state not acquired by clinging but favourable to clinging by root condition.

Dependent on aggregates not acquired by clinging and not favourable to clinging and great primaries, arises mind-produced matter. (1)

(ix) Dependent on state acquired by clinging and favourable to clinging and (state) not acquired by clinging but favourable to clinging, arises state not acquired by clinging but favourable to clinging by root condition.

Dependent on aggregates acquired by clinging and favourable to clinging and great primaries, arises mind-produced matter.

Object 3

2. (i) Dependent on state acquired by clinging and favourable to clinging, arises state acquired by clinging and favourable to clinging by object condition.

Dependent on one aggregate acquired by clinging and favourable to clinging. ... At the moment of conception. ...

(ii) Dependent on state not acquired by clinging but favourable to clinging. ...

(iii) Dependent on state not acquired by clinging and not favourable to clinging ... by object condition. ... three.

Predominance 5

3. (i) Dependent on state not acquired by clinging but favourable to clinging, arises state not acquired by clinging but favourable to clinging by predominance condition.

Dependent on one aggregate not acquired by clinging but favourable to clinging, arise three aggregates and mind-produced matter. ... Dependent on one great primary ... dependent on great primaries, arises mind-produced derived matter. (1)

(ii)–(iv) Dependent on state not acquired by clinging and not favourable to clinging ... three.

(v) Dependent on state not acquired by clinging but favourable to clinging and not acquired by clinging and not favourable to clinging, arises state not acquired by clinging but favourable to clinging by predominance condition.

Dependent on aggregates not acquired by clinging and not favourable to clinging and great primaries, arises mind-produced matter.

Proximity, etc.

4. (i) Dependent on state acquired by clinging and favourable to clinging, arises state acquired by clinging and favourable to clinging by proximity condition ... by contiguity condition ... by conascence condition.

Dependent on one aggregate acquired by clinging and favourable to clinging. ... At the moment of conception. ...

Dependent on one great primary ... dependent on great primaries, arises kamma-produced derived matter ; dependent on one great primary of non-percipient beings ... dependent on great primaries, arises kamma-produced derived matter.

(ii)–(iii) Dependent on state acquired by clinging and favourable to clinging ... three.

(iv) Dependent on state not acquired by clinging but favourable to clinging, arises state not acquired by clinging but favourable to clinging by conascence condition.

Dependent on one aggregate not acquired by clinging but favourable to clinging, arise three aggregates and mind-produced matter. ... Dependent on one great primary ... dependent on great primaries, arises mind-produced derived matter. External ... nutriment-produced ... dependent on one temperature-produced great primary. ....

(v)–(vii) Dependent on state not acquired by clinging and not favourable to clinging ... three.

(viii) Dependent on state not acquired by clinging but favourable to clinging and not acquired by clinging and not favourable to clinging ... not acquired by clinging but favourable to clinging. ...

(ix) Dependent on state acquired by clinging and favourable to clinging and not acquired by clinging but favourable to clinging, (arises state) not acquired by clinging but favourable to clinging. ...

Mutuality 3

5. (i) Dependent on state acquired by clinging and favourable to clinging, arises state acquired by clinging and favourable to clinging by mutuality condition.

Dependent on one aggregate acquired by clinging and favourable to clinging. ... At the moment of conception, dependent on one aggregate acquired by clinging and favourable to clinging, arise three aggregates and (heart-)base ... dependent on aggregates, arises (heart-)base ; dependent on (heart-)base, arise aggregates. Dependent on one great primary ... dependent on two great primaries, arise two great primaries ; dependent on one great primary of non-percipient beings. ...

(ii) Dependent on state not acquired by clinging but favourable to clinging. ... External ... nutriment-produced ... temperature-produced. ...

(iii) Dependent on state not acquired by clinging and not favourable to clinging. ...

Dependence 9, Strong-dependence 3

6. Dependent on state acquired by clinging and favourable to clinging ... by dependence condition. ... nine. ... by strong-dependence condition ... three.

Prenascence 3

7. (i)–(iii) Dependent on state acquired by clinging and favourable to clinging, arises state acquired by clinging and favourable to clinging by prenascence condition. ... three.

Repetition 2

8. (i) Dependent on state not acquired by clinging but favourable to clinging, arises state not acquired by clinging but favourable to clinging by repetition condition.

Dependent on one aggregate not acquired by clinging but favourable to clinging. ...

(ii) Dependent on state not acquired by clinging and not favourable to clinging, arises state not acquired by clinging and not favourable to clinging by repetition condition.

Dependent on one aggregate not acquired by clinging and not favourable to clinging. ...

Kamma 9

9. Dependent on state acquired by clinging and favourable to clinging, arises state acquired by clinging and favourable to clinging by kamma condition. (The same as root condition nine.)

Resultant 9

10. (i)–(iii) Dependent on state acquired by clinging and favourable to clinging, arises state acquired by clinging and favourable to clinging by resultant condition. ... three.

(iv) Dependent on state not acquired by clinging but favourable to clinging, arises state not acquired by clinging but favourable to clinging by resultant condition.

Dependent on one great primary ... dependent on great primaries, arises mind-produced derived matter.

(v)–(ix) Dependent on state not acquired by clinging and not favourable to clinging, arises state not acquired by clinging and not favourable to clinging by resultant condition.

Dependent on one resultant aggregate not acquired by clinging and not favourable to clinging, arise three aggregates ... nine.

Nutriment, etc.

11. Dependent on state acquired by clinging and favourable to clinging, arises state acquired by clinging and favourable to clinging by nutriment condition ... by faculty condition ... by jhāna condition ... by path condition ... by association condition ... by dissociation condition ... by presence condition ... by absence condition ... by disappearance condition ... by non-disappearance condition. ...

(Expand as expanded in " Dependent " Chapter of the Faultless Triplet by way of recital.)

I. CONDITIONS : POSITIVE   (ii) ENUMERATION CHAPTER

By Ones

12. With root 9, object 3, predominance 5, proximity 3, contiguity 3, conascence 9, mutuality 3, dependence 9, strong-dependence 3, prenascence 3, repetition 2, kamma 9, resultant 9, nutriment 9, faculty 9, jhāna 9, path 9, association 3, dissociation 9, presence 9, absence 3, disappearance 3, non-disappearance 9.

By Twos [1]

With root condition and object 3 ... non-disappearance 9.

(Enumerate as enumerated in the " Dependent " Enumeration of the Faultless Triplet by way of recital.)

End of Positive

[1] Cannot be " common " as in the Text.

2. CONDITIONS : NEGATIVE   (i) CLASSIFICATION CHAPTER

Not-root 5

13. (i) Dependent on state acquired by clinging and favourable to clinging, arises state acquired by clinging and favourable to clinging by not-root condition.

Dependent on one rootless aggregate acquired by clinging and favourable to clinging, arise three aggregates . . . dependent on two aggregates, arise two aggregates. At the moment of rootless conception, dependent on one aggregate acquired by clinging and favourable to clinging, arise three aggregates and kamma-produced matter . . . dependent on two aggregates, arise two aggregates and kamma-produced matter ; dependent on aggregates, arises (heart-)base ; dependent on (heart-)base, arise aggregates.

Dependent on one great primary, arise three great primaries . . . dependent on great primaries, arises kamma-produced derived matter. Dependent on one great primary of non-percipient beings . . . dependent on great primaries, arises kamma-produced derived matter. (1)

(ii) Dependent on state acquired by clinging and favourable to clinging, arises state not acquired by clinging but favourable to clinging by not-root condition.

Dependent on rootless aggregates acquired by clinging and favourable to clinging, arises mind-produced matter. (2)

(iii) Dependent on state acquired by clinging and favourable to clinging, arise states, acquired by clinging and favourable to clinging and not acquired by clinging but favourable to clinging, by not-root condition.

Dependent on one rootless aggregate acquired by clinging and favourable to clinging, arise three aggregates and mind-produced matter . . . dependent on two aggregates, arise two aggregates and mind-produced matter. (3)

(iv) Dependent on state not acquired by clinging but favourable to clinging, arises state not acquired by clinging but favourable to clinging by not-root condition.

Dependent on one rootless aggregate not acquired by clinging but favourable to clinging, arise three aggregates and mind-produced matter ... dependent on two aggregates, arise two aggregates and mind-produced matter.

Dependent on one great primary not acquired by clinging but favourable to clinging ... dependent on great primaries, arises mind-produced derived matter. External ... nutriment-produced ... dependent on one temperature-produced great primary ... dependent on great primaries, arises derived matter.

Dependent on doubt-accompanied or restlessness-accompanied aggregates, arises doubt-accompanied or restlessness-accompanied delusion. (1)

(v) Dependent on state acquired by clinging and favourable to clinging and not acquired by clinging but favourable to clinging, arises state not acquired by clinging but favourable to clinging by not-root condition.

Dependent on rootless aggregates acquired by clinging and favourable to clinging and great primaries, arises mind-produced matter. (1)

Not-object 6

14. (i) Dependent on state acquired by clinging and favourable to clinging, arises state acquired by clinging and favourable to clinging by not-object condition.

At the moment of conception, dependent on aggregates acquired by clinging and favourable to clinging, arises kamma-produced matter ; dependent on aggregates, arises (heart-)base. Dependent on one great primary ... dependent on one great primary of non-percipient beings. ... (1)

(ii) Dependent on state acquired by clinging and favourable to clinging, arises state not acquired by clinging but favourable to clinging by not-object condition.

Dependent on aggregates acquired by clinging and favourable to clinging, arises mind-produced matter. (2)

(iii) Dependent on state not acquired by clinging but favourable to clinging, arises state not acquired by clinging but favourable to clinging by not-object condition.

Dependent on aggregates not acquired by clinging but favourable to clinging, arises mind-produced matter. Dependent on one great primary. ... External ... nutriment-produced ... dependent on one temperature-produced great primary. ... (1)

(iv) Dependent on state not acquired by clinging and not favourable to clinging, arises state not acquired by clinging but favourable to clinging by not-object condition.

Dependent on aggregates not acquired by clinging and not favourable to clinging, arises mind-produced matter. (1)

(v) Dependent on state not acquired by clinging but favourable to clinging and not acquired by clinging and not favourable to clinging, arises state not acquired by clinging but favourable to clinging by not-object condition.

Dependent on aggregates not acquired by clinging and not favourable to clinging and great primaries, arises mind-produced matter. (1)

(vi) Dependent on state acquired by clinging and favourable to clinging and not acquired by clinging but favourable to clinging, arises state not acquired by clinging but favourable to clinging by not-object condition.

Dependent on aggregates acquired by clinging and favourable to clinging and great primaries, arises mind-produced matter. (1)

Not-predominance 6

15. (i)–(iii) Dependent on state acquired by clinging and favourable to clinging, arises state acquired by clinging and favourable to clinging by not-predominance condition. (Conception is completed) ... three.

(iv) Dependent on state not acquired by clinging but favourable to clinging ... one.

(v) Dependent on state not acquired by clinging and not favourable to clinging, arises state not acquired by clinging and not favourable to clinging by not-predominance condition.

Dependent on aggregates not acquired by clinging and not favourable to clinging, arises predominance not acquired by clinging and not favourable to clinging. (1)

(vi) Dependent on state acquired by clinging and favourable to clinging and not acquired by clinging but favourable to clinging, arises state not acquired by clinging but favourable to clinging by not-predominance condition.

Dependent on aggregates acquired by clinging and favourable to clinging and great primaries, arises mind-produced matter.

Not-proximity, etc.

16. Dependent on state acquired by clinging and favourable to clinging, arises state acquired by clinging and favourable to clinging by not-proximity condition ... by not-contiguity condition ... by not-mutuality condition ... by not-strong-dependence condition ... by not-prenascence condition ... by not-postnascence condition ... by not-repetition condition. ...

Dependent on state not acquired by clinging and not favourable to clinging, arises state not acquired by clinging and not favourable to clinging by not-repetition condition.

Dependent on one resultant aggregate not acquired by clinging and not favourable to clinging, arise three aggregates. ... (Abbreviated.)

Not-kamma 2

17. (i) Dependent on state not acquired by clinging but favourable to clinging, arises state not acquired by clinging but favourable to clinging by not-kamma condition.

Dependent on aggregates not acquired by clinging but favourable to clinging, arises volition not acquired by clinging but favourable to clinging. External ... nutriment-produced ... dependent on one temperature-produced great primary. ... (1)

(ii) Dependent on state not acquired by clinging and not favourable to clinging, arises state not acquired by clinging and not favourable to clinging by not-kamma condition.

Dependent on faultless aggregates not acquired by clinging and not favourable to clinging, arises volition not acquired by clinging and not favourable to clinging. (1)

Not-resultant 6

18. (i) Dependent on state acquired by clinging and favourable to clinging, arises state acquired by clinging and favourable to clinging by not-resultant condition.

Dependent on one great primary of non-percipient beings ...

dependent on great primaries, arises kamma-produced derived matter.

(ii) Dependent on state not acquired by clinging but favourable to clinging, arises state not acquired by clinging but favourable to clinging by not-resultant condition. ... one.

(iii)–(v) Dependent on state not acquired by clinging and not favourable to clinging, arises state not acquired by clinging and not favourable to clinging by not-resultant condition.

Dependent on one faultless aggregate not acquired by clinging and not favourable to clinging, arise three aggregates ... three.

(vi) Dependent on state, not acquired by clinging but favourable to clinging and not acquired by clinging and not favourable to clinging, arises state not acquired by clinging but favourable to clinging by not-resultant condition.

Dependent on faultless aggregates not acquired by clinging and not favourable to clinging and great primaries, arises mind-produced-matter.

Not-nutriment 2

19. (i) Dependent on state acquired by clinging and favourable to clinging, arises state acquired by clinging and favourable to clinging by not-nutriment condition.

Dependent on one great primary of non-percipient beings. ... (1)

(ii) Dependent on state not acquired by clinging but favourable to clinging, arises state not acquired by clinging but favourable to clinging by not-nutriment condition.

External ... dependent on one temperature-produced great primary. ...

Not-faculty 2

20. (i) Dependent on state acquired by clinging and favourable to clinging, arises state acquired by clinging and favourable to clinging by not-faculty condition.

Dependent on great primaries of non-percipient beings, arises physical life-faculty. (1)

(ii) Dependent on state not acquired by clinging but

favourable to clinging, arises state not acquired by clinging but favourable to clinging by not-faculty condition.

External ... nutriment-produced ... dependent on one temperature-produced great primary. ...

Not-jhāna 2

21. (i) Dependent on state acquired by clinging and favourable to clinging, arises state acquired by clinging and favourable to clinging by not-jhāna condition.

Dependent on one fivefold consciousness-accompanied aggregate, arise three aggregates. ...

Dependent on one great primary of non-percipient beings. ... (1)

(ii) Dependent on state not acquired by clinging but favourable to clinging, arises state not acquired by clinging but favourable to clinging by not-jhāna condition.

External ... nutriment-produced ... dependent on one temperature-produced great primary. ...

Not-path 5

22. Dependent on state acquired by clinging and favourable to clinging, arises state acquired by clinging and favourable to clinging by not-path condition.

Dependent on one rootless aggregate acquired by clinging and favourable to clinging, arise three aggregates ... five.

Not-association 6

23. Dependent on state acquired by clinging and favourable to clinging, arises state acquired by clinging and favourable to clinging by not-association condition. (The same as not-object condition.)

Not-dissociation 3

24. (i) Dependent on state acquired by clinging and favourable to clinging, arises state acquired by clinging and favourable to clinging by not-dissociation condition.

In the immaterial plane, dependent on one aggregate acquired by clinging and favourable to clinging, arise three aggregates. ... Dependent on one great primary of non-percipient beings. ... (1)

(ii) Dependent on state not acquired by clinging but favourable to clinging, arises state not acquired by clinging but favourable to clinging by not-dissociation condition.

In the immaterial plane, dependent on one aggregate not acquired by clinging but favourable to clinging, arise three aggregates. ... External ... nutriment-produced ... dependent on one temperature-produced great primary. ... (1)

(iii) Dependent on state not acquired by clinging and not favourable to clinging, arises state not acquired by clinging and not favourable to clinging by not-dissociation condition.

In the immaterial plane, dependent on one aggregate not acquired by clinging and not favourable to clinging, arise three aggregates ... dependent on two aggregates, arise two aggregates. (1)

Not-absence 6, Not-disappearance 6

25. Dependent on state acquired by clinging and favourable to clinging, arises state acquired by clinging and favourable to clinging by not-absence condition ... by not-disappearance condition.

(Expand in the same way as expanded in the Negative Chapter of Faultless Triplet.)

2. CONDITIONS : NEGATIVE (ii) ENUMERATION CHAPTER

By Ones

26. With not-root 5, not-object 6, not-predominance 6, not-proximity 6, not-contiguity 6, not-mutuality 6, not-strong-dependence 6, not-prenascence 7, not-postnascence 9, not-repetition 9, not-kamma 2, not-resultant 6, not-nutriment 2, not-faculty 2, not-jhāna 2, not-path 5, not-association 6, not-dissociation 3, not-absence 6, not-disappearance 6.

Not-root

By Twos

With not-root condition and not-object 4, not-predominance 5, not-proximity 4 ... not-repetition 5, not-kamma 1, not-resultant 2 ... not-jhāna 2, not-path 5, not-association 4, not-dissociation 2 ... not-disappearance 4.

(Enumerate in the same way as the Faultless Triplet Enumeration.)

End of Negative

3. CONDITIONS : POSITIVE-NEGATIVE

Root

By Twos

27. With root condition, not-object 6 ... not-prenascence 7, not-postnascence 9, not-repetition 9, not-kamma 2, not-resultant 6, not-association 6, not-dissociation 3 ... not-disappearance 6.

(Enumerate in the same way as the Positive-Negative Enumeration of Faultless Triplet.)

End of Positive Negative

4. CONDITIONS : NEGATIVE-POSITIVE

Not-root

By Twos

28. With not-root condition, object 2 ... conascence 5, mutuality 2, dependence 5, strong-dependence 2, prenascence 2, repetition 1, kamma 5 ... jhāna 5, path 1, association 2, dissociation 5 ... non-disappearance 5.

(Enumerate in the same way as the Negative-Positive Enumeration of Faultless Triplet.)

End of Negative-Positive

End of " DEPENDENT " CHAPTER

4. CLINGING TRIPLET   II. " CONASCENT " CHAPTER

1–4. CONDITIONS : THE SET OF FOUR

29. Conascent with state acquired by clinging and favourable to clinging, arises state acquired by clinging and favourable to clinging by root condition.

("Dependent" Chapter and "Conascent" Chapter are the same.)
End of " CONASCENT " CHAPTER

4. CLINGING TRIPLET   III. " CONDITIONED " CHAPTER

I. CONDITIONS : POSITIVE   (i) CLASSIFICATION CHAPTER

Root 11

30. (i) Conditioned by state acquired by clinging and favourable to clinging, arises state acquired by clinging and favourable to clinging by root condition.

Conditioned by one aggregate acquired by clinging and favourable to clinging, arise three aggregates. ... At the moment of conception ... conditioned by aggregates, arises (heart-)base ; conditioned by (heart-)base, arise aggregates. Conditioned by one great primary, arise three great primaries ... conditioned by great primaries, arises kamma-produced derived matter. Conditioned by (heart-)base, arise aggregates acquired by clinging and favourable to clinging. (1)

(ii) Conditioned by state acquired by clinging and favourable to clinging, arises state not acquired by clinging but favourable to clinging by root condition.

Conditioned by aggregates acquired by clinging and favourable to clinging, arises mind-produced matter. Conditioned by (heart-)base, arise aggregates not acquired by clinging but favourable to clinging. (2)

(iii) Conditioned by state acquired by clinging and favourable to clinging, arises state not acquired by clinging and not favourable to clinging by root condition.

Conditioned by (heart-)base, arise aggregates not acquired by clinging and not favourable to clinging. (3)

(iv) Conditioned by state acquired by clinging and favourable to clinging, arise states, acquired by clinging and favourable to clinging and not acquired by clinging but favourable to clinging, by root condition.

Conditioned by one aggregate acquired by clinging and favourable to clinging, arise three aggregates and mind-produced matter. ... (4)

31. (v) Conditioned by state not acquired by clinging but favourable to clinging, arises state not acquired by clinging but favourable to clinging by root condition. ... one.

(vi)–(viii) Conditioned by state not acquired by clinging and not favourable to clinging, arises state not acquired by clinging and not favourable to clinging by root condition. ... three.

(ix) Conditioned by state acquired by clinging and favourable to clinging and not acquired by clinging and not favourable to clinging, arises state not acquired by clinging and not favourable to clinging by root condition.
Conditioned by one aggregate not acquired by clinging and not favourable to clinging and (heart-)base, arise three aggregates ... conditioned by two aggregates and (heart-)base, arise two aggregates. (1)

(x) Conditioned by state not acquired by clinging but favourable to clinging and not acquired by clinging and not favourable to clinging, arises state not acquired by clinging but favourable to clinging by root condition.
Conditioned by aggregates not acquired by clinging and not favourable to clinging and great primaries, arises mind-produced matter. (1)

(xi) Conditioned by state, acquired by clinging and favourable to clinging and not acquired by clinging but favourable to clinging, arises state not acquired by clinging but favourable to clinging by root condition.
Conditioned by aggregates acquired by clinging and favourable to clinging and great primaries, arises mind-produced matter. Conditioned by one aggregate not acquired by clinging but favourable to clinging and (heart-)base, arise three aggregates ... conditioned by two aggregates and (heart-)base, arise two aggregates. (1)

Object 7

32. (i) Conditioned by state acquired by clinging and favourable to clinging, arises state acquired by clinging and favourable to clinging by object condition.
Conditioned by one aggregate acquired by clinging and favourable to clinging, arise three aggregates ... conditioned by

two aggregates, arise two aggregates. At the moment of conception, conditioned by one aggregate acquired by clinging and favourable to clinging, arise three aggregates ... conditioned by two aggregates, arise two aggregates ; conditioned by (heart-)base, arise aggregates.

Conditioned by eye-base, arises eye-consciousness ... conditioned by body-base, arises body-consciousness ; conditioned by (heart-)base, arise aggregates acquired by clinging and favourable to clinging. (1)

(ii) Conditioned by state acquired by clinging and favourable to clinging, arises state not acquired by clinging but favourable to clinging by object condition.

Conditioned by (heart-)base, arise aggregates not acquired by clinging but favourable to clinging. (2)

(iii) Conditioned by state acquired by clinging and favourable to clinging, arises state not acquired by clinging and not favourable to clinging by object condition.

Conditioned by (heart-)base, arise aggregates not acquired by clinging and not favourable to clinging. (3)

(iv) Conditioned by state not acquired by clinging but favourable to clinging, arises state not acquired by clinging but favourable to clinging by object condition.

Conditioned by one aggregate not acquired by clinging but favourable to clinging, arise three aggregates ... conditioned by two aggregates, arise two aggregates. (1)

(v) Conditioned by state not acquired by clinging and not favourable to clinging, arises state not acquired by clinging and not favourable to clinging by object condition.

Conditioned by one aggregate not acquired by clinging and not favourable to clinging, arise three aggregates ... conditioned by two aggregates, arise two aggregates. (1)

(vi) Conditioned by state acquired by clinging and favourable to clinging and not acquired by clinging and not favourable to clinging, arises state not acquired by clinging and not favourable to clinging by object condition.

Conditioned by one aggregate not acquired by clinging and not favourable to clinging and (heart-)base, arise three aggregates ... conditioned by two aggregates and (heart-)base, arise two aggregates. (1)

(vii) Conditioned by state acquired by clinging and favourable to clinging and not acquired by clinging but favourable to clinging, arises state not acquired by clinging but favourable to clinging by object condition.

Conditioned by one aggregate not acquired by clinging but favourable to clinging and (heart-)base, arise three aggregates . . . conditioned by two aggregates and (heart-)base, arise two aggregates. (1)

Predominance 9

33. (i) Conditioned by state acquired by clinging and favourable to clinging, arises state not acquired by clinging but favourable to clinging by predominance condition.

Conditioned by (heart-)base, arise aggregates not acquired by clinging but favourable to clinging. (1)

(ii) Conditioned by state acquired by clinging and favourable to clinging, arises state not acquired by clinging and not favourable to clinging by predominance condition.

Conditioned by (heart-)base, arise aggregates not acquired by clinging and not favourable to clinging. (2)

(iii) Conditioned by state not acquired by clinging but favourable to clinging, arises state not acquired by clinging but favourable to clinging by predominance condition. . . . one.

(iv)–(vi) Conditioned by state not acquired by clinging and not favourable to clinging . . . three.

(vii) Conditioned by state, acquired by clinging and favourable to clinging and not acquired by clinging and not favourable to clinging . . . by predominance condition. . . .

(viii) Conditioned by state, not acquired by clinging but favourable to clinging and not acquired by clinging and not favourable to clinging . . . by predominance condition. . . .

(ix) Conditioned by state, acquired by clinging and favourable to clinging and not acquired by clinging but favourable to clinging, arises state not acquired by clinging but favourable to clinging by predominance condition.

Conditioned by one aggregate not acquired by clinging but favourable to clinging and (heart-)base, arise three aggregates . . . conditioned by two aggregates and (heart-)base, arise two aggregates.

Proximity

34. Conditioned by state acquired by clinging and favourable to clinging, arises state acquired by clinging and favourable to clinging by proximity condition.

(Expand the 24 conditions. ... By non-disappearance condition.)

1. CONDITIONS : POSITIVE   (ii) ENUMERATION CHAPTER

By Ones

35. With root 11, object 7, predominance 9, proximity 7, contiguity 7, conascence 11, mutuality 7, dependence 11, strong-dependence 7, prenascence 7, repetition 6, kamma 11, resultant 11, nutriment 11, faculty 11, jhāna 11, path 11, association 7, dissociation 11, presence 11, absence 7, disappearance 7, non-disappearance 11.

Root

By Twos

With root condition and object 7 ... non-disappearance 11.

(Enumerate in the same way as the enumeration of the Faultless Triplet.)

End of Positive

2. CONDITIONS : NEGATIVE   (i) CLASSIFICATION CHAPTER

Not-root 5

36. Conditioned by state acquired by clinging and favourable to clinging, arises state acquired by clinging and favourable to clinging by not-root condition.

Conditioned by one rootless aggregate acquired by clinging and favourable to clinging. ... At the moment of rootless conception ... one great primary of non-percipient beings. ... Conditioned by eye-base, arises eye-consciousness ... conditioned by body-base, arises body-consciousness ; conditioned by (heart-)base, arise rootless aggregates acquired by clinging and favourable to clinging. (1)

(ii) Conditioned by state acquired by clinging and favourable to clinging, arises state not acquired by clinging but favourable to clinging by not-root condition.

Conditioned by rootless aggregates acquired by clinging and favourable to clinging, arises mind-produced matter. Conditioned by (heart-)base, arise rootless aggregates not acquired by clinging but favourable to clinging. Conditioned by (heart-)base, arises doubt-accompanied or restlessness-accompanied delusion. (2)

(iii) Conditioned by state acquired by clinging and favourable to clinging, arise states, acquired by clinging and favourable to clinging and not acquired by clinging but favourable to clinging, by not-root condition.

Conditioned by one rootless aggregate acquired by clinging and favourable to clinging, arise three aggregates and mind-produced matter. ... (3)

(iv) Conditioned by state not acquired by clinging but favourable to clinging, arises state not acquired by clinging but favourable to clinging by not-root condition.

Conditioned by one rootless aggregate not acquired by clinging but favourable to clinging, arise three aggregates and mind-produced matter. ... External ... nutriment-produced ... one temperature-produced great primary ... matter. Conditioned by doubt-accompanied or restlessness-accompanied aggregates, arises doubt-accompanied or restlessness-accompanied delusion. (1)

(v) Conditioned by state, acquired by clinging and favourable to clinging and not acquired by clinging but favourable to clinging, arises state not acquired by clinging but favourable to clinging by not-root condition.

Conditioned by rootless aggregates acquired by clinging and favourable to clinging and great primaries, arises mind-produced matter. Conditioned by one rootless aggregate not acquired by clinging but favourable to clinging and (heart-)base, arise three aggregates ... conditioned by two aggregates and (heart-)base, arise two aggregates. Conditioned by doubt-accompanied or restlessness-accompanied aggregates and (heart-)base, arises doubt-accompanied or restlessness-accompanied delusion. (1)

Not-object 6

37. Conditioned by state acquired by clinging and favourable to clinging, arises state acquired by clinging and favourable to clinging by not-object condition. . . . (Abbreviated.)

Not-predominance 8

38. (i) Conditioned by state acquired by clinging and favourable to clinging, arises state acquired by clinging and favourable to clinging by not-predominance condition.

Conditioned by one aggregate acquired by clinging and favourable to clinging. . . . (1)

(ii) Conditioned by state acquired by clinging and favourable to clinging, arises state not acquired by clinging but favourable to clinging by not-predominance condition.

Conditioned by aggregates acquired by clinging and favourable to clinging, arises mind-produced matter. Conditioned by (heart-)base, arise aggregates not acquired by clinging but favourable to clinging. (2)

(iii) Conditioned by state acquired by clinging and favourable to clinging, arises state not acquired by clinging and not favourable to clinging by not-predominance condition.

Conditioned by (heart-)base, arises predominance not acquired by clinging and not favourable to clinging. (3)

(iv) Conditioned by state acquired by clinging and favourable to clinging, arise states, acquired by clinging and favourable to clinging and not acquired by clinging but favourable to clinging, by not-predominance condition.

Conditioned by one aggregate acquired by clinging and favourable to clinging, arise three aggregates and mind-produced matter. . . . (4)

(v) Conditioned by state not acquired by clinging but favourable to clinging . . . (one question.)

(vi) Conditioned by state not acquired by clinging and not favourable to clinging, arises state not acquired by clinging and not favourable to clinging by not-predominance condition.

Conditioned by aggregates not acquired by clinging and not favourable to clinging, arises predominance not acquired by clinging and not favourable to clinging. (1)

(vii) Conditioned by state, acquired by clinging and favourable to clinging and not acquired by clinging and not favourable to clinging, arises state not acquired by clinging and not favourable to clinging by not-predominance condition.

Conditioned by aggregates not acquired by clinging and not favourable to clinging and (heart-)base, arises predominance not acquired by clinging and not favourable to clinging. (1)

(viii) Conditioned by state, acquired by clinging and favourable to clinging and not acquired by clinging but favourable to clinging, arises state not acquired by clinging but favourable to clinging by not-predominance condition.

Conditioned by aggregates acquired by clinging and favourable to clinging and great primaries, arises mind-produced matter. Conditioned by one aggregate not acquired by clinging but favourable to clinging and (heart-)base, arise three aggregates . . . conditioned by two aggregates and (heart-)base, arise two aggregates. (1)

Not-proximity, etc.

39. Conditioned by state acquired by clinging and favourable able to clinging, arises state acquired by clinging and favourable to clinging by not-proximity condition . . . by not-contiguity condition . . . by not-mutuality condition . . . by not-strong-dependence condition . . . by not-prenascence condition . . . by not-postnascence condition . . . by not-repetition condition. . . .

Not-kamma 6

40. (i) Conditioned by state acquired by clinging and favourable to clinging, arises state not acquired by clinging but favourable to clinging by not-kamma condition.

Conditioned by (heart-)base, arises volition not acquired by clinging but favourable to clinging. (1)

(ii) Conditioned by state acquired by clinging and favourable to clinging, arises state not acquired by clinging and not favourable to clinging by not-kamma condition.

Conditioned by (heart-)base, arises faultless volition not acquired by clinging and not favourable to clinging. (2)

(iii) Conditioned by state not acquired by clinging but

favourable to clinging, arises state not acquired by clinging but favourable to clinging by not-kamma condition.

Conditioned by aggregates not acquired by clinging but favourable to clinging, arises volition not acquired by clinging but favourable to clinging. External ... nutriment-produced ... conditioned by one temperature-produced great primary. ... (1)

(iv) Conditioned by state not acquired by clinging and not favourable to clinging, arises state not acquired by clinging and not favourable to clinging by not-kamma condition.

Conditioned by faultless aggregates not acquired by clinging and not favourable to clinging, arises volition not acquired by clinging and not favourable to clinging. (1)

(v) Conditioned by state, acquired by clinging and favourable to clinging and not acquired by clinging and not favourable to clinging, arises state not acquired by clinging and not favourable to clinging by not-kamma condition.

Conditioned by faultless aggregates not acquired by clinging and not favourable to clinging and (heart-)base, arises faultless volition not acquired by clinging and not favourable to clinging. (1)

(vi) Conditioned by state, acquired by clinging and favourable to clinging and not acquired by clinging but favourable to clinging, arises state not acquired by clinging but favourable to clinging by not-kamma condition.

Conditioned by aggregates not acquired by clinging but favourable to clinging and (heart-)base, arises volition not acquired by clinging but favourable to clinging.

Not-resultant 10

41. (i) Conditioned by state acquired by clinging and favourable to clinging, arises state acquired by clinging and favourable to clinging by not-resultant condition.

Conditioned by one great primary of non-percipient beings. ... (1)

(ii) Conditioned by state acquired by clinging and favourable to clinging, arises state not acquired by clinging but favourable to clinging by not-resultant condition.

Conditioned by (heart-)base, arise aggregates not acquired by clinging but favourable to clinging. (2)

(iii) Conditioned by state acquired by clinging and favourable to clinging, arises state not acquired by clinging and not favourable to clinging by not-resultant condition.
Conditioned by (heart-)base, arise faultless aggregates not acquired by clinging and not favourable to clinging. (3)

(iv) Conditioned by state not acquired by clinging but favourable to clinging ... one.

(v)–(vii) Conditioned by state not acquired by clinging and not favourable to clinging ... three.

(viii) Conditioned by state, acquired by clinging and favourable to clinging and not acquired by clinging and not favourable to clinging, arises state not acquired by clinging and not favourable to clinging by not-resultant condition. ... (Abbreviated.)

(ix) Conditioned by state, not acquired by clinging but favourable to clinging and not acquired by clinging and not favourable to clinging, arises state not acquired by clinging but favourable to clinging by not-resultant condition. ... (Abbreviated.)

(x) Conditioned by state, acquired by clinging and favourable to clinging and not acquired by clinging but favourable to clinging, arises state not acquired by clinging but favourable to clinging by not-resultant condition.
Conditioned by one aggregate not acquired by clinging but favourable to clinging and (heart-)base, arise three aggregates ... conditioned by two aggregates and (heart-)base, arise two aggregates.

Not-nutriment, etc.

42. Conditioned by state acquired by clinging and favourable to clinging, arises state acquired by clinging and favourable to clinging by not-nutriment condition ... by not-faculty condition ... by not-jhāna condition ... by not-path condition ... by not-association condition ... by not-dissociation condition ... by not-absence condition ... by not-disappearance condition. ... (Abbreviated.)

2. CONDITIONS: NEGATIVE   (ii) ENUMERATION CHAPTER

43. With not-root 5, not-object 6, not-predominance 8, not-proximity 6, not-contiguity 6, not-mutuality 6, not-strong-dependence 6, not-prenascence 7, not-postnascence 11, not-repetition 11, not-kamma 6, not-resultant 10, not-nutriment 2, not-faculty 2, not-jhāna 2, not-path 5, not-association 6, not-dissociation 3, not-absence 6, not-disappearance 6. (Enumerate in detail.)

3. CONDITIONS: POSITIVE-NEGATIVE

44. With root condition, not-object 6 . . . not-disappearance 6. (Enumerate in detail.)

4. CONDITIONS: NEGATIVE-POSITIVE

45. With not-root condition, object 4 . . . non-disappearance 5.

End of " CONDITIONED " CHAPTER

4. CLINGING TRIPLET   IV. " SUPPORTED " CHAPTER

46. Supported by state acquired by clinging and favourable to clinging, arises state acquired by clinging and favourable to clinging by root condition.

Supported by one aggregate acquired by clinging and favourable to clinging, arise three aggregates; supported by three aggregates. . . . (Abbreviated.)

(" Conditioned " Chapter and " Supported " Chapter are the same.)

End of " SUPPORTED " CHAPTER

4. CLINGING TRIPLET   V. " CONJOINED " CHAPTER

I. CONDITIONS: POSITIVE

Root 3

47. (i) Conjoined with state acquired by clinging and favourable to clinging, arises state acquired by clinging and favourable to clinging by root condition.

Conjoined with one aggregate acquired by clinging and favourable to clinging, arise three aggregates ; conjoined with three aggregates, arises one aggregate ; conjoined with two aggregates, arise two aggregates. At the moment of conception, conjoined with one aggregate acquired by clinging and favourable to clinging, arise three aggregates ... conjoined with two aggregates, arise two aggregates. (1)

(ii) Conjoined with state not acquired by clinging but favourable to clinging, arises state not acquired by clinging but favourable to clinging by root condition.

Conjoined with one aggregate not acquired by clinging but favourable to clinging, arise three aggregates ... conjoined with two aggregates, arise two aggregates. (1)

(iii) Conjoined with state not acquired by clinging and not favourable to clinging, arises state not acquired by clinging and not favourable to clinging by root condition.

Conjoined with one aggregate not acquired by clinging and not favourable to clinging, arise three aggregates ... conjoined with two aggregates, arise two aggregates. ... (Abbreviated.)

Enumeration Chapter

48. With root 3 ... predominance 2 ... repetition 2 ... resultant 2 ... non-disappearance 3.

(Enumerate in the same way as enumeration of the Faultless Triplet.)

End of Positive

2. CONDITIONS : NEGATIVE

Not-root 2

49. (i) Conjoined with state acquired by clinging and favourable to clinging, arises state acquired by clinging and favourable to clinging by not-root condition.

Conjoined with one rootless aggregate acquired by clinging and favourable to clinging, arise three aggregates ... conjoined with two aggregates, arise two aggregates. At the moment of rootless conception. ... (1)

(ii) Conjoined with state not acquired by clinging but

favourable to clinging, arises state not acquired by clinging but favourable to clinging by not-root condition.

Conjoined with one rootless aggregate not acquired by clinging but favourable to clinging, arise three aggregates ... conjoined with two aggregates, arise two aggregates. Conjoined with doubt-accompanied or restlessness-accompanied aggregates, arises doubt-accompanied or restlessness-accompanied delusion. ... (Abbreviated.)

With not-root 2, not-predominance 3 ... not-dissociation 3. ... (Abbreviated.)

End of Negative

With root condition, not-predominance 3 ... not-dissociation 3.

With not-root condition, object 2 ... non-disappearance 2.

End of " CONJOINED " CHAPTER

4. CLINGING TRIPLET   VI. " ASSOCIATED " CHAPTER

50. Associated with state acquired by clinging and favourable to clinging, arises state acquired by clinging and favourable to clinging by root condition. ... (Abbreviated.)

With root 3 ... non-disappearance 3.

(" Conjoined " Chapter and " Associated " Chapter are the same.)

End of " ASSOCIATED " CHAPTER

4. CLINGING TRIPLET   VII. " INVESTIGATION " CHAPTER

I. CONDITIONS : POSITIVE   (i) CLASSIFICATION CHAPTER

Root 7

51. (i) State acquired by clinging and favourable to clinging is related to state acquired by clinging and favourable to clinging by root condition.

Roots acquired by clinging and favourable to clinging are related to (their) associated aggregates by root condition. At the moment of conception, roots acquired by clinging and favourable to clinging are related to (their) associated aggregates and kamma-produced matter by root condition. (1)

(ii) State acquired by clinging and favourable to clinging is related to state not acquired by clinging but favourable to clinging by root condition.

Roots acquired by clinging and favourable to clinging are related to mind-produced matter by root condition. (2)

(iii) State acquired by clinging and favourable to clinging is related to state, acquired by clinging and favourable to clinging and not acquired by clinging but favourable to clinging, by root condition.

Roots acquired by clinging and favourable to clinging are related to (their) associated aggregates and mind-produced matter by root condition. (3)

(iv) State not acquired by clinging but favourable to clinging is related to state not acquired by clinging but favourable to clinging by root condition.

Roots not acquired by clinging but favourable to clinging are related to (their) associated aggregates and mind-produced matter by root condition. (1)

(v) State not acquired by clinging and not favourable to clinging is related to state not acquired by clinging and not favourable to clinging by root condition.

Roots not acquired by clinging and not favourable to clinging are related to (their) associated aggregates by root condition. (1)

(vi) State not acquired by clinging and not favourable to clinging is related to state not acquired by clinging but favourable to clinging by root condition.

Roots not acquired by clinging and not favourable to clinging are related to mind-produced matter by root condition. (2)

(vii) State not acquired by clinging and not favourable to clinging is related to state, not acquired by clinging but favourable to clinging and not acquired by clinging and not favourable to clinging, by root condition.

Roots not acquired by clinging and not favourable to clinging are related to (their) associated aggregates and mind-produced matter by root condition. (3)

Object 6

52. (i) State acquired by clinging and favourable to clinging is related to state acquired by clinging and favourable to clinging by object condition.

Learners or common worldlings practise insight into the impermanency, suffering and impersonality of the eye ; enjoy and delight in (the eye). Taking it as object arises lust ... arises grief. When the faultless or faulty has ceased, the resultant arises as registering. ... ear ... nose ... tongue ... body ... visible objects acquired by clinging and favourable to clinging ... smells ... tastes ... tangible objects ... (heart-)-base. ... (They) practise insight into the impermanency, suffering and impersonality of the aggregates acquired by clinging and favourable to clinging ; enjoy and delight in (those aggregates). Taking it as object arises lust ... arises grief. When the faultless or faulty has ceased, the resultant arises as registering.

Visible object-base acquired by clinging and favourable to clinging to eye-consciousness ... smell-base ... taste-base ... tangible object-base acquired by clinging and favourable to clinging is related to body-consciousness by object condition. (1)

(ii) State acquired by clinging and favourable to clinging is related to state not acquired by clinging but favourable to clinging by object condition.

(One) practises insight into the impermanency, suffering and impersonality of the eye ; enjoys and delights in (the eye). Taking it as object arises lust ... arises grief. ... ear ... nose ... tongue ... body ... visible objects acquired by clinging and favourable to clinging ... smells ... tastes ... tangible objects ... (heart-)base. ... (One) practises insight into the impermanency, suffering and impersonality of the aggregates acquired by clinging and favourable to clinging ; enjoys and delights in (those aggregates). Taking it as object arises lust ... arises grief.

By the power of divine-eye, (one) sees the visible object acquired by clinging and favourable to clinging. By the knowledge of penetration into others' minds (he) knows the mind, acquired by clinging and favourable to clinging, of the other being. Aggregates acquired by clinging and favourable to clinging are related to knowledge of supernormal power, knowledge of penetration into others' minds, knowledge of remembrance of past existences, knowledge of future existences, advertence by object condition. (2)

53. (iii) State not acquired by clinging but favourable to clinging is related to state not acquired by clinging but favourable to clinging by object condition.

After having offered the offering, having undertaken the precept, having fulfilled the duty of observance, (one) reviews it. (One) reviews (such acts) formerly well done. Having emerged from jhāna, (one) reviews the jhāna. Noble persons review change-of-lineage. (They) review purification. Noble persons review the eradicated defilements. (They) review the uneradicated defilements. (They) know the defilements addicted to before.

Visible objects not acquired by clinging but favourable to clinging ... sounds ... smells ... tastes ... tangible objects. ... (They) practise insight into the impermanency, suffering and impersonality of the aggregates not acquired by clinging but favourable to clinging; enjoy and delight in (those aggregates). Taking it as object arises lust ... arises grief.

By the power of divine-eye, (they) see the visible object not acquired by clinging but favourable to clinging. By the power of divine-ear element, (they) hear the sound. By the knowledge of penetration into others' minds, (they) know the mind, not acquired by clinging but favourable to clinging, of the other being.

Infinity of space is related to infinity of consciousness by object condition. Nothingness is related to neither-perception-nor-non-perception by object condition.

Aggregates not acquired by clinging but favourable to clinging are related to knowledge of supernormal power, knowledge of penetration into others' minds, knowledge of remembrance of past existences, knowledge of rebirths according to one's kamma, knowledge of future existences, advertence by object condition. (1)

(iv) State not acquired by clinging but favourable to clinging is related to state acquired by clinging and favourable to clinging by object condition.

Learners or common worldlings ... visible objects not acquired by clinging but favourable to clinging ... sounds ... smells ... tastes ... tangible objects ... practise insight into the impermanency, suffering and impersonality of the aggregates not acquired by clinging but favourable to clinging; enjoy and delight in (those aggregates). Taking it as object arises lust ... arises grief. When the faultless or faulty has ceased, the resultant arises as registering.

Faultless infinity of space is related to resultant infinity of consciousness by object condition. Faultless nothingness is related to resultant neither-perception-nor-non-perception by object condition.

Visible object-base not acquired by clinging but favourable to clinging to eye-consciousness ... tangible object-base ... is related to body-consciousness by object condition. (2)

54. (v) State not acquired by clinging and not favourable to clinging is related to state not acquired by clinging and not favourable to clinging by object condition.

Nibbāna is related to Path, Fruition by object condition. (1)

(vi) State not acquired by clinging and not favourable to clinging is related to state not acquired by clinging but favourable to clinging by object condition.

Noble persons, having emerged from Path, review the Path. (They) review Fruition. (They) review Nibbāna. Nibbāna is related to change-of-lineage, purification, advertence by object condition. Noble persons, by the knowledge of penetration into others' minds, know the mind, not acquired by clinging and not favourable to clinging, of the other being.

Aggregates not acquired by clinging and not favourable to clinging are related to knowledge of penetration into others' minds, knowledge of remembrance of past existences, knowledge of future existences, advertence by object condition. (2)

Predominance 5

55. (i) State acquired by clinging and favourable to clinging is related to state not acquired by clinging but favourable to clinging by predominance condition.

Object-predominance : (One) esteems, enjoys and delights in the eye. Taking it as estimable object, arises lust, arises wrong views. ... ear ... nose ... tongue ... body ... visible objects acquired by clinging and favourable to clinging ... smells ... tastes ... tangible objects ... (heart-)base. ... (One) esteems, enjoys and delights in the aggregates acquired by clinging and favourable to clinging. Taking it as estimable object, arises lust, arises wrong views.

(ii) State not acquired by clinging but favourable to clinging is related to state not acquired by clinging but favourable to clinging by predominance condition.

(It is of two kinds, namely :) (*a*) object-predominance, (*b*) conascence-predominance.

(*a*) *Object-predominance* : After having offered the offering, having undertaken the precept, having fulfilled the duty of observance, (one) esteems and reviews it. (One) esteems and reviews (such acts) formerly well done. Having emerged from jhāna, (one) esteems and reviews the jhāna. Learners esteem and review change-of-lineage. (They) esteem and review purification. ... visible objects not acquired by clinging but favourable to clinging ... sounds ... smells ... tastes ... tangible objects. ... (They) esteem and review the aggregates not acquired by clinging but favourable to clinging. Taking it as estimable object, arises lust, arises wrong views.

(*b*) *Conascence-predominance* : Predominance not acquired by clinging but favourable to clinging is related to (its) associated aggregates and mind-produced matter by predominance condition. (1)

(iii) State not acquired by clinging and not favourable to clinging is related to state not acquired by clinging and not favourable to clinging by predominance condition.

(It is of two kinds, namely :) (*a*) object-predominance, (*b*) conascence-predominance.

(*a*) *Object-predominance* : Nibbāna is related to Path, Fruition by predominance condition.

(*b*) *Conascence-predominance* : Predominance not acquired by clinging and not favourable to clinging is related to (its) associated aggregates by predominance condition. (1)

(iv) State not acquired by clinging and not favourable to

clinging is related to state not acquired by clinging but favourable to clinging by predominance condition.

(It is of two kinds, namely :) (*a*) object-predominance, (*b*) conascence-predominance.

(*a*) *Object-predominance* : The Noble persons, having emerged from Path, esteem and review the Path. (They) esteem and review Fruition. (They) esteem and review Nibbāna. Nibbāna is related to change-of-lineage, purification by predominance condition.

(*b*) *Conascence-predominance* : Predominance not acquired by clinging and not favourable to clinging is related to mind-produced matter by predominance condition. (2)

(v) State not acquired by clinging and not favourable to clinging is related to state, not acquired by clinging but favourable to clinging and not acquired by clinging and not favourable to clinging, by predominance condition.

Conascence-predominance : Predominance not acquired by clinging and not favourable to clinging is related to (its) associated aggregates and mind-produced matter by predominance condition. (3)

Proximity 7

56. (i) State acquired by clinging and favourable to clinging is related to state acquired by clinging and favourable to clinging by proximity condition.

Preceding aggregates acquired by clinging and favourable to clinging are related to subsequent aggregates acquired by clinging and favourable to clinging by proximity condition. Five-fold consciousness is related to resultant mind-element by proximity condition. Resultant mind-element is related to resultant mind-consciousness element by proximity condition. (1)

(ii) State acquired by clinging and favourable to clinging is related to state not acquired by clinging but favourable to clinging by proximity condition.

Life-continuum to advertence ; resultant mind-consciousness element is related to functional mind-consciousness element by proximity condition. (2)

(iii) State not acquired by clinging but favourable to clinging is related to state not acquired by clinging but favourable to clinging by proximity condition.

Preceding aggregates not acquired by clinging but favourable to clinging are related to subsequent aggregates not acquired by clinging but favourable to clinging by proximity condition. Adaptation to change-of-lineage ; adaptation to purification ; advertence is related to the aggregates not acquired by clinging but favourable to clinging by proximity condition. (1)

(iv) State not acquired by clinging but favourable to clinging is related to state acquired by clinging and favourable to clinging by proximity condition.

Advertence is related to five-fold consciousness by proximity condition. Aggregates not acquired by clinging but favourable to clinging are related to emergence by proximity condition. (2)

(v) State not acquired by clinging but favourable to clinging is related to state not acquired by clinging and not favourable to clinging by proximity condition.

Change-of-lineage to Path ; purification to Path ; adaptation to attainment of Fruition ; having emerged from the attainment of Extinction, neither-perception-nor-non-perception is related to the attainment of Fruition by proximity condition. (3)

(vi) State not acquired by clinging and not favourable to clinging is related to state not acquired by clinging and not favourable to clinging by proximity condition.

Preceding aggregates not acquired by clinging and not favourable to clinging are related to subsequent aggregates not acquired by clinging and not favourable to clinging by proximity condition. Path to Fruition ; Fruition is related to Fruition by proximity condition. (1)

(vii) State not acquired by clinging and not favourable to clinging is related to state acquired by clinging and favourable to clinging by proximity condition.

Fruition is related to emergence by proximity condition (2).

Contiguity 7

57. State acquired by clinging and favourable to clinging is related to state acquired by clinging and favourable to clinging by contiguity condition. (The same as proximity condition.)

Conascence 9

58. (i) State acquired by clinging and favourable to clinging is related to state acquired by clinging and favourable to clinging by conascence condition.

One aggregate acquired by clinging and favourable to clinging is related to three aggregates by conascence condition ... two aggregates to two aggregates. ... At the moment of conception, one aggregate acquired by clinging and favourable to clinging is related to three aggregates and kamma-produced matter by conascence condition ... two aggregates to two aggregates and kamma-produced matter ... aggregates to (heart-)base ... (heart-)base to aggregates. ...

One great primary to three great primaries ... three great primaries to one great primary ... two great primaries to two great primaries ... great primaries are related to kamma-produced derived matter by conascence condition. One great primary of non-percipient beings. ... (1)

(ii) State acquired by clinging and favourable to clinging is related to state not acquired by clinging but favourable to clinging by conascence condition.

Aggregates acquired by clinging and favourable to clinging are related to mind-produced matter by conascence condition. (2)

(iii) State acquired by clinging and favourable to clinging is related to state, acquired by clinging and favourable to clinging and not acquired by clinging but favourable to clinging, by conascence condition.

One aggregate acquired by clinging and favourable to clinging is related to three aggregates and mind-produced matter by conascence condition ... two aggregates are related to two aggregates and mind-produced matter by conascence condition. (3)

(iv) State not acquired by clinging but favourable to clinging is related to state not acquired by clinging but favourable to clinging by conascence condition.

One aggregate not acquired by clinging but favourable to clinging is related to three aggregates and mind-produced matter by conascence condition ... two aggregates are related to two aggregates and mind-produced matter by conascence condition.

One great primary not acquired by clinging but favourable to clinging ... great primaries to mind-produced matter. ... External ... nutriment-produced ... one temperature-produced great primary ... great primaries are related to derived matter by conascence condition. (1)

(v) State not acquired by clinging and not favourable to clinging is related to state not acquired by clinging and not favourable to clinging by conascence condition.

One aggregate not acquired by clinging and not favourable to clinging is related to three aggregates ... two aggregates are related to two aggregates by conascence condition. (1)

(vi) State not acquired by clinging and not favourable to clinging is related to state not acquired by clinging but favourable to clinging by conascence condition.

Aggregates not acquired by clinging and not favourable to clinging are related to mind-produced matter by conascence condition. (2)

(vii) State not acquired by clinging and not favourable to clinging is related to state, not acquired by clinging but favourable to clinging and not acquired by clinging and not favourable to clinging, by conascence condition.

One aggregate not acquired by clinging and not favourable to clinging is related to three aggregates and mind-produced matter by conascence condition ... two aggregates are related to two aggregates and mind-produced matter by conascence condition. (3)

(viii) States, not acquired by clinging but favourable to clinging and not acquired by clinging and not favourable to clinging, are related to state not acquired by clinging but favourable to clinging by conascence condition.

Aggregates not acquired by clinging and not favourable to clinging and great primaries are related to mind-produced matter by conascence condition. (1)

(ix) States, acquired by clinging and favourable to clinging and not acquired by clinging but favourable to clinging, are related to state not acquired by clinging but favourable to clinging by conascence condition.

Aggregates acquired by clinging and favourable to clinging and great primaries are related to mind-produced matter by conascence condition.

Mutuality 3

59. (i) State acquired by clinging and favourable to clinging is related to state acquired by clinging and favourable to clinging by mutuality condition.

One aggregate acquired by clinging and favourable to clinging is related to three aggregates by mutuality condition ... two aggregates to two aggregates. ... At the moment of conception, one aggregate acquired by clinging and favourable to clinging to three aggregates and (heart-)base ... aggregates to (heart-)base ... (heart-)base to aggregates. ...

One great primary to three great primaries ... two great primaries to two great primaries ... one great primary of non-percipient beings. ... (1)

(ii) State not acquired by clinging but favourable to clinging is related to state not acquired by clinging but favourable to clinging by mutuality condition.

One aggregate not acquired by clinging but favourable to clinging to three aggregates ... two aggregates are related to two aggregates by mutuality condition.

One great primary. ... External ... nutriment-produced ... one temperature-produced great primary. ... (1)

(iii) State not acquired by clinging and not favourable to clinging is related to state not acquired by clinging and not favourable to clinging by mutuality condition.

One aggregate not acquired by clinging and not favourable to clinging to three aggregates ... two aggregates to two aggregates. ... (1)

Dependence 11

60. (i) State acquired by clinging and favourable to clinging is related to state acquired by clinging and favourable to clinging by dependence condition.

One aggregate acquired by clinging and favourable to clinging is related to three aggregates by dependence condition. ... At the moment of conception. . . . One great primary . . . one great primary of non-percipient beings. . . .

Eye-base to eye-consciousness ... body-base to body-consciousness ... (heart-)base is related to the aggregates acquired by clinging and favourable to clinging by dependence condition. (1)

(ii) State acquired by clinging and favourable to clinging is related to state not acquired by clinging but favourable to clinging by dependence condition.

Aggregates acquired by clinging and favourable to clinging are related to mind-produced matter by dependence condition. (Heart-)base is related to the aggregates not acquired by clinging but favourable to clinging by dependence condition. (2)

(iii) State acquired by clinging and favourable to clinging is related to state not acquired by clinging and not favourable to clinging by dependence condition.

(Heart-)base is related to the aggregates not acquired by clinging and not favourable to clinging by dependence condition. (3)

(iv) State acquired by clinging and favourable to clinging is related to state, acquired by clinging and favourable to clinging and not acquired by clinging but favourable to clinging, by dependence condition.

One aggregate acquired by clinging and favourable to clinging is related to three aggregates and mind-produced matter by dependence condition ... two aggregates are related to two aggregates and mind-produced matter by dependence condition. (4)

(v) State not acquired by clinging but favourable to clinging to state not acquired by clinging but favourable to clinging . . . one.

(vi)–(viii) State not acquired by clinging and not favourable to clinging . . . three.

(ix) States, acquired by clinging and favourable to clinging and not acquired by clinging and not favourable to clinging, are related to state not acquired by clinging and not favourable to clinging by dependence condition.

One aggregate not acquired by clinging and not favourable to clinging and (heart-)base are related to three aggregates by dependence condition ... two aggregates and (heart-)base are related to two aggregates by dependence condition. (1)

(x) States, not acquired by clinging but favourable to clinging and not acquired by clinging and not favourable to clinging, are related to state not acquired by clinging but favourable to clinging by dependence condition.
Aggregates not acquired by clinging and not favourable to clinging and great primaries are related to mind-produced matter by dependence condition. (1)

(xi) States, acquired by clinging and favourable to clinging and not acquired by clinging but favourable to clinging, are related to state not acquired by clinging but favourable to clinging by dependence condition.
Aggregates acquired by clinging and favourable to clinging and great primaries are related to mind-produced matter by dependence condition. One aggregate not acquired by clinging but favourable to clinging and (heart-)base are related to three aggregates by dependence condition ... two aggregates and (heart-)base are related to two aggregates by dependence condition. (1)

Strong-dependence 9

61. (i) State acquired by clinging and favourable to clinging is related to state acquired by clinging and favourable to clinging by strong-dependence condition.

(It is of two kinds, namely :) (*a*) proximity-strong-dependence, (*b*) natural strong-dependence. ...

(*b*) *Natural strong-dependence* : Bodily happiness is related to bodily happiness, bodily pain by strong-dependence condition. Bodily pain to bodily happiness, bodily pain ... temperature to bodily happiness, bodily pain ... food to bodily happiness, bodily pain. .... Bodily happiness, bodily pain, temperature, food is related to bodily happiness, bodily pain by strong-dependence condition. (1)

(ii) State acquired by clinging and favourable to clinging is related to state not acquired by clinging but favourable to clinging by strong-dependence condition.

(It is of three kinds, namely :) (*a*) object-strong-dependence,

(b) proximity-strong-dependence, (c) natural strong-dependence. ...

(c) *Natural strong-dependence* : By the strong-dependence of bodily happiness, (one) offers the offering, undertakes the precept, fulfils the duty of observance, develops jhāna, develops insight, develops superknowledge, develops attainment, kills a living being ... causes schism in the Saṅgha. ... bodily pain ... temperature. ... By the strong-dependence of food, (one) offers the offering ... causes schism in the Saṅgha. Bodily happiness, bodily pain, temperature, food is related to confidence not acquired by clinging but favourable to clinging, precept ... learning ... generosity ... wisdom ... lust ... hate ... delusion ... conceit ... wrong views ... wish ... by strong-dependence condition. (2).

(iii) State acquired by clinging and favourable to clinging is related to state not acquired by clinging and not favourable to clinging by strong-dependence condition.

Natural strong-dependence : By the strong-dependence of bodily happiness, (one) develops Path, enters the attainment of Fruition. ... bodily pain ... temperature. ... By the strong-dependence of food, (one) develops Path, enters the attainment of Fruition. Bodily happiness, bodily pain, temperature, food is related to Path, attainment of Fruition by strong-dependence condition. (3)

62. (iv) State not acquired by clinging but favourable to clinging is related to state not acquired by clinging but favourable to clinging by strong-dependence condition.

(It is of three kinds, namely :) (a) object-strong-dependence, (b) proximity-strong-dependence, (c) natural strong-dependence. ...

(c) *Natural strong-dependence* : By the strong-dependence of confidence not acquired by clinging but favourable to clinging, (one) offers the offering, undertakes the precept, fulfils the duty of observance, develops jhāna, develops insight, develops superknowledge, develops attainment ; arouses conceit, adopts wrong views. ... precept not acquired by clinging but favourable to clinging ... learning ... generosity ... wisdom ... lust ... hate ... delusion ... conceit ... wrong views ... wish ... temperature ... food. ... By the strong-dependence of lodging-place ... (one) offers the offering ... develops attainment ; arouses conceit, adopts wrong views, kills a living being ... causes schism in the Saṅgha. Confidence not acquired by clinging but favourable to clinging, precept ... learning ... generosity ... wisdom ... lust ... hate ... delusion ... conceit ... wrong views ... wish ... temperature ... food ... lodging-place ... is related to confidence not acquired by clinging but favourable to clinging, precept ... learning ... generosity ... wisdom ... lust ... hate ... delusion ... conceit ... wrong views ... wish ... by strong-dependence condition.

The preparation for first jhāna to first jhāna ... the preparation for neither-perception-nor-non-perception to neither-perception-nor-non-perception ... first jhāna to second ... nothingness to neither-perception-nor-non-perception ... killing to killing ... wrong views with fixed destiny to wrong views with fixed destiny. ... (1)

(v) State not acquired by clinging but favourable to clinging is related to state acquired by clinging and favourable to clinging by strong-dependence condition.

(It is of two kinds, namely :) (a) proximity-strong-dependence, (b) natural strong-dependence. ...

(b) *Natural strong-dependence* : By the strong-dependence of confidence not acquired by clinging but favourable to clinging, (one) tortures oneself, tortures oneself fully, experiences the suffering caused by searching. ... precept not acquired by clinging but favourable to clinging. ... By the strong-dependence of lodging-place ... (one) tortures onself, tortures oneself fully, experiences the suffering caused by searching. Confidence not acquired by clinging but favourable to clinging ... lodging-place ... is related to bodily happiness, bodily pain by strong-dependence condition. Faultless or faulty kamma is related to (its) resultant by strong-dependence condition. (2)

(vi) State not acquired by clinging but favourable to clinging is related to state not acquired by clinging and not favourable to clinging by strong-dependence condition.

(It is of two kinds, namely :) (a) proximity-strong-dependence, (b) natural strong-dependence. ...

(b) *Natural strong-dependence* : The preparation for first

Path is related to first Path by strong-dependence condition ... for second Path ... for third Path ... the preparation for fourth Path is related to fourth Path by strong-dependence condition. (3)

63. (vii) State not acquired by clinging and not favourable to clinging is related to state not acquired by clinging and not favourable to clinging by strong-dependence condition.

(It is of three kinds, namely:) (*a*) object-strong-dependence, (*b*) proximity-strong-dependence, (*c*) natural strong-dependence. ...

(*c*) *Natural strong-dependence*: First Path is related to second Path by strong-dependence condition; second Path to third Path ... third Path to fourth Path. ... Path is related to attainment of Fruition by strong-dependence condition. (1)

(viii) State not acquired by clinging and not favourable to clinging is related to state acquired by clinging and favourable to clinging by strong-dependence condition.

(It is of two kinds, namely:) (*a*) proximity-strong-dependence, (*b*) natural strong-dependence. ...

(*b*) *Natural strong-dependence*: The attainment of Fruition is related to bodily happiness by strong-dependence condition. (2)

(ix) State not acquired by clinging and not favourable to clinging is related to state not acquired by clinging but favourable to clinging by strong-dependence condition.

(It is of two kinds, namely:) (*a*) object-strong-dependence, (*b*) natural strong-dependence. ...

(*b*) *Natural strong-dependence*: The Noble persons, by the strong-dependence of the Path, generate the attainment which has not yet arisen, enter the attainment which has arisen, practise insight into the impermanency, suffering and impersonality of the formations. The Path is related to the Noble person's analytical knowledge of meaning, analytical knowledge of the Dhamma, analytical knowledge of language, analytical knowledge of the above three, knowledge of correct and faulty conclusion by strong-dependence condition. (3)

Prenascence 7

64. (i) State acquired by clinging and favourable to clinging is related to state acquired by clinging and favourable to clinging by prenascence condition.

(It is of two kinds, namely :) (*a*) object-prenascence, (*b*) base-prenascence.

(*a*) *Object-prenascence* : Learners or common worldlings practise insight into the impermanency, suffering and impersonality of the eye ; enjoy and delight in (the eye). Taking it as object arises lust ... arises grief. When the faultless or faulty has ceased, the resultant arises as registering. ... ear ... nose ... tongue ... body ... visible objects acquired by clinging and favourable to clinging ... smells ... tastes ... tangible objects. ... (They) practise insight into the impermanency, suffering and impersonality of the (heart-)base ... ; enjoy and delight in (the heart-base). Taking it as object arises lust ... arises grief. When the faultless or faulty has ceased, the resultant arises as registering.

Visible object-base acquired by clinging and favourable to clinging to eye-consciousness ... smell-base ... taste-base ... tangible object-base acquired by clinging and favourable to clinging is related to body-consciousness by prenascence condition.

(*b*) *Base-prenascence* : Eye-base to eye-consciousness ... body-base to body-consciousness ... (heart-)base is related to the aggregates acquired by clinging and favourable to clinging by prenascence condition. (1)

(ii) State acquired by clinging and favourable to clinging is related to state not acquired by clinging but favourable to clinging by prenascence condition.

(It is of two kinds, namely :) (*a*) object-prenascence, (*b*) base-prenascence.

(*a*) *Object-prenascence* : (They) practise insight into the impermanency, suffering and impersonality of the eye ; enjoy and delight in (the eye). Taking it as object arises lust ... arises grief. ... ear. ... (They) practise insight into the impermanency, suffering and impersonality of the (heart-)base ; enjoy and delight in (the heart-base). Taking it as object arises lust ... arises grief. By the power of divine-eye, (they) see the visible object acquired by clinging and favourable to clinging.

(*b*) *Base-prenascence* : (Heart-)base is related to the aggregates not acquired by clinging but favourable to clinging by prenascence condition. (2)

(iii) State acquired by clinging and favourable to clinging is related to state not acquired by clinging and not favourable to clinging by prenascence condition.

Base-prenascence: (Heart-)base is related to the aggregates not acquired by clinging and not favourable to clinging by prenascence condition. (3)

65. (iv) State not acquired by clinging but favourable to clinging is related to state not acquired by clinging but favourable to clinging by prenascence condition.

Object-prenascence: Visible objects not acquired by clinging but favourable to clinging ... sounds ... smells ... tastes ... (one) practises insight into the impermanency, suffering and impersonality of tangible objects ... ; enjoys and delights in (them). Taking it as object arises lust ... arises grief. By the power of divine-eye, (one) sees the visible object not acquired by clinging but favourable to clinging. By the power of divine-ear element, (one) hears the sound. (1)

(v) State not acquired by clinging but favourable to clinging is related to state acquired by clinging and favourable to clinging by prenascence condition.

Object-prenascence: Visible objects not acquired by clinging but favourable to clinging, sounds ... smells ... tastes ... (one) practises insight into the impermanency, suffering and impersonality of tangible objects ... ; enjoys and delights in (them). Taking it as object arises lust ... arises grief. When the faultless or faulty has ceased, the resultant arises as registering. Visible object-base not acquired by clinging but favourable to clinging to eye-consciousness ... tangible object-base ... is related to body-consciousness by prenascence condition. (2)

(vi) States, acquired by clinging and favourable to clinging and not acquired by clinging but favourable to clinging, are related to state acquired by clinging and favourable to clinging by prenascence condition.

Object-prenascence and base-prenascence: Visible object-base not acquired by clinging but favourable to clinging and eye-base are related to eye-consciousness by prenascence condition ... tangible object-base not acquired by clinging but favourable to clinging and body-base are related to body-consciousness by prenascence condition. Visible object-base not acquired by clinging but favourable to clinging and (heart-)-base are related to the aggregates acquired by clinging and favourable to clinging by prenascence condition . . . tangible object-base not acquired by clinging but favourable to clinging and (heart-)base are related to the aggregates acquired by clinging and favourable to clinging by prenascence condition. (1)

(vii) States, acquired by clinging and favourable to clinging and not acquired by clinging but favourable to clinging, are related to state not acquired by clinging but favourable to clinging by prenascence condition.

Object-prenascence and base-prenascence : Visible object-base not acquired by clinging but favourable to clinging and (heart-)-base are related to the aggregates not acquired by clinging but favourable to clinging by prenascence condition . . . tangible object-base not acquired by clinging but favourable to clinging and (heart)-base are related to the aggregates not acquired by clinging but favourable to clinging by prenascence condition. (2)

Postnascence 9

66. (i) State acquired by clinging and favourable to clinging is related to state acquired by clinging and favourable to clinging by postnascence condition.

Postnascent aggregates acquired by clinging and favourable to clinging are related to this prenascent body acquired by clinging and favourable to clinging by postnascence condition. (1)

(ii) State acquired by clinging and favourable to clinging is related to state not acquired by clinging but favourable to clinging by postnascence condition.

Postnascent aggregates acquired by clinging and favourable to clinging are related to this prenascent body not acquired by clinging but favourable to clinging by postnascence condition. (2)

(iii) State acquired by clinging and favourable to clinging is related to state, acquired by clinging and favourable to clinging and not acquired by clinging but favourable to clinging, by postnascence condition.

Postnascent aggregates acquired by clinging and favourable to clinging are related to this prenascent body acquired by clinging and favourable to clinging and not acquired by clinging but favourable to clinging by postnascence condition. (3)

(iv) State not acquired by clinging but favourable to clinging is related to state not acquired by clinging but favourable to clinging by postnascence condition.

Postnascent aggregates not acquired by clinging but favourable to clinging are related to this prenascent body not acquired by clinging but favourable to clinging by postnascence condition. (1)

(v) State not acquired by clinging but favourable to clinging is related to state acquired by clinging and favourable to clinging by postnascence condition.

Postnascent aggregates not acquired by clinging but favourable to clinging are related to this prenascent body acquired by clinging and favourable to clinging by postnascence condition. (2)

(vi) State not acquired by clinging but favourable to clinging is related to state, acquired by clinging and favourable to clinging and not acquired by clinging but favourable to clinging, by postnascence condition.

Postnascent aggregates not acquired by clinging but favourable to clinging are related to this prenascent body acquired by clinging and favourable to clinging and not acquired by clinging but favourable to clinging by postnascence condition. (3)

67. (vii) State not acquired by clinging and not favourable to clinging is related to state acquired by clinging and favourable to clinging by postnascence condition.

Postnascent aggregates not acquired by clinging and not favourable to clinging are related to this prenascent body acquired by clinging and favourable to clinging by postnascence condition. (1)

(viii) State not acquired by clinging and not favourable to clinging is related to state not acquired by clinging but favourable to clinging by postnascence condition.

Postnascent aggregates not acquired by clinging and not favourable to clinging are related to this prenascent body not acquired by clinging but favourable to clinging by postnascence condition. (2)

(ix) State not acquired by clinging and not favourable to

clinging is related to state, acquired by clinging and favourable to clinging and not acquired by clinging but favourable to clinging, by postnascence condition.

Postnascent aggregates not acquired by clinging and not favourable to clinging are related to this prenascent body acquired by clinging and favourable to clinging and not acquired by clinging but favourable to clinging by postnascence condition. (3)

Repetition 2

68. (i) State not acquired by clinging but favourable to clinging is related to state not acquired by clinging but favourable to clinging by repetition condition.

Preceding aggregates not acquired by clinging but favourable to clinging are related to subsequent aggregates not acquired by clinging but favourable to clinging by repetition condition. Adaptation to change-of-lineage; adaptation is related to purification by repetition condition. (1)

(ii) State not acquired by clinging but favourable to clinging is related to state not acquired by clinging and not favourable to clinging by repetition condition.

Change-of-lineage to Path; purification is related to Path by repetition condition. (2)

Kamma 8

69. (i) State acquired by clinging and favourable to clinging is related to state acquired by clinging and favourable to clinging by kamma condition.

Volition acquired by clinging and favourable to clinging is related to (its) associated aggregates by kamma condition. At the moment of conception, volition acquired by clinging and favourable to clinging is related to (its) associated aggregates and kamma-produced matter by kamma condition; volition is related to (heart-)base by kamma condition. (1)

(ii) State acquired by clinging and favourable to clinging is related to state not acquired by clinging but favourable to clinging by kamma condition.

Volition acquired by clinging and favourable to clinging is related to mind-produced matter by kamma condition. (2)

(iii) State acquired by clinging and favourable to clinging is related to state, acquired by clinging and favourable to clinging and not acquired by clinging but favourable to clinging, by kamma condition.

Volition acquired by clinging and favourable to clinging is related to (its) associated aggregates and mind-produced matter by kamma condition. (3)

(iv) State not acquired by clinging but favourable to clinging is related to state not acquired by clinging but favourable to clinging by kamma condition.

Volition not acquired by clinging but favourable to clinging is related to (its) associated aggregates and mind-produced matter by kamma condition. (1)

(v) State not acquired by clinging but favourable to clinging is related to state acquired by clinging and favourable to clinging by kamma condition.

Asynchronous volition not acquired by clinging but favourable to clinging is related to resultant aggregates acquired by clinging and favourable to clinging and kamma-produced matter by kamma condition. (2)

70. (vi) State not acquired by clinging and not favourable to clinging is related to state not acquired by clinging and not favourable to clinging by kamma condition.

(It is of two kinds, namely :) (*a*) conascence(-kamma), (*b*) asynchronous (kamma).

(*a*) Conascent volition not acquired by clinging and not favourable to clinging is related to (its) associated aggregates by kamma condition.

(*b*) Asynchronous faultless volition not acquired by clinging and not favourable to clinging is related to resultant aggregates not acquired by clinging and not favourable to clinging by kamma condition. (1)

(vii) State not acquired by clinging and not favourable to clinging is related to state not acquired by clinging but favourable to clinging by kamma condition.

Volition not acquired by clinging and not favourable to clinging is related to mind-produced matter by kamma condition. (2)

(viii) State not acquired by clinging and not favourable to

clinging is related to state, not acquired by clinging but favourable to clinging and not acquired by clinging and not favourable to clinging, by kamma condition.

Volition not acquired by clinging and not favourable to clinging is related to (its) associated aggregates and mind-produced matter by kamma condition. (3)

Resultant 6

71. (i) State acquired by clinging and favourable to clinging is related to state acquired by clinging and favourable to clinging by resultant condition.

One resultant aggregate acquired by clinging and favourable to clinging is related to three aggregates by resultant condition ... two aggregates are related to two aggregates by resultant condition. At the moment of conception, one resultant aggregate acquired by clinging and favourable to clinging is related to three aggregates and kamma-produced matter by resultant condition ... two aggregates are related to two aggregates and kamma-produced matter by resultant condition; aggregates are related to (heart-)base by resultant condition. (1)

(ii) State acquired by clinging and favourable to clinging is related to state not acquired by clinging but favourable to clinging by resultant condition.

Resultant aggregates acquired by clinging and favourable to clinging are related to mind-produced matter by resultant condition. (2)

(iii) State acquired by clinging and favourable to clinging is related to state, acquired by clinging and favourable to clinging and not acquired by clinging but favourable to clinging, by resultant condition.

One resultant aggregate acquired by clinging and favourable to clinging is related to three aggregates and mind-produced matter by resultant condition ... two aggregates are related to two aggregates and mind-produced matter by resultant condition. (3)

(iv) State not acquired by clinging and not favourable to clinging is related to state not acquired by clinging and not favourable to clinging by resultant condition.

One resultant aggregate not acquired by clinging and not favourable to clinging is related to three aggregates by resultant condition . . . two aggregates are related to two aggregates by resultant condition. (1)

(v) State not acquired by clinging and not favourable to clinging is related to state not acquired by clinging but favourable to clinging by resultant condition.

Resultant aggregates not acquired by clinging and not favourable to clinging are related to mind-produced matter by resultant condition. (2)

(vi) State not acquired by clinging and not favourable to clinging is related to state, not acquired by clinging but favourable to clinging and not acquired by clinging and not favourable to clinging, by resultant condition.

One resultant aggregate not acquired by clinging and not favourable to clinging is related to three aggregates and mind-produced matter by resultant condition . . . two aggregates are related to two aggregates and mind-produced matter by resultant condition. (3)

Nutriment 12

72. (i) State acquired by clinging and favourable to clinging is related to state acquired by clinging and favourable to clinging by nutriment condition.

Nutriments acquired by clinging and favourable to clinging are related to (their) associated aggregates by nutriment condition.

At the moment of conception, nutriments acquired by clinging and favourable to clinging are related to (their) associated aggregates and kamma-produced matter by nutriment condition.

Edible food acquired by clinging and favourable to clinging is related to body acquired by clinging and favourable to clinging by nutriment condition. (1)

(ii) State acquired by clinging and favourable to clinging is related to state not acquired by clinging but favourable to clinging by nutriment condition.

Nutriments acquired by clinging and favourable to clinging are related to mind-produced matter by nutriment condition.

Edible food acquired by clinging and favourable to clinging

is related to body not acquired by clinging but favourable to clinging by nutriment condition. (2)

(iii) State acquired by clinging and favourable to clinging is related to state, acquired by clinging and favourable to clinging and not acquired by clinging but favourable to clinging, by nutriment condition.

Nutriments acquired by clinging and favourable to clinging are related to (their) associated aggregates and mind-produced matter by nutriment condition.

Edible food acquired by clinging and favourable to clinging is related to body acquired by clinging and favourable to clinging and not acquired by clinging but favourable to clinging by nutriment condition. (3)

73. (iv) State not acquired by clinging but favourable to clinging is related to state not acquired by clinging but favourable to clinging by nutriment condition.

Nutriments not acquired by clinging but favourable to clinging are related to (their) associated aggregates and mind-produced matter by nutriment condition.

Edible food not acquired by clinging but favourable to clinging is related to body not acquired by clinging but favourable to clinging by nutriment condition. (1)

(v) State not acquired by clinging but favourable to clinging is related to state acquired by clinging and favourable to clinging by nutriment condition.

Edible food not acquired by clinging but favourable to clinging is related to body acquired by clinging and favourable to clinging by nutriment condition. (2)

(vi) State not acquired by clinging but favourable to clinging is related to state, acquired by clinging and favourable to clinging and not acquired by clinging but favourable to clinging, by nutriment condition.

Edible food not acquired by clinging but favourable to clinging is related to body acquired by clinging and favourable to clinging and not acquired by clinging but favourable to clinging by nutriment condition. (3)

(vii) State not acquired by clinging and not favourable to clinging is related to state not acquired by clinging and not favourable to clinging by nutriment condition.

Nutriments not acquired by clinging and not favourable to clinging are related to (their) associated aggregates by nutriment condition. (1)

(viii) State not acquired by clinging and not favourable to clinging is related to state not acquired by clinging but favourable to clinging by nutriment condition.

Nutriments not acquired by clinging and not favourable to clinging are related to mind-produced matter by nutriment condition. (2)

(ix) State not acquired by clinging and not favourable to clinging is related to state, not acquired by clinging but favourable to clinging and not acquired by clinging and not favourable to clinging, by nutriment condition.

Nutriments not acquired by clinging and not favourable to clinging are related to (their) associated aggregates and mind-produced matter by nutriment condition. (3)

74. (x) States, acquired by clinging and favourable to clinging and not acquired by clinging but favourable to clinging, are related to state acquired by clinging and favourable to clinging by nutriment condition.

Edible food acquired by clinging and favourable to clinging and not acquired by clinging but favourable to clinging are related to body acquired by clinging and favourable to clinging by nutriment condition. (1)

(xi) States, acquired by clinging and favourable to clinging and not acquired by clinging but favourable to clinging, are related to state not acquired by clinging but favourable to clinging by nutriment condition.

Edible food acquired by clinging and favourable to clinging and not acquired by clinging but favourable to clinging are related to body not acquired by clinging but favourable to clinging by nutriment condition. (2)

(xii) States, acquired by clinging and favourable to clinging and not acquired by clinging but favourable to clinging, are related to state, acquired by clinging and favourable to clinging and not acquired by clinging but favourable to clinging, by nutriment condition.

Edible food acquired by clinging and favourable to clinging and not acquired by clinging but favourable to clinging are related to body acquired by clinging and favourable to clinging and not acquired by clinging but favourable to clinging by nutriment condition. (3)

Faculty 7

75. (i) State acquired by clinging and favourable to clinging is related to state acquired by clinging and favourable to clinging by faculty condition.

Faculties acquired by clinging and favourable to clinging are related to (their) associated aggregates by faculty condition. At the moment of conception, faculties acquired by clinging and favourable to clinging are related to (their) associated aggregates and kamma-produced matter by faculty condition.

Eye-faculty to eye-consciousness ... body-faculty to body-consciousness. ... Physical life-faculty is related to kamma-produced matter by faculty condition. (1)

(ii) State acquired by clinging and favourable to clinging is related to state not acquired by clinging but favourable to clinging by faculty condition.

Faculties acquired by clinging and favourable to clinging are related to mind-produced matter by faculty condition. (2)

(iii) State acquired by clinging and favourable to clinging is related to state, acquired by clinging and favourable to clinging and not acquired by clinging but favourable to clinging, by faculty condition.

Faculties acquired by clinging and favourable to clinging are related to (their) associated aggregates and mind-produced matter by faculty condition. (3)

(iv) State not acquired by clinging but favourable to clinging is related to state not acquired by clinging but favourable to clinging by faculty condition.

Faculties not acquired by clinging but favourable to clinging are related to (their) associated aggregates and mind-produced matter by faculty condition. (1)

(v) State not acquired by clinging and not favourable to clinging is related to state not acquired by clinging and not favourable to clinging by faculty condition.

Faculties not acquired by clinging and not favourable to

clinging are related to (their) associated aggregates by faculty condition. (1)

(vi) State not acquired by clinging and not favourable to clinging is related to state not acquired by clinging but favourable to clinging by faculty condition.

Faculties not acquired by clinging and not favourable to clinging are related to mind-produced matter by faculty condition. (2)

(vii) State not acquired by clinging and not favourable to clinging is related to state, not acquired by clinging but favourable to clinging and not acquired by clinging and not favourable to clinging, by faculty condition.

Faculties not acquired by clinging and not favourable to clinging are related to (their) associated aggregates and mind-produced matter by faculty condition. (3)

Jhāna 7

76. (i) State acquired by clinging and favourable to clinging is related to state acquired by clinging and favourable to clinging by jhāna condition.

Jhāna factors acquired by clinging and favourable to clinging are related to (their) associated aggregates by jhāna condition.

At the moment of conception, jhāna factors acquired by clinging and favourable to clinging are related to (their) associated aggregates and kamma-produced matter by jhāna condition. (1)

(ii) State acquired by clinging and favourable to clinging is related to state not acquired by clinging but favourable to clinging by jhāna condition.

Jhāna factors acquired by clinging and favourable to clinging are related to mind-produced matter by jhāna condition. (2)

(iii) State acquired by clinging and favourable to clinging is related to state, acquired by clinging and favourable to clinging and not acquired by clinging but favourable to clinging, by jhāna condition.

Jhāna factors acquired by clinging and favourable to clinging are related to (their) associated aggregates and mind-produced matter by jhāna condition. (3)

(iv) State not acquired by clinging but favourable to clinging is related to state not acquired by clinging but favourable to clinging by jhāna condition.

Jhāna factors not acquired by clinging but favourable to clinging are related to (their) associated aggregates and mind-produced matter by jhāna condition. (1)

77. (v) State not acquired by clinging and not favourable to clinging is related to state not acquired by clinging and not favourable to clinging by jhāna condition.

Jhāna factors not acquired by clinging and not favourable to clinging are related to (their) associated aggregates by jhāna condition. (1)

(vi) State not acquired by clinging and not favourable to clinging is related to state not acquired by clinging but favourable to clinging by jhāna condition.

Jhāna factors not acquired by clinging and not favourable to clinging are related to mind-produced matter by jhāna condition. (2)

(vii) State not acquired by clinging and not favourable to clinging is related to state, not acquired by clinging but favourable to clinging and not acquired by clinging and not favourable to clinging, by jhāna condition.

Jhāna factors not acquired by clinging and not favourable to clinging are related to (their) associated aggregates and mind-produced matter by jhāna condition. (3)

Path 7

78. (i) State acquired by clinging and favourable to clinging is related to state acquired by clinging and favourable to clinging by path condition.

Path factors acquired by clinging and favourable to clinging are related to (their) associated aggregates by path condition.

At the moment of conception. ... (1)

(ii) State acquired by clinging and favourable to clinging is related to state not acquired by clinging but favourable to clinging by path condition.

Path factors acquired by clinging and favourable to clinging are related to mind-produced matter by path condition. (2)

(iii) State acquired by clinging and favourable to clinging is related to state, acquired by clinging and favourable to clinging and not acquired by clinging but favourable to clinging, by path condition.

Path factors acquired by clinging and favourable to clinging are related to (their) associated aggregates and mind-produced matter by path condition. (3)

(iv) State not acquired by clinging but favourable to clinging is related to state not acquired by clinging but favourable to clinging by path condition.

Path factors not acquired by clinging but favourable to clinging are related to (their) associated aggregates and mind-produced matter by path condition. (1)

(v) State not acquired by clinging and not favourable to clinging is related to state not acquired by clinging and not favourable to clinging by path condition.

Path factors not acquired by clinging and not favourable to clinging are related to (their) associated aggregates by path condition. (1)

(vi) State not acquired by clinging and not favourable to clinging is related to state not acquired by clinging but favourable to clinging by path condition.

Path factors not acquired by clinging and not favourable to clinging are related to mind-produced matter by path condition. (2)

(vii) State not acquired by clinging and not favourable to clinging is related to state, not acquired by clinging but favourable to clinging and not acquired by clinging and not favourable to clinging, by path condition.

Path factors not acquired by clinging and not favourable to clinging are related to (their) associated aggregates and mind-produced matter by path condition. (3)

Association 3

79. (i) State acquired by clinging and favourable to clinging is related to state acquired by clinging and favourable to clinging by association condition.

One aggregate acquired by clinging and favourable to clinging is related to three aggregates by association condition ... two aggregates to two aggregates. ... At the moment of conception. ... (1)

(ii) State not acquired by clinging but favourable to clinging is related to state not acquired by clinging but favourable to clinging by association condition.

One aggregate not acquired by clinging but favourable to clinging is related to three aggregates by association condition ... two aggregates to two aggregates. ... (1)

(iii) State not acquired by clinging and not favourable to clinging is related to state not acquired by clinging and not favourable to clinging by association condition.

One aggregate not acquired by clinging and not favourable to clinging is related to three aggregates by association condition ... two aggregates to two aggregates. ... (1)

Dissociation 10

80. (i) State acquired by clinging and favourable to clinging is related to state acquired by clinging and favourable to clinging by dissociation condition.

(It is of three kinds, namely :) (*a*) conascence, (*b*) prenascence, (*c*) postnascence.

(*a*) At the moment of conception, conascent aggregates acquired by clinging and favourable to clinging are related to kamma-produced matter by dissociation condition ; aggregates are related to (heart-)base by dissociation condition ; (heart-)base is related to aggregates by dissociation condition.

(*b*) *Prenascence*: Eye-base is related to eye-consciousness by dissociation condition ... body-base is related to body-consciousness by dissociation condition. (Heart-)base is related to the aggregates acquired by clinging and favourable to clinging by dissociation condition.

(*c*) Postnascent aggregates acquired by clinging and favourable to clinging are related to this prenascent body acquired by clinging and favourable to clinging by dissociation condition. (1)

(ii) State acquired by clinging and favourable to clinging is related to state not acquired by clinging but favourable to clinging by dissociation condition.

(It is of three kinds, namely :) (*a*) conascence, (*b*) prenascence, (*c*) postnascence.

(*a*) Conascent aggregates acquired by clinging and favourable to clinging are related to mind-produced matter by dissociation condition.

(*b*) Prenascent (heart-)base is related to the aggregates not acquired by clinging but favourable to clinging by dissociation condition.

(*c*) Postnascent aggregates acquired by clinging and favourable to clinging are related to this prenascent body not acquired by clinging but favourable to clinging by dissociation condition. (2)

(iii) State acquired by clinging and favourable to clinging is related to state not acquired by clinging and not favourable to clinging by dissociation condition.

Prenascent (heart-)base is related to the aggregates not acquired by clinging and not favourable to clinging by dissociation condition. (3)

(iv) State acquired by clinging and favourable to clinging is related to state, acquired by clinging and favourable to clinging and not acquired by clinging but favourable to clinging, by dissociation condition.

Postnascent aggregates acquired by clinging and favourable to clinging are related to this prenascent body acquired by clinging and favourable to clinging and not acquired by clinging but favourable to clinging by dissociation condition. (4)

81. (v) State not acquired by clinging but favourable to clinging is related to state not acquired by clinging but favourable to clinging by dissociation condition.

(It is of two kinds, namely :) (*a*) conascence, (*b*) postnascence.

(*a*) Conascent aggregates not acquired by clinging but favourable to clinging are related to mind-produced matter by dissociation condition.

(*b*) Postnascent aggregates not acquired by clinging but favourable to clinging are related to this prenascent body not acquired by clinging but favourable to clinging by dissociation condition. (1)

(vi) State not acquired by clinging but favourable to clinging is related to state acquired by clinging and favourable to clinging by dissociation condition.

Postnascent aggregates not acquired by clinging but favour-

Clinging Triplet 487

able to clinging are related to this prenascent body acquired by clinging and favourable to clinging by dissociation condition. (2)

(vii) State not acquired by clinging but favourable to clinging is related to state, acquired by clinging and favourable to clinging and not acquired by clinging but favourable to clinging, by dissociation condition.

Postnascent aggregates not acquired by clinging but favourable to clinging are related to this prenascent body acquired by clinging and favourable to clinging and not acquired by clinging but favourable to clinging by dissociation condition. (3)

(viii) State not acquired by clinging and not favourable to clinging is related to state acquired by clinging and favourable to clinging by dissociation condition.

Postnascent aggregates not acquired by clinging and not favourable to clinging are related to this prenascent body acquired by clinging and favourable to clinging by dissociation condition. (1)

(ix) State not acquired by clinging and not favourable to clinging is related to state not acquired by clinging but favourable to clinging by dissociation condition.

(It is of two kinds, namely :) (*a*) conascence, (*b*) postnascence.

(*a*) Conascent aggregates not acquired by clinging and not favourable to clinging are related to mind-produced matter by dissociation condition.

(*b*) Postnascent aggregates not acquired by clinging and not favourable to clinging are related to this prenascent body not acquired by clinging but favourable to clinging by dissociation condition. (2)

(x) State not acquired by clinging and not favourable to clinging is related to state, acquired by clinging and favourable to clinging and not acquired by clinging but favourable to clinging, by dissociation condition.

Postnascent aggregates not acquired by clinging and not favourable to clinging are related to this prenascent body acquired by clinging and favourable to clinging and not acquired by clinging but favourable to clinging by dissociation condition. (3)

Presence 23

82. (i) State acquired by clinging and favourable to clinging is related to state acquired by clinging and favourable to clinging by presence condition.

(It is of five kinds, namely :) (*a*) conascence, (*b*) prenascence, (*c*) postnascence, (*d*) nutriment, (*e*) faculty.

(*a*) One conascent aggregate acquired by clinging and favourable to clinging is related to three aggregates by presence condition ... two aggregates are related to two aggregates by presence condition. At the moment of conception, one aggregate acquired by clinging and favourable to clinging is related to three aggregates and kamma-produced matter by presence condition ... two aggregates are related to two aggregates and kamma-produced matter by presence condition ; aggregates to (heart-)base ... (heart-)base to aggregates. ... One great primary ... great primaries are related to kamma-produced derived matter by presence condition. One great primary of non-percipient beings ... great primaries are related to kamma-produced derived matter by presence condition.

(*b*) *Prenascence* : Learners or common worldlings practise insight into the impermanency, suffering and impersonality of the eye ; enjoy and delight in (the eye). Taking it as object arises lust ... arises grief. When the faultless or faulty has ceased, the resultant arises as registering. ... ear ... nose ... tongue ... body ... visible objects acquired by clinging and favourable to clinging ... smells ... tastes ... tangible objects. ... (They) practise insight into the impermanency, suffering and impersonality of the (heart-)base ; enjoy and delight in (the heart-base). Taking it as object arises lust ... arises grief. When the faultless or faulty has ceased, the resultant arises as registering.

Visible object-base acquired by clinging and favourable to clinging to eye-consciousness ... smell-base ... taste-base ... tangible object-base acquired by clinging and favourable to clinging to body-consciousness. ... Eye-base to eye-consciousness ... body-base to body-consciousness ... (heart-)base is related to the aggregates acquired by clinging and favourable to clinging by presence condition.

(c) Postnascent aggregates acquired by clinging and favourable to clinging are related to this prenascent body acquired by clinging and favourable to clinging by presence condition.

(d) Edible food acquired by clinging and favourable to clinging is related to body acquired by clinging and favourable to clinging by presence condition.

(e) Physical life-faculty is related to kamma-produced matter by presence condition. (1)

(ii) State acquired by clinging and favourable to clinging is related to state not acquired by clinging but favourable to clinging by presence condition.

(It is of four kinds, namely :) (a) conascence, (b) prenascence, (c) postnascence, (d) nutriment.

(a) Conascent aggregates acquired by clinging and favourable to clinging are related to mind-produced matter by presence condition.

(b) *Prenascence* : (One) practises insight into the impermanency, suffering and impersonality of the eye ; enjoys and delights in (the eye). Taking it as object arises lust . . . arises grief. . . . ear . . . nose . . . tongue . . . body . . . visible objects acquired by clinging and favourable to clinging . . . smells . . . tastes . . . tangible objects. . . . (One) practises insight into the impermanency, suffering and impersonality of the (heart-)base ; enjoys and delights in (the heart-base). Taking it as object arises lust . . . arises grief.

By the power of divine-eye, (one) sees the visible object acquired by clinging and favourable to clinging. (Heart-)base is related to the aggregates not acquired by clinging but favourable to clinging by presence condition.

(c) Postnascent aggregates acquired by clinging and favourable to clinging are related to this prenascent body not acquired by clinging but favourable to clinging by presence condition.

(d) Edible food acquired by clinging and favourable to clinging is related to body not acquired by clinging but favourable to clinging by presence condition. (2)

(iii) State acquired by clinging and favourable to clinging is related to state not acquired by clinging and not favourable to clinging by presence condition.

Prenascent (heart-)base is related to the aggregates not

acquired by clinging and not favourable to clinging by presence condition. (3)

(iv) State acquired by clinging and favourable to clinging is related to state, acquired by clinging and favourable to clinging and not acquired by clinging but favourable to clinging, by presence condition.

(It is of three kinds, namely :) (*a*) conascence, (*b*) postnascence, (*c*) nutriment.

(*a*) One conascent aggregate acquired by clinging and favourable to clinging is related to three aggregates and mind-produced matter by presence condition ... two aggregates are related to two aggregates and mind-produced matter by presence condition.

(*b*) Postnascent aggregates acquired by clinging and favourable to clinging are related to this prenascent body acquired by clinging and favourable to clinging and not acquired by clinging but favourable to clinging by presence condition.

(*c*) Edible food acquired by clinging and favourable to clinging is related to body acquired by clinging and favourable to clinging and not acquired by clinging but favourable to clinging by presence condition. (4)

83. (v) State not acquired by clinging but favourable to clinging is related to state not acquired by clinging but favourable to clinging by presence condition.

(It is of four kinds, namely :) (*a*) conascence, (*b*) prenascence, (*c*) postnascence, (*d*) nutriment.

(*a*) One conascent aggregate not acquired by clinging but favourable to clinging is related to three aggregates and mind-produced matter by presence condition ... two aggregates are related to two aggregates and mind-produced matter by presence condition.

One great primary to three great primaries ... great primaries are related to mind-produced derived matter by presence condition. External ... nutriment-produced ... one temperature-produced great primary. ...

(*b*) *Prenascence :* Visible objects not acquired by clinging but favourable to clinging, sounds ... smells ... tastes. ... (One) practises insight into the impermanency, suffering and impersonality of tangible objects ... ; enjoys and delights in (those objects). Taking it as object arises lust ... arises grief. By the power of divine-eye, (one) sees the visible object not acquired by clinging but favourable to clinging. By the power of divine-ear element, hears the sound.

(c) Postnascent aggregates not acquired by clinging but favourable to clinging are related to this prenascent body not acquired by clinging but favourable to clinging by presence condition.

(d) Edible food not acquired by clinging but favourable to clinging is related to body not acquired by clinging but favourable to clinging by presence condition. (1)

(vi) State not acquired by clinging but favourable to clinging is related to state acquired by clinging and favourable to clinging by presence condition.

(It is of three kinds, namely :) (a) prenascence, (b) postnascence, (c) nutriment.

(a) *Prenascence* : Visible objects not acquired by clinging but favourable to clinging, sounds ... smells ... tastes. ... (One) practises insight into the impermanency, suffering and impersonality of tangible objects ... ; enjoys and delights in (those objects). Taking it as object arises lust ... arises grief. When the faultless or faulty has ceased, the resultant arises as registering. Visible object-base not acquired by clinging but favourable to clinging to eye-consciousness ... tangible object-base ... is related to body-consciousness by presence condition.

(b) Postnascent aggregates not acquired by clinging but favourable to clinging are related to this prenascent body acquired by clinging and favourable to clinging by presence condition.

(c) Edible food not acquired by clinging but favourable to clinging is related to body acquired by clinging and favourable to clinging by presence condition. (2)

(vii) State not acquired by clinging but favourable to clinging is related to state, acquired by clinging and favourable to clinging and not acquired by clinging but favourable to clinging, by presence condition.

(It is of two kinds, namely :) (a) postnascence, (b) nutriment.

(a) Postnascent aggregates not acquired by clinging but favourable to clinging are related to this prenascent body acquired by clinging and favourable to clinging and not acquired by clinging but favourable to clinging by presence condition.

(*b*) Edible food not acquired by clinging but favourable to clinging is related to body acquired by clinging and favourable to clinging and not acquired by clinging but favourable to clinging by presence condition. (3)

84. (viii) State not acquired by clinging and not favourable to clinging is related to state not acquired by clinging and not favourable to clinging by presence condition.

One aggregate not acquired by clinging and not favourable to clinging is related to three aggregates by presence condition ... two aggregates are related to two aggregates by presence condition. (1)

(ix) State not acquired by clinging and not favourable to clinging is related to state acquired by clinging and favourable to clinging by presence condition.

Postnascent aggregates not acquired by clinging and not favourable to clinging are related to this prenascent body acquired by clinging and favourable to clinging by presence condition. (2)

(x) State not acquired by clinging and not favourable to clinging is related to state not acquired by clinging but favourable to clinging by presence condition.

(It is of two kinds, namely :) (*a*) conascence, (*b*) postnascence.

(*a*) Conascent aggregates not acquired by clinging and not favourable to clinging are related to mind-produced matter by presence condition.

(*b*) Postnascent aggregates not acquired by clinging and not favourable to clinging are related to this prenascent body not acquired by clinging but favourable to clinging by presence condition. (3)

(xi) State not acquired by clinging and not favourable to clinging is related to state, acquired by clinging and favourable to clinging and not acquired by clinging and not favourable to clinging, by presence condition.

Conascence-postnascence : One conascent aggregate not acquired by clinging and not favourable to clinging is related to three aggregates and this prenascent body acquired by clinging and favourable to clinging by presence condition ; three aggregates are related to one aggregate and this prenascent body acquired by clinging and favourable to clinging by presence condition ; two aggregates are related to two aggregates and this prenascent body acquired by clinging and favourable to clinging by presence condition. (4)

(xii) State not acquired by clinging and not favourable to clinging is related to state, not acquired by clinging but favourable to clinging and not acquired by clinging and not favourable to clinging, by presence condition.

(It is of two kinds, namely :) (*a*) conascence, (*b*) (conascence-) postnascence.

(*a*) One conascent aggregate not acquired by clinging and not favourable to clinging is related to three aggregates and mind-produced matter by presence condition ; three aggregates are related to one aggregate and mind-produced matter by presence condition ; two aggregates are related to two aggregates and mind-produced matter by presence condition.

(*b*) One conascent aggregate not acquired by clinging and not favourable to clinging is related to three aggregates and this prenascent body not acquired by clinging but favourable to clinging by presence condition ; three aggregates are related to one aggregate and this prenascent body not acquired by clinging but favourable to clinging by presence condition ; two aggregates are related to two aggregates and this prenascent body not acquired by clinging but favourable to clinging by presence condition. (5)

(xiii) State not acquired by clinging and not favourable to clinging is related to state, acquired by clinging and favourable to clinging and not acquired by clinging but favourable to clinging, by presence condition.

Postnascent aggregates not acquired by clinging and not favourable to clinging are related to this prenascent body acquired by clinging and favourable to clinging and not acquired by clinging but favourable to clinging by presence condition. (6)

(xiv) State not acquired by clinging and not favourable to clinging is related to state, acquired by clinging and favourable to clinging and not acquired by clinging but favourable to clinging and not acquired by clinging and not favourable to clinging, by presence condition.

Conascence-postnascence : One conascent aggregate not acquired by clinging and not favourable to clinging is related to three aggregates and this prenascent body acquired by clinging and favourable to clinging and not acquired by clinging but favourable to clinging by presence condition ; three aggregates are related to one aggregate and this prenascent body acquired by clinging and favourable to clinging and not acquired by clinging but favourable to clinging by presence condition ; two aggregates are related to two aggregates and this prenascent body acquired by clinging and favourable to clinging and not acquired by clinging but favourable to clinging by presence condition. (7)

85. (xv) States, acquired by clinging and favourable to clinging and not acquired by clinging and not favourable to clinging, are related to state acquired by clinging and favourable to clinging by presence condition.

Postnascence-faculty : Postnascent aggregates not acquired by clinging and not favourable to clinging and physical life-faculty are related to kamma-produced matter by presence condition. (1)

(xvi) States, acquired by clinging and favourable to clinging and not acquired by clinging and not favourable to clinging, are related to state not acquired by clinging and not favourable to clinging by presence condition.

Conascence-prenascence : One conascent aggregate not acquired by clinging and not favourable to clinging and (heart-)-base are related to three aggregates by presence condition ; three aggregates and (heart-)base are related to one aggregate by presence condition ; two aggregates and (heart-)base are related to two aggregates by presence condition. (2)

(xvii) States, not acquired by clinging but favourable to clinging and not acquired by clinging and not favourable to clinging, are related to state acquired by clinging and favourable to clinging by presence condition.

Postnascence-nutriment : Postnascent aggregates not acquired by clinging and not favourable to clinging and edible food not acquired by clinging but favourable to clinging are related to body acquired by clinging and favourable to clinging by presence condition. (1)

(xviii) States, not acquired by clinging but favourable to clinging and not acquired by clinging and not favourable to clinging, are related to state not acquired by clinging but favourable to clinging by presence condition.

(It is of two kinds, namely :) (*a*) conascence, (*b*) postnascence-nutriment.

(*a*) Conascent aggregates not acquired by clinging and not favourable to clinging and great primaries are related to mind-produced matter by presence condition.

(*b*) Postnascent aggregates not acquired by clinging and not favourable to clinging and edible food not acquired by clinging but favourable to clinging are related to body not acquired by clinging but favourable to clinging by presence condition. (2)

(xix) States, not acquired by clinging but favourable to clinging and not acquired by clinging and not favourable to clinging, are related to state, acquired by clinging and favourable to clinging and not acquired by clinging but favourable to clinging, by presence condition.

Postnascence-nutriment : Postnascent aggregates not acquired by clinging and not favourable to clinging and edible food not acquired by clinging but favourable to clinging are related to body acquired by clinging and favourable to clinging and not acquired by clinging but favourable to clinging by presence condition. (3)

86. (xx) States, acquired by clinging and favourable to clinging and not acquired by clinging but favourable to clinging, are related to state acquired by clinging and favourable to clinging by presence condition.

(It is of four kinds, namely :) (*a*) prenascence, (*b*) postnascence(-nutriment), (*c*) nutriment, (*d*) (postnascence-)faculty.

(*a*) *Prenascence* : Visible object-base not acquired by clinging but favourable to clinging and eye-base are related to eye-consciousness by presence condition ... tangible object-base not acquired by clinging but favourable to clinging and body-base are related to body-consciousness by presence condition. Visible object-base not acquired by clinging but favourable to clinging and (heart-)base to the aggregates acquired by clinging and favourable to clinging ... tangible object-base not acquired by clinging but favourable to clinging and (heart-)base are related to the aggregates acquired by clinging and favourable to clinging by presence condition.

(b) Postnascent aggregates acquired by clinging and favourable to clinging and edible food not acquired by clinging but favourable to clinging are related to body acquired by clinging and favourable to clinging by presence condition.

(c) Edible food acquired by clinging and favourable to clinging and not acquired by clinging but favourable to clinging are related to body acquired by clinging and favourable to clinging by presence condition.

(d) Postnascent aggregates not acquired by clinging but favourable to clinging and physical life-faculty are related to kamma-produced matter by presence condition. (1)

(xxi) States, acquired by clinging and favourable to clinging and not acquired by clinging but favourable to clinging, are related to state not acquired by clinging but favourable to clinging by presence condition.

(It is of four kinds, namely :) (a) conascence, (b) prenascence, (c) postnascence(-nutriment), (d) nutriment.

(a) Conascent aggregates acquired by clinging and favourable to clinging and great primaries are related to mind-produced matter by presence condition.

(b) *Prenascence* : Visible object-base not acquired by clinging but favourable to clinging and (heart-)base to the aggregates not acquired by clinging but favourable to clinging ... tangible object-base not acquired by clinging but favourable to clinging and (heart-)base are related to the aggregates not acquired by clinging but favourable to clinging by presence condition.

(c) Postnascent aggregates acquired by clinging and favourable to clinging and edible food not acquired by clinging but favourable to clinging are related to body not acquired by clinging but favourable to clinging by presence condition.

(d) Edible food acquired by clinging and favourable to clinging and not acquired by clinging but favourable to clinging are related to body not acquired by clinging but favourable to clinging by presence condition. (2)

(xxii) States, acquired by clinging and favourable to clinging and not acquired by clinging but favourable to clinging, are related to state, acquired by clinging and favourable to clinging and not acquired by clinging but favourable to clinging, by presence condition.

Nutriment: Edible food acquired by clinging and favourable to clinging and not acquired by clinging but favourable to clinging are related to body acquired by clinging and favourable to clinging and not acquired by clinging but favourable to clinging by presence condition. (3)

(xxiii) States, acquired by clinging and favourable to clinging and not acquired by clinging but favourable to clinging and not acquired by clinging and not favourable to clinging, are related to state acquired by clinging and favourable to clinging by presence condition.

Postnascence-nutriment-faculty: Postnascent aggregates not acquired by clinging and not favourable to clinging, edible food not acquired by clinging but favourable to clinging and physical life-faculty are related to kamma-produced matter by presence condition. (1)

Absence 7, Disappearance 7 and Non-disappearance 23

87. State acquired by clinging and favourable to clinging is related to state acquired by clinging and favourable to clinging by absence condition . . . by disappearance condition . . . by non-disappearance condition. . . . (Abbreviated.)

I. CONDITIONS : POSITIVE   (ii) ENUMERATION CHAPTER

By Ones

88. With root 7, object 6, predominance 5, proximity 7, contiguity 7, conascence 9, mutuality 3, dependence 11, strong-dependence 9, prenascence 7, postnascence 9, repetition 2, kamma 8, resultant 6, nutriment 12, faculty 7, jhāna 7, path 7, association 3, dissociation 10, presence 23, absence 7, disappearance 7, non-disappearance 23.

Common

With root condition and predominance 4, conascence 7, mutuality 3, dependence 7, resultant 6, faculty 7, path 7, association 3, dissociation 4, presence 7, non-disappearance 7. . . . (Abbreviated.)

(Enumerate in the same way as enumerated in Faultless Triplet Enumeration for recital. The Enumeration in Clinging Triplet is more profound and subtle than the Enumeration in Faultless Triplet and therefore it should be enumerated likewise without confusion.)

End of Positive

2. SELECTION OF THE CONDITIONS FOR NEGATIVE

89. (i) State acquired by clinging and favourable to clinging is related to state acquired by clinging and favourable to clinging by object condition, conascence condition, strong-dependence condition, prenascence condition, postnascence condition, nutriment condition, faculty condition. (1)

(ii) State acquired by clinging and favourable to clinging is related to state not acquired by clinging but favourable to clinging by object condition, conascence condition, strong-dependence condition, prenascence condition, postnascence condition, nutriment condition. (2)

(iii) State acquired by clinging and favourable to clinging is related to state not acquired by clinging and not favourable to clinging by strong-dependence condition, prenascence condition. (3)

(iv) State acquired by clinging and favourable to clinging is related to state, acquired by clinging and favourable to clinging and not acquired by clinging but favourable to clinging, by conascence condition, postnascence condition, nutriment condition (4)

(v) State not acquired by clinging but favourable to clinging is related to state not acquired by clinging but favourable to clinging by object condition, conascence condition, strong-dependence condition, prenascence condition, postnascence condition, nutriment condition. (1)

(vi) State not acquired by clinging but favourable to clinging is related to state acquired by clinging and favourable to clinging by object condition, strong-dependence condition, prenascence condition, postnascence condition, kamma condition, nutriment condition. (2)

(vii) State not acquired by clinging but favourable to clinging is related to state not acquired by clinging and not favourable to clinging by strong-dependence condition. (3)

(viii) State not acquired by clinging but favourable to clinging is related to state, acquired by clinging and favourable to clinging and not acquired by clinging but favourable to clinging, by postnascence condition, nutriment condition. (4)

90. (ix) State not acquired by clinging and not favourable to clinging is related to state not acquired by clinging and not favourable to clinging by conascence condition, strong-dependence condition. (1)

(x) State not acquired by clinging and not favourable to clinging is related to state acquired by clinging and favourable to clinging by strong-dependence condition, postnascence condition. (2)

(xi) State not acquired by clinging and not favourable to clinging is related to state not acquired by clinging but favourable to clinging by object condition, conascence condition, strong-dependence condition, postnascence condition. (3)

(xii) State not acquired by clinging and not favourable to clinging is related to state, acquired by clinging and favourable to clinging and not acquired by clinging and not favourable to clinging, by conascence-postnascence. (4)

(xiii) State not acquired by clinging and not favourable to clinging is related to state, not acquired by clinging but favourable to clinging and not acquired by clinging and not favourable to clinging, by conascence-postnascence. (5)

(xiv) State not acquired by clinging and not favourable to clinging is related to state, acquired by clinging and favourable to clinging and not acquired by clinging but favourable to clinging, by postnascence condition. (6)

(xv) State not acquired by clinging and not favourable to clinging is related to state, acquired by clinging and favourable to clinging and not acquired by clinging but favourable to clinging and not acquired by clinging and not favourable to clinging, by conascence-postnascence. (7)

(xvi) States, acquired by clinging and favourable to clinging and not acquired by clinging and not favourable to clinging, are related to state acquired by clinging and favourable to clinging by postnascence-faculty. (1)

(xvii) States, acquired by clinging and favourable to clinging and not acquired by clinging and not favourable to clinging, are related to state not acquired by clinging and not favourable to clinging by conascence-prenascence. (2)

(xviii) States, not acquired by clinging but favourable to clinging and not acquired by clinging and not favourable to clinging, are related to state acquired by clinging and favourable to clinging by postnascence-nutriment. (1)

(xix) States, not acquired by clinging but favourable to clinging and not acquired by clinging and not favourable to clinging, are related to state not acquired by clinging but favourable to clinging by conascence-postnascence-nutriment. (2)

(xx) States, not acquired by clinging but favourable to clinging and not acquired by clinging and not favourable to clinging, are related to state, acquired by clinging and favourable to clinging and not acquired by clinging but favourable to clinging, by postnascence-nutriment. (3)

(xxi) States, acquired by clinging and favourable to clinging and not acquired by clinging but favourable to clinging, are related to state acquired by clinging and favourable to clinging by prenascence-postnascence-nutriment-faculty. (1)

(xxii) States, acquired by clinging and favourable to clinging and not acquired by clinging but favourable to clinging, are related to state not acquired by clinging but favourable to clinging by conascence, prenascence-postnascence-nutriment. (2)

(xxiii) States, acquired by clinging and favourable to clinging and not acquired by clinging but favourable to clinging, are related to state, acquired by clinging and favourable to clinging and not acquired by clinging but favourable to clinging, by nutriment. (3)

(xxiv) States, acquired by clinging and favourable to clinging and not acquired by clinging but favourable to clinging and not acquired by clinging and not favourable to clinging, are related to state acquired by clinging and favourable to clinging by postnascence-nutriment-faculty. (1)

2. CONDITIONS : NEGATIVE (ii) ENUMERATION CHAPTER

By Ones

91. With not-root 24, not-object 24, not-predominance 24, not-proximity 24, not-contiguity 24, not-conascence 20, not-mutuality 20, not-dependence 20, not-strong-dependence 23, not-prenascence 23, not-postnascence 17, not-repetition 24, not-kamma 24, not-resultant 24, not-nutriment 20, not-faculty 22, not-jhāna 24, not-path 24, not-association 20, not-dissociation 14, not-presence 9, not-absence 24, not-disappearance 24, not-non-disappearance 9.

By Twos

92. With not-root condition and not-object 24. ... (Abbreviated.)

(Expand in the same way as expanded in the Negative Enumeration of Faultless Triplet.)

End of Negative

3. CONDITIONS : POSITIVE-NEGATIVE

Root

By Twos

93. With root condition, not-object 7, not-predominance 7, not-proximity 7, not-contiguity 7, not-mutuality 4, not-strong-dependence 7, not-prenascence 7, not-postnascence 7, not-repetition 7, not-kamma 7, not-resultant 4, not-nutriment 7, not-faculty 7, not-jhāna 7, not-path 7, not-association 4, not-dissociation 3, not-absence 7, not-disappearance 7.

Root Combinations

94. Combinations of root, conascence, dependence, presence and non-disappearance (conditions), not-object 7, not-predominance 7, not-proximity 7 ... not-mutuality 4 ... not-resultant 4 ... not-association 4, not-dissociation 3, not-absence 7, not-disappearance 7. ... (Abbreviated.)

(Enumerate in the same way as classified in the Positive-Negative Enumeration of Faultless Triplet.)

End of Positive-Negative

4. CONDITIONS : NEGATIVE-POSITIVE

Not-root

By Twos

95. With not-root condition, object 6, predominance 5, proximity 7, contiguity 7, conascence 9, mutuality 3, dependence 11, strong-dependence 9, prenascence 7, postnascence 9, repetition 2, kamma 8, resultant 6, nutriment 12, faculty 7, jhāna 7, path 7, association 3, dissociation 10, presence 23, absence 7, disappearance 7, non-disappearance 23.   ...
(Abbreviated.)

(Enumerate in the same way as classified in the Negative-Positive Enumeration of Faultless Triplet.)

End of Negative-Positive

END OF CLINGING TRIPLET

5. CORRUPT TRIPLET [1]   I. " DEPENDENT " CHAPTER
I. CONDITIONS : POSITIVE   (i) CLASSIFICATION CHAPTER

Root 9

1. (i) Dependent on corrupt and corrupting state, arises corrupt and corrupting state by root condition.

Dependent on one corrupt and corrupting aggregate, arise three aggregates ... dependent on two aggregates, arise two aggregates. (1)

(ii) Dependent on corrupt and corrupting state, arises not corrupt but corrupting state by root condition.

Dependent on corrupt and corrupting aggregates, arises mind-produced matter. (2)

(iii) Dependent on corrupt and corrupting state, arise corrupt and corrupting and not corrupt but corrupting states by root condition.

Dependent on one corrupt and corrupting aggregate, arise

---

[1] Comprises (1) corrupt and corrupting state, (2) not corrupt but corrupting state, (3) not corrupt and not corrupting state.

three aggregates and mind-produced matter ... dependent on two aggregates, arise two aggregates and mind-produced matter. (3)

(iv) Dependent on not corrupt but corrupting state, arises not corrupt but corrupting state by root condition.

Dependent on one not corrupt but corrupting aggregate, arise three aggregates and mind-produced matter ... dependent on two aggregates, arise two aggregates and mind-produced matter.

At the moment of conception, dependent on one not corrupt but corrupting aggregate, arise three aggregates and kamma-produced matter ... dependent on two aggregates, arise two aggregates and kamma-produced matter; dependent on aggregates, arises (heart-)base; dependent on (heart-)base, arise aggregates.

Dependent on one great primary, arise three great primaries ... dependent on great primaries, arise mind-produced and kamma-produced derived matter. (1)

2. (v) Dependent on not corrupt and not corrupting state, arises not corrupt and not corrupting state by root condition.

Dependent on one not corrupt and not corrupting aggregate, arise three aggregates ... dependent on two aggregates, arise two aggregates. (1)

(vi) Dependent on not corrupt and not corrupting state, arises not corrupt but corrupting state by root condition.

Dependent on not corrupt and not corrupting aggregates, arises mind-produced matter. (2)

(vii) Dependent on not corrupt and not corrupting state, arise not corrupt but corrupting and not corrupt and not corrupting states by root condition.

Dependent on one not corrupt and not corrupting aggregate, arise three aggregates and mind-produced matter ... dependent on two aggregates, arise two aggregates and mind-produced matter. (3)

(viii) Dependent on not corrupt but corrupting (state) [1] and not corrupt and not corrupting state, arises not corrupt but corrupting state by root condition.

---

[1] This is to be understood when the singular is used for denoting two or more states.

Dependent on not corrupt and not corrupting aggregates and great primaries, arises mind-produced matter. (1)

(ix) Dependent on corrupt and corrupting, and not corrupt but corrupting state, arises not corrupt but corrupting state by root condition.

Dependent on corrupt and corrupting aggregates and great primaries, arises mind-produced matter. (1) . . . (Abbreviated.)

1. CONDITIONS : POSITIVE   (ii) ENUMERATION CHAPTER

By Ones

3. With root 9, object 3, predominance 9, proximity 3, contiguity 3, conascence 9, mutuality 3, dependence 9, strong-dependence 3, prenascence 3, repetition 3, kamma 9, resultant 5, nutriment 9 . . . path 9, association 3, dissociation 9 . . . non-disappearance 9. . . . (Abbreviated.)

(Classify in the same way as classified in Faultless Triplet.)

2. CONDITIONS : NEGATIVE

Not-root 2

4. (i) Dependent on corrupt and corrupting state, arises corrupt and corrupting state by not-root condition.

Dependent on doubt-accompanied or restlessness-accompanied aggregates, arises doubt-accompanied or restlessness-accompanied delusion. (1)

(ii) Dependent on not corrupt but corrupting state, arises not corrupt but corrupting state by not-root condition.

Dependent on one not corrupt but corrupting rootless aggregate, arise three aggregates and mind-produced matter. . . . At the moment of rootless conception. . . . One great primary of non-percipient beings. . . . (Abbreviated.)

(Classify in the same way as classified in Faultless Triplet.)

By Ones

5. With not-root 2, not-object 5, not-predominance 6, not-proximity 5 . . . not-strong-dependence 5, not-prenascence 7,

not-postnascence 9, not-repetition 9, not-kamma 3, not-resultant 9, not-nutriment 1 ... not-path 1, not-association 5, not-dissociation 3, not-absence 5, not-disappearance 5. ... (Abbreviated.)

3. CONDITIONS : POSITIVE-NEGATIVE

Root

By Twos

6. With root condition, not-object 5, not-predominance 6 ... not-prenascence 7, not-postnascence 9, not-repetition 9, not-kamma 3, not-resultant 9, not-association 5, not-dissociation 3, not-absence 5, not-disappearance 5. ... (Abbreviated.)

4. CONDITIONS : NEGATIVE-POSITIVE

Not-root

By Twos

7. With not-root condition, object 2 ... resultant 1 ... path 1 ... non-disappearance 2. ... (Abbreviated.)

End of " DEPENDENT " CHAPTER

(Expand "Conascent" Chapter, "Conditioned", "Supported", "Conjoined" and "Associated" Chapter.)

5. CORRUPT TRIPLET   VII. " INVESTIGATION " CHAPTER

1. CONDITIONS : POSITIVE   (i) CLASSIFICATION CHAPTER

Root 7

8. (i) Corrupt and corrupting state is related to corrupt and corrupting state by root condition.

Corrupt and corrupting roots are related to (their) associated aggregates by root condition. (1)

(ii) Corrupt and corrupting state is related to not corrupt but corrupting state by root condition.

Corrupt and corrupting roots are related to mind-produced matter by root condition. (2)

(iii) Corrupt and corrupting state is related to corrupt and corrupting, and not corrupt but corrupting state by root condition.

Corrupt and corrupting roots are related to (their) associated aggregates and mind-produced matter by root condition. (3)

(iv) Not corrupt but corrupting state is related to not corrupt but corrupting state by root condition.

Not corrupt but corrupting roots are related to (their) associated aggregates and mind-produced matter by root condition. At the moment of conception, not corrupt but corrupting roots are related to (their) associated aggregates and kamma-produced matter by root condition. (1)

(v) Not corrupt and not corrupting state is related to not corrupt and not corrupting state by root condition.

Not corrupt and not corrupting roots are related to (their) associated aggregates by root condition. (1)

(vi) Not corrupt and not corrupting state is related to not corrupt but corrupting state by root condition.

Not corrupt and not corrupting roots are related to mind-produced matter by root condition. (2)

(vii) Not corrupt and not corrupting state is related to not corrupt but corrupting, and not corrupt and not corrupting state by root condition.

Not corrupt and not corrupting roots are related to (their) associated aggregates and mind-produced matter by root condition. (3)

Object 6

9. (i) Corrupt and corrupting state is related to corrupt and corrupting state by object condition.

(One) enjoys and delights in lust. Taking it as object arises lust, arises wrong views, arises doubt, arises restlessness, arises grief. (One) enjoys ... wrong views. ... Taking doubt as object. ... Taking restlessness as object. ... Taking grief as object. ... (1)

(Classify in the same way as classified in Faultless Triplet.)

(ii) Corrupt and corrupting state is related to not corrupt but corrupting state by object condition.

The Noble persons review the eradicated defilements, review

the uneradicated defilements, know the defilements addicted to before, practise insight into the impermanency, suffering and impersonality of the corrupt and corrupting aggregates. By the knowledge of penetration into others' minds, (they) know the corrupt and corrupting mind of the other being.

Learners or common worldlings practise insight into the impermanency, suffering and impersonality of the corrupt and corrupting aggregates. When the faultless has ceased, the resultant arises as registering. (They) enjoy and delight in the corrupt and corrupting aggregates ... arises grief. When the faulty has ceased, the resultant arises as registering.

Corrupt and corrupting aggregates are related to knowledge of penetration into others' minds, knowledge of remembrance of past existences, knowledge of rebirths according to one's kamma, knowledge of future existences, advertence by object condition. (2)

10. (iii) Not corrupt but corrupting state is related to not corrupt but corrupting state by object condition.

After having offered the offering, having undertaken the precept, having fulfilled the duty of observance, (one) reviews it. (One) reviews (such acts) formerly well done. Having emerged from jhāna, (one) reviews the jhāna. The Noble persons review change-of-lineage. (They) review purification. (They) practise insight into the impermanency, suffering and impersonality of the eye ; ... ear ... nose ... tongue ... body ... visible objects ... sounds ... smells ... tastes ... tangible objects ... (heart-)base ; (they) practise insight into the impermanency, suffering and impersonality of not corrupt but corrupting aggregates. By the power of divine-eye, (they) see the visible object. By the power of divine-ear element, (they) hear the sound. By the knowledge of penetration into others' minds, (they) know the not corrupt but corrupting mind of the other being.

Infinity of space to infinity of consciousness ... nothingness is related to neither-perception-nor-non-perception by object condition.

Visible object-base is related to eye-consciousness by object condition ... tangible object-base is related to body-consciousness by object condition.

Not corrupt but corrupting aggregates are related to knowledge of supernormal power, knowledge of penetration into others' minds, knowledge of remembrance of past existences, knowledge of rebirths according to one's kamma, knowledge of future existences, advertence by object condition. (1)

(iv) Not corrupt but corrupting state is related to corrupt and corrupting state by object condition.

After having offered the offering, having undertaken the precept, having fulfilled the duty of observance, (one) enjoys and delights in it. Taking it as object arises lust, arises wrong views . . . arises grief. (One) enjoys . . . formerly well done. . . . Having emerged from jhāna, (one) enjoys . . . the jhāna. . . . (One) enjoys . . . the eye . . . tangible objects . . . (heart-)base. . . . (One) enjoys and delights in not corrupt but corrupting aggregates. Taking it as object arises lust . . . arises grief. (2)

(v) Not corrupt and not corrupting state is related to not corrupt and not corrupting state by object condition.

Nibbāna is related to Path, Fruition by object condition. (1)

(vi) Not corrupt and not corrupting state is related to not corrupt but corrupting state by object condition.

The Noble persons, having emerged from Path, review the Path, review Fruition, review Nibbāna. Nibbāna is related to change-of-lineage, purification, advertence by object condition. The Noble persons, by the knowledge of penetration into others' minds, know the not corrupt and not corrupting mind of the other being.

Not corrupt and not corrupting aggregates are related to knowledge of penetration into others' minds, knowledge of remembrance of past existences, knowledge of future existences, advertence by object condition. (2)

Predominance 8

11. (i) Corrupt and corrupting state is related to corrupt and corrupting state by predominance condition.

(It is of two kinds, namely :) (*a*) object-predominance (*b*) conascence-predominance.

(*a*) *Object-predominance* : (One) esteems, enjoys and delights in lust. Taking it as estimable object, arises lust, arises wrong views. (One) esteems, enjoys and delights in wrong views. Taking it as estimable object, arises lust, arises wrong views.

(b) *Conascence-predominance*: Corrupt and corrupting predominance is related to (its) associated aggregates by predominance condition. (1)

(ii) Corrupt and corrupting state is related to not corrupt but corrupting state by predominance condition.

Conascence-predominance: Corrupt and corrupting predominance is related to mind-produced matter by predominance condition. (2)

(iii) Corrupt and corrupting state is related to corrupt and corrupting, and not corrupt but corrupting state by predominance condition.

Conascence-predominance: Corrupt and corrupting predominance is related to (its) associated aggregates and mind-produced matter by predominance condition. (3)

12. (iv) Not corrupt but corrupting state is related to not corrupt but corrupting state by predominance condition.

(It is of two kinds, namely :) (a) object-predominance, (b) conascence-predominance.

(a) *Object-predominance*: After having offered the offering, having undertaken the precept, having fulfilled the duty of observance, (one) esteems and reviews it. (One) esteems and reviews (such acts) formerly well done. Having emerged from jhāna, (one) esteems and reviews the jhāna. Learners esteem and review change-of-lineage. (They) esteem and review purification.

(b) *Conascence-predominance*: Not corrupt but corrupting predominance is related to (its) associated aggregates and mind-produced matter by predominance condition. (1)

(v) Not corrupt but corrupting state is related to corrupt and corrupting state by predominance condition.

Object-predominance: After having offered the offering, having undertaken the precept, having fulfilled the duty of observance, (one) esteems, enjoys and delights in it. Taking it as estimable object, arises lust, arises wrong views. (One) esteems, enjoys and delights in (such acts) formerly well done. ... Having emerged from jhāna, (one) esteems, enjoys and delights in the jhāna. ... (One) esteems, enjoys and delights in the eye ... tangible objects ... (heart-)base. ... (One) esteems, enjoys and delights in the not corrupt but corrupting aggregates. Taking it as estimable object, arises lust, arises wrong views. (2)

(vi) Not corrupt and not corrupting state is related to not corrupt and not corrupting state by predominance condition.

(It is of two kinds, namely :) (a) object-predominance, (b) conascence-predominance.

(a) *Object-predominance* : Nibbāna is related to Path, Fruition by predominance condition.

(b) *Conascence-predominance* : Not corrupt and not corrupting predominance is related to (its) associated aggregates by predominance condition. (1)

(vii) Not corrupt and not corrupting state is related to not corrupt but corrupting state by predominance condition.

(It is of two kinds, namely :) (a) object-predominance, (b) conascence-predominance.

(a) *Object-predominance* : The Noble persons, having emerged from Path, esteem and review the Path, esteem and review Fruition, esteem and review Nibbāna. Nibbāna is related to change-of-lineage, purification by predominance condition.

(b) *Conascence-predominance* : Not corrupt and not corrupting predominance is related to mind-produced matter by predominance condition. (2)

(viii) Not corrupt and not corrupting state is related to not corrupt but corrupting, and not corrupt and not corrupting state by predominance condition.

Conascence-predominance : Not corrupt and not corrupting predominance is related to (its) associated aggregates and mind-produced matter by predominance condition. (3)

Proximity 7

13. (i) Corrupt and corrupting state is related to corrupt and corrupting state by proximity condition.

Preceding corrupt and corrupting aggregates are related to subsequent corrupt and corrupting aggregates by proximity condition. (1)

(ii) Corrupt and corrupting state is related to not corrupt but corrupting state by proximity condition.

Corrupt and corrupting aggregates are related to emergence by proximity condition. (2)

(iii) Not corrupt but corrupting state is related to not corrupt but corrupting state by proximity condition.

Preceding not corrupt but corrupting aggregates are related to subsequent not corrupt but corrupting aggregates by proximity condition. Adaptation to change-of-lineage; adaptation to purification; advertence is related to not corrupt but corrupting aggregates by proximity condition. (1)

(iv) Not corrupt but corrupting state is related to corrupt and corrupting state by proximity condition.

Advertence is related to corrupt and corrupting aggregates by proximity condition. (2)

(v) Not corrupt but corrupting state is related to not corrupt and not corrupting state by proximity condition.

Change-of-lineage to Path; purification to Path; adaptation to attainment of Fruition; having emerged from the attainment of Extinction, neither-perception-nor-non-perception is related to the attainment of Fruition by proximity condition. (3)

(vi) Not corrupt and not corrupting state is related to not corrupt and not corrupting state by proximity condition.

Preceding not corrupt and not corrupting aggregates are related to subsequent not corrupt and not corrupting aggregates by proximity condition. Path to Fruition; Fruition is related to Fruition by proximity condition. (1)

(vii) Not corrupt and not corrupting state is related to not corrupt but corrupting state by proximity condition.

Fruition is related to emergence by proximity condition. (2)

Contiguity, etc.

14. (i) Corrupt and corrupting state is related to corrupt and corrupting state by contiguity condition ... by conascence condition ... by mutuality condition ... by dependence condition ... by strong-dependence condition.

(It is of three kinds, namely:) (*a*) object-strong-dependence, (*b*) proximity-strong-dependence, (*c*) natural strong-dependence. ...

(*c*) *Natural strong-dependence*: By the strong-dependence of

SS*

lust, (one) kills a living being ... causes schism in the Saṅgha. By the strong-dependence of hate, (one) kills a living being ... causes schism in the Saṅgha. ... Lust ... wish is related to lust ... wish by strong-dependence condition.

Killing is related to killing by strong-dependence condition. ... Wrong views with fixed destiny is related to wrong views with fixed destiny by strong-dependence condition. ... (1)

(ii) Corrupt and corrupting state is related to not corrupt but corrupting state by strong-dependence condition.

(It is of two kinds, namely:) (*a*) proximity-strong-dependence, (*b*) natural strong-dependence. ...

(*b*) *Natural strong-dependence* : By the strong-dependence of lust, (one) offers the offering, undertakes the precept, fulfils the duty of observance ... jhāna ... insight, develops superknowledge, develops attainment. ... By the strong-dependence of wish, (one) offers the offering ... develops attainment. Lust ... wish is related to confidence ... bodily happiness, bodily pain by strong-dependence condition.

After having killed, (one) offers the offering, undertakes the precept, fulfils the duty of observance, develops jhāna, develops insight, develops superknowledge, develops attainment to counteract it. ... After having caused schism in the Saṅgha, (one) offers the offering, undertakes the precept, fulfils the duty of observance to counteract it. Faulty kamma is related to resultant by strong-dependence condition. (2)

(iii) Corrupt and corrupting state is related to not corrupt and not corrupting state by strong-dependence condition.

Natural strong-dependence : By the strong-dependence of lust, (one) develops Path, enters the attainment of Fruition. ... hate. ... By the strong-dependence of wish, (one) develops Path, enters the attainment of Fruition. Lust ... wish is related to Path, the attainment of Fruition by strong-dependence condition. (3)

15. (iv) Not corrupt but corrupting state is related to not corrupt but corrupting state by strong-dependence condition.

(It is of three kinds, namely :) (*a*) object-strong-dependence, (*b*) proximity-strong-dependence, (*c*) natural strong-dependence. ...

(*c*) *Natural strong-dependence* : By the strong-dependence of

confidence, (one) offers the offering ... develops attainment. ....
precept ... learning ... generosity ... wisdom ... bodily
happiness ... bodily pain ... temperature ... food. ... By the
strong-dependence of lodging-place, (one) offers the offering ...
develops attainment. Confidence ... lodging-place is related to
confidence ... bodily happiness, bodily pain by strong-
dependence condition. Faultless kamma is related to resultant
by strong-dependence condition. The preparation for first
jhāna to first jhāna ... nothingness to neither-perception-nor-
non-perception. ... (1)

(v) Not corrupt but corrupting state is related to corrupt
and corrupting state by strong-dependence condition.

(It is of three kinds, namely :) (*a*) object-strong-dependence,
(*b*) proximity-strong-dependence, (*c*) natural strong-dependence. ...

(*c*) *Natural strong-dependence* : By the strong-dependence of
confidence, (one) arouses conceit, adopts wrong views. ...
precept. ... By the strong-dependence of lodging-place, (one)
kills a living being ... causes schism in the Saṅgha. Confidence ... lodging-place is related to lust ... ong-wish by str
dependence condition. (2)

(vi) Not corrupt but corrupting state is related to not
corrupt and not corrupting state by strong-dependence
condition.

(It is of two kinds, namely :) (*a*) proximity-strong-dependence,
(*b*) natural strong-dependence. ...

(*b*) *Natural strong-dependence* : The preparation for first
Path is related to first Path ... to second Path ... to third
Path ... to fourth Path by strong-dependence condition. (3)

16. (vii) Not corrupt and not corrupting state is related to not
corrupt and not corrupting state by strong-dependence
condition.

(It is of three kinds, namely :) (*a*) object-strong-dependence,
(*b*) proximity-strong-dependence, (*c*) natural strong-dependence. ...

(*c*) *Natural strong-dependence* : First Path to second Path ...
second Path to third Path ... third Path to fourth Path. ...
Path is related to attainment of Fruition by strong-dependence
condition. (1)

(viii) Not corrupt and not corrupting state is related to not corrupt but corrupting state by strong-dependence condition.

(It is of three kinds, namely :) (*a*) object-strong-dependence, (*b*) proximity-strong-dependence, (*c*) natural strong-dependence. ...

(*c*) *Natural strong-dependence* : The Noble persons, by the strong-dependence of the Path, generate the attainment which has not yet arisen. (They) enter the attainment which has arisen. (They) practise insight into the impermanency, suffering and impersonality of the formations. The Path is related to the Noble person's analytical knowledge of meaning ... knowledge of correct and faulty conclusion by strong-dependence condition. The attainment of Fruition is related to bodily happiness by strong-dependence condition. (2)

Prenascence 3

17. (i) Not corrupt but corrupting state is related to not corrupt but corrupting state by prenascence condition.

(It is of two kinds, namely :) (*a*) object-prenascence, (*b*) base-prenascence.

(*a*) *Object-prenascence* : (One) practises insight into the impermanency, suffering and impersonality of the eye ... ear ... nose ... tongue ... body ... visible objects ... sounds ... smells ... tastes ... tangible objects ; (one) practises insight into the impermanency, suffering and impersonality of the (heart-)base. By the power of divine-eye, sees the visible object. By the power of divine-ear element, hears the sound.

Visible object-base to eye-consciousness ... tangible object-base is related to body-consciousness by prenascence condition.

(*b*) *Base-prenascence* : Eye-base to eye-consciousness ... body-base is related to body-consciousness by prenascence condition. (Heart-)base is related to the not corrupt but corrupting aggregates by prenascence condition. (1)

(ii) Not corrupt but corrupting state is related to corrupt and corrupting state by prenascence condition.

(It is of two kinds, namely :) (*a*) object-prenascence, (*b*) base-prenascence.

(*a*) *Object-prenascence* : (One) enjoys and delights in the eye. Taking it as object arises lust ... arises grief. ... ear ... tangible-objects. ... (One) enjoys and delights in the (heart-)base. Taking it as object arises lust ... arises grief.

(*b*) *Base-prenascence* : (Heart-)base is related to the corrupt and corrupting aggregates by prenascence condition. (2)

(iii) Not corrupt but corrupting state is related to not corrupt and not corrupting state by prenascence condition.

(Heart-)base is related to the not corrupt and not corrupting aggregates by prenascence condition. (3)

Postnascence 3

18. (i) Corrupt and corrupting state is related to not corrupt but corrupting state by postnascence condition.

Corrupt and corrupting postnascent aggregates are related to this prenascent body by postnascence condition. (1)

(ii) Not corrupt but corrupting state is related to not corrupt but corrupting state by postnascence condition.

Not corrupt but corrupting postnascent aggregates are related to this prenascent body by postnascence condition. (1)

(iii) Not corrupt and not corrupting state is related to not corrupt but corrupting state by postnascence condition.

Not corrupt and not corrupting postnascent aggregates are related to this prenascent body by postnascence condition. (1)

Repetition 3

19. (i) Corrupt and corrupting state is related to corrupt and corrupting state by repetition condition.

Preceding corrupt and corrupting aggregates are related to subsequent corrupt and corrupting aggregates by repetition condition. (1)

(ii) Not corrupt but corrupting state is related to not corrupt but corrupting state by repetition condition.

Preceding. ... Adaptation to change-of-lineage ; adaptation is related to purification by repetition condition. (1)

(iii) Not corrupt but corrupting state is related to not corrupt and not corrupting state by repetition condition.

Change-of-lineage to Path ; purification is related to Path by repetition condition. (2)

Kamma 7

20. (i) Corrupt and corrupting state is related to corrupt and corrupting state by kamma condition.

Corrupt and corrupting volition is related to (its) associated aggregates by kamma condition. (1)

(ii) Corrupt and corrupting state is related to not corrupt but corrupting state by kamma condition.

(It is of two kinds, namely :) (*a*) conascence(-kamma), (*b*) asynchronous (kamma).

(*a*) Corrupt and corrupting conascent volition is related to mind-produced matter by kamma condition.

(*b*) Corrupt and corrupting asynchronous volition is related to resultant aggregates and kamma-produced matter by kamma condition. (2)

(iii) Corrupt and corrupting state is related to corrupt and corrupting, and not corrupt but corrupting state by kamma condition.

Corrupt and corrupting volition is related to (its) associated aggregates and mind-produced matter by kamma condition. (3)

(iv) Not corrupt but corrupting state is related to not corrupt but corrupting state by kamma condition.

(It is of two kinds, namely :) conascence(-kamma), (*b*) asynchronous (kamma).

(*a*) Not corrupt but corrupting conascent volition is related to (its) associated aggregates and mind-produced matter by kamma condition. At the moment of conception . . .

(*b*) Not corrupt but corrupting asynchronous volition is related to resultant aggregates and kamma-produced matter by kamma condition. (1)

(v) Not corrupt and not corrupting state is related to not corrupt and not corrupting state by kamma condition.

(It is of two kinds, namely :) (*a*) conascence(-kamma), (*b*) asynchronous (kamma).

(*a*) Not corrupt and not corrupting conascent volition is related to (its) associated aggregates by kamma condition.

(*b*) Not corrupt and not corrupting asynchronous faultless volition is related to not corrupt and not corrupting resultant aggregates by kamma condition. (1)

(vi) Not corrupt and not corrupting state is related to not corrupt but corrupting state by kamma condition.

Not corrupt and not corrupting conascent volition is related to mind-produced matter by kamma condition. (2)

(vii) Not corrupt and not corrupting state is related to not corrupt but corrupting, and not corrupt and not corrupting state by kamma condition.

Not corrupt and not corrupting conascent volition is related to (its) associated aggregates and mind-produced matter by kamma condition. (3)

Resultant 4

21. (i) Not corrupt but corrupting state is related to not corrupt but corrupting state by resultant condition.

One not corrupt but corrupting resultant aggregate is related to three aggregates and mind-produced matter by resultant condition ... two aggregates to two aggregates. ...

At the moment of conception, one not corrupt but corrupting aggregate is related to three aggregates and kamma-produced matter by resultant condition ... two aggregates to two aggregates ... aggregates are related to (heart-)base by resultant condition. (1)

(ii) Not corrupt and not corrupting state is related to not corrupt and not corrupting state by resultant condition.

One not corrupt and not corrupting resultant aggregate is related to three aggregates by resultant condition ... two aggregates to two aggregates. ... (1)

(iii) Not corrupt and not corrupting state is related to not corrupt but corrupting state by resultant condition.

Not corrupt and not corrupting resultant aggregates are related to mind-produced matter by resultant condition. (2)

(iv) Not corrupt and not corrupting state is related to not corrupt but corrupting, and not corrupt and not corrupting state by resultant condition.

One not corrupt and not corrupting resultant aggregate is

related to three aggregates and mind-produced matter by resultant condition . . . two aggregates. . . . (3)

Nutriment 7

22. (i)–(iii) Corrupt and corrupting state is related to corrupt and corrupting state by nutriment condition. . . . three.

(iv) Not corrupt but corrupting state is related to not corrupt but corrupting state by nutriment condition.

Not corrupt but corrupting nutriments are related to (their) associated aggregates and mind-produced matter by nutriment condition. At the moment of conception. . . . Edible food is related to this body by nutriment condition.

(v)–(vii) Not corrupt and not corrupting state is related to not corrupt and not corrupting state by nutriment condition. . . . three.

Faculty 7

23. (i)–(iii) Corrupt and corrupting state is related to corrupt and corrupting state by faculty condition. . . . three.

(iv) Not corrupt but corrupting state is related to not corrupt but corrupting state by faculty condition.

Not corrupt but corrupting faculties are related to (their) associated aggregates and mind-produced matter by faculty condition. At the moment of conception. . . . Eye-faculty to eye-consciousness . . . body-faculty is related to body-consciousness by faculty condition. Physical life-faculty is related to kamma-produced matter by faculty condition.

(v)–(vii) Not corrupt and not corrupting state . . . three.

Jhāna, etc.

24. Corrupt and corrupting state is related to corrupt and corrupting state by jhāna condition . . . by path condition . . . by association condition. . . .

Dissociation 5

25. (i) Corrupt and corrupting state is related to not corrupt but corrupting state by dissociation condition.

(It is of two kinds, namely :) (*a*) conascence, (*b*) postnascence.

(*a*) Corrupt and corrupting conascent aggregates are related to mind-produced matter by dissociation condition.

(*b*) Corrupt and corrupting postnascent aggregates are related to this prenascent body by dissociation condition. (1)

(ii) Not corrupt but corrupting state is related to not corrupt but corrupting state by dissociation condition.

(It is of three kinds, namely :) (*a*) conascence, (*b*) prenascence, (*c*) postnascence.

(*a*) Not corrupt but corrupting conascent aggregates are related to mind-produced matter by dissociation condition. At the moment of conception, not corrupt but corrupting aggregates are related to kamma-produced matter by dissociation condition ; aggregates to (heart-)base . . . (heart-)base is related to aggregates by dissociation condition.

(*b*) *Prenascence*: Eye-base to eye-consciousness . . . body-base is related to body-consciousness by dissociation condition ; (heart-)base is related to not corrupt but corrupting aggregates by dissociation condition.

(*c*) Not corrupt but corrupting postnascent aggregates are related to this prenascent body by dissociation condition. (1)

(iii) Not corrupt but corrupting state is related to corrupt and corrupting state by dissociation condition.

Prenascent (heart-)base is related to corrupt and corrupting aggregates by dissociation condition. (2)

(iv) Not corrupt but corrupting state is related to not corrupt and not corrupting state by dissociation condition.

Prenascent (heart-)base is related to not corrupt and not corrupting aggregates by dissociation condition. (3)

(v) Not corrupt and not corrupting state is related to not corrupt but corrupting state by dissociation condition.

(It is of two kinds, namely :) (*a*) conascence, (*b*) postnascence.

(*a*) Not corrupt and not corrupting conascent aggregates are related to mind-produced matter by dissociation condition.

(*b*) Not corrupt and not corrupting postnascent aggregates are related to this prenascent body by dissociation condition. (1)

Presence 13

26. (i) Corrupt and corrupting state is related to corrupt and corrupting state by presence condition.

One corrupt and corrupting aggregate is related to three aggregates by presence condition. ... (1)

(ii) Corrupt and corrupting state is related to not corrupt but corrupting state by presence condition.

(It is of two kinds, namely :) (*a*) conascence, (*b*) postnascence.

(*a*) Corrupt and corrupting conascent aggregates are related to mind-produced matter by presence condition.

(*b*) Corrupt and corrupting postnascent aggregates are related to this prenascent body by presence condition. (2)

(iii) Corrupt and corrupting state is related to corrupt and corrupting, and not corrupt but corrupting state by presence condition.

One corrupt and corrupting aggregate is related to three aggregates and mind-produced matter by presence condition ... two aggregates. ... (3)

27. (iv) Not corrupt but corrupting state is related to not corrupt but corrupting state by presence condition.

(It is of five kinds, namely :) (*a*) conascence, (*b*) prenascence, (*c*) postnascence, (*d*) nutriment, (*e*) faculty.

(*a*) One not corrupt but corrupting conascent aggregate is related to three aggregates and mind-produced matter by presence condition. ... At the moment of conception. ... One great primary of non-percipient beings is related to three great primaries by presence condition. ...

(*b*) *Prenascence* : (One) practises insight into the impermanency, suffering and impersonality of the eye ... ear ... body ... visible objects ... tangible objects ; (one) practises insight into the impermanency, suffering and impersonality of the (heart-)base. By the power of divine-eye, (one) sees the visible object. By the power of divine-ear element, hears the sound.

Visible object-base to eye-consciousness ... tangible object-base is related to body-consciousness by presence condition.

Eye-base to eye-consciousness ... body-base to body-consciousness ... (heart-)base is related to not corrupt but corrupting aggregates by presence condition.

(*c*) Not corrupt but corrupting postnascent aggregates are related to this prenascent body by presence condition.

(*d*) Edible food to this body. ...

(*e*) Physical life-faculty is related to kamma-produced matter by presence condition. (1)

(v) Not corrupt but corrupting state is related to corrupt and corrupting state by presence condition.

Prenascence : (One) enjoys and delights in the eye. Taking it as object arises lust . . . arises grief. . . . (One) enjoys . . . (heart-)-base. . . . (Heart-)base is related to corrupt and corrupting aggregates by presence condition. (2)

(vi) Not corrupt but corrupting state is related to not corrupt and not corrupting state by presence condition.

Prenascent (heart-)base is related to not corrupt and not corrupting aggregates by presence condition. (3)

28. (vii) Not corrupt and not corrupting state is related to not corrupt and not corrupting state by presence condition.

One not corrupt and not corrupting aggregate is related to three aggregates by presence condition. . . . (1)

(viii) Not corrupt and not corrupting state is related to not corrupt but corrupting state by presence condition.

(It is of two kinds, namely :) (*a*) conascence, (*b*) postnascence.

(*a*) Not corrupt and not corrupting conascent aggregates are related to mind-produced matter by presence condition.

(*b*) Not corrupt and not corrupting postnascent aggregates are related to this prenascent body by presence condition. (2)

(ix) Not corrupt and not corrupting state is related to not corrupt but corrupting, and not corrupt and not corrupting state by presence condition.

One not corrupt and not corrupting aggregate is related to three aggregates and mind-produced matter by presence condition. . . . (3)

29. (x) Not corrupt but corrupting and not corrupt and not corrupting states are related to not corrupt but corrupting state by presence condition.

(It is of three kinds, namely :) (*a*) conascence, (*b*) postnascence-nutriment, (*c*) (postnascence-)faculty.

(*a*) Not corrupt and not corrupting conascent aggregates and great primaries are related to mind-produced matter by presence condition.

(*b*) Not corrupt and not corrupting postnascent aggregates and edible food are related to this body by presence condition.

(c) Not corrupt and not corrupting postnascent aggregates and physical life-faculty are related to kamma-produced matter by presence condition. (1)

(xi) Not corrupt but corrupting and not corrupt and not corrupting states are related to not corrupt and not corrupting state by presence condition.

Conascence-prenascence : One not corrupt and not corrupting conascent aggregate and (heart-)base are related to three aggregates by presence condition. ... (2)

(xii) Corrupt and corrupting and not corrupt but corrupting states are related to corrupt and corrupting state by presence condition.

Conascence-prenascence : One corrupt and corrupting conascent aggregate and (heart-)base are related to three aggregates by presence condition ... two aggregates. ... (1)

(xiii) Corrupt and corrupting and not corrupt but corrupting states are related to not corrupt but corrupting state by presence condition.

(It is of three kinds, namely :) (a) conascence, (b) postnascence-nutriment, (c) (postnascence-)faculty.

(a) Corrupt and corrupting conascent aggregates and great primaries are related to mind-produced matter by presence condition.

(b) Corrupt and corrupting postnascent aggregates and edible food are related to this prenascent body by presence condition.

(c) Corrupt and corrupting postnascent aggregates and physical life-faculty are related to kamma-produced matter by presence condition. (2)

Absence 7, Disappearance 7, and Non-disappearance 13

30. Corrupt and corrupting state is related to corrupt and corrupting state by absence condition ... by disappearance condition ... by non-disappearance condition. ...

I. CONDITIONS : POSITIVE   (ii) ENUMERATION CHAPTER

By Ones

31. With root 7, object 6, predominance 8, proximity 7, contiguity 7, conascence 9, mutuality 3, dependence 13,

strong-dependence 8, prenascence 3, postnascence 3, repetition 3, kamma 7, resultant 4, nutriment 7, faculty 7, jhāna 7, path 7, association 3, dissociation 5, presence 13, absence 7, disappearance 7, non-disappearance 13.

Root

Common 11

With root condition and predominance 4, conascence 7, mutuality 3, dependence 7, resultant 4, faculty 4, path 4, association 3, dissociation 3, presence 7, non-disappearance 7.

Combinations (9)

Without resultant (4)

32. 1. Combination of root, conascence, dependence, presence and non-disappearance (has) 7 (answers) ;

2. Of root, conascence, mutuality, dependence, presence and non-disappearance 3 ;

3. Of root, conascence, mutuality, dependence, association, presence and non-disappearance 3 ;

4. Of root, conascence, dependence, dissociation, presence and non-disappearance 3.

With resultant (5)

5. Of root, conascence, dependence, resultant, presence and non-disappearance 4 ;

6. Of root, conascence, mutuality, dependence, resultant, presence and non-disappearance 2 ;

7. Of root, conascence, mutuality, dependence, resultant, association, presence and non-disappearance 2 ;

8. Of root, conascence, dependence, resultant, dissociation, presence and non-disappearance 2 ;

9. Of root, conascence, mutuality, dependence, resultant, dissociation, presence and non-disappearance 1. (Abbreviated.)

(Expand in the same way as in Faultless Triplet.)

End of Positive

2. SELECTION OF THE CONDITIONS FOR NEGATIVE

33. (i) Corrupt and corrupting state is related to corrupt and corrupting state by object condition, conascence condition, strong-dependence condition. (1)

(ii) Corrupt and corrupting state is related to not corrupt but corrupting state by object condition, conascence condition, strong-dependence condition, postnascence condition, kamma condition. (2)

(iii) Corrupt and corrupting state is related to not corrupt and not corrupting state by strong-dependence condition. (3)

(iv) Corrupt and corrupting state is related to corrupt and corrupting, and not corrupt but corrupting state by conascence condition. (4)

34. (v) Not corrupt but corrupting state is related to not corrupt but corrupting state by object condition, conascence condition, strong-dependence condition, prenascence condition, postnascence condition, kamma condition, nutriment condition, faculty condition. (1)

(vi) Not corrupt but corrupting state is related to corrupt and corrupting state by object condition, strong-dependence condition, prenascence condition. (2)

(vii) Not corrupt but corrupting state is related to not corrupt and not corrupting state by strong-dependence condition, prenascence condition. (3)

(viii) Not corrupt and not corrupting state is related to not corrupt and not corrupting state by conascence condition, strong-dependence condition. (1)

(ix) Not corrupt and not corrupting state is related to not corrupt but corrupting state by object condition, conascence condition, strong-dependence condition, postnascence condition. (2)

(x) Not corrupt and not corrupting state is related to not corrupt but corrupting, and not corrupt and not corrupting state by conascence condition. (3)

(xi) Not corrupt but corrupting and not corrupt and not corrupting states are related to not corrupt but corrupting state by conascence, postnascence-nutriment-faculty. (1)

(xii) Not corrupt but corrupting and not corrupt and not

corrupting states are related to not corrupt and not corrupting state by conascence-prenascence. (2)

(xiii) Corrupt and corrupting and not corrupt but corrupting states are related to corrupt and corrupting state by conascence-prenascence. (1)

(xiv) Corrupt and corrupting and not corrupt but corrupting states are related to not corrupt but corrupting state by conascence, postnascence-nutriment-faculty. (2)

CONDITIONS : NEGATIVE

By Ones

35. With not-root 14, not-object 14, not-predominance 14, not-proximity 14, not-contiguity 14, not-conascence 10, not-mutuality 10, not-dependence 10, not-strong-dependence 13, not-prenascence 12, not-postnascence 14, not-repetition 14, not-kamma 14, not-resultant 14, not-nutriment 14, not-faculty 14, not-jhāna 14, not-path 14, not-association 10, not-dissociation 8, not-presence 8, not-absence 14, not-disappearance 14, not-non-disappearance 8.

By Twos

With not-root condition and not-object 14. . . . (Abbreviated.)

(Enumerate in the same way as the Negative Enumeration of Faultless Triplet.)

End of Negative

3. CONDITIONS : POSITIVE-NEGATIVE

Root

By Twos

36. With root condition, not-object 7, not-predominance 7, not-proximity 7, not-contiguity 7, not-mutuality 3, not-strong-dependence 7, not-prenascence 7, not-postnascence 7, not-repetition 7, not-kamma 7, not-resultant 7, not-nutriment 7, not-faculty 7, not-jhāna 7, not-path 7, not-association 3, not-dissociation 3, not-absence 7, not-disappearance 7.

Combinations

Combinations of root, conascence, dependence, presence and non-disappearance, not-object 7 ... not-mutuality 3 ... not-association 3, not-dissociation 3 ... not-disappearance 7. ... (Abbreviated.)

(Classify in the same way as classified in the Positive-Negative Enumeration of Faultless Triplet.)

End of Positive-Negative

4. CONDITIONS : NEGATIVE-POSITIVE

Not-root

By Twos

37. With not-root condition, object 6, predominance 8, proximity 7, contiguity 7, conascence 9, mutuality 3, dependence 13, strong-dependence 8, prenascence 3, postnascence 3, repetition 3, kamma 7, resultant 4, nutriment 7, faculty 7, jhāna 7, path 7, association 3, dissociation 5, presence 13, absence 7, disappearance 7, non-disappearance 13.

By Threes

With not-root and not-object conditions, predominance 7. ... (Abbreviated.)

(Classify in the same way as classified in the Negative-Positive Enumeration of Faultless Triplet.)

End of Negative-Positive

END OF CORRUPT TRIPLET